AF716413

Revenue Statistics 2019

1965-2018

OECD

BETTER POLICIES FOR BETTER LIVES

This document, as well as any data and map included herein, are without prejudice to the status of or sovereignty over any territory, to the delimitation of international frontiers and boundaries and to the name of any territory, city or area.

The statistical data for Israel are supplied by and under the responsibility of the relevant Israeli authorities. The use of such data by the OECD is without prejudice to the status of the Golan Heights, East Jerusalem and Israeli settlements in the West Bank under the terms of international law.

Please cite this publication as:
OECD (2019), *Revenue Statistics 2019*, OECD Publishing, Paris, *https://doi.org/10.1787/0bbc27da-en*.

ISBN 978-92-64-78222-8 (print)
ISBN 978-92-64-67159-1 (pdf)

Revenue Statistics
ISSN 2522-7696 (print)
ISSN 2522-770X (online)

Photo credits: Cover © some of the graphic elements in the main cover illustration were adapted from Freepik.com.

Corrigenda to publications may be found on line at: *www.oecd.org/about/publishing/corrigenda.htm*.

© OECD 2019

The use of this work, whether digital or print, is governed by the Terms and Conditions to be found at *http://www.oecd.org/termsandconditions*.

Foreword

This annual publication provides information on tax levels and tax structures in OECD countries. It was prepared under the auspices of the Working Party on Tax Policy Analysis and Tax Statistics of the Committee on Fiscal Affairs and is published under the responsibility of the Secretary-General of the OECD.

Acknowledgements

Revenue Statistics 2019 has been produced by the Organisation for Economic Cooperation and Development (OECD)'s Centre for Tax Policy and Administration (CTPA) under the auspices of Working Party No.2 on Tax Policy Analysis and Tax Statistics (WP2) of the Committee on Fiscal Affairs. The authors of this edition were Michelle Harding, Nicolás Miranda and Michael Sharratt. The special feature was written by Miguel Cárdenas Rodríguez and Ivan Haščič in the Environment Directorate and by Michelle Harding.

The authors would like to thank colleagues in the OECD for their invaluable comments and practical support in finalising the publication, including David Bradbury, Karena Garnier, Natalie Lagorce, and Violet Sochay in CTPA; Frederic Parrot and Bettina Wistrom in the Statistics and Data Directorate and the Statistical Editors and Content Management Team in the Press and Communications Directorate. Marie-Aurélie Elkurd at CTPA assisted with the production and publication of this report and Stephanie Coic in the Development Cooperation Directorate (DCD) designed the cover. The authors would also like to thank WP2 delegates and their colleagues working in national administrations for their input and comments.

Table of contents

FIGURES

TABLES

Follow OECD Publications on:

- http://twitter.com/OECD_Pubs
- http://www.facebook.com/OECDPublications
- http://www.linkedin.com/groups/OECD-Publications-4645871
- http://www.youtube.com/oecdilibrary
- http://www.oecd.org/oecddirect/

This book has...

StatLinks
A service that delivers Excel® files from the printed page!

Look for the *StatLinks* at the bottom of the tables or graphs in this book. To download the matching Excel® spreadsheet, just type the link into your Internet browser, starting with the ***https://doi.org*** prefix, or click on the link from the e-book edition.

Executive Summary

In 2018, the average OECD tax-to-GDP ratio remained virtually unchanged compared to 2017, with almost no increase (a change of 0.02 percentage points). This ends the trend of annual increases in the OECD average tax-to-GDP ratio observed since 2009, following the financial crisis. The slowing in the growth of the OECD average was predominantly driven by the impact of the significant fall in the tax-to-GDP ratio of the United States as a result of their tax reforms. However, due to rounding the OECD average tax-to-GDP ratio was 34.3% in 2018 compared to 34.2% in 2017.

In this publication, taxes are defined as compulsory, unrequited payments to general government. They are unrequited in that the benefits provided by governments to taxpayers are not normally allocated in proportion to their payments. Taxes are classified by their base: income, profits and capital gains; payroll; property; goods and services; and other taxes. Compulsory social security contributions (SSCs) paid to general government are also treated as taxes. Revenues are analysed by level of government: federal or central; state; local; and social security funds. Detailed information on the classifications applied is set out in the Interpretative Guide in Annex A.

Tax levels in 2018

Across OECD countries, tax-to-GDP ratios in 2018 ranged from 16.1% in Mexico to 46.1% in France. Half of the OECD countries had tax-to-GDP ratios between 32% and 40% of GDP in 2018, with one-quarter of countries having ratios above this level and one-quarter below. Between 2017 and 2018, the OECD average tax-to-GDP ratio remained virtually unchanged (a change of 0.02 percentage points), although due to rounding the headline figures increased from 34.2% (34.24%) to 34.3% (34.26%).

An increase in tax-to-GDP ratios from 2017 to 2018 is observed in 19 of the 34 countries for which preliminary 2018 data is available. In all of these countries, the increase was due to nominal tax revenues increasing more than the nominal increase in GDP. The increase in the tax-to-GDP ratio was largest in Korea and Luxembourg (1.5 and 1.3 percentage points, respectively) due to higher corporate income taxes in both countries as well as higher revenues from personal income taxes in Luxembourg. There were no other increases above one percentage point.

Fifteen countries experienced a decrease in tax-to-GDP ratios in 2018 relative to 2017. The largest fall was seen in the United States (2.5 percentage points), following the reforms to corporate and personal income taxes and the one-off repatriation tax on foreign earnings implemented in the Tax Cuts and Jobs Act. Falls of over one percentage points were also observed in Hungary and Israel (1.6 and 1.4 percentage points, respectively). Smaller decreases were seen in Denmark, Finland, France, Greece, Iceland, Ireland, Italy, Latvia, the Slovak Republic, Sweden, Switzerland and Turkey. In most countries the decreases were due to nominal tax revenues increasing by less than the increase in GDP, except in the United States and Israel, where nominal tax revenues fell relative to 2017, but nominal GDP rose.

Across the last decade, 26 OECD countries reported higher tax-to-GDP ratios in 2018 than in 2008, with the greatest increases in Greece and the Slovak Republic. Among the remaining 10 countries, tax levels in 2018 remained more than six percentage points lower in Ireland and more than two percentage points lower in Hungary and Norway.

Tax structure in 2017

In 2017, the latest year in which final data is available for all countries, social security contributions (SSCs) amounted to the largest share of tax revenues in the OECD, at just over one-quarter (26.0%) of total revenues, and together with personal income taxes (23.9%) the two categories amounted to nearly one-half of tax revenues in OECD countries, on average. Value Added Tax (VAT) accounted for a further one-fifth of total revenues (20.2%). Other consumption taxes and taxes on corporate income accounted for smaller shares of tax revenues (12.2% and 9.3% respectively), with property taxes (5.8%) and residual taxes accounting for the remaining share.

Since 2016, the share of income taxes to total revenue has increased by 0.7 percentage points. This was relatively evenly split between personal and corporate income taxes (0.4 and 0.3 percentage points, respectively). This continues the recent increase in the share of corporate tax revenues, from 8.8% of total tax revenues in 2014 and 2015, to 9.0% in 2016 and 9.3% in 2017. Since 2016, the share of revenues from taxes on goods and services decreased slightly, with an increase in VAT revenues of 0.2 percentage points outweighed by a fall in the share of revenues from other goods and services taxes (0.3 percentage points). The largest fall between 2016 and 2017 was seen in property tax revenues (0.7 percentage points) although this reflects the impact of the one-off stability contributions in Iceland, which had increased their share in 2016.

Changes by level of government

Tax revenues at different levels of government remained stable in 2017 relative to 2016, both on an OECD average basis and in individual countries. The central share of revenues in 2017 remained at 53.8% of general government revenue in federal countries and at 63.8% in unitary countries. In federal countries, 25.1% of revenues were received at subnational level on average (ranging from 4.6% in Austria to 50.2% in Canada), with roughly two-thirds of revenues being received by state governments and one-third by local governments. In unitary countries, the share of local government revenues was 11.2% on average, ranging from less than 0.9% in Estonia to 35.3% in Sweden.

Environmentally related tax revenues in OECD countries

A special feature in this report details a reconciliation of data on environmentally related taxes in Revenue Statistics with data in the OECD Policy INstruments for the Environment (PINE) database and in Eurostat's National Tax Lists. Reconciling these sources ensures coherence and comparability of the data and thus improves the quality of data available for policy analysis.

The special feature finds that environmentally related tax revenues (ERTRs) in OECD countries in 2017 ranged from 2.8% of total tax revenues in the United States to 12.5% in Slovenia and Turkey, accounting for 6.9% on a simple average basis. Environmentally related tax revenues accounted for 2.3% of GDP, on average, with country shares ranging from 0.7% of GDP in the United States to 4.5% in Slovenia. Since 1995, OECD countries have not moved toward sourcing a greater share of tax revenues from environmentally related tax bases. Across the OECD, the largest share of ERTRs in 2017 was derived from energy taxes, both on average and in nearly every OECD country.

Introduction

The purpose of this annual publication is to provide internationally comparative data on tax levels and tax structures in member countries of the OECD. The taxes imposed in each country are presented in a standardised framework based upon the OECD classification of taxes and its Interpretative Guide as contained in Annex A to this Report.

The data for the Report has, for the most part, been provided by Delegates to Working Party No.2 on Tax Policy Analysis and Tax Statistics of the Committee on Fiscal Affairs. The OECD acknowledges the co-operation of the International Monetary Fund, whose classification of tax revenues — although in a number of respects less detailed — is in many respects similar to that of the OECD.[1] The most important of the other classifications currently in use is the System of National Accounts (henceforth referred to as SNA) and the European System of Integrated Economic Accounts of EU member states (henceforth referred to as ESA), which is primarily an elaboration of SNA, though differing from it in certain respects. Subject to a few exceptions, SNA/ESA figures can be reconciled with the figures in the present Report, since SNA criteria and definitions have been adopted unless the contrary is specifically indicated.

The material is organised in six chapters. Chapter 1 summarises tax trends of the past 50 years focusing in turn on tax-to-GDP ratios (section 1.1), tax structures (section 1.2) and taxes by level of government (section 1.3). Section 1.4 discusses the impact of alternate treatments of non-wastable tax credits. This year's issue also carries in Chapter 2 a special feature on "Identifying environmentally related tax revenues in Revenue Statistics". Chapter 3 contains a set of comparative statistical tables for years 1965 2018. Chapter 4 provides country tables with tax revenue and tax-to-GDP ratios broken down by selected tax categories and by level of government for years between 1990 and 2017 (section 4.1).[2] Two memorandum tables show how countries finance their social benefits, and report taxes and social security contributions paid by general government (section 4.2). Chapter 5, which is available on line only provides statistical tables with a detailed breakdown of tax revenues by country for years between 1965 and 2017 (section 5.1). Two memorandum tables show how countries finance their social benefits, and report taxes and social security contributions paid by general government (section 5.2). Chapter 6, which is also only available on line, attributes tax revenues to general government by the following sub-sectors: central, state; local and social security funds. It contains a set of comparative statistical tables for years 1975 2017 (section 6.1) and a second series of tables with a detailed breakdown of tax revenues by country for years between 1975 and 2017 (section 6.2).

Notes

[1] See IMF, *Government Finance Statistics Manual 2014* (Washington D.C.: International Monetary Fund, 2014).

[2] Because of space limitations, data are shown for selected years between 1965 and 2017. Data for years not shown are available online.

1 Tax revenue trends 1965-2018

Chapter 1 provides information on trends in tax revenues in OECD countries from 1965 to 2018, including changes in tax-to-GDP ratios, tax structures, taxes by level of government and non-wastable tax credits.

Revenue Statistics 2019 presents detailed internationally comparable data on tax revenues of OECD countries for all levels of government. The latest edition provides final data on tax revenues in 1965-2017. In addition, provisional estimates of tax revenues in 2018 are included for almost all OECD countries.[1]

Box 1.1. Revenue Statistics in OECD Countries – definitions & classifications

In *Revenue Statistics 2019*, taxes are defined as compulsory, unrequited payments to general government. Taxes are unrequited in the sense that benefits provided by government are not normally in proportion to their payments.

In the OECD classification, taxes are classified by the base of the tax:

- Income and profits (heading 1000)
- Compulsory social security contributions paid to general government, which are treated as taxes (heading 2000)
- Payroll and workforce (heading 3000)
- Property (heading 4000)
- Goods and services (heading 5000)
- Other (heading 6000)

Much greater detail on the tax concept, the classification of taxes and the accrual basis of reporting is set out in the OECD Interpretative Guide at annex A of *Revenue Statistics 2019*.

All of the averages presented in this summary are unweighted.

Tax-to-GDP ratios

Tax ratios for 2018 (provisional data)

New OECD data in the annual *Revenue Statistics 2019* publication show that on average, tax revenues as a percentage of GDP (i.e. the tax-to-GDP ratio) were virtually unchanged in 2018, with a very slight increase of just under 0.02 p.p. of GDP relative to 2017. This ends the trend of annual increases observed in the OECD average since the financial crisis in 2009, excluding 2016, which was a special case due to the one-off stability contributions in Iceland in that year.[2] The small change in 2018 was largely due to the fall of 2.5 percentage points in the tax-to-GDP ratio of one country (the United States, following the reforms described below) (Figure 1.1). However, due to rounding, the OECD average tax-to-GDP ratio was 34.3% in 2018, compared to 34.2% in 2017 (34.24 % and 34.26%, respectively).

Figure 1.1. Trends in tax-to-GDP ratios, 1965-2018p (as % of GDP)

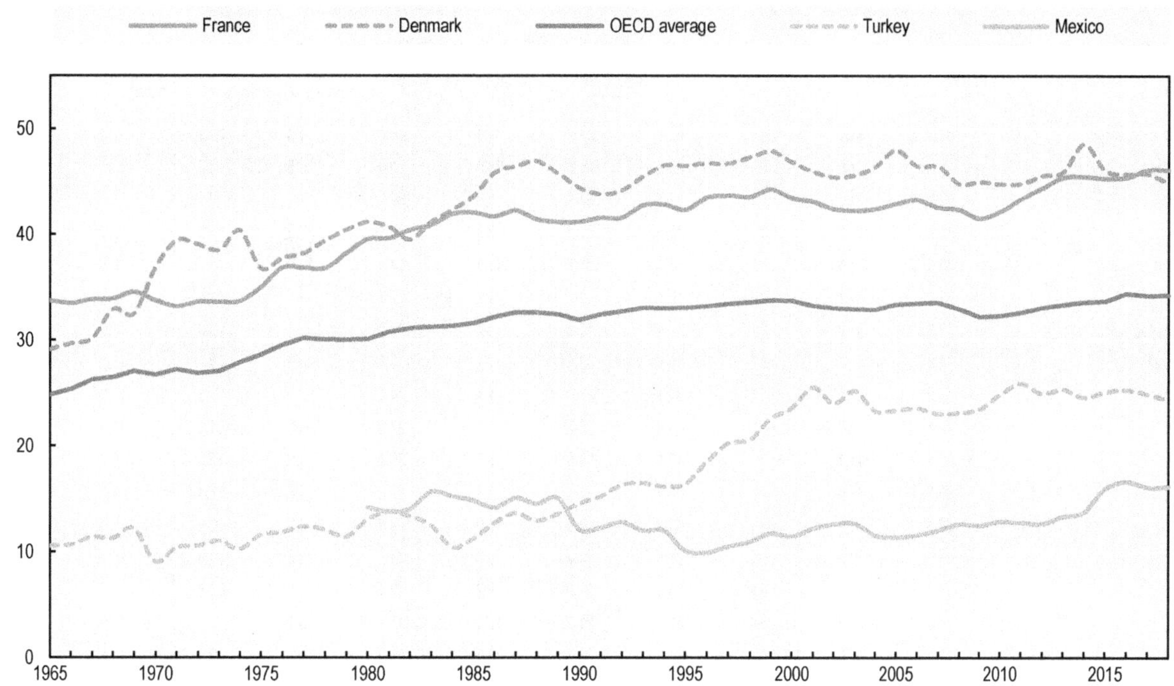

Notes: Data for 2018 are preliminary. The OECD average in 2018 is calculated by applying the unweighted average percentage change for 2018 in the 34 countries providing data for that year to the overall average tax to GDP ratio in 2017.

The 2016 OECD average tax-to-GDP ratio includes the one-off revenues from stability contributions in Iceland. Without these revenues included, the OECD average tax-to-GDP ratio in 2016 would have been 34.0.

Source: Table 3.1.

StatLink http://dx.doi.org/10.1787/888934054474

Table 1.1. Revenue Statistics: overview

	Tax revenue as % of GDP				Tax revenue as % of total tax revenue in 2017						
	2018p	2017	2016	2000	1100 Taxes on income, individuals (PIT)	1200 Taxes on income, corporates (CIT)	2000 Social security contributions (SSC)	4000 Taxes on property	5111 Value added taxes	Other consumption taxes[7]	All other taxes[8]
OECD - Average[1]	**34.3**	**34.2**	**34.4**	**33.8**	**23.9**	**9.3**	**26.0**	**5.8**	**20.2**	**12.2**	**2.6**
Australia	..	28.5	27.6	30.5	40.3	18.5	0.0	10.3	12.2	13.9	4.8
Austria	42.2	41.8	41.9	42.3	21.7	5.9	34.9	1.3	18.3	9.8	8.1
Belgium	44.8	44.5	43.9	43.5	27.2	9.3	30.5	7.9	15.2	9.0	0.9
Canada	33.0	32.8	33.2	34.7	35.7	11.4	14.1	12.0	13.7	9.9	3.2
Chile	21.1	20.1	20.1	18.8	9.7	21.1	7.3	5.4	41.6	13.2	1.8
Czech Republic	35.3	34.9	34.2	32.4	11.5	10.7	43.0	1.4	22.0	10.9	0.5
Denmark[2]	44.9	45.7	45.7	46.9	52.9	7.2	0.1	3.9	20.7	11.1	4.1
Estonia	33.2	32.8	33.5	31.1	17.4	4.7	34.1	0.7	27.8	14.8	0.5
Finland	42.7	43.3	44.0	45.8	29.2	6.3	27.8	3.6	21.0	11.8	0.2
France[2]	46.1	46.1	45.4	43.4	18.6	5.1	36.4	9.5	15.3	9.2	6.0
Germany[3]	38.2	37.6	37.4	36.2	27.1	5.4	37.9	2.7	18.4	7.9	0.6
Greece	38.7	38.9	38.7	33.4	16.0	5.0	29.6	7.9	20.9	18.5	2.1
Hungary	36.6	38.2	39.1	38.5	14.2	5.5	32.1	2.8	24.8	18.2	2.5
Iceland	36.7	37.5	50.8	36.0	38.0	8.2	9.1	5.5	23.8	9.9	5.5
Ireland	22.3	22.5	23.4	30.8	31.2	12.3	17.1	5.7	19.6	12.8	1.3
Israel[4]	31.1	32.5	31.1	34.9	20.7	10.1	16.2	10.0	22.9	11.8	8.4
Italy	42.1	42.1	42.3	40.6	25.7	5.0	30.3	6.2	14.8	13.6	4.4
Japan	..	31.4	30.7	25.8	18.8	11.8	39.9	8.2	13.0	8.0	0.2
Korea	28.4	26.9	26.2	21.5	17.9	14.2	25.7	11.7	16.0	11.8	2.8
Latvia	30.7	31.1	31.2	29.1	21.1	5.1	26.9	3.3	25.7	17.3	0.6
Lithuania[2]	30.3	29.5	29.7	30.8	13.1	5.1	41.5	1.0	26.6	12.0	0.8
Luxembourg	40.1	38.7	37.9	36.9	23.6	13.6	28.6	9.6	15.9	8.4	0.3
Mexico[5]	16.1	16.1	16.6	11.5	21.4	21.8	13.3	1.9	23.1	13.2	5.3
Netherlands	38.8	38.7	38.4	36.9	21.6	8.5	35.7	4.0	17.4	11.7	1.1
New Zealand	32.7	32.1	31.7	32.5	37.8	14.7	0.0	6.0	30.2	8.3	3.1
Norway	39.0	38.8	38.7	41.9	26.5	12.5	26.6	3.3	22.1	8.8	0.1
Poland	35.0	34.1	33.5	32.9	14.6	5.6	37.5	4.0	22.8	14.1	1.3
Portugal	35.4	34.4	34.1	31.1	18.8	9.4	26.8	3.9	25.1	14.9	1.1
Slovak Republic	33.1	33.1	32.3	33.6	10.2	10.4	43.9	1.3	21.1	12.1	1.1
Slovenia	36.4	36.3	36.5	36.6	14.2	4.9	40.0	1.8	22.3	16.3	0.5
Spain[2]	34.4	33.7	33.3	33.2	21.8	6.8	34.0	7.5	19.1	10.2	0.5
Sweden	43.9	44.4	44.2	48.9	29.9	6.3	21.8	2.2	20.9	6.9	11.9
Switzerland[2]	27.9	28.4	27.7	27.6	30.3	10.7	23.6	7.6	12.0	9.1	6.8
Turkey	24.4	24.9	25.3	23.6	14.5	6.8	29.3	4.5	20.1	23.3	1.3
United Kingdom[6]	33.5	33.3	32.7	32.9	27.2	8.5	19.2	12.5	20.7	11.1	0.8
United States	24.3	26.8	25.9	28.3	38.7	6.5	23.0	16.0	0.0	15.7	0.0

1. 2018 provisional average calculated by applying the unweighted average percentage change for 2018 in the 34 countries providing data for that year to the overall average tax to GDP ratio in 2017. The 2016 OECD average tax-to-GDP ratio includes the one-off revenues from stability contributions in Iceland.
2. The total tax revenue has been reduced by the amount of any capital transfer that represents uncollected taxes.
3. From 1991 the figures relate to the united Germany.
4. The data for Israel are supplied by and under the responsibility of the relevant Israeli authorities. The use of such data by the OECD is without prejudice to the status of the Golan Heights, East Jerusalem and Israeli settlements in the West Bank under the terms of international law.
5. 2018 provisional: Secretariat estimate, including expected revenues collected by state and local governments.

6. Corporate income tax revenues for the United Kingdom are based on data provided in July; this was prior to revisions made to the historic Corporation tax data in September, so the revisions are not reflected here. For the latest UK Corporation tax data, please see www.gov.uk/government/statistics/corporation-tax-statistics-2019 the main revisions are explained on page 13 of https://assets.publishing.service.gov.uk/government/uploads/system/uploads/attachment_data/file/833371/Aug19_Receipts_NS_Bulletin_Final.odt.
7. Calculated as 5000 Taxes on goods and services less 5111 Value added taxes.
8. Includes 1300 Unallocable between personal and corporate income tax, 3000 Taxes on payroll and workforce and 6000 Other taxes.

StatLink http://dx.doi.org/10.1787/888934054645

Country tax-to-GDP ratios in 2018 varied considerably (Table 1.1), both across countries and since 2017. Key observations include:

- France had the highest tax-to-GDP ratio in 2018 (46.1%). Denmark, which had the highest tax-to-GDP ratio of OECD countries from 2002 to 2016, had the second-highest tax-to-GDP ratio in 2018 (44.9%). Mexico had the lowest tax-to-GDP ratio (16.1%).
- Of the 34 countries for which data for 2018 are available, the ratio of tax revenues to GDP compared to 2017 rose in 19 and fell in 15.
- Between 2017 and 2018, the largest tax ratio increases were in Korea and Luxembourg at 1.5 p.p. and 1.3 p.p. respectively. In Korea, the rise was due to increases in income taxes (1.1 percentage points, predominantly from corporate tax revenues following the increase in the corporate tax rate from 24.2% in 2017 to 27.5% in 2018), as well as small increases in SSCs and property taxes. In Luxembourg, the increase was predominantly due to higher revenues from income taxes (1.0 percentage points, split between personal and corporate income taxes) and smaller increases in property taxes and VAT. There were no other countries with increases of more than 1 percentage points. (Figure 1.2).
- The largest fall in the tax-to-GDP ratio between 2017 and 2018 was in the United States (2.5 p.p.). The decrease in the United States were due to the tax reforms implemented in the Tax Cuts and Jobs Act, which lowered the corporate tax rate from 38.9% in 2017 to 25.8% in 2018 and also reduced the tax wedge on labour income via reductions to income tax rates and increases in the standard deduction and the child tax credit. These changes lead to a 1.1 percentage point decrease in income taxation (0.5 pp in personal income tax revenues and 0.7 percentage points in corporate income tax revenues). In addition, there was a decrease in property tax revenues of 1.3 percentage points, due to the one-off deemed repatriation tax on foreign earnings under the Tax Cuts and Jobs Act, which increased property tax revenues in 2017.[3]
- Decreases of over 1 percentage points were also seen in Hungary (1.6 p.p.) and Israel (1.4 p.p.). The decrease in Hungary was due to a reduction in revenues from corporate income taxes (0.9 percentage points) as well as slight reductions in personal income taxes, social security contributions and VAT. There were no other countries with a decrease of over one percentage point.

Over a longer timeframe, the OECD average tax-to-GDP ratio was higher in 2018 than in 2008, when it was 32.9% of GDP on average. Across countries, the tax-to-GDP ratio was higher in 2018 than in 2008 in 26 countries. The largest increase was seen in Greece (6.9 percentage points) and increases of over 3 percentage points were also seen in Korea, Luxembourg, Portugal, Mexico, France and the Slovak Republic). Decreases since 2008 were seen in the remaining 10 countries. The largest fall has been in Ireland, from 28.5% in 2008 to 22.3% of GDP in 2018, largely due to the exceptional increase in GDP in 2015. Larger decreases were also seen in Hungary (2.9 percentage points), Norway (2.3) and the United States (1.4) (Figure 1.2).

Figure 1.2. Changes in tax-to-GDP ratios, p.p., 2017-18p and 2008-18p

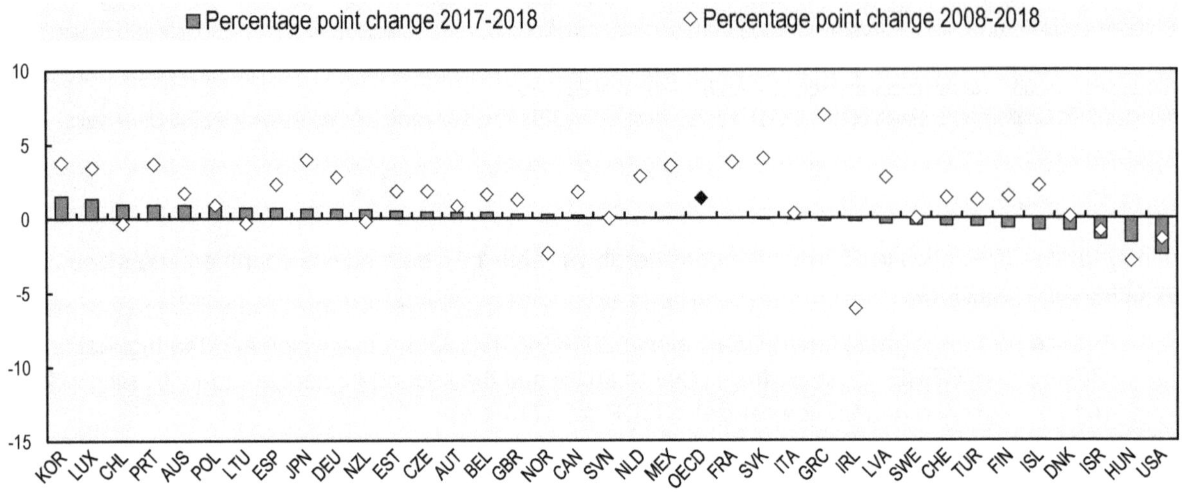

Note: Preliminary data for 2018 was not available for Australia and Japan. For these countries the comparison shown is 2016-2017 and 2008-2017 data.
Source: Secretariat calculations based on Table 3.1.

StatLink http://dx.doi.org/10.1787/888934054493

Changes in the tax-to-GDP ratio are driven by the relative changes in nominal tax revenues and in nominal GDP. From one year to the next, if tax revenues rise more than GDP (or fall less than GDP) the tax-to-GDP ratio will increase. Conversely, if tax revenues rise less than GDP, or fall further, the tax-to-GDP ratio will go down. Therefore, the tax-to-GDP ratio does not necessarily mean that the amount of tax revenues have increased in nominal, or even real, terms.

In 2018, 19 OECD countries had an increase in their tax-to-GDP ratio relative to 2017. In all of these countries, GDP growth was positive, although to a lesser degree than tax revenue growth. Of the 15 OECD countries that experienced a decline in their tax-to-GDP ratio in 2018, thirteen had higher levels of tax revenues in nominal terms than the preceding year, but the increase in nominal tax revenues was less than the increase in nominal GDP levels. Two countries (the United States and Israel) had positive nominal GDP growth and negative tax revenue growth; no countries experienced declines in nominal GDP (Figure 1.3). In Figure 1.3, changes between 2016 and 2017 are shown for Australia and Japan, where the tax-to-GDP ratio is not available in 2018. In both countries, nominal tax revenues grew faster than GDP, leading to increases in the tax-to-GDP ratio.

Box 1.2. Methodology: the tax-to-GDP ratio

The tax-to-GDP ratios shown in *Revenue Statistics 2018* express aggregate tax revenues as a percentage of GDP. The value of this ratio depends on its denominator (GDP) as well as its numerator (tax revenue), and that the denominator – GDP – is subject to historical revision.

The numerator (tax revenue)

- For the numerator, the OECD Secretariat uses revenue figures that are submitted annually by correspondents from national Ministries of Finance, Tax Administrations or National Statistics Offices. Although provisional figures for most countries become available with a lag of about six months, finalised data become available with a lag of around one and a half years. Final revenue data for 2017 were received during the period May-August 2019.
- In thirty-three OECD countries the reporting year coincides with the calendar year. Three countries — Australia, Japan and New Zealand — have different reporting years. Reporting year 2017 includes Q2/2017–Q1/2018 (Japan) and Q3/2017–Q2/2018 (Australia, New Zealand) respectively (Q = quarter).

The denominator (GDP)

- For the denominator, the GDP figures used for *Revenue Statistics 2019* are the most recently available in September 2019. By that time, the 2017 and 2018 GDP figures were available for all OECD countries.
- Using these GDP figures ensures a maximum of consistency and international comparability for the reported tax-to-GDP ratios.
- The GDP figures are based on the OECD Annual National Accounts (ANA – SNA) for the thirty-two OECD countries where the reporting year is the actual calendar year.

Where the reporting year differs from the calendar year, the annual GDP estimates are obtained by aggregating quarterly GDP estimates provided by the OECD Statistics Directorate for those quarters corresponding to each country's fiscal (tax) year.

Figure 1.3. Relative changes in nominal tax revenues and nominal GDP (%), 2017-18p

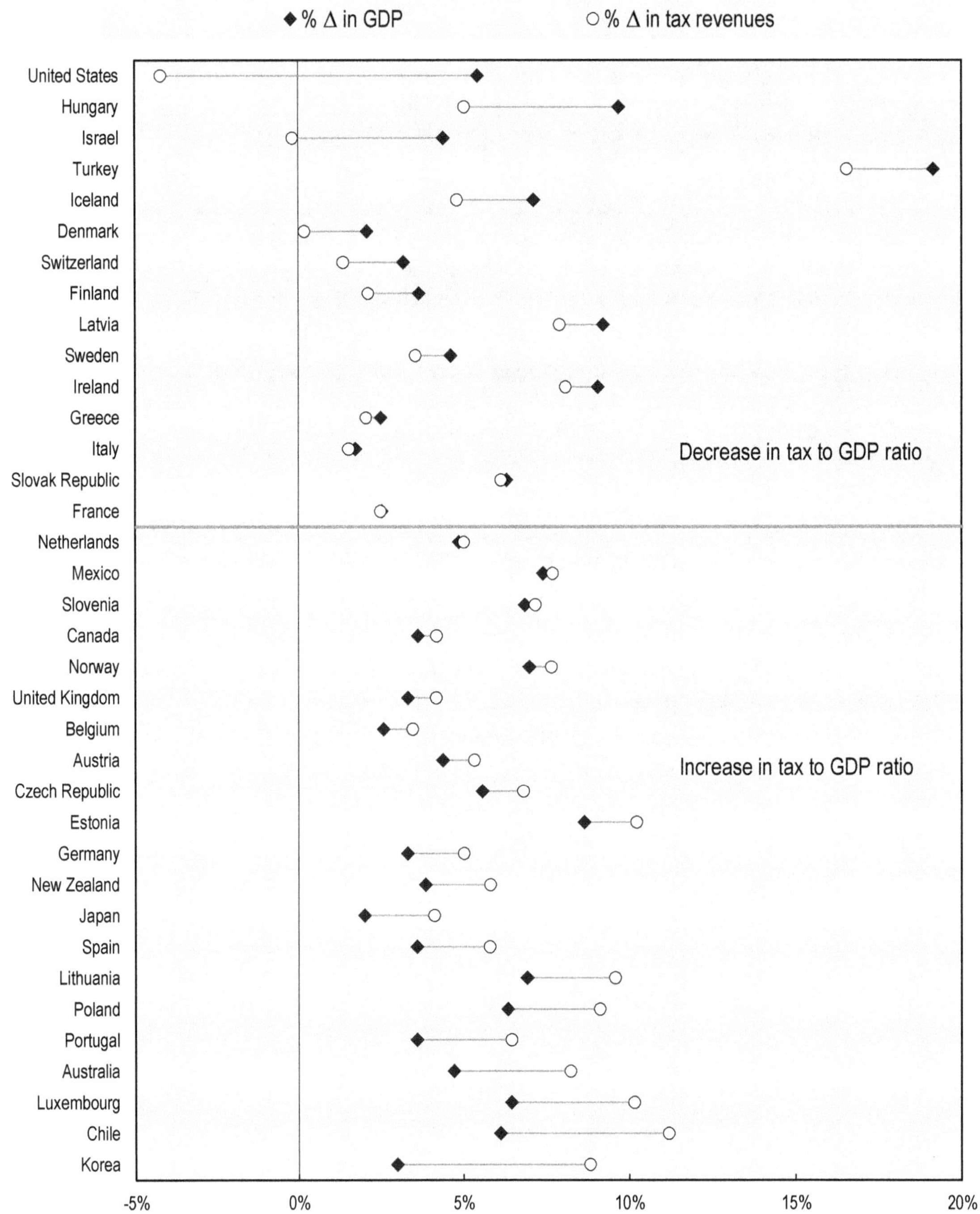

Note: Data for Australia and Japan show the change between 2016 and 2017, as preliminary data for 2018 was not available for Australia and Japan. Data for Mexico in 2018 show a Secretariat estimate, including expected revenues collected by state and local governments.
Source: Secretariat calculations based on chapter 4 (tax revenues) and table 3.19 (GDP).

StatLink http://dx.doi.org/10.1787/888934054512

Figure 1.4. Tax to GDP ratios in 2017 and 2018p (as % of GDP)

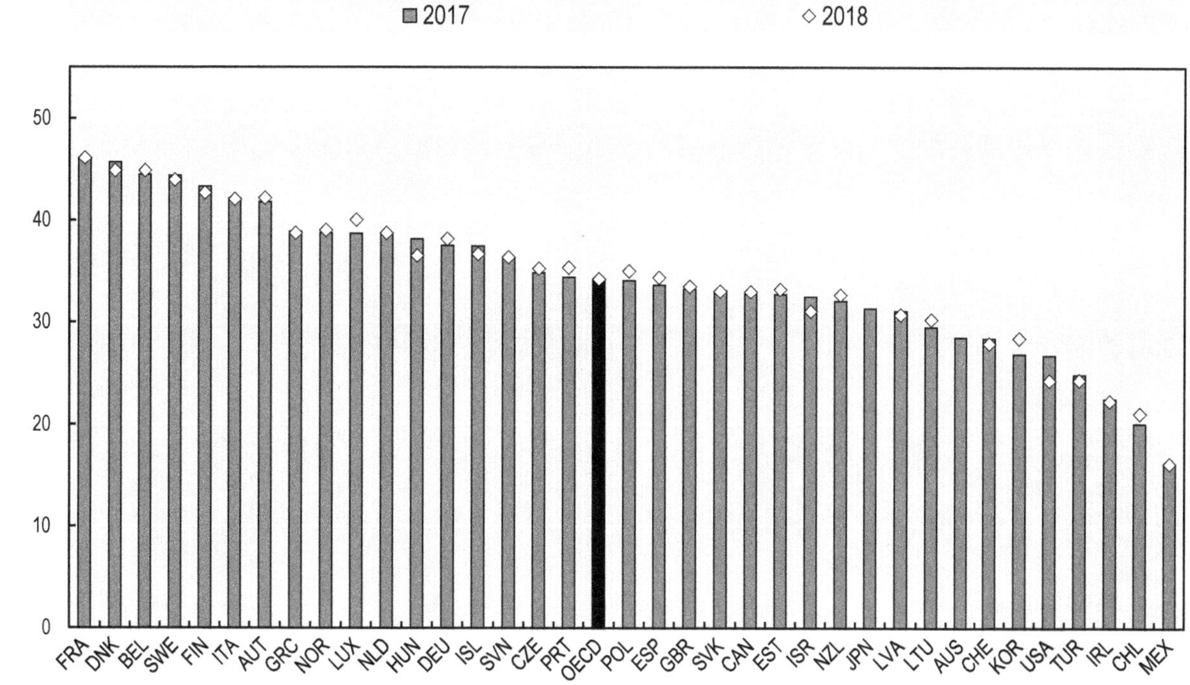

Note: Preliminary data for 2018 were not available for Australia and Japan.
Source: Secretariat calculations based on Table 3.1

StatLink http://dx.doi.org/10.1787/888934054531

Tax-to-GDP ratios for 2017 (final data)

The latest year for which tax-to-GDP ratios are based on final revenue data and available for all OECD countries is 2017 (Figure 1.4). These data show that tax ratios vary considerably across countries:

- In 2017, France had the highest tax-to-GDP ratio (46.1%), followed by Denmark (45.7%). Five other countries also had tax-to-GDP ratios above 40% (Belgium, Sweden, Finland, Italy and Austria).
- Mexico had the lowest ratio at 16.1% followed by Chile (20.1%), Ireland (22.5%) and Turkey (24.9%). No other countries had a tax-to-GDP ratio of less than 25% in 2017, but five other countries had ratios below 30% (United States, Korea, Switzerland, Australia and Lithuania)
- The tax-to-GDP ratio in the OECD area as a whole (un-weighted average) was 34.2% in 2017. In 2016, it was 34.4% when the impact of the one-off stability contributions in Iceland is included, or 34.0% if calculated without including these one-off contributions.[4]
- Relative to 2016, overall tax ratios rose in 22 OECD member countries and fell in 14.
- The largest increases in the tax-to-GDP ratio were in Israel (1.4 percentage points) and in Australia and the United States (0.9).
- The largest reductions were in Iceland (13.3 percentage points, due to the one-off stability contributions received in 2016), Hungary (1.0) and in Estonia and Ireland (0.8).

Between 2016 and 2017, the key changes in the tax-to-GDP ratio were largely driven by increases in revenues from income taxes (0.2 percentage points, evenly split between personal and corporate income taxes). Revenues from social security contributions, taxes on property and taxes on goods and services were unchanged, although within taxes on goods and services, the share of VAT increased slightly and the share of specific goods and services decreased slightly. Revenues from taxes on property decreased by 0.4 percentage points between 2016 and 2017, almost entirely due to the one-off stability contributions in Iceland in 2016.

Table 1.2. Tax structures in the OECD area, selected years (unweighted average as % of GDP)

Per cent

	1965	1990	2000	2007	2010	2013	2015	2016	2017
Total tax revenue	24.9	31.9	33.8	33.6	32.3	33.4	33.7	34.4	34.2
1000 Taxes on income, profits and capital gains	8.7	12.1	11.9	12.1	10.6	11.1	11.3	11.3	11.6
of which:									
1100 Taxes on income, profits and capital gains of individuals	6.8	9.7	8.7	8.2	7.6	8.0	8.3	8.2	8.3
1200 Taxes on income, profits and capital gains of corporates	2.1	2.5	3.2	3.6	2.7	2.8	2.8	2.9	3.0
2000 Social security contributions (SSC)	4.5	7.3	8.6	8.4	8.8	9.0	9.0	9.1	9.1
3000 Taxes on payroll and workforce	0.3	0.3	0.4	0.3	0.3	0.4	0.4	0.4	0.4
4000 Taxes on property	1.9	1.8	1.8	1.8	1.7	1.8	1.9	2.3	1.9
5000 Taxes on goods and services	9.4	10.0	10.9	10.6	10.6	10.8	10.9	11.0	10.9
of which:									
5111 Value added taxes	0.4	5.2	6.4	6.5	6.5	6.6	6.7	6.8	6.8
5121 Excises	3.5	2.6	2.9	2.6	2.7	2.6	2.6	2.6	2.5
6000 Other Taxes	0.1	0.3	0.2	0.2	0.2	0.2	0.2	0.2	0.1

Note: Percentage share of major tax categories in GDP. Data are included from 1965 onwards for Australia, Austria, Belgium, Canada, Denmark, Finland, France, Germany, Greece, Iceland, Ireland, Italy, Japan, Luxembourg, the Netherlands, New Zealand, Norway, Portugal, Spain, Sweden, Switzerland, Turkey, United Kingdom and United States; from 1972 for Korea; from 1980 for Mexico; from 1990 for Chile; from 1991 for Hungary and Poland; from 1993 for the Czech Republic and from 1995 for Estonia, Israel, Latvia, Lithuania, the Slovak Republic and Slovenia. The figures for the 2016 OECD average includes the one-off revenues from stability contributions in Iceland.
Source: OECD (2019), "Revenue Statistics: Comparative tables", OECD Tax Statistics (database), DOI: http://dx.doi.org/10.1787/data-00262-en.

StatLink http://dx.doi.org/10.1787/888934054664

Tax ratio changes between 1965 and 2017

Between 1965 and 2017, the average tax-to-GDP ratio in the OECD area increased from 24.9% to 34.2% (an increase of 9.4 percentage points, with the difference due to rounding) (Figure 1.1).

Before the first oil shock (1973 to 1974), strong, almost uninterrupted income growth enabled tax levels to rise in all OECD countries. In part, tax levels rose automatically through the effect of fiscal drag on personal income tax schedules. From 1975 to 1985, the tax burden in the OECD area increased by 2.9 percentage points. After the mid-1970s, the combination of slower real income growth and higher levels of unemployment apparently limited the revenue raising capacity of governments. But during and after the deep recession following the second oil shock (1980), countries in Europe saw tax levels rise further, to finance higher spending on social security and rein in budget deficits.

After the mid-1980s, most OECD countries substantially reduced the statutory rates of their personal and corporate income tax, but the negative revenue impact of widespread tax reforms was often offset by reducing or abolishing tax reliefs. By 1999, the average OECD tax-to-GDP ratio had risen to 33.8%, the highest recorded level at that time. It fell back slightly between 2001 and 2004, but then rose again between

2005 and 2007 before falling back following the crisis. Taking these changes together the average tax level in the OECD area increased by 1.2 percentage points between 1995 and 2017 (Figure 1.1).

The OECD average conceals the great variety in national tax-to-GDP ratios. In 1965, tax-to-GDP ratios in OECD countries ranged from 10.6% in Turkey to 33.7% in France. By 2017 the corresponding range was from 16.1% in Mexico to 46.1% in France. The trend towards higher tax levels over this period reflects the need to finance a significant increase of public sector outlays in almost all OECD countries.

Tax structures

Tax structures are measured by the share of major taxes in total tax revenue. In 2017, the tax structures of OECD countries varied. Eighteen countries raised the largest part of their revenues from income taxes (both corporate and personal), eleven countries raised the largest part of their revenues from SSCs, and seven countries raised the largest part of their revenues from consumption taxes (including VAT). Taxes on property and payroll taxes played a smaller role in the revenue systems of OECD countries in 2017, both on average and within most countries (Figure 1.5).

Figure 1.5. Tax structures in 2017 (as % of total tax revenue)

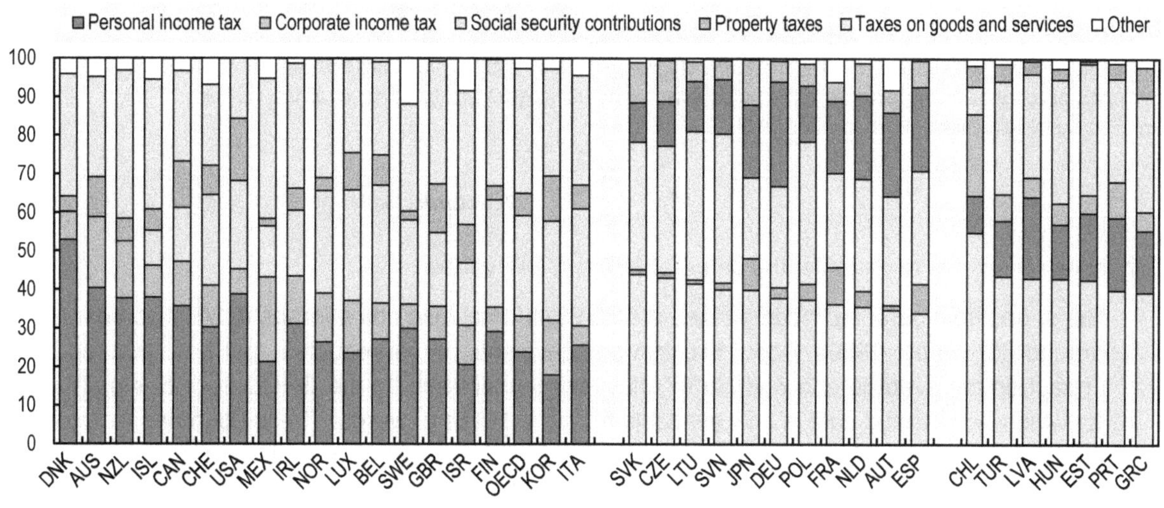

Note: Countries are grouped and ranked by those where income tax revenues (personal and corporate) form the highest share of total tax revenues, followed by those where social security contributions, or taxes on goods and services, form the highest share.
Source: Secretariat calculations based on data in chapter 4.

StatLink http://dx.doi.org/10.1787/888934054550

While on average tax levels have generally been rising, the tax structure or tax 'mix' has been remarkably stable over time. Nevertheless, several trends have emerged up to 2017 – the latest year for which data is available for all 36 OECD countries. These trends are discussed further below.

Taxes on income and profits

On average, in 2017, OECD countries collected 34.0% of their tax revenues through taxes on income and profits (personal and corporate income taxes taken together). Taxes on personal and corporate incomes remain the most important source of revenues used to finance public spending in 18 OECD countries, and in nine of them – Australia, Canada, Denmark, Iceland, Ireland, Mexico, New Zealand, Switzerland and the United States – the share of income taxes in the tax mix in 2017 exceeded 40%.

Figure 1.6. Trends in tax structures (1965-2017, as % of total tax revenue)

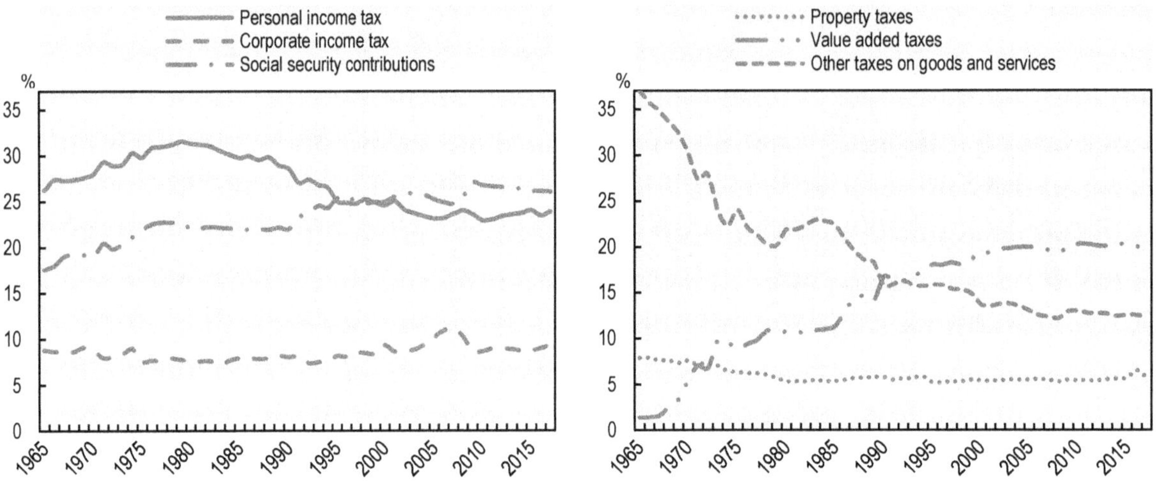

Note: The OECD average tax revenue in 2016 from main categories includes the one-off revenues from stability contributions in Iceland. This predominately affects the average revenues from property taxes, as a percentage of total tax revenues, in that year only.
Source: Secretariat calculations based on tables 3.8 to 3.14.

StatLink http://dx.doi.org/10.1787/888934054569

Within taxes on income and profits, the share of PIT and CIT varies:

- Revenues from personal income taxes are 23.9% of total taxes on average in 2017 compared with around 30% in the 1980s. About two percentage points of this reduction can be attributed to the impact on the average of a number of relatively new entrants to the OECD from Eastern Europe for which tax revenue data is only available from the 1990s onwards. These countries tend to have relatively low personal income tax revenues and high revenues from social security contributions, but this impact is observed in the post 1990 data only.
- The variation in the share of the personal income tax between countries is considerable. In 2017, it ranged from a low of 9.7% in Chile to 40.3% in Australia and 52.9% in Denmark (Figure 1.5).
- Corporate income tax revenues represented between 7% and 9% of total tax revenues, on average, throughout the period 1965 to 2003. They then increased to a high of 11.1% in 2007, before dropping to 8.6% in 2010, directly after the financial crisis. They remained at between 8.6 and 9.0% of total revenues until 2017, when they increased to 9.3% of total tax revenues, on average.
- The share of the corporate income tax in total tax revenues varied considerably across countries from less than 5% (Estonia, Italy and Slovenia) to 21.8% (Mexico) and 21.1% (Chile) in 2017. Apart from the spread in statutory rates of the corporate income tax, these differences are at least partly explained by institutional and country specific factors, for example:
  - the degree to which firms in a country are incorporated,
  - the breadth of the corporate income tax base, for example some narrowing may occur as a consequence of generous depreciation schemes and of tax incentives,

- the degree of cyclicality of the corporate tax system, for which one of the important elements are loss offset provisions,
- the extent of reliance upon tax revenues from the exploitation of oil and/or mineral deposits, and
- other instruments to postpone the taxation of earned profits.

Social security contributions

Social security contributions as a share of total tax revenues on average across the OECD accounted for 26.0% in 2017. They were highest in the Slovak Republic and the Czech Republic (43.9% and 43.0%, respectively). In contrast, Australia and New Zealand do not levy social security contributions.

There is also wide variation across OECD countries in the relative proportions of social security contributions paid by employees and employers (Figure 1.7):

- Seven countries (Chile, Denmark, Greece, Hungary, Israel, Luxembourg, the Netherlands, Poland, and Slovenia) raise more revenues from employee SSCs, whereas the remainder raise more from employer SSCs.
- The highest share of employee SSC revenues are found in Slovenia, at 20.8% of total revenues. Germany, Greece, Hungary, Japan and Poland also have employee SSC revenues of over 15% of total tax revenues. Denmark had the lowest share, at 0.1% of total revenues. Apart from Denmark, only Estonia had revenues from employee SSCs of less than 5% of total revenues.
- The highest share of employer social security contribution revenues are found in Estonia, at 32.4% of total revenues. Lithuania (28.2%), the Czech Republic (27.5%) and the Slovak Republic (25.6%) also had employer SSC revenues of over 25% of total tax revenues. Denmark and Chile had the lowest shares, at 0.03% and 0.2% of total revenues respectively.
- The highest share of self-employed or non-employed social security contribution revenues are found in the Netherlands and the Slovak Republic, at 8.6% and 7.8% of total revenues respectively.

Figure 1.7. Composition of social security contributions, as % of total social security contributions, 2017

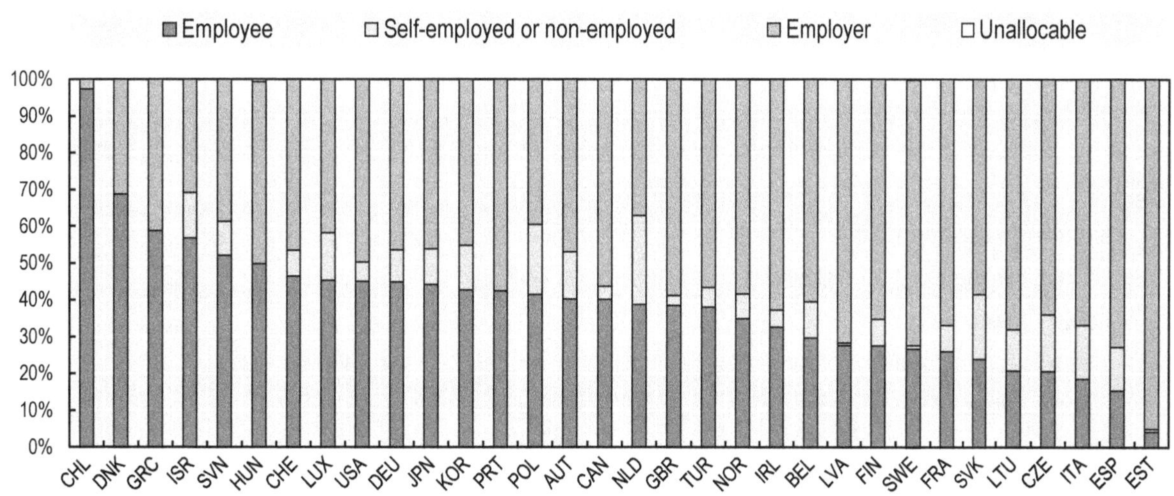

Note: Australia, Iceland, Mexico and New Zealand are not included within figure 1.7. Although Iceland and Mexico collect social security contributions, disaggregated data is not available. New Zealand and Australia do not levy social security contributions.
Source: Secretariat calculations based on data in chapter 4.

StatLink http://dx.doi.org/10.1787/888934054588

Property taxes

Between 1965 and 2017, the share of taxes on property fell from 7.9% to 5.8% of total tax revenues on average across the OECD (Figure 1.6). The United States had the highest share of property tax revenues in 2017 (16.0% of total revenues), although this was due to the one-off deemed repatriation tax which is recorded in 2017.[5] Australia, Canada, the United Kingdom and Korea also had property tax revenues that amounted to more than 10% of total tax revenues. By contrast, property taxes accounted for 0.7% of total revenues in Estonia, the lowest of OECD countries and were also less than 2% in six other countries (Austria, Czech Republic, Lithuania, Mexico, Slovenia and the Slovak Republic).

Consumption taxes

- The share of taxes on consumption (general consumption taxes plus specific consumption taxes) fell from 38.4% to 32.4% between 1965 and 2017 (Figure 1.6).
- During this period, the composition of taxes on goods and services has fundamentally changed. A fast-growing revenue source has been general consumption taxes, especially the value-added tax (VAT) which is now imposed in thirty-five of the thirty-six OECD countries.[6]
- General consumption taxes presently account for 20.8% of total tax revenue, compared with only 11.5% in the mid-1960s. In 2017, the vast majority of this was from VAT (20.2% of total tax revenues) (Figure 1.6)
- The substantially increased importance of the value-added tax has served to counteract the diminishing share of specific consumption taxes, such as excises and custom duties.
- Between 1975 and 2017 the share of specific taxes on consumption (mostly on tobacco, alcoholic drinks and fuels, as well as some environment-related taxes) have almost halved from 17.7% to 9.6% of total revenues. In 2017, excises were the largest single category of total revenues, accounting for 7.6% of total revenues (Figure 1.8).
- Rates of taxes on imported goods were considerably reduced across all OECD countries, reflecting a global trend to remove trade barriers.
- Nevertheless, countries such as Estonia, Mexico, Poland, and Slovenia (around 13%) and Turkey (around 22%) still collect a relatively large proportion of their tax revenues through taxes on specific goods and services.

Taxes by level of government

This section discusses the relative share of tax revenues attributed to the various sub-sectors of general government in 2017. The different sub-sectors are:

- Central government
- State government (federal and regional countries only)
- Local government
- Social security funds
- Supranational (EU countries only)

The guidelines for attributing these revenue shares to the different levels of government are based on the final version of the 2008 System of National Accounts. These guidelines are discussed in the special feature S.1 in the 2011 edition of OECD *Revenue Statistics*.

Figure 1.8. Share of general consumption tax revenues (left panel) and specific consumption revenues (right panel) as % of total revenues, 1975-2017

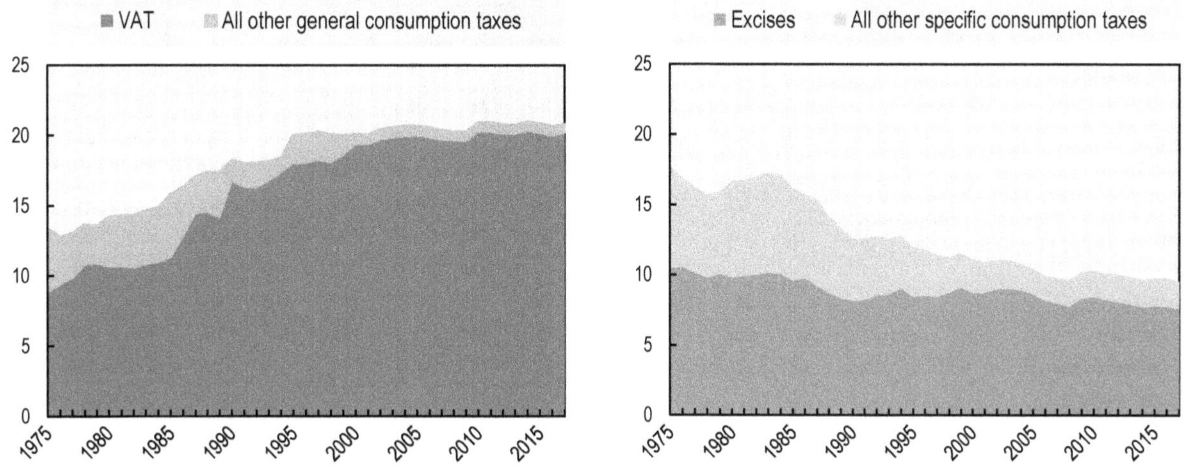

Note: The unweighted average for each year includes all countries which report revenue in the categories shown in that year. The OECD averages for 2016 include the one-off revenues from stability contributions in Iceland.
Source: Secretariat calculations based on chapter 4.

StatLink http://dx.doi.org/10.1787/888934054607

Revenues of sub-national governments

Eight OECD countries have a federal structure. Among these countries, central governments received 53.8% of total revenues in 2017 on average. The second-highest share of revenues on average was received by social security funds, which are a sub-sector of general government, at 21.0% of total revenues, followed by 17.3% at the state level and 7.7% at the local level (Table 1.3). However, within countries there was considerable variation around these means:

- In 2017, the share of central government receipts in the eight federal OECD countries varied from 29.5% in Germany to 80.6% in Australia.
- In 2017, the share of the states varied from 1.6% in Austria, 4.1% in Mexico and 10.8% in Belgium to 39.8% in Canada. The share of local government varied from 1.6% in Mexico to 15.3% in Switzerland.
- Between 1975 and 2017 the share of federal government revenues declined by nearly fifteen percentage points in Belgium and to a lesser extent in Canada and Germany.
- The share of federal government revenues increased in Austria by around 15 and five percentage points respectively. There was little change in Australia and Mexico.
- Of the seven federal countries with social security funds, five increased the share of revenue between 1975 and 2017. The exceptions were Canada and Mexico, where the share slightly declined between 1975 (1980 for Mexico due to data availability) and 2017.

Spain is classified as a regional rather than a unitary country because of its highly decentralised political structure. In 2017 the share of central government receipts was 41.3% compared with 15.2% for the regional government. Between 1975 and 2017, the share of local government receipts increased from around 4% to 10% and the share of social security funds declined from 47.5% to 33.1%.

Table 1.3. Attribution of tax revenues to sub-sectors of general government as % of total tax revenue, federal countries

	Supranational			Central government			State or Regional government			Local government			Social Security Funds		
	1975	1995	2017	1975	1995	2017	1975	1995	2017	1975	1995	2017	1975	1995	2017
Federal countries															
Australia	..	..	..	80.1	77.5	80.6	15.7	19.0	16.0	4.2	3.4	3.4	0.0	0.0	0.0
Austria	..	0.4	0.4	51.7	64.7	65.8	10.6	1.8	1.6	12.4	4.1	3.0	25.3	29.0	29.2
Belgium	1.4	1.0	1.0	65.3	60.1	51.4	..	1.8	10.8	4.4	4.8	4.9	28.8	32.2	32.0
Canada	..	..	..	47.6	39.1	40.9	32.5	37.1	39.8	9.9	9.8	10.3	10.0	14.0	9.1
Germany	1.2	0.6	0.6	33.5	31.4	29.5	22.3	21.6	23.5	9.0	7.4	8.6	34.0	39.0	37.9
Mexico	..	..	..	..	73.9	81.1	..	2.8	4.1	..	1.5	1.6	..	21.8	13.3
Switzerland[2]	..	..	..	30.7	31.2	36.5	27.0	24.3	24.6	20.3	17.7	15.3	22.0	26.8	23.6
United States	..	..	..	45.4	41.4	44.5	19.5	20.0	18.3	14.7	13.3	14.2	20.5	25.2	23.0
Unweighted average	1.3	0.7	0.7	50.6	52.4	53.8	21.3	16.1	17.3	10.7	7.8	7.7	20.1	23.5	21.0
Regional country															
Spain[1,2]	..	0.5	0.7	48.2	51.5	41.3	..	4.7	15.2	4.3	8.6	9.7	47.5	34.7	33.1

1. Spain is constitutionally a non-federal country but has a highly decentralised political structure.
2. The total tax revenue has been reduced by the amount of any capital transfer that represents uncollected taxes.

StatLink http://dx.doi.org/10.1787/888934054683

The remaining twenty-six OECD countries have a unitary structure. In these countries, an average of 63.8% of revenues were derived at the central level, with 24.6% accounted for by social security funds. A further 11.2% were raised by local governments. Among unitary OECD countries:

- The share of central government receipts in 2017 varied from 34.2% in France and 36.5% in Switzerland to 93.4% in New Zealand.
- The local government share varied from 0.9% in Estonia to 35.3% in Sweden.
- Between 1975 and 2017 there have been shifts to local government of 5 percentage points or more in five countries – France, Iceland, Italy, Korea, Portugal and Sweden and a smaller increase in the Netherlands. Shifts of 5 percentage points or more in the other direction occurred in three countries – Ireland, Norway and the United Kingdom.[7]
- Between 1975 and 2017, there were increases in the share of social security funds of 7 or more percentage points in four countries – Finland, France, Japan and Korea and corresponding decreases in four other countries – Italy, Norway, Portugal and Sweden.

Table 1.4. Attribution of tax revenues to sub-sectors of general government as % of total tax revenue, unitary countries

	Supranational			Central government			State or Regional government			Local government			Social Security Funds		
	1975	1995	2017	1975	1995	2017	1975	1995	2017	1975	1995	2017	1975	1995	2017
Unitary countries															
Chile	..	..	..	..	89.9	86.3	..	..	..	..	6.5	7.8	..	3.6	5.9
Czech Republic	..	..	0.5	..	57.7	55.4	..	..	..	..	0.9	1.1	..	41.4	43.0
Denmark[1]	1.0	0.5	0.3	69.1	68.4	73.2	..	..	..	29.8	31.1	26.4	0.1	0.0	0.0
Estonia	..	..	0.6	..	84.3	82.0	..	..	..	..	0.8	0.9	..	14.9	16.6
Finland	..	0.4	0.3	56.0	46.6	48.4	..	..	..	23.5	22.3	23.5	20.4	30.8	27.8
France[1]	0.7	0.4	0.4	51.2	42.6	34.2	..	..	..	7.6	10.9	13.3	40.6	46.0	52.1
Greece	..	0.6	0.5	67.1	66.4	67.4	..	..	..	3.4	2.0	2.4	29.5	31.1	29.6
Hungary	..	..	0.3	..	63.8	62.4	..	..	..	..	2.5	5.8	..	33.6	31.5
Iceland	..	..	..	81.3	79.2	73.5	..	..	..	18.7	20.8	26.5	0.0	0.0	0.0
Ireland	2.3	1.5	0.6	77.4	83.1	82.5	..	..	..	7.3	2.7	2.2	13.1	12.7	14.7
Israel	..	..	..	..	79.6	76.2	..	..	..	..	6.4	7.6	..	14.0	16.2
Italy	..	0.4	0.6	53.2	62.7	53.6	..	..	..	0.9	5.4	15.5	45.9	31.5	30.3
Japan	..	..	..	45.5	41.2	37.4	..	..	..	25.6	25.2	22.7	29.0	33.6	39.9
Korea	..	..	..	89.0	69.2	57.0	..	..	..	10.1	18.7	17.3	0.9	12.1	25.7
Latvia	..	..	0.6	..	43.5	53.2	..	..	..	..	19.5	19.2	..	36.9	26.9
Lithuania[1]	..	..	0.9	..	71.7	56.4	..	..	..	..	2.3	1.2	..	26.1	41.5
Luxembourg	0.8	0.4	0.6	63.6	66.5	67.5	..	..	..	6.7	6.5	4.1	29.0	26.6	27.9
Netherlands	1.5	1.3	1.1	58.9	56.0	60.2	..	..	..	1.2	3.1	3.0	38.4	39.5	35.7
New Zealand	..	..	..	92.3	94.7	93.4	..	..	..	7.7	5.3	6.6	0.0	0.0	0.0
Norway	..	..	..	50.6	58.4	84.1	..	..	..	22.4	19.6	15.9	27.0	22.0	0.0
Poland	..	..	0.5	..	61.2	49.2	..	..	..	..	8.5	12.7	..	30.3	37.5
Portugal	..	0.8	0.5	65.4	72.3	72.9	..	..	..	0.0	5.4	7.1	34.6	21.5	19.5
Slovak Republic	..	..	0.5	..	62.5	55.0	..	..	..	..	1.3	1.9	..	36.2	42.5
Slovenia	..	..	0.4	..	51.8	50.7	..	..	..	..	6.3	9.4	..	41.9	39.6
Sweden	..	0.4	0.3	51.3	46.9	52.4	..	..	..	29.2	30.9	35.3	19.5	21.8	12.1
Turkey	..	..	..	..	75.1	61.2	..	..	..	..	12.8	9.5	..	12.1	29.3
United Kingdom	1.0	1.0	0.5	70.5	77.5	75.5	..	..	..	11.1	3.7	4.9	17.5	17.8	19.2
Unweighted average	1.2	0.7	0.5	65.2	65.7	63.8	..	..	..	12.8	10.4	11.2	21.6	23.6	24.6

1. The total tax revenue has been reduced by the amount of any capital transfer that represents uncollected taxes.

StatLink http://dx.doi.org/10.1787/888934054702

The twenty-three EU member states that are also members of the OECD collect taxes on behalf of the European Union (EU). These include customs duties (Table 1.5) and Single Resolution Fund contributions (Table 1.6). For years prior to 1998, customs duties collected on behalf of the EU by national tax administrations of the EU member states are included under heading 5123. From 1998 onwards they are shown as a memorandum item since they represent a tax imposed by the EU and collected by national administrations.

Table 1.5. Customs duties collected on behalf of the European Union

Millions of national currency

	2000	2005	2007	2010	2013	2014	2015	2016	2017	2018p
Austria[1]	356	325	397	339	328	369	415	449	468	464
Belgium[1]	960	1 208	1 388	1 234	1 185	1 250	1 367	1 575	1 652	1 766
Czech Republic	..	5 586	6 443	6 573	5 556	6 970	7 912	8 033	8 271	8 296
Denmark	2 318	2 823	3 271	3 228	2 775	2 945	3 219	3 039	3 109	3 155
Estonia[1]	..	22	35	24	29	30	34	34	38	43
Finland[1]	129	148	199	151	166	170	165	163	174	174
France[1]	1 505	1 574	1 646	1 741	1 830	1 815	1 919	1 807	1 896	2 056
Germany[1]	3 394	3 433	3 972	4 234	4 251	4 608	5 195	5 089	5 043	5 018
Greece[1]	210	262	307	278	148	163	181	197	266	..
Hungary	..	26 572	27 981	25 004	26 337	31 947	38 960	41 620	45 403	63 431
Ireland[1]	208	226	273	229	247	275	327	311	334	325
Italy[1]	1 536	1 785	2 261	2 225	1 890	2 022	2 246	2 233	2 295	2 295
Latvia[1]	..	26	37	25	28	36	40	47	46	53
Lithuania	..	44	61	52	68	86	99	95	101	116
Luxembourg[1]	27	21	23	18	15	19	23	25	27	24
Netherlands[1]	1 310	1 265	1 679	1 732	1 756	2 046	2 266	2 353	2 420	2 498
Poland	..	1 285	1 760	1 627	1 977	2 316	2 823	3 292	3 485	..
Portugal[1]	204	145	185	177	144	149	158	174	187	226
Slovak Republic[1]	..	75	136	143	115	127	119	124	136	117
Slovenia[1]	..	34	85	59	52	52	52	53	54	57
Spain[1]	956	1 419	1 701	1 472	1 290	1 494	1 779	1 852	1 914	1 903
Sweden	3 450	4 327	5 099	5 412	4 976	5 737	6 243	6 044	6 225	6 498
United Kingdom	1 800	1 908	2 074	2 933	2 914	2 949	3 077	3 318	3 419	3 335

1. For euro area countries, the figures are in euros for all years.

StatLink http://dx.doi.org/10.1787/888934054721

In addition, the Single Resolution Fund (SRF) has been in place since 2015 and countries in the Eurozone are required to make SRF contributions under the Single Resolution Mechanism (Regulation (EU) No 806/2014). Contributions are paid on an ex-ante basis and contributions are transferred from the national authorities to the SRF. So far, contributions have been collected for the years 2015 to 2018. These contributions are included in *Revenue Statistics*, typically under category 5126, and their amounts are summarised in Table 1.6.

Table 1.6. Single resolution fund contributions collected on behalf of the European Union

Millions of national currency

	2015	2016	2017	2018
Austria	198	204	188	199
Belgium	235	278	250	285
Estonia	..	5	5	5
Finland	76	112	122	55
France	910	1565	1910	2277
Germany	1578	1760	1710	1986
Greece	..	98	89	..
Ireland[1]	..	175	98	107
Italy[2]	..	767	2273	1447
Latvia	8	7	7	7
Lithuania	10	7	7	7
Luxembourg	29	77	100	129
Netherlands	454	502	545	621
Portugal	..	145	130	132
Slovak Republic	..	22	18	19
Slovenia	16	13	9	10
Spain	681	719	671	728

Note: These figures may differ slightly from those published on the SRB website. These differences are primarily due to timing.
1. In 2016 the figure includes the 2016 payment of 99.12 and also a payment of 75.89 which was due in quarter 4 of 2015 but was paid in quarter 1 of 2016. The figures in this table were reported by the Central Statistics Office and are gross amounts and therefore due to adjustments will differ from the figures reported on the SRB website, which are net figures.
2. The "Bank contribution to the unique European Resolution Fund" amount includes not only the European but the National resolution fund yet, as required by Eurostat classification.
Source: Revenue Statistics 2019, supplemented by discussions with delegates.

StatLink https://doi.org/10.1787/888934054740

Composition of central and sub central revenues

Figure 1.9 shows the revenues from each major category of tax revenue for central and sub central governments. For federal and regional countries, the sub central level includes revenues received by both state and local governments. Figure 1.9 demonstrates that:

- Central government revenues in almost all OECD countries are predominantly derived from income and goods and services taxes, with a negligible share from property taxes.
- At the subnational level, revenue from property taxes provides a much larger share of revenues than at the central level, and accounts for over 90% of revenues in four countries (Israel, Ireland, Greece and the United Kingdom).
- By contrast, the share of income taxes and goods and services taxes is lower at the sub-central level, the exceptions being Finland, Luxembourg and Sweden, where over 90% of sub-central revenues are derived from income taxes.

Figure 1.9. Composition of revenues of federal or central government (left) and sub-national government (right), 2017

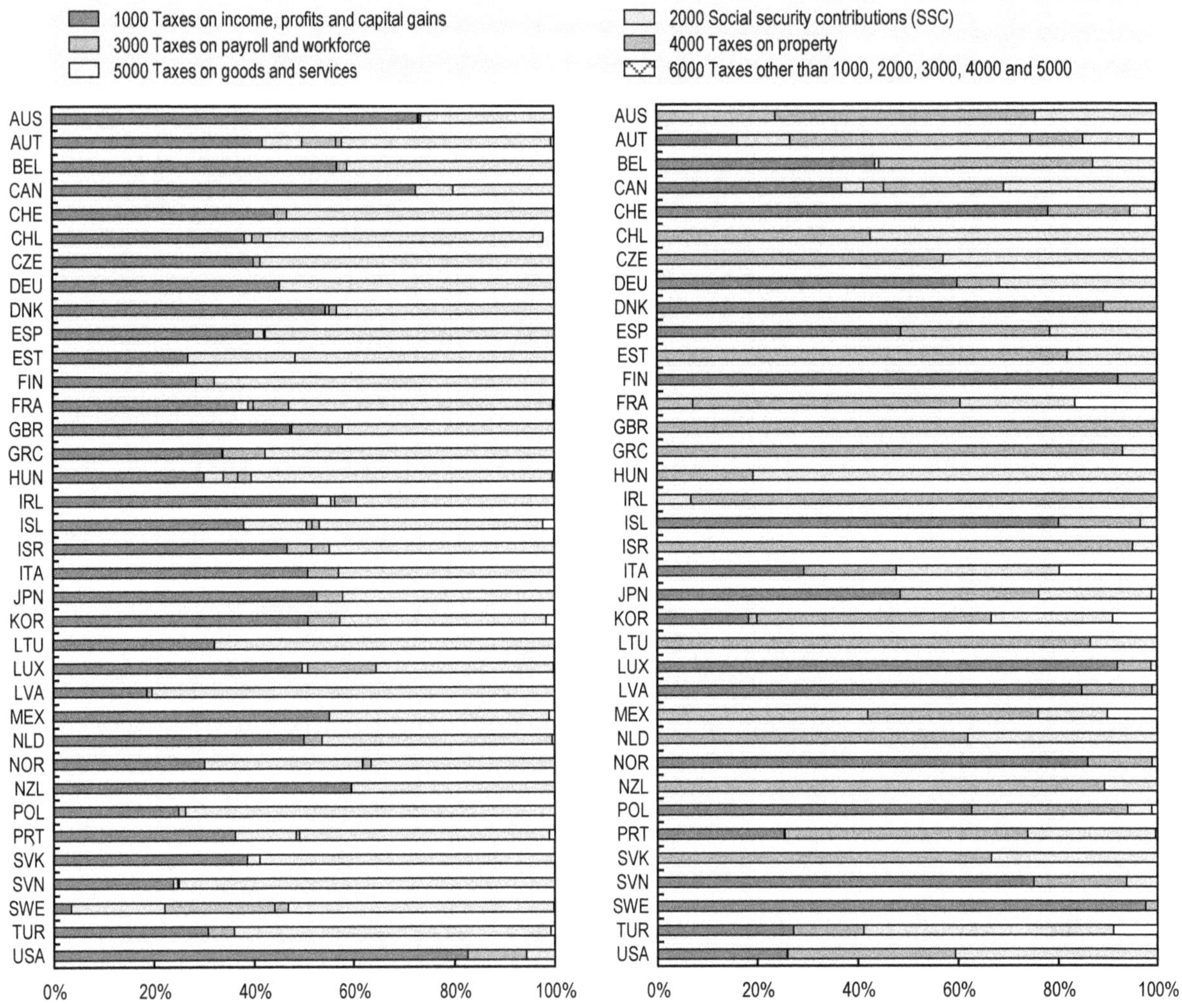

Note: The left-hand panel (a) refers to only those taxes which are classified as central government taxes. Social security contributions paid to social security funds are excluded. The right-hand panel (b) refers only to those taxes which are classified as sub-central taxes (local and (where relevant) state taxes). Social security contributions paid to social security funds are excluded.
Source: Secretariat calculations based on tables 3.16 to 3.18.

StatLink http://dx.doi.org/10.1787/888934054626

Non-wastable tax credits

There are two kinds of tax credits that apply to income taxes (both personal and corporate):

- Non-payable or wastable tax credits are those that can only ever be used to reduce or eliminate a tax liability. They cannot be paid out to either taxpayers or non-tax payers as a benefit. They are, therefore, the same as a tax allowance or relief.
- In contrast, payable or non-wastable tax credits can be partitioned into two parts. One part is used to reduce or eliminate a tax liability in the same way as a wastable tax credit. The other part can be paid directly to recipients as a benefit payment, when the benefit exceeds the tax liability.

The OECD methodology for classifying non-wastable tax credits is set out in paragraphs 19 and 20 of the *Interpretative Guide*. This states that only the part of a non-wastable tax credit that is used to reduce or eliminate a taxpayer's tax liability should be subtracted in the reporting of tax revenues. This is referred to as the 'tax expenditure component' of the credit. In contrast, the part of the tax credit that exceeds the taxpayer's tax liability and is paid to that taxpayer is treated as an expenditure item and not subtracted in the reporting of tax revenues. This part is referred to as the 'transfer component'.

Table 1.7. Effect of alternative treatments of non-wastable tax credits, 2017

	Non-wastable tax credits in billlions of national currency			Total tax revenue in billions of national currency			Total tax revenue as a percentage of GDP		
	Total value	Transfer component	Tax expenditure component	Net basis	Split basis (per current guidance)	Gross basis	Net basis	Split basis (per current guidance)	Gross basis
Australia	9.5	7.0	2.4	520.1	527.2	529.6	28.2	28.5	28.7
Austria[1]	0.3	0.1	0.2	154.5	154.6	154.8	41.8	41.8	41.9
Belgium	0.9	0.3	0.5	195.0	195.3	195.8	44.4	44.5	44.6
Canada[2]	11.6	10.5	1.1	692.2	702.7	703.8	32.3	32.8	32.9
Chile[3]	213.5	151.4	62.1	36 238.6	36 390.0	36 452.1	20.1	20.2	20.2
Czech Republic	35.2	8.9	26.3	1 751.2	1 760.0	1 786.4	34.7	34.9	35.4
Denmark[4]	4.2	0.2	4.0	995.3	995.5	999.5	45.7	45.7	45.9
France[4]	28.9	14.6	14.3	1 043.8	1 058.4	1 072.7	45.5	46.1	46.7
Germany	43.5	15.3	28.2	1 216.0	1 231.3	1 259.4	37.1	37.6	38.4
Iceland	2.8	2.3	0.4	979.0	981.4	981.8	37.4	37.5	37.5
Ireland	0.5	0.0	0.5	..	66.9	67.4	..	22.5	22.7
Israel[5]	1.6	1.6	0.0	411.8	413.4	413.4	32.4	32.5	32.5
Italy	10.3	1.2	9.1	726.6	727.8	736.8	42.1	42.1	42.7
Luxembourg[6]	0.2	..	..	..	..	21.4	..	..	38.7
Mexico	46.8	1.0	45.8	3 526.1	3 527.1	3 572.9	16.1	16.1	16.3
New Zealand	2.2	1.0	1.2	91.7	92.7	93.9	31.7	32.1	32.5
Norway	4.0	3.2	0.8	1 278.7	1 282.0	1 282.7	38.7	38.8	38.8
Slovak Republic[6]	0.3	..	..	..	..	28.1	..	..	33.1
Spain[4]	1.8	1.0	0.8	391.9	392.9	393.7	33.6	33.7	33.8
United Kingdom	29.5	26.0	3.5	655.9	681.9	685.4	32.0	33.3	33.4
United States	177.0	127.6	49.4	5 099.7	5 227.3	5 276.7	26.1	26.8	27.0

Note: In *Revenue Statistics*, the tax revenue data are reported on a split basis, unless indicated otherwise.

1. The children's tax credit is not regarded as a tax credit in the *Revenue Statistics 2018* and is treated entirely as an expenditure provision.
2. Some non-wastable tax credits cannot be split into the transfer and tax expenditure components. Their total values have been added to the transfer component.
3. In *Revenue Statistics*, the tax revenue data for Chile are reported on a net basis.
4. The total tax revenue has been reduced by the amount of any capital transfer that represents uncollected taxes.
5. The data for Israel are supplied by and under the responsibility of the relevant Israeli authorities. The use of such data by the OECD is without prejudice to the status of the Golan Heights, East Jerusalem and Israeli settlements in the West Bank under the terms of international law.
6. In *Revenue Statistics*, the tax revenue data for Luxembourg and Slovak Republic are reported on a gross basis.

StatLink http://dx.doi.org/10.1787/888934054759

Table 1.7 provides information on the non-wastable tax credits in 2017 for those countries reporting them in the *Revenue Statistics 2018* (though it may be that some countries with non-wastable tax credits do not appear in the table). It shows the amounts of the non-wastable tax credits and their two components together with the results of using the figures to calculate tax revenue values and the associated tax-to-GDP ratios. Table 1.7 also shows two alternative treatments:

- The 'net basis' which treats non-wastable tax credits entirely as tax provisions, so that the full value of the tax credit reduces reported tax revenues, as shown in columns 4 and 7.
- The 'gross basis' is the exact opposite, treating non-wastable tax credits entirely as expenditure provisions, with neither the transfer component nor the tax expenditure component being deducted from tax revenue, as shown in columns 6 and 9. This is the approach followed by the GFSM and the SNA.

Table 1.7 shows that, with some exceptions, the choice of method for reporting non-wastable tax credits has only a small impact on the ratio of total tax revenue to GDP. For the countries with available data, the differences between the ratios on a net basis and on a gross basis are one percentage point or more in only France, Germany and the United Kingdom, and between half a percentage point and one percentage point in Australia, Canada, Czech Republic, Italy, New Zealand and the United States.

Notes

[1] Provisional 2018 figures are not available for Australia and provisional figures on social security contributions in Japan are also not available as at the time *Revenue Statistics* was published.

[2] In 2016, Iceland received revenues from one-off stability contributions from entities that previously operated as commercial or savings banks and were concluding operations. The revenue from these contributions led to unusually high tax revenues for a single year and consequently, Iceland's tax-to-GDP ratio rose from 35.4% in 2015 to 50.8% in 2016, before dropping to 37.5% in 2017. This led to an artificial high in the OECD average tax-to-GDP ratio in 2016 of 34.4%. Without these one-off revenues in Iceland, the OECD average tax-to-GDP ratio would have been 34.0%, an increase of 0.2 p.p. relative to 2015.

[3] In 2017, U.S. taxpayers that had un-repatriated accumulated earnings abroad incurred a tax liability on those earnings due to the new tax law. However, U.S. taxpayers may pay any tax on the deemed repatriations in instalments over eight years so there may be a significant difference in the tax liability in 2017 represented in these figures from the actual receipt of tax revenue.

[4] See endnote 2 above.

[5] See endnote 3 above.

[6] The terms "value added tax" and "VAT" are used to refer to any national tax that embodies the basic features of a value added tax by whatever name or acronym it is known e.g. "Goods and Services Tax" ("GST").

[7] For 1975, please see Table 1.4 of *Revenue Statistics*.

2 Special feature: Identifying environmentally-related tax revenues in Revenue Statistics

This chapter provides a special study on identifying environmentally related taxes in OECD countries from 1995-2017.

Introduction

Environmentally related taxes are key policy instruments available to policy makers to influence environmental outcomes, in addition to their function in raising government revenues. They have received increasing attention from policymakers and researchers in recent years. Internalising the external environmental costs that remain unpriced by the market is a key element of cost-effective environmental policy (OECD, 2017[1]). There is a broad consensus in the economics literature that taxes allow this goal to be achieved in a manner that is environmentally effective, economically efficient[1] and socially inclusive (provided possible negative distributional impacts on vulnerable households are addressed through targeted measures). Many countries also use these taxes in complement to other measures to address pollution externalities.

Data on environmentally related tax revenue (ERTR) are used extensively in OECD country reviews (e.g. Environmental Performance Reviews, Economic Surveys), indicator reports (e.g. *Environment at a Glance*, *Green Growth Indicators*) and work on policy integration and structural policies.

This Special Feature builds on the work of the OECD's Environment Policy Committee (EPOC) to reconcile data on environmentally related taxes in the OECD *Policy Instruments for the Environment* (PINE) database with the OECD's *Revenue Statistics* and with Eurostat's National Tax Lists. Related work has focused on developing the OECD methodological guidelines on compiling accounts of ERTRs in line with the System of Environmental Economic Accounting, SEEA (OECD, 2019[2]).

Reconciling the data in *Revenue Statistics* and in the PINE and Eurostat databases will ensure coherence and comparability of data from multiple sources across countries and thus improve the quality of data used for policy analysis.

This chapter discusses differences in reporting and classifications between the key sources of data on ERTRs in OECD countries. It then highlights challenges in identifying ERTRs in *Revenue Statistics*, and presents information on environmentally related taxes in OECD countries based on the *Revenue Statistics* database and the PINE database. The chapter concludes by presenting proposals aimed at facilitating the identification of ERTRs in future editions of *Revenue Statistics*.

Definition of taxes and environmentally-related taxes

The OECD Interpretative Guide (OECD, 2018[3])includes a definition of taxes[2] which is consistent with the System of National Accounts (SNA) ((United Nations, 2009[4])), the System of Environmental Economic Accounting (SEEA) ((United Nations, 2014[5])) as well as the OECD PINE database (http://oe.cd/pine) and the OECD guidelines for compiling ERTR accounts (OECD, 2019[2]):

> *In the OECD classification, the term "taxes" is confined to compulsory unrequited payments to general government. (OECD, 2018[3])*

This definition also includes revenue generated from permit schemes (e.g. auctioning or selling permits or certificates for greenhouse gas emissions or water effluents), which are classified as "non-recurrent taxes on the use of goods and on permission to use goods or perform activities" in the OECD classification.

Identifying environmentally related taxes in Revenue Statistics

The OECD classification of tax revenues used in *Revenue Statistics,* set out in the Interpretative Guide at Annex A of *Revenue Statistics,* classifies taxes according to the economic function of their base (income, property, provision or consumption of goods and services), rather than according to the sector of the economy that they apply to or to the intended purpose of the tax. For example, a tax on fuels is recorded as an excise tax (category 5121) on the basis that it is a tax on a specific good or service, whereas revenues from recurrent motor vehicle taxes are recorded as a recurrent tax on the use of goods (5210). The wide variety of forms taken by environmental taxes means that there is no single, nor even a common set, of classifications that can be used to identify ERTRs in the *Revenue Statistics* classification. It is necessary to look beyond a classification according to the economic function of tax bases to identify these revenues within the *Revenue Statistics* framework.

In the economics literature, *environmental* taxes are motivated by internalising externalities through the alignment of tax rates with marginal external costs, or – more loosely – by using taxes to reduce environmentally harmful behaviour.[3] In practice, the identification of *environmentally related taxes* is made by considering the environmental relevance of tax bases ((OECD, 2006[6])), i.e. independent of the economic function of the base, and without requiring environmental motives for the application of the taxes, or the alignment of tax rates with marginal external costs. These considerations, in line with existing OECD work on this issue, yield the following definition of environmentally related taxes:

> *"Environmentally related taxes are taxes whose tax base is a physical unit (or a proxy of it) of something that has a proven, specific, negative impact on the environment." (United Nations, 2014[5])*

Ideally, environmentally related tax bases will comprise physical units that are directly linked to environmental pressures (e.g. emissions, pollutant concentrations). However, for practical or administrative reasons, these tax bases are sometimes not directly taxed. Instead, inputs or outputs of activities closely linked to environmental pressures (e.g. fuel consumption, ownership of cars) are used. In such cases and in line with existing approaches, these tax bases should be used to identify environmentally related taxes. (Annexe 2.A., drawing on Table 1 in (OECD, 2019[2])) provides a list of tax bases to identify environmentally related taxes. The list describes the currently identified tax bases with environmental relevance. There is no straightforward objective criterion that could be used to define what is "environmentally related" since such taxes cut across the standard tax classifications in the OECD Interpretative Guide.[4] Therefore, the list of environmentally related tax bases is a practical way to identify relevant taxes. The guidelines distinguish four environmentally related tax base categories: energy, transport, pollution and resources; with two sub-categories covering energy-related greenhouse gas (GHG) emissions (under *energy* taxes) and non-energy-related GHG emissions (under *pollution* taxes).

As ERTRs cross-cut the standard tax classification used in *Revenue Statistics*, the four tax base categories are not directly comparable to the tax categories in the SNA and *Revenue Statistics*. However, the large majority of ERTRs are likely to be included in the disaggregated tax categories on production and imports in the SNA (e.g. excise taxes, car registration taxes, pollution taxes) and on goods and services in *Revenue Statistics* (category 5000 of the classification, e.g. excise taxes, recurrent taxes on motor vehicle taxes, and revenues from trading permits).

Existing sources of data on environmentally related tax revenue

The key sources of data on ERTRs include *Revenue Statistics*, the PINE database and the Eurostat National Tax Lists. They are detailed below.

Revenue Statistics

Revenue Statistics provides harmonised and detailed data on all tax revenues for OECD countries from 1965 to 2018, although data for all countries is not available until 1995 and data for 2018 is still preliminary. More recently, the *Revenue Statistics* series has expanded to include three regional publications in Africa, Asia and the Pacific, and Latin America and the Caribbean. Data for all countries from 1990 (where available) is included in the *Global Revenue Statistics Database*. As of 2018, detailed tax revenue statistics are available for over 95 countries.

The wide country coverage and the use of the OECD Interpretative Guide to classify the data in all countries included in the *Global Revenue Statistics Database* provide a unique source of comparable and reliable tax revenue data for use in tax policy analysis and reform.

Although data on ERTRs does not fall within the common tax categories set out in the OECD Interpretative Guide, there is a high level of breakdown shown in country-specific taxes underneath the common categories set out in the Interpretative Guide. These country-specific taxes allow many environmentally related taxes to be identified in each individual country.

OECD PINE database

The OECD *Policy Instruments for the Environment* (PINE) database, which was established in 1998, hosts a unique set of detailed information on more than 3500 environmental policy instruments in over 100 countries. PINE currently contains information on six types of market-based policy instruments (taxes, fees and charges, tradable permits, environmentally motivated subsidies, deposit refund schemes and voluntary agreements) tagged into 12 environmental domains: biodiversity, land management, natural resource management, air pollution, water pollution, waste management, land or soil contamination, noise, ozone layer, climate change, transport and energy efficiency. For more information, see http://oe.cd/pine.

The greatest value of the PINE database is that it collects detailed and structured information at the instrument level, usefully complementing other sources of more aggregated statistics. For tax instruments, in addition to annual revenue, other information is included such as the tax base, tax rate and exemptions. Such information is indispensable for an evaluation of the environmental impacts of the tax. The information is collected via a network of country experts, mostly in government agencies. Identification of environmentally related tax bases and their categorisation follows the guidelines described in (OECD, 2019[2]) see Box 2.1.

Annex 2.B provides an example of the correspondence between data reported to the OECD PINE database and *Revenue Statistics*.

EUROSTAT National Tax Lists

Eurostat publishes revenue data for individual taxes (the National Tax Lists or NTL) imposed by 28 EU-member states as well as Iceland, Norway and Serbia from 1995 onwards.[5] Data are collected based on the European System of National and Regional Accounts (ESA 2010).

Information on the economic functions and categories of individual taxes is particularly helpful for this reconciliation exercise. Eurostat NTLs distinguish different categories of taxes: property taxes, recurrent taxes on immovable property, alcohol and tobacco taxes, and environmentally related taxes.[6] The recording of these data is fully compatible with the OECD definition of environmentally related taxes and the System of National Accounts.

The compilation of Eurostat tax lists is done with the National Tax Lists (the numbers presented here were extracted on 14 January 2019). The identification of the relevant taxes is done using the four different categories of environmentally related taxes: energy, transport, pollution and resources. In total, 650 tax revenue entries out of the 6700 are categorised as environmentally related.

Annex 2.B provides an example of the correspondence between data reported to the OECD PINE database and Eurostat NTLs.

Box 2.1. OECD work on SEEA-compliant ERTR accounts

The System of Environmental Economic Accounting (SEEA) is an internationally agreed statistical framework that integrates economic and environmental data in a systematic, consistent and internationally comparable way to provide a comprehensive and multipurpose view of the interrelationships between the economy and the environment.

Environmentally related tax revenue (ERTR) accounts form part of the SEEA. ERTR accounts can be seamlessly integrated with a large range of conventional economic, environmental and social data, thus facilitating international comparisons and integrated policy analyses. Additionally, ERTR accounts are disaggregated by industries and households and can therefore be used in input-output and other industry-level studies.

The OECD has a long tradition of working on environmentally related taxation and has recently developed practical methodological guidelines for compiling ERTR accounts (OECD, 2019[2]). These guidelines intend to support building global SEEA databases and further advancing the implementation of the SEEA. The OECD guidelines are in line with the SEEA and the System of National Accounts (SNA), and build on existing guidance for applications in countries. They ensure, to the extent possible, coherence with available national and international data sources and manuals, including *Revenue Statistics*, the OECD Policy Instruments for the Environment (PINE) database and the IMF Government Finance Statistics Manual.

Therefore, the ERTR accounts are generally aligned with *Revenue Statistics* by sharing a common definition of taxes, applying accrual accounting and recording revenue acquired at different levels of government. Nevertheless, ERTR accounts cut across the standard tax categories set out in the OECD Interpretative Guide, given their focus on environmentally related taxes. Thus, the tax categories in the ERTR accounts (i.e. energy, transport, pollution and resource taxes) are not directly comparable to most tax categories in *Revenue Statistics*. However, the ERTR are implicitly covered in the more aggregated tax categories on goods and services recorded in *Revenue Statistics* (e.g. excise taxes, recurrent taxes on motor vehicles).

Work on the OECD guidelines started in 2018 and provided an opportunity to reflect on the conceptual foundations of existing accounting methods and identify aspects that might deserve to be further developed in the future:

- greater focus on taxes levied on greenhouse gas (GHG) emissions;
- four *memo items* (i.e. information items not included in the total) on certain land taxes, taxes on oil and natural gas extraction, resource rent taxes, and elevated value-added taxes levied on environmentally related tax bases; and
- a common platform between compilers of the industry-level ERTR accounts and the instrument-level information reported in the PINE database.

The guidelines were successfully tested in four pilot countries. The next steps will involve the collection of ERTR accounts from OECD members and interested accession and partner countries, starting in October 2019, with a view to integrating such reporting into the OECD's regular data collection process under the auspices of the Working Party on Environmental Information.

Identifying environmentally related taxes in *Revenue Statistics*

A reconciliation between data on environmentally related taxes in *Revenue Statistics,* the PINE database and the EU National Tax Lists was conducted in 2018, drawing on ENV/EPOC/WPEI(2018)7. The concordances have been validated by countries (WP2 delegates and PINE contacts) and the revised results on ERTRs in *Revenue Statistics* and the PINE database are summarised below.

Environmentally related tax revenue data reported to Revenue Statistics and PINE

Differences between *Revenue Statistics* and the PINE database arise primarily due to (i) lack of suitable disaggregation of revenue streams in *Revenue Statistics* to allow ERTRs to be identified and (ii) generic labels of taxes in Revenue Statistics that do not permit a match to the more detailed description of the environmentally related tax in the PINE database.

In order to reconcile the differences between these sources, the following approach is adopted:

1. Identify environmentally related taxes in *Revenue Statistics* and, for EU member countries, in National Tax Lists submitted to Eurostat (hereafter Eurostat-NTLs).
2. Compare with the list of taxes in OECD PINE and construct correspondence tables.
3. Compare the level of the revenue reported.

The first step of the exercise is specific to each data source and was done independently. Once the lists of environmentally related taxes were compiled, the comparison with PINE tax lists, the building of the correspondence table and the comparison of revenue levels are done with all data sources simultaneously.

The identification of *environmentally related* taxes in *Revenue Statistics* is done using (i) the hierarchical nomenclature of the OECD Interpretative Guide (set out in Annex A of *Revenue Statistics*) and (ii) a keyword search through the names of the 8250 taxes included in the global *Revenue Statistics* databases (data was extracted on 13 December 2018). The following keywords were used to pre-screen potential *candidates* of environmentally related tax:

- **Energy**, CO_2, Power, Hydro, Oil, Coal, Gas, Diesel, Fuel, Electric, Petrol, Nuclear, Benzol, Pipeline.
- **Transport**, Motor, Car, Road, Air, Driving, Flight, Park, Driver, Highway, Aviation, Departure, Travel, Exit, Automobile, Boat, Vehicle, Passenger, Traffic, Dock, Rail, Ship, Tonnage, Plate, Tractor, Aero.
- **Pollution**, Hazard, Disposable, CFC, Lead, Insect, Plastic, Herb, Ozone, Fertilizer, Pesticide, Manure, Emission, Tyre, Waste, Sulphur, Nitrogen, PVC, Batter, Packaging, Packing, Rubber, Noise.
- **Resources**, Water, Hunt, Fish, Raw, Marine, Mining, Mine, Wood, Timber, Stump, Forest, Wild, Bauxite, Titanium, Gold, Silver, Metal, Logging, Protected, Fur, Animal.
- **Ecology**, Environment, Green, Natural, Climate, Kyoto.

The objective of the keyword search was to identify potential candidates for inclusion in PINE, and to easily spot *new* candidates in future releases of *Revenue Statistics*. Note that these *new* taxes could be either newly introduced, or a disaggregation of taxes that were previously reported under an aggregate heading.

Several categories of the OECD Interpretative Guide are important for the identification of environmentally related taxes. In particular, the classification of *Taxes on goods and services* (5000) is the most relevant. It includes all *Taxes and duties levied on the production, extraction, sale, transfer, leasing or delivery of goods, and the rendering of services* (5100), or *in respect of the use of goods or permission to use goods or to perform activities* (5200). In addition, some taxes of environmental relevance fall under *Other taxes* (6000), and few others concern some *Property taxes* (4000); e.g., forest tax, property tax on boats, payments for the change of use of forest land, forestry levies. Annex 2.B provides an example of the correspondence between data reported to *Revenue Statistics* and to the OECD PINE database.

Challenges and correspondence found

The main challenge for the reconciliation exercise is the aggregation of reported revenue streams in *Revenue Statistics*. Some countries report only at the third or fourth level of the OECD Interpretative Guide classification hierarchy without providing country-specific breakdowns. At these levels, the only environmentally related revenue that can be directly identified in the standard classification is found in the fourth-level classifications 5211 and 5212: *recurrent taxes in respect of motor vehicles*. This aggregation in reporting is partly due to the nature of the OECD classification of taxes which is organised according to the economic characteristics of taxes (e.g. income, payroll, property, goods), whereas the identification of environmentally related taxes is done according to the environmental relevance of the tax base (e.g. freshwater abstraction, pesticide use, energy products, waste management). Ideally, environmentally related information in *Revenue Statistics* should be available at the individual-tax level, with environmentally related taxes reported separately, i.e. the lowest level of the hierarchy, which is country-specific.

Even where country-specific breakdowns are available, some individual-tax revenue streams are reported as aggregates and grouped with other items. For instance, *Revenue Statistics* includes country-specific entries such as "Ecological taxes", "Taxes on pollution/resources", "Other environmental taxes" and "Other taxes on the environment", that do not allow the individual taxes to be easily identified. Similar issues arise in the Eurostat NTLs with generic entries labelled as "Pollution taxes", "Other environmental taxes", "Taxes and charges on environment and pollution". In these cases, the revenue level of multiple PINE entries was compared against these aggregated revenue streams, and a tentative breakdown was developed.

In addition, individual-tax revenue streams are sometimes reported under rather generic labels that do not allow the precise nature of the tax-base (e.g. "Environmental tax", "Environmental charge", "Environmental incentive fee" or "Ecological tax") to be reliably identified. In such cases, revenue streams from *Revenue Statistics* were considered for the reconciliation if they belonged to the OECD Interpretative Guide category 5000, while revenue streams from Eurostat-NTLs were considered only on the basis of their environmental category, independently of the label. The comparison of revenue levels with data in the PINE database allowed for some of the taxes with generic labels to be identified and even some mislabelled data to be detected (e.g., "Excise duties on petrol" in PINE and *Revenue Statistics* correspond to "Excise duties on gas" in Eurostat NTL for the Netherlands).[7] Slightly more descriptive labels of the reported taxes would facilitate the identification of the environmentally related revenue streams.

Another challenge for the reconciliation arises from differences across these data sources on how they report revenue at different levels of government. *Revenue Statistics* reports revenue collected by federal or central government, plus the combined aggregate of states/regions and the combined aggregate of local government revenues. The policy instruments included in the OECD PINE database are entered at the level of the government that introduces and controls the policy. As such, in the OECD PINE database, most of the revenue information is collected at the national level for nation-wide economic instruments (and some supra-national ones, such as European Union Emission Trading System (EU-ETS)), while sub-national tax revenue data are available for individual states or regions in respect of sub-national policies (e.g. Belgium).

The results of the 2018 reconciliation exercise are:

- Construction of a correspondence table, which maps individual tax entries among the three sources: *Revenue Statistics,* OECD PINE and Eurostat NTLs. The table contains about 700 PINE-*Revenue Statistics* and PINE-NTL correspondences. The remainder are unmatched entries, of which, about two thirds are sub-national policy instruments (e.g. India, United States) and one third are national instruments. Annex 2.B includes an example of the correspondences.
- The reconciliation exercise also allowed the inclusion of the revenue from auctioning of tradable permits, which had been previously excluded from the aggregates for most countries. In particular,

this concerns the inclusion of the revenue from auctions of permits under the EU-ETS. It is important to mention that the PINE database captures information on tradable permits separately to taxes; this is different to *Revenue Statistics* and Eurostat NTLs, where such revenue is reported as a tax item.

Calculation of country-level statistics

The reconciled list of taxes is aggregated at the country-level across distinct environmentally related tax categories (see Annex 2.A for a more complete list of tax bases):

- ***Energy***:
  - Energy products (fossil fuels and electricity) including those used in transportation (petrol and diesel).
  - CO_2 taxes
- ***Transport***: One-off import or sales taxes on transport equipment, recurrent taxes on ownership, registration or road use of motor vehicles, and other transport-related taxes. (Note that this definition excludes all taxes on automotive fuels.)
- ***Pollution***:
  - *Air pollution*: Taxes on e.g. SO_x and NO_x emissions.
  - *Ozone-depleting substances*: Taxes on specific substances, such as chlorofluorocarbons (CFCs), carbon tetrachloride, chlorofluoromethane (HCFCs) and other ozone-depleting substances.
  - *Water pollution*: Taxes on discharge of wastewater; pesticides and fertilisers.
  - *Waste management*: Taxes on final disposal of solid waste, on packaging (e.g. plastic bags) and other waste-related taxes (e.g. batteries, tyres).
- ***Resources***:
  - *Mining and quarrying*: Mining royalties, excavation taxes (e.g. sand, gravel).
  - *Freshwater*: Taxes on freshwater abstraction and piped water. (Fees and charges related to water supply are not included.)
  - *Hunting and fishing* taxes.

The correspondence of taxes and tradable permits to the environmental categories presented above is done according to the tax base of each instrument. Information from PINE on the introduction and discontinuation of instruments is used to impute zero revenues. In particular, the field "year of introduction" is used to impute zero revenue before the introduction of the instrument. The last year marked in the "year of revision" is used for those instruments which have been discontinued, and zeros are imputed for subsequent years.

Trends in environmentally related taxes in OECD countries

Environmentally related tax revenues (ERTRs) in OECD countries form a small but important part of total tax revenues, accounting for 5.1% of total tax revenues on a weighted average[8] basis and 6.9% on a simple average basis in 2017, with a range from 2.8% in the United States to 12.5% in Slovenia and Turkey. Similarly, as a share of GDP, ERTRs account for 1.6% of GDP on a weighted average basis and 2.3% on a simple average basis, with their shares in GDP ranging from 0.7% in the United States to 4.5% in Slovenia (Table 2.1).

Since 1995, the earliest year for which Revenue Statistics data is available for all OECD countries, most countries have seen a decline in ERTRs as a share of tax revenues. Because of this, both the weighted and simple average shares of ERTRs to total tax revenue fell significantly (from 7.3% to 6.9% of tax revenues on a simple average basis and from 6.1% to 5.1% on a weighted average basis). In 2017, ERTRs were lower as a share of total taxation than in 1995 in 26 OECD countries, with an average decrease of 1.7 percentage points in these countries. (Figure 2.1, Table 2.1). This fall may be due to a number of factors, discussed further in Box 2.1.

Figure 2.1. Environmentally related tax revenues in OECD countries, 1995 & 2017

% of tax revenues

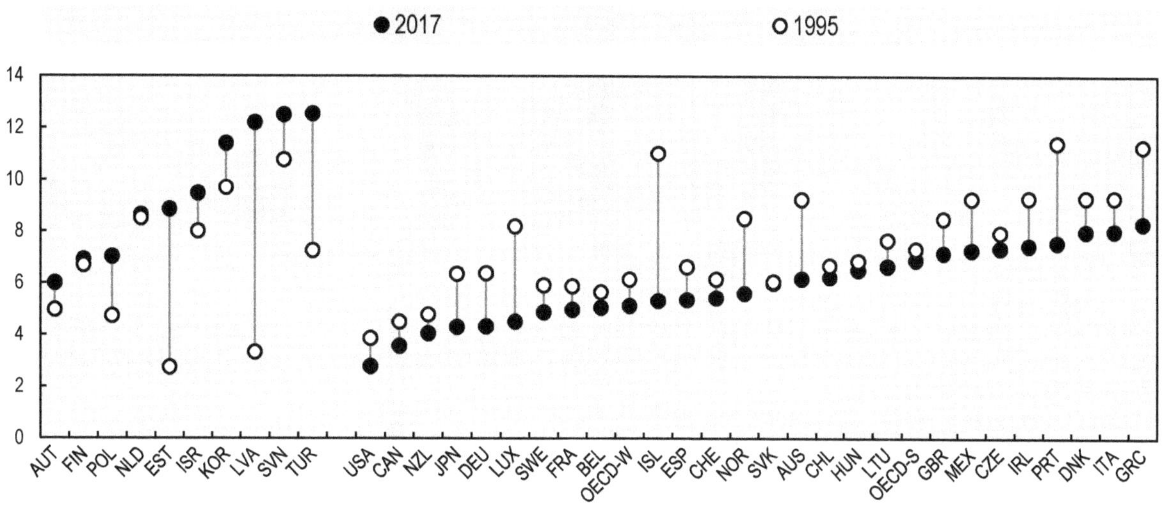

Note: OECD-W refers to the weighted average (as shown in PINE) and OECD-S to the simple average. For Canada, Korea and Israel, data for 2014 are used for subsequent years as data for later years are not available in the PINE database and ERTRs cannot be identified in Revenue Statistics with sufficient precision to be included. For the same reason, data for 2016 are used for 2017 in Australia and the United States.
Source: OECD (2019c) OECD Environment Statistics (database).

StatLink https://doi.org/10.1787/888934054778

The remaining 10 OECD countries had increases in ERTRs over the period as a share of total taxation, with an average increase of 2.9 percentage points in these countries. The largest increases were seen in:

- Latvia, which saw an increase from 3.3% of total tax revenues to 12.2%, due to higher energy taxes;
- Estonia, from 2.7% to 8.8%, entirely from energy tax revenues increasing; and
- Turkey, which saw an increase from 7.2 to 12.5% with roughly equal increases in energy and transport taxes.

Overall, the distribution of OECD countries around these averages has changed slightly. In 2017, the distribution was skewed to the left, with 25 OECD countries having ERTRs of between 4% and 8% of total tax revenues, whereas in 1995, the distribution was more even, with 22 countries having ratios between 6% and 10% (Figure 2.2). This indicates that there has not been a general shift towards ERTRs as a revenue source in OECD countries.

Figure 2.2. Distribution of ERTRs as % of total taxation in OECD countries, 1995 & 2016

Number of countries in each bracket

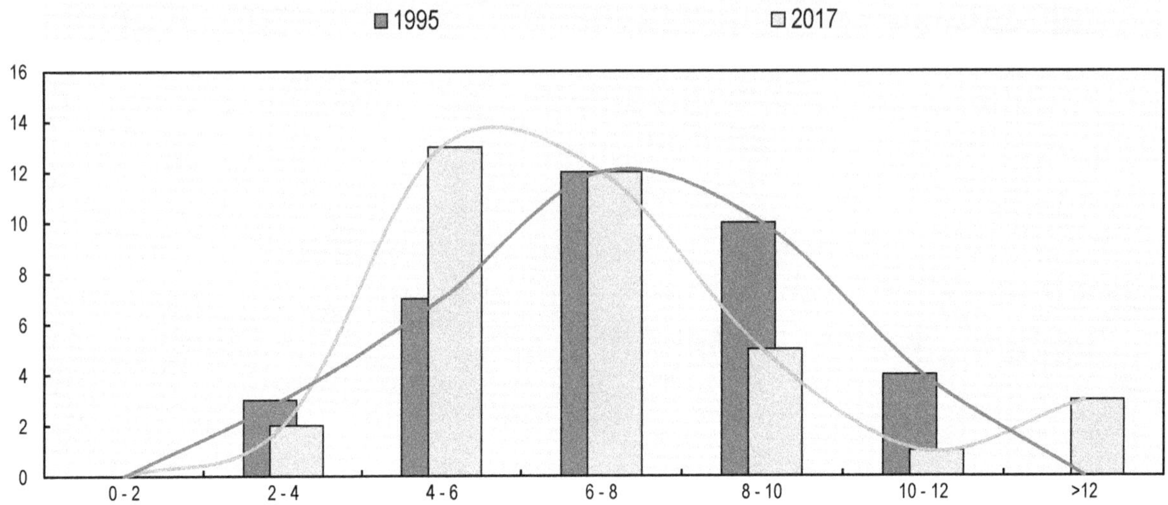

Note: For Canada, Korea and Israel, data for 2014 are used for subsequent years as data for later years are not available in the PINE database and ERTRs cannot be identified in Revenue Statistics with sufficient precision to be included. For the same reason, data for 2016 are used for 2017 in Australia and the United States.
Source: OECD Environment Statistics (database) (OECD, 2019[7]).

StatLink https://doi.org/10.1787/888934054816

As a share of GDP, ERTR in OECD countries have remained relatively steady between 1995 and 2017, with no clear trends emerging. On a simple average basis, ERTRs increased as a share of GDP in the late 1990s to a high point of 2.6% of GDP in 1998 and 1999 (which were was also the high point for the weighted average, at 1.9% of GDP), before decreasing relatively steadily until 2008, picking up in 2009, and slowly increasing since. Half of the OECD countries had ERTRs of between 2.1% and 3.2% of GDP in 1999 and between 1.7% of GDP and 2.9% of GDP in 2017, as shown by the interquartile range in Figure 3. The interquartile range decreased after 1999, before increasing slowly after 2008. The median followed a similar trend to the simple mean across the period, although increased more sharply after the financial crisis to a small peak in 2010, followed by a greater decrease (Figure 2.3).

Box 2.2. Environmentally related taxes as a share of GDP

The tax-to-GDP ratio is the principal indicator used in Revenue Statistics (see Box 1.2 in chapter 1 for further information). Taxes are expressed as a share of GDP both to allow comparability across countries and over time and to provide an indication of the scale of tax revenues against the production of the economy from which they were generated. The indicator is also used for individual tax categories, as unlike the share of total tax revenue, the share of a tax to GDP is not contingent on the levels of other taxes in the economy.

Although the indicator is a useful tool, it has some limitations when applied to ERTRs, as their tax base is not necessarily linked to GDP and may follow quite different trends. Ideally, the tax base for environmentally related taxes is a close proxy for the environmental harm itself such as the emission of CO_2 or a pollutant, or the purchase, import or use of a unit of fuel. Over time, GDP and environmentally related tax bases can decouple, for example as the economy becomes less carbon-intensive as a consequence of environmental policy or other developments. Such a decoupling has been seen, for instance, in several countries that have implemented environmentally related taxation, including Sweden and Norway. This will result in a fall in the share of ERTRs to GDP, but is in fact the intended outcome of such a policy. Similarly, a country with a carbon-intensive economy may have higher ERTRs as a share of GDP than a country with a less carbon-intensive economy, even if the tax rate on environmentally related bases is lower.

Other factors are also important in interpreting changes in ERTRs expressed as a share of GDP, which may result from a shift within the base of the environmentally related tax. For example, a structural shift from a high-taxed fuel to a lower-taxed fuel will result in lower ERTRs. Similarly, deployment of new technologies such as solar and wind power, or fuel-efficient heating technology, could result in a decrease in ERTRs.

Given that environmentally related tax rates are typically defined in physical units (e.g., per tonne) and hence are set in nominal terms. Without inflation adjustment, the value of these rates decreases in real terms over time. While some countries, for example Denmark, the Netherlands and Sweden have implemented such adjustments, most OECD countries do not yet apply inflation adjustments.

Finally, it is important to consider other indicators alongside the ERTRs-to-GDP ratio when evaluating a country's environmental policy. One alternative approach is to compare the level of environmentally related taxes to the environmental harm associated with the tax base. For example, the OECD's Taxing Energy Use and Effective Carbon Rates publications compare taxes on energy use and carbon prices resulting from emissions trading systems against a benchmark value for the climate damage caused by the use of the energy products. Indicators developed in these publications, such as the carbon pricing gap, provide important complementary information in understanding countries' environmental tax and carbon pricing efforts.

In 2017, revenues from ERTR in OECD countries ranged from 0.7% of GDP in the United States to 4.5% in Slovenia (Table 2.1). Across the period, Denmark had the highest level of ERTRs as a percentage of GDP from 1995 to 2011 (with the exception of 1998), and Slovenia had the highest level in 1998 and from 2012 to 2017. The lowest level of ERTRs as a share of GDP was seen in Mexico in 1995 and 1996, the United States from 1997 to 2004, Mexico from 2005 to 2014, during which time this share was negative in several years, [9] and the United States from 2015 onwards.

Table 2.1. Environmentally related tax revenues in OECD countries, selected years

	% of total tax revenue					% of GDP				
	1995	2005	2010	2015	2017	1995	2005	2010	2015	2017
AUS	9.2	7.2	7.4	6.5	6.2	2.6	2.2	1.9	1.8	1.7
AUT	5.0	6.7	6.0	5.8	6.0	2.0	2.8	2.5	2.5	2.5
BEL	5.7	5.7	5.2	4.7	5.0	2.4	2.5	2.2	2.1	2.2
CAN	4.5	3.7	3.8	3.6	3.6	1.6	1.2	1.2	1.1	1.1
CHL	6.7	6.2	5.3	5.9	6.2	1.2	1.3	1.0	1.2	1.3
CZE	7.9	8.1	8.4	7.8	7.3	2.8	2.8	2.7	2.6	2.6
DNK	9.3	10.5	9.2	8.5	8.0	4.3	5.1	4.1	4.0	3.7
EST	2.7	7.6	8.8	8.3	8.8	1.0	2.3	2.9	2.8	2.9
FIN	6.7	7.2	6.7	6.7	6.9	3.0	3.0	2.7	2.9	3.0
FRA	5.9	5.3	5.1	4.9	5.0	2.5	2.3	2.1	2.3	2.3
DEU	6.4	7.1	6.1	5.2	4.3	2.3	2.4	2.1	1.9	1.6
GRC	11.3	6.5	8.1	8.7	8.3	3.2	2.1	2.6	3.2	3.2
HUN	6.8	7.7	7.8	6.7	6.5	2.8	2.8	2.9	2.6	2.5
ISL	11.0	7.7	6.3	5.5	5.3	3.4	3.0	2.0	1.9	2.0
IRL	9.3	8.4	9.0	8.3	7.4	2.9	2.5	2.4	1.9	1.7
ISR	8.0	8.8	10.7	9.5	9.5	2.8	3.0	3.3	2.9	2.9
ITA	9.3	7.5	6.8	8.0	8.0	3.6	2.9	2.8	3.4	3.4
JPN	6.3	6.4	5.8	4.4	4.3	1.7	1.7	1.5	1.4	1.3
KOR	9.7	11.8	11.2	11.4	11.4	1.9	2.7	2.6	2.8	2.8
LVA	3.3	9.3	11.8	13.1	12.2	1.0	2.6	3.3	3.8	3.7
LTU	7.7	8.1	6.5	6.5	6.6	2.1	2.4	1.8	1.9	2.0
LUX	8.2	7.9	6.5	5.0	4.5	2.8	3.0	2.4	1.9	1.7
MEX	9.3	3.4	-1.6	8.6	7.3	0.9	0.4	-0.2	1.4	1.2
NLD	8.5	10.3	9.9	9.2	8.6	3.2	3.6	3.5	3.4	3.3
NZL	4.8	3.9	4.4	4.4	4.0	1.7	1.4	1.3	1.4	1.3
NOR	8.5	6.4	5.9	5.8	5.6	3.4	2.7	2.5	2.2	2.2
POL	4.7	7.7	7.6	7.6	7.0	1.7	2.5	2.4	2.5	2.4
PRT	11.4	9.4	8.0	7.0	7.6	3.3	2.9	2.4	2.4	2.6
SVK	6.1	8.0	7.2	6.2	6.0	2.4	2.5	2.0	2.0	2.0
SVN	10.8	8.6	10.2	12.8	12.5	4.1	3.3	3.8	4.7	4.5
ESP	6.6	5.7	5.5	5.7	5.4	2.1	2.0	1.8	1.9	1.8
SWE	5.9	5.8	6.0	5.1	4.9	2.7	2.7	2.6	2.2	2.1
CHE	6.2	7.6	6.5	6.0	5.4	1.6	2.0	1.7	1.7	1.5
TUR	7.2	17.0	15.0	13.2	12.5	1.2	4.0	3.7	3.3	3.1
GBR	8.5	6.9	7.7	7.6	7.2	2.5	2.3	2.5	2.4	2.4
USA	3.8	3.3	3.4	2.8	2.8	1.0	0.9	0.8	0.7	0.7
OECD-W	6.1	5.9	5.7	5.4	5.1	1.8	1.8	1.6	1.7	1.6
OECD-S	7.3	7.5	7.2	7.1	6.9	2.4	2.5	2.3	2.4	2.3

Note: OECD-W refers to the weighted average and OECD-S to the simple average. For Canada, Korea and Israel, data for 2014 are used for subsequent years as data for later years are not available in the PINE database and ERTRs cannot be identified in Revenue Statistics with sufficient precision to be included. For the same reason, data for 2016 are used for 2017 in Australia and the United States.
Source: OECD Environment Statistics (database) (OECD, 2019[7]).

StatLink https://doi.org/10.1787/888934054797

In monetary terms, the greatest amount of tax revenues, in USD adjusted for purchasing power parity, were raised by the United States, at USD 121 229 million in 2016 (2017 data are not available). Italy had the second highest revenues from ERTRs at USD 69 879 million in 2017, and three other countries (Japan, Turkey and the United Kingdom) also had revenues of greater than USD 60 000 million (Table 2.2).

Figure 2.3. Distribution of ERTRs over time in OECD countries

% of GDP

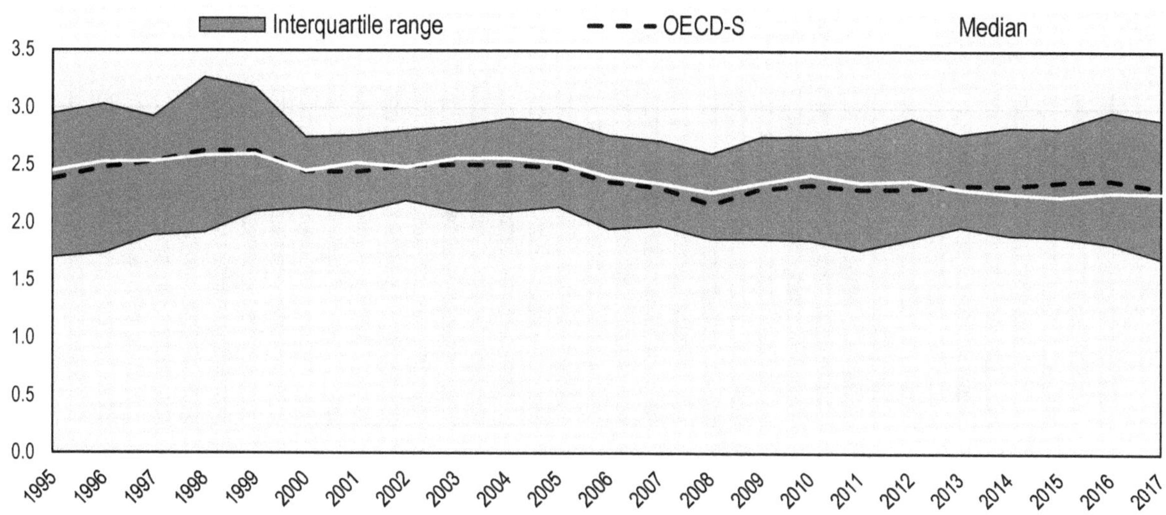

Note: OECD-S refers to the simple average. For Canada, Korea and Israel, data for 2014 are used for subsequent years as data for later years are not available in the PINE database and ERTRs cannot be identified in Revenue Statistics with sufficient precision to be included. For the same reason, data for 2016 are used for 2017 in Australia and the United States.
Source: OECD Environment Statistics (database) (OECD, 2019[7]).

StatLink https://doi.org/10.1787/888934054854

The greatest share of ERTRs in OECD countries in 2017 comes from taxes on energy, predominantly on road fuels, with this share accounting for 71% of total revenues on both a simple and weighted average basis, and over 50% of total ERTRs in all countries (Figure 2.4).

Transport taxes accounted for the second largest share of ERTR in 2017 (both on average, at 26% weighted and 25% unweighted, and in every country except Estonia, France, Lithuania, the Slovak Republic and Slovenia). Pollution and resource taxes play a more minor role: in all but eight OECD countries (Czech Republic, Estonia, France, Iceland, Lithuania, Netherlands, Slovak Republic, Slovenia) they accounted for less than 5% of ERTRs in 2017.

The situation in 1995 was relatively similar: energy taxes then played the biggest role in the composition of ERTRs, at 73% on a weighted average basis and 70% on a simple average basis, although they were under 50% of ERTRs in five countries (Figure 4). Transport taxes accounted for a slightly lower proportion, at 26% (weighted) and 24% (unweighted) on average.

Figure 2.4. Composition of ERTRs in OECD countries in 2017

% of all ERTR

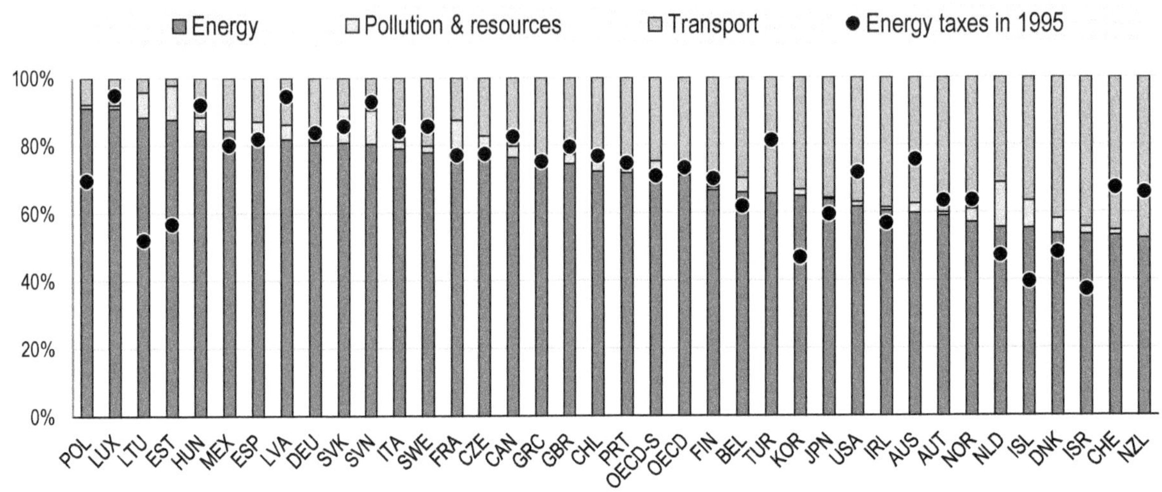

Note: OECD-W refers to the weighted average and OECD-S to the simple average. For Canada, Korea and Israel, data for 2014 are used for subsequent years as data for later years are not available in the PINE database and ERTRs cannot be identified in Revenue Statistics with sufficient precision to be included. For the same reason, data for 2016 are used for 2017 in Australia and the United States.
Source: OECD Environment Statistics (database) (OECD, 2019[7]).

StatLink https://doi.org/10.1787/888934054873

On both a weighted and a simple average basis, there has been a shift towards taxes on energy following the recent financial crisis and away from transport taxes. While revenues from both dropped as a share of GDP in 2008 and 2009, revenues from energy taxes recovered to pre-crisis levels relatively quickly and have increased slowly since. Revenues from transport taxes have not recovered to the same extent and, on a simple average basis, represent a comparatively lower share of total ERTRs, on average, in 2017 than earlier in the period. OECD countries have become more similar, in having a higher share of revenues from energy rather than transport taxes in 2017 compared to 1995.

Finally, taxes on pollution and natural resources represent only a small portion of ERTRs in most countries and on average. This could change in the future if countries start placing a greater emphasis on addressing water pollution, sustainable resource use or conservation of biodiversity.

While comparisons of ERTRs in OECD countries provide a useful starting point for analysing the impact of environmental taxation, comparing only the levels of revenues does not provide the full picture of a country's environmental policy as it does not provide information on the levels of tax rates or the exemptions applied. Other parts of the OECD PINE database, including information on tax rates and exemptions, allows deeper assessment of the environmental impacts of the taxes. In addition, governments may choose to implement environmental policy using a range of other instruments, including fees and charges, expenditures (both direct and subsidies) and regulation, some of which are also detailed in the PINE database (see http://oe.cd/pine for information on the use of alternative instruments in countries).

Figure 2.5. Trends in composition of ERTRs (OECD average), 1995-2017

% of ERTR

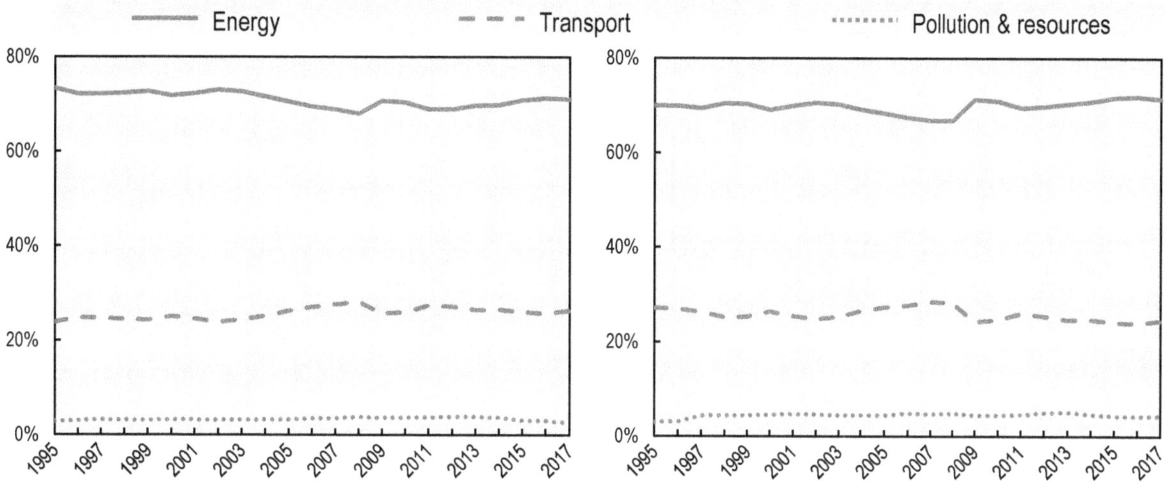

Note: For Canada, Korea and Israel, data for 2014 are used for subsequent years as data for later years are not available in the PINE database and ERTRs cannot be identified in Revenue Statistics with sufficient precision to be included. For the same reason, data for 2016 are used for 2017 in Australia and the United States.
Source: OECD Environment Statistics (database) (OECD, 2019[7]).

StatLink https://doi.org/10.1787/888934054892

Conclusion

Reconciling data on environmentally related tax revenue (ERTRs) in *Revenue Statistics* with the PINE database achieves a greater coherence of data across sources of similar information. This requires identification of environmentally related tax revenue in *Revenue Statistics*, which can be complicated due to (i) aggregation of multiple revenue streams and (ii) generic labels used in countries' submissions. Countries are encouraged to report revenue streams from environmentally related taxes separately as a country specific tax in *Revenue Statistics* (or using a breakdown that follows the ERTR tax categories) and to use labels that allow such taxes to be more clearly identified (e.g. "tax on NO_x emissions" instead for "environmental tax").

Table 2.2. Composition of ERTRs in OECD countries, 2017

	% of ERTRs			USD, adjusted for purchasing power parity			
	Energy	Transport	Pollution and resources	Energy	Transport	Pollution and resources	Total
AUS	59.9	37.3	2.8	11 330	7 055	537	18 922
AUT	59.1	40.0	0.9	5 729	3 881	90	9 701
BEL	66.0	29.8	4.3	7 003	3 159	454	10 615
CAN	76.4	20.3	3.3	12 801	3 398	548	16 748
CHL	72.3	24.2	3.6	3 493	1 167	174	4 834
CZE	76.5	17.2	6.3	6 600	1 484	546	8 630
DNK	53.7	41.9	4.4	5 269	4 106	436	9 812
EST	87.7	2.1	10.2	949	23	110	1 082
FIN	66.7	32.5	0.8	4 393	2 144	53	6 590
FRA	77.2	10.2	12.6	45 089	5 901	7 384	58 374
DEU	81.0	19.0	0.0	47 679	11 185	10	58 874
GRC	75.3	24.7	0.0	6 308	2 072	0	8 380
HUN	84.5	11.5	4.0	5 315	723	251	6 290
ISL	55.4	36.5	8.1	174	115	25	315
IRL	60.6	38.4	1.0	3 114	1 975	53	5 142
ISR	53.5	44.3	2.2	4 009	3 322	167	7 498
ITA	78.9	18.9	2.1	55 166	13 230	1 483	69 879
JPN	64.0	35.6	0.5	41 636	23 167	300	65 102
KOR	65.0	33.1	1.9	30 866	15 749	905	47 520
LVA	81.8	13.8	4.3	1 409	238	75	1 722
LTU	88.4	4.2	7.5	1 385	65	117	1 568
LUX	91.0	7.9	1.1	821	72	9	902
MEX	84.5	12.0	3.5	20 888	2 970	865	24 723
NLD	55.6	31.2	13.2	15 152	8 497	3 601	27 250
NZL	52.4	47.6	0.0	1 150	1 045	0	2 195
NOR	57.1	39.0	3.8	3 970	2 711	267	6 948
POL	91.1	7.8	1.1	21 888	1 868	275	24 030
PRT	71.8	27.1	1.1	5 409	2 042	84	7 535
SVK	80.8	8.9	10.3	2 604	288	333	3 224
SVN	80.4	9.6	9.9	2 284	274	282	2 839
ESP	82.7	12.9	4.4	23 570	3 669	1 268	28 507
SWE	77.9	20.2	1.9	7 657	1 987	188	9 832
CHE	53.2	45.3	1.5	3 845	3 273	107	7 225
TUR	65.6	34.4	0.0	40 275	21 111	0	61 386
GBR	74.5	22.7	2.7	46 081	14 059	1 678	61 819
USA	61.7	36.9	1.4	74 792	44 691	1 745	121 229
OECD-W	71.0	26.4	2.6				807 242[10]
OECD-S	71.2	25.0	3.8	-	-	-	-

Note: OECD-W refers to the weighted average and OECD-S to the simple average. For Canada, Korea and Israel, data for 2014 are used for subsequent years as data for later years are not available in the PINE database and ERTRs cannot be identified in Revenue Statistics with sufficient precision to be included. For the same reason, data for 2016 are used for 2017 in Australia and the United States.
OECD Environment Statistics (database) (OECD, 2019[7]).

StatLink https://doi.org/10.1787/888934054835

The reconciliation of *Revenue Statistics* with the PINE database has allowed several conclusions to be drawn:

- ERTRs in OECD countries in 2017 range from 2.8% of total tax revenues in the United States to 12.5% in Slovenia and Turkey, accounting for 5.1% of total tax revenues on a weighted average basis and 6.9% on a simple average basis. Similarly, as a share of GDP, ERTRs account for 1.6% of GDP on a weighted average basis and 2.3% on a simple average basis, with their shares in GDP ranging from 0.7% in the United States to 4.5% in Slovenia.
- Since 1995, there has been no trend that indicates OECD countries are moving toward sourcing a greater share of tax revenues from environmentally related taxes bases, and OECD countries have not become more similar in the levels of ERTRs observed either as a share of total tax revenues or of GDP.
- The largest share of ERTRs in OECD countries in 2017 was derived from energy taxes, both on average and in nearly every OECD country, accounting for nearly three-quarters of ERTRs.
- On average, the reliance of OECD countries on energy tax revenues (as a share of all ERTRs) increased after the financial crisis, offset by a decrease in revenues from transport taxes.

As part of its work on developing methodological guidelines for compilation of ERTR accounts in line with the SEEA, the OECD is also developing a joint platform to ensure that the instrument-level information in PINE is consistent with the more aggregated statistics reported in ERTR accounts. Similarly, one of the goals of this Special Feature is to achieve consistency between *Revenue Statistics* on the one hand, and the OECD PINE database and ERTR accounts on the other hand, by encouraging a higher disaggregation of ERTR data in *Revenue Statistics*.

References

OECD (2019), “Environmental policy: Environmental policy instruments”, *OECD Environment Statistics* (database), https://dx.doi.org/10.1787/data-00696-en (accessed on 25 November 2019). [7]

OECD (2019), *Environmentally related tax revenue accounts: OECD methodological guidelines in line with the SEEA*, OECD. [2]

OECD (2018), *Revenue Statistics 1965-2017: Interpretative Guide*, http://www.oecd.org/tax/tax-policy/oecd-classification-taxes-interpretative-guide.pdf (accessed on 25 November 2019). [3]

OECD (2017), *Environmental Fiscal Reform: Progress, prospects and pitfalls*, http://www.oecd.org/tax/tax-policy/tax-and-environment.htm. (accessed on 28 November 2019). [1]

OECD (2006), *The Political Economy of Environmentally Related Taxes*, OECD Publishing, Paris, https://dx.doi.org/10.1787/9789264025530-en. [6]

United Nations (2014), *System of Environmental-Economic Accounting 2012 Central Framework*, https://unstats.un.org/unsd/envaccounting/seeaRev/SEEA_CF_Final_en.pdf (accessed on 25 November 2019). [5]

United Nations (2009), *System of National Accounts 2008 European Commission International Monetary Fund*, https://unstats.un.org/unsd/nationalaccount/docs/SNA2008.pdf (accessed on 25 November 2019). [4]

Annex 2.A. List of environmentally related tax bases

Annex Table 2.A.1. List of environmentally related tax bases

Tax base category	Details	Environmentally related tax bases (consumption, production and trade as well as measured and estimated values; if appropriate)
Energy including fuel for transport	*Energy products for transport purposes*	Unleaded petrol, leaded petrol, diesel, other energy products for transport purposes (e.g., LPG, natural gas, kerosene or fuel oil)
	Energy products for stationary purposes	Light fuel oil, heavy fuel oil, natural gas, coal, coke, biofuels, electricity, district heat, other energy products for stationary use
	Energy related GHG emissions	Energy related carbon content, energy related emissions of CO_2 and other GHGs (including proceeds from permit schemes)
Transport excluding fuel for transport		Motor vehicles: production, trade or sale (one off taxes), registration or use (recurrent, e.g., annual taxes), vehicle insurance (excludes general insurance taxes), road: use (e.g., motorway taxes), congestion (e.g., congestion charges and city tolls), other means of transport: railways, water (e.g., taxes on ships), air (e.g., taxes on flights and flight tickets)
Pollution	*Non-energy related GHG emissions*	Non-energy related carbon content (e.g., peat), emissions of CO_2 and other GHGs not related to energy (e.g., cattle-breeding, rice cultivation, synthetic fertilizer application, meat diets, cement; including proceeds from permit schemes)
	Pollutant emissions to air	NOx emissions, SOx emissions, other air pollutants (excluding GHGs)
	Ozone depleting substances	Ozone depleting substances (e.g., CFCs, halons, HCFCs)
	Effluents to water	Effluents of oxidisable matter (BOD, COD), other effluents to water, effluent collection and treatment (fixed annual taxes)
	Non-point sources of water pollution	Pesticides (based on e.g. chemical content, price or volume), artificial fertilisers (based on e.g. phosphorus or nitrogen content or price), manure (based on nitrogen released)
	Waste management	Waste collection, treatment or disposal, individual products (e.g., batteries, tyres, lubricants), packaging (e.g., beverage containers, plastic bags)
	Noise	Noise (e.g., aircraft take-off and landings)
	Radiation	Radiation, radioactive substances
Resources	*Resource extraction, abstraction, harvesting*	Fresh-water abstraction, harvesting of biological resources (e.g., timber, meat, hunted and fished species, wild plants and animals), extraction of raw materials (excluding oil and natural gas; including exploration activity), landscape changes (e.g., cutting of trees)

Source: (OECD, 2019[2])

Annex 2.B. Correspondence table (example)

Annex Table 2.B.1. Correspondence among OECD PINE, OECD Revenue Statistics and Eurostat NTL for the Czech Republic

Instrument	PINE	PINE	Revenue Statistics	Revenue Statistics	Eurostat	Eurostat
	id	Name	id	name	id	name
Tax	344	Electricity tax	5121_L8	On electricity	D2122C-C06	Energy tax on electricity
Tax	344	Electricity tax	5121_L8	On electricity	D214A-C07	Energy tax on electricity
Tax	2107	Fuel excise duty	5121_L1	On mineral oils	D2122C-C01	Excise duty on hydrocarbon fuels and lubricants
Tax	2107	Fuel excise duty	5121_L1	On mineral oils	D214A-C01	Excise duty on hydrocarbon fuels and lubricants
Tax	1407	Natural gas tax	5121_L9	On natural gas	D2122C-C07	Energy tax on natural gas
Tax	1407	Natural gas tax	5121_L9	On natural gas	D214A-C08	Energy tax on natural gas
Tax	2279	Radioactive waste fee	5213_L8	Radioactive waste fee	D29F-C03	Radioactive waste fee
Tax	1399	Solid fuels tax	5121_L10	On solid fuels	D2122C-C08	Energy tax on solid fuels
Tax	1399	Solid fuels tax	5121_L10	On solid fuels	D214A-C09	Energy tax on solid fuels
Tax	1408	Fee for extracted minerals				
Tax	2178	Duty on ozone depleting chemicals	5121_L6	Duty on CFC		
Tax	3166	Air pollution fee	5213_L5	Air pollution fee	D29F-C02	Air pollution fee
Tax	396	Fee for the withdrawal of forest land	5213_L11	Levy on temp. withdrawal of land from forestry		
Tax	396	Fee for the withdrawal of forest land	5220_L2	Levy on withdrawal of land from forestry		
Tax	936	Levy on withdrawal of land from agriculture	5213_L7	Levy on temp. withdrawal of land from agriculture		

Tax	936	Levy on withdrawal of land from agriculture	5220_L1	Levy on withdrawal of land from agriculture		
Tax	3434	Resort and recreation fees on visitors	5213_L1	Resort and recreation fees on visitors		
Tax	2173	Car registration fee for the purposes of support of collection, processing, utilisation and abolition of car wrecks			D214D-C02	Fee for support of collection, processing, reuse and disposal of chosen automobile wrecks.
Tax	351	Electronic road-toll fee				
Tax	2276	Fee for entrance to selected cities and places	5213_L3	Motor vehicle entry fees	D29A-C04	Motor vehicle entry fees
Tax	2276	Fee for entrance to selected cities and places	5213_L3	Motor vehicle entry fees	D59F-C02	Motor vehicle entry fees
Tax	632	Highway fee	5210_L1	Highway fee		
Tax	3897	Licence for lorry transport	5220_L6	Licence for lorry transport		
Tax	677	Road tax	5212_L1	Road tax (commercial)	D29B-C01	Road tax
Tax	1418	Packaging registration and evidence fees	5213_L10	Fees on registration and recording of packaging		
Tax	1418	Waste deposit fee	5213_L6	Waste deposit fee		
Tax	710	Fee for the discharge of waste water into surface water	5213_L4	Water pollution fee	D29F-C01	Water pollution fee
Tax	2175	Fee for permitted discharge of waste water into underground water			D29F-C04	Underground water pollution fee
Tradable permit	4348	EU Emissions Trading System (EU ETS)			D29F-C06	Tax on Emission Allowances

Note: Correspondence table constructed with information extracted on 19 April 2019. The correspondence tables for other countries available upon request.
Source: ENV/EPOC/WPEI(2018)7

Notes

[1] Split incentives (e.g. owner-tenant), steep marginal damage costs (e.g. exposure to hazardous substances), etc., are some of the well-known exceptions when the literature tends to argue in favour of regulatory instruments (e.g. maximum emission limits, minimum efficiency standards and other technology prescriptions) or some combination of the two (i.e. taxes and regulations).

[2] There is on-going work that may lead to the revision of the OECD definition of taxes to include also payments to supra-national institutions.

[3] For a more detailed discussion see OECD (2017).

[4] For instance, in the SNA, taxes are classified regarding taxes on production and imports, income and wealth, and capital. In the OECD *Revenue Statistics*, taxes are classified according to income, profits, capital gains, earnings, payroll, number of employees, property, goods and services, and others. Nevertheless, the large majority of ERTR is likely to be part of taxes on production and imports in the SNA and on goods and services in the OECD *Revenue Statistics*.

[5] Aggregated statistics are also published for Liechtenstein and Switzerland.

[6] Called *environmental taxes* by Eurostat.

[7] This confusion arose because of the similarity of gas and gasoline (or petrol) in English and is being corrected in the National Tax Lists.

[8] The weighted average is calculated using the shares of revenues in USD, adjusted for PPP, for each country. See footnote below for an explanation of why these figures will differ slightly from those reported in PINE.

[9] The OECD *Revenue Statistics* database and the PINE database treat revenues from Mexico's fuel price controlling formula differently, which was in place from 2006 to 2014. *Revenue Statistics* includes only the positive elements of this formula as revenues, whereas the PINE database includes also the implicit subsidy. Data in this Special Feature for Mexico are based on the information provided by delegates for the PINE database and may therefore differ from those reported elsewhere in *Revenue Statistics*.

[10] This figure represents the total, rather than the weighted average.

3 Tax Levels and Tax Structures, 1965-2018

Chapter 3 provides an overview of tax levels and tax structures in OECD countries from 1965-2018.

In all of the following tables the symbol (...) indicates not available/or not applicable. The main series in this chapter cover the years 1965 to 2017. A selection of years are shown in this chapter because of lack of space. The complete series is available on line. Data for 1955 and 1960 (for nineteen OECD countries) are provided in part V of the 1998 edition of this Report.

The Gross Domestic Product (GDP) figures are based on the 2008 System of National Accounts (SNA) for all OECD countries.

In this chapter, the OECD average for 2016 in all tables has been calculated excluding the one-off revenues from stability contributions in Iceland.

Box 3.1. Treatment of capital transfers

Footnotes to Tables 3.1 to 3.18 refer to the treatment of the capital transfers that some countries make to account for taxes that have been assessed but not collected. The capital transfer has been subtracted from the total tax revenue and this reduction has been allocated between tax headings in proportion to their tax revenues.

This applies to the following countries:

- Denmark from 1971.
- France from 1992.
- Lithuania from 1999.
- Spain from 1995.
- Switzerland from 1990.

Table 3.1. Total tax revenue as % of GDP

	1965	1990	2000	2007	2010	2012	2014	2016	2017	2018p
Australia	20.6	28.1	30.5	29.5	25.3	26.9	27.3	27.6	28.5	..
Austria	33.5	39.3	42.3	40.5	41.0	41.8	42.7	41.9	41.8	42.2
Belgium	30.6	41.2	43.5	42.7	42.6	44.2	45.1	43.9	44.5	44.8
Canada	25.0	35.1	34.7	32.5	31.0	31.2	31.3	33.2	32.8	33.0
Chile	..	16.9	18.8	22.7	19.6	21.3	19.6	20.1	20.1	21.1
Czech Republic	..	..	32.4	34.2	32.5	33.7	33.1	34.2	34.9	35.3
Denmark[1]	29.1	44.4	46.9	46.4	44.8	45.5	48.5	45.7	45.7	44.9
Estonia	..	..	31.1	31.3	33.3	31.7	32.1	33.5	32.8	33.2
Finland	30.0	42.9	45.8	41.5	40.8	42.7	43.8	44.0	43.3	42.7
France[1]	33.7	41.2	43.4	42.5	42.1	44.4	45.4	45.4	46.1	46.1
Germany[2]	31.7	34.8	36.2	34.9	35.0	36.4	36.7	37.4	37.6	38.2
Greece	17.1	25.2	33.4	31.8	32.0	35.8	36.0	38.7	38.9	38.7
Hungary	..	..	38.5	39.4	37.3	38.4	38.0	39.1	38.2	36.6
Iceland	25.7	30.4	36.0	38.6	32.3	34.0	37.3	50.8	37.5	36.7
Ireland	24.5	32.4	30.8	30.4	27.0	27.6	28.5	23.4	22.5	22.3
Israel	..	..	34.9	34.2	30.7	30.0	31.0	31.1	32.5	31.1
Italy	24.7	36.4	40.6	41.7	41.9	43.9	43.5	42.3	42.1	42.1
Japan	17.6	28.2	25.8	27.5	26.5	28.2	30.3	30.7	31.4	..
Korea	..	18.8	21.5	24.8	23.4	24.8	24.6	26.2	26.9	28.4
Latvia	..	..	29.1	28.3	28.8	29.2	29.8	31.2	31.1	30.7
Lithuania[1]	..	..	30.8	30.0	28.3	27.0	27.5	29.7	29.5	30.3
Luxembourg	26.4	33.5	36.9	36.1	37.4	38.4	37.6	37.9	38.7	40.1
Mexico	..	12.1	11.5	12.0	12.8	12.6	13.7	16.6	16.1	16.1
Netherlands	30.5	39.7	36.9	35.7	35.7	35.6	37.0	38.4	38.7	38.8
New Zealand	24.5	36.2	32.5	33.9	30.3	31.6	31.3	31.7	32.1	32.7
Norway	29.4	40.2	41.9	42.1	41.9	41.5	38.8	38.7	38.8	39.0
Poland	..	..	32.9	34.6	31.4	32.1	31.9	33.5	34.1	35.0
Portugal	15.7	26.5	31.1	31.8	30.4	31.8	34.3	34.1	34.4	35.4
Slovak Republic	..	..	33.6	29.2	28.1	28.3	31.1	32.3	33.1	33.1
Slovenia	..	..	36.6	37.1	36.9	36.8	36.2	36.5	36.3	36.4
Spain[1]	14.3	31.6	33.2	36.4	31.2	32.1	33.6	33.3	33.7	34.4
Sweden	31.3	49.4	48.9	44.9	43.2	42.5	42.5	44.2	44.4	43.9
Switzerland[1]	16.5	23.7	27.6	26.2	26.6	26.9	26.9	27.7	28.4	27.9
Turkey	10.6	14.5	23.6	23.1	24.8	24.9	24.6	25.3	24.9	24.4
United Kingdom	30.1	32.9	32.9	33.0	32.4	32.4	31.8	32.7	33.3	33.5
United States	23.6	26.0	28.3	26.8	23.5	24.0	25.9	25.9	26.8	24.3
Unweighted average										
OECD Average[3]	**24.9**	**31.9**	**33.8**	**33.6**	**32.3**	**33.1**	**33.6**	**34.4**	**34.2**	**34.3**

.. Not available

Note: Full time series can be accessed at http://oe.cd/full-time-series.

1. The total tax revenue has been reduced by the amount of any capital transfer that represents uncollected taxes. The capital transfer has been allocated between tax headings in proportion to the reported tax revenue.

2. From 1991 the figures relate to the united Germany.

3. 2018: calculated by applying the unweighted average percentage change for 2018 in the 34 countries providing data for that year to the overall average tax to GDP ratio in 2017. The 2016 OECD average tax-to-GDP ratio includes the one-off revenues from stability contributions in Iceland.

StatLink https://doi.org/10.1787/888934054949

Table 3.2. Total tax revenue in billions of US dollars at market exchange rates

	1965	1990	2000	2007	2010	2012	2014	2016	2017	2018p
Australia	5.6	90.9	124.4	290.8	328.3	428.0	399.3	362.0	404.0	..
Austria	..	68.6	83.2	157.6	160.5	171.1	188.7	165.1	174.3	192.2
Belgium	..	89.4	103.6	201.6	206.1	220.0	239.2	206.0	220.1	238.4
Canada	14.2	209.2	262.8	477.2	501.4	570.1	564.6	507.6	541.3	564.8
Chile	..	5.8	14.6	39.4	42.8	57.0	51.1	50.4	55.9	62.8
Czech Republic	..	..	20.0	64.8	67.4	70.0	68.8	66.8	75.3	86.5
Denmark[1]	3.0	61.4	76.9	148.3	144.2	149.0	171.1	142.6	150.8	158.0
Estonia	..	..	1.8	7.0	6.5	7.3	8.5	8.0	8.7	10.1
Finland	..	49.6	57.5	106.0	101.1	109.6	119.4	105.2	109.3	116.9
France[1]	..	550.7	591.8	1 130.7	1 113.7	1 191.0	1 296.4	1 121.0	1 193.1	1 280.1
Germany[2]	..	577.4	706.9	1 200.5	1 196.3	1 290.2	1 429.9	1 307.4	1 388.0	1 526.0
Greece	..	14.6	43.5	101.3	95.9	88.0	85.3	75.5	79.1	84.4
Hungary	..	..	18.2	55.1	48.8	49.1	53.2	49.3	53.3	56.9
Iceland	0.1	2.0	3.2	8.3	4.4	5.0	6.6	10.5	9.2	9.5
Ireland	0.7	15.6	30.7	82.0	60.0	62.1	73.6	70.2	75.4	85.3
Israel	..	..	46.2	61.2	72.0	77.4	96.1	99.4	114.9	114.8
Italy	..	336.6	463.6	918.8	889.9	910.7	935.5	790.6	820.4	871.9
Japan	17.1	903.6	1 263.4	1 242.0	1 509.6	1 749.1	1 482.2	1 516.2	1 531.0	..
Korea	..	52.6	120.5	278.2	256.2	303.2	347.0	371.1	411.7	460.4
Latvia	..	..	1.8	8.8	6.8	8.2	9.3	8.6	9.5	10.7
Lithuania[1]	..	..	3.8	11.9	10.5	11.6	13.3	12.8	14.0	16.1
Luxembourg	..	4.7	7.9	18.4	19.9	21.8	24.8	22.4	24.1	27.8
Mexico	..	35.9	81.2	126.5	135.9	152.2	179.9	179.5	186.9	..
Netherlands	..	132.6	153.7	302.5	301.9	298.7	330.1	300.8	322.0	354.0
New Zealand	1.4	16.4	18.0	47.1	44.9	56.1	63.5	60.3	65.8	67.8
Norway	2.4	48.2	71.8	168.9	179.9	211.7	193.7	143.8	155.0	169.6
Poland	..	..	56.6	148.7	150.6	160.7	173.8	158.3	179.7	205.2
Portugal	..	18.8	36.8	76.4	72.5	68.8	78.7	70.4	75.6	84.2
Slovak Republic	..	..	9.8	25.2	25.1	26.5	31.4	29.0	31.7	35.2
Slovenia	..	..	6.4	17.8	17.7	17.1	18.1	16.3	17.6	19.7
Spain[1]	..	131.6	197.9	538.0	446.8	429.4	462.6	411.9	442.8	490.5
Sweden	7.8	127.7	127.3	219.4	211.2	231.7	244.4	226.6	237.8	242.1
Switzerland[1]	2.6	61.3	75.1	125.8	155.3	179.8	190.9	185.7	193.1	197.1
Turkey	1.3	30.2	64.5	156.2	192.0	218.6	229.6	218.4	212.0	186.2
United Kingdom	30.6	359.4	542.9	1 016.8	794.1	870.1	966.3	869.9	878.0	947.4
United States	167.0	1 552.4	2 900.5	3 868.6	3 517.1	3 887.2	4 544.4	4 841.9	5 227.3	5 007.2
Unweighted average										
OECD Average	**19.5**	**205.4**	**233.0**	**373.5**	**363.5**	**398.8**	**427.0**	**410.6**	**435.8**	..

.. Not available

Note: Full time series can be accessed at http://oe.cd/full-time-series.

1. The total tax revenue has been reduced by the amount of any capital transfer that represents uncollected taxes. The capital transfer has been allocated between tax headings in proportion to the reported tax revenue.
2. From 1991 the figures relate to the united Germany.

StatLink https://doi.org/10.1787/888934054968

Table 3.3. Tax revenue of main headings as % of GDP, 2017

	1000 Income & profits	2000 Social security	3000 Payroll	4000 Property	5000 Goods and services	6000 Others	EU Custom Duties
Australia	16.8	0.0	1.4	3.0	7.4	0.0	..
Austria	11.8	14.6	2.8	0.5	11.8	0.2	0.1
Belgium	16.2	13.6	0.0	3.5	10.8	0.0	0.4
Canada	15.8	4.6	0.7	3.9	7.7	0.0	..
Chile	6.9	1.5	0.0	1.1	11.0	-0.4	..
Czech Republic	7.7	15.0	0.0	0.5	11.5	0.0	0.2
Denmark[1]	28.9	0.0	0.3	1.8	14.5	0.0	0.1
Estonia	7.2	11.2	0.0	0.2	14.0	0.0	0.2
Finland	15.4	12.1	0.0	1.5	14.2	0.0	0.1
France[1]	10.9	16.8	1.5	4.4	11.3	1.2	0.1
Germany[2]	12.2	14.2	0.0	1.0	9.9	0.1	0.2
Greece	8.9	11.5	0.0	3.1	15.3	0.0	0.1
Hungary	7.5	12.3	0.7	1.1	16.4	0.1	0.1
Iceland	18.4	3.4	0.3	2.1	12.6	0.6	..
Ireland	9.8	3.9	0.1	1.3	7.3	0.0	0.1
Israel	11.6	5.3	1.2	3.2	11.3	0.0	..
Italy	13.4	12.8	0.0	2.6	12.0	1.3	0.1
Japan	9.6	12.5	0.0	2.6	6.6	0.1	..
Korea	8.6	6.9	0.1	3.1	7.5	0.7	..
Latvia	8.2	8.4	0.0	1.0	13.4	0.0	0.2
Lithuania[1]	5.4	12.3	0.0	0.3	11.4	0.0	0.2
Luxembourg	14.4	11.1	0.0	3.7	9.4	0.1	0.0
Mexico	7.2	2.1	0.4	0.3	5.9	0.2	..
Netherlands	11.6	13.8	0.0	1.6	11.3	0.1	0.3
New Zealand	17.8	0.0	0.0	1.9	12.3	0.0	..
Norway	15.1	10.3	0.1	1.3	12.0	0.0	..
Poland	6.9	12.8	0.2	1.4	12.6	0.1	0.2
Portugal	9.7	9.2	0.0	1.4	13.8	0.3	0.1
Slovak Republic	7.0	14.5	0.0	0.4	11.0	0.0	0.2
Slovenia	6.9	14.5	0.1	0.6	14.0	0.0	0.1
Spain[1]	9.6	11.5	0.0	2.5	9.9	0.0	0.2
Sweden	16.1	9.7	5.1	1.0	12.3	0.0	0.1
Switzerland[1]	13.5	6.7	0.0	2.2	6.0	0.1	..
Turkey	5.3	7.3	0.0	1.1	10.8	0.3	..
United Kingdom	11.9	6.4	0.1	4.2	10.6	0.0	0.2
United States	12.1	6.2	0.0	4.3	4.2	0.0	..
Unweighted average							
OECD Average	**11.6**	**9.1**	**0.4**	**1.9**	**10.9**	**0.1**	**0.2**

.. Not available

1. The total tax revenue has been reduced by the amount of any capital transfer that represents uncollected taxes. The capital transfer has been allocated between tax headings in proportion to the reported tax revenue.
2. From 1991 the figures relate to the united Germany.

StatLink https://doi.org/10.1787/888934054987

Table 3.4. Tax revenue of main headings as % of total tax revenue, 2017

	1000 Income & profits	2000 Social security	3000 Payroll	4000 Property	5000 Goods and services	6000 Others	EU Custom Duties
Australia	58.8	0.0	4.8	10.3	26.0	0.0	..
Austria	28.3	34.9	6.6	1.3	28.1	0.5	0.3
Belgium	36.5	30.5	0.0	7.9	24.2	0.0	0.8
Canada	48.2	14.1	2.0	12.0	23.5	0.1	..
Chile	34.5	7.3	0.0	5.4	54.8	-2.0	..
Czech Republic	22.2	43.0	0.0	1.4	32.9	0.1	0.5
Denmark[1]	63.3	0.1	0.5	3.9	31.8	0.0	0.3
Estonia	22.1	34.1	0.0	0.7	42.6	0.0	0.5
Finland	35.5	27.8	0.0	3.6	32.9	0.1	0.2
France[1]	23.6	36.4	3.4	9.5	24.5	2.5	0.2
Germany[2]	32.5	37.9	0.0	2.7	26.3	0.2	0.4
Greece	22.8	29.6	0.0	7.9	39.3	0.0	0.4
Hungary	19.6	32.1	1.9	2.8	42.9	0.3	0.3
Iceland	49.2	9.1	0.8	5.5	33.7	1.7	..
Ireland	43.5	17.1	0.6	5.7	32.4	0.0	0.5
Israel	35.5	16.2	3.7	10.0	34.6	0.0	..
Italy	31.7	30.3	0.0	6.2	28.4	3.1	0.3
Japan	30.7	39.9	0.0	8.2	21.0	0.2	..
Korea	32.1	25.7	0.3	11.7	27.7	2.5	..
Latvia	26.2	26.9	0.0	3.3	43.0	0.0	0.5
Lithuania[1]	18.1	41.5	0.0	1.0	38.5	0.0	0.8
Luxembourg	37.2	28.6	0.0	9.6	24.3	0.3	0.1
Mexico	44.6	13.3	2.4	1.9	36.4	1.5	..
Netherlands	30.0	35.7	0.0	4.0	29.1	0.3	0.8
New Zealand	55.6	0.0	0.0	6.0	38.4	0.0	..
Norway	39.0	26.6	0.1	3.3	30.9	0.0	..
Poland	20.2	37.5	0.7	4.0	36.9	0.1	0.5
Portugal	28.2	26.8	0.0	3.9	40.0	0.8	0.3
Slovak Republic	21.2	43.9	0.0	1.3	33.1	0.0	0.5
Slovenia	19.1	40.0	0.1	1.8	38.6	0.0	0.3
Spain[1]	28.6	34.0	0.0	7.5	29.3	0.0	0.5
Sweden	36.3	21.8	11.5	2.2	27.8	0.1	0.3
Switzerland[1]	47.3	23.6	0.0	7.6	21.1	0.5	..
Turkey	21.4	29.3	0.0	4.5	43.5	1.3	..
United Kingdom	35.7	19.2	0.3	12.5	31.9	0.0	0.5
United States	45.2	23.0	0.0	16.0	15.7	0.0	..
Unweighted average							
OECD Average	**34.0**	**26.0**	**1.1**	**5.8**	**32.4**	**0.4**	**0.4**

.. Not available

1. The total tax revenue has been reduced by the amount of any capital transfer that represents uncollected taxes. The capital transfer has been allocated between tax headings in proportion to the reported tax revenue.
2. From 1991 the figures relate to the united Germany.

StatLink https://doi.org/10.1787/888934055006

Table 3.5. Tax revenue of main headings as % of GDP, 2018p

	1000 Income & profits	2000 Social security	3000 Payroll	4000 Property	5000 Goods and services	6000 Others	EU Custom Duties
Australia	..	..	..	..	..	..	..
Austria	12.4	14.7	2.7	0.5	11.6	0.2	0.1
Belgium	16.5	13.5	0.0	3.5	10.9	0.0	0.4
Canada	16.1	4.6	0.7	3.9	7.7	0.0	..
Chile	7.5	1.5	0.0	1.1	11.2	-0.2	..
Czech Republic	7.8	15.6	0.0	0.5	11.3	0.0	0.2
Denmark[1]	27.9	0.0	0.3	1.8	14.7	0.0	0.1
Estonia	7.5	11.6	0.0	0.2	13.7	0.0	0.2
Finland	14.9	11.9	0.0	1.4	14.4	0.0	0.1
France[1]	11.6	16.1	1.5	4.1	11.5	1.2	0.1
Germany[2]	12.5	14.4	0.0	1.0	10.0	0.1	0.1
Greece	8.9	11.6	0.0	3.1	15.1	0.0	0.0
Hungary	6.3	12.1	0.8	1.0	16.1	0.1	0.2
Iceland	18.3	3.5	0.3	2.0	12.0	0.6	..
Ireland	10.2	3.8	0.2	1.3	6.7	0.0	0.1
Israel	10.2	5.2	1.2	3.2	11.3	0.0	..
Italy	13.0	13.1	0.0	2.6	11.9	1.3	0.1
Japan	10.1	..	0.0	2.6	6.2	0.1	..
Korea	9.7	7.2	0.1	3.3	7.5	0.6	..
Latvia	6.9	9.0	0.0	0.9	13.7	0.0	0.2
Lithuania[1]	5.6	12.7	0.0	0.3	11.4	0.0	0.3
Luxembourg	15.4	11.0	0.0	3.9	9.6	0.1	0.0
Mexico	7.1	2.2	..	..	..	..	..
Netherlands	11.5	14.0	0.0	1.6	11.3	0.1	0.3
New Zealand	18.2	0.0	0.0	2.0	12.6	0.0	..
Norway	15.8	10.1	0.1	1.3	11.7	0.0	..
Poland	7.4	13.1	0.2	1.3	12.3	0.6	..
Portugal	10.0	9.5	0.0	1.4	14.0	0.3	0.1
Slovak Republic	7.0	14.6	0.0	0.4	10.9	0.0	0.1
Slovenia	7.2	14.5	0.0	0.6	13.8	0.0	0.1
Spain[1]	10.1	11.6	0.0	2.5	10.0	0.0	0.2
Sweden	15.7	9.7	5.1	1.0	12.3	0.0	0.1
Switzerland[1]	13.3	6.6	0.0	2.1	5.8	0.1	..
Turkey	5.9	7.3	0.0	1.1	9.9	0.3	..
United Kingdom	12.0	6.4	0.1	4.1	10.7	0.0	0.2
United States	11.0	6.1	0.0	3.0	4.3	0.0	..
Unweighted average							
OECD Average	**11.5**	**9.4**	**0.5**	**1.9**	**11.1**	**0.2**	**0.1**

.. Not available

1. The total tax revenue has been reduced by the amount of any capital transfer that represents uncollected taxes. The capital transfer has been allocated between tax headings in proportion to the reported tax revenue.
2. From 1991 the figures relate to the united Germany.

StatLink https://doi.org/10.1787/888934055025

Table 3.6. Tax revenue of main headings as % of total tax revenue, 2018p

	1000 Income & profits	2000 Social security	3000 Payroll	4000 Property	5000 Goods and services	6000 Others	EU Custom Duties
Australia	..	..	..	..	..	..	..
Austria	29.3	34.8	6.4	1.3	27.5	0.5	0.3
Belgium	36.8	30.1	0.0	7.8	24.4	0.0	0.9
Canada	48.8	14.0	2.0	11.7	23.4	0.1	..
Chile	35.8	6.9	0.0	5.1	53.3	-1.1	..
Czech Republic	22.0	44.1	0.0	1.3	32.1	0.0	0.4
Denmark[1]	62.2	0.1	0.6	4.1	32.7	0.0	0.3
Estonia	22.6	34.9	0.0	0.7	41.3	0.0	0.5
Finland	34.8	27.9	0.0	3.4	33.6	0.0	0.2
France[1]	25.1	34.9	3.3	8.9	25.0	2.6	0.2
Germany[2]	32.8	37.7	0.0	2.7	26.2	0.2	0.4
Greece	23.0	30.1	0.0	7.9	39.0	0.0	0.0
Hungary	17.3	33.2	2.1	2.7	44.0	0.2	0.4
Iceland	49.9	9.5	0.8	5.5	32.6	1.7	..
Ireland	45.7	17.0	0.8	5.9	30.0	0.0	0.5
Israel	32.7	16.7	3.8	10.3	36.5	0.0	..
Italy	31.0	31.1	0.0	6.1	28.3	3.2	0.3
Japan	..	..	..	..	..	..	..
Korea	34.1	25.4	0.3	11.6	26.3	2.3	..
Latvia	22.6	29.3	0.0	3.0	44.5	0.0	0.6
Lithuania[1]	18.5	42.1	0.0	1.0	37.5	0.0	0.9
Luxembourg	38.6	27.4	0.0	9.8	24.1	0.2	0.1
Mexico	..	..	..	..	..	..	..
Netherlands	29.6	36.0	0.0	4.0	29.3	0.3	0.8
New Zealand	55.6	0.0	0.0	6.0	38.5	0.0	..
Norway	40.6	25.9	0.1	3.3	30.1	0.0	..
Poland	21.2	37.5	0.6	3.8	35.1	1.8	..
Portugal	28.2	26.8	0.0	4.1	39.6	1.0	0.3
Slovak Republic	21.2	44.1	0.0	1.2	33.1	0.0	0.4
Slovenia	19.9	40.0	0.1	1.7	38.0	0.0	0.3
Spain[1]	29.3	33.8	0.0	7.3	29.1	0.0	0.5
Sweden	35.8	22.0	11.6	2.2	28.0	0.1	0.3
Switzerland[1]	47.5	23.6	0.0	7.6	20.8	0.5	..
Turkey	24.2	30.0	0.0	4.3	40.5	1.1	..
United Kingdom	35.8	19.1	0.4	12.3	32.0	0.0	0.5
United States	45.1	25.1	0.0	12.2	17.6	0.0	..
Unweighted average							
OECD Average	**33.3**	**27.0**	**1.2**	**5.5**	**32.5**	**0.4**	**0.4**

.. Not available

1. The total tax revenue has been reduced by the amount of any capital transfer that represents uncollected taxes. The capital transfer has been allocated between tax headings in proportion to the reported tax revenue.
2. From 1991 the figures relate to the united Germany.

StatLink https://doi.org/10.1787/888934055044

Table 3.7. Taxes on income and profits (1000) as % of GDP and as % of total tax revenue

	% of GDP					% of total tax revenue				
	1990	2000	2010	2016	2017	1990	2000	2010	2016	2017
Australia	16.1	17.6	14.3	15.8	16.8	57.1	57.9	56.5	57.2	58.8
Austria	10.0	12.0	11.5	11.7	11.8	25.5	28.3	28.1	28.0	28.3
Belgium	15.2	16.8	14.6	15.6	16.2	36.9	38.6	34.2	35.6	36.5
Canada	17.0	17.4	14.5	15.9	15.8	48.6	50.1	46.6	48.0	48.2
Chile	3.9	4.4	7.5	6.8	6.9	23.2	23.3	38.1	33.5	34.5
Czech Republic	..	7.4	6.6	7.6	7.7	..	22.8	20.2	22.2	22.2
Denmark[1]	27.1	28.8	27.5	28.7	28.9	61.2	61.4	61.5	62.8	63.3
Estonia	..	7.7	6.6	7.5	7.2	..	24.8	19.8	22.4	22.1
Finland	16.8	19.7	14.5	15.2	15.4	39.2	43.1	35.5	34.6	35.5
France[1]	6.6	10.8	9.5	10.6	10.9	16.1	24.8	22.6	23.3	23.6
Germany[2]	11.3	10.9	10.0	11.9	12.2	32.4	30.1	28.5	31.8	32.5
Greece	5.0	9.0	7.1	9.1	8.9	19.9	26.8	22.0	23.4	22.8
Hungary	..	9.3	7.7	7.6	7.5	..	24.3	20.7	19.3	19.6
Iceland	9.0	14.3	14.3	17.2	18.4	29.7	39.9	44.4	33.9	49.2
Ireland	12.3	13.4	10.5	10.1	9.8	38.0	43.6	38.7	43.1	43.5
Israel	..	13.8	9.0	9.8	11.6	..	39.6	29.1	31.6	35.5
Italy	13.3	13.5	13.7	13.5	13.4	36.5	33.2	32.7	31.9	31.7
Japan	14.2	9.0	8.0	9.4	9.6	50.2	34.8	30.2	30.6	30.7
Korea	6.2	6.2	6.6	8.2	8.6	32.8	28.8	28.0	31.2	32.1
Latvia	..	7.0	7.2	8.0	8.2	..	24.1	25.0	25.7	26.2
Lithuania[1]	..	8.2	4.6	5.6	5.4	..	26.7	16.1	18.8	18.1
Luxembourg	13.5	13.5	13.6	14.0	14.4	40.2	36.5	36.4	36.8	37.2
Mexico	4.1	4.1	5.1	7.1	7.2	34.0	36.0	39.8	42.7	44.6
Netherlands	12.8	9.6	9.9	10.4	11.6	32.3	25.9	27.9	27.2	30.0
New Zealand	21.6	19.5	16.3	17.6	17.8	59.6	60.0	53.8	55.6	55.6
Norway	14.2	18.8	19.7	14.7	15.1	35.2	45.0	47.1	37.9	39.0
Poland	..	6.7	6.3	6.7	6.9	..	20.4	20.0	19.9	20.2
Portugal	6.8	9.1	8.1	9.8	9.7	25.7	29.3	26.8	28.7	28.2
Slovak Republic	..	6.9	5.3	7.0	7.0	..	20.5	19.0	21.6	21.2
Slovenia	..	6.8	7.4	6.9	6.9	..	18.5	20.1	18.8	19.1
Spain[1]	9.7	9.4	8.8	9.4	9.6	30.6	28.3	28.1	28.2	28.6
Sweden	20.6	19.9	15.3	15.9	16.1	41.6	40.8	35.5	36.0	36.3
Switzerland[1]	11.2	12.2	12.1	12.9	13.5	47.1	44.2	45.7	46.6	47.3
Turkey	4.9	7.0	5.3	5.4	5.3	33.5	29.5	21.3	21.1	21.4
United Kingdom	12.9	13.1	12.2	11.7	11.9	39.3	39.6	37.7	35.7	35.7
United States	11.8	14.2	9.9	12.4	12.1	45.2	50.1	42.3	48.0	45.2
Unweighted average										
OECD Average	**12.1**	**11.9**	**10.6**	**11.3**	**11.6**	**37.5**	**34.8**	**32.8**	**33.2**	**34.0**

.. Not available

Note: Full time series can be accessed at http://oe.cd/full-time-series.

1. The total tax revenue has been reduced by the amount of any capital transfer that represents uncollected taxes. The capital transfer has been allocated between tax headings in proportion to the reported tax revenue.
2. From 1991 the figures relate to the united Germany.

StatLink https://doi.org/10.1787/888934055063

Table 3.8. Taxes on personal income (1100) as % of GDP and as % of total tax revenue

	% of GDP					% of total tax revenue				
	1990	2000	2010	2016	2017	1990	2000	2010	2016	2017
Australia	12.1	11.5	9.8	11.3	11.5	43.0	37.7	38.6	40.8	40.3
Austria	8.2	9.3	9.2	9.1	9.1	21.0	22.0	22.4	21.6	21.7
Belgium	13.2	13.7	12.0	12.1	12.1	32.0	31.4	28.2	27.7	27.2
Canada	14.3	12.8	10.9	11.9	11.7	40.8	36.8	35.0	35.8	35.7
Chile	0.9	1.4	1.3	1.8	1.9	5.6	7.6	6.8	8.8	9.7
Czech Republic	..	4.2	3.3	3.8	4.0	..	12.9	10.2	11.2	11.5
Denmark[1]	24.0	24.7	23.2	24.3	24.2	54.0	52.7	51.9	53.1	52.9
Estonia	..	6.8	5.3	5.8	5.7	..	22.0	15.9	17.3	17.4
Finland	14.9	14.0	12.1	13.0	12.6	34.7	30.6	29.5	29.6	29.2
France[1]	4.4	7.8	7.2	8.6	8.6	10.7	18.0	17.0	18.9	18.6
Germany[2]	9.6	9.2	8.5	9.9	10.2	27.6	25.3	24.3	26.5	27.1
Greece	3.6	4.3	4.0	5.9	6.2	14.1	13.0	12.5	15.2	16.0
Hungary	..	7.2	6.5	5.2	5.4	..	18.6	17.4	13.3	14.2
Iceland	8.2	12.5	11.8	13.5	14.3	26.9	34.8	36.5	26.7	38.0
Ireland	10.7	9.8	8.1	7.4	7.0	33.1	31.9	30.0	31.5	31.2
Israel	..	10.2	5.5	6.2	6.7	..	29.1	18.0	19.8	20.7
Italy	9.6	10.1	11.3	10.9	10.8	26.3	24.8	26.9	25.7	25.7
Japan	7.8	5.4	4.9	5.7	5.9	27.8	21.1	18.6	18.6	18.8
Korea	3.8	3.1	3.3	4.6	4.8	20.0	14.6	14.2	17.6	17.9
Latvia	..	5.5	6.2	6.3	6.6	..	18.8	21.6	20.3	21.1
Lithuania[1]	..	7.6	3.6	4.0	3.9	..	24.6	12.6	13.4	13.1
Luxembourg	8.1	6.8	7.9	9.4	9.1	24.1	18.5	21.0	24.6	23.6
Mexico	..	..	2.3	3.4	3.4	..	..	18.3	20.4	21.4
Netherlands	9.8	5.6	7.7	7.1	8.3	24.7	15.1	21.5	18.5	21.6
New Zealand	17.4	14.0	11.4	11.7	12.1	48.0	43.1	37.7	36.8	37.8
Norway	10.5	10.1	9.9	10.7	10.3	26.2	24.1	23.6	27.6	26.5
Poland	..	4.3	4.4	4.8	5.0	..	13.2	13.9	14.4	14.6
Portugal	4.2	5.4	5.4	6.8	6.5	15.9	17.4	17.6	19.8	18.8
Slovak Republic	..	3.3	2.6	3.3	3.4	..	9.9	9.4	10.2	10.2
Slovenia	..	5.5	5.6	5.3	5.1	..	15.0	15.1	14.4	14.2
Spain[1]	6.9	6.4	6.8	7.1	7.3	21.7	19.2	21.9	21.4	21.8
Sweden	19.0	16.3	12.0	13.2	13.3	38.5	33.2	27.9	29.8	29.9
Switzerland[1]	7.7	8.2	8.5	8.6	8.6	32.6	29.7	31.8	31.0	30.3
Turkey	3.9	5.2	3.5	3.7	3.6	26.8	22.2	14.0	14.6	14.5
United Kingdom	9.7	9.6	9.3	9.0	9.1	29.4	29.0	28.6	27.4	27.2
United States	9.8	11.9	8.2	10.4	10.4	37.7	42.2	34.8	40.2	38.7
Unweighted average										
OECD Average	**9.7**	**8.7**	**7.6**	**8.2**	**8.3**	**28.6**	**24.6**	**22.9**	**23.5**	**23.9**

.. Not available

Note: Full time series can be accessed at http://oe.cd/full-time-series.

1. The total tax revenue has been reduced by the amount of any capital transfer that represents uncollected taxes. The capital transfer has been allocated between tax headings in proportion to the reported tax revenue.

2. From 1991 the figures relate to the united Germany.

StatLink https://doi.org/10.1787/888934055082

Table 3.9. Taxes on corporate income (1200) as % of GDP and as % of total tax revenue

	% of GDP					% of total tax revenue				
	1990	2000	2010	2016	2017	1990	2000	2010	2016	2017
Australia	4.0	6.2	4.5	4.5	5.3	14.1	20.2	17.9	16.5	18.5
Austria	1.4	1.9	1.9	2.4	2.5	3.6	4.6	4.6	5.6	5.9
Belgium	2.0	3.1	2.5	3.4	4.1	4.8	7.2	5.9	7.8	9.3
Canada	2.5	4.2	3.2	3.7	3.7	7.0	12.2	10.5	11.3	11.4
Chile	2.1	2.1	4.0	4.2	4.3	12.4	11.2	20.4	20.9	21.1
Czech Republic	..	3.2	3.2	3.7	3.7	..	9.9	10.0	11.0	10.7
Denmark[1]	1.7	3.2	2.3	2.8	3.3	3.8	6.8	5.0	6.2	7.2
Estonia	..	0.9	1.3	1.7	1.5	..	2.8	4.0	5.1	4.7
Finland	1.9	5.7	2.4	2.2	2.7	4.5	12.5	6.0	5.0	6.3
France[1]	2.2	3.0	2.3	2.0	2.3	5.3	6.9	5.5	4.5	5.1
Germany[2]	1.7	1.8	1.5	2.0	2.0	4.8	4.8	4.3	5.3	5.4
Greece	1.4	4.0	2.5	2.5	1.9	5.5	11.9	7.9	6.4	5.0
Hungary	..	2.2	1.2	2.3	2.1	..	5.7	3.3	6.0	5.5
Iceland	0.8	1.2	0.9	2.5	3.1	2.8	3.3	2.7	4.9	8.2
Ireland	1.6	3.6	2.4	2.7	2.8	4.9	11.7	8.7	11.6	12.3
Israel	..	3.3	2.6	3.1	3.3	..	9.6	8.6	9.9	10.1
Italy	3.7	2.8	2.3	2.1	2.1	10.0	6.9	5.5	5.1	5.0
Japan	6.3	3.5	3.1	3.7	3.7	22.4	13.7	11.6	12.0	11.8
Korea	2.4	3.0	3.2	3.6	3.8	12.8	14.1	13.8	13.6	14.2
Latvia	..	1.5	1.0	1.7	1.6	..	5.3	3.4	5.4	5.1
Lithuania[1]	..	0.7	1.0	1.6	1.5	..	2.2	3.5	5.4	5.1
Luxembourg	5.4	6.6	5.8	4.6	5.2	16.1	18.0	15.4	12.2	13.6
Mexico	..	..	1.8	3.5	3.5	..	..	14.4	21.0	21.8
Netherlands	3.0	4.0	2.3	3.3	3.3	7.5	10.9	6.4	8.7	8.5
New Zealand	2.3	4.0	3.7	4.9	4.7	6.5	12.4	12.2	15.5	14.7
Norway	3.6	8.8	9.9	4.0	4.9	9.0	20.9	23.5	10.4	12.5
Poland	..	2.4	1.9	1.8	1.9	..	7.3	6.2	5.5	5.6
Portugal	2.1	3.7	2.7	3.0	3.2	8.0	11.9	9.0	8.9	9.4
Slovak Republic	..	2.6	2.5	3.5	3.4	..	7.7	8.7	10.7	10.4
Slovenia	..	1.1	1.8	1.6	1.8	..	3.1	5.0	4.4	4.9
Spain[1]	2.8	3.0	1.9	2.3	2.3	8.8	9.1	6.2	6.8	6.8
Sweden	1.5	3.7	3.3	2.7	2.8	3.1	7.5	7.6	6.2	6.3
Switzerland[1]	1.8	2.5	2.7	3.1	3.1	7.4	8.9	10.0	11.3	10.7
Turkey	1.0	1.7	1.8	1.6	1.7	6.7	7.3	7.3	6.5	6.8
United Kingdom[3]	3.3	3.5	2.9	2.7	2.8	9.9	10.6	9.1	8.3	8.5
United States	2.0	2.2	1.8	2.0	1.7	7.5	7.9	7.5	7.9	6.5
Unweighted average										
OECD Average	**2.5**	**3.2**	**2.7**	**2.9**	**3.0**	**8.1**	**9.3**	**8.7**	**9.0**	**9.3**

.. Not available

Note: Full time series can be accessed at http://oe.cd/full-time-series.

1. The total tax revenue has been reduced by the amount of any capital transfer that represents uncollected taxes. The capital transfer has been allocated between tax headings in proportion to the reported tax revenue.
2. From 1991 the figures relate to the united Germany.
3. Corporate income tax revenues for the United Kingdom are based on data provided in July; this was prior to revisions made to the historic Corporation tax data in September, so the revisions are not reflected here. For the latest UK Corporation tax data, please see www.gov.uk/government/statistics/corporation-tax-statistics-2019 the main revisions are explained on page 13 of https://assets.publishing.service.gov.uk/government/uploads/system/uploads/attachment_data/file/833371/Aug19_Receipts_NS_Bulletin_Final.odt.

StatLink https://doi.org/10.1787/888934055101

Table 3.10. Social security contributions (2000) as % of GDP and as % of total tax revenue

	% of GDP					% of total tax revenue				
	1990	2000	2010	2016	2017	1990	2000	2010	2016	2017
Australia	0.0	0.0	0.0	0.0	0.0	0.0	0.0	0.0	0.0	0.0
Austria	12.9	14.3	14.0	14.5	14.6	32.9	33.8	34.2	34.7	34.9
Belgium	13.7	13.4	13.8	13.6	13.6	33.2	30.8	32.4	31.1	30.5
Canada	4.3	4.7	4.6	4.9	4.6	12.1	13.6	14.9	14.7	14.1
Chile	1.5	1.4	1.3	1.4	1.5	9.0	7.3	6.8	7.2	7.3
Czech Republic	..	14.4	14.5	14.7	15.0	..	44.3	44.8	42.9	43.0
Denmark[1]	0.0	0.6	0.1	0.1	0.0	0.0	1.4	0.2	0.1	0.1
Estonia	..	10.9	12.8	11.2	11.2	..	35.1	38.4	33.4	34.1
Finland	11.0	11.6	12.1	12.8	12.1	25.6	25.2	29.7	29.1	27.8
France[1]	18.1	15.6	16.1	16.7	16.8	44.1	35.9	38.3	36.8	36.4
Germany[2]	13.0	14.1	13.7	14.1	14.2	37.5	39.0	39.2	37.6	37.9
Greece	7.6	10.1	10.9	10.9	11.5	30.2	30.3	34.2	28.3	29.6
Hungary	..	11.3	11.7	13.0	12.3	..	29.3	31.4	33.2	32.1
Iceland	1.0	2.8	3.8	3.4	3.4	3.1	7.7	11.8	6.7	9.1
Ireland	4.6	3.6	5.0	3.9	3.9	14.1	11.8	18.6	16.9	17.1
Israel	..	5.1	5.2	5.2	5.3	..	14.6	16.9	16.6	16.2
Italy	12.0	11.6	13.0	12.8	12.8	32.9	28.5	31.1	30.2	30.3
Japan	7.5	9.1	10.9	12.4	12.5	26.5	35.2	41.1	40.4	39.9
Korea	1.9	3.6	5.5	6.9	6.9	10.1	16.7	23.3	26.2	25.7
Latvia	..	9.8	8.7	8.3	8.4	..	33.5	30.1	26.5	26.9
Lithuania[1]	..	10.1	11.7	12.1	12.3	..	32.8	41.4	40.8	41.5
Luxembourg	9.2	9.6	10.8	10.8	11.1	27.5	26.1	29.0	28.4	28.6
Mexico	2.0	2.1	2.1	2.2	2.1	16.8	18.0	16.2	13.0	13.3
Netherlands	14.9	14.3	12.9	14.7	13.8	37.4	38.7	36.3	38.2	35.7
New Zealand	0.0	0.0	0.0	0.0	0.0	0.0	0.0	0.0	0.0	0.0
Norway	10.6	8.8	9.4	10.6	10.3	26.3	20.9	22.4	27.4	26.6
Poland	..	12.9	10.8	12.7	12.8	..	39.2	34.4	37.9	37.5
Portugal	7.2	7.9	8.6	9.1	9.2	27.2	25.5	28.3	26.6	26.8
Slovak Republic	..	14.0	12.1	14.1	14.5	..	41.5	43.0	43.5	43.9
Slovenia	..	13.9	14.8	14.5	14.5	..	38.0	40.2	39.7	40.0
Spain[1]	11.2	11.6	11.7	11.3	11.5	35.4	34.9	37.5	33.9	34.0
Sweden	13.5	12.9	10.9	10.0	9.7	27.2	26.3	25.3	22.6	21.8
Switzerland[1]	5.5	6.7	6.3	6.7	6.7	23.3	24.1	23.5	24.2	23.6
Turkey	2.9	4.4	6.2	7.3	7.3	19.7	18.7	24.9	28.8	29.3
United Kingdom	5.6	5.5	6.1	6.2	6.4	17.0	16.8	18.9	18.9	19.2
United States	6.7	6.7	6.1	6.2	6.2	25.6	23.6	26.1	23.8	23.0
Unweighted average										
OECD Average	**7.3**	**8.6**	**8.8**	**9.1**	**9.1**	**22.0**	**25.0**	**26.8**	**26.1**	**26.0**

.. Not available

Note*:* Full time series can be accessed at http://oe.cd/full-time-series.

1. The total tax revenue has been reduced by the amount of any capital transfer that represents uncollected taxes. The capital transfer has been allocated between tax headings in proportion to the reported tax revenue.
2. From 1991 the figures relate to the united Germany.

StatLink https://doi.org/10.1787/888934055120

Table 3.11. Taxes on payroll and workforce (3000) as % of GDP and as % of total tax revenue

	% of GDP					% of total tax revenue				
	1990	2000	2010	2016	2017	1990	2000	2010	2016	2017
Australia	1.7	1.4	1.3	1.3	1.4	6.1	4.5	5.2	4.9	4.8
Austria	2.4	2.7	2.8	2.9	2.8	6.0	6.4	6.9	7.0	6.6
Belgium	0.0	0.0	0.0	0.0	0.0	0.0	0.0	0.0	0.0	0.0
Canada	0.8	0.7	0.6	0.7	0.7	2.3	2.1	2.1	2.1	2.0
Chile	0.0	0.0	0.0	0.0	0.0	0.0	0.0	0.0	0.0	0.0
Czech Republic	..	0.0	0.0	0.0	0.0	..	0.0	0.0	0.0	0.0
Denmark[1]	0.3	0.2	0.2	0.3	0.3	0.7	0.4	0.5	0.6	0.5
Estonia	..	0.0	0.0	0.0	0.0	..	0.0	0.0	0.0	0.0
Finland	0.0	0.0	0.0	0.0	0.0	0.0	0.0	0.0	0.0	0.0
France[1]	0.8	1.0	1.3	1.5	1.5	1.9	2.3	3.2	3.4	3.4
Germany[2]	0.0	0.0	0.0	0.0	0.0	0.0	0.0	0.0	0.0	0.0
Greece	0.2	0.0	0.0	0.0	0.0	0.7	0.0	0.0	0.0	0.0
Hungary	..	1.4	0.4	0.6	0.7	..	3.6	1.1	1.6	1.9
Iceland	1.1	0.0	0.2	0.3	0.3	3.5	0.1	0.5	0.6	0.8
Ireland	0.4	0.0	0.2	0.1	0.1	1.3	0.0	0.7	0.6	0.6
Israel	..	1.3	1.2	1.1	1.2	..	3.6	3.8	3.7	3.7
Italy	0.1	0.0	0.0	0.0	0.0	0.3	0.0	0.0	0.0	0.0
Japan	0.0	0.0	0.0	0.0	0.0	0.0	0.0	0.0	0.0	0.0
Korea	0.1	0.0	0.1	0.1	0.1	0.4	0.2	0.2	0.3	0.3
Latvia	..	0.0	0.0	0.0	0.0	..	0.0	0.1	0.0	0.0
Lithuania[1]	..	0.0	0.0	0.0	0.0	..	0.0	0.0	0.0	0.0
Luxembourg	0.0	0.0	0.0	0.0	0.0	0.0	0.0	0.0	0.0	0.0
Mexico	0.2	0.2	0.3	0.4	0.4	1.8	1.5	2.2	2.3	2.4
Netherlands	0.0	0.0	0.0	0.0	0.0	0.0	0.0	0.0	0.0	0.0
New Zealand	0.0	0.0	0.0	0.0	0.0	0.0	0.0	0.0	0.0	0.0
Norway	0.0	0.0	0.0	0.0	0.1	0.0	0.0	0.0	0.0	0.1
Poland	..	0.2	0.3	0.2	0.2	..	0.7	0.8	0.7	0.7
Portugal	0.0	0.0	0.0	0.0	0.0	0.0	0.0	0.0	0.0	0.0
Slovak Republic	..	0.0	0.0	0.0	0.0	..	0.0	0.0	0.0	0.0
Slovenia	..	1.5	0.1	0.0	0.1	..	4.2	0.2	0.1	0.1
Spain[1]	0.0	0.0	0.0	0.0	0.0	0.0	0.0	0.0	0.0	0.0
Sweden	1.2	2.1	3.1	4.6	5.1	2.5	4.3	7.1	10.5	11.5
Switzerland[1]	0.0	0.0	0.0	0.0	0.0	0.0	0.0	0.0	0.0	0.0
Turkey	0.0	0.0	0.0	0.0	0.0	0.0	0.0	0.0	0.0	0.0
United Kingdom	0.0	0.0	0.0	0.0	0.1	0.0	0.0	0.0	0.0	0.3
United States	0.0	0.0	0.0	0.0	0.0	0.0	0.0	0.1	0.0	0.0
Unweighted average										
OECD Average	**0.3**	**0.4**	**0.3**	**0.4**	**0.4**	**1.0**	**0.9**	**1.0**	**1.1**	**1.1**

.. Not available

Note: Full time series can be accessed at http://oe.cd/full-time-series.

1. The total tax revenue has been reduced by the amount of any capital transfer that represents uncollected taxes. The capital transfer has been allocated between tax headings in proportion to the reported tax revenue.

2. From 1991 the figures relate to the united Germany.

StatLink https://doi.org/10.1787/888934055139

Table 3.12. Taxes on property (4000) as % of GDP and as % of total tax revenue

	% of GDP					% of total tax revenue				
	1990	2000	2010	2016	2017	1990	2000	2010	2016	2017
Australia	2.5	2.7	2.4	3.0	3.0	9.0	8.8	9.4	10.8	10.3
Austria	1.1	0.6	0.5	0.5	0.5	2.7	1.3	1.3	1.3	1.3
Belgium	1.6	2.0	3.1	3.5	3.5	3.8	4.7	7.2	8.0	7.9
Canada	3.5	3.3	3.8	4.0	3.9	10.0	9.5	12.3	12.1	12.0
Chile	1.0	1.3	0.8	1.0	1.1	6.2	7.0	4.1	5.1	5.4
Czech Republic	..	0.5	0.4	0.5	0.5	..	1.4	1.3	1.4	1.4
Denmark[1]	1.9	1.6	1.8	1.8	1.8	4.3	3.3	4.1	4.0	3.9
Estonia	..	0.4	0.3	0.3	0.2	..	1.2	1.0	0.8	0.7
Finland	1.1	1.1	1.1	1.4	1.5	2.4	2.4	2.7	3.2	3.6
France[1]	2.6	3.1	3.6	4.2	4.4	6.3	7.2	8.6	9.3	9.5
Germany[2]	1.2	0.8	0.8	1.1	1.0	3.4	2.3	2.3	2.8	2.7
Greece	1.2	2.6	1.7	3.1	3.1	4.6	7.7	5.2	8.0	7.9
Hungary	..	0.7	1.1	1.1	1.1	..	1.7	3.1	2.8	2.8
Iceland[3]	2.6	2.8	2.3	17.4	2.1	8.4	7.9	7.0	34.2	5.5
Ireland	1.5	1.8	1.4	1.4	1.3	4.6	5.7	5.3	6.1	5.7
Israel	..	3.1	3.3	3.2	3.2	..	9.0	10.7	10.3	10.0
Italy	0.8	1.9	2.0	2.8	2.6	2.3	4.6	4.8	6.6	6.2
Japan	2.7	2.7	2.6	2.6	2.6	9.4	10.5	9.7	8.3	8.2
Korea	2.2	2.7	2.6	3.0	3.1	11.8	12.4	11.3	11.6	11.7
Latvia	..	1.1	0.9	1.1	1.0	..	3.8	3.0	3.4	3.3
Lithuania[1]	..	0.5	0.4	0.3	0.3	..	1.5	1.3	1.1	1.0
Luxembourg	2.8	3.9	2.6	3.5	3.7	8.4	10.7	7.1	9.3	9.6
Mexico	0.2	0.2	0.3	0.3	0.3	1.9	1.8	2.3	1.9	1.9
Netherlands	1.5	1.9	1.4	1.5	1.6	3.7	5.3	3.8	4.0	4.0
New Zealand	2.5	1.7	2.0	1.9	1.9	6.8	5.3	6.6	6.1	6.0
Norway	1.2	1.0	1.2	1.3	1.3	2.9	2.3	2.8	3.2	3.3
Poland	..	1.4	1.3	1.4	1.4	..	4.3	4.2	4.1	4.0
Portugal	0.7	1.1	1.1	1.3	1.4	2.7	3.7	3.5	3.7	3.9
Slovak Republic	..	0.6	0.4	0.4	0.4	..	1.8	1.5	1.3	1.3
Slovenia	..	0.6	0.6	0.6	0.6	..	1.7	1.7	1.7	1.8
Spain[1]	1.7	2.1	2.1	2.6	2.5	5.5	6.4	6.6	7.7	7.5
Sweden	1.7	1.7	1.0	1.1	1.0	3.5	3.4	2.4	2.4	2.2
Switzerland[1]	2.1	2.7	2.0	2.0	2.2	8.9	9.7	7.6	7.4	7.6
Turkey	0.3	0.7	1.0	1.2	1.1	2.3	3.2	4.1	4.8	4.5
United Kingdom	2.7	3.8	3.9	4.1	4.2	8.2	11.5	12.0	12.6	12.5
United States	3.1	2.9	3.2	3.0	4.3	11.8	10.3	13.5	11.5	16.0
Unweighted average										
OECD Average	**1.8**	**1.8**	**1.7**	**2.3**	**1.9**	**5.8**	**5.4**	**5.4**	**6.5**	**5.8**

.. Not available

Note: Full time series can be accessed at http://oe.cd/full-time-series.

1. The total tax revenue has been reduced by the amount of any capital transfer that represents uncollected taxes. The capital transfer has been allocated between tax headings in proportion to the reported tax revenue.
2. From 1991 the figures relate to the united Germany.
3. The 2016 figure for Iceland includes the one-off revenues from stability contributions.

StatLink https://doi.org/10.1787/888934055158

Table 3.13. Taxes on goods and services (5000) as % of GDP and as % of total tax revenue

	% of GDP					% of total tax revenue				
	1990	2000	2010	2016	2017	1990	2000	2010	2016	2017
Australia	7.8	8.8	7.3	7.5	7.4	27.8	28.8	29.0	27.1	26.0
Austria	12.4	12.2	11.6	11.8	11.8	31.5	28.9	28.4	28.2	28.1
Belgium	10.7	10.9	10.8	10.8	10.8	26.1	25.0	25.3	24.5	24.2
Canada	9.1	8.4	7.4	7.6	7.7	25.8	24.2	24.0	23.1	23.5
Chile	10.6	12.0	10.0	11.0	11.0	62.9	63.8	51.2	54.6	54.8
Czech Republic	..	10.2	10.8	11.3	11.5	..	31.5	33.2	33.0	32.9
Denmark[1]	15.1	15.5	14.9	14.7	14.5	33.9	33.1	33.3	32.1	31.8
Estonia	..	12.1	13.4	14.4	14.0	..	38.8	40.2	42.9	42.6
Finland	14.0	13.3	13.0	14.5	14.2	32.5	29.0	31.8	32.8	32.9
France[1]	11.7	11.2	10.5	11.1	11.3	28.4	25.8	24.8	24.4	24.5
Germany[2]	9.3	10.2	10.3	10.1	9.9	26.7	28.1	29.5	27.1	26.3
Greece	11.2	11.6	12.3	15.5	15.3	44.5	34.8	38.2	40.0	39.3
Hungary	..	15.6	16.0	16.6	16.4	..	40.5	42.9	42.4	42.9
Iceland	15.6	15.9	11.4	11.9	12.6	51.3	44.1	35.2	23.4	33.7
Ireland	13.6	11.7	9.8	7.6	7.3	41.9	38.2	36.2	32.5	32.4
Israel	..	11.6	12.1	11.8	11.3	..	33.1	39.4	37.8	34.6
Italy	10.2	11.3	11.0	11.9	12.0	28.0	27.9	26.3	28.2	28.4
Japan	3.9	5.0	5.0	6.3	6.6	13.7	19.3	18.7	20.4	21.0
Korea	8.3	8.2	7.9	7.4	7.5	44.3	38.4	33.7	28.1	27.7
Latvia	..	11.2	11.9	13.6	13.4	..	38.6	41.3	43.7	43.0
Lithuania[1]	..	12.0	11.5	11.4	11.4	..	39.0	40.6	38.4	38.5
Luxembourg	7.9	9.7	10.2	9.6	9.4	23.6	26.3	27.3	25.3	24.3
Mexico	5.3	4.8	4.9	6.4	5.9	44.0	41.7	38.0	38.8	36.4
Netherlands	10.5	10.7	11.0	11.3	11.3	26.4	28.9	30.8	29.5	29.1
New Zealand	12.1	11.3	12.0	12.1	12.3	33.6	34.7	39.6	38.3	38.4
Norway	14.3	13.3	11.6	12.1	12.0	35.5	31.8	27.7	31.4	30.9
Poland	..	11.6	12.6	12.3	12.6	..	35.3	40.1	36.8	36.9
Portugal	11.7	12.5	12.2	13.5	13.8	44.2	40.3	40.2	39.7	40.0
Slovak Republic	..	12.2	10.1	10.7	11.0	..	36.2	35.8	33.1	33.1
Slovenia	..	13.8	13.8	14.4	14.0	..	37.6	37.3	39.3	38.6
Spain[1]	9.0	10.0	8.5	9.9	9.9	28.4	30.0	27.2	29.8	29.3
Sweden	12.3	12.1	12.7	12.4	12.3	25.0	24.8	29.3	28.1	27.8
Switzerland[1]	4.9	6.0	6.1	5.9	6.0	20.6	21.8	22.8	21.4	21.1
Turkey	4.1	9.9	11.8	11.0	10.8	27.9	42.0	47.7	43.6	43.5
United Kingdom	10.2	10.4	10.0	10.6	10.6	31.0	31.6	30.8	32.3	31.9
United States	4.6	4.5	4.2	4.3	4.2	17.5	16.0	18.1	16.6	15.7
Unweighted average										
OECD Average	**10.0**	**10.9**	**10.6**	**11.0**	**10.9**	**32.5**	**33.0**	**33.2**	**32.5**	**32.4**

.. Not available

Note: Full time series can be accessed at http://oe.cd/full-time-series.

1. The total tax revenue has been reduced by the amount of any capital transfer that represents uncollected taxes. The capital transfer has been allocated between tax headings in proportion to the reported tax revenue.
2. From 1991 the figures relate to the united Germany.

StatLink https://doi.org/10.1787/888934055177

Table 3.14. Value added taxes (5111) as % of GDP and as % of total tax revenue

	% of GDP					% of total tax revenue				
	1990	2000	2010	2016	2017	1990	2000	2010	2016	2017
Australia	0.0	3.4	3.4	3.6	3.5	0.0	11.1	13.4	12.9	12.2
Austria	8.2	7.9	7.7	7.7	7.7	20.8	18.7	18.7	18.3	18.3
Belgium	6.8	7.0	6.9	6.8	6.8	16.4	16.1	16.2	15.4	15.2
Canada	0.0	3.2	4.2	4.5	4.5	0.0	9.2	13.7	13.4	13.7
Chile	6.3	7.9	7.5	8.3	8.4	37.4	41.8	38.5	41.2	41.6
Czech Republic	..	5.9	6.6	7.4	7.7	..	18.3	20.5	21.7	22.0
Denmark[1]	8.4	9.2	9.4	9.4	9.5	18.9	19.5	21.1	20.5	20.7
Estonia	..	8.4	8.5	9.1	9.1	..	27.1	25.7	27.2	27.8
Finland	8.3	8.0	8.3	9.1	9.1	19.3	17.4	20.4	20.7	21.0
France[1]	7.6	7.2	6.8	6.9	7.0	18.4	16.7	16.1	15.2	15.3
Germany[2]	5.8	6.7	7.0	6.9	6.9	16.6	18.4	20.0	18.5	18.4
Greece	6.2	6.3	7.1	8.1	8.1	24.6	18.9	22.0	21.0	20.9
Hungary	..	8.6	8.5	9.3	9.5	..	22.4	22.9	23.7	24.8
Iceland	8.7	10.3	7.3	8.2	8.9	28.5	28.5	22.7	16.2	23.8
Ireland	6.6	7.1	6.0	4.7	4.4	20.4	22.9	22.2	20.2	19.6
Israel	..	7.4	7.5	7.5	7.4	..	21.1	24.4	24.1	22.9
Italy	5.3	6.3	6.1	6.1	6.2	14.7	15.4	14.5	14.3	14.8
Japan	1.2	2.3	2.5	4.1	4.1	4.4	9.1	9.6	13.3	13.0
Korea	3.5	3.7	4.1	4.2	4.3	18.7	17.0	17.5	15.8	16.0
Latvia	..	7.0	6.7	8.1	8.0	..	23.9	23.3	26.0	25.7
Lithuania[1]	..	7.4	7.7	7.8	7.8	..	24.2	27.4	26.2	26.6
Luxembourg	4.0	4.9	6.4	6.4	6.2	12.1	13.4	17.0	16.8	15.9
Mexico	3.2	2.8	3.8	3.9	3.7	26.1	24.7	29.4	23.7	23.1
Netherlands	6.5	6.4	6.7	6.8	6.8	16.5	17.3	18.7	17.6	17.4
New Zealand	8.1	8.1	9.3	9.5	9.7	22.4	24.9	30.7	29.8	30.2
Norway	7.6	8.2	7.8	8.6	8.6	18.8	19.7	18.5	22.3	22.1
Poland	..	6.9	7.6	7.2	7.8	..	21.0	24.2	21.6	22.8
Portugal	5.2	7.6	7.5	8.5	8.6	19.6	24.4	24.7	24.8	25.1
Slovak Republic	..	6.9	6.2	6.7	7.0	..	20.4	22.0	20.6	21.1
Slovenia	..	8.5	8.1	8.2	8.1	..	23.3	21.9	22.5	22.3
Spain[1]	5.0	5.9	5.3	6.4	6.4	15.7	17.7	16.9	19.2	19.1
Sweden	7.3	8.3	9.2	9.2	9.3	14.9	16.9	21.2	20.9	20.9
Switzerland[1]	2.7	3.6	3.4	3.4	3.4	11.6	13.0	12.7	12.2	12.0
Turkey	2.7	5.7	5.4	5.0	5.0	18.3	24.2	21.7	19.8	20.1
United Kingdom	5.5	5.9	6.0	6.8	6.9	16.9	17.9	18.7	20.8	20.7
United States	0.0	0.0	0.0	0.0	0.0	0.0	0.0	0.0	0.0	0.0
Unweighted average										
OECD Average	**5.2**	**6.4**	**6.5**	**6.8**	**6.8**	**16.7**	**19.3**	**20.3**	**20.0**	**20.2**

.. Not available

Note*:* Full time series can be accessed at http://oe.cd/full-time-series.

1. The total tax revenue has been reduced by the amount of any capital transfer that represents uncollected taxes. The capital transfer has been allocated between tax headings in proportion to the reported tax revenue.
2. From 1991 the figures relate to the united Germany.

StatLink https://doi.org/10.1787/888934055196

Table 3.15. Tax revenues of sub-sectors of general government as % of total tax revenue

	Supranational			Central government			State or Regional government			Local government			Social Security Funds		
	1975	1995	2017	1975	1995	2017	1975	1995	2017	1975	1995	2017	1975	1995	2017
Federal countries															
Australia	..	..	..	80.1	77.5	80.6	15.7	19.0	16.0	4.2	3.4	3.4	0.0	0.0	0.0
Austria	..	0.4	0.4	51.7	64.7	65.8	10.6	1.8	1.6	12.4	4.1	3.0	25.3	29.0	29.2
Belgium	1.4	1.0	1.0	65.3	60.1	51.4	..	1.8	10.8	4.4	4.8	4.9	28.8	32.2	32.0
Canada	..	..	..	47.6	39.1	40.9	32.5	37.1	39.8	9.9	9.8	10.3	10.0	14.0	9.1
Germany	1.2	0.6	0.6	33.5	31.4	29.5	22.3	21.6	23.5	9.0	7.4	8.6	34.0	39.0	37.9
Mexico	..	..	..	..	73.9	81.1	..	2.8	4.1	..	1.5	1.6	..	21.8	13.3
Switzerland[1]	..	..	..	30.7	31.2	36.5	27.0	24.3	24.6	20.3	17.7	15.3	22.0	26.8	23.6
United States	..	..	..	45.4	41.4	44.5	19.5	20.0	18.3	14.7	13.3	14.2	20.5	25.2	23.0
Unweighted average	1.3	0.7	0.7	50.6	52.4	53.8	21.3	16.1	17.3	10.7	7.8	7.7	20.1	23.5	21.0
Regional country															
Spain[1, 2]	..	0.5	0.7	48.2	51.5	41.3	..	4.7	15.2	4.3	8.6	9.7	47.5	34.7	33.1
Unitary countries															
Chile	..	..	..	..	89.9	86.3	..	..	..	..	6.5	7.8	..	3.6	5.9
Czech Republic	..	..	0.5	..	57.7	55.4	..	..	..	..	0.9	1.1	..	41.4	43.0
Denmark[1]	1.0	0.5	0.3	69.1	68.4	73.2	..	..	..	29.8	31.1	26.4	0.1	0.0	0.0
Estonia	..	..	0.6	..	84.3	82.0	..	..	..	..	0.8	0.9	..	14.9	16.6
Finland	..	0.4	0.3	56.0	46.6	48.4	..	..	..	23.5	22.3	23.5	20.4	30.8	27.8
France[1]	0.7	0.4	0.4	51.2	42.6	34.2	..	..	..	7.6	10.9	13.3	40.6	46.0	52.1
Greece	..	0.6	0.5	67.1	66.4	67.4	..	..	..	3.4	2.0	2.4	29.5	31.1	29.6
Hungary	..	..	0.3	..	63.8	62.4	..	..	..	..	2.5	5.8	..	33.6	31.5
Iceland	..	..	..	81.3	79.2	73.5	..	..	..	18.7	20.8	26.5	0.0	0.0	0.0
Ireland	2.3	1.5	0.6	77.4	83.1	82.5	..	..	..	7.3	2.7	2.2	13.1	12.7	14.7
Israel	..	..	..	..	79.6	76.2	..	..	..	..	6.4	7.6	..	14.0	16.2
Italy	..	0.4	0.6	53.2	62.7	53.6	..	..	..	0.9	5.4	15.5	45.9	31.5	30.3
Japan	..	..	..	45.5	41.2	37.4	..	..	..	25.6	25.2	22.7	29.0	33.6	39.9
Korea	..	..	..	89.0	69.2	57.0	..	..	..	10.1	18.7	17.3	0.9	12.1	25.7
Latvia	..	..	0.6	..	43.5	53.2	..	..	..	..	19.5	19.2	..	36.9	26.9
Lithuania[1]	..	..	0.9	..	71.7	56.4	..	..	..	..	2.3	1.2	..	26.1	41.5
Luxembourg	0.8	0.4	0.6	63.6	66.5	67.5	..	..	..	6.7	6.5	4.1	29.0	26.6	27.9
Netherlands	1.5	1.3	1.1	58.9	56.0	60.2	..	..	..	1.2	3.1	3.0	38.4	39.5	35.7
New Zealand	..	..	..	92.3	94.7	93.4	..	..	..	7.7	5.3	6.6	0.0	0.0	0.0
Norway	..	..	..	50.6	58.4	84.1	..	..	..	22.4	19.6	15.9	27.0	22.0	0.0
Poland	..	..	0.5	..	61.2	49.2	..	..	..	..	8.5	12.7	..	30.3	37.5
Portugal	..	0.8	0.5	65.4	72.3	72.9	..	..	..	0.0	5.4	7.1	34.6	21.5	19.5
Slovak Republic	..	..	0.5	..	62.5	55.0	..	..	..	..	1.3	1.9	..	36.2	42.5
Slovenia	..	..	0.4	..	51.8	50.7	..	..	..	..	6.3	9.4	..	41.9	39.6
Sweden	..	0.4	0.3	51.3	46.9	52.4	..	..	..	29.2	30.9	35.3	19.5	21.8	12.1
Turkey	..	..	..	..	75.1	61.2	..	..	..	..	12.8	9.5	..	12.1	29.3
United Kingdom	1.0	1.0	0.5	70.5	77.5	75.5	..	..	..	11.1	3.7	4.9	17.5	17.8	19.2
Unweighted average	1.2	0.7	0.5	65.2	65.7	63.8	..	..	..	12.8	10.4	11.2	21.6	23.6	24.6

.. Not available

1. The total tax revenue has been reduced by the amount of any capital transfer that represents uncollected taxes.
2. Spain is constitutionally a non-federal country but has a highly decentralised political structure.

StatLink https://doi.org/10.1787/888934055215

Table 3.16. Main central government taxes as % of total tax revenues of central government, 2017

	1000 Income & profits	2000 Social security[2]	3000 Payroll	4000 Property	5000 Goods and services	6000 Others
Federal countries						
Australia	73.0	0.0	0.3	0.4	26.4	0.0
Austria	41.9	7.9	6.7	1.2	41.8	0.5
Belgium	56.6	0.1	0.0	2.1	41.3	0.0
Canada	72.6	7.3	0.0	0.0	20.2	0.0
Germany	45.1	0.0	0.0	0.1	54.8	0.0
Mexico	55.0	0.0	0.0	0.0	43.9	1.1
Switzerland[1]	44.2	0.0	0.0	2.5	53.2	0.1
United States	82.6	0.0	0.0	11.7	5.6	0.0
Unweighted average	58.9	1.9	0.9	2.2	35.9	0.2
Regional country						
Spain[1]	40.0	2.1	0.0	0.3	57.6	0.0
Unitary countries						
Chile	40.0	1.6	0.0	2.4	58.3	-2.3
Czech Republic	40.0	0.0	0.0	1.3	58.5	0.1
Denmark[1]	54.3	0.1	0.7	1.5	43.4	0.0
Estonia	27.0	21.4	0.0	0.0	51.7	0.0
Finland	28.6	0.0	0.0	3.6	67.7	0.1
France[1]	36.6	2.3	1.0	7.0	52.7	0.3
Greece	33.7	0.2	0.0	8.4	57.7	0.0
Hungary	30.1	3.9	2.9	2.7	60.0	0.4
Iceland	38.0	12.4	1.1	1.5	44.7	2.3
Ireland	52.7	2.7	0.8	4.5	39.3	0.0
Israel	46.6	0.0	4.8	3.6	45.0	0.0
Italy	50.7	0.0	0.0	6.2	43.1	0.0
Japan	52.6	0.0	0.0	5.2	42.2	0.0
Korea	50.8	0.0	0.0	6.4	41.2	1.7
Latvia	18.6	0.0	0.1	1.0	80.3	0.0
Lithuania[1]	32.1	0.0	0.0	0.0	67.9	0.0
Luxembourg	49.6	1.1	0.0	13.9	35.3	0.2
Netherlands	49.9	0.0	0.0	3.6	46.0	0.5
New Zealand	59.5	0.0	0.0	0.1	40.4	0.0
Norway	30.1	31.7	0.2	1.5	36.5	0.0
Poland	25.0	0.0	1.3	0.0	73.7	0.0
Portugal	36.2	12.1	0.0	0.7	49.9	1.1
Slovak Republic	38.6	2.5	0.0	0.0	58.9	0.0
Slovenia	23.8	0.8	0.3	0.0	75.0	0.0
Sweden	3.5	18.6	21.9	2.7	53.1	0.2
Turkey	30.7	0.0	0.0	5.2	63.3	0.8
United Kingdom	47.2	0.0	0.4	10.2	42.2	0.0
Unweighted average	38.0	4.3	1.3	3.5	52.9	0.2

Note: Excluding social security contributions accruing to social security funds.

1. The total tax revenue has been reduced by the amount of any capital transfer that represents uncollected taxes. The capital transfer has been allocated between tax headings in proportion to the reported tax revenue.
2. These comprise only social security contributions accruing to central government.

StatLink https://doi.org/10.1787/888934055234

Table 3.17. Main state government taxes as % of total tax revenues of state government, 2017

	1000 Income & profits	2000 Social security	3000 Payroll	4000 Property	5000 Goods and services	6000 Others
Federal countries						
Australia	0.0	0.0	29.0	41.4	29.6	0.0
Austria[1]	47.1	19.8	8.5	2.1	18.2	4.2
Belgium[1]	47.3	1.1	0.0	36.0	15.6	0.0
Canada	46.7	5.3	5.1	4.9	38.0	0.0
Germany[1]	52.9	0.0	0.0	6.7	40.4	0.0
Mexico	0.0	0.0	58.3	18.1	18.6	5.0
Switzerland[2]	76.1	0.0	0.0	16.9	6.3	0.7
United States	41.6	0.0	0.2	3.3	54.9	0.0
Unweighted average	39.0	3.3	12.6	16.2	27.7	1.2
Regional country						
Spain[1, 2, 3]	69.4	0.0	0.0	20.0	10.6	0.0
Unitary countries						
Chile	..	..	..	..	..	..
Czech Republic	..	..	..	..	..	..
Denmark	..	..	..	..	..	..
Estonia	..	..	..	..	..	..
Finland	..	..	..	..	..	..
France	..	..	..	..	..	..
Greece	..	..	..	..	..	..
Hungary	..	..	..	..	..	..
Iceland	..	..	..	..	..	..
Ireland	..	..	..	..	..	..
Israel	..	..	..	..	..	..
Italy	..	..	..	..	..	..
Japan	..	..	..	..	..	..
Korea	..	..	..	..	..	..
Latvia	..	..	..	..	..	..
Lithuania	..	..	..	..	..	..
Luxembourg	..	..	..	..	..	..
Netherlands	..	..	..	..	..	..
New Zealand	..	..	..	..	..	..
Norway	..	..	..	..	..	..
Poland	..	..	..	..	..	..
Portugal	..	..	..	..	..	..
Slovak Republic	..	..	..	..	..	..
Slovenia	..	..	..	..	..	..
Sweden	..	..	..	..	..	..
Turkey	..	..	..	..	..	..
United Kingdom	..	..	..	..	..	..
Unweighted average	..	..	..	..	..	..

.. Not available

1. Payments to the European Union are excluded from these comparisons.
2. The total tax revenue has been reduced by the amount of any capital transfer that represents uncollected taxes. The capital transfer has been allocated between tax headings in proportion to the reported tax revenue.
3. Spain is constitutionally a non-federal country but has a highly decentralised political structure.

StatLink https://doi.org/10.1787/888934055253

Table 3.18. Main local government taxes as % of total tax revenues of local government, 2017

	1000 Income & profits	2000 Social security	3000 Payroll	4000 Property	5000 Goods and services	6000 Others
Federal countries						
Australia	0.0	0.0	0.0	100.0	0.0	0.0
Austria[1]	0.0	5.5	68.5	15.1	7.9	3.0
Belgium[1]	35.4	0.2	0.0	57.6	6.8	0.0
Canada	0.0	0.0	0.0	97.3	1.6	1.0
Germany[1]	79.4	0.0	0.0	13.2	7.2	0.2
Mexico	0.0	0.0	0.0	74.6	2.5	22.9
Switzerland[2]	81.2	0.0	0.0	16.3	0.5	1.9
United States	5.8	0.0	0.0	72.0	22.2	0.0
Unweighted average	25.2	0.7	9.8	55.8	6.1	3.6
Regional country						
Spain[1, 2, 3]	16.3	0.0	0.0	44.7	38.8	0.1
Unitary countries						
Chile	0.0	0.0	0.0	42.6	57.4	0.0
Czech Republic[1]	0.0	0.0	0.0	57.2	42.8	0.0
Denmark[1, 2]	89.3	0.0	0.0	10.7	0.0	0.0
Estonia[1]	0.0	0.0	0.0	81.9	18.1	0.0
Finland[1]	92.1	0.1	0.0	7.8	0.0	0.0
France[1, 2]	0.0	0.0	7.3	53.2	23.0	16.5
Greece[1]	0.0	0.0	0.0	93.2	6.8	0.0
Hungary[1]	0.0	0.0	0.0	19.3	80.7	0.0
Iceland	80.1	0.0	0.0	16.6	3.3	0.0
Ireland[1]	0.0	6.9	0.0	93.1	0.0	0.0
Israel	0.0	0.0	0.0	95.2	4.8	0.0
Italy[1]	29.4	0.0	0.0	18.4	32.5	19.7
Japan	48.5	0.0	0.0	27.6	22.8	1.1
Korea	18.3	0.0	1.7	46.6	24.5	8.9
Latvia[1]	84.8	0.0	0.0	14.1	1.1	0.0
Lithuania[2]	0.0	0.0	0.0	86.5	13.5	0.0
Luxembourg[1]	92.1	0.0	0.0	6.7	1.1	0.2
Netherlands[1]	0.0	0.0	0.0	61.9	38.1	0.0
New Zealand	0.0	0.0	0.0	89.4	10.6	0.0
Norway	86.0	0.0	0.0	12.9	1.1	0.0
Poland[1]	62.7	0.0	0.0	31.4	4.7	1.1
Portugal[1]	25.3	0.2	0.0	48.3	25.8	0.4
Slovak Republic[1]	0.0	0.0	0.0	66.6	33.4	0.0
Slovenia[1]	75.0	0.0	0.0	18.8	6.2	0.0
Sweden[1]	97.6	0.0	0.0	2.4	0.0	0.0
Turkey	27.2	0.0	0.0	13.9	50.1	8.7
United Kingdom[1]	0.0	0.0	0.0	100.0	0.0	0.0
Unweighted average	33.6	0.3	0.3	45.0	18.6	2.1

1. Payments to the European Union are excluded from these comparisons.
2. The total tax revenue has been reduced by the amount of any capital transfer that represents uncollected taxes. The capital transfer has been allocated between tax headings in proportion to the reported tax revenue.
3. Spain is constitutionally a non-federal country but has a highly decentralised political structure.

StatLink https://doi.org/10.1787/888934055272

Table 3.19. Gross domestic product for tax reporting years at market prices, in billions of national currency

		1965	1990	2000	2007	2010	2012	2014	2016	2017	2018p
Australia[1]	AUD	24.3	414.5	705.1	1 177.3	1 416.6	1 536.3	1 624.4	1 764.5	1 847.7	1 938.8
Austria	EUR	18.5	137.5	213.6	284.0	295.9	318.7	333.1	356.2	369.9	386.1
Belgium	EUR	21.0	171.0	258.2	344.7	365.1	387.5	400.1	424.6	439.2	450.5
Canada	CAD	61.3	696.1	1 125.4	1 577.7	1 666.0	1 827.2	1 994.9	2 028.2	2 141.5	2 219.1
Chile	CLP	..	10 522.7	42 005.2	90 702.9	111 508.6	129 947.3	148 599.5	169 469.5	180 211.3	191 248.7
Czech Republic	CZK	..	726.7	2 379.4	3 840.1	3 962.5	4 059.9	4 313.8	4 768.0	5 047.3	5 328.7
Denmark	DKK	71.5	855.6	1 326.9	1 738.8	1 810.9	1 895.0	1 981.2	2 100.2	2 178.1	2 223.1
Estonia	EUR	..	..	6.2	16.2	14.7	17.9	20.1	21.7	23.6	25.7
Finland	EUR	4.5	91.0	136.3	186.6	187.1	199.8	205.5	216.1	223.9	232.1
France	EUR	76.4	1 053.5	1 478.6	1 941.4	1 995.3	2 088.8	2 149.8	2 234.1	2 295.1	2 353.1
Germany	EUR	234.8	1 306.7	2 116.5	2 513.2	2 580.1	2 758.3	2 938.6	3 159.8	3 277.3	3 386.0
Greece	EUR	0.7	45.5	141.2	232.7	226.0	191.2	178.7	176.5	180.2	184.7
Hungary	HUF	..	..	13 350.1	25 680.2	27 224.6	28 781.1	32 583.4	35 474.2	38 355.1	42 072.8
Iceland	ISK	0.2	377.6	707.8	1 378.1	1 672.7	1 841.7	2 073.6	2 490.9	2 616.8	2 803.0
Ireland	EUR	1.3	37.9	108.4	197.2	167.7	175.1	194.8	271.7	297.1	324.0
Israel	ILS	..	118.8	539.2	734.3	873.9	992.6	1 109.2	1 226.6	1 271.6	1 327.4
Italy	EUR	22.3	728.5	1 239.3	1 609.6	1 604.5	1 613.3	1 621.8	1 689.8	1 727.4	1 757.0
Japan[1]	JPY	35 108.0	464 025.4	528 446.7	530 922.8	499 429.1	494 369.7	518 235.1	536 807.9	547 495.7	550 098.7
Korea	KRW	831.3	197 712.3	635 184.6	1 043 257.8	1 265 308.0	1 377 456.7	1 486 079.3	1 641 786.0	1 730 398.5	1 782 268.8
Latvia	EUR	..	..	6.9	22.6	17.9	21.9	23.6	25.0	27.0	29.5
Lithuania	EUR	..	..	13.4	29.0	28.0	33.3	36.6	38.8	42.2	45.1
Luxembourg	EUR	1.0	11.0	23.1	37.2	40.2	44.1	49.8	53.3	55.3	58.9
Mexico	MXN	..	843.6	6 693.7	11 504.1	13 366.4	15 817.8	17 473.8	20 116.7	21 921.2	23 542.7
Netherlands	EUR	35.6	263.0	452.0	619.2	639.2	653.0	671.6	708.3	738.1	774.0
New Zealand[1]	NZD	4.1	75.9	122.2	189.1	205.8	218.8	244.8	273.4	288.8	300.0
Norway	NOK	57.2	749.9	1 507.9	2 351.0	2 593.7	2 968.3	3 146.7	3 119.3	3 304.4	3 535.6
Poland	PLN	..	62.7	747.0	1 187.6	1 445.3	1 629.4	1 720.4	1 861.1	1 989.3	2 115.7
Portugal	EUR	0.6	56.0	128.5	175.5	179.9	168.4	173.1	186.5	194.6	201.6
Slovak Republic	EUR	..	10.0	31.6	63.1	67.6	72.7	76.1	81.2	84.9	90.2
Slovenia	EUR	..	0.9	18.9	35.2	36.3	36.1	37.6	40.4	43.0	45.9
Spain	EUR	8.7	327.8	646.3	1 080.8	1 080.9	1 039.8	1 037.8	1 118.7	1 166.3	1 208.2
Sweden	SEK	127.7	1 529.7	2 383.6	3 301.0	3 523.8	3 688.9	3 940.9	4 385.5	4 578.8	4 789.9
Switzerland	CHF	68.1	358.5	459.4	576.1	608.8	626.4	649.7	660.4	668.6	689.9
Turkey	TRY	0.0	0.5	170.7	880.5	1 160.0	1 569.7	2 044.5	2 608.5	3 106.5	3 701.0
United Kingdom	GBP	36.4	615.7	1 089.3	1 541.4	1 587.5	1 694.4	1 844.3	1 969.5	2 049.6	2 117.7
United States	USD	709.0	5 963.1	10 252.3	14 451.9	14 992.1	16 197.0	17 527.3	18 715.0	19 519.4	20 580.2

.. Not available

Note: This table is based on the archive of the Gross domestic product (GDP) dataset as of the 27th June of 2019, prior to the 2019 benchmark revisions. As it may happen that countries only cover results for a limited time period when first publishing the results of their benchmark revision, this dataset provides users with longer time series based on the methodology as used before the benchmark revision.

1. GDP is fiscal year. The year Y is calculated (at annual rate) as the average of: Q2(Y) to Q1(Y+1) for Japan; and Q3(Y) to Q2(Y+1) for Australia and New Zealand.

Source: OECD National Accounts.

StatLink https://doi.org/10.1787/888934055291

Table 3.20. Exchange rates used, national currency per US dollar at market exchange rates

		1965	1990	2000	2007	2010	2012	2014	2016	2017	2018p
Australia	AUD	0.893	1.282	1.727	1.195	1.090	0.966	1.109	1.345	1.305	1.339
Austria	EUR	..	0.788	1.085	0.730	0.755	0.778	0.754	0.904	0.887	0.847
Belgium	EUR	..	0.788	1.085	0.730	0.755	0.778	0.754	0.904	0.887	0.847
Canada	CAD	1.078	1.167	1.485	1.074	1.030	0.999	1.105	1.325	1.298	1.296
Chile	CLP	0.003	304.903	539.388	522.228	509.982	485.984	570.636	676.541	648.677	641.896
Czech Republic	CZK	..	..	38.637	20.289	19.080	19.538	20.758	24.441	23.385	21.730
Denmark	DKK	6.915	6.186	8.088	5.443	5.622	5.790	5.619	6.731	6.602	6.314
Estonia	EUR	..	0.788	1.085	0.730	0.755	0.778	0.754	0.904	0.887	0.847
Finland	EUR	..	0.788	1.085	0.730	0.755	0.778	0.754	0.904	0.887	0.847
France	EUR	..	0.788	1.085	0.730	0.755	0.778	0.754	0.904	0.887	0.847
Germany	EUR	..	0.788	1.085	0.730	0.755	0.778	0.754	0.904	0.887	0.847
Greece	EUR	..	0.788	1.085	0.730	0.755	0.778	0.754	0.904	0.887	0.847
Hungary	HUF	..	63.206	282.286	183.595	207.764	224.823	232.619	281.521	274.476	270.221
Iceland	ISK	0.431	58.378	78.845	64.075	122.242	125.118	116.688	120.835	106.823	108.269
Ireland	EUR	0.454	0.788	1.085	0.730	0.755	0.778	0.754	0.904	0.887	0.847
Israel	ILS	0.000	2.016	4.077	4.109	3.731	3.850	3.577	3.839	3.599	3.595
Italy	EUR	..	0.788	1.085	0.730	0.755	0.778	0.754	0.904	0.887	0.847
Japan	JPY	361.491	144.796	107.835	117.755	87.761	79.814	105.848	108.803	112.183	110.438
Korea	KRW	266.250	707.995	1 130.640	929.450	1 155.431	1 125.935	1 053.064	1 160.589	1 130.635	1 100.186
Latvia	EUR	..	0.788	1.085	0.730	0.755	0.778	0.754	0.904	0.887	0.847
Lithuania	EUR	..	0.788	1.085	0.730	0.755	0.778	0.754	0.904	0.887	0.847
Luxembourg	EUR	..	0.788	1.085	0.730	0.755	0.778	0.754	0.904	0.887	0.847
Mexico	MXN	0.013	2.841	9.453	10.929	12.632	13.150	13.305	18.627	18.871	19.178
Netherlands	EUR	..	0.788	1.085	0.730	0.755	0.778	0.754	0.904	0.887	0.847
New Zealand	NZD	0.722	1.678	2.205	1.361	1.388	1.235	1.206	1.437	1.407	1.446
Norway	NOK	7.151	6.258	8.797	5.858	6.042	5.815	6.302	8.400	8.271	8.135
Poland	PLN	0.000	0.950	4.346	2.765	3.015	3.252	3.154	3.944	3.779	3.611
Portugal	EUR	..	0.788	1.085	0.730	0.755	0.778	0.754	0.904	0.887	0.847
Slovak Republic	EUR	..	0.788	1.085	0.730	0.755	0.778	0.754	0.904	0.887	0.847
Slovenia	EUR	..	0.788	1.085	0.730	0.755	0.778	0.754	0.904	0.887	0.847
Spain	EUR	..	0.788	1.085	0.730	0.755	0.778	0.754	0.904	0.887	0.847
Sweden	SEK	5.158	5.918	9.161	6.758	7.202	6.769	6.860	8.556	8.547	8.690
Switzerland	CHF	4.328	1.389	1.688	1.200	1.043	0.937	0.915	0.985	0.985	0.978
Turkey	TRY	0.000	0.003	0.624	1.300	1.499	1.792	2.189	3.022	3.649	4.840
United Kingdom	GBP	0.358	0.563	0.661	0.500	0.647	0.631	0.607	0.741	0.777	0.750
United States	USD	1.000	1.000	1.000	1.000	1.000	1.000	1.000	1.000	1.000	1.000

.. Not available

Source: OECD Financial indicators data.

StatLink https://doi.org/10.1787/888934055310

4 Country tables, 1990-2017

Chapter 4 provides a summary of tax revenues by category and by level of government for each OECD country from 1990-2017.

4.1. Tax revenue and % of GDP by selected tax category and by level of government

In all of the following tables the symbol (...) indicates not available/or not applicable. The main series in this chapter cover the years 1990 to 2017. Figures referring to 1965-1989, 1991-1999, 2001-2009 and 2011-2014 have been omitted because of lack of space. A complete series is, however, available on line. Data for 1955 and 1960 (for nineteen OECD countries) are provided in part V of the 1998 edition of this Report.

The Gross Domestic Product (GDP) figures are based on the 2008 System of National Accounts (SNA) for all OECD countries.

Box 1.1. Treatment of capital transfers

Some tables refer to the treatment of the capital transfers that some countries make to account for taxes that have been assessed but not collected. The capital transfer has been subtracted from the total tax revenue and this reduction has been allocated between tax headings in proportion to their tax revenues.

This applies to the following countries:

- Denmark from 1971.
- France from 1992.
- Lithuania from 1999.
- Spain from 1995.
- Switzerland from 1990.

Table 4.1. Australia, tax revenue and % of GDP by selected tax category

	Billion AUD					% of GDP				
	1990	2000	2010	2016	2017	1990	2000	2010	2016	2017
Total tax revenue	**116.5**	**214.8**	**358.0**	**487.1**	**527.2**	**28.1**	**30.5**	**25.3**	**27.6**	**28.5**
1000 Taxes on income, profits and capital gains	**66.5**	**124.4**	**202.2**	**278.8**	**310.0**	**16.1**	**17.6**	**14.3**	**15.8**	**16.8**
1100 Of individuals	50.1	81.0	138.2	198.5	212.5	12.1	11.5	9.8	11.3	11.5
1200 Corporate	16.5	43.4	64.0	80.2	97.5	4.0	6.2	4.5	4.5	5.3
1300 Unallocable between 1100 and 1200	0.0	0.0	0.0	0.0	0.0	0.0	0.0	0.0	0.0	0.0
2000 Social security contributions	**0.0**	**0.0**	**0.0**	**0.0**	**0.0**	**0.0**	**0.0**	**0.0**	**0.0**	**0.0**
2100 Employees	0.0	0.0	0.0	0.0	0.0	0.0	0.0	0.0	0.0	0.0
2200 Employers	0.0	0.0	0.0	0.0	0.0	0.0	0.0	0.0	0.0	0.0
2300 Self-employed or non-employed	0.0	0.0	0.0	0.0	0.0	0.0	0.0	0.0	0.0	0.0
2400 Unallocable between 2100, 2200 and 2300	0.0	0.0	0.0	0.0	0.0	0.0	0.0	0.0	0.0	0.0
3000 Taxes on payroll and workforce	**7.1**	**9.6**	**18.5**	**23.8**	**25.5**	**1.7**	**1.4**	**1.3**	**1.3**	**1.4**
4000 Taxes on property	**10.4**	**18.8**	**33.5**	**52.6**	**54.5**	**2.5**	**2.7**	**2.4**	**3.0**	**3.0**
4100 Recurrent taxes on immovable property	6.1	9.1	19.9	29.2	30.3	1.5	1.3	1.4	1.7	1.6
4200 Recurrent taxes on net wealth	0.0	0.0	0.0	0.0	0.0	0.0	0.0	0.0	0.0	0.0
4300 Estate, inheritance and gift taxes	0.0	0.0	0.0	0.0	0.0	0.0	0.0	0.0	0.0	0.0
4400 Taxes on financial and capital transactions	4.3	9.8	13.6	23.4	24.2	1.0	1.4	1.0	1.3	1.3
4500 Non-recurrent taxes	0.0	0.0	0.0	0.0	0.0	0.0	0.0	0.0	0.0	0.0
4600 Other recurrent taxes on property	0.0	0.0	0.0	0.0	0.0	0.0	0.0	0.0	0.0	0.0
5000 Taxes on goods and services	**32.4**	**61.9**	**103.8**	**131.9**	**137.1**	**7.8**	**8.8**	**7.3**	**7.5**	**7.4**
5100 Taxes on production, sale, transfer, etc	27.2	56.2	92.0	113.2	117.3	6.6	8.0	6.5	6.4	6.4
5110 General taxes	9.4	25.8	49.3	64.3	65.7	2.3	3.7	3.5	3.6	3.6
5111 Value added taxes	0.0	23.9	48.1	62.7	64.1	0.0	3.4	3.4	3.6	3.5
5120 Taxes on specific goods and services	17.8	30.3	42.7	48.9	51.6	4.3	4.3	3.0	2.8	2.8
5121 Excises	12.0	19.8	26.7	22.8	23.7	2.9	2.8	1.9	1.3	1.3
5200 Taxes on use of goods and perform activities	5.2	5.7	11.7	18.8	19.8	1.3	0.8	0.8	1.1	1.1
5300 Unallocable between 5100 and 5200	0.0	0.0	0.0	0.0	0.0	0.0	0.0	0.0	0.0	0.0
6000 Other taxes	**0.0**	**0.0**	**0.0**	**0.0**	**0.0**	**0.0**	**0.0**	**0.0**	**0.0**	**0.0**
Non-wastable tax credits										
Non-wastable tax credits against 1000	..	0.2	6.7	9.1	9.5	..	0.0	0.5	0.5	0.5
Transfer component	..	0.0	4.4	6.7	7.0	..	0.0	0.3	0.4	0.4
Tax expenditure component	..	0.2	2.4	2.4	2.4	..	0.0	0.2	0.1	0.1

.. Not available
Note: More detailed country data and country notes are available in online chapter 5 "Country Tables, 1965-2017": https://doi.org/10.1787/0bbc27da-en.
Full time series can be accessed at http://oe.cd/full-time-series.
Source: Australian Bureau of Statistics.

StatLink https://doi.org/10.1787/888934055329

Table 4.2. Australia, tax revenue and % of GDP by level of government and main taxes

	Billion AUD					% of GDP				
	1990	2000	2010	2016	2017	1990	2000	2010	2016	2017
Federal or Central government										
Total tax revenue	**92.6**	**175.7**	**287.1**	**387.4**	**424.8**	**22.3**	**24.9**	**20.3**	**22.0**	**23.0**
1000 Taxes on income, profits and capital gains	66.5	124.4	202.2	278.8	310.0	16.1	17.6	14.3	15.8	16.8
2000 Social security contributions	0.0	0.0	0.0	0.0	0.0	0.0	0.0	0.0	0.0	0.0
3000 Taxes on payroll and workforce	1.3	0.1	0.5	0.6	1.1	0.3	0.0	0.0	0.0	0.1
4000 Taxes on property	0.2	0.0	0.0	0.0	1.5	0.1	0.0	0.0	0.0	0.1
5000 Taxes on goods and services	24.5	51.1	84.4	108.0	112.1	5.9	7.2	6.0	6.1	6.1
6000 Other taxes	0.0	0.0	0.0	0.0	0.0	0.0	0.0	0.0	0.0	0.0
State/Regional										
Total tax revenue	**19.7**	**32.7**	**58.4**	**82.3**	**84.3**	**4.7**	**4.6**	**4.1**	**4.7**	**4.6**
1000 Taxes on income, profits and capital gains	0.0	0.0	0.0	0.0	0.0	0.0	0.0	0.0	0.0	0.0
2000 Social security contributions	0.0	0.0	0.0	0.0	0.0	0.0	0.0	0.0	0.0	0.0
3000 Taxes on payroll and workforce	5.8	9.5	18.0	23.2	24.4	1.4	1.3	1.3	1.3	1.3
4000 Taxes on property	6.0	12.4	21.1	35.2	34.9	1.4	1.8	1.5	2.0	1.9
5000 Taxes on goods and services	7.9	10.8	19.3	23.9	25.0	1.9	1.5	1.4	1.4	1.4
6000 Other taxes	0.0	0.0	0.0	0.0	0.0	0.0	0.0	0.0	0.0	0.0
Local government										
Total tax revenue	**4.2**	**6.4**	**12.4**	**17.4**	**18.1**	**1.0**	**0.9**	**0.9**	**1.0**	**1.0**
1000 Taxes on income, profits and capital gains	0.0	0.0	0.0	0.0	0.0	0.0	0.0	0.0	0.0	0.0
2000 Social security contributions	0.0	0.0	0.0	0.0	0.0	0.0	0.0	0.0	0.0	0.0
3000 Taxes on payroll and workforce	0.0	0.0	0.0	0.0	0.0	0.0	0.0	0.0	0.0	0.0
4000 Taxes on property	4.2	6.4	12.4	17.4	18.1	1.0	0.9	0.9	1.0	1.0
5000 Taxes on goods and services	0.0	0.0	0.0	0.0	0.0	0.0	0.0	0.0	0.0	0.0
6000 Other taxes	0.0	0.0	0.0	0.0	0.0	0.0	0.0	0.0	0.0	0.0
Social Security Funds										
Total tax revenue	**0.0**	**0.0**	**0.0**	**0.0**	**0.0**	**0.0**	**0.0**	**0.0**	**0.0**	**0.0**
1000 Taxes on income, profits and capital gains	0.0	0.0	0.0	0.0	0.0	0.0	0.0	0.0	0.0	0.0
2000 Social security contributions	0.0	0.0	0.0	0.0	0.0	0.0	0.0	0.0	0.0	0.0
3000 Taxes on payroll and workforce	0.0	0.0	0.0	0.0	0.0	0.0	0.0	0.0	0.0	0.0
4000 Taxes on property	0.0	0.0	0.0	0.0	0.0	0.0	0.0	0.0	0.0	0.0
5000 Taxes on goods and services	0.0	0.0	0.0	0.0	0.0	0.0	0.0	0.0	0.0	0.0
6000 Other taxes	0.0	0.0	0.0	0.0	0.0	0.0	0.0	0.0	0.0	0.0

Note: More detailed country data and country notes are available in online chapter 6 "Tax revenues by sub-sectors of general government": https://doi.org/10.1787/0bbc27da-en. Full time series can be accessed at http://oe.cd/full-time-series.
Source: Australian Bureau of Statistics.

StatLink https://doi.org/10.1787/888934055348

Table 4.3. Austria, tax revenue and % of GDP by selected tax category

	Billion EUR					% of GDP				
	1990	2000	2010	2016	2017	1990	2000	2010	2016	2017
Total tax revenue	**54.0**	**90.3**	**121.2**	**149.3**	**154.6**	**39.3**	**42.3**	**41.0**	**41.9**	**41.8**
1000 Taxes on income, profits and capital gains	**13.8**	**25.6**	**34.0**	**41.8**	**43.7**	**10.0**	**12.0**	**11.5**	**11.7**	**11.8**
1100 Of individuals	11.3	19.9	27.1	32.3	33.5	8.2	9.3	9.2	9.1	9.1
1200 Corporate	1.9	4.2	5.5	8.4	9.1	1.4	1.9	1.9	2.4	2.5
1300 Unallocable between 1100 and 1200	0.5	1.5	1.4	1.1	1.1	0.4	0.7	0.5	0.3	0.3
2000 Social security contributions	**17.8**	**30.5**	**41.4**	**51.8**	**53.9**	**12.9**	**14.3**	**14.0**	**14.5**	**14.6**
2100 Employees	7.5	12.5	16.8	20.9	21.7	5.5	5.8	5.7	5.9	5.9
2200 Employers	8.8	14.7	19.4	24.3	25.3	6.4	6.9	6.6	6.8	6.8
2300 Self-employed or non-employed	1.5	3.4	5.2	6.6	6.9	1.1	1.6	1.7	1.9	1.9
2400 Unallocable between 2100, 2200 and 2300	0.0	0.0	0.0	0.0	0.0	0.0	0.0	0.0	0.0	0.0
3000 Taxes on payroll and workforce	**3.3**	**5.8**	**8.4**	**10.4**	**10.2**	**2.4**	**2.7**	**2.8**	**2.9**	**2.8**
4000 Taxes on property	**1.5**	**1.2**	**1.6**	**2.0**	**1.9**	**1.1**	**0.6**	**0.5**	**0.5**	**0.5**
4100 Recurrent taxes on immovable property	0.4	0.5	0.7	0.8	0.8	0.3	0.2	0.2	0.2	0.2
4200 Recurrent taxes on net wealth	0.6	0.0	0.0	0.0	0.0	0.5	0.0	0.0	0.0	0.0
4300 Estate, inheritance and gift taxes	0.1	0.1	0.0	0.0	0.0	0.1	0.1	0.0	0.0	0.0
4400 Taxes on financial and capital transactions	0.4	0.6	0.8	1.1	1.1	0.3	0.3	0.3	0.3	0.3
4500 Non-recurrent taxes	0.0	0.0	0.0	0.1	0.0	0.0	0.0	0.0	0.0	0.0
4600 Other recurrent taxes on property	0.0	0.0	0.0	0.0	0.0	0.0	0.0	0.0	0.0	0.0
5000 Taxes on goods and services	**17.0**	**26.1**	**34.4**	**42.2**	**43.5**	**12.4**	**12.2**	**11.6**	**11.8**	**11.8**
5100 Taxes on production, sale, transfer, etc	16.2	24.3	31.8	38.7	39.8	11.8	11.4	10.7	10.9	10.8
5110 General taxes	11.2	16.9	22.7	27.3	28.3	8.2	7.9	7.7	7.7	7.7
5111 Value added taxes	11.2	16.9	22.7	27.3	28.3	8.2	7.9	7.7	7.7	7.7
5120 Taxes on specific goods and services	4.9	7.4	9.1	11.3	11.5	3.5	3.4	3.1	3.2	3.1
5121 Excises	3.3	5.5	6.9	7.9	8.3	2.4	2.6	2.3	2.2	2.2
5200 Taxes on use of goods and perform activities	0.9	1.9	2.6	3.5	3.7	0.6	0.9	0.9	1.0	1.0
5300 Unallocable between 5100 and 5200	0.0	0.0	0.0	0.0	0.0	0.0	0.0	0.0	0.0	0.0
6000 Other taxes	**0.7**	**0.8**	**1.1**	**0.8**	**0.8**	**0.5**	**0.4**	**0.4**	**0.2**	**0.2**
Non-wastable tax credits										
Non-wastable tax credits against 1000	..	0.7	0.7	0.5	0.3	..	0.3	0.2	0.2	0.1
Transfer component	..	0.1	0.2	0.3	0.1	..	0.0	0.1	0.1	0.0
Tax expenditure component	..	0.6	0.4	0.2	0.2	..	0.3	0.1	0.1	0.1

.. Not available

Note: More detailed country data and country notes are available in online chapter 5 "Country Tables, 1965-2017": https://doi.org/10.1787/0bbc27da-en.
Full time series can be accessed at http://oe.cd/full-time-series.

Source: Statistics Austria.

StatLink https://doi.org/10.1787/888934055367

Table 4.4. Austria, tax revenue and % of GDP by level of government and main taxes

	Billion EUR					% of GDP				
	1990	2000	2010	2016	2017	1990	2000	2010	2016	2017
Federal or Central government										
Total tax revenue	**27.2**	**60.5**	**80.7**	**98.5**	**101.7**	**19.8**	**28.3**	**27.3**	**27.6**	**27.5**
1000 Taxes on income, profits and capital gains	8.6	24.9	33.1	40.6	42.6	6.3	11.7	11.2	11.4	11.5
2000 Social security contributions	2.4	5.1	6.3	7.8	8.0	1.7	2.4	2.1	2.2	2.2
3000 Taxes on payroll and workforce	2.6	3.9	5.8	7.1	6.8	1.9	1.8	1.9	2.0	1.8
4000 Taxes on property	0.9	0.7	0.9	1.2	1.2	0.6	0.3	0.3	0.3	0.3
5000 Taxes on goods and services	12.3	25.3	33.7	41.2	42.5	8.9	11.8	11.4	11.6	11.5
6000 Other taxes	0.5	0.6	0.9	0.5	0.6	0.4	0.3	0.3	0.1	0.1
State/Regional										
Total tax revenue	**5.8**	**1.4**	**2.0**	**2.4**	**2.5**	**4.2**	**0.7**	**0.7**	**0.7**	**0.7**
1000 Taxes on income, profits and capital gains	2.8	0.6	0.9	1.1	1.2	2.0	0.3	0.3	0.3	0.3
2000 Social security contributions	0.2	0.4	0.5	0.5	0.5	0.2	0.2	0.2	0.1	0.1
3000 Taxes on payroll and workforce	0.0	0.1	0.2	0.2	0.2	0.0	0.1	0.1	0.1	0.1
4000 Taxes on property	0.1	0.0	0.0	0.0	0.1	0.0	0.0	0.0	0.0	0.0
5000 Taxes on goods and services	2.7	0.2	0.3	0.4	0.4	2.0	0.1	0.1	0.1	0.1
6000 Other taxes	0.0	0.1	0.1	0.1	0.1	0.0	0.0	0.0	0.0	0.0
Local government										
Total tax revenue	**6.1**	**3.2**	**3.8**	**4.5**	**4.7**	**4.4**	**1.5**	**1.3**	**1.3**	**1.3**
1000 Taxes on income, profits and capital gains	2.4	0.0	0.0	0.0	0.0	1.8	0.0	0.0	0.0	0.0
2000 Social security contributions	0.2	0.3	0.3	0.3	0.3	0.1	0.1	0.1	0.1	0.1
3000 Taxes on payroll and workforce	0.7	1.8	2.4	3.1	3.2	0.5	0.8	0.8	0.9	0.9
4000 Taxes on property	0.5	0.5	0.6	0.7	0.7	0.4	0.2	0.2	0.2	0.2
5000 Taxes on goods and services	2.1	0.6	0.4	0.4	0.4	1.5	0.3	0.1	0.1	0.1
6000 Other taxes	0.2	0.1	0.1	0.1	0.1	0.1	0.0	0.0	0.0	0.0
Social Security Funds										
Total tax revenue	**15.0**	**24.8**	**34.4**	**43.3**	**45.1**	**10.9**	**11.6**	**11.6**	**12.1**	**12.2**
1000 Taxes on income, profits and capital gains	0.0	0.0	0.0	0.0	0.0	0.0	0.0	0.0	0.0	0.0
2000 Social security contributions	15.0	24.8	34.4	43.3	45.1	10.9	11.6	11.6	12.1	12.2
3000 Taxes on payroll and workforce	0.0	0.0	0.0	0.0	0.0	0.0	0.0	0.0	0.0	0.0
4000 Taxes on property	0.0	0.0	0.0	0.0	0.0	0.0	0.0	0.0	0.0	0.0
5000 Taxes on goods and services	0.0	0.0	0.0	0.0	0.0	0.0	0.0	0.0	0.0	0.0
6000 Other taxes	0.0	0.0	0.0	0.0	0.0	0.0	0.0	0.0	0.0	0.0

Note: More detailed country data and country notes are available in online chapter 6 "Tax revenues by sub-sectors of general government": https://doi.org/10.1787/0bbc27da-en. Full time series can be accessed at http://oe.cd/full-time-series.
Source: Statistics Austria.

StatLink https://doi.org/10.1787/888934055386

Table 4.5. Belgium, tax revenue and % of GDP by selected tax category

	Billion EUR					% of GDP				
	1990	2000	2010	2016	2017	1990	2000	2010	2016	2017
Total tax revenue	**70.4**	**112.4**	**155.6**	**186.3**	**195.3**	**41.2**	**43.5**	**42.6**	**43.9**	**44.5**
1000 Taxes on income, profits and capital gains	**26.0**	**43.4**	**53.2**	**66.2**	**71.3**	**15.2**	**16.8**	**14.6**	**15.6**	**16.2**
1100 Of individuals	22.5	35.3	44.0	51.6	53.1	13.2	13.7	12.0	12.1	12.1
1200 Corporate	3.4	8.1	9.2	14.6	18.1	2.0	3.1	2.5	3.4	4.1
1300 Unallocable between 1100 and 1200	0.0	0.1	0.0	0.1	0.1	0.0	0.0	0.0	0.0	0.0
2000 Social security contributions	**23.4**	**34.6**	**50.4**	**57.9**	**59.6**	**13.7**	**13.4**	**13.8**	**13.6**	**13.6**
2100 Employees	7.2	10.9	15.0	17.1	17.7	4.2	4.2	4.1	4.0	4.0
2200 Employers	14.7	20.8	30.8	35.2	36.0	8.6	8.1	8.4	8.3	8.2
2300 Self-employed or non-employed	1.5	2.9	4.6	5.7	5.8	0.9	1.1	1.3	1.3	1.3
2400 Unallocable between 2100, 2200 and 2300	0.0	0.0	0.0	0.0	0.0	0.0	0.0	0.0	0.0	0.0
3000 Taxes on payroll and workforce	**0.0**	**0.0**	**0.0**	**0.0**	**0.0**	**0.0**	**0.0**	**0.0**	**0.0**	**0.0**
4000 Taxes on property	**2.7**	**5.3**	**11.3**	**14.9**	**15.4**	**1.6**	**2.0**	**3.1**	**3.5**	**3.5**
4100 Recurrent taxes on immovable property	0.6	1.2	4.6	5.6	5.8	0.4	0.5	1.3	1.3	1.3
4200 Recurrent taxes on net wealth	0.0	0.1	0.2	1.0	0.9	0.0	0.0	0.1	0.2	0.2
4300 Estate, inheritance and gift taxes	0.5	1.1	2.3	2.9	3.1	0.3	0.4	0.6	0.7	0.7
4400 Taxes on financial and capital transactions	1.5	2.7	3.5	4.5	4.8	0.9	1.0	1.0	1.1	1.1
4500 Non-recurrent taxes	0.0	0.1	0.3	0.4	0.5	0.0	0.0	0.1	0.1	0.1
4600 Other recurrent taxes on property	0.1	0.2	0.3	0.4	0.3	0.1	0.1	0.1	0.1	0.1
5000 Taxes on goods and services	**18.4**	**28.1**	**39.4**	**45.7**	**47.3**	**10.7**	**10.9**	**10.8**	**10.8**	**10.8**
5100 Taxes on production, sale, transfer, etc	17.4	26.0	37.0	43.2	44.7	10.2	10.1	10.1	10.2	10.2
5110 General taxes	11.6	18.2	25.5	29.0	30.0	6.8	7.1	7.0	6.8	6.8
5111 Value added taxes	11.5	18.1	25.3	28.7	29.8	6.8	7.0	6.9	6.8	6.8
5120 Taxes on specific goods and services	5.8	7.8	11.5	14.3	14.8	3.4	3.0	3.1	3.4	3.4
5121 Excises	3.5	5.7	7.8	9.4	9.9	2.0	2.2	2.1	2.2	2.3
5200 Taxes on use of goods and perform activities	1.0	2.1	2.4	2.5	2.5	0.6	0.8	0.7	0.6	0.6
5300 Unallocable between 5100 and 5200	0.0	0.0	0.0	0.0	0.0	0.0	0.0	0.0	0.0	0.0
6000 Other taxes	**0.0**	**0.0**	**0.0**	**0.0**	**0.0**	**0.0**	**0.0**	**0.0**	**0.0**	**0.0**
Non-wastable tax credits										
Non-wastable tax credits against 1000	..	..	1.0	0.8	0.9	..	..	0.3	0.2	0.2
Transfer component	..	..	0.4	0.3	0.3	..	..	0.1	0.1	0.1
Tax expenditure component	..	..	0.6	0.5	0.5	..	..	0.2	0.1	0.1

.. Not available
Note: More detailed country data and country notes are available in online chapter 5 "Country Tables, 1965-2017": https://doi.org/10.1787/0bbc27da-en.
Full time series can be accessed at http://oe.cd/full-time-series.
Source: Federal Ministry of Finance.

StatLink https://doi.org/10.1787/888934055405

Table 4.6. Belgium, tax revenue and % of GDP by level of government and main taxes

	Billion EUR					% of GDP				
	1990	2000	2010	2016	2017	1990	2000	2010	2016	2017
Federal or Central government										
Total tax revenue	**42.5**	**69.4**	**87.8**	**94.4**	**100.3**	**24.9**	**26.9**	**24.0**	**22.2**	**22.8**
1000 Taxes on income, profits and capital gains	23.9	39.6	49.3	52.0	56.8	13.9	15.3	13.5	12.3	12.9
2000 Social security contributions	0.9	1.3	2.5	0.1	0.1	0.5	0.5	0.7	0.0	0.0
3000 Taxes on payroll and workforce	0.0	0.0	0.0	0.0	0.0	0.0	0.0	0.0	0.0	0.0
4000 Taxes on property	1.1	2.3	0.9	2.1	2.1	0.6	0.9	0.3	0.5	0.5
5000 Taxes on goods and services	16.7	26.3	35.0	40.2	41.4	9.8	10.2	9.6	9.5	9.4
6000 Other taxes	0.0	0.0	0.0	0.0	0.0	0.0	0.0	0.0	0.0	0.0
State/Regional										
Total tax revenue	**1.2**	**2.4**	**8.1**	**19.9**	**21.0**	**0.7**	**0.9**	**2.2**	**4.7**	**4.8**
1000 Taxes on income, profits and capital gains	0.0	0.1	0.0	9.7	9.9	0.0	0.0	0.0	2.3	2.3
2000 Social security contributions	0.0	0.0	0.0	0.2	0.2	0.0	0.0	0.0	0.1	0.1
3000 Taxes on payroll and workforce	0.0	0.0	0.0	0.0	0.0	0.0	0.0	0.0	0.0	0.0
4000 Taxes on property	0.9	1.9	5.6	7.1	7.6	0.5	0.7	1.5	1.7	1.7
5000 Taxes on goods and services	0.2	0.5	2.4	3.0	3.3	0.1	0.2	0.7	0.7	0.7
6000 Other taxes	0.0	0.0	0.0	0.0	0.0	0.0	0.0	0.0	0.0	0.0
Local government										
Total tax revenue	**3.1**	**4.6**	**7.9**	**9.4**	**9.5**	**1.8**	**1.8**	**2.2**	**2.2**	**2.2**
1000 Taxes on income, profits and capital gains	2.1	3.1	2.9	3.3	3.4	1.2	1.2	0.8	0.8	0.8
2000 Social security contributions	0.1	0.0	0.0	0.0	0.0	0.1	0.0	0.0	0.0	0.0
3000 Taxes on payroll and workforce	0.0	0.0	0.0	0.0	0.0	0.0	0.0	0.0	0.0	0.0
4000 Taxes on property	0.6	1.0	4.4	5.3	5.5	0.3	0.4	1.2	1.3	1.2
5000 Taxes on goods and services	0.3	0.4	0.6	0.6	0.6	0.2	0.2	0.2	0.2	0.1
6000 Other taxes	0.0	0.0	0.0	0.0	0.0	0.0	0.0	0.0	0.0	0.0
Social Security Funds										
Total tax revenue	**22.7**	**34.9**	**50.6**	**60.8**	**62.5**	**13.3**	**13.5**	**13.9**	**14.3**	**14.2**
1000 Taxes on income, profits and capital gains	0.0	0.6	1.0	1.2	1.2	0.0	0.2	0.3	0.3	0.3
2000 Social security contributions	22.4	33.3	47.9	57.6	59.3	13.1	12.9	13.1	13.6	13.5
3000 Taxes on payroll and workforce	0.0	0.0	0.0	0.0	0.0	0.0	0.0	0.0	0.0	0.0
4000 Taxes on property	0.1	0.2	0.3	0.3	0.3	0.1	0.1	0.1	0.1	0.1
5000 Taxes on goods and services	0.2	0.8	1.3	1.6	1.7	0.1	0.3	0.4	0.4	0.4
6000 Other taxes	0.0	0.0	0.0	0.0	0.0	0.0	0.0	0.0	0.0	0.0

Note: More detailed country data and country notes are available in online chapter 6 "Tax revenues by sub-sectors of general government": https://doi.org/10.1787/0bbc27da-en. Full time series can be accessed at http://oe.cd/full-time-series.
Source: Federal Ministry of Finance.

StatLink https://doi.org/10.1787/888934055424

Table 4.7. Canada, tax revenue and % of GDP by selected tax category

	Billion CAD					% of GDP				
	1990	2000	2010	2016	2017	1990	2000	2010	2016	2017
Total tax revenue	**244.2**	**390.2**	**516.6**	**672.8**	**702.7**	**35.1**	**34.7**	**31.0**	**33.2**	**32.8**
1000 Taxes on income, profits and capital gains	**118.6**	**195.3**	**241.0**	**323.1**	**338.9**	**17.0**	**17.4**	**14.5**	**15.9**	**15.8**
1100 Of individuals	99.7	143.7	180.9	240.6	251.1	14.3	12.8	10.9	11.9	11.7
1200 Corporate	17.2	47.6	54.1	75.7	80.1	2.5	4.2	3.2	3.7	3.7
1300 Unallocable between 1100 and 1200	1.7	4.0	6.0	6.7	7.7	0.2	0.4	0.4	0.3	0.4
2000 Social security contributions	**29.7**	**53.1**	**76.8**	**99.0**	**99.3**	**4.3**	**4.7**	**4.6**	**4.9**	**4.6**
2100 Employees	10.6	21.4	30.6	39.6	39.9	1.5	1.9	1.8	2.0	1.9
2200 Employers	18.4	30.3	43.5	56.0	55.9	2.7	2.7	2.6	2.8	2.6
2300 Self-employed or non-employed	0.6	1.4	2.6	3.4	3.6	0.1	0.1	0.2	0.2	0.2
2400 Unallocable between 2100, 2200 and 2300	0.0	0.0	0.0	0.0	0.0	0.0	0.0	0.0	0.0	0.0
3000 Taxes on payroll and workforce	**5.5**	**8.0**	**10.8**	**13.8**	**14.3**	**0.8**	**0.7**	**0.6**	**0.7**	**0.7**
4000 Taxes on property	**24.5**	**37.2**	**63.7**	**81.2**	**84.0**	**3.5**	**3.3**	**3.8**	**4.0**	**3.9**
4100 Recurrent taxes on immovable property	20.2	30.2	51.7	65.2	66.8	2.9	2.7	3.1	3.2	3.1
4200 Recurrent taxes on net wealth	1.9	4.2	1.5	0.4	0.4	0.3	0.4	0.1	0.0	0.0
4300 Estate, inheritance and gift taxes	0.0	0.0	0.2	0.3	0.3	0.0	0.0	0.0	0.0	0.0
4400 Taxes on financial and capital transactions	0.0	0.0	3.1	6.3	6.9	0.0	0.0	0.2	0.3	0.3
4500 Non-recurrent taxes	2.4	2.7	7.3	9.0	9.5	0.3	0.2	0.4	0.4	0.4
4600 Other recurrent taxes on property	0.0	0.0	0.0	0.0	0.0	0.0	0.0	0.0	0.0	0.0
5000 Taxes on goods and services	**63.1**	**94.5**	**123.8**	**155.1**	**165.4**	**9.1**	**8.4**	**7.4**	**7.6**	**7.7**
5100 Taxes on production, sale, transfer, etc	59.6	88.9	116.2	146.1	153.7	8.6	7.9	7.0	7.2	7.2
5110 General taxes	34.5	55.3	72.1	93.9	99.9	5.0	4.9	4.3	4.6	4.7
5111 Value added taxes	0.0	35.9	70.7	90.4	96.2	0.0	3.2	4.2	4.5	4.5
5120 Taxes on specific goods and services	25.2	33.6	44.0	52.3	53.8	3.6	3.0	2.6	2.6	2.5
5121 Excises	14.5	18.4	23.3	25.9	27.2	2.1	1.6	1.4	1.3	1.3
5200 Taxes on use of goods and perform activities	3.5	5.6	7.6	9.0	11.7	0.5	0.5	0.5	0.4	0.5
5300 Unallocable between 5100 and 5200	0.0	0.0	0.0	0.0	0.0	0.0	0.0	0.0	0.0	0.0
6000 Other taxes	**2.9**	**2.2**	**0.6**	**0.7**	**0.7**	**0.4**	**0.2**	**0.0**	**0.0**	**0.0**
Non-wastable tax credits										
Non-wastable tax credits against 1000	..	3.4	11.1	11.4	11.6	..	0.3	0.7	0.6	0.5
Transfer component	..	3.1	10.2	10.3	10.5	..	0.3	0.6	0.5	0.5
Tax expenditure component	..	0.3	0.9	1.1	1.1	..	0.0	0.1	0.1	0.1

.. Not available

Note: More detailed country data and country notes are available in online chapter 5 "Country Tables, 1965-2017": https://doi.org/10.1787/0bbc27da-en. Full time series can be accessed at http://oe.cd/full-time-series.

Source: Statistics Canada.

StatLink https://doi.org/10.1787/888934055443

Table 4.8. Canada, tax revenue and % of GDP by level of government and main taxes

	Billion CAD					% of GDP				
	1990	2000	2010	2016	2017	1990	2000	2010	2016	2017
Federal or Central government										
Total tax revenue	**101.7**	**184.4**	**212.8**	**274.9**	**287.3**	**14.6**	**16.4**	**12.8**	**13.6**	**13.4**
1000 Taxes on income, profits and capital gains	73.6	126.3	148.7	195.6	208.5	10.6	11.2	8.9	9.6	9.7
2000 Social security contributions	0.0	18.8	17.9	24.1	20.9	0.0	1.7	1.1	1.2	1.0
3000 Taxes on payroll and workforce	0.0	0.0	0.0	0.0	0.0	0.0	0.0	0.0	0.0	0.0
4000 Taxes on property	0.0	0.0	0.0	0.0	0.0	0.0	0.0	0.0	0.0	0.0
5000 Taxes on goods and services	28.1	39.4	46.2	55.2	58.0	4.0	3.5	2.8	2.7	2.7
6000 Other taxes	0.0	0.0	0.0	0.0	0.0	0.0	0.0	0.0	0.0	0.0
State/Regional										
Total tax revenue	**89.3**	**148.2**	**201.1**	**267.6**	**279.5**	**12.8**	**13.2**	**12.1**	**13.2**	**13.1**
1000 Taxes on income, profits and capital gains	44.9	69.0	92.2	127.5	130.4	6.5	6.1	5.5	6.3	6.1
2000 Social security contributions	0.0	8.3	11.7	14.6	14.9	0.0	0.7	0.7	0.7	0.7
3000 Taxes on payroll and workforce	5.5	8.0	10.8	13.8	14.3	0.8	0.7	0.6	0.7	0.7
4000 Taxes on property	4.2	8.4	9.8	13.0	13.6	0.6	0.7	0.6	0.6	0.6
5000 Taxes on goods and services	34.6	54.5	76.7	98.7	106.2	5.0	4.8	4.6	4.9	5.0
6000 Other taxes	0.0	0.0	0.0	0.0	0.0	0.0	0.0	0.0	0.0	0.0
Local government										
Total tax revenue	**23.5**	**31.5**	**55.4**	**70.1**	**72.3**	**3.4**	**2.8**	**3.3**	**3.5**	**3.4**
1000 Taxes on income, profits and capital gains	0.0	0.0	0.0	0.0	0.0	0.0	0.0	0.0	0.0	0.0
2000 Social security contributions	0.0	0.0	0.0	0.0	0.0	0.0	0.0	0.0	0.0	0.0
3000 Taxes on payroll and workforce	0.0	0.0	0.0	0.0	0.0	0.0	0.0	0.0	0.0	0.0
4000 Taxes on property	20.3	28.8	53.9	68.2	70.4	2.9	2.6	3.2	3.4	3.3
5000 Taxes on goods and services	0.4	0.6	0.9	1.2	1.2	0.1	0.1	0.1	0.1	0.1
6000 Other taxes	2.9	2.2	0.6	0.7	0.7	0.4	0.2	0.0	0.0	0.0
Social Security Funds										
Total tax revenue	**29.7**	**26.0**	**47.2**	**60.3**	**63.6**	**4.3**	**2.3**	**2.8**	**3.0**	**3.0**
1000 Taxes on income, profits and capital gains	0.0	0.0	0.0	0.0	0.0	0.0	0.0	0.0	0.0	0.0
2000 Social security contributions	29.7	26.0	47.2	60.3	63.6	4.3	2.3	2.8	3.0	3.0
3000 Taxes on payroll and workforce	0.0	0.0	0.0	0.0	0.0	0.0	0.0	0.0	0.0	0.0
4000 Taxes on property	0.0	0.0	0.0	0.0	0.0	0.0	0.0	0.0	0.0	0.0
5000 Taxes on goods and services	0.0	0.0	0.0	0.0	0.0	0.0	0.0	0.0	0.0	0.0
6000 Other taxes	0.0	0.0	0.0	0.0	0.0	0.0	0.0	0.0	0.0	0.0

Note: More detailed country data and country notes are available in online chapter 6 "Tax revenues by sub-sectors of general government": https://doi.org/10.1787/0bbc27da-en. Full time series can be accessed at http://oe.cd/full-time-series.
Source: Statistics Canada.

StatLink https://doi.org/10.1787/888934055462

Table 4.9. Chile, tax revenue and % of GDP by selected tax category

	Billion CLP					% of GDP				
	1990	2000	2010	2016	2017	1990	2000	2010	2016	2017
Total tax revenue	**1 777.2**	**7 902.0**	**21 845.7**	**34 129.3**	**36 238.6**	**16.9**	**18.8**	**19.6**	**20.1**	**20.1**
1000 Taxes on income, profits and capital gains	**413.0**	**1 841.6**	**8 329.1**	**11 444.6**	**12 516.2**	**3.9**	**4.4**	**7.5**	**6.8**	**6.9**
1100 Of individuals	99.2	604.1	1 492.8	2 990.7	3 500.0	0.9	1.4	1.3	1.8	1.9
1200 Corporate	219.6	882.9	4 448.7	7 146.7	7 658.4	2.1	2.1	4.0	4.2	4.3
1300 Unallocable between 1100 and 1200	94.2	354.6	2 387.5	1 307.3	1 357.7	0.9	0.8	2.1	0.8	0.8
2000 Social security contributions	**159.6**	**576.8**	**1 494.0**	**2 441.4**	**2 627.6**	**1.5**	**1.4**	**1.3**	**1.4**	**1.5**
2100 Employees	154.0	553.9	1 433.2	2 373.8	2 553.9	1.5	1.3	1.3	1.4	1.4
2200 Employers	5.5	22.8	60.8	67.6	73.6	0.1	0.1	0.1	0.0	0.0
2300 Self-employed or non-employed	0.0	0.0	0.0	0.0	0.0	0.0	0.0	0.0	0.0	0.0
2400 Unallocable between 2100, 2200 and 2300	0.0	0.0	0.0	0.0	0.0	0.0	0.0	0.0	0.0	0.0
3000 Taxes on payroll and workforce	**0.0**	**0.0**	**0.0**	**0.0**	**0.0**	**0.0**	**0.0**	**0.0**	**0.0**	**0.0**
4000 Taxes on property	**109.3**	**554.0**	**898.6**	**1 731.7**	**1 950.2**	**1.0**	**1.3**	**0.8**	**1.0**	**1.1**
4100 Recurrent taxes on immovable property	60.0	302.2	662.4	1 171.4	1 229.2	0.6	0.7	0.6	0.7	0.7
4200 Recurrent taxes on net wealth	0.0	0.0	0.0	0.0	0.0	0.0	0.0	0.0	0.0	0.0
4300 Estate, inheritance and gift taxes	3.4	10.9	39.3	100.5	202.4	0.0	0.0	0.0	0.1	0.1
4400 Taxes on financial and capital transactions	45.9	240.9	196.9	459.8	518.6	0.4	0.6	0.2	0.3	0.3
4500 Non-recurrent taxes	0.0	0.0	0.0	0.0	0.0	0.0	0.0	0.0	0.0	0.0
4600 Other recurrent taxes on property	0.0	0.0	0.0	0.0	0.0	0.0	0.0	0.0	0.0	0.0
5000 Taxes on goods and services	**1 118.7**	**5 041.8**	**11 185.2**	**18 629.6**	**19 858.9**	**10.6**	**12.0**	**10.0**	**11.0**	**11.0**
5100 Taxes on production, sale, transfer, etc	1 074.0	4 789.8	10 532.9	17 449.2	18 597.2	10.2	11.4	9.4	10.3	10.3
5110 General taxes	664.4	3 306.4	8 399.9	14 073.1	15 069.5	6.3	7.9	7.5	8.3	8.4
5111 Value added taxes	664.4	3 306.4	8 399.9	14 073.1	15 069.5	6.3	7.9	7.5	8.3	8.4
5120 Taxes on specific goods and services	409.6	1 483.5	2 133.0	3 376.2	3 527.6	3.9	3.5	1.9	2.0	2.0
5121 Excises	166.0	816.2	1 561.2	2 568.9	2 682.7	1.6	1.9	1.4	1.5	1.5
5200 Taxes on use of goods and perform activities	44.7	251.9	652.3	1 180.4	1 261.7	0.4	0.6	0.6	0.7	0.7
5300 Unallocable between 5100 and 5200	0.0	0.0	0.0	0.0	0.0	0.0	0.0	0.0	0.0	0.0
6000 Other taxes	**-23.4**	**-112.2**	**-61.1**	**-118.0**	**-714.3**	**-0.2**	**-0.3**	**-0.1**	**-0.1**	**-0.4**
Non-wastable tax credits										
Non-wastable tax credits against 1000	0.0	0.0	0.0	179.6	213.5	0.0	0.0	0.0	0.1	0.1
Transfer component	..	..	..	129.6	151.4	..	..	..	0.1	0.1
Tax expenditure component	..	..	..	50.1	62.1	..	..	..	0.0	0.0

.. Not available

Note: More detailed country data and country notes are available in online chapter 5 "Country Tables, 1965-2017": https://doi.org/10.1787/0bbc27da-en. Full time series can be accessed at http://oe.cd/full-time-series.

Source: Servicio de Impuestos internos (Chile's Tax Service).

StatLink https://doi.org/10.1787/888934055481

Table 4.10. Chile, tax revenue and % of GDP by level of government and main taxes

	Billion CLP					% of GDP				
	1990	2000	2010	2016	2017	1990	2000	2010	2016	2017
Federal or Central government										
Total tax revenue	**1 579.7**	**6 936.8**	**19 214.8**	**29 493.6**	**31 274.2**	**15.0**	**16.5**	**17.2**	**17.4**	**17.4**
1000 Taxes on income, profits and capital gains	413.0	1 841.6	8 329.1	11 444.6	12 516.2	3.9	4.4	7.5	6.8	6.9
2000 Social security contributions	66.7	232.7	371.4	483.1	506.0	0.6	0.6	0.3	0.3	0.3
3000 Taxes on payroll and workforce	0.0	0.0	0.0	0.0	0.0	0.0	0.0	0.0	0.0	0.0
4000 Taxes on property	59.7	255.4	245.0	576.8	738.3	0.6	0.6	0.2	0.3	0.4
5000 Taxes on goods and services	1 063.7	4 719.3	10 330.4	17 107.1	18 228.0	10.1	11.2	9.3	10.1	10.1
6000 Other taxes	-23.4	-112.2	-61.1	-118.0	-714.3	-0.2	-0.3	-0.1	-0.1	-0.4
State/Regional										
Total tax revenue	..	..	..	..	..	..	..	..	..	..
1000 Taxes on income, profits and capital gains	..	..	..	..	..	..	..	..	..	..
2000 Social security contributions	..	..	..	..	..	..	..	..	..	..
3000 Taxes on payroll and workforce	..	..	..	..	..	..	..	..	..	..
4000 Taxes on property	..	..	..	..	..	..	..	..	..	..
5000 Taxes on goods and services	..	..	..	..	..	..	..	..	..	..
6000 Other taxes	..	..	..	..	..	..	..	..	..	..
Local government										
Total tax revenue	**104.7**	**621.2**	**1 508.3**	**2 677.4**	**2 842.8**	**1.0**	**1.5**	**1.4**	**1.6**	**1.6**
1000 Taxes on income, profits and capital gains	0.0	0.0	0.0	0.0	0.0	0.0	0.0	0.0	0.0	0.0
2000 Social security contributions	0.0	0.0	0.0	0.0	0.0	0.0	0.0	0.0	0.0	0.0
3000 Taxes on payroll and workforce	0.0	0.0	0.0	0.0	0.0	0.0	0.0	0.0	0.0	0.0
4000 Taxes on property	49.6	298.7	653.6	1 154.9	1 211.9	0.5	0.7	0.6	0.7	0.7
5000 Taxes on goods and services	55.0	322.5	854.8	1 522.5	1 630.9	0.5	0.8	0.8	0.9	0.9
6000 Other taxes	0.0	0.0	0.0	0.0	0.0	0.0	0.0	0.0	0.0	0.0
Social Security Funds										
Total tax revenue	**92.8**	**344.0**	**1 122.6**	**1 958.4**	**2 121.5**	**0.9**	**0.8**	**1.0**	**1.2**	**1.2**
1000 Taxes on income, profits and capital gains	0.0	0.0	0.0	0.0	0.0	0.0	0.0	0.0	0.0	0.0
2000 Social security contributions	92.8	344.0	1 122.6	1 958.4	2 121.5	0.9	0.8	1.0	1.2	1.2
3000 Taxes on payroll and workforce	0.0	0.0	0.0	0.0	0.0	0.0	0.0	0.0	0.0	0.0
4000 Taxes on property	0.0	0.0	0.0	0.0	0.0	0.0	0.0	0.0	0.0	0.0
5000 Taxes on goods and services	0.0	0.0	0.0	0.0	0.0	0.0	0.0	0.0	0.0	0.0
6000 Other taxes	0.0	0.0	0.0	0.0	0.0	0.0	0.0	0.0	0.0	0.0

.. Not available

Note: More detailed country data and country notes are available in online chapter 6 "Tax revenues by sub-sectors of general government": https://doi.org/10.1787/0bbc27da-en. Full time series can be accessed at http://oe.cd/full-time-series.

Source: Servicio de Impuestos internos (Chile's Tax Service).

StatLink https://doi.org/10.1787/888934055500

Table 4.11. Czech Republic, tax revenue and % of GDP by selected tax category

	Billion CZK					% of GDP				
	1990	2000	2010	2016	2017	1990	2000	2010	2016	2017
Total tax revenue	..	**771.6**	**1 286.9**	**1 632.4**	**1 760.0**	..	**32.4**	**32.5**	**34.2**	**34.9**
1000 Taxes on income, profits and capital gains	..	**175.8**	**259.9**	**361.9**	**390.6**	..	**7.4**	**6.6**	**7.6**	**7.7**
1100 Of individuals	..	99.7	131.7	183.1	202.2	..	4.2	3.3	3.8	4.0
1200 Corporate	..	76.2	128.2	178.8	188.3	..	3.2	3.2	3.7	3.7
1300 Unallocable between 1100 and 1200	..	0.0	0.0	0.0	0.0	..	0.0	0.0	0.0	0.0
2000 Social security contributions	..	**341.5**	**576.0**	**699.6**	**757.2**	..	**14.4**	**14.5**	**14.7**	**15.0**
2100 Employees	..	77.3	116.8	143.7	155.8	..	3.2	2.9	3.0	3.1
2200 Employers	..	220.2	363.1	444.2	483.4	..	9.3	9.2	9.3	9.6
2300 Self-employed or non-employed	..	44.1	96.1	111.7	117.9	..	1.9	2.4	2.3	2.3
2400 Unallocable between 2100, 2200 and 2300	..	0.0	0.0	0.0	0.0	..	0.0	0.0	0.0	0.0
3000 Taxes on payroll and workforce	..	**0.0**	**0.0**	**0.0**	**0.0**	..	**0.0**	**0.0**	**0.0**	**0.0**
4000 Taxes on property	..	**10.9**	**16.4**	**23.4**	**23.8**	..	**0.5**	**0.4**	**0.5**	**0.5**
4100 Recurrent taxes on immovable property	..	4.5	8.8	10.6	10.8	..	0.2	0.2	0.2	0.2
4200 Recurrent taxes on net wealth	..	0.0	0.0	0.0	0.0	..	0.0	0.0	0.0	0.0
4300 Estate, inheritance and gift taxes	..	0.6	0.2	0.0	0.0	..	0.0	0.0	0.0	0.0
4400 Taxes on financial and capital transactions	..	5.8	7.4	12.8	13.1	..	0.2	0.2	0.3	0.3
4500 Non-recurrent taxes	..	0.0	0.0	0.0	0.0	..	0.0	0.0	0.0	0.0
4600 Other recurrent taxes on property	..	0.0	0.0	0.0	0.0	..	0.0	0.0	0.0	0.0
5000 Taxes on goods and services	..	**243.0**	**427.8**	**539.0**	**579.3**	..	**10.2**	**10.8**	**11.3**	**11.5**
5100 Taxes on production, sale, transfer, etc	..	226.4	402.1	512.7	552.0	..	9.5	10.1	10.8	10.9
5110 General taxes	..	141.2	263.5	353.9	387.5	..	5.9	6.6	7.4	7.7
5111 Value added taxes	..	141.2	263.5	353.9	387.5	..	5.9	6.6	7.4	7.7
5120 Taxes on specific goods and services	..	85.1	138.6	158.7	164.5	..	3.6	3.5	3.3	3.3
5121 Excises	..	71.4	138.4	158.4	164.1	..	3.0	3.5	3.3	3.3
5200 Taxes on use of goods and perform activities	..	16.6	25.7	26.3	27.2	..	0.7	0.7	0.6	0.5
5300 Unallocable between 5100 and 5200	..	0.0	0.0	0.0	0.0	..	0.0	0.0	0.0	0.0
6000 Other taxes	..	**0.4**	**0.1**	**0.6**	**0.9**	..	**0.0**	**0.0**	**0.0**	**0.0**
Non-wastable tax credits										
Non-wastable tax credits against 1000	..	0.0	25.7	32.8	35.2	..	0.0	0.6	0.7	0.7
Transfer component	..	..	7.8	8.6	8.9	..	..	0.2	0.2	0.2
Tax expenditure component	..	..	17.9	24.2	26.3	..	..	0.5	0.5	0.5

.. Not available

Note: More detailed country data and country notes are available in online chapter 5 "Country Tables, 1965-2017": https://doi.org/10.1787/0bbc27da-en. Full time series can be accessed at http://oe.cd/full-time-series.

Source: Ministry of Finance, Economic Department.

StatLink https://doi.org/10.1787/888934055519

Table 4.12. Czech Republic, tax revenue and % of GDP by level of government and main taxes

	Billion CZK					% of GDP				
	1990	2000	2010	2016	2017	1990	2000	2010	2016	2017
Federal or Central government										
Total tax revenue	..	**423.4**	**687.3**	**906.4**	**975.8**	..	**17.8**	**17.3**	**19.0**	**19.3**
1000 Taxes on income, profits and capital gains	..	175.8	259.9	361.9	390.6	..	7.4	6.6	7.6	7.7
2000 Social security contributions	..	0.0	0.0	0.0	0.0	..	0.0	0.0	0.0	0.0
3000 Taxes on payroll and workforce	..	0.0	0.0	0.0	0.0	..	0.0	0.0	0.0	0.0
4000 Taxes on property	..	6.4	7.6	12.8	13.1	..	0.3	0.2	0.3	0.3
5000 Taxes on goods and services	..	241.0	419.6	531.1	571.2	..	10.1	10.6	11.1	11.3
6000 Other taxes	..	0.1	0.1	0.6	0.9	..	0.0	0.0	0.0	0.0
State/Regional										
Total tax revenue	..	..	..	..	..	..	..	..	..	..
1000 Taxes on income, profits and capital gains	..	..	..	..	..	..	..	..	..	..
2000 Social security contributions	..	..	..	..	..	..	..	..	..	..
3000 Taxes on payroll and workforce	..	..	..	..	..	..	..	..	..	..
4000 Taxes on property	..	..	..	..	..	..	..	..	..	..
5000 Taxes on goods and services	..	..	..	..	..	..	..	..	..	..
6000 Other taxes	..	..	..	..	..	..	..	..	..	..
Local government										
Total tax revenue	..	**6.7**	**17.0**	**18.5**	**18.8**	..	**0.3**	**0.4**	**0.4**	**0.4**
1000 Taxes on income, profits and capital gains	..	0.0	0.0	0.0	0.0	..	0.0	0.0	0.0	0.0
2000 Social security contributions	..	0.0	0.0	0.0	0.0	..	0.0	0.0	0.0	0.0
3000 Taxes on payroll and workforce	..	0.0	0.0	0.0	0.0	..	0.0	0.0	0.0	0.0
4000 Taxes on property	..	4.5	8.7	10.6	10.8	..	0.2	0.2	0.2	0.2
5000 Taxes on goods and services	..	2.0	8.2	7.9	8.0	..	0.1	0.2	0.2	0.2
6000 Other taxes	..	0.3	0.0	0.0	0.0	..	0.0	0.0	0.0	0.0
Social Security Funds										
Total tax revenue	..	**341.5**	**576.0**	**699.6**	**757.2**	..	**14.4**	**14.5**	**14.7**	**15.0**
1000 Taxes on income, profits and capital gains	..	0.0	0.0	0.0	0.0	..	0.0	0.0	0.0	0.0
2000 Social security contributions	..	341.5	576.0	699.6	757.2	..	14.4	14.5	14.7	15.0
3000 Taxes on payroll and workforce	..	0.0	0.0	0.0	0.0	..	0.0	0.0	0.0	0.0
4000 Taxes on property	..	0.0	0.0	0.0	0.0	..	0.0	0.0	0.0	0.0
5000 Taxes on goods and services	..	0.0	0.0	0.0	0.0	..	0.0	0.0	0.0	0.0
6000 Other taxes	..	0.0	0.0	0.0	0.0	..	0.0	0.0	0.0	0.0

.. Not available

Note: More detailed country data and country notes are available in online chapter 6 "Tax revenues by sub-sectors of general government": https://doi.org/10.1787/0bbc27da-en. Full time series can be accessed at http://oe.cd/full-time-series.

Source: Ministry of Finance, Economic Department.

StatLink https://doi.org/10.1787/888934055538

Table 4.13. Denmark, tax revenue and % of GDP by selected tax category

	Billion DKK					% of GDP				
	1990	2000	2010	2016	2017	1990	2000	2010	2016	2017
Total tax revenue	**379.8**	**622.0**	**810.5**	**959.6**	**995.5**	**44.4**	**46.9**	**44.8**	**45.7**	**45.7**
1000 Taxes on income, profits and capital gains	**232.3**	**382.1**	**498.1**	**602.9**	**630.3**	**27.1**	**28.8**	**27.5**	**28.7**	**28.9**
1100 Of individuals	205.2	327.5	420.9	509.5	527.0	24.0	24.7	23.2	24.3	24.2
1200 Corporate	14.6	42.1	40.9	59.8	71.3	1.7	3.2	2.3	2.8	3.3
1300 Unallocable between 1100 and 1200	12.5	12.4	36.4	33.7	32.0	1.5	0.9	2.0	1.6	1.5
2000 Social security contributions	**0.1**	**8.4**	**1.8**	**1.2**	**1.1**	**0.0**	**0.6**	**0.1**	**0.1**	**0.0**
2100 Employees	0.1	8.2	0.9	0.7	0.7	0.0	0.6	0.1	0.0	0.0
2200 Employers	0.0	0.2	0.9	0.5	0.3	0.0	0.0	0.1	0.0	0.0
2300 Self-employed or non-employed	0.0	0.0	0.0	0.0	0.0	0.0	0.0	0.0	0.0	0.0
2400 Unallocable between 2100, 2200 and 2300	0.0	0.0	0.0	0.0	0.0	0.0	0.0	0.0	0.0	0.0
3000 Taxes on payroll and workforce	**2.5**	**2.3**	**4.1**	**5.8**	**5.4**	**0.3**	**0.2**	**0.2**	**0.3**	**0.3**
4000 Taxes on property	**16.2**	**20.7**	**33.4**	**38.3**	**38.9**	**1.9**	**1.6**	**1.8**	**1.8**	**1.8**
4100 Recurrent taxes on immovable property	8.8	13.5	24.1	28.2	28.2	1.0	1.0	1.3	1.3	1.3
4200 Recurrent taxes on net wealth	0.9	0.0	0.0	0.0	0.0	0.1	0.0	0.0	0.0	0.0
4300 Estate, inheritance and gift taxes	2.2	2.9	3.6	4.2	4.3	0.3	0.2	0.2	0.2	0.2
4400 Taxes on financial and capital transactions	4.1	4.2	5.7	6.0	6.4	0.5	0.3	0.3	0.3	0.3
4500 Non-recurrent taxes	0.1	0.1	0.0	0.0	0.0	0.0	0.0	0.0	0.0	0.0
4600 Other recurrent taxes on property	0.0	0.0	0.0	0.0	0.0	0.0	0.0	0.0	0.0	0.0
5000 Taxes on goods and services	**128.8**	**205.9**	**269.6**	**308.0**	**316.4**	**15.1**	**15.5**	**14.9**	**14.7**	**14.5**
5100 Taxes on production, sale, transfer, etc	122.9	195.1	250.0	283.9	291.2	14.4	14.7	13.8	13.5	13.4
5110 General taxes	80.1	121.6	170.9	197.1	205.9	9.4	9.2	9.4	9.4	9.5
5111 Value added taxes	71.7	121.6	170.9	197.1	205.9	8.4	9.2	9.4	9.4	9.5
5120 Taxes on specific goods and services	42.7	73.5	79.1	86.8	85.3	5.0	5.5	4.4	4.1	3.9
5121 Excises	38.1	68.8	73.7	82.2	80.7	4.5	5.2	4.1	3.9	3.7
5200 Taxes on use of goods and perform activities	4.4	7.4	14.7	16.1	16.7	0.5	0.6	0.8	0.8	0.8
5300 Unallocable between 5100 and 5200	1.6	3.4	4.9	8.0	8.5	0.2	0.3	0.3	0.4	0.4
6000 Other taxes	**0.0**	**0.4**	**0.2**	**0.3**	**0.3**	**0.0**	**0.0**	**0.0**	**0.0**	**0.0**
Non-wastable tax credits										
Non-wastable tax credits against 1000	..	..	5.0	4.2	4.2	..	..	0.3	0.2	0.2
Transfer component	..	..	0.2	0.2	0.2	..	..	0.0	0.0	0.0
Tax expenditure component	..	..	4.7	4.0	4.0	..	..	0.3	0.2	0.2

.. Not available

Note: More detailed country data and country notes are available in online chapter 5 "Country Tables, 1965-2017": https://doi.org/10.1787/0bbc27da-en. Full time series can be accessed at http://oe.cd/full-time-series.

The total tax revenue has been reduced by the amount of any capital transfer that represents uncollected taxes. The capital transfer has been allocated between tax headings in proportion to the reported tax revenue. Therefore, the tax revenue amounts are different to those reported in the detailed country data available in online chapter 5 "Country Tables, 1965-2017".

Source: Danmarks Statistik.

StatLink https://doi.org/10.1787/888934055557

Table 4.14. Denmark, tax revenue and % of GDP by level of government and main taxes

	Billion DKK					% of GDP				
	1990	2000	2010	2016	2017	1990	2000	2010	2016	2017
Federal or Central government										
Total tax revenue	**260.3**	**421.2**	**590.0**	**701.1**	**729.1**	**30.4**	**31.7**	**32.6**	**33.4**	**33.5**
1000 Taxes on income, profits and capital gains	124.0	204.5	305.9	376.1	395.6	14.5	15.4	16.9	17.9	18.2
2000 Social security contributions	0.1	1.4	0.9	0.7	0.7	0.0	0.1	0.1	0.0	0.0
3000 Taxes on payroll and workforce	2.5	2.3	4.1	5.8	5.4	0.3	0.2	0.2	0.3	0.3
4000 Taxes on property	7.5	7.2	9.3	10.2	10.7	0.9	0.5	0.5	0.5	0.5
5000 Taxes on goods and services	126.2	205.6	269.6	308.0	316.4	14.7	15.5	14.9	14.7	14.5
6000 Other taxes	0.0	0.4	0.2	0.3	0.3	0.0	0.0	0.0	0.0	0.0
State/Regional										
Total tax revenue	..	..	..	..	..	..	..	..	..	..
1000 Taxes on income, profits and capital gains	..	..	..	..	..	..	..	..	..	..
2000 Social security contributions	..	..	..	..	..	..	..	..	..	..
3000 Taxes on payroll and workforce	..	..	..	..	..	..	..	..	..	..
4000 Taxes on property	..	..	..	..	..	..	..	..	..	..
5000 Taxes on goods and services	..	..	..	..	..	..	..	..	..	..
6000 Other taxes	..	..	..	..	..	..	..	..	..	..
Local government										
Total tax revenue	**116.9**	**191.1**	**216.3**	**255.0**	**262.9**	**13.7**	**14.4**	**11.9**	**12.1**	**12.1**
1000 Taxes on income, profits and capital gains	108.3	177.6	192.3	226.8	234.7	12.7	13.4	10.6	10.8	10.8
2000 Social security contributions	0.0	0.0	0.0	0.0	0.0	0.0	0.0	0.0	0.0	0.0
3000 Taxes on payroll and workforce	0.0	0.0	0.0	0.0	0.0	0.0	0.0	0.0	0.0	0.0
4000 Taxes on property	8.7	13.5	24.1	28.2	28.2	1.0	1.0	1.3	1.3	1.3
5000 Taxes on goods and services	0.0	0.0	0.0	0.0	0.0	0.0	0.0	0.0	0.0	0.0
6000 Other taxes	0.0	0.0	0.0	0.0	0.0	0.0	0.0	0.0	0.0	0.0
Social Security Funds										
Total tax revenue	**0.0**	**7.1**	**0.9**	**0.4**	**0.3**	**0.0**	**0.5**	**0.1**	**0.0**	**0.0**
1000 Taxes on income, profits and capital gains	0.0	0.0	0.0	0.0	0.0	0.0	0.0	0.0	0.0	0.0
2000 Social security contributions	0.0	7.1	0.9	0.4	0.3	0.0	0.5	0.1	0.0	0.0
3000 Taxes on payroll and workforce	0.0	0.0	0.0	0.0	0.0	0.0	0.0	0.0	0.0	0.0
4000 Taxes on property	0.0	0.0	0.0	0.0	0.0	0.0	0.0	0.0	0.0	0.0
5000 Taxes on goods and services	0.0	0.0	0.0	0.0	0.0	0.0	0.0	0.0	0.0	0.0
6000 Other taxes	0.0	0.0	0.0	0.0	0.0	0.0	0.0	0.0	0.0	0.0

.. Not available

Note: More detailed country data and country notes are available in online chapter 6 "Tax revenues by sub-sectors of general government": https://doi.org/10.1787/0bbc27da-en. Full time series can be accessed at http://oe.cd/full-time-series.

The total tax revenue has been reduced by the amount of any capital transfer that represents uncollected taxes. The capital transfer has been allocated between tax headings in proportion to the reported tax revenue. Therefore, the tax revenue amounts are different to those reported in the detailed country data available in online chapter 6 "Tax revenues by sub-sectors of general government".

Source: Danmarks Statistik.

StatLink https://doi.org/10.1787/888934055576

Table 4.15. Estonia, tax revenue and % of GDP by selected tax category

	Billion EUR					% of GDP				
	1990	2000	2010	2016	2017	1990	2000	2010	2016	2017
Total tax revenue	..	**1.9**	**4.9**	**7.3**	**7.7**	..	**31.1**	**33.3**	**33.5**	**32.8**
1000 Taxes on income, profits and capital gains	..	**0.5**	**1.0**	**1.6**	**1.7**	..	**7.7**	**6.6**	**7.5**	**7.2**
1100 Of individuals	..	0.4	0.8	1.3	1.3	..	6.8	5.3	5.8	5.7
1200 Corporate	..	0.1	0.2	0.4	0.4	..	0.9	1.3	1.7	1.5
1300 Unallocable between 1100 and 1200	..	0.0	0.0	0.0	0.0	..	0.0	0.0	0.0	0.0
2000 Social security contributions	..	**0.7**	**1.9**	**2.4**	**2.6**	..	**10.9**	**12.8**	**11.2**	**11.2**
2100 Employees	..	0.0	0.1	0.1	0.1	..	0.0	0.8	0.5	0.5
2200 Employers	..	0.7	1.7	2.3	2.5	..	10.7	11.8	10.6	10.6
2300 Self-employed or non-employed	..	0.0	0.0	0.0	0.0	..	0.2	0.1	0.1	0.1
2400 Unallocable between 2100, 2200 and 2300	..	0.0	0.0	0.0	0.0	..	0.0	0.0	0.0	0.0
3000 Taxes on payroll and workforce	..	**0.0**	**0.0**	**0.0**	**0.0**	..	**0.0**	**0.0**	**0.0**	**0.0**
4000 Taxes on property	..	**0.0**	**0.1**	**0.1**	**0.1**	..	**0.4**	**0.3**	**0.3**	**0.2**
4100 Recurrent taxes on immovable property	..	0.0	0.1	0.1	0.1	..	0.4	0.3	0.3	0.2
4200 Recurrent taxes on net wealth	..	0.0	0.0	0.0	0.0	..	0.0	0.0	0.0	0.0
4300 Estate, inheritance and gift taxes	..	0.0	0.0	0.0	0.0	..	0.0	0.0	0.0	0.0
4400 Taxes on financial and capital transactions	..	0.0	0.0	0.0	0.0	..	0.0	0.0	0.0	0.0
4500 Non-recurrent taxes	..	0.0	0.0	0.0	0.0	..	0.0	0.0	0.0	0.0
4600 Other recurrent taxes on property	..	0.0	0.0	0.0	0.0	..	0.0	0.0	0.0	0.0
5000 Taxes on goods and services	..	**0.7**	**2.0**	**3.1**	**3.3**	..	**12.1**	**13.4**	**14.4**	**14.0**
5100 Taxes on production, sale, transfer, etc	..	0.7	1.9	3.0	3.2	..	11.7	13.0	13.9	13.5
5110 General taxes	..	0.5	1.3	2.0	2.1	..	8.4	8.6	9.1	9.1
5111 Value added taxes	..	0.5	1.3	2.0	2.1	..	8.4	8.5	9.1	9.1
5120 Taxes on specific goods and services	..	0.2	0.7	1.0	1.0	..	3.3	4.4	4.8	4.4
5121 Excises	..	0.2	0.6	1.0	1.0	..	3.0	4.2	4.6	4.2
5200 Taxes on use of goods and perform activities	..	0.0	0.1	0.1	0.1	..	0.4	0.4	0.5	0.5
5300 Unallocable between 5100 and 5200	..	0.0	0.0	0.0	0.0	..	0.0	0.0	0.0	0.0
6000 Other taxes	..	**0.0**	**0.0**	**0.0**	**0.0**	..	**0.0**	**0.0**	**0.0**	**0.0**
Non-wastable tax credits										
Non-wastable tax credits against 1000	..	..	..	..	..	..	..	..	..	..
Transfer component	..	..	..	..	..	..	..	..	..	..
Tax expenditure component	..	..	..	..	..	..	..	..	..	..

.. Not available

Note: More detailed country data and country notes are available in online chapter 5 "Country Tables, 1965-2017": https://doi.org/10.1787/0bbc27da-en. Full time series can be accessed at http://oe.cd/full-time-series.

Source: Statistics Estonia.

StatLink https://doi.org/10.1787/888934055595

Table 4.16. Estonia, tax revenue and % of GDP by level of government and main taxes

	Billion EUR					% of GDP				
	1990	2000	2010	2016	2017	1990	2000	2010	2016	2017
Federal or Central government										
Total tax revenue	..	**1.6**	**3.9**	**6.0**	**6.3**	..	**26.3**	**26.7**	**27.6**	**26.9**
1000 Taxes on income, profits and capital gains	..	0.5	1.0	1.6	1.7	..	7.7	6.6	7.5	7.2
2000 Social security contributions	..	0.4	1.0	1.3	1.4	..	6.6	6.8	5.8	5.7
3000 Taxes on payroll and workforce	..	0.0	0.0	0.0	0.0	..	0.0	0.0	0.0	0.0
4000 Taxes on property	..	0.0	0.0	0.0	0.0	..	0.0	0.0	0.0	0.0
5000 Taxes on goods and services	..	0.7	2.0	3.1	3.3	..	12.0	13.3	14.3	13.9
6000 Other taxes	..	0.0	0.0	0.0	0.0	..	0.0	0.0	0.0	0.0
State/Regional										
Total tax revenue	..	..	..	..	..	..	..	..	..	..
1000 Taxes on income, profits and capital gains	..	..	..	..	..	..	..	..	..	..
2000 Social security contributions	..	..	..	..	..	..	..	..	..	..
3000 Taxes on payroll and workforce	..	..	..	..	..	..	..	..	..	..
4000 Taxes on property	..	..	..	..	..	..	..	..	..	..
5000 Taxes on goods and services	..	..	..	..	..	..	..	..	..	..
6000 Other taxes	..	..	..	..	..	..	..	..	..	..
Local government										
Total tax revenue	..	**0.0**	**0.1**	**0.1**	**0.1**	..	**0.5**	**0.5**	**0.3**	**0.3**
1000 Taxes on income, profits and capital gains	..	0.0	0.0	0.0	0.0	..	0.0	0.0	0.0	0.0
2000 Social security contributions	..	0.0	0.0	0.0	0.0	..	0.0	0.0	0.0	0.0
3000 Taxes on payroll and workforce	..	0.0	0.0	0.0	0.0	..	0.0	0.0	0.0	0.0
4000 Taxes on property	..	0.0	0.1	0.1	0.1	..	0.4	0.3	0.3	0.2
5000 Taxes on goods and services	..	0.0	0.0	0.0	0.0	..	0.1	0.1	0.1	0.1
6000 Other taxes	..	0.0	0.0	0.0	0.0	..	0.0	0.0	0.0	0.0
Social Security Funds										
Total tax revenue	..	**0.3**	**0.9**	**1.2**	**1.3**	..	**4.3**	**5.9**	**5.4**	**5.4**
1000 Taxes on income, profits and capital gains	..	0.0	0.0	0.0	0.0	..	0.0	0.0	0.0	0.0
2000 Social security contributions	..	0.3	0.9	1.2	1.3	..	4.3	5.9	5.4	5.4
3000 Taxes on payroll and workforce	..	0.0	0.0	0.0	0.0	..	0.0	0.0	0.0	0.0
4000 Taxes on property	..	0.0	0.0	0.0	0.0	..	0.0	0.0	0.0	0.0
5000 Taxes on goods and services	..	0.0	0.0	0.0	0.0	..	0.0	0.0	0.0	0.0
6000 Other taxes	..	0.0	0.0	0.0	0.0	..	0.0	0.0	0.0	0.0

.. Not available

Note: More detailed country data and country notes are available in online chapter 6 "Tax revenues by sub-sectors of general government": https://doi.org/10.1787/0bbc27da-en. Full time series can be accessed at http://oe.cd/full-time-series.

Source: Statistics Estonia.

StatLink https://doi.org/10.1787/888934055614

Table 4.17. Finland, tax revenue and % of GDP by selected tax category

	Billion EUR					% of GDP				
	1990	2000	2010	2016	2017	1990	2000	2010	2016	2017
Total tax revenue	**39.1**	**62.4**	**76.3**	**95.1**	**97.0**	**42.9**	**45.8**	**40.8**	**44.0**	**43.3**
1000 Taxes on income, profits and capital gains	**15.3**	**26.9**	**27.1**	**32.9**	**34.4**	**16.8**	**19.7**	**14.5**	**15.2**	**15.4**
1100 Of individuals	13.6	19.1	22.5	28.1	28.3	14.9	14.0	12.1	13.0	12.6
1200 Corporate	1.8	7.8	4.6	4.8	6.1	1.9	5.7	2.4	2.2	2.7
1300 Unallocable between 1100 and 1200	0.0	0.0	0.0	0.0	0.0	0.0	0.0	0.0	0.0	0.0
2000 Social security contributions	**10.0**	**15.8**	**22.6**	**27.6**	**27.0**	**11.0**	**11.6**	**12.1**	**12.8**	**12.1**
2100 Employees	1.2	2.9	4.7	6.8	7.5	1.3	2.1	2.5	3.2	3.3
2200 Employers	8.1	11.6	16.0	18.8	17.6	8.9	8.5	8.6	8.7	7.9
2300 Self-employed or non-employed	0.7	1.3	1.9	2.0	1.9	0.8	0.9	1.0	0.9	0.9
2400 Unallocable between 2100, 2200 and 2300	0.0	0.0	0.0	0.0	0.0	0.0	0.0	0.0	0.0	0.0
3000 Taxes on payroll and workforce	**0.0**	**0.0**	**0.0**	**0.0**	**0.0**	**0.0**	**0.0**	**0.0**	**0.0**	**0.0**
4000 Taxes on property	**1.0**	**1.5**	**2.1**	**3.1**	**3.5**	**1.1**	**1.1**	**1.1**	**1.4**	**1.5**
4100 Recurrent taxes on immovable property	0.1	0.6	1.2	1.7	1.8	0.1	0.4	0.6	0.8	0.8
4200 Recurrent taxes on net wealth	0.0	0.2	0.0	0.0	0.0	0.0	0.1	0.0	0.0	0.0
4300 Estate, inheritance and gift taxes	0.1	0.4	0.4	0.5	0.9	0.2	0.3	0.2	0.2	0.4
4400 Taxes on financial and capital transactions	0.7	0.4	0.5	0.9	0.8	0.8	0.3	0.3	0.4	0.3
4500 Non-recurrent taxes	0.0	0.0	0.0	0.0	0.0	0.0	0.0	0.0	0.0	0.0
4600 Other recurrent taxes on property	0.0	0.0	0.0	0.0	0.0	0.0	0.0	0.0	0.0	0.0
5000 Taxes on goods and services	**12.7**	**18.1**	**24.3**	**31.2**	**31.9**	**14.0**	**13.3**	**13.0**	**14.5**	**14.2**
5100 Taxes on production, sale, transfer, etc	12.6	17.7	23.5	30.0	30.6	13.8	13.0	12.6	13.9	13.7
5110 General taxes	7.5	10.9	15.5	19.7	20.4	8.3	8.0	8.3	9.1	9.1
5111 Value added taxes	7.5	10.9	15.5	19.7	20.4	8.3	8.0	8.3	9.1	9.1
5120 Taxes on specific goods and services	5.0	6.8	8.0	10.3	10.2	5.5	5.0	4.3	4.8	4.5
5121 Excises	3.8	5.6	6.3	8.2	8.0	4.2	4.1	3.4	3.8	3.6
5200 Taxes on use of goods and perform activities	0.2	0.4	0.8	1.2	1.3	0.2	0.3	0.4	0.6	0.6
5300 Unallocable between 5100 and 5200	0.0	0.0	0.0	0.0	0.0	0.0	0.0	0.0	0.0	0.0
6000 Other taxes	**0.0**	**0.0**	**0.1**	**0.1**	**0.1**	**0.1**	**0.0**	**0.0**	**0.0**	**0.0**
Non-wastable tax credits										
Non-wastable tax credits against 1000	..	..	..	..	..	..	..	..	..	..
Transfer component	..	..	..	..	..	..	..	..	..	..
Tax expenditure component	..	..	..	..	..	..	..	..	..	..

.. Not available

Note: More detailed country data and country notes are available in online chapter 5 "Country Tables, 1965-2017": https://doi.org/10.1787/0bbc27da-en. Full time series can be accessed at http://oe.cd/full-time-series.

Source: Bulletin of Statistics; Central Statistical Office (for Central Government revenues); the Annual report of the National Pension Institute and Official Statistics of Finland Series XXIIA published by the Ministry and Social Affairs (for the Social Security and private pension respectively); supplementary information from unpublished sources.

StatLink https://doi.org/10.1787/888934055633

Table 4.18. Finland, tax revenue and % of GDP by level of government and main taxes

	Billion EUR					% of GDP				
	1990	2000	2010	2016	2017	1990	2000	2010	2016	2017
Federal or Central government										
Total tax revenue	**20.7**	**33.1**	**35.0**	**45.3**	**46.9**	**22.7**	**24.3**	**18.7**	**21.0**	**21.0**
1000 Taxes on income, profits and capital gains	7.0	14.0	9.8	12.7	13.4	7.7	10.3	5.2	5.9	6.0
2000 Social security contributions	0.0	0.0	0.0	0.0	0.0	0.0	0.0	0.0	0.0	0.0
3000 Taxes on payroll and workforce	0.0	0.0	0.0	0.0	0.0	0.0	0.0	0.0	0.0	0.0
4000 Taxes on property	0.9	0.9	0.9	1.4	1.7	1.0	0.7	0.5	0.6	0.8
5000 Taxes on goods and services	12.7	18.1	24.3	31.1	31.8	14.0	13.3	13.0	14.4	14.2
6000 Other taxes	0.0	0.0	0.1	0.1	0.1	0.1	0.0	0.0	0.0	0.0
State/Regional										
Total tax revenue	..	..	..	..	..	..	..	..	..	..
1000 Taxes on income, profits and capital gains	..	..	..	..	..	..	..	..	..	..
2000 Social security contributions	..	..	..	..	..	..	..	..	..	..
3000 Taxes on payroll and workforce	..	..	..	..	..	..	..	..	..	..
4000 Taxes on property	..	..	..	..	..	..	..	..	..	..
5000 Taxes on goods and services	..	..	..	..	..	..	..	..	..	..
6000 Other taxes	..	..	..	..	..	..	..	..	..	..
Local government										
Total tax revenue	**8.4**	**13.5**	**18.5**	**22.0**	**22.8**	**9.2**	**9.9**	**9.9**	**10.2**	**10.2**
1000 Taxes on income, profits and capital gains	8.3	12.9	17.3	20.3	21.0	9.1	9.5	9.3	9.4	9.4
2000 Social security contributions	0.0	0.0	0.0	0.0	0.0	0.0	0.0	0.0	0.0	0.0
3000 Taxes on payroll and workforce	0.0	0.0	0.0	0.0	0.0	0.0	0.0	0.0	0.0	0.0
4000 Taxes on property	0.1	0.6	1.2	1.7	1.8	0.1	0.4	0.6	0.8	0.8
5000 Taxes on goods and services	0.0	0.0	0.0	0.0	0.0	0.0	0.0	0.0	0.0	0.0
6000 Other taxes	0.0	0.0	0.0	0.0	0.0	0.0	0.0	0.0	0.0	0.0
Social Security Funds										
Total tax revenue	**10.0**	**15.7**	**22.6**	**27.6**	**27.0**	**11.0**	**11.6**	**12.1**	**12.8**	**12.1**
1000 Taxes on income, profits and capital gains	0.0	0.0	0.0	0.0	0.0	0.0	0.0	0.0	0.0	0.0
2000 Social security contributions	10.0	15.7	22.6	27.6	27.0	11.0	11.6	12.1	12.8	12.1
3000 Taxes on payroll and workforce	0.0	0.0	0.0	0.0	0.0	0.0	0.0	0.0	0.0	0.0
4000 Taxes on property	0.0	0.0	0.0	0.0	0.0	0.0	0.0	0.0	0.0	0.0
5000 Taxes on goods and services	0.0	0.0	0.0	0.0	0.0	0.0	0.0	0.0	0.0	0.0
6000 Other taxes	0.0	0.0	0.0	0.0	0.0	0.0	0.0	0.0	0.0	0.0

.. Not available

Note: More detailed country data and country notes are available in online chapter 6 "Tax revenues by sub-sectors of general government": https://doi.org/10.1787/0bbc27da-en. Full time series can be accessed at http://oe.cd/full-time-series.

Source: Bulletin of Statistics; Central Statistical Office (for Central Government revenues); the Annual report of the National Pension Institute and Official Statistics of Finland Series XXIIA published by the Ministry and Social Affairs (for the Social Security and private pension respectively); supplementary information from unpublished sources.

StatLink https://doi.org/10.1787/888934055652

Table 4.19. France, tax revenue and % of GDP by selected tax category

	Billion EUR					% of GDP				
	1990	2000	2010	2016	2017	1990	2000	2010	2016	2017
Total tax revenue	**433.8**	**642.2**	**840.9**	**1 013.7**	**1 058.4**	**41.2**	**43.4**	**42.1**	**45.4**	**46.1**
1000 Taxes on income, profits and capital gains	**69.6**	**159.5**	**189.9**	**236.6**	**250.1**	**6.6**	**10.8**	**9.5**	**10.6**	**10.9**
1100 Of individuals	46.3	115.3	143.2	191.2	196.6	4.4	7.8	7.2	8.6	8.6
1200 Corporate	23.1	44.2	46.6	45.4	53.5	2.2	3.0	2.3	2.0	2.3
1300 Unallocable between 1100 and 1200	0.3	0.0	0.0	0.0	0.0	0.0	0.0	0.0	0.0	0.0
2000 Social security contributions	**191.1**	**230.7**	**321.7**	**373.1**	**385.0**	**18.1**	**15.6**	**16.1**	**16.7**	**16.8**
2100 Employees	57.3	57.4	77.8	96.0	100.3	5.4	3.9	3.9	4.3	4.4
2200 Employers	118.1	158.6	218.3	249.3	257.0	11.2	10.7	10.9	11.2	11.2
2300 Self-employed or non-employed	15.7	14.6	25.7	27.7	27.7	1.5	1.0	1.3	1.2	1.2
2400 Unallocable between 2100, 2200 and 2300	0.0	0.0	0.0	0.0	0.0	0.0	0.0	0.0	0.0	0.0
3000 Taxes on payroll and workforce	**8.3**	**14.8**	**26.8**	**34.6**	**35.5**	**0.8**	**1.0**	**1.3**	**1.5**	**1.5**
4000 Taxes on property	**27.4**	**45.9**	**72.6**	**94.6**	**100.3**	**2.6**	**3.1**	**3.6**	**4.2**	**4.4**
4100 Recurrent taxes on immovable property	14.8	29.3	49.7	62.3	63.7	1.4	2.0	2.5	2.8	2.8
4200 Recurrent taxes on net wealth	2.6	2.4	4.4	4.8	5.0	0.2	0.2	0.2	0.2	0.2
4300 Estate, inheritance and gift taxes	4.1	6.9	7.7	12.4	14.3	0.4	0.5	0.4	0.6	0.6
4400 Taxes on financial and capital transactions	5.9	7.3	10.8	15.1	17.3	0.6	0.5	0.5	0.7	0.8
4500 Non-recurrent taxes	0.0	0.0	0.0	0.0	0.0	0.0	0.0	0.0	0.0	0.0
4600 Other recurrent taxes on property	0.0	0.0	0.0	0.0	0.0	0.0	0.0	0.0	0.0	0.0
5000 Taxes on goods and services	**123.2**	**165.7**	**208.7**	**247.2**	**259.0**	**11.7**	**11.2**	**10.5**	**11.1**	**11.3**
5100 Taxes on production, sale, transfer, etc	119.2	161.2	202.4	240.1	251.6	11.3	10.9	10.1	10.7	11.0
5110 General taxes	81.3	109.7	140.3	157.9	165.3	7.7	7.4	7.0	7.1	7.2
5111 Value added taxes	80.0	106.9	135.3	154.4	161.7	7.6	7.2	6.8	6.9	7.0
5120 Taxes on specific goods and services	37.9	51.4	62.1	82.1	86.3	3.6	3.5	3.1	3.7	3.8
5121 Excises	26.8	39.6	45.5	58.5	61.6	2.5	2.7	2.3	2.6	2.7
5200 Taxes on use of goods and perform activities	4.0	4.6	6.3	7.2	7.5	0.4	0.3	0.3	0.3	0.3
5300 Unallocable between 5100 and 5200	0.0	0.0	0.0	0.0	0.0	0.0	0.0	0.0	0.0	0.0
6000 Other taxes	**14.1**	**24.0**	**19.5**	**25.9**	**26.6**	**1.3**	**1.6**	**1.0**	**1.2**	**1.2**
Non-wastable tax credits										
Non-wastable tax credits against 1000	..	0.5	17.4	25.9	28.9	..	0.0	0.9	1.2	1.3
Transfer component	..	..	7.9	11.6	14.6	..	..	0.4	0.5	0.6
Tax expenditure component	..	..	9.5	14.3	14.3	..	..	0.5	0.6	0.6

.. Not available

Note: More detailed country data and country notes are available in online chapter 5 "Country Tables, 1965-2017": https://doi.org/10.1787/0bbc27da-en. Full time series can be accessed at http://oe.cd/full-time-series.

The total tax revenue has been reduced by the amount of any capital transfer that represents uncollected taxes. The capital transfer has been allocated between tax headings in proportion to the reported tax revenue. Therefore, the tax revenue amounts are different to those reported in the detailed country data available in online chapter 5 "Country Tables, 1965-2017".

Source: General Account of the Administration of finances for the figures of fiscal receipts. OSCE for the figures of Social Security from 1965 to 1969, and ESA for the following years.

StatLink https://doi.org/10.1787/888934055671

Table 4.20. France, tax revenue and % of GDP by level of government and main taxes

	Billion EUR					% of GDP				
	1990	2000	2010	2016	2017	1990	2000	2010	2016	2017
Federal or Central government										
Total tax revenue	**200.1**	**270.0**	**299.6**	**338.7**	**362.0**	**19.0**	**18.3**	**15.0**	**15.2**	**15.8**
1000 Taxes on income, profits and capital gains	69.6	94.3	97.0	122.8	132.7	6.6	6.4	4.9	5.5	5.8
2000 Social security contributions	3.2	5.4	7.6	8.0	8.3	0.3	0.4	0.4	0.4	0.4
3000 Taxes on payroll and workforce	6.2	10.6	4.2	4.0	3.7	0.6	0.7	0.2	0.2	0.2
4000 Taxes on property	8.6	13.4	15.9	23.1	25.4	0.8	0.9	0.8	1.0	1.1
5000 Taxes on goods and services	112.1	143.3	157.2	179.9	190.8	10.6	9.7	7.9	8.1	8.3
6000 Other taxes	0.4	3.1	17.6	0.9	1.1	0.0	0.2	0.9	0.0	0.0
State/Regional										
Total tax revenue	..	..	..	..	..	..	..	..	..	..
1000 Taxes on income, profits and capital gains	..	..	..	..	..	..	..	..	..	..
2000 Social security contributions	..	..	..	..	..	..	..	..	..	..
3000 Taxes on payroll and workforce	..	..	..	..	..	..	..	..	..	..
4000 Taxes on property	..	..	..	..	..	..	..	..	..	..
5000 Taxes on goods and services	..	..	..	..	..	..	..	..	..	..
6000 Other taxes	..	..	..	..	..	..	..	..	..	..
Local government										
Total tax revenue	**40.2**	**64.4**	**88.7**	**135.8**	**140.7**	**3.8**	**4.4**	**4.4**	**6.1**	**6.1**
1000 Taxes on income, profits and capital gains	0.0	0.0	0.1	0.0	0.0	0.0	0.0	0.0	0.0	0.0
2000 Social security contributions	0.0	0.0	0.0	0.0	0.0	0.0	0.0	0.0	0.0	0.0
3000 Taxes on payroll and workforce	1.7	3.8	7.4	9.6	10.2	0.2	0.3	0.4	0.4	0.4
4000 Taxes on property	18.8	32.5	56.7	71.5	74.9	1.8	2.2	2.8	3.2	3.3
5000 Taxes on goods and services	6.0	7.2	22.9	31.6	32.3	0.6	0.5	1.1	1.4	1.4
6000 Other taxes	13.7	20.8	1.6	23.1	23.2	1.3	1.4	0.1	1.0	1.0
Social Security Funds										
Total tax revenue	**190.9**	**305.9**	**450.6**	**535.6**	**551.8**	**18.1**	**20.7**	**22.6**	**24.0**	**24.0**
1000 Taxes on income, profits and capital gains	0.0	65.2	92.8	113.7	117.4	0.0	4.4	4.7	5.1	5.1
2000 Social security contributions	187.9	225.3	314.1	365.1	376.7	17.8	15.2	15.7	16.3	16.4
3000 Taxes on payroll and workforce	0.4	0.4	15.1	21.0	21.6	0.0	0.0	0.8	0.9	0.9
4000 Taxes on property	0.0	0.0	0.0	0.0	0.0	0.0	0.0	0.0	0.0	0.0
5000 Taxes on goods and services	2.5	14.9	28.4	35.6	35.7	0.2	1.0	1.4	1.6	1.6
6000 Other taxes	0.0	0.1	0.2	0.3	0.4	0.0	0.0	0.0	0.0	0.0

.. Not available

Note: More detailed country data and country notes are available in online chapter 6 "Tax revenues by sub-sectors of general government": https://doi.org/10.1787/0bbc27da-en. Full time series can be accessed at http://oe.cd/full-time-series.

The total tax revenue has been reduced by the amount of any capital transfer that represents uncollected taxes. The capital transfer has been allocated between tax headings in proportion to the reported tax revenue. Therefore, the tax revenue amounts are different to those reported in the detailed country data available in online chapter 6 "Tax revenues by sub-sectors of general government".

Source: General Account of the Administration of finances for the figures of fiscal receipts. OSCE for the figures of Social Security from 1965 to 1969, and ESA for the following years.

StatLink https://doi.org/10.1787/888934055690

Table 4.21. Germany, tax revenue and % of GDP by selected tax category

	Billion EUR					% of GDP				
	1990	2000	2010	2016	2017	1990	2000	2010	2016	2017
Total tax revenue	**454.8**	**767.1**	**903.3**	**1 182.3**	**1 231.3**	**34.8**	**36.2**	**35.0**	**37.4**	**37.6**
1000 Taxes on income, profits and capital gains	**147.3**	**231.2**	**257.8**	**376.3**	**400.6**	**11.3**	**10.9**	**10.0**	**11.9**	**12.2**
1100 Of individuals	125.3	194.2	219.4	313.8	334.1	9.6	9.2	8.5	9.9	10.2
1200 Corporate	22.0	37.1	38.4	62.4	66.5	1.7	1.8	1.5	2.0	2.0
1300 Unallocable between 1100 and 1200	0.0	0.0	0.0	0.0	0.0	0.0	0.0	0.0	0.0	0.0
2000 Social security contributions	**170.4**	**299.4**	**354.0**	**445.0**	**466.5**	**13.0**	**14.1**	**13.7**	**14.1**	**14.2**
2100 Employees	73.6	131.6	155.3	199.4	209.6	5.6	6.2	6.0	6.3	6.4
2200 Employers	86.7	147.4	167.2	206.9	216.4	6.6	7.0	6.5	6.5	6.6
2300 Self-employed or non-employed	10.2	20.4	31.5	38.7	40.5	0.8	1.0	1.2	1.2	1.2
2400 Unallocable between 2100, 2200 and 2300	0.0	0.0	0.0	0.0	0.0	0.0	0.0	0.0	0.0	0.0
3000 Taxes on payroll and workforce	**0.0**	**0.0**	**0.0**	**0.0**	**0.0**	**0.0**	**0.0**	**0.0**	**0.0**	**0.0**
4000 Taxes on property	**15.3**	**17.5**	**21.0**	**33.4**	**33.6**	**1.2**	**0.8**	**0.8**	**1.1**	**1.0**
4100 Recurrent taxes on immovable property	4.5	8.8	11.3	13.7	14.0	0.3	0.4	0.4	0.4	0.4
4200 Recurrent taxes on net wealth	6.2	0.4	0.0	0.4	0.4	0.5	0.0	0.0	0.0	0.0
4300 Estate, inheritance and gift taxes	1.5	3.0	4.4	7.0	6.1	0.1	0.1	0.2	0.2	0.2
4400 Taxes on financial and capital transactions	3.1	5.2	5.3	12.4	13.1	0.2	0.2	0.2	0.4	0.4
4500 Non-recurrent taxes	0.0	0.0	0.0	0.0	0.0	0.0	0.0	0.0	0.0	0.0
4600 Other recurrent taxes on property	0.0	0.0	0.0	0.0	0.0	0.0	0.0	0.0	0.0	0.0
5000 Taxes on goods and services	**121.6**	**215.3**	**266.1**	**320.5**	**323.6**	**9.3**	**10.2**	**10.3**	**10.1**	**9.9**
5100 Taxes on production, sale, transfer, etc	117.2	208.1	256.9	301.6	311.7	9.0	9.8	10.0	9.5	9.5
5110 General taxes	75.5	140.9	180.5	219.1	226.9	5.8	6.7	7.0	6.9	6.9
5111 Value added taxes	75.5	140.9	180.5	219.1	226.9	5.8	6.7	7.0	6.9	6.9
5120 Taxes on specific goods and services	41.7	67.2	76.1	82.3	84.5	3.2	3.2	2.9	2.6	2.6
5121 Excises	31.2	57.2	63.5	64.9	66.5	2.4	2.7	2.5	2.1	2.0
5200 Taxes on use of goods and perform activities	4.4	7.2	9.2	18.8	11.9	0.3	0.3	0.4	0.6	0.4
5300 Unallocable between 5100 and 5200	0.0	0.0	0.0	0.0	0.0	0.0	0.0	0.0	0.0	0.0
6000 Other taxes	**0.2**	**0.2**	**0.2**	**2.0**	**2.0**	**0.0**	**0.0**	**0.0**	**0.1**	**0.1**
Non-wastable tax credits										
Non-wastable tax credits against 1000	..	39.3	46.3	42.9	43.5	..	1.9	1.8	1.4	1.3
Transfer component	..	..	17.7	15.3	15.3	..	..	0.7	0.5	0.5
Tax expenditure component	..	..	28.6	27.6	28.2	..	..	1.1	0.9	0.9

.. Not available

Note: More detailed country data and country notes are available in online chapter 5 "Country Tables, 1965-2017": https://doi.org/10.1787/0bbc27da-en. Full time series can be accessed at http://oe.cd/full-time-series.

Source: Finanzbericht, Bonn; Tax Statistics. Unpublished estimates by the Ministry of Finance.

StatLink https://doi.org/10.1787/888934055709

Table 4.22. Germany, tax revenue and % of GDP by level of government and main taxes

	Billion EUR					% of GDP				
	1990	2000	2010	2016	2017	1990	2000	2010	2016	2017
Federal or Central government										
Total tax revenue	**143.9**	**234.8**	**283.0**	**350.8**	**363.6**	**11.0**	**11.1**	**11.0**	**11.1**	**11.1**
1000 Taxes on income, profits and capital gains	58.2	97.9	104.5	153.4	164.1	4.5	4.6	4.1	4.9	5.0
2000 Social security contributions	0.0	0.0	0.0	0.0	0.0	0.0	0.0	0.0	0.0	0.0
3000 Taxes on payroll and workforce	0.0	0.0	0.0	0.0	0.0	0.0	0.0	0.0	0.0	0.0
4000 Taxes on property	1.2	0.0	0.0	0.4	0.4	0.1	0.0	0.0	0.0	0.0
5000 Taxes on goods and services	84.6	136.9	178.5	197.1	199.1	6.5	6.5	6.9	6.2	6.1
6000 Other taxes	0.0	0.0	0.0	0.0	0.0	0.0	0.0	0.0	0.0	0.0
State/Regional										
Total tax revenue	**97.8**	**172.1**	**190.6**	**279.5**	**289.0**	**7.5**	**8.1**	**7.4**	**8.8**	**8.8**
1000 Taxes on income, profits and capital gains	58.2	88.9	97.6	143.0	152.9	4.5	4.2	3.8	4.5	4.7
2000 Social security contributions	0.0	0.0	0.0	0.0	0.0	0.0	0.0	0.0	0.0	0.0
3000 Taxes on payroll and workforce	0.0	0.0	0.0	0.0	0.0	0.0	0.0	0.0	0.0	0.0
4000 Taxes on property	7.0	8.5	9.7	19.4	19.3	0.5	0.4	0.4	0.6	0.6
5000 Taxes on goods and services	32.6	74.6	83.4	117.1	116.9	2.5	3.5	3.2	3.7	3.6
6000 Other taxes	0.0	0.0	0.0	0.0	0.0	0.0	0.0	0.0	0.0	0.0
Local government										
Total tax revenue	**38.4**	**57.0**	**71.4**	**100.0**	**105.4**	**2.9**	**2.7**	**2.8**	**3.2**	**3.2**
1000 Taxes on income, profits and capital gains	30.9	44.4	55.7	79.9	83.7	2.4	2.1	2.2	2.5	2.6
2000 Social security contributions	0.0	0.0	0.0	0.0	0.0	0.0	0.0	0.0	0.0	0.0
3000 Taxes on payroll and workforce	0.0	0.0	0.0	0.0	0.0	0.0	0.0	0.0	0.0	0.0
4000 Taxes on property	7.2	9.0	11.3	13.7	14.0	0.5	0.4	0.4	0.4	0.4
5000 Taxes on goods and services	0.3	3.4	4.3	6.3	7.5	0.0	0.2	0.2	0.2	0.2
6000 Other taxes	0.2	0.1	0.1	0.2	0.3	0.0	0.0	0.0	0.0	0.0
Social Security Funds										
Total tax revenue	**170.4**	**299.4**	**354.0**	**445.0**	**466.5**	**13.0**	**14.1**	**13.7**	**14.1**	**14.2**
1000 Taxes on income, profits and capital gains	0.0	0.0	0.0	0.0	0.0	0.0	0.0	0.0	0.0	0.0
2000 Social security contributions	170.4	299.4	354.0	445.0	466.5	13.0	14.1	13.7	14.1	14.2
3000 Taxes on payroll and workforce	0.0	0.0	0.0	0.0	0.0	0.0	0.0	0.0	0.0	0.0
4000 Taxes on property	0.0	0.0	0.0	0.0	0.0	0.0	0.0	0.0	0.0	0.0
5000 Taxes on goods and services	0.0	0.0	0.0	0.0	0.0	0.0	0.0	0.0	0.0	0.0
6000 Other taxes	0.0	0.0	0.0	0.0	0.0	0.0	0.0	0.0	0.0	0.0

Note: More detailed country data and country notes are available in online chapter 6 "Tax revenues by sub-sectors of general government": https://doi.org/10.1787/0bbc27da-en. Full time series can be accessed at http://oe.cd/full-time-series.
Source: Finanzbericht, Bonn; Tax Statistics. Unpublished estimates by the Ministry of Finance.

StatLink https://doi.org/10.1787/888934055728

Table 4.23. Greece, tax revenue and % of GDP by selected tax category

	Billion EUR					% of GDP				
	1990	2000	2010	2016	2017	1990	2000	2010	2016	2017
Total tax revenue	**11.5**	**47.2**	**72.4**	**68.3**	**70.1**	**25.2**	**33.4**	**32.0**	**38.7**	**38.9**
1000 Taxes on income, profits and capital gains	**2.3**	**12.7**	**16.0**	**16.0**	**16.0**	**5.0**	**9.0**	**7.1**	**9.1**	**8.9**
1100 Of individuals	1.6	6.1	9.0	10.4	11.2	3.6	4.3	4.0	5.9	6.2
1200 Corporate	0.6	5.6	5.7	4.4	3.5	1.4	4.0	2.5	2.5	1.9
1300 Unallocable between 1100 and 1200	0.0	0.9	1.2	1.2	1.2	0.1	0.6	0.5	0.7	0.7
2000 Social security contributions	**3.5**	**14.3**	**24.7**	**19.3**	**20.7**	**7.6**	**10.1**	**10.9**	**10.9**	**11.5**
2100 Employees	1.7	7.6	13.3	11.6	12.2	3.8	5.4	5.9	6.6	6.8
2200 Employers	1.7	6.7	11.5	7.7	8.5	3.8	4.7	5.1	4.4	4.7
2300 Self-employed or non-employed	0.0	0.0	0.0	0.0	0.0	0.0	0.0	0.0	0.0	0.0
2400 Unallocable between 2100, 2200 and 2300	0.0	0.0	0.0	0.0	0.0	0.0	0.0	0.0	0.0	0.0
3000 Taxes on payroll and workforce	**0.1**	**0.0**	**0.0**	**0.0**	**0.0**	**0.2**	**0.0**	**0.0**	**0.0**	**0.0**
4000 Taxes on property	**0.5**	**3.6**	**3.7**	**5.5**	**5.6**	**1.2**	**2.6**	**1.7**	**3.1**	**3.1**
4100 Recurrent taxes on immovable property	0.0	0.4	0.6	3.7	3.7	0.0	0.3	0.2	2.1	2.0
4200 Recurrent taxes on net wealth	0.0	0.7	1.3	1.1	1.2	0.0	0.5	0.6	0.6	0.6
4300 Estate, inheritance and gift taxes	0.1	0.4	0.2	0.1	0.2	0.3	0.3	0.1	0.1	0.1
4400 Taxes on financial and capital transactions	0.4	2.0	1.1	0.5	0.6	0.8	1.4	0.5	0.3	0.3
4500 Non-recurrent taxes	0.0	0.0	0.0	0.0	0.0	0.0	0.0	0.0	0.0	0.0
4600 Other recurrent taxes on property	0.0	0.1	0.6	0.0	0.0	0.0	0.1	0.3	0.0	0.0
5000 Taxes on goods and services	**5.1**	**16.4**	**27.7**	**27.3**	**27.6**	**11.2**	**11.6**	**12.3**	**15.5**	**15.3**
5100 Taxes on production, sale, transfer, etc	4.9	14.6	25.2	23.2	23.3	10.7	10.3	11.2	13.1	12.9
5110 General taxes	3.0	9.2	16.5	14.6	14.9	6.7	6.5	7.3	8.3	8.3
5111 Value added taxes	2.8	8.9	16.0	14.3	14.6	6.2	6.3	7.1	8.1	8.1
5120 Taxes on specific goods and services	1.8	5.3	8.6	8.4	8.2	3.9	3.8	3.8	4.8	4.6
5121 Excises	1.4	4.1	7.6	7.1	6.9	3.0	2.9	3.3	4.0	3.8
5200 Taxes on use of goods and perform activities	0.2	1.3	1.7	3.2	3.4	0.5	0.9	0.7	1.8	1.9
5300 Unallocable between 5100 and 5200	0.0	0.5	0.8	1.0	0.9	0.0	0.4	0.3	0.5	0.5
6000 Other taxes	**0.0**	**0.0**	**0.0**	**0.0**	**0.0**	**0.0**	**0.0**	**0.0**	**0.0**	**0.0**
Non-wastable tax credits										
Non-wastable tax credits against 1000	..	..	..	..	..	..	..	..	..	..
Transfer component	..	..	..	..	..	..	..	..	..	..
Tax expenditure component	..	..	..	..	..	..	..	..	..	..

.. Not available

Note: More detailed country data and country notes are available in online chapter 5 "Country Tables, 1965-2017": https://doi.org/10.1787/0bbc27da-en. Full time series can be accessed at http://oe.cd/full-time-series.

The total tax revenue has been reduced by the amount of any capital transfer that represents uncollected taxes. The capital transfer has been allocated between tax headings in proportion to the reported tax revenue. Therefore, the tax revenue amounts are different to those reported in the detailed country data available in online chapter 5 "Country Tables, 1965-2017".

Source: Ministry of Finance, General accounting Office, 20th Directorate of Budget except the heading 2000 provided by the National Statistics Bureau.

StatLink https://doi.org/10.1787/888934055747

Table 4.24. Greece, tax revenue and % of GDP by level of government and main taxes

	Billion EUR					% of GDP				
	1990	2000	2010	2016	2017	1990	2000	2010	2016	2017
Federal or Central government										
Total tax revenue	**7.8**	**31.9**	**46.5**	**47.6**	**47.3**	**17.1**	**22.6**	**20.6**	**27.0**	**26.2**
1000 Taxes on income, profits and capital gains	2.3	12.7	15.9	16.0	16.0	5.0	9.0	7.0	9.1	8.9
2000 Social security contributions	0.0	0.7	1.3	0.7	0.1	0.1	0.5	0.6	0.4	0.0
3000 Taxes on payroll and workforce	0.0	0.0	0.0	0.0	0.0	0.0	0.0	0.0	0.0	0.0
4000 Taxes on property	0.5	2.6	2.1	3.9	4.0	1.2	1.8	0.9	2.2	2.2
5000 Taxes on goods and services	4.9	16.0	27.1	27.0	27.3	10.9	11.3	12.0	15.3	15.1
6000 Other taxes	0.0	0.0	0.0	0.0	0.0	0.0	0.0	0.0	0.0	0.0
State/Regional										
Total tax revenue	..	..	..	..	..	..	..	..	..	..
1000 Taxes on income, profits and capital gains	..	..	..	..	..	..	..	..	..	..
2000 Social security contributions	..	..	..	..	..	..	..	..	..	..
3000 Taxes on payroll and workforce	..	..	..	..	..	..	..	..	..	..
4000 Taxes on property	..	..	..	..	..	..	..	..	..	..
5000 Taxes on goods and services	..	..	..	..	..	..	..	..	..	..
6000 Other taxes	..	..	..	..	..	..	..	..	..	..
Local government										
Total tax revenue	**0.1**	**1.0**	**1.7**	**1.6**	**1.7**	**0.3**	**0.7**	**0.8**	**0.9**	**0.9**
1000 Taxes on income, profits and capital gains	0.0	0.0	0.0	0.0	0.0	0.0	0.0	0.0	0.0	0.0
2000 Social security contributions	0.0	0.0	0.0	0.0	0.0	0.0	0.0	0.0	0.0	0.0
3000 Taxes on payroll and workforce	0.1	0.0	0.0	0.0	0.0	0.2	0.0	0.0	0.0	0.0
4000 Taxes on property	0.0	0.8	1.5	1.5	1.6	0.0	0.6	0.7	0.9	0.9
5000 Taxes on goods and services	0.1	0.2	0.2	0.1	0.1	0.1	0.1	0.1	0.1	0.1
6000 Other taxes	0.0	0.0	0.0	0.0	0.0	0.0	0.0	0.0	0.0	0.0
Social Security Funds										
Total tax revenue	**3.4**	**14.1**	**24.0**	**18.7**	**20.8**	**7.5**	**10.0**	**10.6**	**10.6**	**11.5**
1000 Taxes on income, profits and capital gains	0.0	0.0	0.0	0.0	0.0	0.0	0.0	0.0	0.0	0.0
2000 Social security contributions	3.4	13.6	23.4	18.6	20.7	7.5	9.6	10.4	10.5	11.5
3000 Taxes on payroll and workforce	0.0	0.0	0.0	0.0	0.0	0.0	0.0	0.0	0.0	0.0
4000 Taxes on property	0.0	0.2	0.1	0.0	0.0	0.0	0.1	0.1	0.0	0.0
5000 Taxes on goods and services	0.0	0.3	0.4	0.1	0.1	0.0	0.2	0.2	0.1	0.1
6000 Other taxes	0.0	0.0	0.0	0.0	0.0	0.0	0.0	0.0	0.0	0.0

.. Not available

Note: More detailed country data and country notes are available in online chapter 6 "Tax revenues by sub-sectors of general government": https://doi.org/10.1787/0bbc27da-en. Full time series can be accessed at http://oe.cd/full-time-series.

The total tax revenue has been reduced by the amount of any capital transfer that represents uncollected taxes. The capital transfer has been allocated between tax headings in proportion to the reported tax revenue. Therefore, the tax revenue amounts are different to those reported in the detailed country data available in online chapter 6 "Tax revenues by sub-sectors of general government".

Source: Ministry of Finance, General accounting Office, 20th Directorate of Budget except the heading 2000 provided by the National Statistics Bureau.

StatLink https://doi.org/10.1787/888934055766

Table 4.25. Hungary, tax revenue and % of GDP by selected tax category

	Billion HUF					% of GDP				
	1990	2000	2010	2016	2017	1990	2000	2010	2016	2017
Total tax revenue	..	**5 140.6**	**10 145.5**	**13 887.6**	**14 642.3**	..	**38.5**	**37.3**	**39.1**	**38.2**
1000 Taxes on income, profits and capital gains	..	**1 247.4**	**2 098.6**	**2 684.6**	**2 873.6**	..	**9.3**	**7.7**	**7.6**	**7.5**
1100 Of individuals	..	954.7	1 768.8	1 853.4	2 075.2	..	7.2	6.5	5.2	5.4
1200 Corporate	..	292.7	329.7	831.1	798.3	..	2.2	1.2	2.3	2.1
1300 Unallocable between 1100 and 1200	..	0.0	0.0	0.0	0.0	..	0.0	0.0	0.0	0.0
2000 Social security contributions	..	**1 506.8**	**3 184.2**	**4 613.9**	**4 704.1**	..	**11.3**	**11.7**	**13.0**	**12.3**
2100 Employees	..	275.3	1 069.1	1 989.8	2 344.7	..	2.1	3.9	5.6	6.1
2200 Employers	..	1 213.2	2 047.6	2 594.2	2 329.0	..	9.1	7.5	7.3	6.1
2300 Self-employed or non-employed	..	0.9	21.2	0.0	0.0	..	0.0	0.1	0.0	0.0
2400 Unallocable between 2100, 2200 and 2300	..	17.4	46.3	30.0	30.4	..	0.1	0.2	0.1	0.1
3000 Taxes on payroll and workforce	..	**183.4**	**116.0**	**220.8**	**275.6**	..	**1.4**	**0.4**	**0.6**	**0.7**
4000 Taxes on property	..	**89.0**	**312.1**	**391.9**	**410.7**	..	**0.7**	**1.1**	**1.1**	**1.1**
4100 Recurrent taxes on immovable property	..	30.8	92.5	210.3	218.1	..	0.2	0.3	0.6	0.6
4200 Recurrent taxes on net wealth	..	0.0	135.7	59.8	53.4	..	0.0	0.5	0.2	0.1
4300 Estate, inheritance and gift taxes	..	5.5	6.3	8.3	9.4	..	0.0	0.0	0.0	0.0
4400 Taxes on financial and capital transactions	..	52.8	77.6	113.6	129.8	..	0.4	0.3	0.3	0.3
4500 Non-recurrent taxes	..	0.0	0.0	0.0	0.0	..	0.0	0.0	0.0	0.0
4600 Other recurrent taxes on property	..	0.0	0.0	0.0	0.0	..	0.0	0.0	0.0	0.0
5000 Taxes on goods and services	..	**2 081.1**	**4 350.3**	**5 882.8**	**6 285.4**	..	**15.6**	**16.0**	**16.6**	**16.4**
5100 Taxes on production, sale, transfer, etc	..	2 052.4	4 238.8	5 735.5	6 136.1	..	15.4	15.6	16.2	16.0
5110 General taxes	..	1 340.6	3 010.8	4 104.6	4 460.3	..	10.0	11.1	11.6	11.6
5111 Value added taxes	..	1 153.7	2 325.6	3 297.2	3 625.1	..	8.6	8.5	9.3	9.5
5120 Taxes on specific goods and services	..	711.8	1 228.0	1 630.9	1 675.8	..	5.3	4.5	4.6	4.4
5121 Excises	..	533.5	929.9	1 150.6	1 157.6	..	4.0	3.4	3.2	3.0
5200 Taxes on use of goods and perform activities	..	28.7	111.6	147.3	149.3	..	0.2	0.4	0.4	0.4
5300 Unallocable between 5100 and 5200	..	0.0	0.0	0.0	0.0	..	0.0	0.0	0.0	0.0
6000 Other taxes	..	**32.9**	**59.4**	**52.1**	**47.6**	..	**0.2**	**0.2**	**0.1**	**0.1**
Non-wastable tax credits										
Non-wastable tax credits against 1000	..	..	..	..	..	..	..	..	..	..
Transfer component	..	..	..	..	..	..	..	..	..	..
Tax expenditure component	..	..	..	..	..	..	..	..	..	..

.. Not available

Note: More detailed country data and country notes are available in online chapter 5 "Country Tables, 1965-2017": https://doi.org/10.1787/0bbc27da-en.
Full time series can be accessed at http://oe.cd/full-time-series.

Source: Ministry of Finance, Economic Department.

StatLink https://doi.org/10.1787/888934055785

Table 4.26. Hungary, tax revenue and % of GDP by level of government and main taxes

	Billion HUF					% of GDP				
	1990	2000	2010	2016	2017	1990	2000	2010	2016	2017
Federal or Central government										
Total tax revenue	**..**	**3 316.0**	**6 391.5**	**8 409.8**	**9 134.9**	**..**	**24.8**	**23.5**	**23.7**	**23.8**
1000 Taxes on income, profits and capital gains	..	1 230.8	2 064.3	2 551.8	2 750.2	..	9.2	7.6	7.2	7.2
2000 Social security contributions	..	136.6	182.0	244.4	353.2	..	1.0	0.7	0.7	0.9
3000 Taxes on payroll and workforce	..	15.4	103.1	212.2	262.9	..	0.1	0.4	0.6	0.7
4000 Taxes on property	..	29.1	182.8	236.7	247.7	..	0.2	0.7	0.7	0.6
5000 Taxes on goods and services	..	1 878.3	3 799.9	5 126.1	5 483.3	..	14.1	14.0	14.5	14.3
6000 Other taxes	..	25.8	59.4	38.6	37.7	..	0.2	0.2	0.1	0.1
State/Regional										
Total tax revenue	**..**	**..**	**..**	**..**	**..**	**..**	**..**	**..**	**..**	**..**
1000 Taxes on income, profits and capital gains	..	..	..	..	..	..	..	..	..	..
2000 Social security contributions	..	..	..	..	..	..	..	..	..	..
3000 Taxes on payroll and workforce	..	..	..	..	..	..	..	..	..	..
4000 Taxes on property	..	..	..	..	..	..	..	..	..	..
5000 Taxes on goods and services	..	..	..	..	..	..	..	..	..	..
6000 Other taxes	..	..	..	..	..	..	..	..	..	..
Local government										
Total tax revenue	**..**	**266.0**	**652.2**	**805.7**	**846.2**	**..**	**2.0**	**2.4**	**2.3**	**2.2**
1000 Taxes on income, profits and capital gains	..	2.2	0.1	0.0	0.0	..	0.0	0.0	0.0	0.0
2000 Social security contributions	..	0.0	0.0	0.0	0.0	..	0.0	0.0	0.0	0.0
3000 Taxes on payroll and workforce	..	1.2	1.2	0.0	0.0	..	0.0	0.0	0.0	0.0
4000 Taxes on property	..	59.9	129.3	155.2	163.0	..	0.4	0.5	0.4	0.4
5000 Taxes on goods and services	..	202.8	521.6	650.4	683.2	..	1.5	1.9	1.8	1.8
6000 Other taxes	..	0.0	0.0	0.0	0.0	..	0.0	0.0	0.0	0.0
Social Security Funds										
Total tax revenue	**..**	**1 558.6**	**3 076.2**	**4 629.7**	**4 614.9**	**..**	**11.7**	**11.3**	**13.1**	**12.0**
1000 Taxes on income, profits and capital gains	..	14.5	34.2	132.7	123.4	..	0.1	0.1	0.4	0.3
2000 Social security contributions	..	1 370.2	3 002.2	4 369.5	4 350.9	..	10.3	11.0	12.3	11.3
3000 Taxes on payroll and workforce	..	166.9	11.7	8.6	12.8	..	1.3	0.0	0.0	0.0
4000 Taxes on property	..	0.0	0.0	0.0	0.0	..	0.0	0.0	0.0	0.0
5000 Taxes on goods and services	..	0.0	28.1	105.4	118.0	..	0.0	0.1	0.3	0.3
6000 Other taxes	..	7.0	0.0	13.4	9.9	..	0.1	0.0	0.0	0.0

.. Not available

Note: More detailed country data and country notes are available in online chapter 6 "Tax revenues by sub-sectors of general government": https://doi.org/10.1787/0bbc27da-en. Full time series can be accessed at http://oe.cd/full-time-series.

Source: Ministry of Finance, Economic Department.

StatLink https://doi.org/10.1787/888934055804

Table 4.27. Iceland, tax revenue and % of GDP by selected tax category

	Billion ISK					% of GDP				
	1990	2000	2010	2016	2017	1990	2000	2010	2016	2017
Total tax revenue	**114.9**	**254.6**	**540.3**	**1 265.6**	**981.4**	**30.4**	**36.0**	**32.3**	**50.8**	**37.5**
1000 Taxes on income, profits and capital gains	**34.1**	**101.5**	**239.7**	**429.5**	**482.6**	**9.0**	**14.3**	**14.3**	**17.2**	**18.4**
1100 Of individuals	30.9	88.5	197.3	337.5	373.0	8.2	12.5	11.8	13.5	14.3
1200 Corporate	3.2	8.4	14.6	62.2	80.0	0.8	1.2	0.9	2.5	3.1
1300 Unallocable between 1100 and 1200	0.0	4.6	27.7	29.9	29.6	0.0	0.7	1.7	1.2	1.1
2000 Social security contributions	**3.6**	**19.7**	**63.6**	**85.4**	**89.6**	**1.0**	**2.8**	**3.8**	**3.4**	**3.4**
2100 Employees	0.3	..	..	..	..	0.1	..	..	..	..
2200 Employers	3.3	..	..	..	..	0.9	..	..	..	..
2300 Self-employed or non-employed	0.0	..	..	..	..	0.0	..	..	..	..
2400 Unallocable between 2100, 2200 and 2300	0.0	19.7	63.6	85.4	89.6	0.0	2.8	3.8	3.4	3.4
3000 Taxes on payroll and workforce	**4.1**	**0.2**	**2.8**	**7.4**	**7.9**	**1.1**	**0.0**	**0.2**	**0.3**	**0.3**
4000 Taxes on property	**9.7**	**20.0**	**38.1**	**432.6**	**54.0**	**2.6**	**2.8**	**2.3**	**17.4**	**2.1**
4100 Recurrent taxes on immovable property	4.1	10.1	28.5	38.7	43.4	1.1	1.4	1.7	1.6	1.7
4200 Recurrent taxes on net wealth	2.4	5.2	3.8	0.4	0.3	0.6	0.7	0.2	0.0	0.0
4300 Estate, inheritance and gift taxes	0.2	0.8	2.6	3.7	4.3	0.1	0.1	0.2	0.1	0.2
4400 Taxes on financial and capital transactions	2.9	3.1	2.7	4.9	4.6	0.8	0.4	0.2	0.2	0.2
4500 Non-recurrent taxes	0.0	0.1	0.1	384.6	0.5	0.0	0.0	0.0	15.4	0.0
4600 Other recurrent taxes on property	0.0	0.7	0.3	0.4	0.9	0.0	0.1	0.0	0.0	0.0
5000 Taxes on goods and services	**58.9**	**112.2**	**190.1**	**295.8**	**330.8**	**15.6**	**15.9**	**11.4**	**11.9**	**12.6**
5100 Taxes on production, sale, transfer, etc	56.6	100.7	179.0	277.1	311.2	15.0	14.2	10.7	11.1	11.9
5110 General taxes	37.1	72.7	122.4	205.4	234.0	9.8	10.3	7.3	8.2	8.9
5111 Value added taxes	32.7	72.7	122.4	205.4	234.0	8.7	10.3	7.3	8.2	8.9
5120 Taxes on specific goods and services	19.5	28.0	56.6	71.7	77.2	5.2	4.0	3.4	2.9	3.0
5121 Excises	2.3	23.6	46.7	61.7	67.7	0.6	3.3	2.8	2.5	2.6
5200 Taxes on use of goods and perform activities	2.4	11.6	11.1	18.8	19.6	0.6	1.6	0.7	0.8	0.7
5300 Unallocable between 5100 and 5200	0.0	0.0	0.0	0.0	0.0	0.0	0.0	0.0	0.0	0.0
6000 Other taxes	**4.5**	**1.0**	**6.0**	**14.9**	**16.4**	**1.2**	**0.1**	**0.4**	**0.6**	**0.6**
Non-wastable tax credits										
Non-wastable tax credits against 1000	..	..	..	1.6	2.8	..	..	..	0.1	0.1
Transfer component	..	..	..	1.3	2.3	..	..	..	0.1	0.1
Tax expenditure component	..	..	..	0.3	0.4	..	..	..	0.0	0.0

.. Not available

Note: More detailed country data and country notes are available in online chapter 5 "Country Tables, 1965-2017": https://doi.org/10.1787/0bbc27da-en. Full time series can be accessed at http://oe.cd/full-time-series.

The 2016 figure for Iceland includes the one-off revenues from stability contributions.

Source: Ministry of Finance, Economic Department.

StatLink https://doi.org/10.1787/888934055823

Table 4.28. Iceland, tax revenue and % of GDP by level of government and main taxes

	Billion ISK					% of GDP				
	1990	2000	2010	2016	2017	1990	2000	2010	2016	2017
Federal or Central government										
Total tax revenue	**91.6**	**195.1**	**402.3**	**1 030.2**	**721.7**	**24.3**	**27.6**	**24.1**	**41.4**	**27.6**
1000 Taxes on income, profits and capital gains	19.9	55.5	132.9	240.8	274.6	5.3	7.8	7.9	9.7	10.5
2000 Social security contributions	3.6	19.7	63.6	85.4	89.6	1.0	2.8	3.8	3.4	3.4
3000 Taxes on payroll and workforce	4.1	0.2	2.8	7.4	7.9	1.1	0.0	0.2	0.3	0.3
4000 Taxes on property	6.0	9.9	9.7	394.1	10.8	1.6	1.4	0.6	15.8	0.4
5000 Taxes on goods and services	57.7	108.9	187.4	287.6	322.3	15.3	15.4	11.2	11.5	12.3
6000 Other taxes	0.4	1.0	6.0	14.9	16.4	0.1	0.1	0.4	0.6	0.6
State/Regional										
Total tax revenue	..	..	..	..	..	..	..	..	..	..
1000 Taxes on income, profits and capital gains	..	..	..	..	..	..	..	..	..	..
2000 Social security contributions	..	..	..	..	..	..	..	..	..	..
3000 Taxes on payroll and workforce	..	..	..	..	..	..	..	..	..	..
4000 Taxes on property	..	..	..	..	..	..	..	..	..	..
5000 Taxes on goods and services	..	..	..	..	..	..	..	..	..	..
6000 Other taxes	..	..	..	..	..	..	..	..	..	..
Local government										
Total tax revenue	**23.3**	**59.4**	**138.0**	**235.4**	**259.7**	**6.2**	**8.4**	**8.2**	**9.5**	**9.9**
1000 Taxes on income, profits and capital gains	14.2	46.0	106.8	188.7	208.0	3.8	6.5	6.4	7.6	7.9
2000 Social security contributions	0.0	0.0	0.0	0.0	0.0	0.0	0.0	0.0	0.0	0.0
3000 Taxes on payroll and workforce	0.0	0.0	0.0	0.0	0.0	0.0	0.0	0.0	0.0	0.0
4000 Taxes on property	3.7	10.1	28.4	38.5	43.2	1.0	1.4	1.7	1.5	1.7
5000 Taxes on goods and services	1.2	3.3	2.8	8.2	8.5	0.3	0.5	0.2	0.3	0.3
6000 Other taxes	4.1	0.0	0.0	0.0	0.0	1.1	0.0	0.0	0.0	0.0
Social Security Funds										
Total tax revenue	**0.0**	**0.0**	**0.0**	**0.0**	**0.0**	**0.0**	**0.0**	**0.0**	**0.0**	**0.0**
1000 Taxes on income, profits and capital gains	0.0	0.0	0.0	0.0	0.0	0.0	0.0	0.0	0.0	0.0
2000 Social security contributions	0.0	0.0	0.0	0.0	0.0	0.0	0.0	0.0	0.0	0.0
3000 Taxes on payroll and workforce	0.0	0.0	0.0	0.0	0.0	0.0	0.0	0.0	0.0	0.0
4000 Taxes on property	0.0	0.0	0.0	0.0	0.0	0.0	0.0	0.0	0.0	0.0
5000 Taxes on goods and services	0.0	0.0	0.0	0.0	0.0	0.0	0.0	0.0	0.0	0.0
6000 Other taxes	0.0	0.0	0.0	0.0	0.0	0.0	0.0	0.0	0.0	0.0

.. Not available

Note: More detailed country data and country notes are available in online chapter 5 "Country Tables, 1965-2017": https://doi.org/10.1787/0bbc27da-en. Full time series can be accessed at http://oe.cd/full-time-series.

The 2016 figure for Iceland includes the one-off revenues from stability contributions.

Source: Ministry of Finance, Economic Department.

StatLink https://doi.org/10.1787/888934055842

Table 4.29. Ireland, tax revenue and % of GDP by selected tax category

	Billion EUR					% of GDP				
	1990	2000	2010	2016	2017	1990	2000	2010	2016	2017
Total tax revenue	**12.3**	**33.3**	**45.3**	**63.5**	**66.9**	**32.4**	**30.8**	**27.0**	**23.4**	**22.5**
1000 Taxes on income, profits and capital gains	**4.7**	**14.6**	**17.5**	**27.4**	**29.1**	**12.3**	**13.4**	**10.5**	**10.1**	**9.8**
1100 Of individuals	4.1	10.6	13.6	20.0	20.9	10.7	9.8	8.1	7.4	7.0
1200 Corporate	0.6	3.9	3.9	7.4	8.2	1.6	3.6	2.4	2.7	2.8
1300 Unallocable between 1100 and 1200	0.0	0.0	0.0	0.0	0.0	0.0	0.0	0.0	0.0	0.0
2000 Social security contributions	**1.7**	**3.9**	**8.4**	**10.7**	**11.4**	**4.6**	**3.6**	**5.0**	**3.9**	**3.9**
2100 Employees	0.6	0.9	3.2	3.5	3.7	1.5	0.9	1.9	1.3	1.3
2200 Employers	1.1	2.8	4.9	6.7	7.2	2.9	2.6	2.9	2.4	2.4
2300 Self-employed or non-employed	0.1	0.2	0.3	0.6	0.5	0.2	0.2	0.2	0.2	0.2
2400 Unallocable between 2100, 2200 and 2300	0.0	0.0	0.0	0.0	0.0	0.0	0.0	0.0	0.0	0.0
3000 Taxes on payroll and workforce	**0.2**	**0.0**	**0.3**	**0.4**	**0.4**	**0.4**	**0.0**	**0.2**	**0.1**	**0.1**
4000 Taxes on property	**0.6**	**1.9**	**2.4**	**3.8**	**3.8**	**1.5**	**1.8**	**1.4**	**1.4**	**1.3**
4100 Recurrent taxes on immovable property	0.3	0.6	1.3	1.8	1.8	0.8	0.5	0.8	0.7	0.6
4200 Recurrent taxes on net wealth	0.0	0.0	0.0	0.0	0.0	0.0	0.0	0.0	0.0	0.0
4300 Estate, inheritance and gift taxes	0.0	0.2	0.2	0.4	0.4	0.1	0.2	0.1	0.2	0.2
4400 Taxes on financial and capital transactions	0.2	1.1	0.8	1.6	1.5	0.6	1.0	0.5	0.6	0.5
4500 Non-recurrent taxes	0.0	0.0	0.0	0.0	0.0	0.0	0.0	0.0	0.0	0.0
4600 Other recurrent taxes on property	0.0	0.0	0.0	0.0	0.0	0.0	0.0	0.0	0.0	0.0
5000 Taxes on goods and services	**5.1**	**12.7**	**16.4**	**20.7**	**21.7**	**13.6**	**11.7**	**9.8**	**7.6**	**7.3**
5100 Taxes on production, sale, transfer, etc	4.9	12.2	15.1	18.7	19.7	13.0	11.2	9.0	6.9	6.6
5110 General taxes	2.5	7.6	10.1	12.8	13.1	6.6	7.1	6.0	4.7	4.4
5111 Value added taxes	2.5	7.6	10.1	12.8	13.1	6.6	7.1	6.0	4.7	4.4
5120 Taxes on specific goods and services	2.4	4.5	5.0	5.9	6.6	6.4	4.2	3.0	2.2	2.2
5121 Excises	2.1	4.4	4.9	5.8	6.2	5.5	4.1	2.9	2.1	2.1
5200 Taxes on use of goods and perform activities	0.2	0.6	1.3	1.9	2.0	0.5	0.5	0.8	0.7	0.7
5300 Unallocable between 5100 and 5200	0.0	0.0	0.0	0.0	0.0	0.0	0.0	0.0	0.0	0.0
6000 Other taxes	**0.0**	**0.0**	**0.0**	**0.0**	**0.0**	**0.0**	**0.0**	**0.0**	**0.0**	**0.0**
Non-wastable tax credits										
Non-wastable tax credits against 1000	..	..	1.1	0.5	0.5	..	..	0.6	0.2	0.2
Transfer component	..	..	0.0	0.0	0.0	..	..	0.0	0.0	0.0
Tax expenditure component	..	..	1.1	0.5	0.5	..	..	0.6	0.2	0.2

.. Not available

Note: More detailed country data and country notes are available in online chapter 5 "Country Tables, 1965-2017": https://doi.org/10.1787/0bbc27da-en. Full time series can be accessed at http://oe.cd/full-time-series.

Source: Annual Report of he Revenue Commissioners, Financial Accounts and National Income and Expenditure Accounts.

StatLink https://doi.org/10.1787/888934055861

Table 4.30. Ireland, tax revenue and % of GDP by level of government and main taxes

	Billion EUR					% of GDP				
	1990	2000	2010	2016	2017	1990	2000	2010	2016	2017
Federal or Central government										
Total tax revenue	**10.1**	**28.7**	**36.9**	**52.3**	**55.2**	**26.7**	**26.5**	**22.0**	**19.3**	**18.6**
1000 Taxes on income, profits and capital gains	4.7	14.6	17.5	27.4	29.1	12.3	13.4	10.5	10.1	9.8
2000 Social security contributions	0.1	0.1	1.5	1.4	1.5	0.2	0.1	0.9	0.5	0.5
3000 Taxes on payroll and workforce	0.2	0.0	0.3	0.4	0.4	0.4	0.0	0.2	0.1	0.1
4000 Taxes on property	0.3	1.3	1.1	2.5	2.5	0.7	1.2	0.6	0.9	0.8
5000 Taxes on goods and services	5.0	12.7	16.4	20.7	21.7	13.1	11.7	9.8	7.6	7.3
6000 Other taxes	0.0	0.0	0.0	0.0	0.0	0.0	0.0	0.0	0.0	0.0
State/Regional										
Total tax revenue	..	..	..	..	..	..	..	..	..	..
1000 Taxes on income, profits and capital gains	..	..	..	..	..	..	..	..	..	..
2000 Social security contributions	..	..	..	..	..	..	..	..	..	..
3000 Taxes on payroll and workforce	..	..	..	..	..	..	..	..	..	..
4000 Taxes on property	..	..	..	..	..	..	..	..	..	..
5000 Taxes on goods and services	..	..	..	..	..	..	..	..	..	..
6000 Other taxes	..	..	..	..	..	..	..	..	..	..
Local government										
Total tax revenue	**0.3**	**0.7**	**1.5**	**1.4**	**1.4**	**0.9**	**0.6**	**0.9**	**0.5**	**0.5**
1000 Taxes on income, profits and capital gains	0.0	0.0	0.0	0.0	0.0	0.0	0.0	0.0	0.0	0.0
2000 Social security contributions	0.0	0.1	0.2	0.1	0.1	0.1	0.1	0.1	0.0	0.0
3000 Taxes on payroll and workforce	0.0	0.0	0.0	0.0	0.0	0.0	0.0	0.0	0.0	0.0
4000 Taxes on property	0.3	0.6	1.3	1.4	1.3	0.8	0.5	0.8	0.5	0.5
5000 Taxes on goods and services	0.0	0.0	0.0	0.0	0.0	0.0	0.0	0.0	0.0	0.0
6000 Other taxes	0.0	0.0	0.0	0.0	0.0	0.0	0.0	0.0	0.0	0.0
Social Security Funds										
Total tax revenue	**1.6**	**3.8**	**6.7**	**9.2**	**9.8**	**4.3**	**3.5**	**4.0**	**3.4**	**3.3**
1000 Taxes on income, profits and capital gains	0.0	0.0	0.0	0.0	0.0	0.0	0.0	0.0	0.0	0.0
2000 Social security contributions	1.6	3.8	6.7	9.2	9.8	4.3	3.5	4.0	3.4	3.3
3000 Taxes on payroll and workforce	0.0	0.0	0.0	0.0	0.0	0.0	0.0	0.0	0.0	0.0
4000 Taxes on property	0.0	0.0	0.0	0.0	0.0	0.0	0.0	0.0	0.0	0.0
5000 Taxes on goods and services	0.0	0.0	0.0	0.0	0.0	0.0	0.0	0.0	0.0	0.0
6000 Other taxes	0.0	0.0	0.0	0.0	0.0	0.0	0.0	0.0	0.0	0.0

.. Not available

Note: More detailed country data and country notes are available in online chapter 6 "Tax revenues by sub-sectors of general government": https://doi.org/10.1787/0bbc27da-en. Full time series can be accessed at http://oe.cd/full-time-series.

Source: Annual Report of he Revenue Commissioners, Financial Accounts and National Income and Expenditure Accounts.

StatLink https://doi.org/10.1787/888934055880

Table 4.31. Israel, tax revenue and % of GDP by selected tax category

	Billion ILS					% of GDP				
	1990	2000	2010	2016	2017	1990	2000	2010	2016	2017
Total tax revenue	..	**188.3**	**268.6**	**381.6**	**413.4**	..	**34.9**	**30.7**	**31.1**	**32.5**
1000 Taxes on income, profits and capital gains	..	**74.6**	**78.3**	**120.5**	**146.9**	..	**13.8**	**9.0**	**9.8**	**11.6**
1100 Of individuals	..	54.8	48.2	75.6	85.4	..	10.2	5.5	6.2	6.7
1200 Corporate	..	18.0	23.1	37.8	41.9	..	3.3	2.6	3.1	3.3
1300 Unallocable between 1100 and 1200	..	1.8	6.9	7.1	19.6	..	0.3	0.8	0.6	1.5
2000 Social security contributions	..	**27.6**	**45.3**	**63.5**	**66.8**	..	**5.1**	**5.2**	**5.2**	**5.3**
2100 Employees	..	15.8	27.8	35.9	37.9	..	2.9	3.2	2.9	3.0
2200 Employers	..	8.2	11.4	19.5	20.6	..	1.5	1.3	1.6	1.6
2300 Self-employed or non-employed	..	3.6	6.1	8.1	8.3	..	0.7	0.7	0.7	0.7
2400 Unallocable between 2100, 2200 and 2300	..	0.0	0.0	0.0	0.0	..	0.0	0.0	0.0	0.0
3000 Taxes on payroll and workforce	..	**6.8**	**10.3**	**14.1**	**15.2**	..	**1.3**	**1.2**	**1.1**	**1.2**
4000 Taxes on property	..	**16.9**	**28.8**	**39.2**	**41.3**	..	**3.1**	**3.3**	**3.2**	**3.2**
4100 Recurrent taxes on immovable property	..	11.3	18.8	24.4	24.9	..	2.1	2.1	2.0	2.0
4200 Recurrent taxes on net wealth	..	0.0	0.0	0.0	0.0	..	0.0	0.0	0.0	0.0
4300 Estate, inheritance and gift taxes	..	0.0	0.0	0.0	0.0	..	0.0	0.0	0.0	0.0
4400 Taxes on financial and capital transactions	..	3.2	4.1	6.6	6.6	..	0.6	0.5	0.5	0.5
4500 Non-recurrent taxes	..	2.4	6.0	8.2	9.8	..	0.5	0.7	0.7	0.8
4600 Other recurrent taxes on property	..	0.0	0.0	0.0	0.0	..	0.0	0.0	0.0	0.0
5000 Taxes on goods and services	..	**62.4**	**105.9**	**144.3**	**143.2**	..	**11.6**	**12.1**	**11.8**	**11.3**
5100 Taxes on production, sale, transfer, etc	..	57.9	98.1	134.4	133.3	..	10.7	11.2	11.0	10.5
5110 General taxes	..	49.9	79.9	112.9	111.0	..	9.3	9.1	9.2	8.7
5111 Value added taxes	..	39.8	65.5	92.0	94.5	..	7.4	7.5	7.5	7.4
5120 Taxes on specific goods and services	..	8.0	18.1	21.6	22.3	..	1.5	2.1	1.8	1.8
5121 Excises	..	6.6	15.5	18.3	19.3	..	1.2	1.8	1.5	1.5
5200 Taxes on use of goods and perform activities	..	4.5	7.8	9.9	9.9	..	0.8	0.9	0.8	0.8
5300 Unallocable between 5100 and 5200	..	0.0	0.0	0.0	0.0	..	0.0	0.0	0.0	0.0
6000 Other taxes	..	**0.0**	**0.0**	**0.0**	**0.0**	..	**0.0**	**0.0**	**0.0**	**0.0**
Non-wastable tax credits										
Non-wastable tax credits against 1000	..	..	0.1	1.3	1.6	..	..	0.0	0.1	0.1
Transfer component	..	..	0.1	1.2	1.6	..	..	0.0	0.1	0.1
Tax expenditure component	..	..	0.0	0.1	0.0	..	..	0.0	0.0	0.0

.. Not available
Note: More detailed country data and country notes are available in online chapter 5 "Country Tables, 1965-2017": https://doi.org/10.1787/0bbc27da-en.
Full time series can be accessed at http://oe.cd/full-time-series.
The data for Israel are supplied by and under the responsibility of the relevant Israeli authorities. The use of such data by the OECD is without prejudice to the status of the Golan Heights, East Jerusalem and Israeli settlements in the West Bank under the terms of international law.
Source: Israel Central Bureau of Statistics and Israel Ministry of Finance.

StatLink https://doi.org/10.1787/888934055899

Table 4.32. Israel, tax revenue and % of GDP by level of government and main taxes

	Billion ILS					% of GDP				
	1990	2000	2010	2016	2017	1990	2000	2010	2016	2017
Federal or Central government										
Total tax revenue	..	**148.0**	**199.9**	**288.1**	**315.1**	..	**27.5**	**22.9**	**23.5**	**24.8**
1000 Taxes on income, profits and capital gains	..	74.6	78.3	120.5	146.9	..	13.8	9.0	9.8	11.6
2000 Social security contributions	..	0.0	0.0	0.0	0.0	..	0.0	0.0	0.0	0.0
3000 Taxes on payroll and workforce	..	6.8	10.3	14.1	15.2	..	1.3	1.2	1.1	1.2
4000 Taxes on property	..	4.8	6.6	10.7	11.3	..	0.9	0.8	0.9	0.9
5000 Taxes on goods and services	..	61.8	104.7	142.9	141.7	..	11.5	12.0	11.6	11.1
6000 Other taxes	..	0.0	0.0	0.0	0.0	..	0.0	0.0	0.0	0.0
State/Regional										
Total tax revenue	..	..	..	..	..	..	..	..	..	..
1000 Taxes on income, profits and capital gains	..	..	..	..	..	..	..	..	..	..
2000 Social security contributions	..	..	..	..	..	..	..	..	..	..
3000 Taxes on payroll and workforce	..	..	..	..	..	..	..	..	..	..
4000 Taxes on property	..	..	..	..	..	..	..	..	..	..
5000 Taxes on goods and services	..	..	..	..	..	..	..	..	..	..
6000 Other taxes	..	..	..	..	..	..	..	..	..	..
Local government										
Total tax revenue	..	**12.7**	**23.4**	**30.0**	**31.5**	..	**2.4**	**2.7**	**2.4**	**2.5**
1000 Taxes on income, profits and capital gains	..	0.0	0.0	0.0	0.0	..	0.0	0.0	0.0	0.0
2000 Social security contributions	..	0.0	0.0	0.0	0.0	..	0.0	0.0	0.0	0.0
3000 Taxes on payroll and workforce	..	0.0	0.0	0.0	0.0	..	0.0	0.0	0.0	0.0
4000 Taxes on property	..	12.1	22.2	28.5	30.0	..	2.2	2.5	2.3	2.4
5000 Taxes on goods and services	..	0.6	1.1	1.5	1.5	..	0.1	0.1	0.1	0.1
6000 Other taxes	..	0.0	0.0	0.0	0.0	..	0.0	0.0	0.0	0.0
Social Security Funds										
Total tax revenue	..	**27.6**	**45.3**	**63.5**	**66.8**	..	**5.1**	**5.2**	**5.2**	**5.3**
1000 Taxes on income, profits and capital gains	..	0.0	0.0	0.0	0.0	..	0.0	0.0	0.0	0.0
2000 Social security contributions	..	27.6	45.3	63.5	66.8	..	5.1	5.2	5.2	5.3
3000 Taxes on payroll and workforce	..	0.0	0.0	0.0	0.0	..	0.0	0.0	0.0	0.0
4000 Taxes on property	..	0.0	0.0	0.0	0.0	..	0.0	0.0	0.0	0.0
5000 Taxes on goods and services	..	0.0	0.0	0.0	0.0	..	0.0	0.0	0.0	0.0
6000 Other taxes	..	0.0	0.0	0.0	0.0	..	0.0	0.0	0.0	0.0

.. Not available

Note: More detailed country data and country notes are available in online chapter 6 "Tax revenues by sub-sectors of general government": https://doi.org/10.1787/0bbc27da-en. Full time series can be accessed at http://oe.cd/full-time-series.

The data for Israel are supplied by and under the responsibility of the relevant Israeli authorities. The use of such data by the OECD is without prejudice to the status of the Golan Heights, East Jerusalem and Israeli settlements in the West Bank under the terms of international law.

Source: Israel Central Bureau of Statistics and Israel Ministry of Finance.

StatLink https://doi.org/10.1787/888934055918

Table 4.33. Italy, tax revenue and % of GDP by selected tax category

	Billion EUR					% of GDP				
	1990	2000	2010	2016	2017	1990	2000	2010	2016	2017
Total tax revenue	**265.1**	**503.1**	**671.9**	**714.9**	**727.8**	**36.4**	**40.6**	**41.9**	**42.3**	**42.1**
1000 Taxes on income, profits and capital gains	**96.7**	**166.9**	**219.5**	**228.4**	**230.9**	**13.3**	**13.5**	**13.7**	**13.5**	**13.4**
1100 Of individuals	69.7	124.9	180.5	183.7	187.0	9.6	10.1	11.3	10.9	10.8
1200 Corporate	26.6	34.7	36.7	36.3	36.3	3.7	2.8	2.3	2.1	2.1
1300 Unallocable between 1100 and 1200	0.4	7.3	2.3	8.3	7.6	0.1	0.6	0.1	0.5	0.4
2000 Social security contributions	**87.3**	**143.6**	**209.1**	**215.9**	**220.6**	**12.0**	**11.6**	**13.0**	**12.8**	**12.8**
2100 Employees	16.8	27.3	37.6	40.0	40.9	2.3	2.2	2.3	2.4	2.4
2200 Employers	62.5	99.9	144.3	144.0	147.3	8.6	8.1	9.0	8.5	8.5
2300 Self-employed or non-employed	8.0	16.4	27.2	31.9	32.4	1.1	1.3	1.7	1.9	1.9
2400 Unallocable between 2100, 2200 and 2300	0.0	0.0	0.0	0.0	0.0	0.0	0.0	0.0	0.0	0.0
3000 Taxes on payroll and workforce	**0.9**	**0.0**	**0.0**	**0.0**	**0.0**	**0.1**	**0.0**	**0.0**	**0.0**	**0.0**
4000 Taxes on property	**6.0**	**23.4**	**32.4**	**46.9**	**44.9**	**0.8**	**1.9**	**2.0**	**2.8**	**2.6**
4100 Recurrent taxes on immovable property	0.0	9.4	9.7	21.7	22.1	0.0	0.8	0.6	1.3	1.3
4200 Recurrent taxes on net wealth	0.0	0.0	2.1	0.4	0.4	0.0	0.0	0.1	0.0	0.0
4300 Estate, inheritance and gift taxes	0.4	1.0	0.5	0.7	0.8	0.1	0.1	0.0	0.0	0.0
4400 Taxes on financial and capital transactions	5.6	12.3	17.4	17.7	17.7	0.8	1.0	1.1	1.0	1.0
4500 Non-recurrent taxes	0.0	0.1	0.9	4.2	1.1	0.0	0.0	0.1	0.3	0.1
4600 Other recurrent taxes on property	0.0	0.6	1.9	2.2	2.8	0.0	0.0	0.1	0.1	0.2
5000 Taxes on goods and services	**74.3**	**140.3**	**176.6**	**201.3**	**206.9**	**10.2**	**11.3**	**11.0**	**11.9**	**12.0**
5100 Taxes on production, sale, transfer, etc	67.1	125.7	158.5	176.4	181.5	9.2	10.1	9.9	10.4	10.5
5110 General taxes	38.9	77.5	97.6	102.4	107.9	5.3	6.3	6.1	6.1	6.2
5111 Value added taxes	38.9	77.5	97.6	102.4	107.9	5.3	6.3	6.1	6.1	6.2
5120 Taxes on specific goods and services	28.0	48.3	61.0	74.0	73.6	3.9	3.9	3.8	4.4	4.3
5121 Excises	20.3	31.5	36.4	48.4	46.8	2.8	2.5	2.3	2.9	2.7
5200 Taxes on use of goods and perform activities	4.5	8.5	10.5	13.3	13.2	0.6	0.7	0.7	0.8	0.8
5300 Unallocable between 5100 and 5200	2.7	6.1	7.6	11.7	12.2	0.4	0.5	0.5	0.7	0.7
6000 Other taxes	**0.0**	**27.3**	**31.9**	**20.2**	**22.3**	**0.0**	**2.2**	**2.0**	**1.2**	**1.3**
Non-wastable tax credits										
Non-wastable tax credits against 1000	..	..	0.0	12.6	10.3	..	..	0.0	0.7	0.6
Transfer component	..	..	0.1	3.7	1.2	..	..	0.0	0.2	0.1
Tax expenditure component	..	..	-0.1	8.9	9.1	..	..	0.0	0.5	0.5

.. Not available

Note: More detailed country data and country notes are available in online chapter 5 "Country Tables, 1965-2017": https://doi.org/10.1787/0bbc27da-en. Full time series can be accessed at http://oe.cd/full-time-series.

Source: Ministero dell'economia e delle finanze; Istituto nazionale di statistica.

StatLink https://doi.org/10.1787/888934055937

Table 4.34. Italy, tax revenue and % of GDP by level of government and main taxes

	Billion EUR					% of GDP				
	1990	2000	2010	2016	2017	1990	2000	2010	2016	2017
Federal or Central government										
Total tax revenue	**168.9**	**280.8**	**357.3**	**388.4**	**389.9**	**23.2**	**22.7**	**22.3**	**23.0**	**22.6**
1000 Taxes on income, profits and capital gains	92.7	154.2	193.9	197.6	197.7	12.7	12.4	12.1	11.7	11.4
2000 Social security contributions	0.0	0.0	0.0	0.0	0.0	0.0	0.0	0.0	0.0	0.0
3000 Taxes on payroll and workforce	0.9	0.0	0.0	0.0	0.0	0.1	0.0	0.0	0.0	0.0
4000 Taxes on property	6.0	12.9	21.0	26.5	24.1	0.8	1.0	1.3	1.6	1.4
5000 Taxes on goods and services	69.3	113.6	142.5	164.4	168.0	9.5	9.2	8.9	9.7	9.7
6000 Other taxes	0.0	0.0	0.0	0.0	0.0	0.0	0.0	0.0	0.0	0.0
State/Regional										
Total tax revenue	..	..	..	..	..	..	..	..	..	..
1000 Taxes on income, profits and capital gains	..	..	..	..	..	..	..	..	..	..
2000 Social security contributions	..	..	..	..	..	..	..	..	..	..
3000 Taxes on payroll and workforce	..	..	..	..	..	..	..	..	..	..
4000 Taxes on property	..	..	..	..	..	..	..	..	..	..
5000 Taxes on goods and services	..	..	..	..	..	..	..	..	..	..
6000 Other taxes	..	..	..	..	..	..	..	..	..	..
Local government										
Total tax revenue	**7.7**	**77.2**	**103.2**	**107.7**	**112.7**	**1.1**	**6.2**	**6.4**	**6.4**	**6.5**
1000 Taxes on income, profits and capital gains	4.0	12.7	25.6	30.8	33.1	0.6	1.0	1.6	1.8	1.9
2000 Social security contributions	0.0	0.0	0.0	0.0	0.0	0.0	0.0	0.0	0.0	0.0
3000 Taxes on payroll and workforce	0.0	0.0	0.0	0.0	0.0	0.0	0.0	0.0	0.0	0.0
4000 Taxes on property	0.0	10.5	11.5	20.4	20.8	0.0	0.8	0.7	1.2	1.2
5000 Taxes on goods and services	3.7	26.7	34.2	36.2	36.6	0.5	2.2	2.1	2.1	2.1
6000 Other taxes	0.0	27.3	31.9	20.2	22.3	0.0	2.2	2.0	1.2	1.3
Social Security Funds										
Total tax revenue	**87.3**	**143.6**	**209.1**	**215.9**	**220.6**	**12.0**	**11.6**	**13.0**	**12.8**	**12.8**
1000 Taxes on income, profits and capital gains	0.0	0.0	0.0	0.0	0.0	0.0	0.0	0.0	0.0	0.0
2000 Social security contributions	87.3	143.6	209.1	215.9	220.6	12.0	11.6	13.0	12.8	12.8
3000 Taxes on payroll and workforce	0.0	0.0	0.0	0.0	0.0	0.0	0.0	0.0	0.0	0.0
4000 Taxes on property	0.0	0.0	0.0	0.0	0.0	0.0	0.0	0.0	0.0	0.0
5000 Taxes on goods and services	0.0	0.0	0.0	0.0	0.0	0.0	0.0	0.0	0.0	0.0
6000 Other taxes	0.0	0.0	0.0	0.0	0.0	0.0	0.0	0.0	0.0	0.0

.. Not available

Note: More detailed country data and country notes are available in online chapter 6 "Tax revenues by sub-sectors of general government": https://doi.org/10.1787/0bbc27da-en. Full time series can be accessed at http://oe.cd/full-time-series.

Source: Ministero dell'economia e delle finanze; Istituto nazionale di statistica.

StatLink https://doi.org/10.1787/888934055956

Table 4.35. Japan, tax revenue and % of GDP by selected tax category

	Billion JPY					% of GDP				
	1990	2000	2010	2016	2017	1990	2000	2010	2016	2017
Total tax revenue	**130 842.7**	**136 235.8**	**132 484.3**	**164 962.9**	**171 751.4**	**28.2**	**25.8**	**26.5**	**30.7**	**31.4**
1000 Taxes on income, profits and capital gains	**65 681.6**	**47 398.2**	**40 034.3**	**50 447.7**	**52 657.9**	**14.2**	**9.0**	**8.0**	**9.4**	**9.6**
1100 Of individuals	36 393.6	28 677.3	24 662.7	30 669.6	32 324.6	7.8	5.4	4.9	5.7	5.9
1200 Corporate	29 288.0	18 720.9	15 371.6	19 778.1	20 333.3	6.3	3.5	3.1	3.7	3.7
1300 Unallocable between 1100 and 1200	0.0	0.0	0.0	0.0	0.0	0.0	0.0	0.0	0.0	0.0
2000 Social security contributions	**34 612.6**	**47 968.3**	**54 460.6**	**66 614.3**	**68 561.7**	**7.5**	**9.1**	**10.9**	**12.4**	**12.5**
2100 Employees	13 895.0	19 829.9	23 592.6	29 311.4	30 339.9	3.0	3.8	4.7	5.5	5.5
2200 Employers	16 648.8	22 455.5	24 674.2	30 560.4	31 636.6	3.6	4.2	4.9	5.7	5.8
2300 Self-employed or non-employed	4 068.8	5 682.9	6 193.8	6 742.5	6 585.2	0.9	1.1	1.2	1.3	1.2
2400 Unallocable between 2100, 2200 and 2300	0.0	0.0	0.0	0.0	0.0	0.0	0.0	0.0	0.0	0.0
3000 Taxes on payroll and workforce	**0.0**	**0.0**	**0.0**	**0.0**	**0.0**	**0.0**	**0.0**	**0.0**	**0.0**	**0.0**
4000 Taxes on property	**12 296.3**	**14 294.4**	**12 878.3**	**13 772.3**	**14 073.1**	**2.7**	**2.7**	**2.6**	**2.6**	**2.6**
4100 Recurrent taxes on immovable property	7 098.5	10 413.7	10 225.0	10 165.1	10 323.1	1.5	2.0	2.0	1.9	1.9
4200 Recurrent taxes on net wealth	0.0	0.0	0.0	0.0	0.0	0.0	0.0	0.0	0.0	0.0
4300 Estate, inheritance and gift taxes	1 918.0	1 782.2	1 250.4	2 131.4	2 292.0	0.4	0.3	0.3	0.4	0.4
4400 Taxes on financial and capital transactions	3 279.8	2 098.5	1 402.9	1 475.8	1 458.0	0.7	0.4	0.3	0.3	0.3
4500 Non-recurrent taxes	0.0	0.0	0.0	0.0	0.0	0.0	0.0	0.0	0.0	0.0
4600 Other recurrent taxes on property	0.0	0.0	0.0	0.0	0.0	0.0	0.0	0.0	0.0	0.0
5000 Taxes on goods and services	**17 916.8**	**26 227.2**	**24 730.2**	**33 711.0**	**36 031.3**	**3.9**	**5.0**	**5.0**	**6.3**	**6.6**
5100 Taxes on production, sale, transfer, etc	15 646.5	23 180.2	22 160.4	31 254.2	33 581.7	3.4	4.4	4.4	5.8	6.1
5110 General taxes	5 778.3	12 350.3	12 675.2	21 931.0	22 249.2	1.2	2.3	2.5	4.1	4.1
5111 Value added taxes	5 778.3	12 350.3	12 675.2	21 931.0	22 249.2	1.2	2.3	2.5	4.1	4.1
5120 Taxes on specific goods and services	9 868.2	10 829.9	9 485.2	9 323.2	11 332.5	2.1	2.0	1.9	1.7	2.1
5121 Excises	8 637.2	9 837.0	8 622.4	8 315.9	10 241.0	1.9	1.9	1.7	1.5	1.9
5200 Taxes on use of goods and perform activities	2 270.3	3 047.0	2 569.8	2 456.8	2 449.6	0.5	0.6	0.5	0.5	0.4
5300 Unallocable between 5100 and 5200	0.0	0.0	0.0	0.0	0.0	0.0	0.0	0.0	0.0	0.0
6000 Other taxes	**335.4**	**347.7**	**381.1**	**417.6**	**427.4**	**0.1**	**0.1**	**0.1**	**0.1**	**0.1**
Non-wastable tax credits										
Non-wastable tax credits against 1000	..	..	..	..	..	..	..	..	..	..
Transfer component	..	..	..	..	..	..	..	..	..	..
Tax expenditure component	..	..	..	..	..	..	..	..	..	..

.. Not available

Note: More detailed country data and country notes are available in online chapter 5 "Country Tables, 1965-2017": https://doi.org/10.1787/0bbc27da-en. Full time series can be accessed at http://oe.cd/full-time-series.

Source: Tax Bureau, Ministry of Finance.

StatLink https://doi.org/10.1787/888934055975

Table 4.36. Japan, tax revenue and % of GDP by level of government and main taxes

	Billion JPY					% of GDP				
	1990	2000	2010	2016	2017	1990	2000	2010	2016	2017
Federal or Central government										
Total tax revenue	**62 779.7**	**52 720.8**	**43 707.4**	**58 956.3**	**64 284.1**	**13.5**	**10.0**	**8.8**	**11.0**	**11.7**
1000 Taxes on income, profits and capital gains	44 379.1	30 536.2	23 372.1	30 721.4	33 782.5	9.6	5.8	4.7	5.7	6.2
2000 Social security contributions	0.0	0.0	0.0	0.0	0.0	0.0	0.0	0.0	0.0	0.0
3000 Taxes on payroll and workforce	0.0	0.0	0.0	0.0	0.0	0.0	0.0	0.0	0.0	0.0
4000 Taxes on property	4 601.6	3 314.9	2 274.5	3 210.5	3 343.5	1.0	0.6	0.5	0.6	0.6
5000 Taxes on goods and services	13 799.0	18 869.7	18 060.9	25 024.4	27 158.1	3.0	3.6	3.6	4.7	5.0
6000 Other taxes	0.0	0.0	0.0	0.0	0.0	0.0	0.0	0.0	0.0	0.0
State/Regional										
Total tax revenue	..	..	..	..	..	..	..	..	..	..
1000 Taxes on income, profits and capital gains	..	..	..	..	..	..	..	..	..	..
2000 Social security contributions	..	..	..	..	..	..	..	..	..	..
3000 Taxes on payroll and workforce	..	..	..	..	..	..	..	..	..	..
4000 Taxes on property	..	..	..	..	..	..	..	..	..	..
5000 Taxes on goods and services	..	..	..	..	..	..	..	..	..	..
6000 Other taxes	..	..	..	..	..	..	..	..	..	..
Local government										
Total tax revenue	**33 450.4**	**35 546.7**	**34 316.3**	**39 392.3**	**38 905.6**	**7.2**	**6.7**	**6.9**	**7.3**	**7.1**
1000 Taxes on income, profits and capital gains	21 302.5	16 862.0	16 662.3	19 726.3	18 875.4	4.6	3.2	3.3	3.7	3.4
2000 Social security contributions	0.0	0.0	0.0	0.0	0.0	0.0	0.0	0.0	0.0	0.0
3000 Taxes on payroll and workforce	0.0	0.0	0.0	0.0	0.0	0.0	0.0	0.0	0.0	0.0
4000 Taxes on property	7 694.7	10 979.5	10 603.8	10 561.8	10 729.6	1.7	2.1	2.1	2.0	2.0
5000 Taxes on goods and services	4 117.8	7 357.5	6 669.2	8 686.6	8 873.2	0.9	1.4	1.3	1.6	1.6
6000 Other taxes	335.4	347.7	381.1	417.6	427.4	0.1	0.1	0.1	0.1	0.1
Social Security Funds										
Total tax revenue	**34 612.6**	**47 968.3**	**54 460.6**	**66 614.3**	**68 561.7**	**7.5**	**9.1**	**10.9**	**12.4**	**12.5**
1000 Taxes on income, profits and capital gains	0.0	0.0	0.0	0.0	0.0	0.0	0.0	0.0	0.0	0.0
2000 Social security contributions	34 612.6	47 968.3	54 460.6	66 614.3	68 561.7	7.5	9.1	10.9	12.4	12.5
3000 Taxes on payroll and workforce	0.0	0.0	0.0	0.0	0.0	0.0	0.0	0.0	0.0	0.0
4000 Taxes on property	0.0	0.0	0.0	0.0	0.0	0.0	0.0	0.0	0.0	0.0
5000 Taxes on goods and services	0.0	0.0	0.0	0.0	0.0	0.0	0.0	0.0	0.0	0.0
6000 Other taxes	0.0	0.0	0.0	0.0	0.0	0.0	0.0	0.0	0.0	0.0

.. Not available

Note: More detailed country data and country notes are available in online chapter 6 "Tax revenues by sub-sectors of general government": https://doi.org/10.1787/0bbc27da-en. Full time series can be accessed at http://oe.cd/full-time-series.

Source: Tax Bureau, Ministry of Finance.

StatLink https://doi.org/10.1787/888934055994

Table 4.37. Korea, tax revenue and % of GDP by selected tax category

	Billion KRW					% of GDP				
	1990	2000	2010	2016	2017	1990	2000	2010	2016	2017
Total tax revenue	**37 261.7**	**136 295.0**	**295 968.0**	**430 752.0**	**465 470.0**	**18.8**	**21.5**	**23.4**	**26.2**	**26.9**
1000 Taxes on income, profits and capital gains	**12 203.5**	**39 254.0**	**82 905.0**	**134 503.0**	**149 420.0**	**6.2**	**6.2**	**6.6**	**8.2**	**8.6**
1100 Of individuals	7 440.4	19 950.0	42 098.0	75 711.0	83 121.0	3.8	3.1	3.3	4.6	4.8
1200 Corporate	4 756.6	19 271.0	40 807.0	58 792.0	66 299.0	2.4	3.0	3.2	3.6	3.8
1300 Unallocable between 1100 and 1200	6.5	33.0	0.0	0.0	0.0	0.0	0.0	0.0	0.0	0.0
2000 Social security contributions	**3 760.0**	**22 759.0**	**69 090.0**	**112 658.0**	**119 676.0**	**1.9**	**3.6**	**5.5**	**6.9**	**6.9**
2100 Employees	1 464.0	8 578.0	28 213.0	48 077.0	51 125.0	0.7	1.4	2.2	2.9	3.0
2200 Employers	1 694.0	9 409.0	30 856.0	51 190.0	54 063.0	0.9	1.5	2.4	3.1	3.1
2300 Self-employed or non-employed	602.0	4 772.0	10 021.0	13 391.0	14 488.0	0.3	0.8	0.8	0.8	0.8
2400 Unallocable between 2100, 2200 and 2300	0.0	0.0	0.0	0.0	0.0	0.0	0.0	0.0	0.0	0.0
3000 Taxes on payroll and workforce	**152.8**	**258.0**	**714.0**	**1 293.0**	**1 376.0**	**0.1**	**0.0**	**0.1**	**0.1**	**0.1**
4000 Taxes on property	**4 388.9**	**16 846.0**	**33 516.0**	**49 820.0**	**54 406.0**	**2.2**	**2.7**	**2.6**	**3.0**	**3.1**
4100 Recurrent taxes on immovable property	980.0	3 385.0	9 270.0	13 095.0	14 319.0	0.5	0.5	0.7	0.8	0.8
4200 Recurrent taxes on net wealth	0.0	0.0	0.0	0.0	0.0	0.0	0.0	0.0	0.0	0.0
4300 Estate, inheritance and gift taxes	353.9	989.0	3 076.0	5 350.0	6 785.0	0.2	0.2	0.2	0.3	0.4
4400 Taxes on financial and capital transactions	2 959.7	11 935.0	21 170.0	31 375.0	33 302.0	1.5	1.9	1.7	1.9	1.9
4500 Non-recurrent taxes	95.3	537.0	0.0	0.0	0.0	0.0	0.1	0.0	0.0	0.0
4600 Other recurrent taxes on property	0.0	0.0	0.0	0.0	0.0	0.0	0.0	0.0	0.0	0.0
5000 Taxes on goods and services	**16 497.5**	**52 271.0**	**99 769.0**	**121 197.0**	**129 065.0**	**8.3**	**8.2**	**7.9**	**7.4**	**7.5**
5100 Taxes on production, sale, transfer, etc	16 023.5	50 023.0	96 573.0	113 644.0	121 293.0	8.1	7.9	7.6	6.9	7.0
5110 General taxes	6 964.4	23 212.0	51 800.0	68 229.0	74 361.0	3.5	3.7	4.1	4.2	4.3
5111 Value added taxes	6 964.4	23 212.0	51 800.0	68 229.0	74 361.0	3.5	3.7	4.1	4.2	4.3
5120 Taxes on specific goods and services	9 059.1	26 811.0	44 773.0	45 415.0	46 932.0	4.6	4.2	3.5	2.8	2.7
5121 Excises	4 923.7	18 155.0	31 340.0	34 762.0	35 779.0	2.5	2.9	2.5	2.1	2.1
5200 Taxes on use of goods and perform activities	473.9	2 248.0	3 196.0	7 553.0	7 772.0	0.2	0.4	0.3	0.5	0.4
5300 Unallocable between 5100 and 5200	0.0	0.0	0.0	0.0	0.0	0.0	0.0	0.0	0.0	0.0
6000 Other taxes	**259.1**	**4 907.0**	**9 974.0**	**11 281.0**	**11 527.0**	**0.1**	**0.8**	**0.8**	**0.7**	**0.7**
Non-wastable tax credits										
Non-wastable tax credits against 1000	..	..	..	..	..	..	..	..	..	..
Transfer component	..	..	..	..	..	..	..	..	..	..
Tax expenditure component	..	..	..	..	..	..	..	..	..	..

.. Not available

Note: More detailed country data and country notes are available in online chapter 5 "Country Tables, 1965-2017": https://doi.org/10.1787/0bbc27da-en. Full time series can be accessed at http://oe.cd/full-time-series.

Source: Ministry of Finance and Economy, Ministry of Home Affairs.

StatLink https://doi.org/10.1787/888934056013

Table 4.38. Korea, tax revenue and % of GDP by level of government and main taxes

	Billion KRW					% of GDP				
	1990	2000	2010	2016	2017	1990	2000	2010	2016	2017
Federal or Central government										
Total tax revenue	**27 140.8**	**92 935.0**	**177 718.0**	**242 562.0**	**265 385.0**	**13.7**	**14.6**	**14.0**	**14.8**	**15.3**
1000 Taxes on income, profits and capital gains	11 655.2	35 824.0	75 352.0	121 127.0	134 685.0	5.9	5.6	6.0	7.4	7.8
2000 Social security contributions	0.0	0.0	0.0	0.0	0.0	0.0	0.0	0.0	0.0	0.0
3000 Taxes on payroll and workforce	29.3	0.0	0.0	0.0	0.0	0.0	0.0	0.0	0.0	0.0
4000 Taxes on property	866.3	5 866.0	11 288.0	14 849.0	16 946.0	0.4	0.9	0.9	0.9	1.0
5000 Taxes on goods and services	14 377.5	46 812.0	86 629.0	102 439.0	109 365.0	7.3	7.4	6.8	6.2	6.3
6000 Other taxes	212.5	4 433.0	4 449.0	4 147.0	4 389.0	0.1	0.7	0.4	0.3	0.3
State/Regional										
Total tax revenue	..	..	..	..	..	..	..	..	..	..
1000 Taxes on income, profits and capital gains	..	..	..	..	..	..	..	..	..	..
2000 Social security contributions	..	..	..	..	..	..	..	..	..	..
3000 Taxes on payroll and workforce	..	..	..	..	..	..	..	..	..	..
4000 Taxes on property	..	..	..	..	..	..	..	..	..	..
5000 Taxes on goods and services	..	..	..	..	..	..	..	..	..	..
6000 Other taxes	..	..	..	..	..	..	..	..	..	..
Local government										
Total tax revenue	**6 360.9**	**20 601.0**	**49 160.0**	**75 532.0**	**80 409.0**	**3.2**	**3.2**	**3.9**	**4.6**	**4.6**
1000 Taxes on income, profits and capital gains	548.3	3 430.0	7 553.0	13 376.0	14 735.0	0.3	0.5	0.6	0.8	0.9
2000 Social security contributions	0.0	0.0	0.0	0.0	0.0	0.0	0.0	0.0	0.0	0.0
3000 Taxes on payroll and workforce	123.5	258.0	714.0	1 293.0	1 376.0	0.1	0.0	0.1	0.1	0.1
4000 Taxes on property	3 522.6	10 980.0	22 228.0	34 971.0	37 460.0	1.8	1.7	1.8	2.1	2.2
5000 Taxes on goods and services	2 120.0	5 459.0	13 140.0	18 758.0	19 700.0	1.1	0.9	1.0	1.1	1.1
6000 Other taxes	46.6	474.0	5 525.0	7 134.0	7 138.0	0.0	0.1	0.4	0.4	0.4
Social Security Funds										
Total tax revenue	**3 760.0**	**22 759.0**	**69 090.0**	**112 658.0**	**119 676.0**	**1.9**	**3.6**	**5.5**	**6.9**	**6.9**
1000 Taxes on income, profits and capital gains	0.0	0.0	0.0	0.0	0.0	0.0	0.0	0.0	0.0	0.0
2000 Social security contributions	3 760.0	22 759.0	69 090.0	112 658.0	119 676.0	1.9	3.6	5.5	6.9	6.9
3000 Taxes on payroll and workforce	0.0	0.0	0.0	0.0	0.0	0.0	0.0	0.0	0.0	0.0
4000 Taxes on property	0.0	0.0	0.0	0.0	0.0	0.0	0.0	0.0	0.0	0.0
5000 Taxes on goods and services	0.0	0.0	0.0	0.0	0.0	0.0	0.0	0.0	0.0	0.0
6000 Other taxes	0.0	0.0	0.0	0.0	0.0	0.0	0.0	0.0	0.0	0.0

.. Not available

Note: More detailed country data and country notes are available in online chapter 6 "Tax revenues by sub-sectors of general government": https://doi.org/10.1787/0bbc27da-en. Full time series can be accessed at http://oe.cd/full-time-series.

Source: Ministry of Finance and Economy, Ministry of Home Affairs.

StatLink https://doi.org/10.1787/888934056032

Table 4.39. Latvia, tax revenue and % of GDP by selected tax category

	Billion EUR					% of GDP				
	1990	2000	2010	2016	2017	1990	2000	2010	2016	2017
Total tax revenue	..	**2.0**	**5.2**	**7.8**	**8.4**	..	**29.1**	**28.8**	**31.2**	**31.1**
1000 Taxes on income, profits and capital gains	..	**0.5**	**1.3**	**2.0**	**2.2**	..	**7.0**	**7.2**	**8.0**	**8.2**
1100 Of individuals	..	0.4	1.1	1.6	1.8	..	5.5	6.2	6.3	6.6
1200 Corporate	..	0.1	0.2	0.4	0.4	..	1.5	1.0	1.7	1.6
1300 Unallocable between 1100 and 1200	..	0.0	0.0	0.0	0.0	..	0.0	0.0	0.0	0.0
2000 Social security contributions	..	**0.7**	**1.6**	**2.1**	**2.3**	..	**9.8**	**8.7**	**8.3**	**8.4**
2100 Employees	..	0.2	0.4	0.5	0.6	..	2.4	2.2	2.1	2.3
2200 Employers	..	0.5	1.2	1.5	1.6	..	7.3	6.4	6.1	6.0
2300 Self-employed or non-employed	..	0.0	0.0	0.0	0.0	..	0.0	0.1	0.1	0.1
2400 Unallocable between 2100, 2200 and 2300	..	0.0	0.0	0.0	0.0	..	0.0	0.0	0.0	0.0
3000 Taxes on payroll and workforce	..	**0.0**	**0.0**	**0.0**	**0.0**	..	**0.0**	**0.0**	**0.0**	**0.0**
4000 Taxes on property	..	**0.1**	**0.2**	**0.3**	**0.3**	..	**1.1**	**0.9**	**1.1**	**1.0**
4100 Recurrent taxes on immovable property	..	0.1	0.1	0.2	0.2	..	0.9	0.7	0.9	0.8
4200 Recurrent taxes on net wealth	..	0.0	0.0	0.0	0.0	..	0.0	0.0	0.0	0.0
4300 Estate, inheritance and gift taxes	..	0.0	0.0	0.0	0.0	..	0.0	0.0	0.0	0.0
4400 Taxes on financial and capital transactions	..	0.0	0.0	0.0	0.0	..	0.2	0.1	0.2	0.2
4500 Non-recurrent taxes	..	0.0	0.0	0.0	0.0	..	0.0	0.0	0.0	0.0
4600 Other recurrent taxes on property	..	0.0	0.0	0.0	0.0	..	0.0	0.0	0.0	0.0
5000 Taxes on goods and services	..	**0.8**	**2.1**	**3.4**	**3.6**	..	**11.2**	**11.9**	**13.6**	**13.4**
5100 Taxes on production, sale, transfer, etc	..	0.7	2.0	3.2	3.4	..	10.8	11.2	12.9	12.7
5110 General taxes	..	0.5	1.3	2.3	2.4	..	7.0	7.3	9.2	9.0
5111 Value added taxes	..	0.5	1.2	2.0	2.2	..	7.0	6.7	8.1	8.0
5120 Taxes on specific goods and services	..	0.3	0.7	0.9	1.0	..	3.8	3.9	3.8	3.7
5121 Excises	..	0.2	0.6	0.9	0.9	..	3.4	3.6	3.5	3.4
5200 Taxes on use of goods and perform activities	..	0.0	0.1	0.2	0.2	..	0.5	0.7	0.7	0.7
5300 Unallocable between 5100 and 5200	..	0.0	0.0	0.0	0.0	..	0.0	0.0	0.0	0.0
6000 Other taxes	..	**0.0**	**0.0**	**0.0**	**0.0**	..	**0.0**	**0.0**	**0.0**	**0.0**
Non-wastable tax credits										
Non-wastable tax credits against 1000	..	..	..	..	..	..	..	..	..	..
Transfer component	..	..	..	..	..	..	..	..	..	..
Tax expenditure component	..	..	..	..	..	..	..	..	..	..

.. Not available
Note: More detailed country data and country notes are available in online chapter 5 "Country Tables, 1965-2017": https://doi.org/10.1787/0bbc27da-en. Full time series can be accessed at http://oe.cd/full-time-series.
Source: Ministry of Finance.

StatLink https://doi.org/10.1787/888934056051

Table 4.40. Latvia, tax revenue and % of GDP by level of government and main taxes

	Billion EUR					% of GDP				
	1990	2000	2010	2016	2017	1990	2000	2010	2016	2017
Federal or Central government										
Total tax revenue	..	**1.0**	**2.5**	**4.2**	**4.5**	..	**14.4**	**14.2**	**16.8**	**16.6**
1000 Taxes on income, profits and capital gains	..	0.2	0.4	0.8	0.8	..	3.1	2.2	3.1	3.1
2000 Social security contributions	..	0.0	0.0	0.0	0.0	..	0.0	0.0	0.0	0.0
3000 Taxes on payroll and workforce	..	0.0	0.0	0.0	0.0	..	0.0	0.0	0.0	0.0
4000 Taxes on property	..	0.0	0.0	0.0	0.0	..	0.2	0.2	0.2	0.2
5000 Taxes on goods and services	..	0.8	2.1	3.4	3.6	..	11.2	11.8	13.5	13.3
6000 Other taxes	..	0.0	0.0	0.0	0.0	..	0.0	0.0	0.0	0.0
State/Regional										
Total tax revenue	..	..	..	..	..	..	..	..	..	..
1000 Taxes on income, profits and capital gains	..	..	..	..	..	..	..	..	..	..
2000 Social security contributions	..	..	..	..	..	..	..	..	..	..
3000 Taxes on payroll and workforce	..	..	..	..	..	..	..	..	..	..
4000 Taxes on property	..	..	..	..	..	..	..	..	..	..
5000 Taxes on goods and services	..	..	..	..	..	..	..	..	..	..
6000 Other taxes	..	..	..	..	..	..	..	..	..	..
Local government										
Total tax revenue	..	**0.3**	**1.0**	**1.5**	**1.6**	..	**4.9**	**5.8**	**5.9**	**6.0**
1000 Taxes on income, profits and capital gains	..	0.3	0.9	1.2	1.4	..	3.9	5.0	4.9	5.1
2000 Social security contributions	..	0.0	0.0	0.0	0.0	..	0.0	0.0	0.0	0.0
3000 Taxes on payroll and workforce	..	0.0	0.0	0.0	0.0	..	0.0	0.0	0.0	0.0
4000 Taxes on property	..	0.1	0.1	0.2	0.2	..	0.9	0.7	0.9	0.8
5000 Taxes on goods and services	..	0.0	0.0	0.0	0.0	..	0.1	0.1	0.1	0.1
6000 Other taxes	..	0.0	0.0	0.0	0.0	..	0.0	0.0	0.0	0.0
Social Security Funds										
Total tax revenue	..	**0.7**	**1.6**	**2.1**	**2.3**	..	**9.8**	**8.7**	**8.3**	**8.4**
1000 Taxes on income, profits and capital gains	..	0.0	0.0	0.0	0.0	..	0.0	0.0	0.0	0.0
2000 Social security contributions	..	0.7	1.6	2.1	2.3	..	9.8	8.7	8.3	8.4
3000 Taxes on payroll and workforce	..	0.0	0.0	0.0	0.0	..	0.0	0.0	0.0	0.0
4000 Taxes on property	..	0.0	0.0	0.0	0.0	..	0.0	0.0	0.0	0.0
5000 Taxes on goods and services	..	0.0	0.0	0.0	0.0	..	0.0	0.0	0.0	0.0
6000 Other taxes	..	0.0	0.0	0.0	0.0	..	0.0	0.0	0.0	0.0

.. Not available

Note: More detailed country data and country notes are available in online chapter 6 "Tax revenues by sub-sectors of general government": https://doi.org/10.1787/0bbc27da-en. Full time series can be accessed at http://oe.cd/full-time-series.

Source: Ministry of Finance.

StatLink https://doi.org/10.1787/888934056070

Table 4.41. Lithuania, tax revenue and % of GDP by selected tax category

	Billion EUR					% of GDP				
	1990	2000	2010	2016	2017	1990	2000	2010	2016	2017
Total tax revenue	..	**4.1**	**7.9**	**11.5**	**12.5**	..	**30.8**	**28.3**	**29.7**	**29.5**
1000 Taxes on income, profits and capital gains	..	**1.1**	**1.3**	**2.2**	**2.3**	..	**8.2**	**4.6**	**5.6**	**5.4**
1100 Of individuals	..	1.0	1.0	1.5	1.6	..	7.6	3.6	4.0	3.9
1200 Corporate	..	0.1	0.3	0.6	0.6	..	0.7	1.0	1.6	1.5
1300 Unallocable between 1100 and 1200	..	0.0	0.0	0.0	0.0	..	0.0	0.0	0.0	0.0
2000 Social security contributions	..	**1.3**	**3.3**	**4.7**	**5.2**	..	**10.1**	**11.7**	**12.1**	**12.3**
2100 Employees	..	0.1	0.6	1.0	1.1	..	0.8	2.3	2.5	2.5
2200 Employers	..	1.1	2.1	3.2	3.5	..	8.3	7.5	8.2	8.3
2300 Self-employed or non-employed	..	0.1	0.5	0.5	0.6	..	1.0	1.9	1.4	1.4
2400 Unallocable between 2100, 2200 and 2300	..	0.0	0.0	0.0	0.0	..	0.0	0.0	0.0	0.0
3000 Taxes on payroll and workforce	..	**0.0**	**0.0**	**0.0**	**0.0**	..	**0.0**	**0.0**	**0.0**	**0.0**
4000 Taxes on property	..	**0.1**	**0.1**	**0.1**	**0.1**	..	**0.5**	**0.4**	**0.3**	**0.3**
4100 Recurrent taxes on immovable property	..	0.1	0.1	0.1	0.1	..	0.5	0.4	0.3	0.3
4200 Recurrent taxes on net wealth	..	0.0	0.0	0.0	0.0	..	0.0	0.0	0.0	0.0
4300 Estate, inheritance and gift taxes	..	0.0	0.0	0.0	0.0	..	0.0	0.0	0.0	0.0
4400 Taxes on financial and capital transactions	..	0.0	0.0	0.0	0.0	..	0.0	0.0	0.0	0.0
4500 Non-recurrent taxes	..	0.0	0.0	0.0	0.0	..	0.0	0.0	0.0	0.0
4600 Other recurrent taxes on property	..	0.0	0.0	0.0	..	..	0.0	0.0	0.0	..
5000 Taxes on goods and services	..	**1.6**	**3.2**	**4.4**	**4.8**	..	**12.0**	**11.5**	**11.4**	**11.4**
5100 Taxes on production, sale, transfer, etc	..	1.5	3.1	4.4	4.7	..	11.5	11.2	11.2	11.2
5110 General taxes	..	1.1	2.2	3.0	3.3	..	8.0	7.8	7.8	7.9
5111 Value added taxes	..	1.0	2.2	3.0	3.3	..	7.4	7.7	7.8	7.8
5120 Taxes on specific goods and services	..	0.5	1.0	1.3	1.4	..	3.5	3.4	3.4	3.3
5121 Excises	..	0.4	0.9	1.2	1.3	..	3.2	3.2	3.2	3.2
5200 Taxes on use of goods and perform activities	..	0.1	0.1	0.1	0.1	..	0.5	0.3	0.2	0.2
5300 Unallocable between 5100 and 5200	..	0.0	0.0	0.0	0.0	..	0.0	0.0	0.0	0.0
6000 Other taxes	..	**0.0**	**0.0**	**0.0**	**0.0**	..	**0.0**	**0.0**	**0.0**	**0.0**
Non-wastable tax credits										
Non-wastable tax credits against 1000	..	..	..	..	..	..	..	..	..	..
Transfer component	..	..	..	..	..	..	..	..	..	..
Tax expenditure component	..	..	..	..	..	..	..	..	..	..

.. Not available

Note: More detailed country data and country notes are available in online chapter 5 "Country Tables, 1965-2017": https://doi.org/10.1787/0bbc27da-en. Full time series can be accessed at http://oe.cd/full-time-series.

The total tax revenue has been reduced by the amount of any capital transfer that represents uncollected taxes. The capital transfer has been allocated between tax headings in proportion to the reported tax revenue. Therefore, the tax revenue amounts are different to those reported in the detailed country data available in online chapter 5 "Country Tables, 1965-2017".

Source: Ministry of Finance.

StatLink https://doi.org/10.1787/888934056089

Table 4.42. Lithuania, tax revenue and % of GDP by level of government and main taxes

	Billion EUR					% of GDP				
	1990	2000	2010	2016	2017	1990	2000	2010	2016	2017
Federal or Central government										
Total tax revenue	..	**2.7**	**4.5**	**6.6**	**7.0**	..	**20.1**	**15.9**	**16.9**	**16.7**
1000 Taxes on income, profits and capital gains	..	1.1	1.3	2.2	2.3	..	8.2	4.6	5.6	5.4
2000 Social security contributions	..	0.0	0.0	0.0	0.0	..	0.0	0.0	0.0	0.0
3000 Taxes on payroll and workforce	..	0.0	0.0	0.0	0.0	..	0.0	0.0	0.0	0.0
4000 Taxes on property	..	0.0	0.0	0.0	0.0	..	0.0	0.0	0.0	0.0
5000 Taxes on goods and services	..	1.6	3.2	4.4	4.8	..	11.9	11.4	11.3	11.3
6000 Other taxes	..	0.0	0.0	0.0	0.0	..	0.0	0.0	0.0	0.0
State/Regional										
Total tax revenue	..	..	..	..	..	..	..	..	..	..
1000 Taxes on income, profits and capital gains	..	..	..	..	..	..	..	..	..	..
2000 Social security contributions	..	..	..	..	..	..	..	..	..	..
3000 Taxes on payroll and workforce	..	..	..	..	..	..	..	..	..	..
4000 Taxes on property	..	..	..	..	..	..	..	..	..	..
5000 Taxes on goods and services	..	..	..	..	..	..	..	..	..	..
6000 Other taxes	..	..	..	..	..	..	..	..	..	..
Local government										
Total tax revenue	..	**0.1**	**0.1**	**0.1**	**0.1**	..	**0.6**	**0.5**	**0.4**	**0.4**
1000 Taxes on income, profits and capital gains	..	0.0	0.0	0.0	0.0	..	0.0	0.0	0.0	0.0
2000 Social security contributions	..	0.0	0.0	0.0	0.0	..	0.0	0.0	0.0	0.0
3000 Taxes on payroll and workforce	..	0.0	0.0	0.0	0.0	..	0.0	0.0	0.0	0.0
4000 Taxes on property	..	0.1	0.1	0.1	0.1	..	0.5	0.4	0.3	0.3
5000 Taxes on goods and services	..	0.0	0.0	0.0	0.0	..	0.1	0.1	0.0	0.0
6000 Other taxes	..	0.0	0.0	0.0	0.0	..	0.0	0.0	0.0	0.0
Social Security Funds										
Total tax revenue	..	**1.3**	**3.3**	**4.7**	**5.2**	..	**10.1**	**11.7**	**12.1**	**12.3**
1000 Taxes on income, profits and capital gains	..	0.0	0.0	0.0	0.0	..	0.0	0.0	0.0	0.0
2000 Social security contributions	..	1.3	3.3	4.7	5.2	..	10.1	11.7	12.1	12.3
3000 Taxes on payroll and workforce	..	0.0	0.0	0.0	0.0	..	0.0	0.0	0.0	0.0
4000 Taxes on property	..	0.0	0.0	0.0	0.0	..	0.0	0.0	0.0	0.0
5000 Taxes on goods and services	..	0.0	0.0	0.0	0.0	..	0.0	0.0	0.0	0.0
6000 Other taxes	..	0.0	0.0	0.0	0.0	..	0.0	0.0	0.0	0.0

.. Not available

Note: More detailed country data and country notes are available in online chapter 6 "Tax revenues by sub-sectors of general government": https://doi.org/10.1787/0bbc27da-en. Full time series can be accessed at http://oe.cd/full-time-series.

The total tax revenue has been reduced by the amount of any capital transfer that represents uncollected taxes. The capital transfer has been allocated between tax headings in proportion to the reported tax revenue. Therefore, the tax revenue amounts are different to those reported in the detailed country data available in online chapter 6 "Tax revenues by sub-sectors of general government".

Source: Ministry of Finance.

StatLink https://doi.org/10.1787/888934056108

Table 4.43. Luxembourg, tax revenue and % of GDP by selected tax category

	Billion EUR					% of GDP				
	1990	2000	2010	2016	2017	1990	2000	2010	2016	2017
Total tax revenue	**3.7**	**8.5**	**15.0**	**20.2**	**21.4**	**33.5**	**36.9**	**37.4**	**37.9**	**38.7**
1000 Taxes on income, profits and capital gains	**1.5**	**3.1**	**5.5**	**7.4**	**8.0**	**13.5**	**13.5**	**13.6**	**14.0**	**14.4**
1100 Of individuals	0.9	1.6	3.2	5.0	5.1	8.1	6.8	7.9	9.4	9.1
1200 Corporate	0.6	1.5	2.3	2.5	2.9	5.4	6.6	5.8	4.6	5.2
1300 Unallocable between 1100 and 1200	0.0	0.0	0.0	0.0	0.0	0.0	0.0	0.0	0.0	0.0
2000 Social security contributions	**1.0**	**2.2**	**4.4**	**5.7**	**6.1**	**9.2**	**9.6**	**10.8**	**10.8**	**11.1**
2100 Employees	0.4	1.0	2.0	2.6	2.8	3.5	4.3	5.0	4.9	5.0
2200 Employers	0.5	1.0	1.9	2.4	2.6	4.5	4.2	4.7	4.5	4.6
2300 Self-employed or non-employed	0.1	0.3	0.5	0.7	0.8	1.2	1.2	1.2	1.4	1.4
2400 Unallocable between 2100, 2200 and 2300	0.0	0.0	0.0	0.0	0.0	0.0	0.0	0.0	0.0	0.0
3000 Taxes on payroll and workforce	**0.0**	**0.0**	**0.0**	**0.0**	**0.0**	**0.0**	**0.0**	**0.0**	**0.0**	**0.0**
4000 Taxes on property	**0.3**	**0.9**	**1.1**	**1.9**	**2.1**	**2.8**	**3.9**	**2.6**	**3.5**	**3.7**
4100 Recurrent taxes on immovable property	0.0	0.0	0.0	0.0	0.0	0.1	0.1	0.1	0.1	0.1
4200 Recurrent taxes on net wealth	0.2	0.6	0.8	1.4	1.5	1.6	2.7	2.1	2.7	2.7
4300 Estate, inheritance and gift taxes	0.0	0.0	0.1	0.1	0.1	0.1	0.1	0.1	0.2	0.2
4400 Taxes on financial and capital transactions	0.1	0.2	0.2	0.3	0.4	1.0	1.0	0.4	0.6	0.7
4500 Non-recurrent taxes	0.0	0.0	0.0	0.0	0.0	0.0	0.0	0.0	0.0	0.0
4600 Other recurrent taxes on property	0.0	0.0	0.0	0.0	0.0	0.0	0.0	0.0	0.0	0.0
5000 Taxes on goods and services	**0.9**	**2.2**	**4.1**	**5.1**	**5.2**	**7.9**	**9.7**	**10.2**	**9.6**	**9.4**
5100 Taxes on production, sale, transfer, etc	0.8	2.2	4.0	5.0	5.1	7.7	9.6	10.0	9.4	9.3
5110 General taxes	0.4	1.1	2.6	3.4	3.4	4.0	4.9	6.4	6.4	6.2
5111 Value added taxes	0.4	1.1	2.6	3.4	3.4	4.0	4.9	6.4	6.4	6.2
5120 Taxes on specific goods and services	0.4	1.1	1.5	1.6	1.7	3.7	4.7	3.7	3.1	3.1
5121 Excises	0.4	1.0	1.4	1.4	1.4	3.3	4.5	3.5	2.7	2.6
5200 Taxes on use of goods and perform activities	0.0	0.0	0.1	0.1	0.1	0.2	0.1	0.2	0.2	0.2
5300 Unallocable between 5100 and 5200	0.0	0.0	0.0	0.0	0.0	0.0	0.0	0.0	0.0	0.0
6000 Other taxes	**0.0**	**0.0**	**0.0**	**0.1**	**0.1**	**0.1**	**0.1**	**0.1**	**0.1**	**0.1**
Non-wastable tax credits										
Non-wastable tax credits against 1000	..	..	..	0.2	0.2	..	..	..	0.4	0.4
Transfer component	..	..	..	..	..	..	..	..	..	..
Tax expenditure component	..	..	..	..	..	..	..	..	..	..

.. Not available

Note: More detailed country data and country notes are available in online chapter 5 "Country Tables, 1965-2017": https://doi.org/10.1787/0bbc27da-en. Full time series can be accessed at http://oe.cd/full-time-series.

Source: General account of the State.

StatLink https://doi.org/10.1787/888934056127

Table 4.44. Luxembourg, tax revenue and % of GDP by level of government and main taxes

	Billion EUR					% of GDP				
	1990	2000	2010	2016	2017	1990	2000	2010	2016	2017
Federal or Central government										
Total tax revenue	**2.4**	**5.8**	**10.1**	**13.7**	**14.4**	**22.1**	**25.3**	**25.2**	**25.8**	**26.1**
1000 Taxes on income, profits and capital gains	1.3	2.6	4.9	6.7	7.2	11.6	11.5	12.1	12.6	12.9
2000 Social security contributions	0.0	0.1	0.1	0.2	0.2	0.1	0.3	0.3	0.3	0.3
3000 Taxes on payroll and workforce	0.0	0.0	0.0	0.0	0.0	0.0	0.0	0.0	0.0	0.0
4000 Taxes on property	0.3	0.9	1.0	1.8	2.0	2.6	3.8	2.5	3.4	3.6
5000 Taxes on goods and services	0.8	2.2	4.1	5.0	5.1	7.7	9.7	10.2	9.4	9.2
6000 Other taxes	0.0	0.0	0.0	0.0	0.0	0.1	0.0	0.0	0.1	0.0
State/Regional										
Total tax revenue	**..**	**..**	**..**	**..**	**..**	**..**	**..**	**..**	**..**	**..**
1000 Taxes on income, profits and capital gains	..	..	..	..	..	..	..	..	..	..
2000 Social security contributions	..	..	..	..	..	..	..	..	..	..
3000 Taxes on payroll and workforce	..	..	..	..	..	..	..	..	..	..
4000 Taxes on property	..	..	..	..	..	..	..	..	..	..
5000 Taxes on goods and services	..	..	..	..	..	..	..	..	..	..
6000 Other taxes	..	..	..	..	..	..	..	..	..	..
Local government										
Total tax revenue	**0.2**	**0.5**	**0.7**	**0.8**	**0.9**	**2.1**	**2.1**	**1.6**	**1.5**	**1.6**
1000 Taxes on income, profits and capital gains	0.2	0.5	0.6	0.7	0.8	1.9	2.0	1.5	1.3	1.5
2000 Social security contributions	0.0	0.0	0.0	0.0	0.0	0.0	0.0	0.0	0.0	0.0
3000 Taxes on payroll and workforce	0.0	0.0	0.0	0.0	0.0	0.0	0.0	0.0	0.0	0.0
4000 Taxes on property	0.0	0.0	0.0	0.1	0.1	0.2	0.1	0.1	0.1	0.1
5000 Taxes on goods and services	0.0	0.0	0.0	0.0	0.0	0.0	0.0	0.0	0.0	0.0
6000 Other taxes	0.0	0.0	0.0	0.0	0.0	0.0	0.0	0.0	0.0	0.0
Social Security Funds										
Total tax revenue	**1.0**	**2.2**	**4.2**	**5.6**	**6.0**	**9.1**	**9.3**	**10.5**	**10.5**	**10.8**
1000 Taxes on income, profits and capital gains	0.0	0.0	0.0	0.0	0.0	0.0	0.0	0.0	0.0	0.0
2000 Social security contributions	1.0	2.2	4.2	5.6	6.0	9.1	9.3	10.5	10.5	10.8
3000 Taxes on payroll and workforce	0.0	0.0	0.0	0.0	0.0	0.0	0.0	0.0	0.0	0.0
4000 Taxes on property	0.0	0.0	0.0	0.0	0.0	0.0	0.0	0.0	0.0	0.0
5000 Taxes on goods and services	0.0	0.0	0.0	0.0	0.0	0.0	0.0	0.0	0.0	0.0
6000 Other taxes	0.0	0.0	0.0	0.0	0.0	0.0	0.0	0.0	0.0	0.0

.. Not available

Note: More detailed country data and country notes are available in online chapter 6 "Tax revenues by sub-sectors of general government": https://doi.org/10.1787/0bbc27da-en. Full time series can be accessed at http://oe.cd/full-time-series.

Source: General account of the State.

StatLink https://doi.org/10.1787/888934056146

Table 4.45. Mexico, tax revenue and % of GDP by selected tax category

	Billion MXN					% of GDP				
	1990	2000	2010	2016	2017	1990	2000	2010	2016	2017
Total tax revenue	**102.0**	**767.2**	**1 716.2**	**3 343.3**	**3 527.1**	**12.1**	**11.5**	**12.8**	**16.6**	**16.1**
1000 Taxes on income, profits and capital gains	**34.7**	**276.5**	**683.6**	**1 427.1**	**1 572.0**	**4.1**	**4.1**	**5.1**	**7.1**	**7.2**
1100 Of individuals	..	..	313.5	681.8	754.1	..	..	2.3	3.4	3.4
1200 Corporate	..	..	246.7	700.9	769.2	..	..	1.8	3.5	3.5
1300 Unallocable between 1100 and 1200	34.7	276.5	123.4	44.4	48.7	4.1	4.1	0.9	0.2	0.2
2000 Social security contributions	**17.2**	**138.2**	**277.5**	**435.0**	**467.7**	**2.0**	**2.1**	**2.1**	**2.2**	**2.1**
2100 Employees	..	..	..	..	..	..	..	..	..	..
2200 Employers	..	..	..	..	..	..	..	..	..	..
2300 Self-employed or non-employed	..	..	..	..	..	..	..	..	..	..
2400 Unallocable between 2100, 2200 and 2300	17.2	138.2	277.5	435.0	467.7	2.0	2.1	2.1	2.2	2.1
3000 Taxes on payroll and workforce	**1.8**	**11.2**	**36.9**	**76.8**	**84.1**	**0.2**	**0.2**	**0.3**	**0.4**	**0.4**
4000 Taxes on property	**1.9**	**14.0**	**39.0**	**63.3**	**67.8**	**0.2**	**0.2**	**0.3**	**0.3**	**0.3**
4100 Recurrent taxes on immovable property	1.0	9.9	25.7	40.4	44.7	0.1	0.1	0.2	0.2	0.2
4200 Recurrent taxes on net wealth	0.0	0.0	0.0	0.0	0.0	0.0	0.0	0.0	0.0	0.0
4300 Estate, inheritance and gift taxes	0.0	0.0	0.0	0.0	0.0	0.0	0.0	0.0	0.0	0.0
4400 Taxes on financial and capital transactions	0.9	4.0	13.2	22.9	23.2	0.1	0.1	0.1	0.1	0.1
4500 Non-recurrent taxes	0.0	0.0	0.0	0.0	0.0	0.0	0.0	0.0	0.0	0.0
4600 Other recurrent taxes on property	0.0	0.0	0.0	0.0	0.0	0.0	0.0	0.0	0.0	0.0
5000 Taxes on goods and services	**44.8**	**319.6**	**651.9**	**1 295.7**	**1 283.0**	**5.3**	**4.8**	**4.9**	**6.4**	**5.9**
5100 Taxes on production, sale, transfer, etc	44.2	310.3	630.1	1 274.7	1 262.8	5.2	4.6	4.7	6.3	5.8
5110 General taxes	26.6	189.6	504.5	791.7	816.0	3.2	2.8	3.8	3.9	3.7
5111 Value added taxes	26.6	189.6	504.5	791.7	816.0	3.2	2.8	3.8	3.9	3.7
5120 Taxes on specific goods and services	17.5	120.7	125.6	483.0	446.7	2.1	1.8	0.9	2.4	2.0
5121 Excises	10.1	86.2	86.1	420.4	378.5	1.2	1.3	0.6	2.1	1.7
5200 Taxes on use of goods and perform activities	0.7	9.3	21.8	20.9	20.3	0.1	0.1	0.2	0.1	0.1
5300 Unallocable between 5100 and 5200	0.0	0.0	0.0	0.0	0.0	0.0	0.0	0.0	0.0	0.0
6000 Other taxes	**1.6**	**7.7**	**27.4**	**45.5**	**52.5**	**0.2**	**0.1**	**0.2**	**0.2**	**0.2**
Non-wastable tax credits										
Non-wastable tax credits against 1000	..	..	40.3	44.9	46.8	..	..	0.3	0.2	0.2
Transfer component	..	..	9.7	1.1	1.0	..	..	0.1	0.0	0.0
Tax expenditure component	..	..	30.6	43.7	45.8	..	..	0.2	0.2	0.2

.. Not available

Note: More detailed country data and country notes are available in online chapter 5 "Country Tables, 1965-2017": https://doi.org/10.1787/0bbc27da-en. Full time series can be accessed at http://oe.cd/full-time-series.

Source: Ministry of Finance, Economic Department.

StatLink https://doi.org/10.1787/888934056165

Table 4.46. Mexico, tax revenue and % of GDP by level of government and main taxes

	Billion MXN					% of GDP				
	1990	2000	2010	2016	2017	1990	2000	2010	2016	2017
Federal or Central government										
Total tax revenue	**81.4**	**600.5**	**1 351.5**	**2 724.3**	**2 859.3**	**9.7**	**9.0**	**10.1**	**13.5**	**13.0**
1000 Taxes on income, profits and capital gains	34.7	276.5	683.6	1 427.1	1 572.0	4.1	4.1	5.1	7.1	7.2
2000 Social security contributions	0.0	0.0	0.0	0.0	0.0	0.0	0.0	0.0	0.0	0.0
3000 Taxes on payroll and workforce	0.8	0.0	0.0	0.0	0.0	0.1	0.0	0.0	0.0	0.0
4000 Taxes on property	0.0	0.0	0.0	0.0	0.0	0.0	0.0	0.0	0.0	0.0
5000 Taxes on goods and services	44.6	318.1	645.6	1 268.4	1 254.9	5.3	4.8	4.8	6.3	5.7
6000 Other taxes	1.3	5.9	22.2	28.8	32.4	0.2	0.1	0.2	0.1	0.1
State/Regional										
Total tax revenue	**2.2**	**20.5**	**58.3**	**133.0**	**144.2**	**0.3**	**0.3**	**0.4**	**0.7**	**0.7**
1000 Taxes on income, profits and capital gains	0.0	0.0	0.0	0.0	0.0	0.0	0.0	0.0	0.0	0.0
2000 Social security contributions	0.0	0.0	0.0	0.0	0.0	0.0	0.0	0.0	0.0	0.0
3000 Taxes on payroll and workforce	1.0	11.2	36.8	76.8	84.1	0.1	0.2	0.3	0.4	0.4
4000 Taxes on property	0.9	7.0	13.1	23.6	26.1	0.1	0.1	0.1	0.1	0.1
5000 Taxes on goods and services	0.1	1.3	5.8	25.9	26.8	0.0	0.0	0.0	0.1	0.1
6000 Other taxes	0.2	0.9	2.5	6.7	7.2	0.0	0.0	0.0	0.0	0.0
Local government										
Total tax revenue	**1.3**	**8.0**	**29.0**	**50.9**	**56.0**	**0.1**	**0.1**	**0.2**	**0.3**	**0.3**
1000 Taxes on income, profits and capital gains	0.0	0.0	0.0	0.0	0.0	0.0	0.0	0.0	0.0	0.0
2000 Social security contributions	0.0	0.0	0.0	0.0	0.0	0.0	0.0	0.0	0.0	0.0
3000 Taxes on payroll and workforce	0.0	0.0	0.1	0.0	0.0	0.0	0.0	0.0	0.0	0.0
4000 Taxes on property	1.0	6.9	25.8	39.6	41.8	0.1	0.1	0.2	0.2	0.2
5000 Taxes on goods and services	0.1	0.2	0.5	1.3	1.4	0.0	0.0	0.0	0.0	0.0
6000 Other taxes	0.1	0.9	2.6	10.0	12.8	0.0	0.0	0.0	0.1	0.1
Social Security Funds										
Total tax revenue	**17.2**	**138.2**	**277.5**	**435.0**	**467.7**	**2.0**	**2.1**	**2.1**	**2.2**	**2.1**
1000 Taxes on income, profits and capital gains	0.0	0.0	0.0	0.0	0.0	0.0	0.0	0.0	0.0	0.0
2000 Social security contributions	17.2	138.2	277.5	435.0	467.7	2.0	2.1	2.1	2.2	2.1
3000 Taxes on payroll and workforce	0.0	0.0	0.0	0.0	0.0	0.0	0.0	0.0	0.0	0.0
4000 Taxes on property	0.0	0.0	0.0	0.0	0.0	0.0	0.0	0.0	0.0	0.0
5000 Taxes on goods and services	0.0	0.0	0.0	0.0	0.0	0.0	0.0	0.0	0.0	0.0
6000 Other taxes	0.0	0.0	0.0	0.0	0.0	0.0	0.0	0.0	0.0	0.0

Note: More detailed country data and country notes are available in online chapter 6 "Tax revenues by sub-sectors of general government": https://doi.org/10.1787/0bbc27da-en. Full time series can be accessed at http://oe.cd/full-time-series.
Source: Ministry of Finance, Economic Department.

StatLink https://doi.org/10.1787/888934056184

Table 4.47. Netherlands, tax revenue and % of GDP by selected tax category

	Billion EUR					% of GDP				
	1990	2000	2010	2016	2017	1990	2000	2010	2016	2017
Total tax revenue	**104.4**	**166.8**	**227.9**	**272.0**	**285.7**	**39.7**	**36.9**	**35.7**	**38.4**	**38.7**
1000 Taxes on income, profits and capital gains	**33.7**	**43.3**	**63.6**	**74.0**	**85.8**	**12.8**	**9.6**	**9.9**	**10.4**	**11.6**
1100 Of individuals	25.8	25.1	49.0	50.3	61.6	9.8	5.6	7.7	7.1	8.3
1200 Corporate	7.9	18.1	14.6	23.7	24.2	3.0	4.0	2.3	3.3	3.3
1300 Unallocable between 1100 and 1200	0.0	0.0	0.0	0.0	0.0	0.0	0.0	0.0	0.0	0.0
2000 Social security contributions	**39.1**	**64.5**	**82.7**	**103.9**	**101.9**	**14.9**	**14.3**	**12.9**	**14.7**	**13.8**
2100 Employees	24.1	35.3	41.6	42.0	39.6	9.2	7.8	6.5	5.9	5.4
2200 Employers	7.8	18.7	29.4	36.6	37.7	3.0	4.1	4.6	5.2	5.1
2300 Self-employed or non-employed	7.1	10.5	11.7	25.3	24.6	2.7	2.3	1.8	3.6	3.3
2400 Unallocable between 2100, 2200 and 2300	0.0	0.0	0.0	0.0	0.0	0.0	0.0	0.0	0.0	0.0
3000 Taxes on payroll and workforce	**0.0**	**0.0**	**0.0**	**0.0**	**0.0**	**0.0**	**0.0**	**0.0**	**0.0**	**0.0**
4000 Taxes on property	**3.8**	**8.8**	**8.8**	**10.8**	**11.5**	**1.5**	**1.9**	**1.4**	**1.5**	**1.6**
4100 Recurrent taxes on immovable property	1.7	3.1	4.2	6.6	6.9	0.7	0.7	0.7	0.9	0.9
4200 Recurrent taxes on net wealth	0.6	0.8	0.0	0.0	0.0	0.2	0.2	0.0	0.0	0.0
4300 Estate, inheritance and gift taxes	0.5	1.5	1.7	1.8	1.8	0.2	0.3	0.3	0.3	0.2
4400 Taxes on financial and capital transactions	1.0	3.4	2.8	2.3	2.7	0.4	0.8	0.4	0.3	0.4
4500 Non-recurrent taxes	0.0	0.0	0.0	0.0	0.0	0.0	0.0	0.0	0.0	0.0
4600 Other recurrent taxes on property	0.0	0.0	0.0	0.0	0.0	0.0	0.0	0.0	0.0	0.0
5000 Taxes on goods and services	**27.6**	**48.2**	**70.1**	**80.3**	**83.2**	**10.5**	**10.7**	**11.0**	**11.3**	**11.3**
5100 Taxes on production, sale, transfer, etc	25.1	43.6	62.5	71.6	74.4	9.5	9.6	9.8	10.1	10.1
5110 General taxes	17.2	28.9	42.7	47.9	49.9	6.5	6.4	6.7	6.8	6.8
5111 Value added taxes	17.2	28.8	42.7	47.8	49.8	6.5	6.4	6.7	6.8	6.8
5120 Taxes on specific goods and services	7.9	14.7	19.8	23.7	24.5	3.0	3.3	3.1	3.3	3.3
5121 Excises	6.0	13.8	18.4	19.0	19.7	2.3	3.0	2.9	2.7	2.7
5200 Taxes on use of goods and perform activities	2.5	4.6	7.6	8.7	8.8	1.0	1.0	1.2	1.2	1.2
5300 Unallocable between 5100 and 5200	0.0	0.0	0.0	0.0	0.0	0.0	0.0	0.0	0.0	0.0
6000 Other taxes	**0.3**	**0.8**	**1.0**	**0.7**	**0.9**	**0.1**	**0.2**	**0.2**	**0.1**	**0.1**
Non-wastable tax credits										
Non-wastable tax credits against 1000	..	..	..	..	..	..	..	..	..	..
Transfer component	..	..	..	..	..	..	..	..	..	..
Tax expenditure component	..	..	..	..	..	..	..	..	..	..

.. Not available

Note: More detailed country data and country notes are available in online chapter 5 "Country Tables, 1965-2017": https://doi.org/10.1787/0bbc27da-en. Full time series can be accessed at http://oe.cd/full-time-series.

Source: Social security contributions and local taxes: Central Bureau of Statistics. Other taxes: Ministry of Finance.

StatLink https://doi.org/10.1787/888934056203

Table 4.48. Netherlands, tax revenue and % of GDP by level of government and main taxes

	Billion EUR					% of GDP				
	1990	2000	2010	2016	2017	1990	2000	2010	2016	2017
Federal or Central government										
Total tax revenue	**61.4**	**95.1**	**135.1**	**156.7**	**172.0**	**23.3**	**21.0**	**21.1**	**22.1**	**23.3**
1000 Taxes on income, profits and capital gains	33.7	43.3	63.6	74.0	85.8	12.8	9.6	9.9	10.4	11.6
2000 Social security contributions	0.0	0.0	0.0	0.0	0.0	0.0	0.0	0.0	0.0	0.0
3000 Taxes on payroll and workforce	0.0	0.0	0.0	0.0	0.0	0.0	0.0	0.0	0.0	0.0
4000 Taxes on property	2.1	5.7	4.6	5.6	6.2	0.8	1.3	0.7	0.8	0.8
5000 Taxes on goods and services	25.3	45.4	66.2	76.4	79.2	9.6	10.0	10.4	10.8	10.7
6000 Other taxes	0.3	0.8	0.8	0.7	0.9	0.1	0.2	0.1	0.1	0.1
State/Regional										
Total tax revenue	..	..	..	..	..	..	..	..	..	..
1000 Taxes on income, profits and capital gains	..	..	..	..	..	..	..	..	..	..
2000 Social security contributions	..	..	..	..	..	..	..	..	..	..
3000 Taxes on payroll and workforce	..	..	..	..	..	..	..	..	..	..
4000 Taxes on property	..	..	..	..	..	..	..	..	..	..
5000 Taxes on goods and services	..	..	..	..	..	..	..	..	..	..
6000 Other taxes	..	..	..	..	..	..	..	..	..	..
Local government										
Total tax revenue	**2.5**	**5.6**	**8.1**	**8.3**	**8.6**	**0.9**	**1.2**	**1.3**	**1.2**	**1.2**
1000 Taxes on income, profits and capital gains	0.0	0.0	0.0	0.0	0.0	0.0	0.0	0.0	0.0	0.0
2000 Social security contributions	0.0	0.0	0.0	0.0	0.0	0.0	0.0	0.0	0.0	0.0
3000 Taxes on payroll and workforce	0.0	0.0	0.0	0.0	0.0	0.0	0.0	0.0	0.0	0.0
4000 Taxes on property	1.7	3.1	4.2	5.2	5.3	0.7	0.7	0.7	0.7	0.7
5000 Taxes on goods and services	0.8	2.5	3.7	3.2	3.3	0.3	0.6	0.6	0.4	0.4
6000 Other taxes	0.0	0.0	0.2	0.0	0.0	0.0	0.0	0.0	0.0	0.0
Social Security Funds										
Total tax revenue	**39.1**	**64.5**	**82.7**	**103.9**	**101.9**	**14.9**	**14.3**	**12.9**	**14.7**	**13.8**
1000 Taxes on income, profits and capital gains	0.0	0.0	0.0	0.0	0.0	0.0	0.0	0.0	0.0	0.0
2000 Social security contributions	39.1	64.5	82.7	103.9	101.9	14.9	14.3	12.9	14.7	13.8
3000 Taxes on payroll and workforce	0.0	0.0	0.0	0.0	0.0	0.0	0.0	0.0	0.0	0.0
4000 Taxes on property	0.0	0.0	0.0	0.0	0.0	0.0	0.0	0.0	0.0	0.0
5000 Taxes on goods and services	0.0	0.0	0.0	0.0	0.0	0.0	0.0	0.0	0.0	0.0
6000 Other taxes	0.0	0.0	0.0	0.0	0.0	0.0	0.0	0.0	0.0	0.0

.. Not available

Note: More detailed country data and country notes are available in online chapter 6 "Tax revenues by sub-sectors of general government": https://doi.org/10.1787/0bbc27da-en. Full time series can be accessed at http://oe.cd/full-time-series.

Source: Social security contributions and local taxes: Central Bureau of Statistics. Other taxes: Ministry of Finance.

StatLink https://doi.org/10.1787/888934056222

Table 4.49. New Zealand, tax revenue and % of GDP by selected tax category

	Billion NZD					% of GDP				
	1990	2000	2010	2016	2017	1990	2000	2010	2016	2017
Total tax revenue	**27.5**	**39.8**	**62.3**	**86.6**	**92.7**	**36.2**	**32.5**	**30.3**	**31.7**	**32.1**
1000 Taxes on income, profits and capital gains	**16.4**	**23.9**	**33.5**	**48.1**	**51.5**	**21.6**	**19.5**	**16.3**	**17.6**	**17.8**
1100 Of individuals	13.2	17.1	23.5	31.9	35.0	17.4	14.0	11.4	11.7	12.1
1200 Corporate	1.8	4.9	7.6	13.5	13.6	2.3	4.0	3.7	4.9	4.7
1300 Unallocable between 1100 and 1200	1.4	1.8	2.4	2.8	2.9	1.9	1.5	1.1	1.0	1.0
2000 Social security contributions	**0.0**	**0.0**	**0.0**	**0.0**	**0.0**	**0.0**	**0.0**	**0.0**	**0.0**	**0.0**
2100 Employees	0.0	0.0	0.0	0.0	0.0	0.0	0.0	0.0	0.0	0.0
2200 Employers	0.0	0.0	0.0	0.0	0.0	0.0	0.0	0.0	0.0	0.0
2300 Self-employed or non-employed	0.0	0.0	0.0	0.0	0.0	0.0	0.0	0.0	0.0	0.0
2400 Unallocable between 2100, 2200 and 2300	0.0	0.0	0.0	0.0	0.0	0.0	0.0	0.0	0.0	0.0
3000 Taxes on payroll and workforce	**0.0**	**0.0**	**0.0**	**0.0**	**0.0**	**0.0**	**0.0**	**0.0**	**0.0**	**0.0**
4000 Taxes on property	**1.9**	**2.1**	**4.1**	**5.3**	**5.5**	**2.5**	**1.7**	**2.0**	**1.9**	**1.9**
4100 Recurrent taxes on immovable property	1.7	2.0	4.0	5.2	5.4	2.3	1.7	2.0	1.9	1.9
4200 Recurrent taxes on net wealth	0.0	0.0	0.0	0.0	0.0	0.0	0.0	0.0	0.0	0.0
4300 Estate, inheritance and gift taxes	0.1	0.0	0.0	0.0	0.0	0.1	0.0	0.0	0.0	0.0
4400 Taxes on financial and capital transactions	0.1	0.1	0.1	0.1	0.1	0.1	0.1	0.0	0.0	0.0
4500 Non-recurrent taxes	0.0	0.0	0.0	0.0	0.0	0.0	0.0	0.0	0.0	0.0
4600 Other recurrent taxes on property	0.0	0.0	0.0	0.0	0.0	0.0	0.0	0.0	0.0	0.0
5000 Taxes on goods and services	**9.2**	**13.8**	**24.7**	**33.2**	**35.6**	**12.1**	**11.3**	**12.0**	**12.1**	**12.3**
5100 Taxes on production, sale, transfer, etc	8.7	12.9	23.1	30.9	33.2	11.4	10.5	11.2	11.3	11.5
5110 General taxes	6.2	9.9	19.1	25.8	28.0	8.1	8.1	9.3	9.5	9.7
5111 Value added taxes	6.2	9.9	19.1	25.8	28.0	8.1	8.1	9.3	9.5	9.7
5120 Taxes on specific goods and services	2.5	3.0	4.0	5.1	5.3	3.3	2.5	1.9	1.9	1.8
5121 Excises	1.9	2.1	1.8	2.2	2.2	2.5	1.8	0.9	0.8	0.8
5200 Taxes on use of goods and perform activities	0.5	0.9	1.6	2.3	2.4	0.7	0.7	0.8	0.8	0.8
5300 Unallocable between 5100 and 5200	0.0	0.0	0.0	0.0	0.0	0.0	0.0	0.0	0.0	0.0
6000 Other taxes	**0.0**	**0.0**	**0.0**	**0.0**	**0.0**	**0.0**	**0.0**	**0.0**	**0.0**	**0.0**
Non-wastable tax credits										
Non-wastable tax credits against 1000	..	1.1	2.8	2.3	2.2	..	0.9	1.4	0.8	0.8
Transfer component	..	0.7	1.8	1.1	1.0	..	0.6	0.9	0.4	0.3
Tax expenditure component	..	0.3	1.0	1.2	1.2	..	0.3	0.5	0.5	0.4

.. Not available

Note: More detailed country data and country notes are available in online chapter 5 "Country Tables, 1965-2017": https://doi.org/10.1787/0bbc27da-en. Full time series can be accessed at http://oe.cd/full-time-series.

Source: Local Authorities Statistics, Department of Statistics, Wellington.

StatLink https://doi.org/10.1787/888934056241

Table 4.50. New Zealand, tax revenue and % of GDP by level of government and main taxes

	Billion NZD					% of GDP				
	1990	2000	2010	2016	2017	1990	2000	2010	2016	2017
Federal or Central government										
Total tax revenue	**25.8**	**37.5**	**57.9**	**80.8**	**86.6**	**34.0**	**30.7**	**28.1**	**29.6**	**30.0**
1000 Taxes on income, profits and capital gains	16.4	23.9	33.5	48.1	51.5	21.6	19.5	16.3	17.6	17.8
2000 Social security contributions	0.0	0.0	0.0	0.0	0.0	0.0	0.0	0.0	0.0	0.0
3000 Taxes on payroll and workforce	0.0	0.0	0.0	0.0	0.0	0.0	0.0	0.0	0.0	0.0
4000 Taxes on property	0.3	0.1	0.1	0.1	0.1	0.4	0.1	0.0	0.0	0.0
5000 Taxes on goods and services	9.1	13.6	24.3	32.6	35.0	12.0	11.1	11.8	11.9	12.1
6000 Other taxes	0.0	0.0	0.0	0.0	0.0	0.0	0.0	0.0	0.0	0.0
State/Regional										
Total tax revenue	..	..	..	..	..	..	..	..	..	..
1000 Taxes on income, profits and capital gains	..	..	..	..	..	..	..	..	..	..
2000 Social security contributions	..	..	..	..	..	..	..	..	..	..
3000 Taxes on payroll and workforce	..	..	..	..	..	..	..	..	..	..
4000 Taxes on property	..	..	..	..	..	..	..	..	..	..
5000 Taxes on goods and services	..	..	..	..	..	..	..	..	..	..
6000 Other taxes	..	..	..	..	..	..	..	..	..	..
Local government										
Total tax revenue	**1.7**	**2.3**	**4.5**	**5.8**	**6.1**	**2.2**	**1.9**	**2.2**	**2.1**	**2.1**
1000 Taxes on income, profits and capital gains	0.0	0.0	0.0	0.0	0.0	0.0	0.0	0.0	0.0	0.0
2000 Social security contributions	0.0	0.0	0.0	0.0	0.0	0.0	0.0	0.0	0.0	0.0
3000 Taxes on payroll and workforce	0.0	0.0	0.0	0.0	0.0	0.0	0.0	0.0	0.0	0.0
4000 Taxes on property	1.6	2.0	4.0	5.2	5.4	2.0	1.7	2.0	1.9	1.9
5000 Taxes on goods and services	0.1	0.2	0.4	0.6	0.6	0.2	0.2	0.2	0.2	0.2
6000 Other taxes	0.0	0.0	0.0	0.0	0.0	0.0	0.0	0.0	0.0	0.0
Social Security Funds										
Total tax revenue	**0.0**	**0.0**	**0.0**	**0.0**	**0.0**	**0.0**	**0.0**	**0.0**	**0.0**	**0.0**
1000 Taxes on income, profits and capital gains	0.0	0.0	0.0	0.0	0.0	0.0	0.0	0.0	0.0	0.0
2000 Social security contributions	0.0	0.0	0.0	0.0	0.0	0.0	0.0	0.0	0.0	0.0
3000 Taxes on payroll and workforce	0.0	0.0	0.0	0.0	0.0	0.0	0.0	0.0	0.0	0.0
4000 Taxes on property	0.0	0.0	0.0	0.0	0.0	0.0	0.0	0.0	0.0	0.0
5000 Taxes on goods and services	0.0	0.0	0.0	0.0	0.0	0.0	0.0	0.0	0.0	0.0
6000 Other taxes	0.0	0.0	0.0	0.0	0.0	0.0	0.0	0.0	0.0	0.0

.. Not available

Note: More detailed country data and country notes are available in online chapter 6 "Tax revenues by sub-sectors of general government": https://doi.org/10.1787/0bbc27da-en. Full time series can be accessed at http://oe.cd/full-time-series.

Source: Local Authorities Statistics, Department of Statistics, Wellington.

StatLink https://doi.org/10.1787/888934056260

Table 4.51. Norway, tax revenue and % of GDP by selected tax category

	Billion NOK					% of GDP				
	1990	2000	2010	2016	2017	1990	2000	2010	2016	2017
Total tax revenue	**301.8**	**631.6**	**1 086.7**	**1 207.6**	**1 282.0**	**40.2**	**41.9**	**41.9**	**38.7**	**38.8**
1000 Taxes on income, profits and capital gains	**106.3**	**284.2**	**512.0**	**458.2**	**499.7**	**14.2**	**18.8**	**19.7**	**14.7**	**15.1**
1100 Of individuals	79.1	152.0	256.5	332.8	339.1	10.5	10.1	9.9	10.7	10.3
1200 Corporate	27.2	132.2	255.5	125.4	160.6	3.6	8.8	9.9	4.0	4.9
1300 Unallocable between 1100 and 1200	0.0	0.0	0.0	0.0	0.0	0.0	0.0	0.0	0.0	0.0
2000 Social security contributions	**79.4**	**132.2**	**243.0**	**331.4**	**341.6**	**10.6**	**8.8**	**9.4**	**10.6**	**10.3**
2100 Employees	25.3	45.2	81.0	115.4	119.3	3.4	3.0	3.1	3.7	3.6
2200 Employers	50.1	79.2	148.1	193.8	199.3	6.7	5.3	5.7	6.2	6.0
2300 Self-employed or non-employed	3.9	7.8	13.9	22.3	23.0	0.5	0.5	0.5	0.7	0.7
2400 Unallocable between 2100, 2200 and 2300	0.0	0.0	0.0	0.0	0.0	0.0	0.0	0.0	0.0	0.0
3000 Taxes on payroll and workforce	**0.0**	**0.0**	**0.0**	**0.0**	**1.9**	**0.0**	**0.0**	**0.0**	**0.0**	**0.1**
4000 Taxes on property	**8.9**	**14.5**	**30.9**	**39.2**	**42.9**	**1.2**	**1.0**	**1.2**	**1.3**	**1.3**
4100 Recurrent taxes on immovable property	2.2	2.8	8.5	13.7	14.6	0.3	0.2	0.3	0.4	0.4
4200 Recurrent taxes on net wealth	5.1	7.7	14.1	16.7	19.0	0.7	0.5	0.5	0.5	0.6
4300 Estate, inheritance and gift taxes	0.4	1.3	2.4	0.2	0.1	0.1	0.1	0.1	0.0	0.0
4400 Taxes on financial and capital transactions	1.1	2.7	5.9	8.6	9.2	0.1	0.2	0.2	0.3	0.3
4500 Non-recurrent taxes	0.0	0.0	0.0	0.0	0.0	0.0	0.0	0.0	0.0	0.0
4600 Other recurrent taxes on property	0.0	0.0	0.0	0.0	0.0	0.0	0.0	0.0	0.0	0.0
5000 Taxes on goods and services	**107.3**	**200.7**	**300.7**	**378.8**	**395.9**	**14.3**	**13.3**	**11.6**	**12.1**	**12.0**
5100 Taxes on production, sale, transfer, etc	102.9	185.9	284.9	358.8	376.6	13.7	12.3	11.0	11.5	11.4
5110 General taxes	56.7	125.0	201.8	270.1	284.7	7.6	8.3	7.8	8.7	8.6
5111 Value added taxes	56.7	124.2	201.2	269.2	282.8	7.6	8.2	7.8	8.6	8.6
5120 Taxes on specific goods and services	46.2	60.9	83.1	88.8	91.9	6.2	4.0	3.2	2.8	2.8
5121 Excises	37.5	54.9	76.3	79.5	81.3	5.0	3.6	2.9	2.5	2.5
5200 Taxes on use of goods and perform activities	4.4	14.8	15.8	19.9	19.4	0.6	1.0	0.6	0.6	0.6
5300 Unallocable between 5100 and 5200	0.0	0.0	0.0	0.0	0.0	0.0	0.0	0.0	0.0	0.0
6000 Other taxes	**0.0**	**0.0**	**0.0**	**0.0**	**0.0**	**0.0**	**0.0**	**0.0**	**0.0**	**0.0**
Non-wastable tax credits										
Non-wastable tax credits against 1000	..	..	1.2	3.6	4.0	..	..	0.0	0.1	0.1
Transfer component	..	..	1.0	3.0	3.2	..	..	0.0	0.1	0.1
Tax expenditure component	..	..	0.3	0.6	0.8	..	..	0.0	0.0	0.0

.. Not available

Note: More detailed country data and country notes are available in online chapter 5 "Country Tables, 1965-2017": https://doi.org/10.1787/0bbc27da-en.
Full time series can be accessed at http://oe.cd/full-time-series.

Source: Statistics Norway; National Accounts.

StatLink https://doi.org/10.1787/888934056279

Table 4.52. Norway, tax revenue and % of GDP by level of government and main taxes

	Billion NOK					% of GDP				
	1990	2000	2010	2016	2017	1990	2000	2010	2016	2017
Federal or Central government										
Total tax revenue	**165.4**	**536.1**	**938.4**	**1 012.1**	**1 078.4**	**22.1**	**35.6**	**36.2**	**32.4**	**32.6**
1000 Taxes on income, profits and capital gains	50.6	198.4	380.8	288.9	324.7	6.8	13.2	14.7	9.3	9.8
2000 Social security contributions	4.7	132.2	243.0	331.4	341.6	0.6	8.8	9.4	10.6	10.3
3000 Taxes on payroll and workforce	0.0	0.0	0.0	0.0	1.9	0.0	0.0	0.0	0.0	0.1
4000 Taxes on property	3.4	7.0	16.0	15.4	16.5	0.5	0.5	0.6	0.5	0.5
5000 Taxes on goods and services	106.7	198.6	298.6	376.5	393.7	14.2	13.2	11.5	12.1	11.9
6000 Other taxes	0.0	0.0	0.0	0.0	0.0	0.0	0.0	0.0	0.0	0.0
State/Regional										
Total tax revenue	..	..	..	..	..	..	..	..	..	..
1000 Taxes on income, profits and capital gains	..	..	..	..	..	..	..	..	..	..
2000 Social security contributions	..	..	..	..	..	..	..	..	..	..
3000 Taxes on payroll and workforce	..	..	..	..	..	..	..	..	..	..
4000 Taxes on property	..	..	..	..	..	..	..	..	..	..
5000 Taxes on goods and services	..	..	..	..	..	..	..	..	..	..
6000 Other taxes	..	..	..	..	..	..	..	..	..	..
Local government										
Total tax revenue	**61.6**	**95.5**	**148.2**	**195.4**	**203.5**	**8.2**	**6.3**	**5.7**	**6.3**	**6.2**
1000 Taxes on income, profits and capital gains	55.7	85.8	131.2	169.3	175.0	7.4	5.7	5.1	5.4	5.3
2000 Social security contributions	0.0	0.0	0.0	0.0	0.0	0.0	0.0	0.0	0.0	0.0
3000 Taxes on payroll and workforce	0.0	0.0	0.0	0.0	0.0	0.0	0.0	0.0	0.0	0.0
4000 Taxes on property	5.5	7.6	14.9	23.9	26.3	0.7	0.5	0.6	0.8	0.8
5000 Taxes on goods and services	0.4	2.1	2.2	2.3	2.2	0.1	0.1	0.1	0.1	0.1
6000 Other taxes	0.0	0.0	0.0	0.0	0.0	0.0	0.0	0.0	0.0	0.0
Social Security Funds										
Total tax revenue	**74.8**	**0.0**	**0.0**	**0.0**	**0.0**	**10.0**	**0.0**	**0.0**	**0.0**	**0.0**
1000 Taxes on income, profits and capital gains	0.0	0.0	0.0	0.0	0.0	0.0	0.0	0.0	0.0	0.0
2000 Social security contributions	74.6	0.0	0.0	0.0	0.0	10.0	0.0	0.0	0.0	0.0
3000 Taxes on payroll and workforce	0.0	0.0	0.0	0.0	0.0	0.0	0.0	0.0	0.0	0.0
4000 Taxes on property	0.0	0.0	0.0	0.0	0.0	0.0	0.0	0.0	0.0	0.0
5000 Taxes on goods and services	0.2	0.0	0.0	0.0	0.0	0.0	0.0	0.0	0.0	0.0
6000 Other taxes	0.0	0.0	0.0	0.0	0.0	0.0	0.0	0.0	0.0	0.0

.. Not available

Note: More detailed country data and country notes are available in online chapter 6 "Tax revenues by sub-sectors of general government": https://doi.org/10.1787/0bbc27da-en. Full time series can be accessed at http://oe.cd/full-time-series.

Source: Statistics Norway; National Accounts.

StatLink https://doi.org/10.1787/888934056298

Table 4.53. Poland, tax revenue and % of GDP by selected tax category

	Billion PLN					% of GDP				
	1990	2000	2010	2016	2017	1990	2000	2010	2016	2017
Total tax revenue	..	**246.0**	**454.0**	**624.2**	**679.1**	..	**32.9**	**31.4**	**33.5**	**34.1**
1000 Taxes on income, profits and capital gains	..	**50.3**	**91.0**	**124.3**	**137.5**	..	**6.7**	**6.3**	**6.7**	**6.9**
1100 Of individuals	..	32.4	62.9	90.1	99.1	..	4.3	4.4	4.8	5.0
1200 Corporate	..	17.9	28.1	34.2	38.4	..	2.4	1.9	1.8	1.9
1300 Unallocable between 1100 and 1200	..	0.0	0.0	0.0	0.0	..	0.0	0.0	0.0	0.0
2000 Social security contributions	..	**96.4**	**156.0**	**236.3**	**255.0**	..	**12.9**	**10.8**	**12.7**	**12.8**
2100 Employees	..	42.4	60.2	97.1	105.8	..	5.7	4.2	5.2	5.3
2200 Employers	..	41.1	65.4	91.9	100.9	..	5.5	4.5	4.9	5.1
2300 Self-employed or non-employed	..	12.9	30.4	47.3	48.3	..	1.7	2.1	2.5	2.4
2400 Unallocable between 2100, 2200 and 2300	..	0.0	0.0	0.0	0.0	..	0.0	0.0	0.0	0.0
3000 Taxes on payroll and workforce	..	**1.6**	**3.7**	**4.2**	**4.5**	..	**0.2**	**0.3**	**0.2**	**0.2**
4000 Taxes on property	..	**10.6**	**19.1**	**25.6**	**27.1**	..	**1.4**	**1.3**	**1.4**	**1.4**
4100 Recurrent taxes on immovable property	..	8.4	16.4	22.7	23.8	..	1.1	1.1	1.2	1.2
4200 Recurrent taxes on net wealth	..	0.0	0.0	0.0	0.0	..	0.0	0.0	0.0	0.0
4300 Estate, inheritance and gift taxes	..	0.2	0.3	0.3	0.3	..	0.0	0.0	0.0	0.0
4400 Taxes on financial and capital transactions	..	2.0	2.4	2.6	3.0	..	0.3	0.2	0.1	0.2
4500 Non-recurrent taxes	..	0.0	0.0	0.0	0.0	..	0.0	0.0	0.0	0.0
4600 Other recurrent taxes on property	..	0.0	0.0	0.0	0.0	..	0.0	0.0	0.0	0.0
5000 Taxes on goods and services	..	**86.9**	**182.0**	**229.6**	**250.6**	..	**11.6**	**12.6**	**12.3**	**12.6**
5100 Taxes on production, sale, transfer, etc	..	84.9	175.2	221.5	243.2	..	11.4	12.1	11.9	12.2
5110 General taxes	..	51.6	109.7	134.6	154.7	..	6.9	7.6	7.2	7.8
5111 Value added taxes	..	51.6	109.7	134.6	154.7	..	6.9	7.6	7.2	7.8
5120 Taxes on specific goods and services	..	33.3	65.5	87.0	88.6	..	4.5	4.5	4.7	4.5
5121 Excises	..	27.2	62.0	75.6	79.0	..	3.6	4.3	4.1	4.0
5200 Taxes on use of goods and perform activities	..	2.0	6.8	8.1	7.4	..	0.3	0.5	0.4	0.4
5300 Unallocable between 5100 and 5200	..	0.0	0.0	0.0	0.0	..	0.0	0.0	0.0	0.0
6000 Other taxes	..	**0.3**	**0.6**	**0.9**	**1.0**	..	**0.0**	**0.0**	**0.1**	**0.1**
Non-wastable tax credits										
Non-wastable tax credits against 1000	..	..	..	..	..	..	..	..	..	..
Transfer component	..	..	..	..	..	..	..	..	..	..
Tax expenditure component	..	..	..	..	..	..	..	..	..	..

.. Not available

Note: More detailed country data and country notes are available in online chapter 5 "Country Tables, 1965-2017": https://doi.org/10.1787/0bbc27da-en. Full time series can be accessed at http://oe.cd/full-time-series.

Source: Ministry of Finance, Economic Department.

StatLink https://doi.org/10.1787/888934056317

Table 4.54. Poland, tax revenue and % of GDP by level of government and main taxes

	Billion PLN					% of GDP				
	1990	2000	2010	2016	2017	1990	2000	2010	2016	2017
Federal or Central government										
Total tax revenue	..	**126.9**	**239.2**	**304.7**	**334.3**	..	**17.0**	**16.6**	**16.4**	**16.8**
1000 Taxes on income, profits and capital gains	..	40.0	57.7	75.2	83.4	..	5.3	4.0	4.0	4.2
2000 Social security contributions	..	0.0	0.0	0.0	0.0	..	0.0	0.0	0.0	0.0
3000 Taxes on payroll and workforce	..	1.6	3.7	4.2	4.5	..	0.2	0.3	0.2	0.2
4000 Taxes on property	..	0.0	0.0	0.0	0.0	..	0.0	0.0	0.0	0.0
5000 Taxes on goods and services	..	85.3	177.8	225.3	246.4	..	11.4	12.3	12.1	12.4
6000 Other taxes	..	0.0	0.0	0.0	0.0	..	0.0	0.0	0.0	0.0
State/Regional										
Total tax revenue	..	..	..	..	..	..	..	..	..	..
1000 Taxes on income, profits and capital gains	..	..	..	..	..	..	..	..	..	..
2000 Social security contributions	..	..	..	..	..	..	..	..	..	..
3000 Taxes on payroll and workforce	..	..	..	..	..	..	..	..	..	..
4000 Taxes on property	..	..	..	..	..	..	..	..	..	..
5000 Taxes on goods and services	..	..	..	..	..	..	..	..	..	..
6000 Other taxes	..	..	..	..	..	..	..	..	..	..
Local government										
Total tax revenue	..	**22.7**	**57.1**	**79.8**	**86.2**	..	**3.0**	**4.0**	**4.3**	**4.3**
1000 Taxes on income, profits and capital gains	..	10.3	33.3	49.0	54.1	..	1.4	2.3	2.6	2.7
2000 Social security contributions	..	0.0	0.0	0.0	0.0	..	0.0	0.0	0.0	0.0
3000 Taxes on payroll and workforce	..	0.0	0.0	0.0	0.0	..	0.0	0.0	0.0	0.0
4000 Taxes on property	..	10.6	19.1	25.6	27.1	..	1.4	1.3	1.4	1.4
5000 Taxes on goods and services	..	1.5	4.1	4.2	4.1	..	0.2	0.3	0.2	0.2
6000 Other taxes	..	0.3	0.6	0.9	1.0	..	0.0	0.0	0.1	0.1
Social Security Funds										
Total tax revenue	..	**96.4**	**156.0**	**236.3**	**255.0**	..	**12.9**	**10.8**	**12.7**	**12.8**
1000 Taxes on income, profits and capital gains	..	0.0	0.0	0.0	0.0	..	0.0	0.0	0.0	0.0
2000 Social security contributions	..	96.4	156.0	236.3	255.0	..	12.9	10.8	12.7	12.8
3000 Taxes on payroll and workforce	..	0.0	0.0	0.0	0.0	..	0.0	0.0	0.0	0.0
4000 Taxes on property	..	0.0	0.0	0.0	0.0	..	0.0	0.0	0.0	0.0
5000 Taxes on goods and services	..	0.0	0.0	0.0	0.0	..	0.0	0.0	0.0	0.0
6000 Other taxes	..	0.0	0.0	0.0	0.0	..	0.0	0.0	0.0	0.0

.. Not available

Note: More detailed country data and country notes are available in online chapter 6 "Tax revenues by sub-sectors of general government": https://doi.org/10.1787/0bbc27da-en. Full time series can be accessed at http://oe.cd/full-time-series.

Source: Ministry of Finance, Economic Department.

StatLink https://doi.org/10.1787/888934056336

Table 4.55. Portugal, tax revenue and % of GDP by selected tax category

	Billion EUR					% of GDP				
	1990	2000	2010	2016	2017	1990	2000	2010	2016	2017
Total tax revenue	**14.8**	**39.9**	**54.7**	**63.6**	**67.0**	**26.5**	**31.1**	**30.4**	**34.1**	**34.4**
1000 Taxes on income, profits and capital gains	**3.8**	**11.7**	**14.6**	**18.3**	**18.9**	**6.8**	**9.1**	**8.1**	**9.8**	**9.7**
1100 Of individuals	2.4	6.9	9.6	12.6	12.6	4.2	5.4	5.4	6.8	6.5
1200 Corporate	1.2	4.7	4.9	5.7	6.3	2.1	3.7	2.7	3.0	3.2
1300 Unallocable between 1100 and 1200	0.3	0.0	0.1	0.0	0.0	0.5	0.0	0.0	0.0	0.0
2000 Social security contributions	**4.0**	**10.2**	**15.5**	**16.9**	**17.9**	**7.2**	**7.9**	**8.6**	**9.1**	**9.2**
2100 Employees	1.5	4.3	6.7	7.2	7.6	2.6	3.3	3.7	3.9	3.9
2200 Employers	2.4	5.9	8.8	9.7	10.3	4.3	4.6	4.9	5.2	5.3
2300 Self-employed or non-employed	0.1	0.0	0.0	0.0	0.0	0.3	0.0	0.0	0.0	0.0
2400 Unallocable between 2100, 2200 and 2300	0.0	0.0	0.0	0.0	0.0	0.0	0.0	0.0	0.0	0.0
3000 Taxes on payroll and workforce	**0.0**	**0.0**	**0.0**	**0.0**	**0.0**	**0.0**	**0.0**	**0.0**	**0.0**	**0.0**
4000 Taxes on property	**0.4**	**1.5**	**1.9**	**2.4**	**2.6**	**0.7**	**1.1**	**1.1**	**1.3**	**1.4**
4100 Recurrent taxes on immovable property	0.1	0.5	1.1	1.5	1.6	0.2	0.4	0.6	0.8	0.8
4200 Recurrent taxes on net wealth	0.0	0.0	0.0	0.0	0.0	0.0	0.0	0.0	0.0	0.0
4300 Estate, inheritance and gift taxes	0.1	0.1	0.0	0.0	0.0	0.1	0.1	0.0	0.0	0.0
4400 Taxes on financial and capital transactions	0.2	0.9	0.8	0.9	1.1	0.3	0.7	0.5	0.5	0.5
4500 Non-recurrent taxes	0.0	0.0	0.0	0.0	0.0	0.0	0.0	0.0	0.0	0.0
4600 Other recurrent taxes on property	0.0	0.0	0.0	0.0	0.0	0.0	0.0	0.0	0.0	0.0
5000 Taxes on goods and services	**6.6**	**16.1**	**22.0**	**25.3**	**26.8**	**11.7**	**12.5**	**12.2**	**13.5**	**13.8**
5100 Taxes on production, sale, transfer, etc	6.4	15.6	21.2	24.0	25.5	11.5	12.2	11.8	12.9	13.1
5110 General taxes	2.9	9.7	13.5	15.8	16.8	5.2	7.6	7.5	8.5	8.6
5111 Value added taxes	2.9	9.7	13.5	15.8	16.8	5.2	7.6	7.5	8.5	8.6
5120 Taxes on specific goods and services	3.5	5.9	7.7	8.3	8.7	6.3	4.6	4.3	4.4	4.5
5121 Excises	2.1	4.5	5.7	5.8	6.1	3.7	3.5	3.1	3.1	3.1
5200 Taxes on use of goods and perform activities	0.1	0.4	0.7	1.1	1.2	0.2	0.3	0.4	0.6	0.6
5300 Unallocable between 5100 and 5200	0.0	0.1	0.0	0.1	0.0	0.0	0.0	0.0	0.1	0.0
6000 Other taxes	**0.0**	**0.3**	**0.5**	**0.6**	**0.6**	**0.1**	**0.2**	**0.3**	**0.3**	**0.3**
Non-wastable tax credits										
Non-wastable tax credits against 1000	..	..	..	..	..	..	..	..	..	..
Transfer component	..	..	..	..	..	..	..	..	..	..
Tax expenditure component	..	..	..	..	..	..	..	..	..	..

.. Not available

Note: More detailed country data and country notes are available in online chapter 5 "Country Tables, 1965-2017": https://doi.org/10.1787/0bbc27da-en. Full time series can be accessed at http://oe.cd/full-time-series.

Source: Instituto Nacionale de Estatistica; Conta do Estado, Contas de Gerência dos Fundos e Serviços Autonomos da Administraçao Central; Estatisticas das Financas publicas; Relatorio do Instituto de Gestao Financeira da Seguranta Social, Contas de Gerência das Regioes Autonomas da Madeira e dos Atores.

StatLink https://doi.org/10.1787/888934056355

Table 4.56. Portugal, tax revenue and % of GDP by level of government and main taxes

	Billion EUR					% of GDP				
	1990	2000	2010	2016	2017	1990	2000	2010	2016	2017
Federal or Central government										
Total tax revenue	**9.8**	**27.8**	**36.5**	**46.3**	**48.9**	**17.6**	**21.6**	**20.3**	**24.8**	**25.1**
1000 Taxes on income, profits and capital gains	3.6	11.1	13.6	17.0	17.7	6.4	8.7	7.5	9.1	9.1
2000 Social security contributions	0.0	1.3	1.9	5.5	5.9	0.0	1.0	1.1	3.0	3.0
3000 Taxes on payroll and workforce	0.0	0.0	0.0	0.0	0.0	0.0	0.0	0.0	0.0	0.0
4000 Taxes on property	0.1	0.3	0.2	0.2	0.3	0.1	0.2	0.1	0.1	0.2
5000 Taxes on goods and services	6.1	14.8	20.3	22.9	24.4	10.9	11.5	11.3	12.3	12.5
6000 Other taxes	0.0	0.3	0.5	0.6	0.5	0.1	0.2	0.3	0.3	0.3
State/Regional										
Total tax revenue	..	..	..	..	..	..	..	..	..	..
1000 Taxes on income, profits and capital gains	..	..	..	..	..	..	..	..	..	..
2000 Social security contributions	..	..	..	..	..	..	..	..	..	..
3000 Taxes on payroll and workforce	..	..	..	..	..	..	..	..	..	..
4000 Taxes on property	..	..	..	..	..	..	..	..	..	..
5000 Taxes on goods and services	..	..	..	..	..	..	..	..	..	..
6000 Other taxes	..	..	..	..	..	..	..	..	..	..
Local government										
Total tax revenue	**0.8**	**2.5**	**3.6**	**4.6**	**4.8**	**1.5**	**2.0**	**2.0**	**2.5**	**2.4**
1000 Taxes on income, profits and capital gains	0.2	0.6	1.1	1.3	1.2	0.4	0.4	0.6	0.7	0.6
2000 Social security contributions	0.0	0.0	0.0	0.0	0.0	0.0	0.0	0.0	0.0	0.0
3000 Taxes on payroll and workforce	0.0	0.0	0.0	0.0	0.0	0.0	0.0	0.0	0.0	0.0
4000 Taxes on property	0.3	1.2	1.7	2.2	2.3	0.6	0.9	0.9	1.2	1.2
5000 Taxes on goods and services	0.3	0.7	0.8	1.2	1.2	0.5	0.6	0.5	0.6	0.6
6000 Other taxes	0.0	0.0	0.0	0.0	0.0	0.0	0.0	0.0	0.0	0.0
Social Security Funds										
Total tax revenue	**4.0**	**9.4**	**14.4**	**12.4**	**13.1**	**7.2**	**7.3**	**8.0**	**6.6**	**6.7**
1000 Taxes on income, profits and capital gains	0.0	0.0	0.0	0.0	0.0	0.0	0.0	0.0	0.0	0.0
2000 Social security contributions	4.0	8.8	13.5	11.4	12.0	7.2	6.9	7.5	6.1	6.2
3000 Taxes on payroll and workforce	0.0	0.0	0.0	0.0	0.0	0.0	0.0	0.0	0.0	0.0
4000 Taxes on property	0.0	0.0	0.0	0.0	0.0	0.0	0.0	0.0	0.0	0.0
5000 Taxes on goods and services	0.0	0.5	0.8	1.0	1.0	0.0	0.4	0.5	0.5	0.5
6000 Other taxes	0.0	0.0	0.0	0.0	0.0	0.0	0.0	0.0	0.0	0.0

.. Not available

Note: More detailed country data and country notes are available in online chapter 6 "Tax revenues by sub-sectors of general government": https://doi.org/10.1787/0bbc27da-en. Full time series can be accessed at http://oe.cd/full-time-series.

Source: Instituto Nacionale de Estatistica; Conta do Estado, Contas de Gerência dos Fundos e Serviços Autonomos da Administraçao Central; Estatisticas das Financas publicas; Relatorio do Instituto de Gestao Financeira da Seguranta Social, Contas de Gerência das Regioes Autonomas da Madeira e dos Atores.

StatLink https://doi.org/10.1787/888934056374

Table 4.57. Slovak Republic, tax revenue and % of GDP by selected tax category

	Billion EUR					% of GDP				
	1990	2000	2010	2016	2017	1990	2000	2010	2016	2017
Total tax revenue	..	**10.6**	**19.0**	**26.3**	**28.1**	..	**33.6**	**28.1**	**32.3**	**33.1**
1000 Taxes on income, profits and capital gains	..	**2.2**	**3.6**	**5.7**	**6.0**	..	**6.9**	**5.3**	**7.0**	**7.0**
1100 Of individuals	..	1.1	1.8	2.7	2.9	..	3.3	2.6	3.3	3.4
1200 Corporate	..	0.8	1.7	2.8	2.9	..	2.6	2.5	3.5	3.4
1300 Unallocable between 1100 and 1200	..	0.3	0.2	0.2	0.2	..	1.0	0.2	0.2	0.2
2000 Social security contributions	..	**4.4**	**8.2**	**11.4**	**12.3**	..	**14.0**	**12.1**	**14.1**	**14.5**
2100 Employees	..	0.9	2.1	2.6	2.9	..	2.9	3.1	3.3	3.5
2200 Employers	..	2.9	4.6	6.5	7.2	..	9.0	6.8	8.0	8.5
2300 Self-employed or non-employed	..	0.7	1.5	2.3	2.2	..	2.1	2.2	2.9	2.6
2400 Unallocable between 2100, 2200 and 2300	..	0.0	0.0	0.0	0.0	..	0.0	0.0	0.0	0.0
3000 Taxes on payroll and workforce	..	**0.0**	**0.0**	**0.0**	**0.0**	..	**0.0**	**0.0**	**0.0**	**0.0**
4000 Taxes on property	..	**0.2**	**0.3**	**0.3**	**0.4**	..	**0.6**	**0.4**	**0.4**	**0.4**
4100 Recurrent taxes on immovable property	..	0.1	0.3	0.3	0.4	..	0.5	0.4	0.4	0.4
4200 Recurrent taxes on net wealth	..	0.0	0.0	0.0	0.0	..	0.0	0.0	0.0	0.0
4300 Estate, inheritance and gift taxes	..	0.0	0.0	0.0	0.0	..	0.0	0.0	0.0	0.0
4400 Taxes on financial and capital transactions	..	0.0	0.0	0.0	0.0	..	0.1	0.0	0.0	0.0
4500 Non-recurrent taxes	..	0.0	0.0	0.0	0.0	..	0.0	0.0	0.0	0.0
4600 Other recurrent taxes on property	..	0.0	0.0	0.0	0.0	..	0.0	0.0	0.0	0.0
5000 Taxes on goods and services	..	**3.8**	**6.8**	**8.7**	**9.3**	..	**12.2**	**10.1**	**10.7**	**11.0**
5100 Taxes on production, sale, transfer, etc	..	3.6	6.3	8.0	8.6	..	11.5	9.3	9.8	10.1
5110 General taxes	..	2.2	4.2	5.4	5.9	..	6.9	6.2	6.7	7.0
5111 Value added taxes	..	2.2	4.2	5.4	5.9	..	6.9	6.2	6.7	7.0
5120 Taxes on specific goods and services	..	1.5	2.1	2.5	2.7	..	4.6	3.1	3.1	3.1
5121 Excises	..	1.0	1.9	2.2	2.3	..	3.1	2.9	2.7	2.7
5200 Taxes on use of goods and perform activities	..	0.2	0.4	0.6	0.6	..	0.7	0.6	0.7	0.7
5300 Unallocable between 5100 and 5200	..	0.0	0.1	0.2	0.2	..	0.0	0.2	0.2	0.2
6000 Other taxes	..	**0.0**	**0.0**	**0.0**	**0.0**	..	**0.0**	**0.0**	**0.0**	**0.0**
Non-wastable tax credits										
Non-wastable tax credits against 1000	..	..	0.3	0.3	0.3	..	..	0.4	0.3	0.3
Transfer component	..	..	..	..	..	..	..	..	..	..
Tax expenditure component	..	..	..	..	..	..	..	..	..	..

.. Not available

Note: More detailed country data and country notes are available in online chapter 5 "Country Tables, 1965-2017": https://doi.org/10.1787/0bbc27da-en.
Full time series can be accessed at http://oe.cd/full-time-series.

Source: Ministry of Finance.

StatLink https://doi.org/10.1787/888934056393

Table 4.58. Slovak Republic, tax revenue and % of GDP by level of government and main taxes

	Billion EUR					% of GDP				
	1990	2000	2010	2016	2017	1990	2000	2010	2016	2017
Federal or Central government										
Total tax revenue	..	**6.2**	**10.3**	**14.4**	**15.5**	..	**19.5**	**15.3**	**17.8**	**18.2**
1000 Taxes on income, profits and capital gains	..	2.2	3.6	5.7	6.0	..	6.9	5.3	7.0	7.0
2000 Social security contributions	..	0.1	0.2	0.3	0.4	..	0.3	0.3	0.3	0.5
3000 Taxes on payroll and workforce	..	0.0	0.0	0.0	0.0	..	0.0	0.0	0.0	0.0
4000 Taxes on property	..	0.1	0.0	0.0	0.0	..	0.2	0.0	0.0	0.0
5000 Taxes on goods and services	..	3.8	6.5	8.5	9.1	..	12.1	9.7	10.5	10.7
6000 Other taxes	..	0.0	0.0	0.0	0.0	..	0.0	0.0	0.0	0.0
State/Regional										
Total tax revenue	..	..	..	..	..	..	..	..	..	..
1000 Taxes on income, profits and capital gains	..	..	..	..	..	..	..	..	..	..
2000 Social security contributions	..	..	..	..	..	..	..	..	..	..
3000 Taxes on payroll and workforce	..	..	..	..	..	..	..	..	..	..
4000 Taxes on property	..	..	..	..	..	..	..	..	..	..
5000 Taxes on goods and services	..	..	..	..	..	..	..	..	..	..
6000 Other taxes	..	..	..	..	..	..	..	..	..	..
Local government										
Total tax revenue	..	**0.1**	**0.5**	**0.5**	**0.5**	..	**0.5**	**0.8**	**0.6**	**0.6**
1000 Taxes on income, profits and capital gains	..	0.0	0.0	0.0	0.0	..	0.0	0.0	0.0	0.0
2000 Social security contributions	..	0.0	0.0	0.0	0.0	..	0.0	0.0	0.0	0.0
3000 Taxes on payroll and workforce	..	0.0	0.0	0.0	0.0	..	0.0	0.0	0.0	0.0
4000 Taxes on property	..	0.1	0.3	0.3	0.4	..	0.4	0.4	0.4	0.4
5000 Taxes on goods and services	..	0.0	0.3	0.2	0.2	..	0.0	0.4	0.2	0.2
6000 Other taxes	..	0.0	0.0	0.0	0.0	..	0.0	0.0	0.0	0.0
Social Security Funds										
Total tax revenue	..	**4.3**	**7.9**	**11.2**	**11.9**	..	**13.7**	**11.7**	**13.7**	**14.1**
1000 Taxes on income, profits and capital gains	..	0.0	0.0	0.0	0.0	..	0.0	0.0	0.0	0.0
2000 Social security contributions	..	4.3	7.9	11.2	11.9	..	13.7	11.7	13.7	14.1
3000 Taxes on payroll and workforce	..	0.0	0.0	0.0	0.0	..	0.0	0.0	0.0	0.0
4000 Taxes on property	..	0.0	0.0	0.0	0.0	..	0.0	0.0	0.0	0.0
5000 Taxes on goods and services	..	0.0	0.0	0.0	0.0	..	0.0	0.0	0.0	0.0
6000 Other taxes	..	0.0	0.0	0.0	0.0	..	0.0	0.0	0.0	0.0

.. Not available

Note: More detailed country data and country notes are available in online chapter 6 "Tax revenues by sub-sectors of general government": https://doi.org/10.1787/0bbc27da-en. Full time series can be accessed at http://oe.cd/full-time-series.

Source: Ministry of Finance.

StatLink https://doi.org/10.1787/888934056412

Table 4.59. Slovenia, tax revenue and % of GDP by selected tax category

	Billion EUR					% of GDP				
	1990	2000	2010	2016	2017	1990	2000	2010	2016	2017
Total tax revenue	..	**6.9**	**13.4**	**14.7**	**15.6**	..	**36.6**	**36.9**	**36.5**	**36.3**
1000 Taxes on income, profits and capital gains	..	**1.3**	**2.7**	**2.8**	**3.0**	..	**6.8**	**7.4**	**6.9**	**6.9**
1100 Of individuals	..	1.0	2.0	2.1	2.2	..	5.5	5.6	5.3	5.1
1200 Corporate	..	0.2	0.7	0.6	0.8	..	1.1	1.8	1.6	1.8
1300 Unallocable between 1100 and 1200	..	0.0	0.0	0.0	0.0	..	0.1	0.0	0.0	0.0
2000 Social security contributions	..	**2.6**	**5.4**	**5.8**	**6.2**	..	**13.9**	**14.8**	**14.5**	**14.5**
2100 Employees	..	1.4	2.8	3.0	3.2	..	7.7	7.7	7.5	7.6
2200 Employers	..	1.0	2.1	2.2	2.4	..	5.3	5.7	5.6	5.6
2300 Self-employed or non-employed	..	0.2	0.5	0.6	0.6	..	0.9	1.5	1.4	1.4
2400 Unallocable between 2100, 2200 and 2300	..	0.0	0.0	0.0	0.0	..	0.0	0.0	0.0	0.0
3000 Taxes on payroll and workforce	..	**0.3**	**0.0**	**0.0**	**0.0**	..	**1.5**	**0.1**	**0.0**	**0.1**
4000 Taxes on property	..	**0.1**	**0.2**	**0.3**	**0.3**	..	**0.6**	**0.6**	**0.6**	**0.6**
4100 Recurrent taxes on immovable property	..	0.1	0.2	0.2	0.2	..	0.4	0.5	0.5	0.5
4200 Recurrent taxes on net wealth	..	0.0	0.0	0.0	0.0	..	0.0	0.0	0.0	0.0
4300 Estate, inheritance and gift taxes	..	0.0	0.0	0.0	0.0	..	0.0	0.0	0.0	0.0
4400 Taxes on financial and capital transactions	..	0.0	0.0	0.0	0.0	..	0.1	0.1	0.1	0.1
4500 Non-recurrent taxes	..	0.0	0.0	0.0	0.0	..	0.1	0.0	0.0	0.0
4600 Other recurrent taxes on property	..	0.0	0.0	0.0	0.0	..	0.0	0.0	0.0	0.0
5000 Taxes on goods and services	..	**2.6**	**5.0**	**5.8**	**6.0**	..	**13.8**	**13.8**	**14.4**	**14.0**
5100 Taxes on production, sale, transfer, etc	..	2.5	4.8	5.4	5.6	..	13.1	13.2	13.4	13.1
5110 General taxes	..	1.6	2.9	3.3	3.5	..	8.7	8.1	8.2	8.1
5111 Value added taxes	..	1.6	2.9	3.3	3.5	..	8.5	8.1	8.2	8.1
5120 Taxes on specific goods and services	..	0.8	1.9	2.1	2.1	..	4.4	5.1	5.2	5.0
5121 Excises	..	0.6	1.6	1.7	1.7	..	3.1	4.3	4.1	4.0
5200 Taxes on use of goods and perform activities	..	0.1	0.2	0.4	0.4	..	0.6	0.6	0.9	0.9
5300 Unallocable between 5100 and 5200	..	0.0	0.0	0.0	0.0	..	0.0	0.0	0.0	0.0
6000 Other taxes	..	**0.0**	**0.0**	**0.0**	**0.0**	..	**0.0**	**0.0**	**0.0**	**0.0**
Non-wastable tax credits										
Non-wastable tax credits against 1000	..	..	..	..	..	..	..	..	..	..
Transfer component	..	..	..	..	..	..	..	..	..	..
Tax expenditure component	..	..	..	..	..	..	..	..	..	..

.. Not available
Note: More detailed country data and country notes are available in online chapter 5 "Country Tables, 1965-2017": https://doi.org/10.1787/0bbc27da-en.
Full time series can be accessed at http://oe.cd/full-time-series.
Source: Statistical Office of the Republic of Slovenia.

StatLink https://doi.org/10.1787/888934056431

Table 4.60. Slovenia, tax revenue and % of GDP by level of government and main taxes

	Billion EUR					% of GDP				
	1990	2000	2010	2016	2017	1990	2000	2010	2016	2017
Federal or Central government										
Total tax revenue	**..**	**3.8**	**6.5**	**7.5**	**7.9**	**..**	**20.2**	**18.0**	**18.6**	**18.4**
1000 Taxes on income, profits and capital gains	..	0.9	1.6	1.7	1.9	..	4.8	4.3	4.2	4.4
2000 Social security contributions	..	0.0	0.1	0.1	0.1	..	0.1	0.2	0.2	0.2
3000 Taxes on payroll and workforce	..	0.3	0.0	0.0	0.0	..	1.5	0.1	0.0	0.1
4000 Taxes on property	..	0.0	0.0	0.0	0.0	..	0.1	0.0	0.0	0.0
5000 Taxes on goods and services	..	2.6	4.9	5.7	5.9	..	13.7	13.5	14.1	13.8
6000 Other taxes	..	0.0	0.0	0.0	0.0	..	0.0	0.0	0.0	0.0
State/Regional										
Total tax revenue	**..**	**..**	**..**	**..**	**..**	**..**	**..**	**..**	**..**	**..**
1000 Taxes on income, profits and capital gains	..	..	..	..	..	..	..	..	..	..
2000 Social security contributions	..	..	..	..	..	..	..	..	..	..
3000 Taxes on payroll and workforce	..	..	..	..	..	..	..	..	..	..
4000 Taxes on property	..	..	..	..	..	..	..	..	..	..
5000 Taxes on goods and services	..	..	..	..	..	..	..	..	..	..
6000 Other taxes	..	..	..	..	..	..	..	..	..	..
Local government										
Total tax revenue	**..**	**0.5**	**1.5**	**1.4**	**1.5**	**..**	**2.7**	**4.0**	**3.5**	**3.4**
1000 Taxes on income, profits and capital gains	..	0.4	1.1	1.1	1.1	..	2.0	3.1	2.6	2.5
2000 Social security contributions	..	0.0	0.0	0.0	0.0	..	0.0	0.0	0.0	0.0
3000 Taxes on payroll and workforce	..	0.0	0.0	0.0	0.0	..	0.0	0.0	0.0	0.0
4000 Taxes on property	..	0.1	0.2	0.3	0.3	..	0.6	0.6	0.6	0.6
5000 Taxes on goods and services	..	0.0	0.1	0.1	0.1	..	0.1	0.3	0.2	0.2
6000 Other taxes	..	0.0	0.0	0.0	0.0	..	0.0	0.0	0.0	0.0
Social Security Funds										
Total tax revenue	**..**	**2.6**	**5.3**	**5.8**	**6.2**	**..**	**13.8**	**14.7**	**14.3**	**14.4**
1000 Taxes on income, profits and capital gains	..	0.0	0.0	0.0	0.0	..	0.0	0.0	0.0	0.0
2000 Social security contributions	..	2.6	5.3	5.8	6.2	..	13.8	14.7	14.3	14.4
3000 Taxes on payroll and workforce	..	0.0	0.0	0.0	0.0	..	0.0	0.0	0.0	0.0
4000 Taxes on property	..	0.0	0.0	0.0	0.0	..	0.0	0.0	0.0	0.0
5000 Taxes on goods and services	..	0.0	0.0	0.0	0.0	..	0.0	0.0	0.0	0.0
6000 Other taxes	..	0.0	0.0	0.0	0.0	..	0.0	0.0	0.0	0.0

.. Not available

Note: More detailed country data and country notes are available in online chapter 6 "Tax revenues by sub-sectors of general government": https://doi.org/10.1787/0bbc27da-en. Full time series can be accessed at http://oe.cd/full-time-series.

Source: Statistical Office of the Republic of Slovenia.

StatLink https://doi.org/10.1787/888934056450

Table 4.61. Spain, tax revenue and % of GDP by selected tax category

	Billion EUR					% of GDP				
	1990	2000	2010	2016	2017	1990	2000	2010	2016	2017
Total tax revenue	**103.7**	**214.7**	**337.4**	**372.4**	**392.9**	**31.6**	**33.2**	**31.2**	**33.3**	**33.7**
1000 Taxes on income, profits and capital gains	**31.8**	**60.8**	**94.8**	**104.8**	**112.5**	**9.7**	**9.4**	**8.8**	**9.4**	**9.6**
1100 Of individuals	22.5	41.2	73.9	79.5	85.6	6.9	6.4	6.8	7.1	7.3
1200 Corporate	9.1	19.6	21.0	25.3	26.9	2.8	3.0	1.9	2.3	2.3
1300 Unallocable between 1100 and 1200	0.1	0.0	0.0	0.0	0.0	0.0	0.0	0.0	0.0	0.0
2000 Social security contributions	**36.7**	**74.8**	**126.5**	**126.2**	**133.6**	**11.2**	**11.6**	**11.7**	**11.3**	**11.5**
2100 Employees	6.0	12.1	20.0	19.4	20.5	1.8	1.9	1.9	1.7	1.8
2200 Employers	26.4	53.9	88.5	91.0	97.1	8.0	8.3	8.2	8.1	8.3
2300 Self-employed or non-employed	4.4	8.8	18.1	15.8	16.0	1.3	1.4	1.7	1.4	1.4
2400 Unallocable between 2100, 2200 and 2300	0.0	0.0	0.0	0.0	0.0	0.0	0.0	0.0	0.0	0.0
3000 Taxes on payroll and workforce	**0.0**	**0.0**	**0.0**	**0.0**	**0.0**	**0.0**	**0.0**	**0.0**	**0.0**	**0.0**
4000 Taxes on property	**5.7**	**13.8**	**22.3**	**28.5**	**29.4**	**1.7**	**2.1**	**2.1**	**2.6**	**2.5**
4100 Recurrent taxes on immovable property	1.5	3.9	9.4	12.7	13.1	0.5	0.6	0.9	1.1	1.1
4200 Recurrent taxes on net wealth	0.6	1.4	0.7	2.0	2.1	0.2	0.2	0.1	0.2	0.2
4300 Estate, inheritance and gift taxes	0.4	1.4	2.4	2.7	2.7	0.1	0.2	0.2	0.2	0.2
4400 Taxes on financial and capital transactions	2.5	6.0	8.0	7.4	8.5	0.8	0.9	0.7	0.7	0.7
4500 Non-recurrent taxes	0.6	1.1	1.8	3.7	3.0	0.2	0.2	0.2	0.3	0.3
4600 Other recurrent taxes on property	0.0	0.0	0.0	0.0	0.0	0.0	0.0	0.0	0.0	0.0
5000 Taxes on goods and services	**29.4**	**64.3**	**91.8**	**110.8**	**115.3**	**9.0**	**10.0**	**8.5**	**9.9**	**9.9**
5100 Taxes on production, sale, transfer, etc	26.7	58.3	84.6	102.4	106.7	8.2	9.0	7.8	9.2	9.1
5110 General taxes	16.6	38.0	57.3	71.7	75.3	5.1	5.9	5.3	6.4	6.5
5111 Value added taxes	16.3	37.9	57.0	71.5	75.1	5.0	5.9	5.3	6.4	6.4
5120 Taxes on specific goods and services	10.1	20.4	27.3	30.7	31.4	3.1	3.2	2.5	2.7	2.7
5121 Excises	6.0	17.7	23.8	25.5	26.2	1.8	2.7	2.2	2.3	2.2
5200 Taxes on use of goods and perform activities	2.6	6.0	7.2	8.4	8.6	0.8	0.9	0.7	0.7	0.7
5300 Unallocable between 5100 and 5200	0.1	0.0	0.0	0.0	0.0	0.0	0.0	0.0	0.0	0.0
6000 Other taxes	**0.0**	**0.0**	**0.5**	**0.2**	**0.1**	**0.0**	**0.0**	**0.0**	**0.0**	**0.0**
Non-wastable tax credits										
Non-wastable tax credits against 1000	..	0.0	1.9	1.7	1.8	..	0.0	0.2	0.2	0.2
Transfer component	..	..	1.2	0.9	1.0	..	..	0.1	0.1	0.1
Tax expenditure component	..	..	0.7	0.8	0.8	..	..	0.1	0.1	0.1

.. Not available

Note: More detailed country data and country notes are available in online chapter 5 "Country Tables, 1965-2017": https://doi.org/10.1787/0bbc27da-en. Full time series can be accessed at http://oe.cd/full-time-series.

The total tax revenue has been reduced by the amount of any capital transfer that represents uncollected taxes. The capital transfer has been allocated between tax headings in proportion to the reported tax revenue. Therefore, the tax revenue amounts are different to those reported in the detailed country data available in online chapter 5 "Country Tables, 1965-2017".

Source: Informacion Estatistica del Ministerio de Hacienda (for national taxes). Cuentas de las Administraciones Publicas (for local taxes and social security) both published by Secretaria General Tecnica del Ministerio de Hacienda.

StatLink https://doi.org/10.1787/888934056469

Table 4.62. Spain, tax revenue and % of GDP by level of government and main taxes

	Billion EUR					% of GDP				
	1990	2000	2010	2016	2017	1990	2000	2010	2016	2017
Federal or Central government										
Total tax revenue	**53.7**	**105.6**	**139.4**	**156.1**	**162.3**	**16.4**	**16.3**	**12.9**	**14.0**	**13.9**
1000 Taxes on income, profits and capital gains	29.5	51.8	62.4	61.7	64.9	9.0	8.0	5.8	5.5	5.6
2000 Social security contributions	0.4	2.3	3.4	3.5	3.4	0.1	0.3	0.3	0.3	0.3
3000 Taxes on payroll and workforce	0.0	0.0	0.0	0.0	0.0	0.0	0.0	0.0	0.0	0.0
4000 Taxes on property	0.4	0.3	0.1	1.1	0.4	0.1	0.1	0.0	0.1	0.0
5000 Taxes on goods and services	23.4	51.2	73.0	89.8	93.5	7.2	7.9	6.8	8.0	8.0
6000 Other taxes	0.0	0.0	0.5	0.1	0.1	0.0	0.0	0.0	0.0	0.0
State/Regional										
Total tax revenue	**5.0**	**16.5**	**43.3**	**54.2**	**59.7**	**1.5**	**2.5**	**4.0**	**4.8**	**5.1**
1000 Taxes on income, profits and capital gains	0.4	5.5	27.4	37.4	41.4	0.1	0.9	2.5	3.3	3.6
2000 Social security contributions	0.0	0.0	0.0	0.0	0.0	0.0	0.0	0.0	0.0	0.0
3000 Taxes on payroll and workforce	0.0	0.0	0.0	0.0	0.0	0.0	0.0	0.0	0.0	0.0
4000 Taxes on property	3.0	7.8	10.1	10.7	11.9	0.9	1.2	0.9	1.0	1.0
5000 Taxes on goods and services	1.6	3.2	5.8	6.0	6.3	0.5	0.5	0.5	0.5	0.5
6000 Other taxes	0.0	0.0	0.0	0.0	0.0	0.0	0.0	0.0	0.0	0.0
Local government										
Total tax revenue	**8.1**	**19.2**	**30.1**	**36.7**	**38.1**	**2.5**	**3.0**	**2.8**	**3.3**	**3.3**
1000 Taxes on income, profits and capital gains	1.9	3.5	5.1	5.8	6.2	0.6	0.5	0.5	0.5	0.5
2000 Social security contributions	0.0	0.0	0.0	0.0	0.0	0.0	0.0	0.0	0.0	0.0
3000 Taxes on payroll and workforce	0.0	0.0	0.0	0.0	0.0	0.0	0.0	0.0	0.0	0.0
4000 Taxes on property	2.3	5.7	12.1	16.7	17.0	0.7	0.9	1.1	1.5	1.5
5000 Taxes on goods and services	3.9	10.0	12.9	14.3	14.8	1.2	1.5	1.2	1.3	1.3
6000 Other taxes	0.0	0.0	0.0	0.0	0.0	0.0	0.0	0.0	0.0	0.0
Social Security Funds										
Total tax revenue	**36.4**	**72.6**	**123.1**	**122.8**	**130.2**	**11.1**	**11.2**	**11.4**	**11.0**	**11.2**
1000 Taxes on income, profits and capital gains	0.0	0.0	0.0	0.0	0.0	0.0	0.0	0.0	0.0	0.0
2000 Social security contributions	36.4	72.6	123.1	122.8	130.2	11.1	11.2	11.4	11.0	11.2
3000 Taxes on payroll and workforce	0.0	0.0	0.0	0.0	0.0	0.0	0.0	0.0	0.0	0.0
4000 Taxes on property	0.0	0.0	0.0	0.0	0.0	0.0	0.0	0.0	0.0	0.0
5000 Taxes on goods and services	0.0	0.0	0.0	0.0	0.0	0.0	0.0	0.0	0.0	0.0
6000 Other taxes	0.0	0.0	0.0	0.0	0.0	0.0	0.0	0.0	0.0	0.0

Note: More detailed country data and country notes are available in online chapter 6 "Tax revenues by sub-sectors of general government": https://doi.org/10.1787/0bbc27da-en. Full time series can be accessed at http://oe.cd/full-time-series.

The total tax revenue has been reduced by the amount of any capital transfer that represents uncollected taxes. The capital transfer has been allocated between tax headings in proportion to the reported tax revenue. Therefore, the tax revenue amounts are different to those reported in the detailed country data available in online chapter 6 "Tax revenues by sub-sectors of general government".

Source: Informacion Estatistica del Ministerio de Hacienda (for national taxes). Cuentas de las Administraciones Publicas (for local taxes and social security) both published by Secretaria General Tecnica del Ministerio de Hacienda.

StatLink https://doi.org/10.1787/888934056488

Table 4.63. Sweden, tax revenue and % of GDP by selected tax category

	Billion SEK					% of GDP				
	1990	2000	2010	2016	2017	1990	2000	2010	2016	2017
Total tax revenue	**756.0**	**1 166.0**	**1 521.3**	**1 938.7**	**2 032.3**	**49.4**	**48.9**	**43.2**	**44.2**	**44.4**
1000 Taxes on income, profits and capital gains	**314.8**	**475.3**	**539.7**	**697.6**	**736.9**	**20.6**	**19.9**	**15.3**	**15.9**	**16.1**
1100 Of individuals	291.1	387.5	423.9	577.1	608.3	19.0	16.3	12.0	13.2	13.3
1200 Corporate	23.7	87.8	115.8	120.5	128.6	1.5	3.7	3.3	2.7	2.8
1300 Unallocable between 1100 and 1200	0.0	0.0	0.0	0.0	0.0	0.0	0.0	0.0	0.0	0.0
2000 Social security contributions	**205.9**	**307.0**	**384.7**	**438.9**	**443.1**	**13.5**	**12.9**	**10.9**	**10.0**	**9.7**
2100 Employees	0.8	63.1	89.2	113.3	118.7	0.1	2.6	2.5	2.6	2.6
2200 Employers	196.9	237.5	288.4	321.4	320.4	12.9	10.0	8.2	7.3	7.0
2300 Self-employed or non-employed	8.1	5.6	7.5	5.1	4.8	0.5	0.2	0.2	0.1	0.1
2400 Unallocable between 2100, 2200 and 2300	0.0	0.8	-0.4	-1.0	-0.8	0.0	0.0	0.0	0.0	0.0
3000 Taxes on payroll and workforce	**18.7**	**50.1**	**107.5**	**203.4**	**233.2**	**1.2**	**2.1**	**3.1**	**4.6**	**5.1**
4000 Taxes on property	**26.6**	**39.9**	**36.5**	**46.3**	**45.5**	**1.7**	**1.7**	**1.0**	**1.1**	**1.0**
4100 Recurrent taxes on immovable property	8.9	23.3	26.4	33.4	32.9	0.6	1.0	0.7	0.8	0.7
4200 Recurrent taxes on net wealth	3.2	8.2	0.0	0.0	0.0	0.2	0.3	0.0	0.0	0.0
4300 Estate, inheritance and gift taxes	1.4	2.5	0.0	0.0	0.0	0.1	0.1	0.0	0.0	0.0
4400 Taxes on financial and capital transactions	13.1	5.8	10.1	12.8	12.6	0.9	0.2	0.3	0.3	0.3
4500 Non-recurrent taxes	0.0	0.0	0.0	0.0	0.0	0.0	0.0	0.0	0.0	0.0
4600 Other recurrent taxes on property	0.0	0.0	0.0	0.0	0.0	0.0	0.0	0.0	0.0	0.0
5000 Taxes on goods and services	**188.7**	**288.8**	**446.1**	**544.4**	**565.1**	**12.3**	**12.1**	**12.7**	**12.4**	**12.3**
5100 Taxes on production, sale, transfer, etc	181.6	281.4	429.7	524.7	545.2	11.9	11.8	12.2	12.0	11.9
5110 General taxes	112.4	199.6	326.7	409.4	427.7	7.3	8.4	9.3	9.3	9.3
5111 Value added taxes	112.4	197.5	322.6	405.0	425.1	7.3	8.3	9.2	9.2	9.3
5120 Taxes on specific goods and services	69.2	81.8	103.0	115.3	117.5	4.5	3.4	2.9	2.6	2.6
5121 Excises	55.3	70.3	91.5	95.5	97.9	3.6	3.0	2.6	2.2	2.1
5200 Taxes on use of goods and perform activities	7.1	7.4	16.4	19.7	19.9	0.5	0.3	0.5	0.4	0.4
5300 Unallocable between 5100 and 5200	0.0	0.0	0.0	0.0	0.0	0.0	0.0	0.0	0.0	0.0
6000 Other taxes	**1.3**	**1.5**	**1.4**	**2.2**	**2.3**	**0.1**	**0.1**	**0.0**	**0.0**	**0.0**
Non-wastable tax credits										
Non-wastable tax credits against 1000	..	..	..	..	..	..	..	..	..	..
Transfer component	..	..	..	..	..	..	..	..	..	..
Tax expenditure component	..	..	..	..	..	..	..	..	..	..

.. Not available

Note: More detailed country data and country notes are available in online chapter 5 "Country Tables, 1965-2017": https://doi.org/10.1787/0bbc27da-en. Full time series can be accessed at http://oe.cd/full-time-series.

Source: Monthly reports of central Government Revenues (unpublished) National Audit Bureau, Stockholm. Local Government Finance (SOS), Tax assessment statistics (SOS) , National Central Bureau of Statistics, Stockholm.National Accounts (Statistical Reports), National Bureau of Statistics, Stockholm.

StatLink https://doi.org/10.1787/888934056507

Table 4.64. Sweden, tax revenue and % of GDP by level of government and main taxes

	Billion SEK					% of GDP				
	1990	2000	2010	2016	2017	1990	2000	2010	2016	2017
Federal or Central government										
Total tax revenue	**383.9**	**699.1**	**795.2**	**1 012.8**	**1 064.0**	**25.1**	**29.3**	**22.6**	**23.1**	**23.2**
1000 Taxes on income, profits and capital gains	94.7	139.0	16.9	28.0	36.9	6.2	5.8	0.5	0.6	0.8
2000 Social security contributions	54.8	180.2	201.2	205.0	198.1	3.6	7.6	5.7	4.7	4.3
3000 Taxes on payroll and workforce	18.7	50.1	107.5	203.4	233.2	1.2	2.1	3.1	4.6	5.1
4000 Taxes on property	26.6	39.9	22.4	29.9	28.5	1.7	1.7	0.6	0.7	0.6
5000 Taxes on goods and services	187.8	288.5	445.8	544.3	565.1	12.3	12.1	12.7	12.4	12.3
6000 Other taxes	1.3	1.5	1.4	2.2	2.3	0.1	0.1	0.0	0.0	0.0
State/Regional										
Total tax revenue	..	..	..	..	..	..	..	..	..	..
1000 Taxes on income, profits and capital gains	..	..	..	..	..	..	..	..	..	..
2000 Social security contributions	..	..	..	..	..	..	..	..	..	..
3000 Taxes on payroll and workforce	..	..	..	..	..	..	..	..	..	..
4000 Taxes on property	..	..	..	..	..	..	..	..	..	..
5000 Taxes on goods and services	..	..	..	..	..	..	..	..	..	..
6000 Other taxes	..	..	..	..	..	..	..	..	..	..
Local government										
Total tax revenue	**221.0**	**336.3**	**537.0**	**685.9**	**717.0**	**14.4**	**14.1**	**15.2**	**15.6**	**15.7**
1000 Taxes on income, profits and capital gains	220.1	336.3	522.9	669.6	700.1	14.4	14.1	14.8	15.3	15.3
2000 Social security contributions	0.0	0.0	0.0	0.0	0.0	0.0	0.0	0.0	0.0	0.0
3000 Taxes on payroll and workforce	0.0	0.0	0.0	0.0	0.0	0.0	0.0	0.0	0.0	0.0
4000 Taxes on property	0.0	0.0	14.1	16.3	16.9	0.0	0.0	0.4	0.4	0.4
5000 Taxes on goods and services	0.9	0.0	0.0	0.0	0.0	0.1	0.0	0.0	0.0	0.0
6000 Other taxes	0.0	0.0	0.0	0.0	0.0	0.0	0.0	0.0	0.0	0.0
Social Security Funds										
Total tax revenue	**151.1**	**126.8**	**183.5**	**233.9**	**245.0**	**9.9**	**5.3**	**5.2**	**5.3**	**5.4**
1000 Taxes on income, profits and capital gains	0.0	0.0	0.0	0.0	0.0	0.0	0.0	0.0	0.0	0.0
2000 Social security contributions	151.1	126.8	183.5	233.9	245.0	9.9	5.3	5.2	5.3	5.4
3000 Taxes on payroll and workforce	0.0	0.0	0.0	0.0	0.0	0.0	0.0	0.0	0.0	0.0
4000 Taxes on property	0.0	0.0	0.0	0.0	0.0	0.0	0.0	0.0	0.0	0.0
5000 Taxes on goods and services	0.0	0.0	0.0	0.0	0.0	0.0	0.0	0.0	0.0	0.0
6000 Other taxes	0.0	0.0	0.0	0.0	0.0	0.0	0.0	0.0	0.0	0.0

.. Not available

Note: More detailed country data and country notes are available in online chapter 6 "Tax revenues by sub-sectors of general government": https://doi.org/10.1787/0bbc27da-en. Full time series can be accessed at http://oe.cd/full-time-series.

Source: Monthly reports of central Government Revenues (unpublished) National Audit Bureau, Stockholm. Local Government Finance (SOS), Tax assessment statistics (SOS) , National Central Bureau of Statistics, Stockholm.National Accounts (Statistical Reports), National Bureau of Statistics, Stockholm.

StatLink https://doi.org/10.1787/888934056526

Table 4.65. Switzerland, tax revenue and % of GDP by selected tax category

	Billion CHF					% of GDP				
	1990	2000	2010	2016	2017	1990	2000	2010	2016	2017
Total tax revenue	**85.1**	**126.8**	**161.9**	**183.0**	**190.2**	**23.7**	**27.6**	**26.6**	**27.7**	**28.4**
1000 Taxes on income, profits and capital gains	**40.1**	**56.1**	**73.9**	**85.2**	**90.0**	**11.2**	**12.2**	**12.1**	**12.9**	**13.5**
1100 Of individuals	27.7	37.7	51.5	56.8	57.6	7.7	8.2	8.5	8.6	8.6
1200 Corporate	6.3	11.3	16.3	20.7	20.4	1.8	2.5	2.7	3.1	3.1
1300 Unallocable between 1100 and 1200	6.1	7.1	6.2	7.7	12.0	1.7	1.5	1.0	1.2	1.8
2000 Social security contributions	**19.8**	**30.6**	**38.1**	**44.3**	**44.8**	**5.5**	**6.7**	**6.3**	**6.7**	**6.7**
2100 Employees	9.3	14.3	17.5	20.5	20.8	2.6	3.1	2.9	3.1	3.1
2200 Employers	9.3	14.3	17.5	20.6	20.8	2.6	3.1	2.9	3.1	3.1
2300 Self-employed or non-employed	1.3	2.0	3.2	3.2	3.2	0.4	0.4	0.5	0.5	0.5
2400 Unallocable between 2100, 2200 and 2300	0.0	0.0	0.0	0.0	0.0	0.0	0.0	0.0	0.0	0.0
3000 Taxes on payroll and workforce	**0.0**	**0.0**	**0.0**	**0.0**	**0.0**	**0.0**	**0.0**	**0.0**	**0.0**	**0.0**
4000 Taxes on property	**7.6**	**12.3**	**12.3**	**13.5**	**14.4**	**2.1**	**2.7**	**2.0**	**2.0**	**2.2**
4100 Recurrent taxes on immovable property	0.4	0.7	1.0	1.2	1.3	0.1	0.2	0.2	0.2	0.2
4200 Recurrent taxes on net wealth	3.4	5.2	7.1	8.6	9.0	0.9	1.1	1.2	1.3	1.3
4300 Estate, inheritance and gift taxes	0.9	1.2	1.0	1.1	1.2	0.2	0.3	0.2	0.2	0.2
4400 Taxes on financial and capital transactions	2.2	4.3	2.4	1.5	2.0	0.6	0.9	0.4	0.2	0.3
4500 Non-recurrent taxes	0.0	0.0	0.0	0.0	0.0	0.0	0.0	0.0	0.0	0.0
4600 Other recurrent taxes on property	0.6	0.8	0.9	0.9	1.0	0.2	0.2	0.2	0.1	0.2
5000 Taxes on goods and services	**17.5**	**27.7**	**37.0**	**39.1**	**40.1**	**4.9**	**6.0**	**6.1**	**5.9**	**6.0**
5100 Taxes on production, sale, transfer, etc	15.9	25.2	32.0	33.6	34.2	4.4	5.5	5.3	5.1	5.1
5110 General taxes	9.8	16.8	20.9	22.6	23.2	2.7	3.7	3.4	3.4	3.5
5111 Value added taxes	9.8	16.5	20.5	22.3	22.8	2.7	3.6	3.4	3.4	3.4
5120 Taxes on specific goods and services	6.0	8.3	11.1	10.9	11.0	1.7	1.8	1.8	1.7	1.6
5121 Excises	4.6	6.8	8.2	8.0	8.1	1.3	1.5	1.4	1.2	1.2
5200 Taxes on use of goods and perform activities	1.6	2.5	4.9	5.5	5.8	0.4	0.6	0.8	0.8	0.9
5300 Unallocable between 5100 and 5200	0.0	0.0	0.0	0.0	0.0	0.0	0.0	0.0	0.0	0.0
6000 Other taxes	**0.1**	**0.2**	**0.6**	**0.9**	**1.0**	**0.0**	**0.0**	**0.1**	**0.1**	**0.1**
Non-wastable tax credits										
Non-wastable tax credits against 1000	..	..	..	..	..	..	..	..	..	..
Transfer component	..	..	..	..	..	..	..	..	..	..
Tax expenditure component	..	..	..	..	..	..	..	..	..	..

.. Not available

Note: More detailed country data and country notes are available in online chapter 5 "Country Tables, 1965-2017": https://doi.org/10.1787/0bbc27da-en. Full time series can be accessed at http://oe.cd/full-time-series.

The total tax revenue has been reduced by the amount of any capital transfer that represents uncollected taxes. The capital transfer has been allocated between tax headings in proportion to the reported tax revenue. Therefore, the tax revenue amounts are different to those reported in the detailed country data available in online chapter 5 "Country Tables, 1965-2017".

Source: Financial Statistics, Federal Finance Administration.

StatLink https://doi.org/10.1787/888934056545

Table 4.66. Switzerland, tax revenue and % of GDP by level of government and main taxes

	Billion CHF					% of GDP				
	1990	2000	2010	2016	2017	1990	2000	2010	2016	2017
Federal or Central government										
Total tax revenue	**28.9**	**46.6**	**59.0**	**64.2**	**69.4**	**8.1**	**10.1**	**9.7**	**9.7**	**10.4**
1000 Taxes on income, profits and capital gains	10.9	17.0	22.6	26.7	30.7	3.0	3.7	3.7	4.0	4.6
2000 Social security contributions	0.0	0.0	0.0	0.0	0.0	0.0	0.0	0.0	0.0	0.0
3000 Taxes on payroll and workforce	0.0	0.0	0.0	0.0	0.0	0.0	0.0	0.0	0.0	0.0
4000 Taxes on property	2.1	4.1	2.2	1.3	1.7	0.6	0.9	0.4	0.2	0.3
5000 Taxes on goods and services	16.0	25.5	34.2	36.1	36.9	4.5	5.6	5.6	5.5	5.5
6000 Other taxes	0.0	0.0	0.0	0.1	0.1	0.0	0.0	0.0	0.0	0.0
State/Regional										
Total tax revenue	**21.4**	**29.1**	**40.2**	**45.9**	**46.8**	**6.0**	**6.3**	**6.6**	**7.0**	**7.0**
1000 Taxes on income, profits and capital gains	16.5	21.9	31.1	35.2	35.6	4.6	4.8	5.1	5.3	5.3
2000 Social security contributions	0.0	0.0	0.0	0.0	0.0	0.0	0.0	0.0	0.0	0.0
3000 Taxes on payroll and workforce	0.0	0.0	0.0	0.0	0.0	0.0	0.0	0.0	0.0	0.0
4000 Taxes on property	3.5	5.1	6.3	7.6	7.9	1.0	1.1	1.0	1.2	1.2
5000 Taxes on goods and services	1.4	2.1	2.7	2.9	3.0	0.4	0.5	0.4	0.4	0.4
6000 Other taxes	0.0	0.0	0.0	0.2	0.3	0.0	0.0	0.0	0.0	0.0
Local government										
Total tax revenue	**15.0**	**20.6**	**24.7**	**28.6**	**29.1**	**4.2**	**4.5**	**4.1**	**4.3**	**4.4**
1000 Taxes on income, profits and capital gains	12.8	17.2	20.2	23.3	23.7	3.6	3.7	3.3	3.5	3.5
2000 Social security contributions	0.0	0.0	0.0	0.0	0.0	0.0	0.0	0.0	0.0	0.0
3000 Taxes on payroll and workforce	0.0	0.0	0.0	0.0	0.0	0.0	0.0	0.0	0.0	0.0
4000 Taxes on property	2.0	3.1	3.8	4.5	4.8	0.6	0.7	0.6	0.7	0.7
5000 Taxes on goods and services	0.1	0.1	0.1	0.1	0.2	0.0	0.0	0.0	0.0	0.0
6000 Other taxes	0.1	0.2	0.6	0.6	0.6	0.0	0.0	0.1	0.1	0.1
Social Security Funds										
Total tax revenue	**19.8**	**30.6**	**38.1**	**44.3**	**44.8**	**5.5**	**6.7**	**6.3**	**6.7**	**6.7**
1000 Taxes on income, profits and capital gains	0.0	0.0	0.0	0.0	0.0	0.0	0.0	0.0	0.0	0.0
2000 Social security contributions	19.8	30.6	38.1	44.3	44.8	5.5	6.7	6.3	6.7	6.7
3000 Taxes on payroll and workforce	0.0	0.0	0.0	0.0	0.0	0.0	0.0	0.0	0.0	0.0
4000 Taxes on property	0.0	0.0	0.0	0.0	0.0	0.0	0.0	0.0	0.0	0.0
5000 Taxes on goods and services	0.0	0.0	0.0	0.0	0.0	0.0	0.0	0.0	0.0	0.0
6000 Other taxes	0.0	0.0	0.0	0.0	0.0	0.0	0.0	0.0	0.0	0.0

Note: More detailed country data and country notes are available in online chapter 6 "Tax revenues by sub-sectors of general government": https://doi.org/10.1787/0bbc27da-en. Full time series can be accessed at http://oe.cd/full-time-series.
The total tax revenue has been reduced by the amount of any capital transfer that represents uncollected taxes. The capital transfer has been allocated between tax headings in proportion to the reported tax revenue. Therefore, the tax revenue amounts are different to those reported in the detailed country data available in online chapter 5 "Country Tables, 1965-2017".
Source: Financial Statistics, Federal Finance Administration.

StatLink https://doi.org/10.1787/888934056564

Table 4.67. Turkey, tax revenue and % of GDP by selected tax category

	Billion TRY					% of GDP				
	1990	2000	2010	2016	2017	1990	2000	2010	2016	2017
Total tax revenue	**0.1**	**40.3**	**287.9**	**660.0**	**773.4**	**14.5**	**23.6**	**24.8**	**25.3**	**24.9**
1000 Taxes on income, profits and capital gains	**0.0**	**11.9**	**61.3**	**139.6**	**165.3**	**4.9**	**7.0**	**5.3**	**5.4**	**5.3**
1100 Of individuals	0.0	9.0	40.4	96.6	112.4	3.9	5.2	3.5	3.7	3.6
1200 Corporate	0.0	2.9	20.9	43.0	52.9	1.0	1.7	1.8	1.6	1.7
1300 Unallocable between 1100 and 1200	0.0	0.0	0.0	0.0	0.0	0.0	0.0	0.0	0.0	0.0
2000 Social security contributions	**0.0**	**7.5**	**71.7**	**190.2**	**226.7**	**2.9**	**4.4**	**6.2**	**7.3**	**7.3**
2100 Employees	0.0	2.7	26.9	72.8	86.4	1.1	1.6	2.3	2.8	2.8
2200 Employers	0.0	3.6	39.4	107.9	128.3	1.6	2.1	3.4	4.1	4.1
2300 Self-employed or non-employed	0.0	1.2	5.4	9.5	12.0	0.2	0.7	0.5	0.4	0.4
2400 Unallocable between 2100, 2200 and 2300	0.0	0.0	0.0	0.0	0.0	0.0	0.0	0.0	0.0	0.0
3000 Taxes on payroll and workforce	**0.0**	**0.0**	**0.0**	**0.0**	**0.0**	**0.0**	**0.0**	**0.0**	**0.0**	**0.0**
4000 Taxes on property	**0.0**	**1.3**	**11.7**	**31.9**	**34.9**	**0.3**	**0.7**	**1.0**	**1.2**	**1.1**
4100 Recurrent taxes on immovable property	0.0	0.2	2.7	6.7	6.8	0.0	0.1	0.2	0.3	0.2
4200 Recurrent taxes on net wealth	0.0	0.0	0.0	0.0	0.0	0.0	0.0	0.0	0.0	0.0
4300 Estate, inheritance and gift taxes	0.0	0.0	0.2	0.6	0.7	0.0	0.0	0.0	0.0	0.0
4400 Taxes on financial and capital transactions	0.0	1.1	8.8	24.5	27.3	0.3	0.6	0.8	0.9	0.9
4500 Non-recurrent taxes	0.0	0.0	0.0	0.0	0.0	0.0	0.0	0.0	0.0	0.0
4600 Other recurrent taxes on property	0.0	0.0	0.0	0.0	0.0	0.0	0.0	0.0	0.0	0.0
5000 Taxes on goods and services	**0.0**	**16.9**	**137.3**	**287.9**	**336.3**	**4.1**	**9.9**	**11.8**	**11.0**	**10.8**
5100 Taxes on production, sale, transfer, etc	0.0	16.3	131.9	277.6	324.9	4.0	9.6	11.4	10.6	10.5
5110 General taxes	0.0	9.7	62.5	130.8	155.7	2.9	5.7	5.4	5.0	5.0
5111 Value added taxes	0.0	9.7	62.5	130.8	155.7	2.7	5.7	5.4	5.0	5.0
5120 Taxes on specific goods and services	0.0	6.6	69.3	146.8	169.3	1.1	3.9	6.0	5.6	5.4
5121 Excises	0.0	4.7	57.3	120.4	138.3	0.1	2.8	4.9	4.6	4.5
5200 Taxes on use of goods and perform activities	0.0	0.6	5.4	10.4	11.3	0.1	0.3	0.5	0.4	0.4
5300 Unallocable between 5100 and 5200	0.0	0.0	0.0	0.0	0.0	0.0	0.0	0.0	0.0	0.0
6000 Other taxes	**0.0**	**2.7**	**5.9**	**10.4**	**10.3**	**2.4**	**1.6**	**0.5**	**0.4**	**0.3**
Non-wastable tax credits										
Non-wastable tax credits against 1000	..	..	..	..	..	..	..	..	..	..
Transfer component	..	..	..	..	..	..	..	..	..	..
Tax expenditure component	..	..	..	..	..	..	..	..	..	..

.. Not available

Note: More detailed country data and country notes are available in online chapter 5 "Country Tables, 1965-2017": https://doi.org/10.1787/0bbc27da-en.
Full time series can be accessed at http://oe.cd/full-time-series.

Source: Bulletin of national accounts and the Budget revenue Bulletin.

StatLink https://doi.org/10.1787/888934056583

Table 4.68. Turkey, tax revenue and % of GDP by level of government and main taxes

	Billion TRY					% of GDP				
	1990	2000	2010	2016	2017	1990	2000	2010	2016	2017
Federal or Central government										
Total tax revenue	**0.1**	**29.1**	**189.4**	**405.8**	**473.2**	**10.4**	**17.1**	**16.3**	**15.6**	**15.2**
1000 Taxes on income, profits and capital gains	0.0	10.5	54.6	122.5	145.3	4.3	6.2	4.7	4.7	4.7
2000 Social security contributions	0.0	0.0	0.0	0.0	0.0	0.0	0.0	0.0	0.0	0.0
3000 Taxes on payroll and workforce	0.0	0.0	0.0	0.0	0.0	0.0	0.0	0.0	0.0	0.0
4000 Taxes on property	0.0	0.9	8.1	22.2	24.6	0.3	0.5	0.7	0.9	0.8
5000 Taxes on goods and services	0.0	15.2	124.0	256.2	299.4	3.6	8.9	10.7	9.8	9.6
6000 Other taxes	0.0	2.5	2.7	4.9	3.8	2.2	1.5	0.2	0.2	0.1
State/Regional										
Total tax revenue	..	..	..	..	..	..	..	..	..	..
1000 Taxes on income, profits and capital gains	..	..	..	..	..	..	..	..	..	..
2000 Social security contributions	..	..	..	..	..	..	..	..	..	..
3000 Taxes on payroll and workforce	..	..	..	..	..	..	..	..	..	..
4000 Taxes on property	..	..	..	..	..	..	..	..	..	..
5000 Taxes on goods and services	..	..	..	..	..	..	..	..	..	..
6000 Other taxes	..	..	..	..	..	..	..	..	..	..
Local government										
Total tax revenue	**0.0**	**3.6**	**26.8**	**64.0**	**73.5**	**1.3**	**2.1**	**2.3**	**2.5**	**2.4**
1000 Taxes on income, profits and capital gains	0.0	1.4	6.7	17.0	20.0	0.6	0.8	0.6	0.7	0.6
2000 Social security contributions	0.0	0.0	0.0	0.0	0.0	0.0	0.0	0.0	0.0	0.0
3000 Taxes on payroll and workforce	0.0	0.0	0.0	0.0	0.0	0.0	0.0	0.0	0.0	0.0
4000 Taxes on property	0.0	0.3	3.6	9.7	10.2	0.0	0.2	0.3	0.4	0.3
5000 Taxes on goods and services	0.0	1.7	13.3	31.8	36.8	0.5	1.0	1.1	1.2	1.2
6000 Other taxes	0.0	0.2	3.2	5.5	6.4	0.2	0.1	0.3	0.2	0.2
Social Security Funds										
Total tax revenue	**0.0**	**7.5**	**71.7**	**190.2**	**226.7**	**2.9**	**4.4**	**6.2**	**7.3**	**7.3**
1000 Taxes on income, profits and capital gains	0.0	0.0	0.0	0.0	0.0	0.0	0.0	0.0	0.0	0.0
2000 Social security contributions	0.0	7.5	71.7	190.2	226.7	2.9	4.4	6.2	7.3	7.3
3000 Taxes on payroll and workforce	0.0	0.0	0.0	0.0	0.0	0.0	0.0	0.0	0.0	0.0
4000 Taxes on property	0.0	0.0	0.0	0.0	0.0	0.0	0.0	0.0	0.0	0.0
5000 Taxes on goods and services	0.0	0.0	0.0	0.0	0.0	0.0	0.0	0.0	0.0	0.0
6000 Other taxes	0.0	0.0	0.0	0.0	0.0	0.0	0.0	0.0	0.0	0.0

.. Not available

Note: More detailed country data and country notes are available in online chapter 6 "Tax revenues by sub-sectors of general government": https://doi.org/10.1787/0bbc27da-en. Full time series can be accessed at http://oe.cd/full-time-series.

Source: Bulletin of national accounts and the Budget revenue Bulletin.

StatLink https://doi.org/10.1787/888934056602

Table 4.69. United Kingdom, tax revenue and % of GDP by selected tax category

	Billion GBP					% of GDP				
	1990	2000	2010	2016	2017	1990	2000	2010	2016	2017
Total tax revenue	**202.4**	**358.7**	**514.1**	**644.6**	**681.9**	**32.9**	**32.9**	**32.4**	**32.7**	**33.3**
1000 Taxes on income, profits and capital gains	**79.6**	**142.2**	**193.8**	**229.9**	**243.2**	**12.9**	**13.1**	**12.2**	**11.7**	**11.9**
1100 Of individuals	59.5	104.1	147.0	176.6	185.6	9.7	9.6	9.3	9.0	9.1
1200 Corporate	20.1	38.1	46.8	53.3	57.6	3.3	3.5	2.9	2.7	2.8
1300 Unallocable between 1100 and 1200	0.0	0.0	0.0	0.0	0.0	0.0	0.0	0.0	0.0	0.0
2000 Social security contributions	**34.5**	**60.3**	**97.3**	**121.9**	**130.6**	**5.6**	**5.5**	**6.1**	**6.2**	**6.4**
2100 Employees	13.3	24.2	38.7	47.3	50.4	2.2	2.2	2.4	2.4	2.5
2200 Employers	20.0	34.0	55.9	71.4	76.7	3.2	3.1	3.5	3.6	3.7
2300 Self-employed or non-employed	1.2	2.0	2.8	3.2	3.4	0.2	0.2	0.2	0.2	0.2
2400 Unallocable between 2100, 2200 and 2300	0.0	0.0	0.0	0.0	0.0	0.0	0.0	0.0	0.0	0.0
3000 Taxes on payroll and workforce	**0.0**	**0.0**	**0.0**	**0.0**	**1.8**	**0.0**	**0.0**	**0.0**	**0.0**	**0.1**
4000 Taxes on property	**16.5**	**41.1**	**61.8**	**81.3**	**85.6**	**2.7**	**3.8**	**3.9**	**4.1**	**4.2**
4100 Recurrent taxes on immovable property	13.5	30.6	50.0	60.3	62.8	2.2	2.8	3.2	3.1	3.1
4200 Recurrent taxes on net wealth	0.0	0.0	0.0	0.0	0.0	0.0	0.0	0.0	0.0	0.0
4300 Estate, inheritance and gift taxes	1.3	2.2	2.6	4.8	5.4	0.2	0.2	0.2	0.2	0.3
4400 Taxes on financial and capital transactions	1.8	8.4	9.1	16.0	17.1	0.3	0.8	0.6	0.8	0.8
4500 Non-recurrent taxes	0.0	0.0	0.0	0.3	0.3	0.0	0.0	0.0	0.0	0.0
4600 Other recurrent taxes on property	0.0	0.0	0.0	0.0	0.0	0.0	0.0	0.0	0.0	0.0
5000 Taxes on goods and services	**62.8**	**113.3**	**158.3**	**208.1**	**217.3**	**10.2**	**10.4**	**10.0**	**10.6**	**10.6**
5100 Taxes on production, sale, transfer, etc	59.4	108.3	150.8	200.5	209.5	9.6	9.9	9.5	10.2	10.2
5110 General taxes	34.1	64.3	95.9	133.9	141.3	5.5	5.9	6.0	6.8	6.9
5111 Value added taxes	34.1	64.3	95.9	133.9	141.3	5.5	5.9	6.0	6.8	6.9
5120 Taxes on specific goods and services	25.2	44.0	54.9	66.6	68.1	4.1	4.0	3.5	3.4	3.3
5121 Excises	19.7	37.3	45.5	48.0	48.7	3.2	3.4	2.9	2.4	2.4
5200 Taxes on use of goods and perform activities	3.4	5.0	7.4	7.6	7.8	0.6	0.5	0.5	0.4	0.4
5300 Unallocable between 5100 and 5200	0.0	0.0	0.0	0.0	0.0	0.0	0.0	0.0	0.0	0.0
6000 Other taxes	**9.0**	**0.0**	**0.0**	**0.0**	**0.0**	**1.5**	**0.0**	**0.0**	**0.0**	**0.0**
Non-wastable tax credits										
Non-wastable tax credits against 1000	7.5	4.7	30.1	30.1	29.5	1.2	0.4	1.9	1.5	1.4
Transfer component	0.5	3.4	23.7	26.7	26.0	0.1	0.3	1.5	1.4	1.3
Tax expenditure component	7.0	1.2	6.5	3.4	3.5	1.1	0.1	0.4	0.2	0.2

Note: More detailed country data and country notes are available in online chapter 5 "Country Tables, 1965-2017": https://doi.org/10.1787/0bbc27da-en. Full time series can be accessed at http://oe.cd/full-time-series.

Corporate income tax revenues for the United Kingdom are based on data provided in July; this was prior to revisions made to the historic Corporation tax data in September, so the revisions are not reflected here. For the latest UK Corporation tax data, please see www.gov.uk/government/statistics/corporation-tax-statistics-2019 the main revisions are explained on page 13 of https://assets.publishing.service.gov.uk/government/uploads/system/uploads/attachment_data/file/833371/Aug19_Receipts_NS_Bulletin_Final.odt.

Source: National Income and Expenditure; Central Statistical Office; Annual reports of Her Majesty's Revenue and Customs.

StatLink https://doi.org/10.1787/888934056621

Table 4.70. United Kingdom, tax revenue and % of GDP by level of government and main taxes

	Billion GBP					% of GDP				
	1990	2000	2010	2016	2017	1990	2000	2010	2016	2017
Federal or Central government										
Total tax revenue	**151.9**	**282.1**	**387.6**	**488.0**	**514.7**	**24.7**	**25.9**	**24.4**	**24.8**	**25.1**
1000 Taxes on income, profits and capital gains	79.6	142.2	193.8	229.9	243.2	12.9	13.1	12.2	11.7	11.9
2000 Social security contributions	0.0	0.0	0.0	0.0	0.0	0.0	0.0	0.0	0.0	0.0
3000 Taxes on payroll and workforce	0.0	0.0	0.0	0.0	1.8	0.0	0.0	0.0	0.0	0.1
4000 Taxes on property	11.4	26.9	35.5	50.0	52.4	1.9	2.5	2.2	2.5	2.6
5000 Taxes on goods and services	60.9	112.9	158.3	208.0	217.3	9.9	10.4	10.0	10.6	10.6
6000 Other taxes	0.0	0.0	0.0	0.0	0.0	0.0	0.0	0.0	0.0	0.0
State/Regional										
Total tax revenue	..	..	..	..	..	..	..	..	..	..
1000 Taxes on income, profits and capital gains	..	..	..	..	..	..	..	..	..	..
2000 Social security contributions	..	..	..	..	..	..	..	..	..	..
3000 Taxes on payroll and workforce	..	..	..	..	..	..	..	..	..	..
4000 Taxes on property	..	..	..	..	..	..	..	..	..	..
5000 Taxes on goods and services	..	..	..	..	..	..	..	..	..	..
6000 Other taxes	..	..	..	..	..	..	..	..	..	..
Local government										
Total tax revenue	**14.1**	**14.2**	**26.2**	**31.3**	**33.1**	**2.3**	**1.3**	**1.7**	**1.6**	**1.6**
1000 Taxes on income, profits and capital gains	0.0	0.0	0.0	0.0	0.0	0.0	0.0	0.0	0.0	0.0
2000 Social security contributions	0.0	0.0	0.0	0.0	0.0	0.0	0.0	0.0	0.0	0.0
3000 Taxes on payroll and workforce	0.0	0.0	0.0	0.0	0.0	0.0	0.0	0.0	0.0	0.0
4000 Taxes on property	5.1	14.2	26.2	31.3	33.1	0.8	1.3	1.7	1.6	1.6
5000 Taxes on goods and services	0.0	0.0	0.0	0.0	0.0	0.0	0.0	0.0	0.0	0.0
6000 Other taxes	9.0	0.0	0.0	0.0	0.0	1.5	0.0	0.0	0.0	0.0
Social Security Funds										
Total tax revenue	**34.5**	**60.3**	**97.3**	**121.9**	**130.6**	**5.6**	**5.5**	**6.1**	**6.2**	**6.4**
1000 Taxes on income, profits and capital gains	0.0	0.0	0.0	0.0	0.0	0.0	0.0	0.0	0.0	0.0
2000 Social security contributions	34.5	60.3	97.3	121.9	130.6	5.6	5.5	6.1	6.2	6.4
3000 Taxes on payroll and workforce	0.0	0.0	0.0	0.0	0.0	0.0	0.0	0.0	0.0	0.0
4000 Taxes on property	0.0	0.0	0.0	0.0	0.0	0.0	0.0	0.0	0.0	0.0
5000 Taxes on goods and services	0.0	0.0	0.0	0.0	0.0	0.0	0.0	0.0	0.0	0.0
6000 Other taxes	0.0	0.0	0.0	0.0	0.0	0.0	0.0	0.0	0.0	0.0

.. Not available

Note: More detailed country data and country notes are available in online chapter 6 "Tax revenues by sub-sectors of general government": https://doi.org/10.1787/0bbc27da-en. Full time series can be accessed at http://oe.cd/full-time-series.

Source: National Income and Expenditure; Central Statistical Office; Annual reports of Her Majesty's Revenue and Customs.

StatLink https://doi.org/10.1787/888934056640

Table 4.71. United States, tax revenue and % of GDP by selected tax category

	Billion USD					% of GDP				
	1990	2000	2010	2016	2017	1990	2000	2010	2016	2017
Total tax revenue	**1 552.4**	**2 900.5**	**3 517.1**	**4 841.9**	**5 227.3**	**26.0**	**28.3**	**23.5**	**25.9**	**26.8**
1000 Taxes on income, profits and capital gains	**701.7**	**1 453.9**	**1 488.7**	**2 325.8**	**2 363.1**	**11.8**	**14.2**	**9.9**	**12.4**	**12.1**
1100 Of individuals	584.7	1 224.5	1 223.2	1 944.8	2 025.5	9.8	11.9	8.2	10.4	10.4
1200 Corporate	117.0	229.3	265.5	381.0	337.6	2.0	2.2	1.8	2.0	1.7
1300 Unallocable between 1100 and 1200	0.0	0.0	0.0	0.0	0.0	0.0	0.0	0.0	0.0	0.0
2000 Social security contributions	**397.0**	**683.1**	**917.4**	**1 153.6**	**1 204.5**	**6.7**	**6.7**	**6.1**	**6.2**	**6.2**
2100 Employees	173.9	305.6	406.4	517.0	542.9	2.9	3.0	2.7	2.8	2.8
2200 Employers	204.1	343.2	461.7	574.3	598.2	3.4	3.3	3.1	3.1	3.1
2300 Self-employed or non-employed	19.0	34.4	49.3	62.3	63.3	0.3	0.3	0.3	0.3	0.3
2400 Unallocable between 2100, 2200 and 2300	0.0	0.0	0.0	0.0	0.0	0.0	0.0	0.0	0.0	0.0
3000 Taxes on payroll and workforce	**0.0**	**0.0**	**2.3**	**1.9**	**2.1**	**0.0**	**0.0**	**0.0**	**0.0**	**0.0**
4000 Taxes on property	**182.4**	**299.5**	**473.4**	**559.1**	**837.7**	**3.1**	**2.9**	**3.2**	**3.0**	**4.3**
4100 Recurrent taxes on immovable property	161.5	254.7	438.6	508.4	532.2	2.7	2.5	2.9	2.7	2.7
4200 Recurrent taxes on net wealth	0.0	0.0	0.0	0.0	0.0	0.0	0.0	0.0	0.0	0.0
4300 Estate, inheritance and gift taxes	15.8	35.6	19.7	25.3	28.1	0.3	0.3	0.1	0.1	0.1
4400 Taxes on financial and capital transactions	2.1	4.4	7.5	16.5	18.2	0.0	0.0	0.1	0.1	0.1
4500 Non-recurrent taxes	0.0	0.0	0.0	0.0	250.0	0.0	0.0	0.0	0.0	1.3
4600 Other recurrent taxes on property	3.0	4.8	7.7	8.9	9.2	0.1	0.0	0.1	0.0	0.0
5000 Taxes on goods and services	**271.3**	**464.0**	**635.3**	**801.6**	**820.0**	**4.6**	**4.5**	**4.2**	**4.3**	**4.2**
5100 Taxes on production, sale, transfer, etc	235.2	404.1	546.7	703.9	717.8	3.9	3.9	3.6	3.8	3.7
5110 General taxes	125.6	221.4	295.1	380.9	395.7	2.1	2.2	2.0	2.0	2.0
5111 Value added taxes	0.0	0.0	0.0	0.0	0.0	0.0	0.0	0.0	0.0	0.0
5120 Taxes on specific goods and services	109.7	182.7	251.6	322.9	322.1	1.8	1.8	1.7	1.7	1.7
5121 Excises	65.0	108.6	146.6	158.9	160.9	1.1	1.1	1.0	0.8	0.8
5200 Taxes on use of goods and perform activities	36.1	59.9	88.6	97.7	102.2	0.6	0.6	0.6	0.5	0.5
5300 Unallocable between 5100 and 5200	0.0	0.0	0.0	0.0	0.0	0.0	0.0	0.0	0.0	0.0
6000 Other taxes	**0.0**	**0.0**	**0.0**	**0.0**	**0.0**	**0.0**	**0.0**	**0.0**	**0.0**	**0.0**
Non-wastable tax credits										
Non-wastable tax credits against 1000	6.2	36.5	171.9	165.6	177.0	0.1	0.4	1.1	0.9	0.9
Transfer component	4.4	26.9	101.8	121.1	127.6	0.1	0.3	0.7	0.6	0.7
Tax expenditure component	1.8	9.6	70.1	44.6	49.4	0.0	0.1	0.5	0.2	0.3

Note: More detailed country data and country notes are available in online chapter 5 "Country Tables, 1965-2017": https://doi.org/10.1787/0bbc27da-en. Full time series can be accessed at http://oe.cd/full-time-series.
Source: Federal estimates are derived from the US Budget, the Final Monthly Treasury Statement and the Annual Report of the US Treasury Department. The State and Local estimates are derived from Government Finances, published by the Bureau of the Census.

StatLink https://doi.org/10.1787/888934056659

Table 4.72. United States, tax revenue and % of GDP by level of government and main taxes

	Billion USD					% of GDP				
	1990	2000	2010	2016	2017	1990	2000	2010	2016	2017
Federal or Central government										
Total tax revenue	**632.2**	**1 316.6**	**1 288.7**	**2 054.5**	**2 328.1**	**10.6**	**12.8**	**8.6**	**11.0**	**11.9**
1000 Taxes on income, profits and capital gains	569.7	1 201.3	1 176.8	1 896.8	1 923.5	9.6	11.7	7.9	10.1	9.9
2000 Social security contributions	0.0	0.0	0.0	0.0	0.0	0.0	0.0	0.0	0.0	0.0
3000 Taxes on payroll and workforce	0.0	0.0	0.0	0.0	0.0	0.0	0.0	0.0	0.0	0.0
4000 Taxes on property	11.6	28.1	15.1	20.1	273.2	0.2	0.3	0.1	0.1	1.4
5000 Taxes on goods and services	50.9	87.3	96.8	137.7	131.5	0.9	0.9	0.6	0.7	0.7
6000 Other taxes	0.0	0.0	0.0	0.0	0.0	0.0	0.0	0.0	0.0	0.0
State/Regional										
Total tax revenue	**309.7**	**547.6**	**723.9**	**928.1**	**954.9**	**5.2**	**5.3**	**4.8**	**5.0**	**4.9**
1000 Taxes on income, profits and capital gains	120.2	231.0	279.4	388.0	396.9	2.0	2.3	1.9	2.1	2.0
2000 Social security contributions	0.0	0.0	0.0	0.0	0.0	0.0	0.0	0.0	0.0	0.0
3000 Taxes on payroll and workforce	0.0	0.0	2.3	1.9	2.1	0.0	0.0	0.0	0.0	0.0
4000 Taxes on property	12.2	21.9	23.1	31.1	31.9	0.2	0.2	0.2	0.2	0.2
5000 Taxes on goods and services	177.3	294.7	419.1	507.1	524.1	3.0	2.9	2.8	2.7	2.7
6000 Other taxes	0.0	0.0	0.0	0.0	0.0	0.0	0.0	0.0	0.0	0.0
Local government										
Total tax revenue	**213.6**	**353.2**	**587.2**	**705.7**	**739.9**	**3.6**	**3.4**	**3.9**	**3.8**	**3.8**
1000 Taxes on income, profits and capital gains	11.9	21.6	32.5	41.0	42.8	0.2	0.2	0.2	0.2	0.2
2000 Social security contributions	0.0	0.0	0.0	0.0	0.0	0.0	0.0	0.0	0.0	0.0
3000 Taxes on payroll and workforce	0.0	0.0	0.0	0.0	0.0	0.0	0.0	0.0	0.0	0.0
4000 Taxes on property	158.6	249.5	435.3	507.9	532.7	2.7	2.4	2.9	2.7	2.7
5000 Taxes on goods and services	43.1	82.0	119.4	156.8	164.4	0.7	0.8	0.8	0.8	0.8
6000 Other taxes	0.0	0.0	0.0	0.0	0.0	0.0	0.0	0.0	0.0	0.0
Social Security Funds										
Total tax revenue	**397.0**	**683.1**	**917.4**	**1 153.6**	**1 204.5**	**6.7**	**6.7**	**6.1**	**6.2**	**6.2**
1000 Taxes on income, profits and capital gains	0.0	0.0	0.0	0.0	0.0	0.0	0.0	0.0	0.0	0.0
2000 Social security contributions	397.0	683.1	917.4	1 153.6	1 204.5	6.7	6.7	6.1	6.2	6.2
3000 Taxes on payroll and workforce	0.0	0.0	0.0	0.0	0.0	0.0	0.0	0.0	0.0	0.0
4000 Taxes on property	0.0	0.0	0.0	0.0	0.0	0.0	0.0	0.0	0.0	0.0
5000 Taxes on goods and services	0.0	0.0	0.0	0.0	0.0	0.0	0.0	0.0	0.0	0.0
6000 Other taxes	0.0	0.0	0.0	0.0	0.0	0.0	0.0	0.0	0.0	0.0

Note: More detailed country data and country notes are available in online chapter 6 "Tax revenues by sub-sectors of general government": https://doi.org/10.1787/0bbc27da-en. Full time series can be accessed at http://oe.cd/full-time-series.
Source: Federal estimates are derived from the US Budget, the Final Monthly Treasury Statement and the Annual Report of the US Treasury Department. The State and Local estimates are derived from Government Finances, published by the Bureau of the Census.

StatLink https://doi.org/10.1787/888934056678

4.2. Memorandum tables

Table 4.73 shows different sources for financing social benefits, beyond compulsory social security contributions reported in section 4.1. In addition, this table shows also data on other taxes, on voluntary contributions to government and on compulsory contributions to private sector.

Table 4.74 shows social security contributions and payroll taxes paid by government. During the revision of the Interpretative Guide in 1984, the question arose of how to treat taxes paid by government. The two most prominent examples of such taxes are social security contributions and payroll taxes paid by government in respect of its employees. After a long discussion it was decided that the data shown in this publication should continue to include taxes paid by government (see §5 of the Interpretative Guide in annex A).

Whilst it was recognised that for certain purposes (e.g. to show the cash flow to the government sector from the private sector) it would be appropriate to eliminate taxes paid by one sector of government to another or tax payments between different units of the same sector of government, the view was taken that to record tax flows in the context of the economy as a whole required that taxes paid by government should be included in the data. This treatment ensures that the different resource flows of an economy, including the calculation of the output of government, are measured consistently in after-tax units. Nevertheless, it was decided that data on identifiable taxes paid by government should be separately identified in a memorandum item and this is the purpose of the country tables which follow.

The data that are reproduced in the following tables refer to actual compulsory payments made by general government in respect of their employees. Fictive, voluntary and imputed contributions are excluded from these data. The definitions of social security contributions, payroll taxes and general government are those set out in §35 to §41, §42 and §3 to §4 of the Interpretative Guide. Information on the other taxes paid by government (namely property taxes and consumption taxes) is not available in most countries, although it is believed that in all countries taxes based upon payroll are the most important taxes paid by government. In many cases, the data are estimates and are not always constructed on a basis consistent with that used in the main tables.

Table 4.73. Financing of social security benefits

National currency

	Currency	Total 1990	Total 2000	Total 2010	Total 2016	Total 2017	2017 Social security contributions	2017 Other taxes	2017 Voluntary contributions to government	2017 Compulsory contributions to private sector	2017 Total
Australia	Million AUD	0	0	0	0	0	..	..	..	..	**0**
Austria	Million EUR	17 904	30 716	41 762	52 148	54 235	53 917	0	318	0	**54 235**
Belgium	Million EUR	24 082	40 065	67 281	71 044	76 587	59 594	16 920	73	0	**76 587**
Canada	Million CAD	29 653	53 109	76 787	98 954	99 346	99 346	0	0	0	**99 346**
Chile	Million CLP	487 661	2598 389	6902 690	12090 176	12891 280	2627 558	0	0	10263 722	**12891 280**
Czech Republic	Million CZK	..	345 480	582 784	707 132	765 231	757 183	0	463	7 585	**765 231**
Denmark	Million DKK	9 466	26 531	22 854	18 852	18 730	1 060	0	14 891	2 779	**18 730**
Estonia	Million EUR	..	674	1 918	2 841	3 065	2 636	0	0	429	**3 065**
Finland	Million EUR	11 070	16 904	23 479	28 562	27 899	27 000	0	302	597	**27 899**
France	Million EUR	194 091	312 876	461 199	547 061	563 652	387 443	176 209	0	0	**563 652**
Germany	Million EUR	184 914	328 889	369 783	465 409	487 493	466 470	0	9 324	11 699	**487 493**
Greece	Million EUR	3 466	14 284	24 748	19 313	20 746	20 746	0	0	0	**20 746**
Hungary	Million HUF	..	1759 277	3539 643	4932 246	5022 039	4704 101	316 775	1 163	0	**5022 039**
Iceland	Million ISK	37 632	95 260	236 509	471 834	466 655	89 649	133 273	0	243 733	**466 655**
Ireland	Million EUR	1 729	3 947	8 442	10 717	11 439	11 439	0	0	0	**11 439**
Israel	Million ILS	..	27 565	54 443	94 152	100 783	66 783	0	0	34 000	**100 783**
Italy	Million EUR	87 256	144 093	209 683	216 636	221 405	220 622	0	783	0	**221 405**
Japan	Billion JPY	34 613	47 968	54 461	66 614	68 562	68 562	0	0	0	**68 562**
Korea	Billion KRW	3 760	22 759	69 090	112 658	119 676	119 676	0	0	0	**119 676**
Latvia	Million EUR	..	682	1 590	2 154	2 356	2 259	97	0	0	**2 356**
Lithuania	Million EUR	..	1 362	3 391	4 872	5 345	5 170	0	2	173	**5 345**
Luxembourg	Million EUR	1 015	2 240	4 380	5 776	6 169	6 125	0	44	0	**6 169**
Mexico	Million MXN	21 005	205 575	423 569	659 803	711 436	467 710	0	0	243 726	**711 436**
Netherlands	Million EUR	44 965	101 610	82 732	103 902	101 913	101 913	0	0	..	**101 913**
New Zealand	Million NZD	0	0	0	0	0	..	..	..	..	**0**
Norway	Million NOK	79 701	132 170	243 015	331 389	341 591	341 591	0	0	0	**341 591**
Poland	Million PLN	..	96 386	156 026	236 292	254 968	254 968	0	0	0	**254 968**
Portugal	Million EUR	4 055	10 602	16 154	17 699	18 747	17 950	797	0	0	**18 747**
Slovak Republic	Million EUR	..	4 409	8 904	11 871	12 839	12 325	0	10	504	**12 839**
Slovenia	Million EUR	..	2 631	5 382	5 842	6 240	6 240	0	0	0	**6 240**
Spain	Million EUR	36 722	76 046	129 733	128 672	135 831	134 698	0	1 133	0	**135 831**
Sweden	Million SEK	205 867	315 082	399 552	456 856	462 335	443 110	0	19 225	0	**462 335**
Switzerland	Million CHF	41 865	64 791	90 541	106 892	109 655	44 998	7 722	0	56 934	**109 655**
Turkey	Million TRY	15	7 543	71 696	190 247	226 720	226 720	0	0	0	**226 720**
United Kingdom	Million GBP	45 690	76 663	128 219	149 861	157 321	130 595	0	26 678	48	**157 321**
United States	Million USD	408 691	705 666	979 242	1235 853	1294 619	1204 453	0	90 166	0	**1294 619**

.. Not available

StatLink https://doi.org/10.1787/888934056697

Table 4.74. Social security contributions and payroll taxes paid by government

National currency

		Total					2017				
	Currency	1990	2000	2010	2016	2017	Federal or Central government	State/Regional	Local government	Social security Funds	**Total**
Australia[1]	Million AUD	92	301	579	796	840	0	0	42	0	**840**
Austria	Million EUR	1 341	2 949	5 618	6 878	7 076	2 657	2 027	2 046	346	**7 076**
Belgium	Million EUR	1 769	3 105	5 261	7 473	7 774	744	2 424	4 184	423	**7 774**
Canada	Million CAD	..	6 365	10 185	12 648	12 784	1 575	6 808	4 401	0	**12 784**
Chile	Million CLP	..	54 633	189 974	298 964	319 933	236 530	..	82 601	801	**319 933**
Czech Republic	Million CZK	..	34 220	55 771	85 085	92 538	43 564	..	47 919	1 056	**92 538**
Denmark	Million DKK	0	0	0	0	0	..	..	..	..	**0**
Estonia	Million EUR	..	177	532	762	827	486	..	277	64	**827**
Finland	Million EUR	1 938	3 769	5 579	6 079	5 442	997	..	4 327	118	**5 442**
France	Million EUR	23 380	36 256	53 670	60 741	62 689	15 772	..	23 330	23 587	**62 689**
Germany	Million EUR	13 581	15 738	20 319	24 291	25 455	1 983	8 150	12 222	3 100	**25 455**
Greece	Million EUR	124	1 742	3 604	2 663	1 637	1 282	..	0	355	**1 637**
Hungary	Million HUF	..	366 958	544 870	739 505	707 308	552 059	..	153 231	2 017	**707 308**
Iceland	Million ISK	..	..	..	..	..	..	..	..	..	**..**
Ireland	Million EUR	149	447	1 205	1 536	1 657	574	..	1 077	6	**1 657**
Israel	Million ILS	..	4 110	6 710	9 900	10 350	8 250	..	2 100	0	**10 350**
Italy	Million EUR	..	36 679	50 627	49 881	50 628	0	..	0	50 628	**50 628**
Japan	Billion JPY	2 017	2 900	2 981	3 459	3 463	908	..	2 555	0	**3 463**
Korea	Billion KRW	..	..	..	..	..	..	..	..	..	**..**
Latvia	Million EUR	..	40	174	230	252	..	..	..	..	**252**
Lithuania	Million EUR	..	358	700	865	909	479	..	414	16	**909**
Luxembourg	Million EUR	267	287	507	706	749	725	..	4	20	**749**
Mexico	Million MXN	2 952	44 879	103 440	150 386	159 491	159 491	0	0	0	**159 491**
Netherlands	Million EUR	345	2 006	0	0	0	..	..	..	..	**0**
New Zealand	Million NZD	0	0	0	0	0	..	..	..	..	**0**
Norway	Million NOK	17 887	36 726	77 588	113 081	118 314	54 686	..	63 628	0	**118 314**
Poland	Million PLN	..	11 601	18 553	26 357	27 695	11 096	..	16 009	590	**27 695**
Portugal	Million EUR	33	197	0	0	0	..	..	..	..	**0**
Slovak Republic	Million EUR	..	642	1 322	1 798	1 899	1 120	..	739	40	**1 899**
Slovenia	Million EUR	..	335	613	623	652	429	..	215	7	**652**
Spain	Million EUR	4 010	9 620	18 506	19 232	20 082	2 325	12 464	4 802	491	**20 082**
Sweden	Million SEK	69 315	101 628	136 740	177 588	187 340	42 143	..	145 197	0	**187 340**
Switzerland	Million CHF	1 458	1 873	2 809	3 266	3 359	522	1 858	952	26	**3 359**
Turkey	Million TRY	9	3 619	39 363	107 905	128 331	128 331	..	0	0	**128 331**
United Kingdom	Million GBP	4 091	6 035	11 732	13 215	14 086	9 301	..	4 785	0	**14 086**
United States	Million USD	28 861	44 137	71 370	77 654	79 866	27 616	52 250	0	0	**79 866**

.. Not available

1. For Australia, the total differs from the sum of the four levels of government. The difference is due to a multi-jurisdictional (University) sector specific to this country. This sector contains units where jurisdiction is shared between two or more governments, or where classification of a unit to a jurisdiction is otherwise unclear. The main type of units currently falling into this category is public universities.

StatLink https://doi.org/10.1787/888934056716

5 Detailed country tables, 1965-2017

Chapter 5 provides detailed country information on tax revenues for each OECD country from 1965-2017.

5.1. Tax revenues

In all of the following tables the symbol (...) indicates not available/or not applicable. The main series in this chapter cover the years 1965 to 2017. For reasons of space, a selection of years are shown in these tables. A complete series is, however, available on line. Data for 1955 and 1960 (for nineteen OECD countries) are provided in part V of the 1998 edition of this Report.

Table 5.1. Australia: Detailed country table, 1965-2017

Million AUD

	1965	1980	1990	2000	2007	2010	2013	2015	2016	2017
Total tax revenue	**5 024**	**39 878**	**116 500**	**214 752**	**347 545**	**357 958**	**433 342**	**463 350**	**487 078**	**527 185**
1000 Taxes on income, profits and capital gains	**2 547**	**22 383**	**66 542**	**124 427**	**206 134**	**202 184**	**246 073**	**262 357**	**278 764**	**310 041**
1100 Of individuals	1 729	17 532	50 062	80 991	127 587	138 163	169 972	191 747	198 534	212 520
1110 On income and profits	1 729	17 532	49 888	80 991	127 587	138 163	169 972	191 747	198 534	212 520
1120 On capital gains	0	0	174	0	0	0	0	0	0	0
1200 Corporate	818	4 851	16 480	43 436	78 547	64 021	76 101	70 610	80 230	97 521
1210 On profits	818	4 851	16 315	43 436	78 547	64 021	76 101	70 610	80 230	97 521
Income tax on companies	791	4 574	15 220	42 221	76 655	62 549	74 535	68 779	78 254	95 539
Dividend and interest taxes	17	161	899	846	1 892	1 472	1 566	1 831	1 976	1 982
Other withholding taxes	0	116	196	369	0	0	0	0	0	0
1220 On capital gains	0	0	165	0	0	0	0	0	0	0
1300 Unallocable between 1100 and 1200	0	0	0	0	0	0	0	0	0	0
2000 Social security contributions	**0**	**0**	**0**	**0**	**0**	**0**	**0**	**0**	**0**	**0**
2100 Employees	0	0	0	0	0	0	0	0	0	0
2110 On a payroll basis	..	..	..	..	..	..	..	..	..	..
2120 On an income tax basis	..	..	..	..	..	..	..	..	..	..
2200 Employers	0	0	0	0	0	0	0	0	0	0
2210 On a payroll basis	..	..	..	..	..	..	..	..	..	..
2220 On an income tax basis	..	..	..	..	..	..	..	..	..	..
2300 Self-employed or non-employed	0	0	0	0	0	0	0	0	0	0
2310 On a payroll basis	..	..	..	..	..	..	..	..	..	..
2320 On an income tax basis	..	..	..	..	..	..	..	..	..	..
2400 Unallocable between 2100, 2200 and 2300	0	0	0	0	0	0	0	0	0	0
2410 On a payroll basis	..	..	..	..	..	..	..	..	..	..
2420 On an income tax basis	..	..	..	..	..	..	..	..	..	..
3000 Taxes on payroll and workforce	**157**	**1 988**	**7 115**	**9 624**	**16 407**	**18 492**	**22 210**	**23 354**	**23 799**	**25 520**
4000 Taxes on property	**576**	**3 105**	**10 427**	**18 825**	**31 156**	**33 526**	**40 963**	**49 641**	**52 585**	**54 533**
4100 Recurrent taxes on immovable property	341	1 886	6 148	9 067	15 615	19 907	23 603	27 093	29 232	30 344
4110 Households	..	..	..	..	..	..	..	..	..	..
4120 Others	..	..	..	..	..	..	..	..	..	..
4200 Recurrent taxes on net wealth	0	0	0	0	0	0	0	0	0	0
4210 Individual	..	..	..	..	..	..	..	..	..	..
4220 Corporate	..	..	..	..	..	..	..	..	..	..
4300 Estate, inheritance and gift taxes	137	175	0	0	0	0	0	0	0	0
4310 Estate and inheritance taxes	131	174	..	..	..	..	..	..	..	..
Estate duty central government	36	17	..	..	..	..	..	..	..	..
St. and loc. estate probate and succession	95	157	..	..	..	..	..	..	..	..
4320 Gift taxes	7	1	..	..	..	..	..	..	..	..
4400 Taxes on financial and capital transactions	98	1 044	4 279	9 758	15 541	13 619	17 360	22 548	23 353	24 189
4500 Non-recurrent taxes	0	0	0	0	0	0	0	0	0	0
4510 On net wealth	..	..	..	..	..	..	..	..	..	..
4520 Other non-recurrent taxes	..	..	..	..	..	..	..	..	..	..
4600 Other recurrent taxes on property	0	0	0	0	0	0	0	0	0	0
5000 Taxes on goods and services	**1 744**	**12 402**	**32 416**	**61 876**	**93 848**	**103 756**	**124 096**	**127 998**	**131 930**	**137 091**
5100 Taxes on production, sale, transfer, etc.	1 508	11 097	27 213	56 178	84 851	92 007	103 419	110 185	113 155	117 340
5110 General taxes	370	2 102	9 365	25 830	45 486	49 329	56 819	61 815	64 251	65 700
5111 Value added taxes	0	0	0	23 854	44 381	48 093	55 517	60 312	62 727	64 062
5112 Sales tax	370	2 102	9 365	1 976	1 105	1 236	1 302	1 503	1 524	1 638
5113 Other	0	0	0	0	0	0	0	0	0	0
5120 Taxes on specific goods and services	1 138	8 995	17 848	30 348	39 365	42 678	46 600	48 370	48 904	51 640
5121 Excise duties	781	6 183	11 975	19 768	24 357	26 689	26 472	22 541	22 773	23 673
Excises central government	752	5 834	10 359	19 019	23 526	25 803	25 648	21 625	21 895	22 763
Statutory corporate payments	0	83	378	295	231	452	343	405	335	346
Primary production charges	29	266	1 238	454	600	434	481	511	543	564
5122 Profits of fiscal monopolies	0	0	0	0	0	0	0	0	0	0
5123 Customs and import duties	271	1 799	3 319	4 606	6 070	5 828	9 280	14 046	14 196	15 690
Customs duties central government	271	1 799	3 319	4 606	6 070	5 828	9 280	14 046	14 196	15 690
5124 Taxes on exports	1	117	57	0	10	11	10	11	11	0
Customs duties on coal exports	0	85	54	..	0	0	0	0	0	0
Other	1	32	3	..	10	11	10	11	11	0
5125 Taxes on investment goods	0	0	0	0	0	0	0	0	0	0
5126 Taxes on specific services	85	896	2 497	5 974	8 928	10 150	10 838	11 772	11 924	12 277
Taxes race meetings	31	240	651	300	358	366	318	257	225	265
Poker machines	16	140	295	2 074	3 009	3 125	3 238	3 684	3 717	3 881
Lotteries	7	122	325	890	1 118	1 147	1 257	1 369	1 293	1 330
Levies on fire insurance companies	16	157	363	574	937	1 232	740	786	803	812
Other	15	237	863	2 136	3 506	4 280	5 285	5 676	5 886	5 989
5127 Other taxes on internat. trade and transactions	0	0	0	0	0	0	0	0	0	0
5128 Other taxes	0	0	0	0	0	0	0	0	0	0

	1965	1980	1990	2000	2007	2010	2013	2015	2016	2017
5130 Unallocable between 5110 and 5120	0	0	0	0	0	0	0	0	0	0
5200 Taxes on use of goods and perform activities	236	1 305	5 203	5 698	8 997	11 749	20 677	17 813	18 775	19 751
5210 Recurrent taxes	197	1 260	5 109	5 698	8 997	11 749	20 677	17 813	18 775	19 751
5211 Paid by households: motor vehicles	65	448	1 373	3 908	6 196	7 229	8 591	9 586	9 930	7 695
5212 Paid by others: motor vehicles	65	351	937	125	189	232	301	318	344	3 108
Fees on motor vehicle registry	46	312	794	0	0	0	0	0	0	1 851
Drivers licences	12	30	111	0	0	0	0	0	0	0
Stamp duty on vehicle registry	6	9	32	125	189	232	301	318	344	1 257
5213 Paid in respect of other goods	67	461	2 799	1 665	2 611	4 288	11 786	7 910	8 501	8 947
Broadcasting tv licences	37	21	125	210	288	150	157	128	0	0
Business franchise lic. tobac. fuel	0	221	2 016	227	0	0	2	1	0	1
Other taxes	2	12	33	1 129	2 321	4 136	11 603	7 760	8 478	8 923
Liquor taxes	28	206	603	97	2	1	24	22	23	24
Dog licenses	0	1	22	0	0	0	0	0	0	0
5220 Non-recurrent taxes	39	45	94	0	0	0	0	0	0	0
5300 Unallocable between 5100 and 5200	0	0	0	0	0	0	0	0	0	0
6000 Other taxes	**0**	**0**	**0**	**0**	**0**	**0**	**0**	**0**	**0**	**0**
6100 Paid solely by business	..	..	..	..	..	..	..	..	..	..
6200 Other	..	..	..	..	..	..	..	..	..	..
Non-wastable tax credits										
Non-wastable tax credits against 1110	0	0	..	195	2 585	991	323	453	429	402
Tax expenditure component	..	..	..	175	178	110	215	307	287	267
Transfer component	..	..	..	20	2 407	881	108	146	142	135
Non-wastable tax credits against 1210	..	..	..	0	4 564	5 726	7 914	8 966	8 644	9 069
Tax expenditure component	..	..	..	..	1 922	2 253	2 147	2 453	2 106	2 166
Transfer component	..	..	..	..	2 642	3 473	5 767	6 513	6 538	6 903
Total tax revenue on cash basis	**5 024**	**39 878**	**116 500**	**..**	**..**	**..**	**..**	**..**	**..**	**..**
Total tax revenue on accrual basis	**..**	**..**	**..**	**214 752**	**347 545**	**357 958**	**433 342**	**463 350**	**487 078**	**527 185**
Conciliation with National Accounts										
Additional taxes included in National Accounts	..	..	..	0	0	0	0	0	0	0
Taxes excluded from National Accounts	..	..	..	0	0	0	0	0	0	0
Difference in treatment of tax credits	..	..	..	175	2 100	2 363	2 362	2 760	2 393	2 433
Capital transfer for uncollected revenue	..	..	..	0	0	0	0	0	0	0
Voluntary social security contributions	..	..	..	0	0	0	0	0	0	0
Miscellaneous differences	..	..	..	0	0	0	0	0	0	0
National Accounts: Taxes and actual social contributions	..	..	..	214 927	349 645	360 321	435 704	466 110	489 471	529 618
Imputed social contributions	..	..	..	0	0	0	0	0	0	0
National Accounts: Taxes and all social contributions	..	..	..	214 927	349 645	360 321	435 704	466 110	489 471	529 618

.. Not available

Note: Data are on a fiscal year basis beginning 1st July.

From 1998 taxes are recorded on an accrual basis; prior to that they were on a cash basis.

Direct taxes paid by public trading enterprises are excluded from receipts.

The figures for total tax revenue do not match the published totals in Taxation Revenue Australia. The latter is based on an accrual IMF GFS methodology and there are some differences between that and the OECD equivalent.

Heading 5213 includes radio and television licenses fees, though these are usually not regarded as a tax revenue in the OECD list.

Headings for non-wastable tax credits 1110 and 1210 include the private health insurance tax offset, family benefit, baby bonus tax offsets (paid during the 2003-04 budget year), film tax offset, and research and development tax offsets. The estimation of non-wastable credits into the expenditure and transfer components is in accordance with the OECD guidelines on the treatment and the data for this memorandum item has been provided by the Australian Taxation Office.

Source: Australian Bureau of Statistics.

StatLink https://doi.org/10.1787/888934056735

Table 5.2. Austria: Detailed country table, 1965-2017

Million EUR

	1965	1980	1990	2000	2007	2010	2013	2015	2016	2017
Total tax revenue	**6 210**	**29 759**	**54 040**	**90 324**	**115 146**	**121 192**	**138 099**	**148 174**	**149 312**	**154 611**
Total tax revenue exclusive of custom duties	..	..	..	**89 968**	**114 749**	**120 853**	**137 771**	**147 760**	**148 863**	**154 143**
1000 Taxes on income, profits and capital gains	**1 584**	**7 959**	**13 797**	**25 553**	**34 319**	**34 021**	**39 792**	**44 501**	**41 775**	**43 729**
1100 Of individuals	1 240	6 899	11 326	19 890	25 741	27 098	31 474	35 546	32 250	33 521
1110 On income and profits	1 240	6 899	11 326	19 890	25 741	27 098	31 474	35 546	32 250	33 521
Income tax	415	1 576	2 501	3 202	3 253	3 358	3 737	3 979	4 630	4 502
Special income tax	0	0	0	0	0	0	0	0	0	0
Wage tax	417	4 626	7 823	15 630	20 607	21 783	25 669	28 429	25 435	26 459
Tax on industry and trade	196	402	454	7	0	0	0	0	0	0
Tax on capital yields	2	14	46	354	970	938	981	1 979	963	1 305
Contribution to chambers	60	279	501	697	910	1 018	1 087	1 159	1 222	1 254
Water supply fund	151	0	0	0	0	0	0	0	0	0
Contribution emergency fund	0	0	0	0	0	0	0	0	0	0
1120 On capital gains	0	0	0	0	0	0	0	0	0	0
1200 Corporate	334	1 049	1 930	4 157	6 622	5 519	6 963	7 659	8 388	9 117
1210 On profits	334	1 049	1 930	4 157	6 622	5 519	6 963	7 659	8 388	9 117
Corporation tax	195	698	998	3 865	6 094	4 978	6 377	6 752	7 812	8 438
Tax on industry and trade	83	254	624	10	0	1	0	0	0	0
Special tax on income	0	0	0	0	0	0	0	0	0	0
Tax on capital yields	5	33	108	118	346	347	370	684	344	447
Water supply fund	35	0	0	0	0	0	0	0	0	0
Contribution emergency fund	0	0	0	0	0	0	0	0	0	0
Contribution to chambers	14	58	200	164	182	193	216	224	232	232
Directors tax	2	6	0	0	0	0	0	0	0	0
1220 On capital gains	0	0	0	0	0	0	0	0	0	0
1300 Unallocable between 1100 and 1200	10	12	540	1 506	1 956	1 405	1 354	1 295	1 137	1 091
Fines related to tax offences	10	12	18	33	77	99	73	70	66	77
Tax on interest	0	0	522	1 473	1 879	1 305	1 282	1 225	1 071	1 014
2000 Social security contributions	**1 548**	**9 200**	**17 763**	**30 510**	**38 453**	**41 423**	**46 845**	**49 867**	**51 827**	**53 917**
2100 Employees	686	3 792	7 512	12 477	15 612	16 846	18 931	20 115	20 919	21 718
2110 On a payroll basis	..	..	..	12 477	15 612	16 846	18 931	20 115	20 919	21 718
Health insurance contributions	..	..	..	2 606	3 326	3 675	4 082	4 347	4 531	4 733
Pension insurance contributions	..	..	..	6 410	8 274	8 986	10 183	10 896	11 378	11 865
Pension contributions, civil servants	..	..	..	1 489	1 579	1 625	1 672	1 629	1 636	1 596
Unemployment insurance contributions	..	..	..	1 854	2 284	2 385	2 803	3 040	3 167	3 307
Health insurance contributions, local government employees	..	..	..	100	130	156	169	181	185	191
Special unemployment insurance contributions	..	..	..	17	19	20	22	23	23	25
2120 On an income tax basis	..	..	..	0	0	0	0	0	0	0
2200 Employers	721	4 563	8 768	14 651	18 091	19 421	21 922	23 281	24 275	25 286
2210 On a payroll basis	..	..	..	14 651	18 091	19 421	21 922	23 281	24 275	25 286
Health insurance contributions	..	..	..	2 667	3 395	3 669	4 075	4 339	4 523	4 724
Pension insurance contributions	..	..	..	7 888	10 214	11 144	12 642	13 549	14 154	14 764
Pension contributions, civil servants	..	..	..	438	376	361	297	298	296	276
Accident insurance contributions	..	..	..	952	1 157	1 254	1 409	1 394	1 446	1 498
Unemployment insurance contributions	..	..	..	1 854	2 284	2 385	2 803	3 040	3 167	3 307
Health insurance contributions, local government employees	..	..	..	101	141	157	170	181	185	192
Contributions to sickness benefit fund	..	..	..	341	0	0	0	0	0	0
Special pension contributions, nightshift workers	..	..	..	11	18	15	31	38	37	38
Contributions to insolvency fund	..	..	..	381	488	416	473	419	342	355
Special unemployment insurance contributions construction workers	..	..	..	17	19	20	22	23	126	132
2220 On an income tax basis	..	..	..	0	0	0	0	0	0	0
2300 Self-employed or non-employed	141	845	1 482	3 382	4 750	5 155	5 993	6 470	6 633	6 913
2310 On a payroll basis	..	..	..	3 382	4 750	5 155	5 993	6 470	6 633	6 913
Health insurance contributions	..	..	..	1 971	2 724	3 090	3 441	3 664	3 721	3 857
Pension insurance contributions	..	..	..	1 117	1 527	1 524	1 973	2 210	2 321	2 451
Pension contributions, civil servants (retired)	..	..	..	116	274	297	315	317	314	311
Accident insurance contributions	..	..	..	77	85	88	95	98	92	103
Health insurance contributions, local government employees	..	..	..	101	140	156	169	181	185	191
2320 On an income tax basis	..	..	..	0	0	0	0	0	0	0
2400 Unallocable between 2100, 2200 and 2300	0	0	0	0	0	0	0	0	0	0
2410 On a payroll basis	..	..	..	..	..	..	..	..	..	..
2420 On an income tax basis	..	..	..	..	..	..	..	..	..	..

	1965	1980	1990	2000	2007	2010	2013	2015	2016	2017
3000 Taxes on payroll and workforce	**472**	**2 097**	**3 259**	**5 788**	**7 266**	**8 359**	**9 489**	**10 040**	**10 401**	**10 238**
Emplr. contr. equaliz. of family.burdens	318	1 397	2 147	3 140	3 915	4 762	5 319	5 623	5 821	5 487
Tax on sum of wages	82	375	669	1 735	2 238	2 402	2 742	2 911	3 015	3 126
Promotion residential buildings	44	217	389	595	754	811	915	965	1 003	1 068
Tax on employment (Vienna undergr.)	0	20	21	21	22	22	67	65	67	66
Special levy for households allowances	26	80	0	0	0	0	0	0	0	0
Disabled persons equalization levy	2	8	34	54	83	91	138	148	157	154
Contributions to chambers	0	0	0	242	253	271	308	327	337	337
4000 Taxes on property	**246**	**858**	**1 473**	**1 206**	**1 572**	**1 555**	**2 341**	**1 965**	**1 953**	**1 942**
4100 Recurrent taxes on immovable property	92	231	355	526	626	682	736	761	771	805
4110 Households	47	66	84	87	92	93	105	107	107	125
Duty on farms	9	15	20	20	20	20	29	30	30	37
Farm contr. equaliz. of family burdens	5	6	6	6	6	6	6	6	6	8
Farm contribution to chambers	14	23	32	32	39	40	43	44	44	52
Contr. residential buildings reconstruction	4	0	0	0	0	0	0	0	0	0
Land tax A	16	22	25	28	26	26	26	26	26	28
4120 Others	45	165	271	440	534	589	631	654	664	681
Tax on vacant plots	1	4	5	5	5	6	6	6	6	6
Land tax B	44	161	266	435	529	583	625	649	658	675
4200 Recurrent taxes on net wealth	103	401	642	1	0	0	0	0	0	0
4210 Individual	37	140	189	1	..	..	..	..	..	..
Capital tax	25	109	189	1	..	..	..	..	..	..
Contribution emergency fund	0	0	0	0	..	..	..	..	..	..
Tax on industry and trade	10	26	0	0	..	..	..	..	..	..
Contribution to chambers	2	6	0	0	..	..	..	..	..	..
4220 Corporate	66	260	453	0	..	..	..	..	..	..
Capital tax	24	139	322	0	..	..	..	..	..	..
Capital death duty	20	53	131	0	..	..	..	..	..	..
Contribution emergency fund	0	0	0	0	..	..	..	..	..	..
Tax on industry and trade	19	56	0	0	..	..	..	..	..	..
Contribution to chambers	3	13	0	0	..	..	..	..	..	..
4300 Estate, inheritance and gift taxes	16	50	77	111	155	35	19	12	2	1
4310 Estate and inheritance taxes	..	..	..	..	..	..	..	..	..	..
4320 Gift taxes	..	..	..	..	..	..	..	..	..	..
4400 Taxes on financial and capital transactions	35	176	399	568	791	828	858	1 116	1 127	1 110
Land transfer tax	30	150	251	452	644	727	790	1 014	1 118	1 105
Capital transfer tax	5	27	148	115	147	102	67	102	9	5
4500 Non-recurrent taxes	0	0	0	0	0	10	728	76	52	27
4510 On net wealth	..	..	..	..	..	0	717	4	30	10
Withholding tax	..	..	..	..	..	..	717	4	30	10
4520 Other non-recurrent taxes	..	..	..	..	..	10	11	72	22	16
Foundation tax	..	..	..	..	..	10	11	72	22	16
4600 Other recurrent taxes on property	0	0	0	0	0	0	0	0	0	0
5000 Taxes on goods and services	**2 321**	**9 379**	**17 034**	**26 140**	**32 211**	**34 400**	**38 373**	**40 649**	**42 157**	**43 521**
5100 Taxes on production, sale, transfer, etc.	2 275	9 006	16 169	24 260	29 783	31 774	35 393	37 218	38 660	39 790
5110 General taxes	1 160	5 984	11 229	16 857	20 941	22 711	24 920	26 282	27 308	28 312
5111 Value added taxes	0	5 984	11 229	16 857	20 941	22 711	24 920	26 282	27 308	28 312
5112 Sales tax	0	0	0	0	0	0	0	0	0	0
5113 Other	1 160	0	0	0	0	0	0	0	0	0
Turnover tax	664	..	..	..	..	..	..	..	..	..
Additional federal levy-turnover	332	..	..	..	..	..	..	..	..	..
Additional lieu invoice stp.	164	..	..	..	..	..	..	..	..	..
5120 Taxes on specific goods and services	1 115	2 996	4 873	7 365	8 839	9 060	10 472	10 933	11 348	11 474

	1965	1980	1990	2000	2007	2010	2013	2015	2016	2017
5121 Excise duties	610	2 219	3 290	5 484	6 760	6 921	7 598	7 749	7 920	8 272
Tax on beer	39	44	56	161	200	198	193	189	196	192
Tax on wine	7	0	0	0	0	0	0	0	0	0
Tax on sparkling wine	1	7	25	25	1	1	1	19	23	23
Tax on tobacco	188	519	820	1 197	1 446	1 502	1 664	1 782	1 829	1 896
Tax on mineral oils	50	136	1 426	2 726	3 689	3 854	4 173	4 218	4 338	4 551
Additional federal levy mineral oils	202	876	0	0	0	0	0	0	0	0
Special duty alcoholic drinks	0	142	193	0	0	0	0	0	0	0
Special duty vehicles	0	0	0	0	0	0	0	0	0	0
Duty on starch products	0	4	13	0	0	0	0	0	0	0
Beverage tax	46	216	364	178	3	-1	-1	0	0	0
Other receipts-Market Organisation Act	26	35	9	0	1	0	0	0	0	0
Transport equality levy	0	5	1	0	0	0	0	0	0	0
Market Organisation Act - milk	35	177	192	0	0	0	0	0	0	0
Market Organisation Act - livestock	0	0	0	0	0	0	0	0	0	0
Market Organisation Act - grain	16	23	142	0	0	0	0	0	0	0
Duty promotion milk distrib.	0	34	13	0	0	0	0	0	0	0
Special tax on mineral oils	0	0	37	0	0	0	0	0	0	0
Duty on vehicles (fuel consumption)	0	0	0	433	457	453	455	395	429	473
Agricultural fund	0	0	0	23	16	18	18	17	17	17
Tax on energy	0	0	0	562	764	726	886	931	899	926
Social contributions to the artists' fund	0	0	0	0	11	6	7	13	8	7
Duty on exceeding milk-quota	0	0	0	36	24	6	26	11	0	0
Car registration taxes	0	0	0	143	148	158	175	174	182	188
5122 Profits of fiscal monopolies	37	57	52	130	122	129	324	328	390	384
Duty on spirits	5	14	17	130	122	129	130	120	142	142
Federal monopolies salt	1	0	0	0	0	0	0	0	0	0
Federal monopolies spirits	30	43	35	0	0	0	0	0	0	0
Federal monopolies gambling	0	0	0	0	0	0	194	208	248	242
5123 Customs and import duties	332	354	677	-5	-8	0	0	0	0	0
Customs duties	310	237	418	-5	-8	0	..	..	..	..
Other import duties	0	21	61	0	0	0	..	..	..	..
Contribution promote foreign trade	10	63	171	0	0	0	..	..	..	..
Import equalization duties	12	33	27	0	0	0	..	..	..	..
5124 Taxes on exports	8	36	1	0	0	0	0	0	0	0
Contribution to promote foreign trade	8	36	1	..	..	..	..	..	..	..
5125 Taxes on investment goods	0	33	0	0	0	0	0	0	0	0
5126 Taxes on specific services	129	297	854	1 720	1 967	2 005	2 545	2 852	3 033	2 814
Insurance tax	25	135	384	745	993	1 017	1 056	1 122	1 147	1 128
Transport tax	63	0	0	0	0	0	0	0	0	0
Duty on casinos	2	28	64	105	71	55	45	70	89	99
Fire protection tax	5	24	50	45	54	56	57	61	62	62
Advertisement tax	7	31	65	62	0	0	0	0	0	0
Entertainment tax	2	2	2	5	8	9	21	18	6	1
Tax on tourism	8	43	71	103	142	171	182	186	220	233
Amusement tax	13	17	51	73	94	107	84	30	23	18
Announcement tax	3	18	40	81	0	1	0	0	0	0
Tax on interest yields	0	0	0	0	0	0	0	0	0	0
Tax on gambling stakes - licences	0	0	116	197	202	221	251	254	253	250
Tax on advertisement	0	0	0	33	108	110	110	107	107	110
Levy on dangerous waste	0	0	10	71	72	51	53	56	58	62
Duty for airways security	0	0	0	28	56	30	0	0	0	0
Tax on gambling stakes - gains	0	0	0	171	166	176	0	0	0	0
Flight Charge	0	0	0	0	0	0	98	109	109	115
Financial Institutions Stability Fees	0	0	0	0	0	0	588	838	959	734
5127 Other taxes on internat. trade and transactions	0	0	0	0	0	0	0	0	0	0
5128 Other taxes	0	0	0	34	-3	4	4	4	4	4
Levy on sugar	..	..	..	34	-3	4	4	4	4	4
5130 Unallocable between 5110 and 5120	0	26	66	38	3	4	2	4	5	4
Fines related to tax offenses	..	26	66	38	3	4	2	4	5	4
5200 Taxes on use of goods and perform activities	46	373	865	1 881	2 429	2 626	2 980	3 431	3 497	3 731
5210 Recurrent taxes	38	335	757	1 733	2 253	2 416	2 715	3 124	3 208	3 412
5211 Paid by households: motor vehicles	22	156	366	811	1 173	1 293	1 482	1 814	1 870	1 986
5212 Paid by others: motor vehicles	13	41	97	298	370	334	352	421	432	460
5213 Paid in respect of other goods	3	138	294	624	710	789	881	890	905	966
Hunting and fishing duties	1	4	7	10	10	10	19	22	22	21
Dog tax	1	4	6	8	10	11	17	18	19	20
Contribution to promotion of arts	1	3	8	71	120	132	147	143	156	183
Tax on radio and tv - licenses	0	15	46	450	571	636	698	708	709	742
Road transport duty	0	112	226	84	0	0	0	0	0	0
5220 Non-recurrent taxes	8	38	108	147	175	210	265	307	289	319
Certain user fees; taxes on emission of noxious	8	38	108	147	175	210	265	307	289	319

	1965	1980	1990	2000	2007	2010	2013	2015	2016	2017
gases										
5300 Unallocable between 5100 and 5200	0	0	0	0	0	0	0	0	0	0
6000 Other taxes	**38**	**266**	**714**	**770**	**928**	**1 095**	**931**	**737**	**750**	**796**
Tax on financial institutions	0	0	123	-3	0	0	0	0	0	0
Administration duties	4	17	32	278	366	521	517	302	304	315
Stamp fees	7	46	76	135	92	84	27	32	35	37
Contributions of interested persons	0	0	130	0	0	0	0	0	0	0
Parking duty	0	0	6	0	0	0	0	0	0	0
Contrbutions to students' associations	0	0	0	4	8	11	12	11	12	12
Duty on contribution to political parties	0	0	0	0	-1	1	0	0	1	0
Other fees, taxes on production n.e.c.	0	0	0	272	346	353	227	252	253	279
Embossing fee	0	0	0	0	1	1	1	1	1	1
Other taxes	28	202	347	82	115	124	145	139	144	150
Compensation levy according to the Vienna Tree Protection Act	..	..	..	1	1	2	1	0	2	3
6100 Paid solely by business	..	..	..	..	..	..	..	..	..	..
6200 Other	..	..	..	..	..	..	..	..	..	..
Custom duties collected for the EU	**..**	**..**	**..**	**356**	**397**	**339**	**328**	**415**	**449**	**468**
Non-wastable tax credits										
Non-wastable tax credits against 1110	..	..	..	650	650	650	570	540	540	330
Tax expenditure component	..	..	..	590	450	422	341	295	224	228
Transfer component	..	..	..	60	200	228	229	245	316	102
Non-wastable tax credits against 1210	..	..	..	0	0	0	0	0	0	0
Tax expenditure component	..	..	..	..	..	..	..	..	..	..
Transfer component	..	..	..	..	..	..	..	..	..	..
Total tax revenue on cash basis	**6 210**	**29 759**	**54 040**	**90 299**	**115 045**	**120 735**	**137 970**	**147 741**	**149 241**	**154 388**
Total tax revenue on accrual basis	**..**	**..**	**..**	**90 324**	**115 146**	**121 192**	**138 099**	**148 174**	**149 312**	**154 611**
Conciliation with National Accounts										
Additional taxes included in National Accounts	..	..	..	0	0	0	0	0	0	0
Taxes excluded from National Accounts	..	..	..	0	0	0	0	0	0	0
Difference in treatment of tax credits	..	..	..	590	450	422	341	295	224	228
Capital transfer for uncollected revenue	..	..	..	0	0	0	0	0	0	0
Voluntary social security contributions	..	..	..	206	256	339	299	321	321	318
Miscellaneous differences	..	..	..	0	0	0	0	0	0	0
National Accounts: Taxes and actual social contributions	..	..	..	91 120	115 853	121 953	138 739	148 790	149 856	155 157
Imputed social contributions	..	..	..	2 485	2 177	2 106	1 972	1 925	1 865	1 807
National Accounts: Taxes and all social contributions	..	..	..	93 605	118 030	124 060	140 711	150 715	151 722	156 964

.. Not available

Note: Year ending 31st December.

From 1995 data are on accrual basis.

Following national practice, one-third of the revenues from stamp fees (heading 6000) and fifty percent of the revenues from administration duties (heading 6000) are treated as tax revenues, the remainder being treated as non-tax revenue.

From 1988 onwards promoting residential building is being mainly financed by capital transfers from the Federal Government to the Länder. For the years 1985 to 1987 legally fixed shares of some taxes have been transmitted automatically from Federal Government to the Länder for this purpose and these funds have been classified as tax receipts of the Länder in those years. From 1988, they are classified as Federal Government tax revenues. This break in the time series (1987/1988) affects only the shares of the different subsectors and not total tax revenues.

From 1998 contributions of interested persons and parking duties are classified as non-tax revenues (sales) and no longer reported under heading 6000.

Source: Statistics Austria.

StatLink https://doi.org/10.1787/888934056754

Table 5.3. Belgium: Detailed country table, 1965-2017

Million EUR

	1965	1980	1990	2000	2007	2010	2013	2015	2016	2017
Total tax revenue	**6 421**	**37 443**	**70 408**	**112 423**	**147 262**	**155 610**	**176 969**	**183 864**	**186 323**	**195 270**
Total tax revenue exclusive of custom duties	..	..	..	**111 463**	**145 874**	**154 377**	**175 784**	**182 498**	**184 748**	**193 618**
1000 Taxes on income, profits and capital gains	**1 774**	**15 379**	**25 983**	**43 421**	**52 801**	**53 243**	**62 739**	**65 573**	**66 249**	**71 319**
1100 Of individuals	1 317	13 626	22 538	35 260	40 967	43 956	50 471	51 879	51 565	53 130
1110 On income and profits	1 317	13 626	22 538	35 260	40 967	43 956	50 471	51 879	51 565	53 130
Immovable income withholding tax	148	532	1 053	1 857	0	0	0	0	0	0
Movable income withholding tax	119	1 062	3 014	1 737	2 351	2 426	4 314	4 104	3 993	3 741
Earned income withholding tax	740	9 119	15 422	27 738	35 969	39 758	44 639	45 609	45 273	46 878
Advance payments PIT	125	1 776	2 144	1 959	1 747	1 611	1 508	1 547	1 513	1 591
Non residents tax	0	-2	4	585	792	810	841	976	980	928
Assessments PIT	183	1 128	878	774	-915	-1 697	-1 988	-1 512	-1 421	-1 261
Special social contributions	0	0	19	602	957	1 032	1 117	1 106	1 198	1 209
Other income taxes	0	12	2	8	65	17	41	48	29	45
1120 On capital gains	0	0	0	0	0	0	0	0	0	0
1200 Corporate	397	1 744	3 405	8 083	11 749	9 249	12 218	13 643	14 620	18 127
1210 On profits	397	1 744	3 405	8 083	11 749	9 249	12 218	13 643	14 620	18 127
Immovable income withholding tax (corporate)	33	0	0	0	0	0	0	0	0	0
Movable income withholding tax (corporate)	41	367	1 206	544	686	315	478	466	407	319
Advance payments (corporate)	262	1 273	2 735	7 112	9 733	7 691	7 930	8 538	8 594	11 586
Assessments (corporate)	60	79	-553	404	1 270	1 196	3 662	4 466	5 571	5 936
Non residents tax (corporate)	0	-6	18	17	41	43	138	154	38	270
Other income taxes (corporate)	0	32	-2	5	19	4	10	19	9	15
1220 On capital gains	0	0	0	0	0	0	0	0	0	0
1300 Unallocable between 1100 and 1200	61	9	40	78	85	38	51	51	64	63
Former income taxes	51	0	0	0	0	0	0	0	0	0
Penalties	3	0	0	0	0	0	0	0	0	0
Other	7	9	40	78	85	38	51	51	64	63
2000 Social security contributions	**2 018**	**10 798**	**23 386**	**34 636**	**45 659**	**50 447**	**56 355**	**58 628**	**57 931**	**59 594**
2100 Employees	569	3 130	7 152	10 936	13 851	14 998	16 481	16 962	17 110	17 742
2110 On a payroll basis	..	3 130	7 152	10 936	13 851	14 998	16 481	16 962	17 110	17 742
On gross wages	..	3 130	7 062	10 936	13 851	14 998	16 481	16 962	17 110	17 742
On social benefits	..	0	89	0	0	0	0	0	0	0
2120 On an income tax basis	..	0	0	0	0	0	0	0	0	0
2200 Employers	1 320	6 791	14 689	20 794	27 943	30 811	34 807	36 207	35 152	36 021
2210 On a payroll basis	..	6 791	14 689	20 794	27 943	30 811	34 807	36 207	35 152	36 021
Contributions by government	..	1 059	1 769	3 105	4 493	5 261	6 535	7 437	7 473	7 774
Contributions by other sectors	..	5 732	12 920	17 689	23 450	25 550	28 273	28 769	27 679	28 247
2220 On an income tax basis	..	0	0	0	0	0	0	0	0	0
2300 Self-employed or non-employed	129	877	1 546	2 906	3 866	4 637	5 066	5 459	5 669	5 831
Self-employed	..	803	1 230	2 053	2 678	3 342	3 703	3 975	4 071	4 153
Unemployed	..	0	0	0	0	0	0	0	0	0
Retired	..	29	198	709	1 012	1 134	1 254	1 371	1 483	1 568
Other	..	45	118	144	176	161	109	113	115	110
2310 On a payroll basis	..	877	1 546	2 906	3 866	4 637	5 066	5 459	5 669	5 831
2320 On an income tax basis	..	0	0	0	0	0	0	0	0	0
2400 Unallocable between 2100, 2200 and 2300	0	0	0	0	0	0	0	0	0	0
2410 On a payroll basis	..	..	..	..	..	..	..	..	..	..
2420 On an income tax basis	..	..	..	..	..	..	..	..	..	..
3000 Taxes on payroll and workforce	**0**	**0**	**0**	**0**	**6**	**7**	**8**	**8**	**8**	**8**
Levy on public mandates	..	..	..	..	6	7	8	8	8	8
4000 Taxes on property	**240**	**1 161**	**2 679**	**5 282**	**10 550**	**11 252**	**13 805**	**14 407**	**14 856**	**15 394**
4100 Recurrent taxes on immovable property	2	210	599	1 164	4 146	4 632	5 187	5 433	5 635	5 754
4110 Households	0	26	63	102	2 779	3 115	3 478	3 651	3 784	3 876
4120 Others	2	184	536	1 063	1 367	1 517	1 710	1 782	1 851	1 879
Tax on non profit institutions	2	7	17	41	32	33	38	41	43	45
Immovable income withholding tax (corporate)	0	177	519	929	1 269	1 416	1 584	1 651	1 715	1 746
Regional tax (Brussels)	0	0	0	94	66	68	88	90	93	89
4200 Recurrent taxes on net wealth	0	0	0	92	253	237	451	661	968	929
4210 Individual	..	..	..	0	0	0	0	0	0	0
4220 Corporate	..	..	..	92	253	237	451	661	968	929
4300 Estate, inheritance and gift taxes	75	309	504	1 101	2 053	2 269	3 096	3 002	2 932	3 131
4310 Estate and inheritance taxes	69	281	475	1 042	1 702	1 939	2 634	2 510	2 365	2 526
4320 Gift taxes	6	29	29	59	351	330	463	492	567	604

	1965	1980	1990	2000	2007	2010	2013	2015	2016	2017
4400 Taxes on financial and capital transactions	163	633	1 478	2 669	3 704	3 493	3 886	4 358	4 464	4 800
Registration duties	153	527	1 213	1 967	3 325	3 210	3 542	3 899	4 065	4 342
Mortgage duties	2	10	29	37	76	75	72	93	89	83
Court duties	2	8	29	38	31	34	37	41	47	40
Economic expansion fund	0	0	0	0	0	0	0	0	0	0
Tax on stock exchange transactions	4	31	92	386	234	134	193	287	219	296
Tax on stock exchange listings	2	4	21	0	0	0	0	0	0	0
Tax on bearer securities	0	0	0	79	3	0	6	0	0	0
Stamp duties	0	53	94	161	35	40	36	38	44	40
4500 Non-recurrent taxes	0	0	0	74	163	328	877	635	415	487
4510 On net wealth	..	..	..	0	0	0	0	0	0	0
4520 Other non-recurrent taxes	..	..	..	74	163	328	877	635	415	487
Tax on long term savings	..	..	..	74	163	194	207	413	382	369
Voluntary disclosure tax	..	..	..	0	0	0	0	0	0	0
Voluntary disclosure tax (Diamond)	..	..	..	0	0	0	0	0	0	0
Voluntary disclosure tax (bis)	..	..	..	0	0	134	614	145	8	12
Voluntary disclosure tax (ter)	..	..	..	0	0	0	54	78	24	106
Special contribution on credit associations	..	..	..	0	0	0	2	0	0	0
4600 Other recurrent taxes on property	0	8	99	182	232	294	309	318	443	293
Levy for fighting the non-use of an electric power production site by a producer	..	..	..	..	..	..	..	0	120	0
Transfer to the Fund for Industrial Accidents of recognized private insurance corporations	..	..	..	..	..	..	..	318	323	293
Tax on securities accounts	..	..	..	..	..	..	..	0	0	0
5000 Taxes on goods and services	**2 386**	**10 105**	**18 360**	**28 125**	**36 798**	**39 393**	**42 830**	**43 843**	**45 703**	**47 303**
5100 Taxes on production, sale, transfer, etc.	2 187	9 606	17 387	26 021	34 427	37 004	40 400	41 351	43 211	44 748
5110 General taxes	1 355	6 321	11 570	18 240	24 135	25 515	27 491	27 796	28 956	29 957
5111 Value added taxes	0	6 321	11 547	18 114	23 864	25 262	27 250	27 578	28 722	29 763
VAT	..	6 293	11 491	18 114	23 864	25 262	27 250	27 578	28 722	29 763
Vehicle immatriculation tax	..	28	56	0	0	0	0	0	0	0
5112 Sales tax	0	0	23	126	271	253	241	219	235	194
5113 Other	1 355	0	0	0	0	0	0	0	0	0
Taxes assimilated to stamp duties	1 355	..	..	..	..	..	..	..	..	..
5120 Taxes on specific goods and services	832	3 285	5 818	7 781	10 292	11 489	12 910	13 555	14 254	14 791
5121 Excise duties	531	1 997	3 478	5 690	7 367	7 783	8 036	8 649	9 442	9 906
Mineral oil	278	1 109	2 017	3 392	3 891	4 148	4 072	4 556	4 963	5 195
Liquified gases and benzol	0	4	0	0	0	0	0	0	0	0
Tobacco	132	501	868	1 342	1 821	1 885	2 197	2 262	2 306	2 245
Spirits	23	123	191	206	225	235	272	318	323	320
Consumption tax on alcohol and spirits	26	54	0	0	0	0	0	0	0	0
Fermented sparkling beverages	1	7	11	24	39	57	77	92	104	103
Fermented fruit beverages	18	57	88	101	115	116	132	148	174	172
Beer	38	93	170	208	191	188	183	194	202	201
Non-alcoholic beverages	10	44	113	148	49	54	58	56	100	103
Coffee, sugar and syrup	5	5	22	13	12	13	15	14	14	15
Levy on energy	0	0	0	193	341	383	337	343	340	340
Intermediate alcoholic products	0	0	0	32	28	26	26	26	28	28
Inspection fee on domestic fuel oil	0	0	0	29	43	51	41	36	33	32
Ecotax	0	0	0	2	1	0	1	0	1	0
Levy on packaging	0	0	0	0	296	320	332	336	338	341
Federal contribution on electricity and natural gas	0	0	0	0	311	292	281	269	518	812
Environmental charge	0	0	0	0	5	15	14	1	0	0
5122 Profits of fiscal monopolies	0	0	0	0	0	0	0	0	0	0
5123 Customs and import duties	272	627	809	0	0	0	0	0	0	0
Import duties	206	0	0	..	..	..	..	..	..	..
Levies on agricultural products	63	0	0	..	..	..	..	..	..	..
ECSC levies	2	0	0	..	..	..	..	..	..	..
EU levies, import duties	0	383	716	..	..	..	..	..	..	..
EU levies on agricultural products	0	244	93	..	..	..	..	..	..	..
5124 Taxes on exports	0	1	0	0	0	0	0	0	0	0
5125 Taxes on investment goods	0	0	0	0	0	0	0	0	0	0
5126 Taxes on specific services	29	452	937	1 365	2 044	2 455	3 137	3 210	3 164	3 170
Gambling and betting tax	9	47	51	45	64	77	73	80	90	94
Insurance levy	19	404	885	1 282	1 930	2 123	2 285	2 307	2 353	2 382
Bill-posting tax	0	0	1	1	3	3	3	3	2	3
Deposit insurance	0	0	0	36	48	252	609	441	441	440
Resolution fund	0	0	0	0	0	0	167	380	278	252
5127 Other taxes on internat. trade and transactions	0	0	0	0	0	0	0	0	0	0
5128 Other taxes	0	208	593	726	881	1 252	1 737	1 695	1 649	1 715
5130 Unallocable between 5110 and 5120	0	0	0	0	0	0	0	0	0	0
5200 Taxes on use of goods and perform activities	199	496	966	2 096	2 363	2 384	2 420	2 482	2 482	2 540

	1965	1980	1990	2000	2007	2010	2013	2015	2016	2017
5210 Recurrent taxes	199	496	966	1 887	2 032	2 005	2 023	2 032	1 959	1 993
Traffic tax	100	368	712	1 413	1 693	1 702	1 830	1 851	1 767	1 802
5211 Paid by households: motor vehicles	0	204	458	889	1 051	1 054	1 148	1 163	1 169	1 210
5212 Paid by others: motor vehicles	0	164	254	525	642	648	683	689	598	591
5213 Paid in respect of other goods	99	127	254	474	338	303	193	181	192	191
Tax on entertainment devices	6	20	20	71	56	58	74	56	52	54
Tax on pubs	1	5	24	18	0	0	0	0	0	0
Hunting tax	2	0	0	0	0	0	0	0	0	0
Local taxes	90	15	19	38	99	112	10	22	22	22
Radio and television licence fees	0	87	191	347	184	133	108	103	118	115
5220 Non-recurrent taxes	0	0	0	209	332	379	397	451	523	548
Vehicle registration tax	..	..	..	209	332	379	360	349	388	435
Vehicle registration tax (households)	..	..	..	139	221	252	240	233	259	290
Vehicle registration tax (others)	..	..	..	70	111	126	120	116	130	145
Emission permits	..	..	..	0	0	0	36	101	135	112
5300 Unallocable between 5100 and 5200	0	3	7	7	7	6	10	9	11	15
6000 Other taxes	**2**	**0**	**0**	**0**	**61**	**36**	**46**	**40**	**0**	**0**
6100 Paid solely by business	0	..	..	..	0	0	0	0	0	0
6200 Other	2	..	..	..	61	36	46	40	0	0
Fines and interest	2	..	..	..	0	0	0	0	0	0
Custom duties collected for the EU	**..**	**..**	**..**	**960**	**1 388**	**1 234**	**1 185**	**1 367**	**1 575**	**1 652**
Non-wastable tax credits										
Non-wastable tax credits against 1110	..	..	..	..	348	1 037	1 492	830	761	852
Tax expenditure component	..	..	..	..	78	588	1 077	537	460	542
Transfer component	..	..	..	..	270	449	415	293	301	310
Non-wastable tax credits against 1210	..	..	..	..	0	0	0	0	0	0
Tax expenditure component	..	..	..	..	..	..	..	..	..	..
Transfer component	..	..	..	..	..	..	..	..	..	..
Total tax revenue on cash basis	**6 421**	**37 438**	**70 268**	**..**	**..**	**..**	**..**	**..**	**..**	**..**
Total tax revenue on accrual basis	**..**	**37 443**	**70 408**	**112 423**	**147 262**	**155 610**	**176 969**	**183 864**	**186 323**	**195 270**
Conciliation with National Accounts										
Additional taxes included in National Accounts	..	107	447	1 300	1 387	1 646	1 578	1 657	1 786	1 807
National lottery profits	..	107	262	279	225	243	215	206	201	185
Water levies	..	0	66	378	119	137	122	104	136	119
Sanitel levy	..	0	0	14	13	15	14	6	7	12
Levy on industrial waste	..	0	27	74	68	54	46	55	84	79
Levy on manure	..	0	0	11	11	5	5	1	3	2
Levy on household waste	..	0	0	20	0	0	0	0	0	0
Earned income withholding tax (EU)	..	0	93	174	270	345	336	370	392	408
Social contributions (EU)	..	0	0	136	250	340	330	360	381	396
Imputed social contributions (EU)	..	0	0	213	431	508	511	554	582	606
Taxes excluded from National Accounts	..	0	0	0	0	0	0	0	0	0
Deposit insurance	..	..	..	..	..	..	..	..	..	..
Difference in treatment of tax credits	..	0	0	0	78	588	1 077	537	460	542
Capital transfer for uncollected revenue	..	0	0	0	0	0	0	0	0	0
Voluntary social security contributions	..	41	52	54	55	62	74	72	72	73
Miscellaneous differences	..	0	0	0	0	0	0	0	0	0
Reallocation national levels of government	..	..	..	..	..	..	..	..	..	..
Reallocation EU	..	..	..	..	..	..	..	..	..	..
National Accounts: Taxes and actual social contributions	..	37 590	70 907	113 564	148 351	157 399	179 186	185 576	188 058	197 086
Imputed social contributions	..	1 497	2 886	5 377	7 568	8 713	10 071	9 799	10 108	10 541
National Accounts: Taxes and all social contributions	..	39 087	73 793	118 940	155 919	166 112	189 257	195 375	198 166	207 627

.. Not available

Note: Year ending 31st December. From 1970, data are on accrual basis

Source: Federal Ministry of Finance.

StatLink https://doi.org/10.1787/888934056773

Table 5.4. Canada: Detailed country table, 1965-2017

Million CAD

	1965	1980	1990	2000	2007	2010	2013	2015	2016	2017
Total tax revenue	**15 318**	**101 015**	**244 152**	**390 234**	**512 663**	**516 591**	**592 206**	**653 264**	**672 809**	**702 704**
1000 Taxes on income, profits and capital gains	**5 910**	**47 064**	**118 566**	**195 320**	**251 198**	**240 961**	**281 787**	**314 841**	**323 053**	**338 866**
1100 Of individuals	3 464	34 451	99 722	143 652	190 025	180 894	214 054	240 304	240 585	251 092
1110 On income and profits	3 464	34 451	99 722	143 652	190 025	180 894	214 054	240 304	240 585	251 092
Taxes federal government	2 635	21 231	60 252	90 694	116 395	109 341	127 655	143 315	142 511	150 989
Taxes on individuals - province	829	13 220	39 470	52 958	73 630	71 553	86 399	96 989	98 074	100 103
1120 On capital gains	0	0	0	0	0	0	0	0	0	0
1200 Corporate	2 276	11 741	17 190	47 643	54 272	54 101	62 359	67 894	75 720	80 071
1210 On profits	2 276	11 741	17 190	47 643	54 272	54 101	62 359	67 894	75 720	80 071
Taxes federal government	1 752	8 110	11 726	31 570	37 093	33 419	38 142	41 726	46 299	49 769
Taxes on corporations - province	524	3 631	5 464	16 073	17 179	20 682	24 217	26 168	29 421	30 302
1220 On capital gains	0	0	0	0	0	0	0	0	0	0
1300 Unallocable between 1100 and 1200	170	872	1 654	4 025	6 901	5 966	5 374	6 643	6 748	7 703
Non-resident withhold taxes - federal	170	872	1 654	4 025	6 901	5 966	5 374	6 643	6 748	7 703
2000 Social security contributions	**854**	**10 649**	**29 653**	**53 109**	**73 722**	**76 787**	**90 394**	**96 371**	**98 954**	**99 346**
2100 Employees	318	3 756	10 634	21 361	29 361	30 626	36 057	38 685	39 623	39 917
Canada pension plan	47	1 265	3 745	9 401	16 194	16 852	20 021	21 491	21 905	23 025
Quebec pension plan	15	431	1 108	2 897	4 124	5 450	5 815	6 293	6 539	6 991
Employment insurance	164	1 393	5 284	7 782	7 084	7 388	9 198	9 772	9 966	8 623
Hospital insurance premiums	92	667	496	1 281	1 959	937	1 023	1 128	1 213	1 278
2110 On a payroll basis	..	..	10 634	20 976	28 654	29 689	35 034	37 557	38 410	38 639
2120 On an income tax basis	..	..	0	385	707	937	1 023	1 128	1 213	1 278
2200 Employers	536	6 697	18 449	30 307	41 922	43 525	51 261	54 380	55 950	55 866
Canada pension plan	48	1 266	3 745	9 401	16 194	16 852	20 021	21 491	21 905	23 025
Quebec pension plan	15	432	1 108	2 897	4 124	5 450	5 815	6 293	6 539	6 991
Employment insurance	164	2 006	7 398	10 894	9 917	10 343	12 877	13 681	13 953	12 072
Hospital insurance premiums	92	1 270	496	897	1 252	0	0	0	0	0
Social insurance levies	217	1 723	5 702	6 218	10 434	10 881	12 548	12 914	13 554	13 778
2210 On a payroll basis	..	..	18 449	30 307	41 922	43 525	51 261	54 380	55 950	55 866
2220 On an income tax basis	..	..	0	0	0	0	0	0	0	0
2300 Self-employed or non-employed	0	196	570	1 442	2 440	2 636	3 076	3 307	3 381	3 563
Canada pension plan	..	153	478	1 200	2 096	2 181	2 591	2 781	2 835	2 979
Quebec pension plan	..	43	92	242	344	455	486	525	546	584
2310 On a payroll basis	..	196	570	1 442	2 440	2 636	3 076	3 307	3 381	3 563
2320 On an income tax basis	..	0	0	0	0	0	0	0	0	0
2400 Unallocable between 2100, 2200 and 2300	0	0	0	0	0	0	0	0	0	0
2410 On a payroll basis	..	..	..	..	..	..	..	..	..	..
2420 On an income tax basis	..	..	..	..	..	..	..	..	..	..
3000 Taxes on payroll and workforce	**0**	**0**	**5 499**	**8 013**	**10 038**	**10 760**	**12 482**	**13 256**	**13 792**	**14 331**
4000 Taxes on property	**2 186**	**9 195**	**24 467**	**37 157**	**54 507**	**63 735**	**70 451**	**77 778**	**81 178**	**84 021**
4100 Recurrent taxes on immovable property	1 830	8 315	20 189	30 242	44 567	51 702	57 769	62 651	65 191	66 839
On property provincial government	11	133	1 645	3 078	3 164	4 476	4 946	5 410	5 778	5 838
Personal property local government	17	0	18 544	27 165	41 403	47 226	52 823	57 241	59 413	61 001
Real property local government	1 802	8 182	0	0	0	0	0	0	0	0
4110 Households	..	..	..	..	..	..	..	..	..	..
4120 Others	..	..	..	..	..	..	..	..	..	..
4200 Recurrent taxes on net wealth	25	512	1 911	4 171	2 970	1 523	414	372	424	440
4210 Individual	0	0	0	0	0	0	0	0	0	0
4220 Corporate	25	512	1 911	4 171	2 970	1 523	414	372	424	440
4300 Estate, inheritance and gift taxes	223	75	3	2	0	178	221	268	260	304
4310 Estate and inheritance taxes	216	75	3	2	..	178	221	268	260	304
On inheritances federal government	108	0	0	0	..	0	0	0	0	0
Succession duties provincial government	108	75	3	2	..	178	221	268	260	304
4320 Gift taxes	7	0	0	0	..	0	0	0	0	0
On gifts federal government	7	..	..	..	..	..	..	..	..	..
4400 Taxes on financial and capital transactions	0	0	0	0	2 868	3 077	3 646	4 975	6 315	6 939
4500 Non-recurrent taxes	108	293	2 365	2 742	4 102	7 254	8 401	9 512	8 988	9 499
4510 On net wealth	0	0	0	0	0	0	0	0	0	0
4520 Other non-recurrent taxes	108	293	2 365	2 742	4 102	7 254	8 401	9 512	8 988	9 499
Special assessments and charges local govt.	108	293	2 365	2 742	4 102	7 254	8 401	9 512	8 988	9 499
4600 Other recurrent taxes on property	0	0	0	0	0	0	0	0	0	0
5000 Taxes on goods and services	**6 202**	**32 909**	**63 092**	**94 468**	**122 855**	**123 752**	**136 396**	**150 270**	**155 091**	**165 395**
5100 Taxes on production, sale, transfer, etc.	5 310	24 808	59 627	88 879	114 701	116 160	128 554	140 745	146 128	153 721
5110 General taxes	2 730	11 658	34 475	55 313	71 242	72 130	81 452	90 593	93 851	99 938
5111 Value added taxes	0	0	0	35 884	46 072	70 712	78 292	86 694	90 392	96 159
5112 Sales tax	2 730	11 658	34 475	19 429	25 170	1 418	3 160	3 899	3 459	3 779
Sales taxes federal government	813	5 429	16 866	0	0	0	0	0	0	0
Sales taxes provincial, local govt.	1 917	6 229	17 609	19 429	25 170	1 418	3 160	3 899	3 459	3 779
5113 Other	0	0	0	0	0	0	0	0	0	0

	1965	1980	1990	2000	2007	2010	2013	2015	2016	2017
5120 Taxes on specific goods and services	2 580	13 150	25 153	33 565	43 459	44 030	47 102	50 152	52 278	53 783
5121 Excise duties	1 499	6 805	14 473	18 417	22 759	23 281	24 470	25 284	25 926	27 171
Excises federal government	740	3 850	6 405	8 377	9 249	10 244	10 261	10 372	10 649	10 887
Liquor	..	..	926	1 103	1 224	1 554	1 488	1 521	1 563	1 700
Tobacco	..	..	2 247	2 176	2 466	3 025	3 019	2 875	3 298	3 117
Gasoline and motive fuel	..	..	2 472	4 807	5 272	5 306	5 460	5 678	5 482	5 759
Remitted gaming profits	..	..	45	0	0	0	0	0	0	0
Miscellaneous consumption taxes	..	..	715	291	287	358	294	297	306	311
Excises provincial government	759	2 955	8 067	10 039	13 510	13 037	14 209	14 912	15 277	16 284
Motor fuel	680	1 863	4 674	7 031	8 065	8 198	9 094	9 727	10 139	10 343
Tobacco	53	772	2 776	2 279	4 181	4 620	4 879	5 108	5 120	5 006
Other	26	320	617	730	1 264	219	236	77	18	935
5122 Profits of fiscal monopolies	294	1 406	3 758	8 756	11 565	11 565	12 059	13 016	13 623	13 863
Own enterprises contributions	294	1 406	3 758	8 756	11 565	11 565	12 059	13 016	13 623	13 863
5123 Customs and import duties	686	3 199	4 021	2 824	3 829	3 441	4 193	5 181	5 461	5 593
Customs and import duties federal govt.	686	3 199	4 021	2 824	3 829	3 441	4 193	5 181	5 461	5 593
5124 Taxes on exports	0	842	0	0	0	0	0	0	0	0
5125 Taxes on investment goods	0	0	0	0	0	0	0	0	0	0
5126 Taxes on specific services	84	575	2 385	2 524	4 088	4 489	5 087	5 213	5 935	5 966
Tax on insurance premiums, provincial govt.	45	261	1 141	1 740	2 796	3 305	3 901	3 962	4 587	4 503
Tax on insurance premiums, federal govt.	0	1	1	1	11	28	13	10	7	1
Amusement and admission taxes	4	25	126	538	537	322	280	291	330	355
Air transportation taxes	0	166	488	0	403	600	662	722	768	823
Racetrack betting	35	122	155	55	36	36	32	33	26	25
Tax on meals and hotels	0	0	473	191	305	198	199	195	217	259
5127 Other taxes on internat. trade and transactions	0	0	0	0	0	0	0	0	0	0
5128 Other taxes	17	323	517	1 045	1 217	1 255	1 292	1 458	1 333	1 190
Other taxes federal government	0	98	272	758	762	557	439	544	421	417
Other taxes provincial government	17	225	245	287	455	698	853	914	912	773
5130 Unallocable between 5110 and 5120	0	0	0	0	0	0	0	0	0	0
5200 Taxes on use of goods and perform activities	892	8 101	3 465	5 589	8 154	7 592	7 842	9 525	8 963	11 674
5210 Recurrent taxes	306	1 500	2 393	3 644	4 368	4 452	5 017	5 589	5 777	6 022
5211 Paid by households: motor vehicles	103	666	1 056	1 696	2 241	1 986	2 237	2 478	2 612	2 739
5212 Paid by others: motor vehicles	141	509	697	1 039	1 242	1 153	1 343	1 552	1 587	1 682
5213 Paid in respect of other goods	62	325	640	909	885	1 313	1 437	1 559	1 578	1 601
5220 Non-recurrent taxes	586	6 601	1 072	1 945	3 786	3 140	2 825	3 936	3 186	5 652
Licences and permits local govt.	36	132	317	499	889	807	952	1 023	1 026	1 028
Licences and permits provincial govt.	550	6 469	755	1 446	2 897	2 333	1 873	2 913	2 160	4 624
5300 Unallocable between 5100 and 5200	0	0	0	0	0	0	0	0	0	0
6000 Other taxes	**166**	**1 198**	**2 875**	**2 167**	**342**	**596**	**696**	**748**	**740**	**745**
6100 Paid solely by business	139	943	2 386	1 280	0	0	0	0	0	0
6200 Other	27	255	489	887	342	596	696	748	740	745
Poll tax local government	5	0	0	0	0	0	0	0	0	0
Miscellaneous local government	11	358	489	887	342	596	696	748	740	745
Other federal government	11	-103	0	0	0	0	0	0	0	0
Non-wastable tax credits										
Non-wastable tax credits against 1110	..	..	..	1 633	5 550	6 415	7 326	7 510	7 681	7 997
Tax expenditure component	..	..	..	276	824	875	965	968	1 113	1 051
Transfer component	..	..	..	1 357	4 726	5 540	6 361	6 542	6 568	6 946
Non-wastable tax credits against 1210	..	..	..	1 758	3 445	4 726	3 754	3 768	3 758	3 575
Tax expenditure component	..	..	..	20	12	19	17	15	16	16
Transfer component	..	..	..	1 738	3 433	4 707	3 737	3 753	3 742	3 559
Total tax revenue on cash basis	**15 318**	**101 015**	**244 152**	**388 833**	**527 734**	**..**	**..**	**..**	**..**	**..**
Total tax revenue on accrual basis	**..**	**..**	**..**	**390 234**	**512 663**	**516 591**	**592 206**	**653 264**	**672 809**	**702 704**
Conciliation with National Accounts										
Additional taxes included in National Accounts	..	..	..	0	0	0	0	0	0	0
Taxes excluded from National Accounts	..	..	..	0	0	0	0	0	0	0
Difference in treatment of tax credits	..	..	..	296	836	894	982	983	1 129	1 068
Capital transfer for uncollected revenue	..	..	..	0	0	0	0	0	0	0
Voluntary social security contributions	..	..	..	0	0	0	0	0	0	0
Miscellaneous differences	..	..	..	0	0	0	0	0	0	0
National Accounts: Taxes and actual social contributions	..	..	..	390 234	513 499	517 485	593 188	654 247	673 938	703 771
Imputed social contributions	..	..	..	0	0	0	0	0	0	0
National Accounts: Taxes and all social contributions	..	..	..	390 234	513 499	517 485	593 188	654 247	673 938	703 771

.. Not available

Note: From 2001, all data are for the year ending 31st December. For 2000 and earlier years, data for the Federal, Provincial and Territorial governments and Social security funds are on a fiscal year basis commencing 1st April. Data for local government are on a fiscal year basis commencing 1st January.
From 1999 data are on accrual basis except that personal income taxes are on a modified cash basis.
There are some minor differences between the data for the years 1965 to 1978 and those for subsequent years. These mostly relate to the inclusion of fines and penalities or late payment of taxes and deductions for the child tax credits in the data for the years 1979 to 1983.
Heading 1210 - Taxes federal government: Federal corporate taxes include capital taxes.
Heading 2000: Includes receipts from the Canadian Pension Plan, Quebec Pension Plan, Unemployement Insurance Fund and Provincial Health Insurance. Premiums, Medicare Premiums and Social Insurance levies but excludes that part of the taxes on income and sales taxes earmarked for old age security. The practice of earmarking these taxes was discontinued in June 1975.
Heading 4400: From 2002 onward includes land transfer taxes of the provincial, territorial and local governments. Prior to 2002 land transfer taxes of the local government were included in line 6000 and those provincial and territorial governments were included in line 4520.
Heading 5121: The large increase in this heading between 1980 and 1981 is due to the introduction of a 'special petroleum compensation charge', a 'Canadian ownership special charge' and to an increase in the natural gas tax of C$ 2399 millions.
Heading 5122: From 1988, profits on fiscal monopolies include lottery profits.
Heading 5128: From 1988, other taxes of Federal Government include the annual fees for managing the spectrum (airwaves) allocation to the cellular industry.
Heading 5211: Some Québec motor vehicle licence administrative fees are included in sales of goods and services for the period 1988-89 to 1997-98. From 1998-99 onward, these fees are included under other taxes - motor vehicle licences.
Source: Statistics Canada.

StatLink https://doi.org/10.1787/888934056792

Table 5.5. Chile: Detailed country table, 1965-2017

Million CLP

	1965	1980	1990	2000	2007	2010	2013	2015	2016	2017
Total tax revenue	..	..	**1 777 218**	**7 901 998**	**20 598 963**	**21 845 693**	**27 381 686**	**32 532 354**	**34 129 307**	**36 238 557**
1000 Taxes on income, profits and capital gains	..	..	**412 974**	**1 841 630**	**9 412 056**	**8 329 060**	**9 520 709**	**11 840 521**	**11 444 570**	**12 516 154**
1100 Of individuals	..	..	99 154	604 100	989 348	1 492 837	1 964 172	3 199 876	2 990 653	3 500 023
Second category tax	..	..	65 552	490 980	993 129	1 449 099	1 981 699	2 350 120	2 458 249	2 585 694
Global complementary tax	..	..	33 603	113 120	-3 781	43 738	-17 527	-36 757	-213 365	50 495
Other	..	..	0	0	0	0	0	886 513	745 769	863 834
1110 On income and profits	..	..	..	..	..	..	..	..	..	..
1120 On capital gains	..	..	..	..	..	..	..	..	..	..
1200 Corporate	..	..	219 586	882 896	6 054 487	4 448 745	6 041 089	6 839 133	7 146 657	7 658 420
First category tax	..	..	200 891	815 747	5 084 996	3 913 870	5 473 355	6 183 830	6 689 101	7 049 471
Surtax on state owned enterprises	..	..	16 074	47 634	113 334	194 203	124 220	132 352	88 362	193 058
Mining tax	..	..	0	0	835 452	298 558	324 577	323 507	105 653	101 970
Other	..	..	2 621	19 516	20 705	42 114	118 937	199 444	263 541	313 921
1210 On profits	..	..	..	..	..	..	..	..	..	..
1220 On capital gains	..	..	..	..	..	..	..	..	..	..
1300 Unallocable between 1100 and 1200	..	..	94 233	354 634	2 368 221	2 387 478	1 515 449	1 801 512	1 307 260	1 357 711
Additional tax	..	..	59 082	350 301	1 462 715	1 414 057	1 337 721	1 429 758	1 331 564	1 453 577
Other	..	..	35 151	4 332	905 507	973 421	177 727	371 755	-24 304	-95 865
2000 Social security contributions	..	..	**159 559**	**576 758**	**1 148 647**	**1 493 987**	**1 968 973**	**2 252 489**	**2 441 419**	**2 627 558**
2100 Employees	..	..	154 021	553 937	1 098 620	1 433 159	1 906 340	2 188 575	2 373 777	2 553 916
2110 On a payroll basis	..	..	154 021	553 937	1 098 620	1 433 159	1 906 340	2 188 575	2 373 777	2 553 916
2120 On an income tax basis	..	..	0	0	0	0	0	0	0	0
2200 Employers	..	..	5 538	22 821	50 027	60 828	62 633	63 914	67 642	73 643
2210 On a payroll basis	..	..	5 538	22 821	50 027	60 828	62 633	63 914	67 642	73 643
2220 On an income tax basis	..	..	0	0	0	0	0	0	0	0
2300 Self-employed or non-employed	..	..	0	0	0	0	0	0	0	0
2310 On a payroll basis	..	..	..	..	..	..	..	..	..	..
2320 On an income tax basis	..	..	..	..	..	..	..	..	..	..
2400 Unallocable between 2100, 2200 and 2300	..	..	0	0	0	0	0	0	0	0
2410 On a payroll basis	..	..	..	..	..	..	..	..	..	..
2420 On an income tax basis	..	..	..	..	..	..	..	..	..	..
3000 Taxes on payroll and workforce	..	..	**0**	**0**	**0**	**0**	**0**	**0**	**0**	**0**
4000 Taxes on property	..	..	**109 319**	**554 037**	**1 013 571**	**898 607**	**1 133 765**	**1 421 274**	**1 731 723**	**1 950 217**
4100 Recurrent taxes on immovable property	..	..	59 968	302 244	496 311	662 368	840 842	1 056 920	1 171 399	1 229 195
4110 Households	..	..	..	..	..	..	..	..	..	..
4120 Others	..	..	..	..	..	..	..	..	..	..
4200 Recurrent taxes on net wealth	..	..	0	0	0	0	0	0	0	0
4210 Individual	..	..	..	..	..	..	..	..	..	..
4220 Corporate	..	..	..	..	..	..	..	..	..	..
4300 Estate, inheritance and gift taxes	..	..	3 444	10 906	28 501	39 338	45 550	92 236	100 490	202 376
4310 Estate and inheritance taxes	..	..	..	..	..	..	..	..	..	..
4320 Gift taxes	..	..	..	..	..	..	..	..	..	..
4400 Taxes on financial and capital transactions	..	..	45 907	240 886	488 759	196 901	247 373	272 118	459 834	518 645
4500 Non-recurrent taxes	..	..	0	0	0	0	0	0	0	0
4510 On net wealth	..	..	..	..	..	..	..	..	..	..
4520 Other non-recurrent taxes	..	..	..	..	..	..	..	..	..	..
4600 Other recurrent taxes on property	..	..	0	0	0	0	0	0	0	0
5000 Taxes on goods and services	..	..	**1 118 722**	**5 041 769**	**9 023 666**	**11 185 156**	**14 779 915**	**17 597 378**	**18 629 617**	**19 858 881**
5100 Taxes on production, sale, transfer, etc.	..	..	1 074 009	4 789 827	8 578 636	10 532 904	13 869 529	16 515 485	17 449 222	18 597 180
5110 General taxes	..	..	664 421	3 306 350	6 781 501	8 399 926	11 170 794	13 273 958	14 073 050	15 069 540
5111 Value added taxes	..	..	664 421	3 306 350	6 781 501	8 399 926	11 170 794	13 273 958	14 073 050	15 069 540
5112 Sales tax	..	..	0	0	0	0	0	0	0	0
5113 Other	..	..	0	0	0	0	0	0	0	0
5120 Taxes on specific goods and services	..	..	409 588	1 483 477	1 797 135	2 132 978	2 698 735	3 241 527	3 376 172	3 527 640
5121 Excise duties	..	..	166 050	816 160	1 299 844	1 561 205	1 987 475	2 412 773	2 568 863	2 682 659
Cigarettes and tobacco	..	..	60 604	283 275	455 595	647 637	815 991	981 422	1 009 034	978 696
Gasolene and diesel	..	..	105 445	532 885	844 249	913 568	1 171 483	1 388 218	1 502 039	1 629 561
Oil stabilisation fund	..	..	0	0	0	0	0	0	0	0
Fisheries Law Extraction Rights	..	..	0	0	0	0	0	8 558	9 998	11 749
Additional tax on new motor vehicles	..	..	0	0	0	0	0	34 575	47 792	62 654
5122 Profits of fiscal monopolies	..	..	0	0	0	0	0	0	0	0
5123 Customs and import duties	..	..	222 486	548 571	300 416	267 331	303 393	343 491	308 871	321 156
5124 Taxes on exports	..	..	0	0	0	0	0	0	0	0
5125 Taxes on investment goods	..	..	0	0	0	0	0	0	0	0
5126 Taxes on specific services	..	..	21 052	118 746	196 875	304 442	407 867	485 263	498 438	523 824
5127 Other taxes on internat. trade and transactions	..	..	0	0	0	0	0	0	0	0
5128 Other taxes	..	..	0	0	0	0	0	0	0	0
5130 Unallocable between 5110 and 5120	..	..	0	0	0	0	0	0	0	0
5200 Taxes on use of goods and perform activities	..	..	44 714	251 942	445 030	652 252	910 386	1 081 893	1 180 395	1 261 702

	1965	1980	1990	2000	2007	2010	2013	2015	2016	2017
5210 Recurrent taxes	..	..	44 714	251 942	445 030	652 252	910 386	1 081 893	1 180 395	1 261 702
Motor vehicles	..	..	24 469	93 880	155 158	218 219	330 754	397 608	434 137	482 009
5211 Paid by households: motor vehicles	..	..	0	0	0	0	0	0	0	0
5212 Paid by others: motor vehicles	..	..	0	0	0	0	0	0	0	0
5213 Paid in respect of other goods	..	..	20 245	158 062	289 872	434 033	579 632	684 285	746 258	779 693
Municipal permits	..	..	18 401	136 138	263 996	396 944	527 955	630 943	692 974	725 954
Mining patents	..	..	3 374	34 730	25 184	36 213	50 094	51 767	51 641	52 254
Other	..	..	-1 530	-12 806	692	876	1 583	1 575	1 643	1 485
5220 Non-recurrent taxes	..	..	0	0	0	0	0	0	0	0
Tax on Polluting Fixed Sources	..	..	0	0	0	0	0	0	0	0
5300 Unallocable between 5100 and 5200	..	..	0	0	0	0	0	0	0	0
6000 Other taxes	**..**	**..**	**-23 356**	**-112 195**	**1 023**	**-61 117**	**-21 676**	**-579 308**	**-118 021**	**-714 253**
6100 Paid solely by business	..	..	0	0	0	0	0	0	0	0
6200 Other	..	..	-23 356	-112 195	1 023	-61 117	-21 676	-579 308	-118 021	-714 253
Non-wastable tax credits										
Non-wastable tax credits against 1110	..	..	0	0	0	0	0	0	0	0
Tax expenditure component	..	..	..	..	..	..	..	..	..	..
Transfer component	..	..	..	..	..	..	..	..	..	..
Non-wastable tax credits against 1210	..	..	0	0	0	0	0	175 468	179 642	213 519
Tax expenditure component	..	..	..	..	..	..	..	45 774	50 061	62 076
Transfer component	..	..	..	..	..	..	..	129 694	129 580	151 443
Total tax revenue on cash basis	**..**	**..**	**1 777 218**	**7 901 998**	**20 598 963**	**21 845 693**	**27 381 686**	**32 532 354**	**34 129 307**	**36 238 557**
Total tax revenue on accrual basis	**..**	**..**	**..**	**..**	**..**	**..**	**..**	**..**	**..**	**..**
Conciliation with National Accounts										
Additional taxes included in National Accounts	..	..	..	..	..	..	..	..	..	..
Taxes excluded from National Accounts	..	..	..	..	..	..	..	..	..	..
Difference in treatment of tax credits	..	..	..	..	..	..	..	..	..	..
Capital transfer for uncollected revenue	..	..	..	..	..	..	..	..	..	..
Voluntary social security contributions	..	..	..	..	..	..	..	..	..	..
Miscellaneous differences	..	..	..	..	..	..	..	..	..	..
National Accounts: Taxes and actual social contributions	..	..	..	..	..	..	..	..	..	..
Imputed social contributions	..	..	..	..	..	..	..	..	..	..
National Accounts: Taxes and all social contributions	..	..	..	..	..	..	..	..	..	..

.. Not available

Note: Year ending 31st December.

The data are on a cash basis.

Source: Servicio de Impuestos internos (Chile's Tax Service).

StatLink https://doi.org/10.1787/888934056811

Table 5.6. Czech Republic: Detailed country table, 1965-2017

Million CZK

	1965	1980	1990	2000	2007	2010	2013	2015	2016	2017
Total tax revenue	..	..	..	**771 596**	**1 313 753**	**1 286 861**	**1 396 555**	**1 532 565**	**1 632 447**	**1 760 047**
Total tax revenue exclusive of custom duties	..	..	..	..	**1 307 310**	**1 280 288**	**1 390 999**	**1 524 653**	**1 624 414**	**1 751 777**
1000 Taxes on income, profits and capital gains	..	..	..	**175 846**	**325 328**	**259 934**	**290 263**	**329 768**	**361 857**	**390 566**
1100 Of individuals	..	..	..	99 668	153 374	131 706	149 831	164 678	183 103	202 244
1110 On income and profits	..	..	..	99 668	153 374	131 706	149 831	164 678	183 103	202 244
Wages and salaries withholding	..	..	..	73 474	126 736	115 755	129 793	139 888	156 271	175 301
Of unincorporated individuals	..	..	..	17 254	17 825	5 747	7 437	9 100	10 860	10 974
Withheld on interest and dividends paid to individuals	..	..	..	8 940	8 813	10 204	12 602	15 691	15 972	15 969
1120 On capital gains	..	..	..	0	0	0	0	0	0	0
1200 Corporate	..	..	..	76 178	171 954	128 228	140 432	165 090	178 754	188 322
1210 On profits	..	..	..	76 178	171 954	128 228	140 432	165 090	178 754	188 322
Profit tax	..	..	..	68 945	164 016	118 248	124 820	147 157	158 862	167 120
Withheld on interest and dividends paid to corporations	..	..	..	7 233	7 162	9 156	7 736	9 415	8 306	8 760
Levy on lottery revenue	..	..	..	0	776	824	7 876	8 518	11 586	12 442
1220 On capital gains	..	..	..	0	0	0	0	0	0	0
1300 Unallocable between 1100 and 1200	..	..	..	0	0	0	0	0	0	0
2000 Social security contributions	..	..	..	**341 544**	**573 417**	**576 029**	**603 072**	**659 743**	**699 604**	**757 183**
2100 Employees	..	..	..	77 272	127 662	116 818	123 353	133 878	143 730	155 827
2110 On a payroll basis	..	..	..	77 272	127 662	116 818	123 353	133 878	143 730	155 827
Retirement	..	..	..	40 489	66 644	69 272	71 871	78 120	83 738	91 414
State employment policy	..	..	..	2 492	4 101	0	0	0	0	0
Sick leave	..	..	..	6 852	11 279	0	0	0	0	0
Health insurance	..	..	..	27 439	45 638	47 546	51 482	55 758	59 992	64 413
2120 On an income tax basis	..	..	..	0	0	0	0	0	0	0
2200 Employers	..	..	..	220 207	359 493	363 074	382 498	417 778	444 201	483 437
2210 On a payroll basis	..	..	..	220 207	359 493	363 074	382 498	417 778	444 201	483 437
Retirement	..	..	..	121 547	220 591	229 450	239 248	261 786	277 562	302 926
State employment policy	..	..	..	19 933	12 303	12 756	13 345	14 604	15 484	16 897
Sick leave	..	..	..	20 555	33 834	24 332	25 454	27 851	29 533	32 231
Health insurance	..	..	..	54 879	91 275	95 095	102 964	111 517	119 983	128 825
Penalties	..	..	..	3 293	1 490	1 441	1 487	2 020	1 639	2 558
2220 On an income tax basis	..	..	..	0	0	0	0	0	0	0
2300 Self-employed or non-employed	..	..	..	44 065	86 262	96 137	97 221	108 088	111 674	117 919
2310 On a payroll basis	..	..	..	44 065	86 262	96 137	97 221	108 088	111 674	117 919
Retirement	..	..	..	7 819	19 508	20 510	21 262	22 472	23 674	25 197
State employment policy	..	..	..	1 082	1 114	1 173	911	962	1 013	1 080
Sick leave	..	..	..	0	0	0	0	0	0	0
Health insurance	..	..	..	34 992	65 483	74 299	74 908	84 460	86 834	91 027
Self-employed	..	..	..	7 328	15 921	17 603	18 732	20 748	21 278	22 075
Non-employed	..	..	..	200	2 103	3 996	2 500	2 768	3 303	3 699
Government	..	..	..	27 464	47 459	52 700	53 676	60 944	62 253	65 253
Penalties	..	..	..	172	157	155	140	193	153	615
2320 On an income tax basis	..	..	..	0	0	0	0	0	0	0
2400 Unallocable between 2100, 2200 and 2300	..	..	..	0	0	0	0	0	0	0
2410 On a payroll basis	..	..	..	..	..	..	..	..	..	..
2420 On an income tax basis	..	..	..	..	..	..	..	..	..	..
3000 Taxes on payroll and workforce	..	..	..	**0**	**0**	**0**	**0**	**0**	**0**	**0**
4000 Taxes on property	..	..	..	**10 890**	**15 495**	**16 364**	**19 210**	**21 920**	**23 425**	**23 850**
4100 Recurrent taxes on immovable property	..	..	..	4 469	5 126	8 752	9 852	10 333	10 609	10 783
4110 Households	..	..	..	1 452	2 228	4 302	5 387	5 433	5 545	5 660
Real property tax	..	..	..	1 452	2 228	4 302	5 387	5 433	5 545	5 660
4120 Others	..	..	..	3 017	2 898	4 450	4 465	4 900	5 064	5 123
Levy collected by Winery Fund	..	..	..	0	2	5	5	20	27	25
Real property tax	..	..	..	3 017	2 895	4 445	4 461	4 880	5 037	5 098
4200 Recurrent taxes on net wealth	..	..	..	0	0	0	0	0	0	0
4210 Individual	..	..	..	..	..	..	..	..	..	..
4220 Corporate	..	..	..	..	..	..	..	..	..	..
4300 Estate, inheritance and gift taxes	..	..	..	587	460	218	215	20	11	13
4310 Estate and inheritance taxes	..	..	..	112	115	78	76	10	5	3
Inheritance tax	..	..	..	112	115	78	76	10	5	3
4320 Gift taxes	..	..	..	475	345	140	139	10	6	9
Gift tax	..	..	..	475	345	140	139	10	6	9
4400 Taxes on financial and capital transactions	..	..	..	5 834	9 909	7 394	9 143	11 566	12 805	13 054
Real property transfer tax	..	..	..	5 834	9 909	7 394	9 143	11 566	12 805	13 054
4500 Non-recurrent taxes	..	..	..	0	0	0	0	0	0	0
4510 On net wealth	..	..	..	..	..	..	..	..	..	..
4520 Other non-recurrent taxes	..	..	..	..	..	..	..	..	..	..
4600 Other recurrent taxes on property	..	..	..	0	0	0	0	0	0	0

	1965	1980	1990	2000	2007	2010	2013	2015	2016	2017
5000 Taxes on goods and services	..	..	..	**242 960**	**393 041**	**427 813**	**478 386**	**512 835**	**538 972**	**579 274**
5100 Taxes on production, sale, transfer, etc.	..	..	..	226 354	365 998	402 072	453 863	487 378	512 659	552 033
5110 General taxes	..	..	..	141 235	232 288	263 457	303 822	333 274	353 915	387 537
5111 Value added taxes	..	..	..	141 235	232 288	263 457	303 822	333 274	353 915	387 537
5112 Sales tax	..	..	..	0	0	0	0	0	0	0
5113 Other	..	..	..	0	0	0	0	0	0	0
Previous turnover tax	..	..	..	..	..	..	..	..	..	..
5120 Taxes on specific goods and services	..	..	..	85 119	133 710	138 615	150 041	154 105	158 744	164 496
5121 Excise duties	..	..	..	71 404	133 492	138 401	149 760	153 785	158 401	164 114
On mineral oils	..	..	..	46 998	81 661	80 508	77 160	83 460	87 557	88 878
On alcohol and liquor	..	..	..	5 629	7 201	5 820	6 658	7 203	7 169	7 354
On beer	..	..	..	3 410	3 564	4 396	4 545	4 648	4 642	4 657
On wine	..	..	..	350	342	317	288	332	348	368
On tobacco products	..	..	..	14 984	40 713	44 062	52 193	53 380	53 678	57 524
Duty on CFC	..	..	..	33	0	0	0	0	0	0
Levy collected by Winery Fund	..	..	..	0	11	24	21	0	5	5
On electricity	..	..	..	0	0	1 433	1 305	1 229	1 478	1 537
On natural gas	..	..	..	0	0	1 347	1 256	1 146	1 191	1 301
On solid fuels	..	..	..	0	0	495	469	415	426	452
Fee on electricity from solar radiation	..	..	..	0	0	0	5 866	1 972	1 906	2 038
5122 Profits of fiscal monopolies	..	..	..	0	0	0	0	0	0	0
5123 Customs and import duties	..	..	..	13 572	0	0	0	0	0	0
Customs duties	..	..	..	13 572	..	..	..	..	..	..
Previous import surcharge	..	..	..	0	..	..	..	..	..	..
5124 Taxes on exports	..	..	..	0	0	0	0	0	0	0
5125 Taxes on investment goods	..	..	..	0	0	0	0	0	0	0
5126 Taxes on specific services	..	..	..	143	218	214	281	320	343	382
Fees on entry tickets	..	..	..	65	61	53	56	53	62	69
Fees on recreational units (based on capacity)	..	..	..	69	144	147	213	240	252	279
Fees on advertising facilities	..	..	..	0	0	0	0	0	0	0
Restaurant sale alcoh. beverages and tobac. products	..	..	..	0	0	0	0	0	0	0
Fees collected by the cinematography EBF	..	..	..	9	13	14	12	27	29	34
Fees on advertisement	..	..	..	0	0	0	126	191	151	150
5127 Other taxes on internat. trade and transactions	..	..	..	0	0	0	0	0	0	0
5128 Other taxes	..	..	..	0	0	0	0	0	0	0
5130 Unallocable between 5110 and 5120	..	..	..	0	0	0	0	0	0	0
5200 Taxes on use of goods and perform activities	..	..	..	16 606	27 043	25 740	24 523	25 456	26 313	27 241
5210 Recurrent taxes	..	..	..	10 788	18 100	18 461	18 176	19 023	19 493	20 278
Highway fee	..	..	..	1 753	2 429	3 061	3 803	4 397	4 757	4 991
5211 Paid by households: motor vehicles	..	..	..	0	0	0	0	0	0	0
5212 Paid by others: motor vehicles	..	..	..	5 456	5 882	5 138	5 323	5 868	6 012	6 245
Road tax (commercial)	..	..	..	5 456	5 882	5 138	5 323	5 868	6 012	6 245
5213 Paid in respect of other goods	..	..	..	3 579	9 790	10 262	9 050	8 758	8 724	9 042
Resort and recreation fees on visitors	..	..	..	232	312	284	301	327	351	387
Dog fees	..	..	..	191	277	281	281	277	274	274
Motor vehicle entry fees	..	..	..	32	25	23	14	13	18	19
Water pollution fee	..	..	..	520	404	202	208	173	203	193
Air pollution fee	..	..	..	685	525	399	268	283	270	171
Waste deposit fee	..	..	..	454	5 728	5 948	6 162	6 218	6 278	6 361
Levy on temp. withdrawal of land from agriculture	..	..	..	94	40	34	52	39	69	59
Radioactive waste fee	..	..	..	642	1 310	1 430	1 563	1 393	1 225	1 547
Fees on operated gambling machines	..	..	..	722	1 145	927	131	0	0	0
Fees on registration and recording of packaging	..	..	..	0	17	17	16	18	17	17
Levy on temp. withdrawal of land from forestry	..	..	..	7	6	6	6	7	10	7
Other environmental fees	..	..	..	0	0	710	47	11	9	7
5220 Non-recurrent taxes	..	..	..	5 818	8 943	7 280	6 348	6 433	6 820	6 963
Levy on withdrawal of land from agriculture	..	..	..	532	361	306	469	348	620	534
Levy on withdrawal of land from forestry	..	..	..	40	57	57	55	59	88	60
Tax on use of public space	..	..	..	645	639	626	629	632	621	635
Misc. licence and permit fees	..	..	..	4 601	7 881	6 279	5 187	5 382	5 475	5 705
Land betterment fee	..	..	..	0	4	11	7	11	17	29
Licence for lorry transport	..	..	..	0	1	1	0	1	0	0
5300 Unallocable between 5100 and 5200	..	..	..	0	0	0	0	0	0	0
6000 Other taxes	..	..	..	**356**	**29**	**149**	**67**	**387**	**556**	**904**
Unallocated previous taxes and levies	..	..	..	0	0	0	0	0	0	0
6100 Paid solely by business	..	..	..	0	0	0	0	0	0	0
6200 Other	..	..	..	356	29	149	67	387	556	904
Other taxes, fees and related payments	..	..	..	356	29	149	67	387	556	904
Custom duties collected for the EU	..	..	..	..	**6 443**	**6 573**	**5 556**	**7 912**	**8 033**	**8 271**

	1965	1980	1990	2000	2007	2010	2013	2015	2016	2017
Non-wastable tax credits										
Non-wastable tax credits against 1110	..	..	..	0	16 022	25 727	28 696	31 415	32 833	35 216
Tax expenditure component	..	..	..	..	13 416	17 922	20 203	22 532	24 234	26 334
Transfer component	..	..	..	..	2 606	7 805	8 493	8 883	8 599	8 882
Total tax revenue on cash basis	..	..	..	**772 272**	**1 310 618**	**1 273 676**	**1 353 469**	**1 478 758**	**1 606 157**	**1 712 822**
Total tax revenue on accrual basis	..	..	..	**771 596**	**1 313 753**	**1 286 861**	**1 396 555**	**1 532 565**	**1 632 447**	**1 760 047**
Conciliation with National Accounts										
Additional taxes included in National Accounts	..	..	..	2 837	5 757	6 094	6 424	0	0	0
Compulsory injury insurance	..	..	..	2 837	5 757	6 094	6 424	0	0	0
Driving licence fees	..	..	..	0	0	0	0	0	0	0
Taxes excluded from National Accounts	..	..	..	-9 488	-17 797	-20 096	-18 893	-20 314	-20 712	-23 258
Tax on use of public space	..	..	..	-645	-639	-632	-629	-632	-621	-635
Waste deposit fee	..	..	..	-454	-5 728	-5 948	-6 162	-6 218	-6 278	-6 361
Misc. licence and permit fees	..	..	..	-2 301	-3 940	-3 139	-2 593	-2 691	-2 737	-2 852
Radioactive waste fee	..	..	..	-642	-1 310	-1 430	-1 563	-1 393	-1 225	-1 547
Health insurance: non-employed	..	..	..	-200	-2 103	-3 996	-2 500	-2 768	-3 303	-3 699
Health insurance: government	..	..	..	0	0	0	0	0	0	0
Soc. Security contr. employers: Penalties	..	..	..	-3 293	-1 490	-1 441	-1 487	-2 020	-1 639	-2 558
Soc. Security contr. Self-employed or non-employed: Penalties	..	..	..	-200	-157	-155	-140	-193	-153	-615
Licence for lorry transport	..	..	..	0	-1	-1	0	-1	0	0
Highway fee	..	..	..	-1 753	-2 429	-3 061	-3 803	-4 397	-4 757	-4 991
Other environmental fees	..	..	..	0	0	-105	-14	0	0	0
Levy on loterry revenue	..	..	..	0	0	-187	0	0	0	0
Value added taxes	..	..	..	0	0	0	0	0	0	0
Difference in treatment of tax credits	..	..	..	0	127	-451	778	-118	-47	-455
Capital transfer for uncollected revenue	..	..	..	0	0	0	0	0	0	0
Voluntary social security contributions	..	..	..	1 099	974	661	337	386	418	463
Miscellaneous differences	..	..	..	2 162	0	0	0	0	0	0
National Accounts: Taxes and actual social contributions	..	..	..	768 206	1 302 815	1 273 070	1 385 202	1 512 520	1 612 105	1 736 797
Imputed social contributions	..	..	..	423	299	600	934	1 027	1 008	1 170
National Accounts: Taxes and all social contributions	..	..	..	768 629	1 303 114	1 273 670	1 386 136	1 513 547	1 613 113	1 737 967

.. Not available
Note: Year ending 31st December.
From 1995 data are on accrual basis.
Source: Ministry of Finance, Economic Department.

StatLink https://doi.org/10.1787/888934056830

Table 5.7. Denmark: Detailed country table, 1965-2017

Million DKK

	1965	1980	1990	2000	2007	2010	2013	2015	2016	2017
Total tax revenue	**20 821**	**166 358**	**382 232**	**623 911**	**809 988**	**813 972**	**901 001**	**957 281**	**969 153**	**1 004 418**
Total tax revenue exclusive of custom duties	..	..	..	**621 586**	**806 707**	**810 730**	**898 177**	**953 996**	**966 084**	**1 001 281**
1000 Taxes on income, profits and capital gains	**9 712**	**92 404**	**233 739**	**383 244**	**486 845**	**500 276**	**564 937**	**605 698**	**608 916**	**635 959**
1100 Of individuals	8 758	86 958	206 478	328 532	427 412	422 685	490 887	525 144	514 544	531 747
1110 On income and profits	8 758	86 909	206 335	328 305	427 070	422 364	490 627	524 856	514 302	531 453
Central government income tax	5 020	33 351	91 638	77 491	155 540	124 943	141 399	169 059	172 820	178 554
County income tax	0	10 742	31 361	56 135	0	0	0	0	0	0
Municipality income tax	2 948	33 555	77 571	121 975	173 114	193 111	209 303	220 815	229 085	236 796
Seaman's income tax	66	457	0	0	0	0	0	0	0	0
Old-age pension fund contributions	592	2 163	0	0	0	0	0	0	0	0
Social pension fund contributions	0	3 340	0	0	0	0	0	0	0	0
Sickness benefit fund contributions	0	1 804	0	0	0	0	0	0	0	0
Pension schemes and annuity insurance	22	355	2 627	6 923	8 948	9 842	42 974	22 842	6 251	5 663
Special income tax	101	1 054	2 810	0	0	0	0	0	0	0
Duty on canceled pension schemes	9	82	0	0	0	0	0	0	0	0
Duty on feed rent increases	0	8	5	0	0	0	0	0	0	0
Duty on employees' remuneration compens. fund releases	0	0	325	654	1 144	982	1 129	11 177	1 935	2 198
Duty on interest on consumer loans	0	0	0	0	0	0	0	0	0	0
Labour market contributions	0	0	0	56 729	76 609	80 863	82 599	87 359	90 334	94 070
Imputed income from owner-occupied dwelling	0	0	0	8 399	11 716	12 623	13 223	13 604	13 879	14 173
1120 On capital gains	0	49	144	226	343	321	260	289	241	294
Tax on winnings from lotteries, pools, etc.	..	49	144	226	343	321	260	289	241	294
1200 Corporate	954	5 446	14 660	42 279	54 871	41 057	54 066	57 723	60 379	71 928
1210 On profits	954	5 446	14 660	42 279	54 871	41 057	54 066	57 723	60 379	71 928
1220 On capital gains	0	0	0	0	0	0	0	0	0	0
1300 Unallocable between 1100 and 1200	0	0	12 601	12 434	4 562	36 535	19 984	22 832	33 994	32 284
2000 Social security contributions	**690**	**710**	**101**	**8 453**	**1 286**	**1 815**	**1 618**	**1 378**	**1 197**	**1 060**
2100 Employees	567	1	98	8 209	1 057	900	879	826	737	729
Sickness benefit fund contributions	30	0	0	0	0	0	0	0	0	0
Sickday benefit contributions, ordinary	534	0	0	0	0	0	0	0	0	0
Sickday benefit contributions, special	3	0	0	0	0	0	0	0	0	0
Contribution to merchant marine's welf. board	0	1	1	0	0	0	0	0	0	0
Special pension scheme savings	0	0	0	6 846	0	0	0	0	0	0
Contr. to pension funds from officials in companies	0	0	0	879	555	450	476	438	386	377
Contr. to pension funds from officials in non-profit institutions	0	0	96	485	502	450	403	388	351	352
2110 On a payroll basis	..	..	..	..	..	..	..	..	..	..
2120 On an income tax basis	..	..	..	..	..	..	..	..	..	..
2200 Employers	123	709	3	244	229	914	739	552	460	331
Unemployment insurance contributions	41	598	0	0	0	0	0	0	0	0
Disablement insurance contributions	21	58	0	0	0	0	0	0	0	0
Sickness benefit fund contributions	61	0	0	0	0	0	0	0	0	0
Contribution to employee's wage guarantee fund	0	50	0	241	227	908	731	542	450	323
Contribution to merchant marine's welf. board	0	1	1	0	0	0	0	0	0	0
Shipping owners contr. sickness assist. seamen	0	1	2	3	2	6	8	10	10	8
2210 On a payroll basis	..	..	..	..	..	..	..	..	..	..
2220 On an income tax basis	..	..	..	..	..	..	..	..	..	..
2300 Self-employed or non-employed	0	0	0	0	0	0	0	0	0	0
2310 On a payroll basis	..	..	..	..	..	..	..	..	..	..
2320 On an income tax basis	..	..	..	..	..	..	..	..	..	..
2400 Unallocable between 2100, 2200 and 2300	0	0	0	0	0	0	0	0	0	0
2410 On a payroll basis	..	..	..	..	..	..	..	..	..	..
2420 On an income tax basis	..	..	..	..	..	..	..	..	..	..
3000 Taxes on payroll and workforce	**0**	**0**	**2 494**	**2 258**	**3 975**	**4 160**	**6 130**	**5 894**	**5 903**	**5 494**
4000 Taxes on property	**1 691**	**9 806**	**16 269**	**20 738**	**31 556**	**33 533**	**34 995**	**39 169**	**38 692**	**39 258**
4100 Recurrent taxes on immovable property	1 029	5 676	8 891	13 565	18 996	24 161	26 370	28 085	28 436	28 465
Central government land tax	130	264	0	0	0	0	0	0	0	0
County land tax	169	2 315	2 915	4 070	0	0	0	0	0	0
Municipal land tax	408	2 257	4 123	7 049	15 601	19 645	22 580	24 707	25 110	25 233
Centr. Govt. fixed tax on real property	32	11	0	0	0	0	0	0	0	0
County fixed tax on real property	45	0	0	0	0	0	0	0	0	0
Municipal fixed tax on real property	190	91	0	0	0	0	0	0	0	0
County duty on land (public property)	4	22	22	25	0	0	0	0	0	0
County duty on buildings (public property)	0	53	88	97	0	0	0	0	0	0
Municipal duty on land (public property)	26	103	244	383	393	434	359	364	360	374
Municipal duty on buildings (residential)	0	195	335	381	757	814	641	599	596	594
Municipal duty on buildings (business)	25	366	1 165	1 560	2 244	3 269	2 789	2 416	2 370	2 264
4110 Households	..	..	..	..	..	..	..	..	..	..

	1965	1980	1990	2000	2007	2010	2013	2015	2016	2017
4120 Others	..	..	..	..	..	..	..	..	..	..
4200 Recurrent taxes on net wealth	306	963	934	0	0	0	0	0	0	0
4210 Individual	306	963	934	..	..	..	..	..	..	..
4220 Corporate	0	0	0	..	..	..	..	..	..	..
4300 Estate, inheritance and gift taxes	137	738	2 197	2 863	3 896	3 646	3 940	5 177	4 240	4 368
4310 Estate and inheritance taxes	..	..	..	..	..	..	..	..	..	..
4320 Gift taxes	..	..	..	..	..	..	..	..	..	..
4400 Taxes on financial and capital transactions	219	2 313	4 166	4 171	8 659	5 726	4 685	5 907	6 017	6 426
Stamp duties	214	2 243	2 829	4 125	8 574	5 695	4 664	5 879	5 986	6 386
Duty on share capital creation	0	32	500	0	0	0	0	0	0	0
Duty to land registry office	5	38	28	46	85	30	21	28	31	40
Duty on transfers of shares	0	0	809	0	0	0	0	0	0	0
4500 Non-recurrent taxes	0	116	81	140	6	0	0	0	0	0
4510 On net wealth	..	0	0	0	0	0	..	..	..	..
4520 Other non-recurrent taxes	..	116	81	140	6	0	..	..	..	..
4600 Other recurrent taxes on property	0	0	0	0	0	0	0	0	0	0
5000 Taxes on goods and services	**8 727**	**63 437**	**129 630**	**206 502**	**282 855**	**270 741**	**290 347**	**301 538**	**311 102**	**319 238**
5100 Taxes on production, sale, transfer, etc.	8 239	60 545	123 645	195 666	264 043	251 061	267 670	277 824	286 681	293 808
5110 General taxes	2 139	37 727	80 650	121 955	174 639	171 583	181 378	191 479	199 046	207 768
5111 Value added taxes	2 139	37 727	72 120	121 955	174 639	171 583	181 378	191 479	199 046	207 768
5112 Sales tax	0	0	0	0	0	0	0	0	0	0
5113 Other	0	0	8 530	0	0	0	0	0	0	0
Labour market contrib. concerning imports	..	..	4 903	..	..	..	..	..	..	..
Labour market contrib. concerning value added	..	..	3 627	..	..	..	..	..	..	..
5120 Taxes on specific goods and services	6 100	22 817	42 995	73 711	89 405	79 479	86 292	86 345	87 635	86 040
5121 Excise duties	5 466	20 473	38 339	68 977	82 861	74 032	81 894	81 893	82 984	81 376
Duty on petrol	1 016	3 713	5 637	10 005	9 154	8 029	7 286	7 348	7 496	7 499
Motor vehicle registration duty	818	2 989	7 917	13 858	24 289	13 586	15 218	17 988	19 444	19 976
Cigarettes and tobacco duties	1 469	4 472	6 516	7 489	7 201	8 283	8 417	7 658	7 063	7 547
Duties on cigars, cheroots and cigarillos	234	220	128	80	40	32	47	113	57	66
Sale of revenue labels	0	3	10	13	13	5	4	4	1	2
Sales duties on chocolate and sugar	254	331	801	1 205	1 289	1 470	2 020	2 156	2 231	2 184
Raw material duty on chocolate and sugar	11	14	54	60	93	144	180	187	139	169
Special tax on chocolate and sugar	0	2	13	76	46	51	68	103	99	126
Duty on ice-cream	33	58	135	168	180	201	297	297	330	308
Duty on coffee	5	249	224	266	250	243	271	280	287	254
Duty on mineral water	68	195	466	505	418	383	374	0	0	0
Duty on beer	622	1 983	3 100	1 510	1 080	895	977	916	947	918
Duty on wine	122	611	1 448	1 166	1 032	1 071	1 674	1 764	1 772	1 724
Duty on spirits	412	1 432	1 982	1 756	1 213	1 028	1 127	1 201	1 197	1 212
Duty on restaurant sales of alcoholic bev.	150	0	0	0	0	0	0	0	0	0
Duty on wireless sets	55	67	0	0	0	0	0	0	0	0
Duty on television sets	0	93	-18	0	0	0	0	0	0	0
Duty on video recorders	0	17	-15	0	0	0	0	0	0	0
Duty on major household appliances	0	199	-10	0	0	0	0	0	0	0
Duty on grammophone records	10	46	84	0	0	0	0	0	0	0
Duty on playing cards	1	2	0	0	0	0	0	0	0	0
Duty on matches	5	3	-1	0	0	0	0	0	0	0
Duty on lighters	1	8	-4	0	0	0	0	0	0	0
Duty on electric bulbs	36	67	152	176	211	117	95	86	76	65
Duty on perfumery and toilet articles	91	214	506	0	0	0	0	0	0	0
Duty on almanacs	3	0	0	0	0	0	0	0	0	0
Duty on salmon	0	1	0	0	0	0	0	0	0	0
Duty on paper and cardboard	45	0	0	0	0	0	0	0	0	0
Duty on sugar	0	174	-8	0	0	0	0	0	0	0
Duty on tea	0	12	10	8	8	8	8	8	8	5
Duty on electricity	0	1 222	4 317	7 430	8 665	10 195	10 013	11 501	11 657	12 164
Duty on certain oil products	0	1 719	2 938	6 757	8 549	8 623	9 306	9 347	9 705	9 804
Duty on certain retail containers	0	100	397	594	727	706	715	316	331	335
Duty on gas	0	56	47	0	0	0	0	0	0	0
Duty on extraction and import of raw materials	0	16	129	172	220	119	132	148	150	165
Duty on disposable tableware	0	0	72	65	126	120	121	138	144	141
Duty on insecticides, herbicides, etc.	0	0	13	366	449	466	656	598	516	532
Duty on videotapes	0	0	0	0	0	0	0	0	0	0
Duty on coal, etc.	0	0	849	1 217	1 450	2 587	2 991	2 255	2 064	1 916
Other duties on goods and services	5	186	20	53	147	189	-13	186	156	160
Duty on waste	0	0	404	1 025	1 225	51	167	130	155	161
Duty on CFC	0	0	27	0	53	56	82	65	70	58
Duty on CO2	0	0	0	4 883	5 108	5 822	5 762	3 652	3 577	3 632
Duty on cigarette paper	0	0	0	68	32	28	36	38	35	32
Duty on rechargeable Ni-Cd batteries	0	0	0	21	17	4	3	2	1	1
Duty on piped water	0	0	0	1 357	1 371	1 334	1 584	1 688	1 595	1 571

	1965	1980	1990	2000	2007	2010	2013	2015	2016	2017
Duty on carrier bags made of paper, plastic, etc.	0	0	0	178	210	201	186	208	196	190
Duty on tires	0	0	0	29	45	62	50	57	56	54
Duty on sulphur	0	0	0	165	108	48	51	42	38	39
Duty on chlorinated solvents	0	0	0	2	0	0	0	0	0	0
Duty on natural gas	0	0	0	2 532	3 375	4 524	5 255	3 160	3 213	3 002
Duty on nitrogen	0	0	0	30	27	26	21	17	19	15
Duty on specific growth stimulants	0	0	0	0	0	0	0	0	0	0
Duty on PVC-film	0	0	0	7	12	11	10	11	12	11
Duty on PVC and phathalates	0	0	0	31	42	23	18	19	18	16
Duty on lead accumulators	0	0	0	14	0	0	0	0	0	0
Duty on mineral phosphorus	0	0	0	0	51	51	49	52	52	52
Surcharge on alcoholic soft drinks	0	0	0	0	17	26	33	33	35	33
Duty on nitrogen oxides	0	0	0	0	0	212	870	820	490	159
Duty on saturated fat	0	0	0	0	0	0	0	0	0	0
Duty on PSO (Public Service Obligations)	0	0	0	3 641	4 319	3 004	5 734	7 302	7 553	5 078
5122 Profits of fiscal monopolies	16	183	404	1 402	1 648	1 481	1 339	1 230	1 333	1 282
5123 Customs and import duties	556	1 113	1 849	0	0	0	0	0	0	0
Customs duties	0	1 032	1 779	..	..	..	..	0	0	0
Temporary import surcharge	556	0	0	..	..	..	..	..	..	..
Import duties on agricultural produce	0	81	70	..	..	..	..	0	0	0
5124 Taxes on exports	0	0	0	0	0	0	0	0	0	0
5125 Taxes on investment goods	0	0	0	0	0	0	0	0	0	0
5126 Taxes on specific services	62	771	1 567	3 019	4 525	3 932	3 008	3 189	3 286	3 348
Sales tax on gambling stakes races	17	28	20	12	18	16	15	14	13	13
Tax on football pools	31	152	284	942	1 143	1 071	0	0	0	0
Tax on cinema tickets	14	0	0	0	0	0	0	0	0	0
Duty on motor vehicle compl. insurance	0	470	923	1 327	2 104	1 854	1 598	1 529	1 535	1 519
Duty on insurance on pleasure boats	0	13	57	66	100	122	127	126	122	124
Duty on charter flight	0	109	283	0	0	0	0	0	0	0
Turnover tax on 6-win horse race betting	0	0	0	0	0	0	0	0	0	0
Duty on casinos	0	0	0	180	261	173	192	200	219	216
Passenger duty	0	0	0	477	6	0	0	0	0	0
Duty on the Danish State Lottery	0	0	0	16	35	41	42	44	45	46
Duty on slot machines	0	0	0	0	858	656	545	618	658	627
Duty on gambling	0	0	0	0	0	0	288	397	405	450
Duty on online casinos	0	0	0	0	0	0	202	261	289	354
5127 Other taxes on internat. trade and transactions	0	0	0	0	0	0	0	0	0	0
5128 Other taxes	0	277	837	312	370	33	51	33	33	33
Duty paid to ECSC	..	4	5	0	0	0	0	0	0	0
Sugar storing duty	..	83	113	62	0	0	0	0	0	0
Duty on the production of sugar	..	81	145	249	-26	33	51	33	33	33
Duty on milk co-reponsibility levy	..	109	255	0	0	0	0	0	0	0
Grain co-reponsibility levy	..	0	319	0	0	0	0	0	0	0
Restructuring scheme for EU sugar system	..	0	0	0	397	0	0	0	0	0
5130 Unallocable between 5110 and 5120	0	0	0	0	0	0	0	0	0	0
5200 Taxes on use of goods and perform activities	488	2 893	4 410	7 468	14 088	14 731	16 180	16 537	16 299	16 895
5210 Recurrent taxes	488	2 893	4 410	7 468	14 088	14 731	15 966	16 171	15 891	16 490
5211 Paid by households: motor vehicles	199	1 874	2 922	5 485	7 105	7 614	8 094	8 136	7 850	8 207
Weight duty automobiles	199	1 874	2 922	5 318	6 954	7 467	7 936	7 859	7 565	7 937
Recycling fee on cars	0	0	0	167	151	147	158	277	285	270
5212 Paid by others: motor vehicles	287	1 014	1 441	1 919	3 125	2 980	3 336	3 483	3 567	3 757
Weight duty automobiles	287	1 014	1 441	1 612	2 652	2 611	2 952	3 088	3 133	3 287
Road charges	0	0	0	307	473	370	383	395	434	471
5213 Paid in respect of other goods	2	5	47	64	3 858	4 137	4 537	4 552	4 474	4 527
5220 Non-recurrent taxes	0	0	0	0	0	0	214	365	408	405
5300 Unallocable between 5100 and 5200	0	0	1 575	3 368	4 724	4 948	6 497	7 177	8 122	8 536
6000 Other taxes	**0**	**0**	**0**	**391**	**190**	**206**	**152**	**320**	**275**	**272**
6100 Paid solely by business	..	..	..	391	190	206	152	320	275	272
6200 Other	..	..	..	0	0	0	0	0	0	0
Custom duties collected for the EU	**..**	**..**	**..**	**2 325**	**3 282**	**3 242**	**2 824**	**3 285**	**3 069**	**3 136**
Non-wastable tax credits										
Non-wastable tax credits against 1110	..	..	..	..	..	4 960	5 515	4 228	4 227	4 198
Tax expenditure component	..	..	..	..	..	4 712	5 240	4 016	4 016	3 988
Transfer component	..	..	..	..	..	248	276	211	211	210
Non-wastable tax credits against 1210	..	..	..	..	..	0	0	0	0	0
Tax expenditure component	..	..	..	..	..	..	..	..	..	..
Transfer component	..	..	..	..	..	..	..	..	..	..
Total tax revenue on cash basis	**..**	**..**	**..**	**..**	**..**	**..**	**..**	**..**	**..**	**..**
Total tax revenue on accrual basis	**20 821**	**166 358**	**382 232**	**623 911**	**809 988**	**813 972**	**901 001**	**957 281**	**969 153**	**1 004 418**
Conciliation with National Accounts										
Additional taxes included in National Accounts	0	0	0	0	0	0	0	0	0	0
Taxes excluded from National Accounts	0	0	0	0	0	0	0	0	0	0

	1965	1980	1990	2000	2007	2010	2013	2015	2016	2017
Difference in treatment of tax credits	0	0	0	0	0	4 712	5 240	4 016	4 016	3 988
Capital transfer for uncollected revenue	0	-1 374	-2 387	-1 917	-2 726	-3 475	-15 512	-19 396	-9 519	-8 926
Voluntary social security contributions	0	1 673	8 087	16 633	17 061	17 192	14 655	14 721	14 833	14 891
Miscellaneous differences	0	0	0	0	0	0	0	0	0	0
National Accounts: Taxes and actual social contributions	20 821	166 657	387 932	638 626	824 324	832 401	905 384	956 623	978 483	1 014 371
Imputed social contributions	0	5 958	4 592	6 223	5 693	5 356	4 520	4 067	3 668	3 507
National Accounts: Taxes and all social contributions	20 821	172 615	392 525	644 849	830 017	837 757	909 904	960 690	982 151	1 017 878

.. Not available
Note: Year ending 31st December.
The figures are on an accrual basis.
Heading 2300 includes a small amount of voluntary contributions which cannot be isolated.
Source: Danmarks Statistik.

StatLink https://doi.org/10.1787/888934056849

Table 5.8. Estonia: Detailed country table, 1965-2017

Million EUR

	1965	1980	1990	2000	2007	2010	2013	2015	2016	2017
Total tax revenue	..	..	..	**1 919**	**5 082**	**4 894**	**5 988**	**6 864**	**7 271**	**7 738**
Total tax revenue exclusive of customs duties	..	..	..	..	**5 047**	**4 870**	**5 960**	**6 830**	**7 237**	**7 700**
1000 Taxes on income, profits and capital gains	..	..	..	**476**	**1 197**	**970**	**1 357**	**1 607**	**1 628**	**1 710**
1100 Of individuals	..	..	..	421	936	776	1 031	1 182	1 259	1 344
1110 On income and profits	..	..	..	421	936	776	1 031	1 182	1 259	1 344
1120 On capital gains	..	..	..	0	0	0	0	0	0	0
1200 Corporate	..	..	..	55	261	194	327	424	369	366
1210 On profits	..	..	..	55	65	35	62	38	38	40
1220 On capital gains	..	..	..	0	196	159	265	386	331	325
1300 Unallocable between 1100 and 1200	..	..	..	0	0	0	0	0	0	0
2000 Social security contributions	..	..	..	**674**	**1 683**	**1 879**	**2 077**	**2 290**	**2 429**	**2 636**
2100 Employees	..	..	..	0	28	116	109	99	103	112
2110 On a payroll basis	..	..	..	..	28	116	109	99	103	112
2120 On an income tax basis	..	..	..	..	0	0	0	0	0	0
2200 Employers	..	..	..	662	1 635	1 742	1 949	2 171	2 306	2 503
2210 On a payroll basis	..	..	..	662	1 635	1 742	1 949	2 171	2 306	2 503
2220 On an income tax basis	..	..	..	0	0	0	0	0	0	0
2300 Self-employed or non-employed	..	..	..	12	21	21	19	20	20	21
2310 On a payroll basis	..	..	..	12	21	21	19	20	20	21
2320 On an income tax basis	..	..	..	0	0	0	0	0	0	0
2400 Unallocable between 2100, 2200 and 2300	..	..	..	0	0	0	0	0	0	0
2410 On a payroll basis	..	..	..	..	..	..	..	..	..	..
2420 On an income tax basis	..	..	..	..	..	..	..	..	..	..
3000 Taxes on payroll and workforce	..	..	..	**0**	**0**	**0**	**0**	**0**	**0**	**0**
4000 Taxes on property	..	..	..	**24**	**35**	**51**	**57**	**58**	**59**	**58**
4100 Recurrent taxes on immovable property	..	..	..	24	35	51	57	58	59	58
Land tax	..	..	..	24	35	51	57	58	59	58
4110 Households	..	..	..	..	..	..	..	..	..	..
4120 Others	..	..	..	..	..	..	..	..	..	..
4200 Recurrent taxes on net wealth	..	..	..	0	0	0	0	0	0	0
4210 Individual	..	..	..	..	..	..	..	..	..	..
4220 Corporate	..	..	..	..	..	..	..	..	..	..
4300 Estate, inheritance and gift taxes	..	..	..	0	0	0	0	0	0	0
4310 Estate and inheritance taxes	..	..	..	..	..	..	..	..	..	..
4320 Gift taxes	..	..	..	..	..	..	..	..	..	..
4400 Taxes on financial and capital transactions	..	..	..	0	0	0	0	0	0	0
4500 Non-recurrent taxes	..	..	..	0	0	0	0	0	0	0
4510 On net wealth	..	..	..	..	..	..	..	..	..	..
4520 Other non-recurrent taxes	..	..	..	..	..	..	..	..	..	..
4600 Other recurrent taxes on property	..	..	..	0	0	0	0	0	0	0
5000 Taxes on goods and services	..	..	..	**745**	**2 131**	**1 969**	**2 468**	**2 875**	**3 121**	**3 296**
5100 Taxes on production, sale, transfer, etc.	..	..	..	723	2 064	1 914	2 402	2 794	3 020	3 189
5110 General taxes	..	..	..	521	1 423	1 263	1 558	1 872	1 974	2 148
5111 Value added taxes	..	..	..	520	1 423	1 257	1 558	1 872	1 974	2 148
5112 Sales tax	..	..	..	0	0	6	0	0	0	0
5113 Other	..	..	..	0	0	0	0	0	0	0
5120 Taxes on specific goods and services	..	..	..	202	640	651	844	922	1 046	1 040
5121 Excise duties	..	..	..	183	577	619	796	869	997	990
Alcohol	..	..	..	62	153	154	212	207	254	222
Tobacco	..	..	..	36	134	91	169	183	201	197
Fuel	..	..	..	76	290	343	383	444	506	535
Motor vehicle	..	..	..	9	0	0	0	0	0	0
Package	..	..	..	0	0	0	0	1	0	0
Fur	..	..	..	0	0	0	0	0	0	0
Electricity	..	..	..	0	0	31	33	34	35	36
5122 Profits of fiscal monopolies	..	..	..	0	0	0	0	0	0	0
5123 Customs and import duties	..	..	..	2	0	0	0	0	0	0
5124 Taxes on exports	..	..	..	0	0	0	0	0	0	0
5125 Taxes on investment goods	..	..	..	0	0	0	0	0	0	0
5126 Taxes on specific services	..	..	..	17	64	33	48	53	48	51
Gambling tax	..	..	..	7	30	21	22	23	26	27
Advertising tax	..	..	..	1	3	2	4	4	5	6
Postal service payment	..	..	..	0	0	0	0	0	0	0
Liquid fuel stockpiling fee	..	..	..	0	2	5	6	5	4	5
Contributions to the Guarantee Fund	..	..	..	9	29	5	17	20	13	13
5127 Other taxes on internat. trade and transactions	..	..	..	0	0	0	0	0	0	0
5128 Other taxes	..	..	..	0	0	0	0	0	0	0
5130 Unallocable between 5110 and 5120	..	..	..	0	0	0	0	0	0	0
5200 Taxes on use of goods and perform activities	..	..	..	22	68	55	65	80	101	107

	1965	1980	1990	2000	2007	2010	2013	2015	2016	2017
5210 Recurrent taxes	..	..	..	22	68	55	65	73	80	84
Car registration fee	..	..	..	2	5	4	7	7	7	8
Heavy vehicle tax	..	..	..	0	4	4	4	5	5	5
5211 Paid by households: motor vehicles	..	..	..	..	..	..	..	..	..	..
5212 Paid by others: motor vehicles	..	..	..	..	..	..	..	..	..	..
5213 Paid in respect of other goods	..	..	..	20	58	47	55	61	68	71
Business and professional licenses	..	..	..	3	2	1	1	1	1	1
Pollution fee	..	..	..	10	44	31	37	44	50	53
Specific use of water	..	..	..	4	9	13	14	13	13	15
Fees for closure of roads, streets and squares	..	..	..	0	1	1	1	2	2	1
Fishing fees	..	..	..	1	1	1	2	2	2	1
Tax on motor vehicle	..	..	..	2	0	0	0	0	0	0
Boat tax	..	..	..	0	0	0	0	0	0	0
Animal tax	..	..	..	0	0	0	0	0	0	0
5220 Non-recurrent taxes	..	..	..	0	0	0	0	7	21	24
Revenue from the sale of emission permits	..	..	..	..	..	..	..	7	21	24
5300 Unallocable between 5100 and 5200	..	..	..	0	0	0	0	0	0	0
6000 Other taxes	**..**	**..**	**..**	**0**	**0**	**0**	**0**	**0**	**0**	**0**
6100 Paid solely by business	..	..	..	..	..	..	..	..	..	..
6200 Other	..	..	..	..	..	..	..	..	..	..
Other taxes	..	..	..	..	..	..	..	..	..	..
Custom duties collected for the EU	**..**	**..**	**..**	**..**	**35**	**24**	**29**	**34**	**34**	**38**
Total tax revenue on cash basis	**..**	**..**	**..**	**1 907**	**5 003**	**4 921**	**5 964**	**6 833**	**7 213**	**7 694**
Total tax revenue on accrual basis	**..**	**..**	**..**	**1 919**	**5 082**	**4 894**	**5 988**	**6 864**	**7 271**	**7 738**
Conciliation with National Accounts										
Additional taxes included in National Accounts	..	..	..	0	0	0	0	0	0	0
Taxes excluded from National Accounts	..	..	..	0	0	0	0	0	0	0
Difference in treatment of tax credits	..	..	..	0	0	0	0	0	0	0
Capital transfer for uncollected revenue	..	..	..	0	0	0	0	0	0	0
Voluntary social security contributions	..	..	..	0	0	0	0	0	0	0
Miscellaneous differences	..	..	..	0	0	0	0	0	0	0
National Accounts: Taxes and actual social contributions	..	..	..	1 919	5 082	4 894	5 988	6 864	7 271	7 738
Imputed social contributions	..	..	..	4	20	30	38	49	52	62
National Accounts: Taxes and all social contributions	..	..	..	1 922	5 102	4 924	6 026	6 913	7 323	7 800

.. Not available
Note: Year ending 31st December.
Data on an accrual basis.
Source: Statistics Estonia.

StatLink https://doi.org/10.1787/888934056868

Table 5.9. Finland: Detailed country table, 1965-2017

Million EUR

	1965	1980	1990	2000	2007	2010	2013	2015	2016	2017
Total tax revenue	**1 362**	**11 895**	**39 050**	**62 435**	**77 447**	**76 315**	**88 688**	**92 074**	**95 126**	**96 985**
Total tax revenue exclusive of custom duties	..	..	..	**62 306**	**77 248**	**76 164**	**88 522**	**91 909**	**94 963**	**96 811**
1000 Taxes on income, profits and capital gains	**564**	**4 654**	**15 323**	**26 911**	**30 358**	**27 104**	**30 797**	**32 371**	**32 934**	**34 404**
1100 Of individuals	453	4 248	13 562	19 118	23 396	22 545	25 998	27 824	28 136	28 277
1110 On income and profits	453	4 234	13 521	19 118	23 396	22 545	25 998	27 824	28 136	28 277
Tax on income	125	1 827	5 918	9 036	9 086	6 465	7 903	9 138	9 312	9 109
The final withdrawal tax on interest income	0	0	0	92	254	205	207	110	90	66
Communal tax	279	2 376	7 603	9 990	14 056	15 875	17 888	18 576	18 734	19 102
Seaman's tax	3	31	0	0	0	0	0	0	0	0
National pension contributions	32	0	0	0	0	0	0	0	0	0
National health insurance contributions	15	0	0	0	0	0	0	0	0	0
1120 On capital gains	0	14	42	0	0	0	0	0	0	0
Tax on lottery prizes	..	14	42	..	..	..	..	..	..	..
1200 Corporate	111	405	1 761	7 792	6 962	4 559	4 799	4 547	4 798	6 127
1210 On profits	111	405	1 761	7 792	6 962	4 559	4 799	4 547	4 798	6 127
Tax on income	72	202	1 001	4 758	5 298	2 972	3 227	2 761	3 268	4 238
Communal tax	36	187	699	2 900	1 541	1 471	1 456	1 668	1 530	1 889
Church tax	3	16	61	134	123	116	116	118	0	0
1220 On capital gains	0	0	0	0	0	0	0	0	0	0
1300 Unallocable between 1100 and 1200	0	0	0	0	0	0	0	0	0	0
2000 Social security contributions	**93**	**2 776**	**10 012**	**15 756**	**21 384**	**22 648**	**25 632**	**26 639**	**27 641**	**27 000**
2100 Employees	1	394	1 152	2 926	4 050	4 710	5 811	6 364	6 836	7 467
For employment pension schemes	1	10	23	2 120	2 950	3 386	4 235	4 714	4 773	5 182
For unemployment schemes	0	0	0	435	369	267	457	489	870	1 242
2110 On a payroll basis	..	10	23	2 565	3 319	3 653	4 692	5 203	5 643	6 424
2120 On an income tax basis	..	384	1 129	361	731	1 057	1 119	1 161	1 193	1 043
National pension contributions	..	251	502	2	0	0	0	0	0	0
National health insurance contributions	..	133	627	359	731	1 057	1 119	1 161	1 193	1 043
2200 Employers	93	2 230	8 127	11 571	15 715	16 041	17 888	18 232	18 763	17 585
For national pension schemes	29	685	1 502	1 566	1 331	0	0	0	0	0
For national health insurance	10	244	792	839	1 142	1 590	1 612	1 662	1 712	914
For unemployment schemes	3	106	206	1 143	1 346	1 377	1 775	1 676	2 110	1 817
For employment pension schemes	50	1 195	5 627	8 023	11 896	13 074	14 501	14 894	14 941	14 854
For accident and group life insurance premiums	0	0	0	0	0	0	0	0	0	0
2210 On a payroll basis	..	2 230	8 127	11 571	15 715	16 041	17 888	18 232	18 763	17 585
2220 On an income tax basis	..	0	0	0	0	0	0	0	0	0
2300 Self-employed or non-employed	0	152	733	1 259	1 619	1 897	1 933	2 043	2 042	1 948
For employment pension schemes	..	84	394	576	817	932	1 187	1 269	1 247	1 252
2310 On a payroll basis	..	84	394	576	817	932	1 187	1 269	1 247	1 252
2320 On an income tax basis	..	68	339	683	802	965	746	774	795	696
National pension contributions	..	43	151	5	0	0	0	0	0	0
National health insurance contributions	..	25	188	678	802	965	746	774	795	696
2400 Unallocable between 2100, 2200 and 2300	0	0	0	0	0	0	0	0	0	0
2410 On a payroll basis	..	..	..	..	..	..	..	..	..	..
2420 On an income tax basis	..	..	..	..	..	..	..	..	..	..
3000 Taxes on payroll and workforce	**70**	**22**	**0**	**0**	**0**	**0**	**0**	**0**	**0**	**0**
Soc. Sec. contr. for children allowance	70	22	..	..	..	..	..	..	..	..
4000 Taxes on property	**54**	**221**	**956**	**1 518**	**2 012**	**2 087**	**2 599**	**3 017**	**3 066**	**3 459**
4100 Recurrent taxes on immovable property	0	0	76	569	855	1 169	1 363	1 603	1 670	1 774
4110 Households	..	..	46	273	405	576	623	733	764	811
4120 Others	..	..	30	296	450	593	740	870	906	963
4200 Recurrent taxes on net wealth	24	24	26	179	0	0	0	0	0	0
4210 Individual	11	23	25	175	..	..	..	..	..	..
4220 Corporate	13	2	1	4	..	..	..	..	..	..
4300 Estate, inheritance and gift taxes	3	26	146	368	459	387	646	631	522	909
4310 Estate and inheritance taxes	3	21	121	307	384	324	541	528	437	761
4320 Gift taxes	1	5	25	61	75	63	105	103	85	148
4400 Taxes on financial and capital transactions	27	170	707	401	698	531	590	783	874	776
Stamp duty excluded entertainment	27	170	688	-20	0	0	0	0	0	0
Credit tax	0	0	19	0	0	0	0	0	0	0
Transfer tax	0	0	0	421	698	531	590	783	874	776
4500 Non-recurrent taxes	0	0	0	0	0	0	0	0	0	0
4510 On net wealth	..	..	..	..	..	..	..	..	..	..
4520 Other non-recurrent taxes	..	..	..	..	..	..	..	..	..	..
4600 Other recurrent taxes on property	0	0	0	0	0	0	0	0	0	0
5000 Taxes on goods and services	**578**	**4 202**	**12 710**	**18 091**	**23 425**	**24 256**	**29 430**	**29 801**	**31 223**	**31 887**
5100 Taxes on production, sale, transfer, etc.	570	4 158	12 553	17 651	22 754	23 491	28 496	28 744	29 979	30 577
5110 General taxes	251	2 062	7 519	10 869	15 207	15 533	18 888	18 974	19 694	20 404

	1965	1980	1990	2000	2007	2010	2013	2015	2016	2017
5111 Value added taxes	251	2 062	7 519	10 869	15 207	15 533	18 888	18 974	19 694	20 404
Value added taxes	251	2 062	7 519	9 616	13 657	13 691	16 561	16 680	17 206	17 707
VAT repayments of local government	0	0	0	849	1 550	1 842	2 327	2 294	2 488	2 697
Social Insur. Institutions' part of VAT revenue	0	0	0	404	0	0	0	0	0	0
5112 Sales tax	0	0	0	0	0	0	0	0	0	0
5113 Other	0	0	0	0	0	0	0	0	0	0
Suppl. sales tax on consumer durables	..	..	..	..	..	..	..	..	..	..
5120 Taxes on specific goods and services	319	2 096	5 034	6 782	7 547	7 958	9 608	9 770	10 285	10 173
5121 Excise duties	183	1 615	3 811	5 613	6 013	6 286	7 511	7 678	8 195	8 002
Excise on tobacco products	52	206	473	561	622	655	852	885	983	962
Excise on sweetments	6	23	26	0	0	0	0	0	0	0
Excise on medium, strong beer	3	109	419	0	0	0	0	0	0	0
Excise on non-alcoholic beverages	2	17	22	32	35	37	204	250	255	151
Excise on certain foodstuffs	3	218	36	0	0	0	0	0	0	0
Excise on liquid fuels	58	504	983	2 582	2 907	3 167	3 925	4 054	4 407	4 324
Excise on motor cars	28	238	697	1 059	1 217	941	931	882	959	972
Tax on alcoholic beverages	29	353	813	1 239	1 016	1 279	1 355	1 356	1 344	1 340
Levies on pharmacy	2	16	46	86	113	122	153	165	174	182
Levies for price reduction on butter	0	3	0	0	0	0	0	0	0	0
Levies for marketing of milk	0	12	58	0	0	0	0	0	0	0
Excise on margarines	0	18	55	0	0	0	0	0	0	0
Stock-building levies on liquid fuels	0	15	44	46	50	48	45	43	44	43
Excise on sugar products	0	18	34	0	0	0	0	0	0	0
Excise on feeding stuffs	0	0	0	0	0	0	0	0	0	0
Excise on fertilizers	0	21	21	0	0	0	0	0	0	0
Excise on oil-based concentrated feed	0	1	0	0	0	0	0	0	0	0
Excise on protein feed	0	0	0	0	0	0	0	0	0	0
Equalization fee agricultural products	0	8	29	0	0	0	0	0	0	0
Excise on albumen	0	0	30	0	0	0	0	0	0	0
Tax on electricity	0	65	0	0	0	0	0	0	0	0
Oil damage levy	0	0	7	5	8	20	27	24	10	8
Oil waste levy	0	0	4	3	4	4	4	4	4	4
Price difference compensations	0	-231	0	0	0	0	0	0	0	0
The milk quota charge	0	0	6	0	0	0	0	0	0	0
Levies for marketing of special agric. prod.	0	0	0	0	0	0	0	0	0	0
Excise on phosphorous fertilizers	0	0	7	0	0	0	0	0	0	0
Excise on certain beverage packages	0	0	0	0	41	13	15	15	15	16
5122 Profits of fiscal monopolies	38	86	202	0	0	0	0	0	0	0
Excess profits on alcohol	38	86	202	..	..	..	..	..	..	..
5123 Customs and import duties	88	235	423	0	0	0	0	0	0	0
Import duties	62	126	232	..	..	..	..	..	..	..
Import levies on agricultural products	26	6	12	..	..	..	..	..	..	..
Local import duties (Town dues)	1	0	0	..	..	..	..	..	..	..
Import levies price stabilisation fund	0	3	0	..	..	..	..	..	..	..
Custom duties and levies on agricultural goods	0	0	0	..	..	..	..	..	..	..
Equalization tax	0	100	179	..	..	..	..	..	..	..
5124 Taxes on exports	0	0	0	0	0	0	0	0	0	0
Export duties	..	..	..	..	..	..	..	..	..	..
Levies on export	..	..	..	..	..	..	..	..	..	..
Counter-cyclical tax exports	..	..	..	..	..	..	..	..	..	..
5125 Taxes on investment goods	0	0	0	0	0	0	0	0	0	0
Investment tax on buildings	..	..	..	..	..	..	..	..	..	..
5126 Taxes on specific services	9	161	599	1 160	1 533	1 671	2 096	2 091	2 089	2 170
Net revenue of betting	8	94	329	703	807	874	948	967	966	1 060
Tax on motion pictures	0	0	0	0	0	0	0	0	0	0
Stamp duties on entertainment	2	5	0	0	0	0	0	0	0	0
Fire protection levy	0	3	7	6	8	9	10	11	11	11
Tax on waste	0	0	0	33	56	42	56	32	21	12
Rail tax	0	0	0	0	18	18	19	6	6	5
Tax on insurance premiums	0	58	263	337	509	584	712	777	785	768
Tax on lottery prizes	0	0	0	80	135	144	217	222	231	228
Tax on telecommunications	0	0	0	0	0	0	0	0	0	0
Bank tax	0	0	0	0	0	0	134	0	-43	-36
Contributions to the Resolution Fund	0	0	0	0	0	0	0	76	112	122
5127 Other taxes on internat. trade and transactions	0	0	0	0	0	0	0	0	0	0
Tax on charter flights	..	..	..	..	..	..	..	..	..	..
5128 Other taxes	0	0	0	9	1	1	1	1	1	1
Sugar levy	..	..	..	9	1	1	1	1	1	1
Steel and coal levy	..	..	..	0	0	0	0	0	0	0
5130 Unallocable between 5110 and 5120	0	0	0	0	0	0	0	0	0	0
5200 Taxes on use of goods and perform activities	8	44	157	440	671	765	934	1 057	1 244	1 310
5210 Recurrent taxes	8	44	157	423	637	725	897	960	1 118	1 204

	1965	1980	1990	2000	2007	2010	2013	2015	2016	2017
5211 Paid by households: motor vehicles	0	2	5	165	486	541	696	748	886	960
5212 Paid by others: motor vehicles	7	32	135	235	126	150	170	182	197	209
5213 Paid in respect of other goods	1	10	17	22	25	34	31	30	35	35
Dog licenses	1	2	4	5	3	2	2	1	1	1
Hunting and fishing licenses	1	7	13	17	17	24	23	22	23	22
Seamens welfare and rescue levy	0	0	0	1	1	1	1	0	0	0
Nuclear energy research levy	0	0	0	0	4	7	5	7	11	12
5220 Non-recurrent taxes	0	0	0	17	34	40	37	97	126	106
Vehicle registration tax	..	..	..	17	34	40	37	36	36	31
Income from auction of emission allowances	..	..	..	0	0	0	0	61	90	75
5300 Unallocable between 5100 and 5200	0	0	0	0	0	0	0	0	0	0
6000 Other taxes	**2**	**21**	**50**	**30**	**69**	**69**	**64**	**81**	**99**	**61**
6100 Paid solely by business	0	0	0	0	0	0	0	0	0	0
6200 Other	2	21	50	30	69	69	64	81	99	61
Custom duties collected for the EU	**..**	**..**	**..**	**129**	**199**	**151**	**166**	**165**	**163**	**174**
Total tax revenue on cash basis	**1 362**	**11 895**	**39 398**	**61 639**	**77 110**	**76 214**	**88 416**	**91 917**	**95 191**	**96 563**
Total tax revenue on accrual basis	**..**	**..**	**39 050**	**62 435**	**77 447**	**76 315**	**88 688**	**92 074**	**95 126**	**96 985**
Conciliation with National Accounts										
Additional taxes included in National Accounts	..	0	0	0	0	0	0	0	0	0
Taxes excluded from National Accounts	..	0	0	0	0	0	0	0	0	0
Difference in treatment of tax credits	..	0	0	0	0	0	0	0	0	0
Capital transfer for uncollected revenue	..	0	0	0	0	0	0	0	0	0
Voluntary social security contributions	..	262	632	235	228	254	270	303	308	302
Miscellaneous differences	..	0	0	0	0	0	0	0	0	0
National Accounts: Taxes and actual social contributions	..	12 157	39 682	62 671	77 675	76 569	88 958	92 377	95 434	97 287
Imputed social contributions	..	513	688	30	0	0	0	0	0	0
National Accounts: Taxes and all social contributions	..	12 670	40 370	62 701	77 675	76 569	88 958	92 377	95 434	97 287

.. Not available

Note: Year ending 31st December.

From 1988 data are on accrual basis.

Finland has an imputation system where the full credit is taken into account in shareholders taxation. According to estimates made by the National Board of Taxation, the credit given to shareholders was 193 millions euros in 1991; the effects on personal income taxation are estimated.

Headings 2120 and 2320: The breakdown of contributions paid by employees and self-employed or non-employed is estimated.

Heading 4200: All figures in this subheading are estimated.

Heading 4400: Stamp duties include payment for some government services where the levy can be regarded as requited (the levy is linked to the cost of providing the service). However they are classified as taxes and recorded under this subheading as taxes on financial and capital transactions because the amounts involved cannot be identified.

Heading 5121: The negative item under the title 'Price difference compensations' refers to the subsidies paid out on agricultural products under the price compensation scheme which can be offset against any positive tax liability which arising under the same scheme. From 1983 this item has been offset against revenues from excises on certain foodstuffs, on medium and stronger beer and on non-alcoholic beverages.

Heading 5126: Prior to 1979, no figures are available for amounts paid under the Fire protection levy .

Heading 5212: Prior to 1990, a part of the tax is paid by 'households'.

Source: Bulletin of Statistics; Central Statistical Office (for Central Government revenues); the Annual report of the National Pension Institute and Official Statistics of Finland Series XXIIA published by the Ministry and Social Affairs (for the Social Security and private pension respectively); supplementary information from unpublished sources.

StatLink https://doi.org/10.1787/888934056887

Table 5.10. France: Detailed country table, 1965-2017

Million EUR

	1965	1980	1990	2000	2007	2010	2013	2015	2016	2017
Total tax revenue	**25 776**	**178 576**	**433 771**	**645 528**	**831 226**	**846 318**	**966 817**	**1 002 131**	**1 020 206**	**1 065 242**
Total tax revenue exclusive of custom duties	**0**	**0**	**0**	**644 015**	**829 569**	**844 566**	**964 975**	**1 000 199**	**1 018 387**	**1 063 334**
1000 Taxes on income, profits and capital gains	**4 095**	**30 019**	**69 649**	**160 363**	**197 939**	**191 085**	**235 964**	**234 532**	**238 091**	**251 708**
1100 Of individuals	2 736	20 734	46 272	115 885	141 405	144 165	179 715	188 357	192 421	197 910
1110 On income and profits	2 723	20 674	46 252	115 884	141 405	144 165	179 715	188 357	192 421	197 910
Tax on individual income	..	18 207	39 237	49 548	48 597	49 575	70 098	72 750	75 571	76 748
Tax on non business profits	..	51	189	293	559	446	598	927	617	800
Tax on financial assets	..	2 333	3 971	0	0	0	0	0	0	0
CSG, CRDS, social security contributions for the benefit of the FSV, FNAL and / or the FS	..	0	0	65 953	92 204	93 972	108 247	113 065	111 751	115 440
Flat-rate tax on precious metals	..	70	58	47	37	52	69	71	70	72
Tax on multiple wages	..	7	20	38	0	0	0	0	0	0
Social solidarity contribution	..	0	2 207	5	0	82	381	0	2 486	2 633
Others	..	6	571	0	8	38	322	1 544	1 926	2 217
1120 On capital gains	14	59	20	1	0	0	0	0	0	0
On capital gains	..	0	0	0	0	0	0	0	0	0
Levies on construction profits	..	59	20	1	0	0	0	0	0	0
1200 Corporate	1 358	9 158	23 117	44 478	56 534	46 920	56 249	46 175	45 670	53 798
1210 On profits	1 358	9 158	23 117	44 478	56 534	46 920	56 249	46 175	45 670	53 798
Corporations' tax (excluding tax credits to reduce or remove the taxation)	..	8 524	20 804	39 755	51 063	39 095	46 474	39 579	39 521	47 834
3% tax on dividends	..	0	0	0	0	0	1 943	2 165	2 038	1 677
Tax on financial assets	..	487	1 333	1 460	3 492	5 952	5 894	3 325	3 037	3 062
Precount on distributed profits (exceptional levy of 25% since 2005)	..	36	247	1 135	88	28	-6	4	0	1
Exceptional levies on temporary work corporations	..	0	0	0	0	0	0	0	0	0
Social contribution on corporation profits	..	0	0	589	158	842	1 160	971	978	1 142
Annual flat-rate tax	..	111	658	1 484	1 656	599	680	4	2	2
Exceptionnal levies on insurances	..	0	61	55	64	94	104	127	94	80
Other	..	0	14	0	13	310	0	0	0	0
1220 On capital gains	0	0	0	0	0	0	0	0	0	0
1300 Unallocable between 1100 and 1200	0	127	260	0	0	0	0	0	0	0
2000 Social security contributions	**8 804**	**76 235**	**191 141**	**231 875**	**307 663**	**323 816**	**356 934**	**370 375**	**375 441**	**387 443**
2100 Employees	1 701	19 851	57 347	57 686	76 815	78 268	88 097	93 767	96 643	100 910
Actual cotisations	0	19 851	57 347	57 686	76 815	78 268	88 097	93 767	96 643	100 910
2110 On a payroll basis	0	0	0	57 686	76 815	78 268	88 097	93 767	96 643	100 910
2120 On an income tax basis	0	0	0	0	0	0	0	0	0	0
2200 Employers	6 525	50 742	118 079	159 476	208 688	219 687	240 672	248 173	250 928	258 691
Actual cotisations	0	50 742	118 079	159 476	208 688	219 687	240 672	248 173	250 928	258 691
2210 On a payroll basis	0	0	0	159 476	208 688	219 687	240 672	248 173	250 928	258 691
2220 On an income tax basis	0	0	0	0	0	0	0	0	0	0
2300 Self-employed or non-employed	578	5 642	15 714	14 713	22 160	25 861	28 165	28 435	27 870	27 842
Actual cotisations	..	5 642	15 714	14 713	22 160	25 861	28 165	28 435	27 870	27 842
2310 On a payroll basis	0	0	0	14 713	22 160	25 861	28 165	28 435	27 870	27 842
2320 On an income tax basis	0	0	0	0	0	0	0	0	0	0
2400 Unallocable between 2100, 2200 and 2300	0	0	0	0	0	0	0	0	0	0
2410 On a payroll basis	0	0	0	0	0	0	0	0	0	0
2420 On an income tax basis	0	0	0	0	0	0	0	0	0	0
3000 Taxes on payroll and workforce	**1 189**	**3 935**	**8 254**	**14 916**	**22 874**	**26 926**	**33 595**	**34 574**	**34 801**	**35 715**
Tax on wages	0	2 413	5 208	7 583	10 272	11 440	13 127	13 165	13 515	13 845
Corporate social contributions	0	0	0	0	0	657	4 654	5 019	5 245	5 497
Apprenticeship tax	0	172	101	102	964	430	554	29	30	31
Tax benefitting the wage garantee scheme (AGS): royalties for concessions, patents, licenses, trademarks, processes, rights and similar values	0	263	379	551	736	1 759	1 435	1 479	1 259	966
Tax on vocational training	0	236	30	97	19	13	17	17	17	21
Tax benefitting the FNAL: ACOSS (employer contributions)	0	120	754	1 506	2 412	2 465	3 123	2 929	2 674	2 683
Tax benefitting the transports union	0	731	1 600	3 786	5 738	7 044	8 089	9 249	9 679	10 244
Payment benefitting the UNEDIC	0	0	23	24	0	0	0	0	0	0
Tax on re-employed pensioners income	0	0	0	0	0	0	0	0	0	0
Providence contribution	0	0	0	415	773	1 120	496	415	423	397
Others	0	0	159	851	100	81	49	27	23	21
Taxes benefitting the national solidarity fund for autonomy (CNSA)	0	0	0	0	1 860	1 917	2 051	1 891	1 920	1 994
Employers' contribution to the early retirement of asbestos workers regime (FCAATA)	0	0	0	0	0	0	0	0	0	0
Exceptional levy on high wages	0	0	0	0	0	0	0	354	16	16
4000 Taxes on property	**1 105**	**8 591**	**27 434**	**46 169**	**67 573**	**73 085**	**84 209**	**92 323**	**95 200**	**100 989**
4100 Recurrent taxes on immovable property	506	5 358	14 808	29 439	42 130	50 061	57 411	60 443	62 672	64 152

	1965	1980	1990	2000	2007	2010	2013	2015	2016	2017
4110 Households	198	4 454	11 493	22 285	32 839	38 952	44 684	46 873	48 425	49 557
Council tax	0	2 306	5 100	8 366	12 433	15 254	17 470	18 424	18 807	19 311
Tax on real-estate properties	0	1 034	4 040	8 460	11 983	14 403	16 539	17 557	18 465	18 926
Waste collection tax	0	534	1 219	3 103	5 117	5 699	6 552	6 567	6 703	6 803
Contribution to public broadcasting	0	0	0	2 099	2 255	2 472	2 866	3 012	3 210	3 248
Tax on non-developped land	0	506	979	172	851	919	955	980	955	971
Chamber of Agriculture tax	0	0	0	53	59	61	62	61	59	61
Street-cleaning tax	0	0	0	68	74	75	109	109	109	113
Other taxes	0	74	156	-36	67	69	131	163	117	124
4120 Others	308	904	3 315	7 154	9 291	11 109	12 727	13 570	14 247	14 595
Tax on real-estate properties	0	759	3 032	6 256	9 054	10 865	12 477	13 246	13 930	14 277
Tax on non-developped land	0	127	245	688	0	0	0	0	0	0
Chamber of Agriculture tax	0	18	39	210	237	244	250	242	234	243
Other taxes	0	0	0	0	0	0	0	82	83	75
4200 Recurrent taxes on net wealth	0	0	2 615	2 440	4 390	4 461	4 372	5 224	4 837	5 068
4210 Individual	..	..	938	2 440	4 390	4 461	4 372	5 224	4 837	5 068
4220 Corporate	..	..	1 677	0	0	0	..	..	..	..
4300 Estate, inheritance and gift taxes	145	1 010	4 124	6 907	8 910	7 738	10 456	12 317	12 489	14 344
4310 Estate and inheritance taxes	140	875	3 490	5 508	7 853	6 862	9 368	10 690	10 863	11 898
Inheritance taxes	0	861	3 453	5 428	7 794	6 806	8 433	10 540	10 689	11 785
Various receipts and tax fines	0	14	37	80	59	56	935	150	174	113
4320 Gift taxes	5	135	634	1 399	1 057	876	1 088	1 627	1 626	2 446
Donations	0	113	568	1 399	1 057	876	1 088	1 627	1 626	2 446
Various receipts and tax fines	0	0	0	0	0	0	0	0	0	0
Other taxes	0	22	66	0	0	0	0	0	0	0
4400 Taxes on financial and capital transactions	447	2 224	5 886	7 383	12 143	10 825	11 970	14 339	15 202	17 425
Debts, annuities, offices	0	30	209	279	443	279	359	335	375	325
Business assets	0	253	518	199	268	154	135	132	137	153
Tangible movable assets	0	14	18	0	0	1	0	1	1	1
Properties and real property rights	0	63	4	2	2	3	1	1	2	1
Agreements and civil acts between companies	0	95	218	4	5	8	6	7	7	4
Various receipts and tax fines	0	35	60	367	179	253	4	6	5	10
Judicial and extra-judicial documents	0	6	10	0	0	0	0	0	0	0
Land registration tax	0	781	38	68	130	140	703	770	805	897
Various stamps and fees	0	94	242	0	0	0	0	0	0	0
Taxes on stock exchange transactions	0	168	525	407	271	0	0	0	0	0
Tax on financial transactions	0	0	0	0	0	0	697	917	715	964
Additional registration taxes	0	679	4 002	5 339	10 396	9 567	9 538	11 618	12 533	14 536
Other taxes and receipts	0	5	44	718	449	420	527	552	622	534
4500 Non-recurrent taxes	8	0	0	0	0	0	0	0	0	0
4510 On net wealth	8	..	..	0	0	0	..	..	..	..
4520 Other non-recurrent taxes	0	..	..	0	0	0	..	..	..	..
4600 Other recurrent taxes on property	0	0	0	0	0	0	0	0	0	0
5000 Taxes on goods and services	**9 902**	**54 317**	**123 235**	**166 608**	**206 293**	**210 067**	**231 413**	**242 920**	**248 824**	**260 689**
5100 Taxes on production, sale, transfer, etc.	9 676	52 719	119 201	162 007	200 452	203 746	224 764	235 972	241 589	253 175
5110 General taxes	5 994	37 760	81 341	110 296	142 033	141 219	150 935	156 940	158 921	166 354
5111 Value added taxes	5 173	37 282	79 972	107 511	137 137	136 129	145 264	152 550	155 370	162 793
VAT (general budget)	0	36 895	78 902	103 054	136 927	135 578	144 490	151 680	154 490	161 932
VAT (BAPSA)	0	62	101	4 111	0	0	0	0	0	0
Other VAT	0	325	969	0	0	0	0	0	0	0
Sub-compensations of agricultural VAT	0	0	0	346	138	330	462	381	373	364
Value added taxes on subsidies	0	0	0	0	72	221	312	489	507	497
5112 Sales tax	822	0	0	0	0	0	0	0	0	0
5113 Other	0	477	1 369	2 784	4 896	5 090	5 671	4 390	3 551	3 561
Social solidarity contribution	..	477	1 369	2 784	4 896	5 090	5 671	4 390	3 551	3 561
5120 Taxes on specific goods and services	3 682	14 960	37 860	51 712	58 419	62 527	73 829	79 032	82 668	86 821

	1965	1980	1990	2000	2007	2010	2013	2015	2016	2017
5121 Excise duties	2 775	11 013	26 834	39 850	44 013	45 770	52 343	56 660	58 916	62 012
Excise tax on energy products	0	7 136	17 476	23 493	24 318	23 577	23 693	26 238	27 926	29 587
Exceptional levies on oil product corporations	0	0	0	0	0	0	0	0	0	0
Taxes on wines, ciders and meads	0	97	174	0	121	121	486	501	497	495
Taxes on alcohol	0	1 238	1 593	3 025	484	2 482	2 950	2 956	2 965	2 974
Taxes on beer and mineral water	0	58	91	20	409	538	803	931	957	999
Other taxes and receipts	0	136	38	19	2 169	100	90	110	110	72
Taxes on tobaccos and matches	0	1 188	2 989	7 965	9 659	11 083	12 227	12 318	12 058	12 441
Fines and confiscations	0	2	1	0	0	0	0	0	0	0
Gold and silver warranty	0	6	19	29	2	0	0	0	0	0
ANDA taxes	0	84	147	89	0	0	0	0	0	0
Tax on health protection and the organisation of meat markets	0	0	0	48	46	43	41	43	43	42
Tax on cereals	0	147	275	19	19	24	18	14	4	8
Fees on tobacco stores	0	0	0	0	0	0	0	0	0	0
Fees on potash salt	0	0	0	0	0	0	0	0	0	0
Tax on flour	0	0	0	38	0	0	0	0	0	0
Fees included in fuel price	0	36	32	453	485	495	499	493	533	539
National Book Fund tax	0	7	17	0	0	0	0	0	0	0
Tax on logging products	0	11	0	0	0	0	0	0	0	0
Mining fees	0	16	59	43	23	25	22	16	15	15
Tax on electricity and heating	0	426	1 340	1 061	2 990	3 717	7 253	8 703	9 350	9 993
Surtax on appetizers	0	12	17	0	0	0	0	0	0	0
Pharmaceutical taxes	0	4	559	0	0	0	0	0	0	0
Tax on beet, sugar and alcohol	0	22	400	0	0	0	0	0	0	0
Solidarity tax on oil seeds	0	8	41	0	0	0	0	0	0	0
Tax on food fats	0	32	89	99	0	0	0	0	0	0
National Literature Fund tax	0	23	0	0	0	0	0	0	0	0
Tax on water consumption	0	34	51	74	5	11	1	2	1	2
Tax on meat	0	25	36	0	19	1	1	0	0	0
Tax on pollution, distribution, collection and extraction of water	0	217	609	1 624	1 821	1 763	2 175	2 268	2 332	2 364
Sugar market fund tax	0	0	0	0	0	0	0	0	0	0
Exceptional contribution on pharmacies and laboratories	0	16	0	522	0	0	0	0	0	0
Local tax	0	5	8	241	247	325	127	126	118	145
Contribution of low voltage electric energy suppliers	0	0	0	183	322	324	374	375	377	378
ADEME tax	0	0	0	80	212	489	499	449	449	449
Dock dues	0	0	0	449	544	581	386	422	439	439
General tax on polluting activities	0	0	0	6	16	16	205	117	87	81
Tax on oil products	0	0	0	0	0	0	367	379	364	377
Other taxes	0	30	772	78	102	55	126	199	291	612
Tax benefitting the French petrol institute (IFP)	0	0	0	193	0	0	0	0	0	0
5122 Profits of fiscal monopolies	0	0	0	0	0	0	0	0	0	0
5123 Customs and import duties	471	966	1 669	297	386	428	763	733	768	755
Import duties (State)	0	0	0	0	0	0	0	0	0	0
Import duties (UE)	0	873	1 623	0	0	0	0	0	0	0
Dock dues	0	0	0	267	327	361	627	678	706	707
Other taxes	0	94	46	30	59	67	136	55	62	48
5124 Taxes on exports	0	75	15	0	0	0	0	0	0	0
Agricultural levies (State part)	..	0	0	0	0	0	0	0	0	0
Agricultural levies (EU part)	..	75	15	0	0	0	0	0	0	0
5125 Taxes on investment goods	0	0	0	0	0	0	0	0	0	0

	1965	1980	1990	2000	2007	2010	2013	2015	2016	2017
5126 Taxes on specific services	431	2 690	8 373	11 204	14 007	16 274	20 656	21 585	22 925	24 000
Levies on horse-race bets	0	446	545	502	719	626	434	446	431	434
Levies on gambling casinos	0	0	0	727	1 022	748	708	691	719	741
Levies on the French national lottery	0	200	702	1 305	1 982	1 800	1 941	2 118	2 245	2 290
Exceptionnal levies on banks and lending institutions	0	0	0	0	0	0	0	0	0	0
Tax on insurance policies	0	1 292	4 782	5 097	6 571	7 099	9 973	10 386	10 763	10 503
Tax on leases	0	264	633	573	29	-5	-1	0	0	0
Taxes on funerals	0	11	32	14	11	12	12	12	13	13
Stamp taxes for transportation contracts	0	9	77	10	0	0	0	0	0	0
Tax on expertise and technical checks	0	0	0	0	0	0	0	0	0	0
ANAEM tax	0	0	0	33	58	129	145	146	150	150
Tax on the use of inland waterways	0	0	0	104	157	169	192	183	174	178
Other various taxes	0	98	272	273	449	1 007	547	798	1 392	1 912
Taxes on entertainment	0	75	195	274	372	425	799	785	865	867
Insurances contributions to the guarantee funds	0	32	135	223	274	323	387	450	555	755
Tax on automobile insurance	0	0	0	55	0	0	0	0	0	0
Additional contribution on insurance contracts to the FNGCA	0	0	0	261	96	101	120	125	58	60
National fund for housing improvement, 5% levy	0	114	258	678	604	604	726	932	946	1 145
Movie-making corporations contributions to the CNC	0	52	207	397	144	766	735	695	707	697
Agricultural insurances fund tax on food	0	0	0	0	0	0	0	0	0	0
National Sports Fund tax	0	3	0	0	0	0	0	0	0	0
Annuities and pensions upgrading fund tax	0	15	0	0	0	0	0	0	0	0
Annual tax on outstanding loans	0	0	0	0	0	0	0	0	0	0
Tax on advertisement	0	0	26	52	38	156	219	232	237	235
Levies on mortgage recording officers wages	0	67	188	0	0	0	0	0	0	0
Tax on safety and security	0	0	0	220	353	459	521	574	607	655
Tax on systemic risk	0	0	0	0	0	0	899	591	529	436
CMU tax on mutual insurances	0	0	0	247	560	1 637	1 851	1 909	1 972	2 370
Major natural disasters prevention fund (FPRNM) tax	0	0	0	0	0	0	197	205	205	211
Other taxes	0	10	320	159	568	218	251	307	357	348
5127 Other taxes on internat. trade and transactions	0	0	0	0	0	0	..	..	..	..
5128 Other taxes	5	215	970	360	13	55	67	54	59	54
Co-responsibility tax on milk	0	48	119	0	0	0	0	0	0	0
Co-responsibility tax on cereals	0	0	520	0	0	0	0	0	0	0
European Coal and Steel Community levy	0	14	0	0	0	0	0	0	0	0
Collector of customs	0	9	24	0	0	0	0	0	0	0
Various taxes (local government)	0	0	0	0	0	0	0	0	0	0
Contributions on sugar	0	68	185	270	0	42	54	41	41	41
Sugar market fund tax	0	76	120	76	0	0	0	0	0	0
Other taxes	0	0	2	14	13	13	13	13	18	13
5130 Unallocable between 5110 and 5120	0	0	0	0	0	0	0	0	0	0
5200 Taxes on use of goods and perform activities	226	1 598	4 034	4 601	5 841	6 321	6 649	6 948	7 235	7 514
5210 Recurrent taxes	178	1 226	3 024	2 810	3 009	2 866	2 849	2 669	2 870	2 859
5211 Paid by households: motor vehicles	27	545	1 236	126	0	0	0	0	0	0
Tax differential (central and local government)	0	545	1 236	126	0	0	0	0	0	0
5212 Paid by others: motor vehicles	79	545	1 086	1 280	1 559	1 269	1 181	1 028	909	780
Tax on corporation vehicles	0	197	345	644	891	992	876	753	692	638
Tax on vehicles (central and local government)	0	348	741	636	668	277	305	275	217	142
5213 Paid in respect of other goods	72	136	702	1 404	1 450	1 597	1 668	1 641	1 961	2 079
Special tax on use of roads	0	0	0	420	526	539	573	574	596	608
Weighing tax	0	17	14	0	0	0	0	0	0	0
Various taxes (local government)	0	7	33	0	0	0	0	0	0	0
Tax on video recorders	0	0	0	0	0	0	0	0	0	0
Fee on nuclear power plants monitoring	0	8	41	0	0	0	0	0	0	0
Tax on use of slaughterhouses	0	19	13	0	0	0	0	0	0	0
Corporation contributions on medicines preparation	0	0	20	238	0	379	213	255	265	296
Tax on electric pylons	0	1	66	128	183	213	244	231	241	251
Beverage licences	0	8	22	23	0	0	0	0	0	0
Gallicisation and navigation annual right (DAFN)	0	0	0	0	0	39	37	37	39	38
Fees on radio frequencies use	0	0	0	191	280	275	262	187	283	307
Other taxes	0	75	493	404	461	152	339	357	537	579
5220 Non-recurrent taxes	47	372	1 010	1 791	2 832	3 455	3 800	4 279	4 365	4 655
Entry into service receipt	0	75	0	0	0	0	0	0	0	0
Beverage taxes and licences	0	0	0	3	0	0	0	0	0	0
Fee for the right to build	0	79	53	72	0	18	18	0	0	0
Local tax on the equipement	0	146	263	305	848	1 252	1 381	1 839	1 912	2 074
Car registration tax	0	0	0	1 373	1 939	1 917	2 042	2 086	2 187	2 229
Tax on exceeding the density legal ceiling	0	38	270	38	45	82	82	52	0	0
Additional tax on car registration	0	0	0	0	0	186	277	302	266	352
Other taxes	0	35	423	0	0	0	0	0	0	0
5300 Unallocable between 5100 and 5200	0	0	0	0	0	0	0	0	0	0

	1965	1980	1990	2000	2007	2010	2013	2015	2016	2017
6000 Other taxes	**681**	**5 480**	**14 060**	**24 084**	**27 227**	**19 587**	**22 860**	**25 475**	**26 030**	**26 790**
6100 Paid solely by business	678	5 480	14 060	22 398	27 219	19 581	22 854	25 469	26 024	26 784
National Institute of intellectual property (INPI) tax on services	0	43	67	115	156	165	180	193	197	204
Tax on general charges	0	0	0	0	0	0	0	0	0	0
Tax on the use of fixed assets	0	5 152	13 381	19 641	22 035	0	0	0	0	0
Tax on union benefits (local government)	0	36	197	293	0	0	0	0	0	0
Various taxes (central government)	0	0	0	61	236	255	478	649	660	637
Annual tax on outstanding loans	0	110	0	0	0	0	0	0	0	0
Exceptionnal levies on insurance corporations	0	0	0	0	0	0	0	0	0	0
Fees of the chambers of commerce and industry	0	36	125	155	203	275	233	253	228	229
Payments of industrial enterprises to the benefit of the FNE	0	4	240	204	33	10	3	0	0	1
Other taxes	0	98	50	1 127	3 721	1 078	775	2 400	2 482	2 802
(ANDA) and (ADAR) tax	0	0	0	32	0	0	0	0	0	0
Property contributions of the corporations	0	0	0	0	0	4 941	5 908	6 356	6 525	6 659
Contributions on the value added of the corporations	0	0	0	0	0	10 346	12 168	12 973	13 542	13 526
Flat-rate tax on network corporations	0	0	0	0	0	1 223	1 206	1 297	1 324	1 329
Exit tax on insurance	0	0	0	0	0	0	0	0	0	0
Fees of the chambers of commerce and industry	0	0	0	770	835	1 103	1 323	458	860	871
Employers' contribution on stock options	0	0	0	0	0	185	380	490	206	300
Tax on railway companies profit	0	0	0	0	0	0	200	400	0	226
6200 Other	3	0	0	1 686	8	6	6	6	6	6
Other taxes	0	..	..	1 686	8	6	6	6	6	6
Sectors accounts differential	0	..	..	0	0	0	0	0	0	0
Customs duties collected for EU	**0**	**0**	**0**	**1 513**	**1 657**	**1 752**	**1 842**	**1 932**	**1 819**	**1 908**
Non-wastable tax credits										
Non-wastable tax credits against 1110	0	0	0	0	7 663	10 761	8 214	8 041	6 526	6 248
Tax component	0	0	0	0	0	8 234	6 755	5 669	3 830	3 623
Transfer component	0	0	0	0	0	2 527	1 459	2 372	2 696	2 625
Non-wastable tax credits against 1210	0	0	0	457	1 860	6 655	5 466	18 618	19 352	22 639
Tax component	0	0	0	0	0	1 277	3 572	10 560	10 461	10 662
Transfer component	0	0	0	0	0	5 378	1 894	8 058	8 891	11 977
Non-wastable tax credits against 3000	0	0	0	0	0	0	0	0	0	0
Tax expenditure component	0	0	0	0	0	0	0	0	0	0
Transfer component	0	0	0	0	0	0	0	0	0	0
Total tax revenue on cash basis	**25 776**	**178 576**	**433 771**	**642 156**	**825 954**	**840 905**	**960 513**	**995 462**	**1 013 710**	**1 058 413**
Total tax revenue on accrual basis	**0**	**0**	**0**	**645 528**	**831 226**	**846 318**	**966 817**	**1 002 131**	**1 020 206**	**1 065 242**
Conciliation with National Accounts										
Additional taxes included in national accounts	0	0	0	0	0	0	0	0	0	0
Tax excluded from national accounts	0	0	0	-3 171	-5 191	-5 774	-6 661	-6 676	-6 812	-6 916
Waste collection tax	..	..	..	-3 103	-5 117	-5 699	-6 552	-6 567	-6 703	-6 803
Tax on electric pylons	..	..	..	0	0	0	0	0	0	0
Street-cleaning tax	..	..	..	-68	-74	-75	-109	-109	-109	-113
Difference in treatment of tax credits	0	0	0	0	0	9 511	10 327	16 229	14 291	14 285
Capital transfer for uncollected revenue	0	0	0	-3 372	-5 272	-5 413	-6 304	-6 669	-6 496	-6 829
Voluntary social security contributions	0	0	0	0	0	0	0	0	0	0
Miscellaneous differences	0	0	0	0	0	0	0	0	0	0
National Accounts: taxes and actual social contributions	0	0	0	638 985	820 763	844 642	964 179	1 005 015	1 021 189	1 065 782
Imputed social contributions	0	0	0	25 875	33 510	38 028	41 947	42 655	42 930	43 038
National Accounts: taxes and all social contributions	0	0	0	664 860	854 273	882 670	1 006 126	1 047 670	1 064 119	1 108 820

.. Not available

Note: Calendar year ending on December 31st.

From 1992, the data are on an accrual basis.

From 1970, figures were calculated according to the new System of National Accounts and are not, therefore, comparable to those of the previous years.

The section 2000 includes certain voluntary contributions.

The section 4220 corresponds to the remuneration for the guarantee of the State given to savings banks.

Source: General Account of the Administration of finances for the figures of fiscal receipts. OSCE for the figures of Social Security from 1965 to 1969, and ESA for the following years.

StatLink https://doi.org/10.1787/888934056906

Table 5.11. Germany: Detailed country table, 1965-2017

Million EUR

	1965	1980	1990	2000	2007	2010	2013	2015	2016	2017
Total tax revenue	**74 359**	**287 373**	**454 777**	**767 052**	**876 915**	**903 285**	**1 039 213**	**1 127 408**	**1 182 264**	**1 231 275**
Total tax revenue exclusive of customs duties	..	..	..	**763 658**	**872 943**	**899 051**	**1 034 962**	**1 122 213**	**1 177 175**	**1 226 232**
1000 Taxes on income, profits and capital gains	**25 059**	**100 821**	**147 257**	**231 249**	**273 596**	**257 817**	**320 228**	**351 387**	**376 251**	**400 605**
1100 Of individuals	19 254	85 134	125 296	194 173	218 848	219 387	270 481	298 846	313 835	334 069
1110 On income and profits	19 254	85 134	125 296	194 173	218 848	219 387	270 481	298 846	313 835	334 069
Taxes on wages and salaries	8 558	57 039	90 801	135 733	146 365	145 202	174 814	194 116	201 405	211 685
Assessed income tax	7 567	18 813	18 672	12 225	25 341	31 346	42 586	48 902	54 035	59 784
Withholding tax on dividends	691	2 135	5 538	13 515	13 572	12 982	17 258	17 944	19 452	20 918
Supplementary tax	0	0	0	10 347	10 907	10 706	13 085	14 555	15 204	16 144
Enterprise tax	2 438	7 147	10 285	16 486	14 630	13 709	17 305	18 037	19 956	20 693
Stabilisation tax	0	0	0	0	0	0	0	0	0	0
Withholding tax on interest	0	0	0	5 867	8 033	5 442	5 433	5 292	3 783	4 845
1120 On capital gains	0	0	0	0	0	0	0	0	0	0
1200 Corporate	5 806	15 686	21 961	37 076	54 748	38 430	49 747	52 541	62 416	66 536
1210 On profits	5 806	15 686	21 961	37 076	54 748	38 430	49 747	52 541	62 416	66 536
Corporation tax	4 177	10 902	15 385	23 575	23 386	12 516	19 762	20 178	27 552	29 782
Supplementary tax	0	20	1	1 494	1 550	982	1 337	1 409	1 733	1 902
Sacrifice for Berlin	3	0	0	0	0	0	0	0	0	0
Enterprise tax	1 625	4 765	6 576	10 540	25 486	22 002	25 722	28 106	31 095	32 244
Stabilisation tax	0	0	0	0	0	0	0	0	0	0
Withholding tax on interest	0	0	0	1 467	4 326	2 930	2 926	2 848	2 036	2 608
1220 On capital gains	0	0	0	0	0	0	0	0	0	0
1300 Unallocable between 1100 and 1200	0	0	0	0	0	0	0	0	0	0
2000 Social security contributions	**19 876**	**98 659**	**170 449**	**299 440**	**320 594**	**353 955**	**392 295**	**424 633**	**445 013**	**466 470**
2100 Employees	8 723	43 833	73 580	131 610	141 079	155 283	174 333	188 972	199 378	209 593
Payments by employees total	8 723	43 833	73 580	131 610	141 079	155 283	174 333	188 972	199 378	209 593
2110 On a payroll basis	..	..	..	131 610	141 079	155 283	174 333	188 972	199 378	209 593
2120 On an income tax basis	..	..	..	0	0	0	0	0	0	0
2200 Employers	10 693	52 985	86 659	147 410	152 198	167 206	184 217	199 153	206 925	216 423
Payments by employers total	10 693	52 985	86 659	147 410	152 198	167 206	184 217	199 153	206 925	216 423
2210 On a payroll basis	..	..	..	147 410	152 198	167 206	184 217	199 153	206 925	216 423
2220 On an income tax basis	..	..	..	0	0	0	0	0	0	0
2300 Self-employed or non-employed	460	1 841	10 210	20 420	27 317	31 466	33 745	36 508	38 710	40 454
Payments total	460	1 841	10 210	20 420	27 317	31 466	33 745	36 508	38 710	40 454
2310 On a payroll basis	..	..	..	20 420	27 317	31 466	33 745	36 508	38 710	40 454
2320 On an income tax basis	..	..	..	0	0	0	0	0	0	0
2400 Unallocable between 2100, 2200 and 2300	0	0	0	0	0	0	0	0	0	0
2410 On a payroll basis	..	..	..	..	..	..	..	..	..	..
2420 On an income tax basis	..	..	..	..	..	..	..	..	..	..
3000 Taxes on payroll and workforce	**477**	**445**	**0**	**0**	**0**	**0**	**0**	**0**	**0**	**0**
Payroll tax	477	445	..	..	..	..	..	..	..	..
4000 Taxes on property	**4 313**	**9 414**	**15 321**	**17 505**	**21 873**	**21 012**	**26 104**	**31 076**	**33 439**	**33 600**
4100 Recurrent taxes on immovable property	1 079	2 968	4 461	8 849	10 713	11 315	12 377	13 215	13 654	13 965
4110 Households	644	1 187	1 784	3 540	4 285	4 526	4 951	5 286	5 462	5 586
4120 Others	435	1 780	2 676	5 309	6 428	6 789	7 426	7 929	8 192	8 379
4200 Recurrent taxes on net wealth	2 530	4 362	6 213	433	5	2	700	322	370	382
4210 Individual	973	977	1 425	191	2	1	0	-1	0	0
General wealth tax	471	954	1 425	191	2	1	..	-1	..	..
Equalization of war burden	502	23	0	0	0	0	..	0	..	..
4220 Corporate	1 557	3 385	4 788	242	3	1	700	323	370	382
General wealth tax	490	1 431	1 813	242	3	1	0	-1	0	0
Equalization of war burden	350	15	0	0	0	0	0	0	0	0
Enterprise tax	717	1 939	2 975	0	0	0	0	0	0	0
Bank levy	0	0	0	0	0	0	520	0	14	10
Contribution to Deposit Protection Fund	0	0	0	0	0	0	180	324	356	372
4300 Estate, inheritance and gift taxes	162	520	1 545	2 982	4 203	4 405	4 633	6 290	7 007	6 114
4310 Estate and inheritance taxes	134	416	1 359	2 624	3 699	3 876	4 077	5 535	6 166	5 380
4320 Gift taxes	28	104	186	358	504	529	556	755	841	734
4400 Taxes on financial and capital transactions	542	1 564	3 103	5 241	6 952	5 290	8 394	11 249	12 408	13 139
Real property transfer tax	150	521	1 999	5 081	6 952	5 290	8 394	11 249	12 408	13 139
Additional real property transfer	198	680	148	160	0	0	0	0	0	0
Capital transfer tax	111	200	807	0	0	0	0	0	0	0
Bill of exchange tax	83	163	149	0	0	0	0	0	0	0
4500 Non-recurrent taxes	0	0	0	0	0	0	0	0	0	0
4510 On net wealth	..	..	..	..	..	..	..	..	..	..
4520 Other non-recurrent taxes	..	..	..	..	..	..	..	..	..	..
4600 Other recurrent taxes on property	0	0	0	0	0	0	0	0	0	0
5000 Taxes on goods and services	**24 462**	**77 863**	**121 577**	**215 292**	**256 708**	**266 095**	**296 163**	**313 323**	**320 480**	**323 595**
5100 Taxes on production, sale, transfer, etc.	23 079	74 406	117 209	208 050	247 547	256 940	277 725	294 292	301 634	311 680

	1965	1980	1990	2000	2007	2010	2013	2015	2016	2017
5110 General taxes	12 235	47 779	75 459	140 871	170 387	180 533	197 326	211 936	219 100	226 901
5111 Value added taxes	0	47 779	75 459	140 871	170 387	180 533	197 326	211 936	219 100	226 901
5112 Sales tax	0	0	0	0	0	0	0	0	0	0
5113 Other	12 235	0	0	0	0	0	0	0	0	0
Turnover tax old	11 028	..	..	..	..	..	..	..	..	..
Old turnover tax on import	1 208	..	..	..	..	..	..	..	..	..
5120 Taxes on specific goods and services	10 844	26 627	41 750	67 179	76 808	76 067	80 111	82 064	82 254	84 495
5121 Excise duties	8 213	20 566	31 158	57 224	63 811	63 452	64 624	65 320	64 924	66 509
Duty on mineral oils	3 798	10 917	17 701	37 826	38 877	39 601	39 260	39 605	40 135	40 998
Duty on power	0	0	0	3 356	6 439	6 167	6 987	6 560	6 507	7 003
Duty on tobacco	2 402	5 771	8 898	11 443	14 108	13 453	14 131	14 963	14 062	14 299
Duty on alcohol	771	1 986	2 162	2 151	2 169	2 049	2 098	2 073	2 089	2 090
Duty on beer	501	645	693	843	750	708	675	679	673	664
Duty on coffee	488	756	986	1 087	1 016	1 012	1 033	1 024	1 039	1 054
Duty on sugar	59	72	79	0	0	0	0	0	0	0
Duty on tea	16	32	31	0	0	0	0	0	0	0
Duty on salt	20	20	23	0	0	0	0	0	0	0
Duty on electric lamps	34	63	83	0	0	0	0	0	0	0
Duty on playing cards	2	4	0	0	0	0	0	0	0	0
Duty on beverages	46	22	8	6	1	0	0	0	0	0
Duty on acetic acid	3	2	0	0	0	0	0	0	0	0
Duty on champagne	69	274	494	512	451	462	440	416	419	401
Duty on matches	5	2	0	0	0	0	0	0	0	0
Duty on ice cream	1	0	0	0	0	0	0	0	0	0
5122 Profits of fiscal monopolies	8	2	0	0	0	0	0	0	0	0
5123 Customs and import duties	1 658	3 125	3 847	0	0	0	0	0	0	0
Monetary compensation accounts	0	368	1	..	..	..	..	..	..	..
Customs (mainly EU)	1 294	2 353	3 662	..	..	..	..	..	..	..
Agricultural levies EU	364	404	184	..	..	..	..	..	..	..
5124 Taxes on exports	0	0	0	0	0	0	0	0	0	0
5125 Taxes on investment goods	0	0	0	0	0	0	0	0	0	0
5126 Taxes on specific services	942	2 689	6 443	9 599	13 025	12 583	15 421	16 704	17 292	17 950
Duty transport goods on residents	0	0	0	0	0	0	0	0	0	0
Transport tax	452	0	0	0	0	0	0	0	0	0
Insurance tax	198	910	2 266	7 243	10 410	10 261	11 588	12 445	12 822	13 317
Fire insurance tax	33	124	200	288	319	326	392	413	442	451
Entertainment tax	55	44	140	267	210	376	708	881	985	1 048
Taxes on betting and gambling	204	655	1 046	1 801	1 702	1 412	1 635	1 711	1 808	1 834
Tax on electricity bills	0	956	2 792	0	0	0	0	0	0	0
Aviation tax	0	0	0	0	0	0	955	1 027	1 075	1 116
Gaming casinos levy	0	0	0	0	384	208	143	227	160	184
5127 Other taxes on internat. trade and transactions	0	0	4	5	1	2	2	2	2	2
5128 Other taxes	24	244	298	351	-29	30	64	38	36	34
Levies CECA	24	56	36	0	0	0	0	0	0	0
Cotisation sugar EU	0	112	224	351	-29	30	64	38	36	34
Levy on milk	0	75	38	0	0	0	0	0	0	0
5130 Unallocable between 5110 and 5120	0	0	0	0	352	340	288	292	280	284
Contributions to the German National Petroleum Stockpiling Agency	..	..	..	..	352	340	288	292	280	284
5200 Taxes on use of goods and perform activities	1 383	3 457	4 368	7 242	9 161	9 155	18 438	19 031	18 846	11 915
5210 Recurrent taxes	1 369	3 454	4 368	7 239	9 161	8 765	17 766	18 286	17 778	11 015
5211 Paid by households: motor vehicles	614	1 892	2 950	5 177	6 823	6 447	6 393	6 855	6 946	6 908
5212 Paid by others: motor vehicles	728	1 475	1 300	1 838	2 075	2 041	2 097	1 950	2 006	2 040
5213 Paid in respect of other goods	27	87	118	224	263	277	9 276	9 481	8 826	2 067
Dog taxes	24	75	101	198	240	258	299	322	336	349
Hunting and fishing taxes	4	13	17	26	23	19	10	10	9	9
Nuclear fuel tax	0	0	0	0	0	0	1 285	1 018	422	-6 284
Licence fee (private households)	0	0	0	0	0	0	6 975	7 383	7 318	7 258
Licence fee (companies)	0	0	0	0	0	0	707	748	741	735
5220 Non-recurrent taxes	14	3	1	3	0	390	672	745	1 068	900
Non-recurrent taxes	..	..	..	..	..	0	0	0	0	0
CO2 emission certificates	..	..	..	..	..	390	672	745	1 068	900
5300 Unallocable between 5100 and 5200	0	0	0	0	0	0	0	0	0	0
6000 Other taxes	**172**	**172**	**172**	**172**	**172**	**172**	**172**	**1 794**	**1 992**	**1 962**
6100 Paid solely by business	0	0	0	0	0	0	0	0	0	0
6200 Other	172	172	172	172	172	172	172	216	232	252
SRF bank levy	0	0	0	0	0	0	0	1 578	1 760	1 710
Custom duties collected for the EU	**..**	**..**	**..**	**3 394**	**3 972**	**4 234**	**4 251**	**5 195**	**5 089**	**5 043**

	1965	1980	1990	2000	2007	2010	2013	2015	2016	2017
Non-wastable tax credits										
Non-wastable tax credits against 1110	..	..	..	38 356	43 602	45 475	41 890	41 951	42 842	43 440
Tax expenditure component	..	..	..	..	29 499	28 268	25 972	26 817	27 576	28 141
Transfer component	..	..	..	..	14 104	17 207	15 920	15 134	15 266	15 297
Non-wastable tax credits against 1210	..	..	..	962	804	802	426	200	98	24
Tax expenditure component	..	..	..	..	348	326	172	120	52	18
Transfer component	..	..	..	..	456	474	254	80	46	8
Total tax revenue on cash basis	**74 359**	**287 373**	**454 777**	**767 052**	**874 109**	**903 192**	**1 037 871**	**1 125 631**	**1 179 022**	**1 229 636**
Total tax revenue on accrual basis	**..**	**..**	**..**	**..**	**876 915**	**903 285**	**1 039 213**	**1 127 408**	**1 182 264**	**1 231 275**
Conciliation with National Accounts										
Additional taxes included in National Accounts	..	..	..	..	2 348	2 009	2 404	2 864	2 614	2 617
Several duties, administrative fees and other revenues	..	..	..	..	2 348	2 009	2 404	2 864	2 614	2 617
Taxes excluded from National Accounts	..	..	..	..	0	0	0	0	0	0
Difference in treatment of tax credits	..	..	..	..	12 623	9 230	6 054	5 598	5 598	5 534
Capital transfer for uncollected revenue	..	..	..	..	0	0	0	0	0	0
Voluntary social security contributions	..	..	..	..	20 930	6 442	7 354	8 226	8 781	9 324
Miscellaneous differences	..	..	..	..	33 538	33 056	31 883	33 433	34 187	42 064
National Accounts: Taxes and actual social contributions	..	..	..	..	946 354	954 022	1 086 908	1 177 529	1 233 444	1 290 814
Imputed social contributions	..	..	..	..	29 424	32 584	33 444	34 510	36 074	37 043
National Accounts: Taxes and all social contributions	..	..	..	..	975 778	986 606	1 120 352	1 212 039	1 269 518	1 327 857

.. Not available
Note: Year ending 31st December.
From 2002 data are on accrual basis.
The tax revenues for Germany refer to the old Länder until 1990 and to all Germany beginning in 1991.
Heading 1000: In the years up to 2000, the revenues shown take into account the whole amount of non-wastable tax credits including that part paid out by the tax authorities which should, under the OECD criteria, be treated as expenditure. From 2001, the data necessary to make the adjustment have become available and the revenue figures comply with the OECD criteria from that year. The impact of this change is shown in Table D in Part I of this Report.
Heading for non-wastable tax credits against 1110 comprise child tax credits (paid out of wage tax revenue), tax credits for owner occupied housing (paid out of assessed income tax revenue) and investment tax credits for unincorporated businesses (for investment in former East Germany; paid out of assessed income tax revenue).
Heading for non-wastable tax credits against 1210 are investment tax credits for incorporated businesses (for investment in former East Germany; paid out of corporate income tax revenue).
Source: Finanzbericht, Bonn; Tax Statistics. Unpublished estimates by the Ministry of Finance.

StatLink https://doi.org/10.1787/888934056925

Table 5.12. Greece: Detailed country table, 1965-2017

Million EUR

	1965	1980	1990	2000	2007	2010	2013	2015	2016	2017
Total tax revenue	**116**	**1 475**	**11 472**	**47 200**	**73 990**	**72 412**	**64 558**	**64 938**	**68 294**	**70 126**
Total tax revenue exclusive of custom duties	..	..	..	**46 990**	**73 683**	**72 134**	**64 410**	**64 757**	**68 097**	**69 860**
1000 Taxes on income, profits and capital gains	**11**	**286**	**2 283**	**12 662**	**17 176**	**15 953**	**14 015**	**14 904**	**15 988**	**15 965**
1100 Of individuals	8	220	1 619	6 127	10 554	9 015	10 780	10 155	10 404	11 227
1110 On income and profits	8	220	1 619	6 102	10 500	8 948	10 698	10 047	10 320	11 148
Personal income tax	..	..	1 414	..	..	..	..	..	..	..
Receipts from previous years	..	..	62	..	..	..	..	..	..	..
Agricultural social security fund	..	..	143	..	..	..	..	..	..	..
1120 On capital gains	0	0	0	25	54	67	82	108	84	79
1200 Corporate	2	56	631	5 625	5 304	5 717	2 071	3 800	4 388	3 510
1210 On profits	2	56	631	5 625	5 304	5 717	2 071	3 800	4 388	3 510
Corporation income tax	2	39	553	..	..	..	..	..	..	..
Receipts from previous years	0	8	33	..	..	..	..	..	..	..
Agricultural social security fund	0	9	46	..	..	..	..	..	..	..
1220 On capital gains	0	0	0	0	0	0	0	0	0	0
1300 Unallocable between 1100 and 1200	1	10	32	910	1 318	1 221	1 164	949	1 196	1 228
Extraordinary taxes	0	10	32	..	..	..	..	..	..	..
Other taxes on income and profits	1	0	0	..	..	..	..	..	..	..
2000 Social security contributions	**37**	**485**	**3 466**	**14 284**	**24 940**	**24 748**	**19 354**	**18 807**	**19 313**	**20 746**
2100 Employees	15	214	1 735	7 629	13 417	13 292	10 881	11 095	11 597	12 201
2110 On a payroll basis	..	..	..	..	..	..	..	..	..	..
2120 On an income tax basis	..	..	..	..	..	..	..	..	..	..
2200 Employers	14	213	1 728	6 655	11 523	11 456	8 473	7 712	7 716	8 545
2210 On a payroll basis	..	..	..	..	..	..	..	..	..	..
2220 On an income tax basis	..	..	..	..	..	..	..	..	..	..
2300 Self-employed or non-employed	0	0	3	0	0	0	0	0	0	0
2310 On a payroll basis	..	..	..	..	..	..	..	..	..	..
2320 On an income tax basis	..	..	..	..	..	..	..	..	..	..
2400 Unallocable between 2100, 2200 and 2300	7	58	0	0	0	0	0	0	0	0
2410 On a payroll basis	..	..	..	..	..	..	..	..	..	..
2420 On an income tax basis	..	..	..	..	..	..	..	..	..	..
3000 Taxes on payroll and workforce	**1**	**27**	**79**	**0**	**0**	**0**	**0**	**0**	**0**	**0**
4000 Taxes on property	**11**	**68**	**532**	**3 631**	**4 908**	**3 741**	**5 698**	**5 418**	**5 491**	**5 559**
4100 Recurrent taxes on immovable property	0	4	22	372	709	553	2 619	3 592	3 672	3 653
4110 Households	0	3	22	..	..	..	..	..	..	..
4120 Others	0	1	0	..	..	..	..	..	..	..
Taxes on immovable property	0	0	..	..	..	..	..	..	..	..
4200 Recurrent taxes on net wealth	0	0	0	714	1 208	1 272	1 084	1 083	1 144	1 166
4210 Individual	..	..	..	..	..	..	..	..	..	..
4220 Corporate	..	..	..	..	..	..	..	..	..	..
4300 Estate, inheritance and gift taxes	1	18	141	372	208	165	99	134	115	154
4310 Estate and inheritance taxes	1	13	85	..	..	..	..	..	..	..
4320 Gift taxes	0	4	55	..	..	..	..	..	..	..
4400 Taxes on financial and capital transactions	10	44	368	2 035	2 556	1 146	615	547	543	577
Stamp and transaction taxes	10	41	368	2 035	2 556	1 146	615	547	543	577
Receipts from previous years	0	3	0	0	0	0	0	0	0	0
4500 Non-recurrent taxes	0	2	1	27	0	1	0	0	0	0
4510 On net wealth	0	0	0	..	..	..	..	..	..	..
4520 Other non-recurrent taxes	0	2	1	..	..	..	..	..	..	..
4600 Other recurrent taxes on property	0	0	0	111	227	604	1 281	62	17	9
5000 Taxes on goods and services	**57**	**608**	**5 109**	**16 413**	**26 659**	**27 692**	**25 343**	**25 628**	**27 305**	**27 590**
5100 Taxes on production, sale, transfer, etc.	51	564	4 881	14 576	24 234	25 225	21 386	21 317	23 151	23 265
5110 General taxes	12	194	3 040	9 234	17 020	16 504	13 100	13 190	14 595	14 905
5111 Value added taxes	0	0	2 821	8 927	16 511	15 958	12 593	12 885	14 333	14 642
5112 Sales tax	9	185	123	0	0	0	0	0	0	0
5113 Other	2	9	96	307	509	546	507	305	262	263
Other taxes on goods and services	1	9	34	307	509	546	507	305	262	263
Receipts from previous years	1	0	62	0	0	0	0	0	0	0
5120 Taxes on specific goods and services	39	370	1 789	5 305	7 100	8 642	8 177	8 027	8 426	8 224
5121 Excise duties	20	165	1 372	4 058	5 876	7 565	6 995	6 927	7 129	6 876
Duty on tobacco products	8	45	357	1 769	2 657	2 712	2 506	2 365	2 563	2 028
Duty on alcohol and spirits	1	7	50	262	334	501	417	393	493	535
Duty on mineral oil	7	75	637	2 016	2 878	4 242	3 894	3 971	3 888	4 085
Duty on sugar	3	6	0	0	0	0	0	0	0	0
Duty on coton and other products	0	30	328	11	7	110	178	198	185	228
5122 Profits of fiscal monopolies	2	6	0	0	0	0	0	0	0	0
5123 Customs and import duties	12	94	112	10	7	1	5	0	0	0
Import duties	11	90	111	10	7	1	5	..	..	..
Agricultural social security fund	1	5	1	0	0	0	0	..	0	0

	1965	1980	1990	2000	2007	2010	2013	2015	2016	2017
5124 Taxes on exports	0	1	1	0	0	0	0	0	0	0
5125 Taxes on investment goods	0	0	0	0	0	0	0	0	0	0
5126 Taxes on specific services	2	47	293	1 237	1 217	1 076	1 177	1 100	1 297	1 348
5127 Other taxes on internat. trade and transactions	0	0	0	0	0	0	0	0	0	0
5128 Other taxes	4	58	10	0	0	0	0	0	0	0
Agricultural social security fund	2	..	..	..	..	..	..	..	..	..
Other taxes	2	..	..	..	..	..	..	..	..	..
5130 Unallocable between 5110 and 5120	0	0	52	37	114	79	109	100	130	136
5200 Taxes on use of goods and perform activities	6	44	228	1 320	2 169	1 682	2 954	3 217	3 190	3 444
5210 Recurrent taxes	5	24	219	1 320	2 169	1 682	2 954	3 217	3 190	3 444
Motor vehicle tax	5	0	..	..	..	..	..	..	..	..
5211 Paid by households: motor vehicles	..	23	210	281	598	825	781	780	788	795
5212 Paid by others: motor vehicles	..	0	8	735	1 182	272	120	207	232	264
5213 Paid in respect of other goods	0	1	1	304	389	585	2 053	2 230	2 170	2 385
Taxes on boats/ships	0	0	1	..	..	..	..	..	..	..
5220 Non-recurrent taxes	1	20	9	0	0	0	0	0	0	0
Exceptional tax on construction of buildings	0	..	9	..	..	..	..	..	..	..
Building permits	0	..	0	..	..	..	..	..	..	..
5300 Unallocable between 5100 and 5200	0	0	0	517	256	785	1 003	1 094	964	881
6000 Other taxes	**0**	**1**	**3**	**0**	**0**	**0**	**0**	**0**	**0**	**0**
6100 Paid solely by business	..	0	0	..	..	..	..	..	..	..
6200 Other	..	1	3	..	..	..	..	..	..	..
Custom duties collected for the EU	**..**	**..**	**..**	**210**	**307**	**278**	**148**	**181**	**197**	**266**
Total tax revenue on cash basis	**116**	**1 475**	**11 472**	**45 979**	**72 429**	**73 083**	**62 632**	**63 230**	**66 808**	**67 618**
Total tax revenue on accrual basis	**..**	**..**	**..**	**47 200**	**73 990**	**72 412**	**64 558**	**64 938**	**68 294**	**70 126**
Conciliation with National Accounts										
Additional taxes included in National Accounts	..	..	..	0	0	0	0	0	0	0
Taxes excluded from National Accounts	..	..	..	0	0	0	0	0	0	0
Difference in treatment of tax credits	..	..	..	0	0	0	0	0	0	0
Capital transfer for uncollected revenue	..	..	..	0	0	0	0	0	0	0
Tax (Employer's actual social contributions)	..	..	..	..	..	..	..	..	..	..
Tax (Employee's actual social contributions)	..	..	..	..	..	..	..	..	..	..
Voluntary social security contributions	..	..	..	0	0	0	0	0	0	0
Miscellaneous differences	..	..	..	0	0	0	0	0	0	0
National Accounts: Taxes and actual social contributions	..	..	..	47 200	73 990	72 412	64 558	64 938	68 294	70 126
Imputed social contributions	..	..	..	2 055	3 952	4 952	5 101	5 615	5 595	5 220
National Accounts: Taxes and all social contributions	..	..	..	49 255	77 942	77 364	69 659	70 553	73 889	75 346

.. Not available

Note: Year ending 31st December.

From 1998 data are on accrual basis.

Source: Ministry of Finance, General accounting Office, 20th Directorate of Budget except the heading 2000 provided by the National Statistics Bureau.

StatLink https://doi.org/10.1787/888934056944

Table 5.13. Hungary: Detailed country table, 1965-2017

Million HUF

	1965	1980	1990	2000	2007	2010	2013	2015	2016	2017
Total tax revenue	..	..	..	**5 140 592**	**10 114 322**	**10 145 488**	**11 480 591**	**13 288 991**	**13 887 642**	**14 642 332**
Total tax revenue exclusive of custom duties	..	..	..	..	**10 086 341**	**10 120 484**	**11 454 253**	**13 250 031**	**13 846 022**	**14 596 929**
1000 Taxes on income, profits and capital gains	..	..	..	**1 247 420**	**2 539 389**	**2 098 578**	**2 026 518**	**2 428 430**	**2 684 571**	**2 873 577**
1100 Of individuals	..	..	..	954 698	1 838 563	1 768 830	1 610 329	1 814 908	1 853 431	2 075 248
1110 On income and profits	..	..	..	954 698	1 838 563	1 768 830	1 610 329	1 814 908	1 853 431	2 075 248
1120 On capital gains	..	..	..	0	0	0	0	0	0	0
1200 Corporate	..	..	..	292 722	700 826	329 748	416 189	613 522	831 140	798 329
Corporate income tax	..	..	..	292 722	510 781	323 370	322 467	539 777	756 652	710 069
Research and development fund levy	..	..	..	0	0	0	0	0	0	0
Financial institutions' special tax	..	..	..	0	10 890	21 618	27 686	19 995	14 513	10 859
Separate tax for companies	..	..	..	0	178 598	-32 390	0	0	0	0
Medicine tax	..	..	..	0	558	163	111	0	0	0
Energy corporations' special tax	..	..	..	0	0	16 987	54 060	41 608	46 218	53 124
Small business tax	..	..	..	0	0	0	11 865	12 142	13 757	24 277
1210 On profits	..	..	..	..	..	..	..	..	..	..
1220 On capital gains	..	..	..	..	..	..	..	..	..	..
1300 Unallocable between 1100 and 1200	..	..	..	0	0	0	0	0	0	0
Interest withholding	..	..	..	..	..	..	..	..	..	..
2000 Social security contributions	..	..	..	**1 506 755**	**3 402 194**	**3 184 209**	**3 745 638**	**4 293 731**	**4 613 936**	**4 704 101**
2100 Employees	..	..	..	275 323	941 682	1 069 050	1 593 836	1 784 485	1 989 780	2 344 708
Pensions	..	..	..	150 585	336 855	488 670	875 707	983 459	1 043 209	1 190 212
Health	..	..	..	81 874	513 633	472 561	591 729	656 158	703 226	802 505
Unemployment	..	..	..	42 864	91 194	107 819	126 400	144 868	243 345	351 991
2110 On a payroll basis	..	..	..	..	..	..	..	..	..	..
2120 On an income tax basis	..	..	..	..	..	..	..	..	..	..
2200 Employers	..	..	..	1 213 190	2 402 941	2 047 626	2 126 488	2 480 101	2 594 178	2 329 000
Pensions	..	..	..	734 456	1 508 490	1 857 334	2 101 798	2 087 117	2 032 688	1 797 898
Health	..	..	..	385 019	693 705	116 587	24 690	389 808	560 395	529 899
Unemployment	..	..	..	93 715	200 746	73 705	0	3 176	1 095	1 203
2210 On a payroll basis	..	..	..	..	..	..	..	..	..	..
2220 On an income tax basis	..	..	..	..	..	..	..	..	..	..
2300 Self-employed or non-employed	..	..	..	873	2 534	21 232	0	0	0	0
Pensions: of which	..	..	..	0	0	0	..	..	..	..
Self-employed	..	..	..	..	..	..	..	..	..	..
Unemployed	..	..	..	..	..	..	..	..	..	..
Retired	..	..	..	..	..	..	..	..	..	..
Other	..	..	..	..	..	..	..	..	..	..
Health: of which	..	..	..	873	2 534	21 232	..	..	..	..
Self-employed	..	..	..	873	2 534	21 232	..	..	..	..
Unemployed	..	..	..	0	0	0	..	..	..	..
Retired	..	..	..	0	0	0	..	..	..	..
Other	..	..	..	0	0	0	..	..	..	..
2310 On a payroll basis	..	..	..	..	..	..	..	..	..	..
2320 On an income tax basis	..	..	..	..	..	..	..	..	..	..
2400 Unallocable between 2100, 2200 and 2300	..	..	..	17 368	55 037	46 301	25 314	29 145	29 978	30 393
2410 On a payroll basis	..	..	..	..	..	..	..	..	..	..
2420 On an income tax basis	..	..	..	..	..	..	..	..	..	..
3000 Taxes on payroll and workforce	..	..	..	**183 430**	**82 068**	**115 951**	**168 749**	**199 334**	**220 784**	**275 643**
Rehabilitation contribution	..	..	..	2 184	13 559	56 004	64 400	67 460	70 496	80 661
Training levy	..	..	..	13 186	36 612	47 083	63 536	66 153	70 295	81 224
Wage guarantee contribution	..	..	..	0	0	0	0	0	0	0
Communal tax on enterprises	..	..	..	1 192	1 261	1 170	2	0	0	0
Health contribution	..	..	..	166 869	20 427	2 262	0	0	0	0
Medicine tax	..	..	..	0	10 209	9 431	9 547	10 283	8 631	12 757
Tax on home-workers	..	..	..	0	0	1	23	29	32	29
Lump sum tax for small taxpayers	..	..	..	0	0	0	31 241	55 409	71 330	100 972
4000 Taxes on property	..	..	..	**89 024**	**202 711**	**312 058**	**388 824**	**437 952**	**391 912**	**410 674**
4100 Recurrent taxes on immovable property	..	..	..	30 810	72 071	92 525	190 249	200 908	210 279	218 058
Land tax	..	..	..	0	0	0	0	0	0	0
Building tax	..	..	..	22 262	54 556	71 025	102 719	111 965	117 522	123 130
Development land tax	..	..	..	3 099	6 900	9 861	19 395	19 102	22 112	24 018
Communal tax on recreational howes	..	..	..	893	1 412	1 515	21	26	8	8
Communal tax on households	..	..	..	4 557	9 069	10 124	13 175	13 451	14 589	14 765
Luxury tax	..	..	..	0	134	0	0	0	0	0
Public utility tax	..	..	..	0	0	0	54 939	55 906	55 032	55 042
Community tax	..	..	..	0	0	0	0	458	1 016	1 095
4110 Households	..	..	..	..	..	..	..	..	..	..
4120 Others	..	..	..	..	..	..	..	..	..	..

	1965	1980	1990	2000	2007	2010	2013	2015	2016	2017
4200 Recurrent taxes on net wealth	..	..	..	0	0	135 652	128 560	136 282	59 791	53 392
Surtax payable by financial institutions	..	..	..	..	..	135 652	128 560	136 282	59 791	53 392
4210 Individual	..	..	..	..	..	..	..	..	..	..
4220 Corporate	..	..	..	..	..	..	..	..	..	..
4300 Estate, inheritance and gift taxes	..	..	..	5 460	13 175	6 264	5 307	7 373	8 278	9 393
4310 Estate and inheritance taxes	..	..	..	4 020	10 775	4 242	4 097	6 230	6 980	8 164
Inheritance tax-local	..	..	..	2 010	4 658	1 858	0	0	0	0
Inheritance tax-central	..	..	..	2 010	6 117	2 385	4 097	6 230	6 980	8 164
4320 Gift taxes	..	..	..	1 440	2 400	2 021	1 210	1 143	1 298	1 229
Gift tax-local	..	..	..	720	1 038	885	0	0	0	0
Gift tax-central	..	..	..	720	1 363	1 136	1 210	1 143	1 298	1 229
4400 Taxes on financial and capital transactions	..	..	..	52 754	117 465	77 618	64 708	93 389	113 564	129 831
Property transfer tax-local	..	..	..	26 349	50 783	33 990	0	0	0	0
Property transfer tax-central	..	..	..	26 405	66 682	43 628	64 708	93 389	113 564	129 831
4500 Non-recurrent taxes	..	..	..	0	0	0	0	0	0	0
4510 On net wealth	..	..	..	..	..	..	..	..	..	..
4520 Other non-recurrent taxes	..	..	..	..	..	..	..	..	..	..
4600 Other recurrent taxes on property	..	..	..	0	0	0	0	0	0	0
5000 Taxes on goods and services	**..**	**..**	**..**	**2 081 107**	**3 803 630**	**4 350 310**	**5 048 359**	**5 833 760**	**5 882 758**	**6 285 353**
5100 Taxes on production, sale, transfer, etc.	..	..	..	2 052 380	3 722 487	4 238 757	4 923 663	5 695 624	5 735 486	6 136 059
5110 General taxes	..	..	..	1 340 572	2 622 027	3 010 781	3 414 342	4 097 513	4 104 591	4 460 258
5111 Value added taxes	..	..	..	1 153 750	2 013 271	2 325 608	2 693 555	3 307 312	3 297 156	3 625 111
5112 Sales tax	..	..	..	0	0	37 795	47 927	50 635	51 719	65 133
Public health product tax	..	..	..	..	..	0	19 090	29 882	28 983	34 171
Hydrocarbons stockholding fee	..	..	..	..	..	37 795	28 837	20 753	22 736	30 962
5113 Other	..	..	..	186 823	608 756	647 378	672 860	739 566	755 716	770 014
Local tax on company sales	..	..	..	186 823	427 134	443 093	500 868	584 380	608 981	638 731
Simplified business tax	..	..	..	0	152 812	181 880	110 021	89 406	81 138	63 641
Research and development contribution	..	..	..	0	28 810	22 405	61 971	65 780	65 597	67 642
5120 Taxes on specific goods and services	..	..	..	711 808	1 100 461	1 227 976	1 509 321	1 598 111	1 630 895	1 675 801
5121 Excise duties	..	..	..	533 502	969 730	929 881	992 270	1 119 189	1 150 550	1 157 642
Road fund petrol tax	..	..	..	0	0	0	0	0	0	0
Alcohol production duty	..	..	..	3 848	5 621	3 021	196	8 007	2 249	6 803
Water fund tax	..	..	..	6 017	13 171	14 444	13 164	12 305	13 021	12 225
Forestry fund tax	..	..	..	2 858	3 353	284	0	0	0	0
Environment petrol tax	..	..	..	14 837	19 447	17 274	46 711	65 534	70 894	77 792
Budget excises (central budget)	..	..	..	505 942	916 869	877 778	915 547	1 015 555	1 045 887	1 041 979
Coffee	..	..	..	3 200	0	0	0	0	0	0
Alcohol	..	..	..	53 500	88 600	83 078	85 487	87 369	101 515	86 315
Tobacco	..	..	..	107 000	252 400	251 778	312 509	321 922	298 080	294 071
Petrol	..	..	..	156 000	218 200	216 728	189 755	206 220	216 079	221 662
Diesel	..	..	..	157 000	256 600	293 588	308 736	375 026	402 943	411 037
Other oil	..	..	..	6 000	2 200	2 567	3 451	3 608	3 623	3 873
Other budget excises	..	..	..	30 343	93 442	30 039	15 608	21 410	23 647	25 021
Energy tax	..	..	..	0	11 269	17 080	16 652	17 788	18 499	18 843
5122 Profits of fiscal monopolies	..	..	..	0	0	0	0	0	0	0
5123 Customs and import duties	..	..	..	137 730	9 193	8 425	8 970	13 392	12 944	15 148
Customs duties	..	..	..	137 730	9 193	8 425	8 970	13 392	12 944	15 148
5124 Taxes on exports	..	..	..	0	0	0	0	0	0	0
5125 Taxes on investment goods	..	..	..	0	0	0	0	0	0	0
5126 Taxes on specific services	..	..	..	40 576	105 879	289 020	507 201	464 765	466 533	502 157
Gambling tax	..	..	..	27 935	71 804	62 718	41 316	44 972	33 126	38 067
Tourism tax	..	..	..	4 379	0	0	0	0	0	0
Communal tourism tax	..	..	..	2 943	4 935	5 798	8 411	10 475	11 676	13 602
Cultural contribution	..	..	..	4 387	8 432	1 096	105	127	172	93
Pork slaughterhouse tax	..	..	..	32	0	0	0	0	0	0
Breeding contribution	..	..	..	899	919	0	0	0	0	0
Medicine tax	..	..	..	0	19 789	28 104	40 496	45 529	43 580	45 940
Surtax payable by financial institutions	..	..	..	0	0	39 611	1 217	3 441	3 966	1 857
Specific sectors' surtax	..	..	..	0	0	151 693	9 815	285	-870	1 112
Telecommunication services tax	..	..	..	0	0	0	50 176	54 516	53 162	53 609
Accident tax	..	..	..	0	0	0	23 313	27 694	32 876	37 904
Insurance tax	..	..	..	0	0	0	28 088	30 108	32 870	35 729
Financial transaction levy	..	..	..	0	0	0	289 321	205 616	201 600	216 336
Waste dumping contribution	..	..	..	0	0	0	6 639	11 123	8 742	12 036
Advertising tax	..	..	..	0	0	0	0	5 675	13 010	4 730
Protection Fund levies (BEVA)	..	..	..	0	0	0	1 000	2 600	9 343	10 221
Protection Fund levies (OBA)	..	..	..	0	0	0	7 299	14 391	14 750	15 613
Protection Fund levies (Resolution Fund)	..	..	..	0	0	0	0	7 290	7 397	8 712
Protection Fund levies (SZHTKA)	..	..	..	0	0	0	5	923	1 133	1 023
Protection Fund levies (KA)	..	..	..	0	0	0	0	0	0	5 573
Tourism development contribution	..	..	..	0	0	0	0	0	0	0

	1965	1980	1990	2000	2007	2010	2013	2015	2016	2017
5127 Other taxes on internat. trade and transactions	..	..	..	0	0	0	0	0	0	0
Previous differential producer's turnover tax	..	..	..	..	..	..	..	..	..	..
5128 Other taxes	..	..	..	0	15 659	650	881	765	868	854
Sugar duty	..	..	..	..	15 659	650	881	765	868	854
5130 Unallocable between 5110 and 5120	..	..	..	0	0	0	0	0	0	0
5200 Taxes on use of goods and perform activities	..	..	..	28 727	81 143	111 553	124 696	138 136	147 271	149 294
5210 Recurrent taxes	..	..	..	25 454	74 268	106 903	121 126	130 237	137 559	136 129
Tax on domestically registered vehicles-local	..	..	..	12 622	62 432	71 112	69 248	73 247	73 130	76 361
Tax on domestically registered vehicles-extra budget	..	..	..	0	0	0	0	0	0	0
Tax on domestically registered vehicles-central	..	..	..	8 250	0	79	0	0	0	0
Tax on foreign registered vehicles extra budget fund	..	..	..	0	0	0	0	0	0	0
Tax on foreign registered vehicles-central	..	..	..	3 078	1 655	1 397	0	0	0	0
Company car tax	..	..	..	0	0	25 867	32 935	31 570	32 085	33 339
5211 Paid by households: motor vehicles	..	..	..	0	0	0	0	0	0	0
5212 Paid by others: motor vehicles	..	..	..	0	0	0	0	0	0	0
5213 Paid in respect of other goods	..	..	..	1 504	10 181	8 448	18 943	25 420	32 344	26 429
Environmental protection charge	..	..	..	5	13	27	0	0	0	0
Fishing development contribution	..	..	..	40	104	0	0	0	0	0
Environmental pollution charge	..	..	..	0	8 785	7 653	7 861	6 680	5 276	5 109
Air pollution levy	..	..	..	751	610	53	0	0	0	0
Water pollution levy	..	..	..	225	186	0	0	0	0	0
Toxic waste levy	..	..	..	65	42	130	0	0	0	0
Noise abatement levy	..	..	..	13	8	19	0	0	0	0
Unidentified environmental protection levies paid to local governments	..	..	..	404	433	566	521	265	241	274
Sale of emission allowances	..	..	..	0	0	0	10 561	17 479	25 754	19 830
Concession fees (tobacco shops)	..	..	..	0	0	0	0	996	1 073	1 216
5220 Non-recurrent taxes	..	..	..	3 273	6 875	4 650	3 570	7 899	9 712	13 165
Land protection levy	..	..	..	1 640	3 777	2 488	1 881	3 610	5 450	8 771
Vehicle weight fee	..	..	..	805	1 288	820	624	0	0	0
Game protection contribution	..	..	..	178	176	1	0	0	0	0
Casino license fee	..	..	..	650	1 635	1 341	1 065	4 289	4 262	4 394
5300 Unallocable between 5100 and 5200	..	..	..	0	0	0	0	0	0	0
6000 Other taxes	**..**	**..**	**..**	**32 857**	**56 348**	**59 378**	**76 165**	**56 824**	**52 061**	**47 581**
Unallocable tax penalties	..	..	..	23 546	33 321	36 250	56 836	35 530	30 767	24 783
6100 Paid solely by business	..	..	..	9 311	23 028	23 128	19 329	21 294	21 294	22 798
Nuclear contribution	..	..	..	9 311	22 828	23 128	19 329	21 294	21 294	22 798
Medicine tax	..	..	..	0	200	0	0	0	0	0
6200 Other	..	..	..	0	0	0	0	0	0	0
Custom duties collected for the EU	**..**	**..**	**..**	**..**	**27 981**	**25 004**	**26 337**	**38 960**	**41 620**	**45 403**
Total tax revenue on cash basis	**..**	**..**	**..**	**5 140 592**	**10 020 734**	**10 051 249**	**11 554 613**	**13 227 403**	**13 747 176**	**14 400 054**
Total tax revenue on accrual basis	**..**	**..**	**..**	**..**	**10 114 322**	**10 145 488**	**11 480 591**	**13 288 991**	**13 887 642**	**14 642 332**

	1965	1980	1990	2000	2007	2010	2013	2015	2016	2017
Conciliation with National Accounts										
Additional taxes included in National Accounts	..	..	..	..	45 120	37 453	67 094	85 587	92 787	87 181
Social security contributions	..	..	..	..	0	71	29 592	49 911	56 886	52 736
Duty for state procedures	..	..	..	..	45 084	37 331	37 417	35 653	35 875	34 424
Other taxes	..	..	..	..	36	51	85	23	26	21
Taxes excluded from National Accounts	..	..	..	..	-49 439	-53 707	-71 167	-48 414	-43 192	-37 311
Water fund tax	..	..	..	..	-13 171	-14 444	-13 164	-12 305	-13 021	-12 225
Tax on foreign registered vehicles	..	..	..	..	-1 655	-1 397	0	0	0	0
Environmental protection fee	..	..	..	..	-446	-593	-520	-265	-241	-274
Air pollution levy	..	..	..	..	-610	-53	0	0	0	0
Water pollution levy	..	..	..	..	-186	0	0	0	0	0
Toxic waste levy	..	..	..	..	-42	-130	0	0	0	0
Noise abatement levy	..	..	..	..	-8	-19	0	0	0	0
Vehicle weight fee	..	..	..	..	0	-820	-624	0	0	0
Unallocable tax penalties	..	..	..	..	-33 320	-36 250	-56 836	-35 530	-30 767	-24 783
Tax on home-workers	..	..	..	..	0	-1	-23	-29	-32	-29
Specific sectors' surtax correction	..	..	..	..	0	0	0	-285	870	0
Difference in treatment of tax credits	..	..	..	..	0	0	0	0	0	0
Capital transfer for uncollected revenue	..	..	..	..	0	0	0	0	0	0
Voluntary social security contributions	..	..	..	..	1 762	1 585	1 503	1 229	1 235	1 163
Miscellaneous differences	..	..	..	..	-2 687	-9	-2	-1	-16	0
Inheritance tax	..	..	..	..	0	0	0	0	0	0
Gift tax	..	..	..	..	0	0	0	0	0	0
Property transfer tax	..	..	..	..	0	0	0	0	0	0
Rounding	..	..	..	..	4	0	-2	-1	4	0
Taxes on income and profits	..	..	..	..	-2 087	0	0	0	0	0
Corporate income tax	..	..	..	..	0	0	0	0	0	0
Customs duties	..	..	..	..	-603	-9	0	0	-20	0
Vehicle weight fee	..	..	..	..	0	0	0	0	0	0
Environment petrol tax	..	..	..	..	0	0	0	0	0	0
Social security contributions	..	..	..	..	0	0	0	0	0	0
Credit institutions' special tax	..	..	..	..	0	0	0	0	0	0
National Accounts: Taxes and actual social contributions	..	..	..	..	10 109 078	10 130 810	11 478 019	13 327 392	13 938 456	14 693 365
Imputed social contributions	..	..	..	..	21 113	24 841	21 669	28 783	15 438	18 607
National Accounts: Taxes and all social contributions	..	..	..	..	10 130 191	10 155 651	11 499 688	13 356 175	13 953 894	14 711 972

.. Not available

Note: Year ending 31st December.

From 2002, data are on accrual basis.

Heading 5121: the aggregate figure for excise tax revenues is on a cash basis. Revenue from specific excises is in several cases reported on an accrual basis. Tax base for "Environment petrol tax" is broader than petrol only.

Heading 5123: part of environmentally related payments is attributable to Local government. It is not possible to present a more detailed breakdown of these figures.

Source: Ministry of Finance, Economic Department.

StatLink https://doi.org/10.1787/888934056963

Table 5.14. Iceland: Detailed country table, 1965-2017

Million ISK

	1965	1980	1990	2000	2007	2010	2013	2015	2016	2017
Total tax revenue	**60**	**4 731**	**114 932**	**254 556**	**531 760**	**540 276**	**676 142**	**812 002**	**1 265 609**	**981 364**
1000 Taxes on income, profits and capital gains	**13**	**1 211**	**34 106**	**101 473**	**241 378**	**239 664**	**315 577**	**380 979**	**429 545**	**482 568**
1100 Of individuals	12	1 092	30 908	88 492	180 070	197 318	258 623	297 979	337 457	373 009
1110 On income and profits	..	..	..	88 492	180 070	197 318	258 623	297 979	337 457	373 009
1120 On capital gains	..	..	..	0	0	..	0	0	0	0
1200 Corporate	1	119	3 198	8 356	32 555	14 609	40 479	52 544	62 152	79 993
1210 On profits	..	..	..	8 356	32 555	14 609	40 479	52 544	62 152	79 993
1220 On capital gains	..	..	..	0	0	..	0	0	0	0
1300 Unallocable between 1100 and 1200	0	0	0	4 625	28 754	27 737	16 475	30 457	29 936	29 566
2000 Social security contributions	**5**	**102**	**3 607**	**19 680**	**39 594**	**63 599**	**69 899**	**79 707**	**85 370**	**89 649**
2100 Employees	0	0	315	..	..	..	..	..	..	..
2110 On a payroll basis	..	..	..	..	..	..	..	..	..	..
2120 On an income tax basis	..	..	..	..	..	..	..	..	..	..
2200 Employers	5	102	3 292	..	..	..	..	..	..	..
2210 On a payroll basis	..	..	..	..	..	..	..	..	..	..
2220 On an income tax basis	..	..	..	..	..	..	..	..	..	..
2300 Self-employed or non-employed	0	0	0	..	..	..	..	..	..	..
2310 On a payroll basis	..	..	..	..	..	..	..	..	..	..
2320 On an income tax basis	..	..	..	..	..	..	..	..	..	..
2400 Unallocable between 2100, 2200 and 2300	0	0	0	19 680	39 594	63 599	69 899	79 707	85 370	89 649
2410 On a payroll basis	..	..	..	19 680	39 594	63 599	69 899	79 707	85 370	89 649
2420 On an income tax basis	..	..	..	0	0	..	0	0	0	0
3000 Taxes on payroll and workforce	**1**	**180**	**4 071**	**184**	**1 519**	**2 827**	**6 534**	**6 638**	**7 375**	**7 946**
4000 Taxes on property	**2**	**297**	**9 689**	**19 983**	**32 523**	**38 068**	**46 493**	**43 487**	**432 554**	**53 958**
4100 Recurrent taxes on immovable property	1	138	4 131	10 107	20 567	28 542	30 664	34 879	38 654	43 364
4110 Households	0	50	1 862	..	..	..	..	..	..	..
4120 Others	1	88	2 269	..	..	..	..	..	..	..
4200 Recurrent taxes on net wealth	0	69	2 402	5 173	-8	3 849	8 886	657	359	346
4210 Individual	..	29	1 476	..	..	..	..	..	..	..
4220 Corporate	..	40	926	..	..	..	..	..	..	..
4300 Estate, inheritance and gift taxes	0	6	235	765	1 663	2 613	2 437	2 919	3 719	4 268
4310 Estate and inheritance taxes	0	6	235	765	1 663	2 613	2 437	2 919	3 719	4 268
4320 Gift taxes	0	0	0	0	0	..	0	0	0	0
4400 Taxes on financial and capital transactions	1	84	2 921	3 143	9 484	2 656	3 973	4 327	4 853	4 581
4500 Non-recurrent taxes	0	0	0	113	460	146	233	362	384 594	528
4510 On net wealth	..	..	..	0	0	..	0	0	0	0
4520 Other non-recurrent taxes	..	..	..	113	460	146	233	362	384 594	528
4600 Other recurrent taxes on property	0	0	0	681	356	263	299	343	376	871
5000 Taxes on goods and services	**37**	**2 834**	**58 943**	**112 245**	**214 988**	**190 131**	**226 619**	**262 828**	**295 844**	**330 795**
5100 Taxes on production, sale, transfer, etc.	37	2 778	56 564	100 669	191 957	178 995	215 271	250 095	277 088	311 200
5110 General taxes	10	1 368	37 084	72 667	137 593	122 393	149 828	183 674	205 435	233 951
5111 Value added taxes	0	0	32 698	72 667	137 593	122 393	149 828	183 674	205 435	233 951
5112 Sales tax	10	1 368	4 386	0	0	0	0	0	0	0
5113 Other	0	0	0	0	0	0	0	0	0	0
5120 Taxes on specific goods and services	27	1 410	19 480	28 002	54 364	56 603	65 444	66 421	71 653	77 249
5121 Excise duties	1	311	2 346	23 585	45 891	46 711	55 171	56 909	61 710	67 717
5122 Profits of fiscal monopolies	5	263	5 986	..	0	0	..	..	..	..
5123 Customs and import duties	20	715	9 181	2 702	5 446	5 950	5 815	4 989	5 087	3 912
5124 Taxes on exports	1	2	0	1	0	2	0	0	0	0
5125 Taxes on investment goods	0	0	0	0	0	0	0	0	0	0
5126 Taxes on specific services	1	69	1 404	1 715	3 026	3 940	4 457	4 523	4 856	5 620
5127 Other taxes on internat. trade and transactions	0	50	563	0	0	0	0	0	0	0
5128 Other taxes	0	0	0	0	0	0	0	0	0	0
5130 Unallocable between 5110 and 5120	0	0	0	0	0	0	0	0	0	0
5200 Taxes on use of goods and perform activities	1	56	2 379	11 576	23 032	11 135	11 347	12 733	18 756	19 595
5210 Recurrent taxes	1	56	2 379	..	..	..	..	..	..	..
5211 Paid by households: motor vehicles	0	10	970	..	..	..	..	..	..	..
5212 Paid by others: motor vehicles	0	41	1 331	..	..	..	..	..	..	..
5213 Paid in respect of other goods	0	5	78	..	..	..	..	..	..	..
5220 Non-recurrent taxes	0	0	0	..	..	..	..	..	..	..
5300 Unallocable between 5100 and 5200	0	0	0	0	0	0	0	0	0	0
6000 Other taxes	**2**	**107**	**4 516**	**991**	**1 758**	**5 988**	**11 020**	**38 364**	**14 921**	**16 448**
6100 Paid solely by business	2	107	4 145	418	628	763	5 255	32 477	9 099	10 331
6200 Other	0	0	371	573	1 130	5 225	5 766	5 887	5 822	6 117

	1965	1980	1990	2000	2007	2010	2013	2015	2016	2017
Non-wastable tax credits										
Non-wastable tax credits against 1110	..	..	..	..	..	..	0	0	0	0
Tax expenditure component	..	..	..	..	..	..	0	0	0	0
Transfer component	..	..	..	..	..	..	0	0	0	0
Non-wastable tax credits against 1210	..	..	..	..	..	..	1 085	1 304	1 558	2 780
Tax expenditure component	..	..	..	..	..	..	148	176	261	438
Transfer component	..	..	..	..	..	..	937	1 128	1 297	2 341
Total tax revenue on cash basis	**60**	**4 731**	**114 932**	**..**	**..**	**..**	**..**	**..**	**..**	**..**
Total tax revenue on accrual basis	**..**	**..**	**..**	**254 556**	**531 760**	**540 276**	**676 142**	**812 002**	**1 265 609**	**981 364**
Conciliation with National Accounts										
Additional taxes included in National Accounts	..	..	..	0	0	0	0	0	0	0
Taxes excluded from National Accounts	..	..	..	-765	-1 663	-2 613	-2 437	-2 919	-3 719	-4 268
Estate and inheritance taxes (4310)	..	..	..	-765	-1 663	-2 613	-2 437	-2 919	-3 719	-4 268
Difference in treatment of tax credits	..	..	..	0	0	0	0	0	0	0
Capital transfer for uncollected revenue	..	..	..	0	0	0	0	0	0	0
Voluntary social security contributions	..	..	..	0	0	0	0	0	0	0
Miscellaneous differences	..	..	..	0	0	0	0	0	0	0
National Accounts: Taxes and actual social contributions	..	..	..	253 791	530 097	537 662	673 704	809 084	1 261 890	977 096
Imputed social contributions	..	..	..	0	0	0	0	0	0	0
National Accounts: Taxes and all social contributions	..	..	..	253 791	530 097	537 662	673 704	809 084	1 261 890	977 096

.. Not available

Note: Year ending 31st December.

From 1998 data are on accrual basis.

The 2016 figure for Iceland includes the one-off revenues from stability contributions.

Source: Ministry of Finance, Economic Department.

StatLink https://doi.org/10.1787/888934056982

Table 5.15. Ireland: Detailed country table, 1965-2017

Million EUR

	1965	1980	1990	2000	2007	2010	2013	2015	2016	2017
Total tax revenue	**317**	**4 046**	**12 260**	**33 344**	**59 930**	**45 311**	**50 788**	**60 657**	**63 470**	**66 916**
Total tax revenue exclusive of custom duties	..	..	..	**33 136**	**59 657**	**45 082**	**50 542**	**60 331**	**63 160**	**66 581**
1000 Taxes on income, profits and capital gains	**82**	**1 478**	**4 662**	**14 551**	**24 521**	**17 544**	**20 482**	**26 044**	**27 370**	**29 078**
1100 Of individuals	53	1 294	4 059	10 650	18 127	13 592	16 204	19 167	20 013	20 876
1110 On income and profits	53	1 286	4 023	9 876	15 029	13 247	15 836	18 498	19 193	20 050
Income tax	66	1 286	4 023	9 876	15 029	13 247	15 836	18 498	19 193	20 050
Surtax	3	0	0	0	0	0	0	0	0	0
Income tax paid by corporations	-17	0	0	0	0	0	0	0	0	0
1120 On capital gains	0	8	36	774	3 097	345	369	669	820	826
1200 Corporate	29	184	603	3 900	6 395	3 945	4 273	6 873	7 353	8 198
1210 On profits	29	184	603	3 900	6 395	3 945	4 273	6 873	7 353	8 198
Corporation profits tax	12	2	0	0	0	0	0	0	0	0
Corporation tax	0	176	603	3 885	6 393	3 944	4 272	6 872	7 352	8 197
Income tax paid by corporation	17	0	0	0	0	0	0	0	0	0
Agricultural produce duty	0	6	0	14	1	1	1	1	1	1
1220 On capital gains	0	0	0	0	0	0	0	0	0	0
1300 Unallocable between 1100 and 1200	0	0	0	2	0	7	4	4	4	4
2000 Social security contributions	**21**	**578**	**1 729**	**3 947**	**8 126**	**8 442**	**9 019**	**10 218**	**10 717**	**11 439**
2100 Employees	10	190	570	943	1 909	3 179	3 290	3 547	3 461	3 740
2110 On a payroll basis	..	..	570	943	1 909	3 179	3 290	3 547	3 461	3 740
2120 On an income tax basis	..	..	0	0	0	0	0	0	0	0
2200 Employers	10	380	1 092	2 814	5 796	4 932	5 326	6 211	6 653	7 177
2210 On a payroll basis	..	..	1 092	2 814	5 796	4 932	5 326	6 211	6 653	7 177
2220 On an income tax basis	..	..	0	0	0	0	0	0	0	0
2300 Self-employed or non-employed	0	8	67	190	421	331	403	460	603	522
2310 On a payroll basis	..	..	67	190	421	331	403	460	603	522
2320 On an income tax basis	..	..	0	0	0	0	0	0	0	0
2400 Unallocable between 2100, 2200 and 2300	0	0	0	0	0	0	0	0	0	0
2410 On a payroll basis	..	..	..	..	..	..	..	..	..	..
2420 On an income tax basis	..	..	..	..	..	..	..	..	..	..
3000 Taxes on payroll and workforce	**0**	**9**	**159**	**15**	**411**	**310**	**314**	**357**	**390**	**431**
4000 Taxes on property	**48**	**213**	**569**	**1 902**	**4 789**	**2 389**	**3 632**	**3 918**	**3 842**	**3 821**
4100 Recurrent taxes on immovable property	39	139	312	587	1 233	1 322	1 724	1 864	1 817	1 826
4110 Households	..	..	..	..	..	..	..	..	..	..
4120 Others	..	..	..	..	..	..	..	..	..	..
4200 Recurrent taxes on net wealth	0	1	0	0	0	0	536	169	0	0
4210 Individual	..	..	..	..	..	..	0	0	0	0
4220 Corporate	..	..	..	0	0	0	536	169	0	0
4300 Estate, inheritance and gift taxes	6	14	48	225	405	235	278	401	411	448
4310 Estate and inheritance taxes	6	14	45	210	337	192	259	365	376	417
Estate duty	5	..	..	..	..	..	..	..	..	..
Legacy duty	1	..	..	..	..	..	..	..	..	..
Succession duty	0	..	..	..	..	..	..	..	..	..
4320 Gift taxes	0	0	3	15	68	43	20	36	34	31
4400 Taxes on financial and capital transactions	3	59	209	1 090	3 151	832	1 093	1 484	1 613	1 547
Stamp duty	3	59	209	1 090	3 151	832	1 093	1 484	1 613	1 547
4500 Non-recurrent taxes	0	0	0	0	0	0	0	0	0	0
4510 On net wealth	..	..	..	..	..	..	..	..	..	..
4520 Other non-recurrent taxes	..	..	..	..	..	..	..	..	..	..
4600 Other recurrent taxes on property	0	0	0	0	0	0	0	0	0	0
5000 Taxes on goods and services	**167**	**1 769**	**5 141**	**12 721**	**21 809**	**16 390**	**17 071**	**19 781**	**20 654**	**21 706**
5100 Taxes on production, sale, transfer, etc.	155	1 741	4 940	12 166	20 710	15 090	15 542	17 834	18 749	19 697
5110 General taxes	18	597	2 500	7 643	14 355	10 067	10 372	11 956	12 802	13 111
5111 Value added taxes	0	597	2 500	7 643	14 355	10 067	10 372	11 956	12 802	13 111
Value added tax	..	597	2 500	7 643	14 355	10 067	10 372	11 956	12 802	13 111
5112 Sales tax	18	0	0	0	0	0	0	0	0	0
Turnover tax	18	..	..	..	..	..	..	..	..	..
Wholesale tax	0	..	..	..	..	..	..	..	..	..
5113 Other	0	0	0	0	0	0	0	0	0	0
5120 Taxes on specific goods and services	137	1 143	2 440	4 523	6 354	5 023	5 170	5 878	5 948	6 585
5121 Excise duties	124	1 045	2 084	4 402	6 125	4 859	5 013	5 474	5 766	6 163
Beer	19	192	356	475	459	316	363	418	429	419
Oils	31	330	745	1 491	2 204	2 099	2 035	2 120	2 179	2 233
Spirits	16	148	153	241	363	244	282	313	343	352
Table waters	0	11	23	0	0	0	0	0	0	0
Tobacco	50	187	419	1 035	1 192	1 160	1 064	1 055	1 098	1 397
Wine, cider, perry	1	18	46	154	297	266	354	414	440	446
Motor vehicle (incl. tyres)	7	148	331	985	1 554	395	459	702	814	850
Others	1	11	11	20	57	379	457	451	464	467

	1965	1980	1990	2000	2007	2010	2013	2015	2016	2017
5122 Profits of fiscal monopolies	0	0	0	0	0	0	0	0	0	0
5123 Customs and import duties	10	62	147	0	0	0	0	0	0	0
5124 Taxes on exports	0	0	0	0	0	0	0	0	0	0
UE agriculture levies	..	..	..	..	..	..	..	..	..	..
5125 Taxes on investment goods	0	0	0	0	0	0	0	0	0	0
5126 Taxes on specific services	3	21	171	122	229	164	157	404	357	520
Duty on betting	2	19	37	59	36	30	26	37	50	52
Sweepstakes duty	1	1	0	0	0	0	0	0	0	0
Bank levy	0	0	46	61	66	-70	-23	190	96	247
Other	0	1	88	2	127	204	154	178	210	221
5127 Other taxes on internat. trade and transactions	0	0	0	0	0	0	0	0	0	0
5128 Other taxes	0	14	37	0	0	0	0	0	0	0
5130 Unallocable between 5110 and 5120	0	0	0	0	0	0	0	0	0	0
5200 Taxes on use of goods and perform activities	11	28	201	555	1 100	1 300	1 530	1 947	1 904	2 009
5210 Recurrent taxes	11	28	201	555	1 100	1 300	1 530	1 947	1 904	2 009
5211 Paid by households: motor vehicles	6	14	100	373	723	768	885	890	833	809
5212 Paid by others: motor vehicles	5	11	82	124	239	256	284	281	263	255
5213 Paid in respect of other goods	0	3	20	58	138	276	360	776	809	944
5220 Non-recurrent taxes	0	0	0	0	0	0	0	0	0	0
5300 Unallocable between 5100 and 5200	0	0	0	0	0	0	0	0	0	0
6000 Other taxes	**0**	**0**	**0**	**0**	**0**	**6**	**23**	**12**	**12**	**8**
6100 Paid solely by business	..	..	..	..	..	0	0	0	0	0
6200 Other	..	..	..	0	0	6	23	12	12	8
Custom duties collected for the EU	**..**	**..**	**..**	**208**	**273**	**229**	**247**	**327**	**311**	**334**
Non-wastable tax credits										
Non-wastable tax credits against 1110	..	..	..	..	843	1 073	816	555	523	523
Tax expenditure component	..	..	..	..	843	1 073	816	555	523	523
Transfer component	..	..	..	..	0	0	0	0	..	0
Total tax revenue on cash basis	**317**	**4 046**	**12 260**	**32 978**	**59 976**	**45 342**	**50 642**	**60 324**	**62 927**	**66 793**
Total tax revenue on accrual basis	**..**	**..**	**..**	**33 344**	**59 930**	**45 311**	**50 788**	**60 657**	**63 470**	**66 916**
Conciliation with National Accounts										
Additional taxes included in National Accounts	..	..	..	0	0	178	178	177	177	178
Taxes excluded from National Accounts	..	..	..	0	0	0	0	0	0	0
Difference in treatment of tax credits	..	..	..	0	843	1 073	816	555	523	523
Capital transfer for uncollected revenue	..	..	..	0	0	0	0	0	0	0
Voluntary social security contributions	..	..	..	0	0	0	0	0	0	0
Miscellaneous differences	..	..	..	0	0	0	0	0	0	0
National Accounts: Taxes and actual social contributions	..	..	..	33 344	60 773	46 561	51 782	61 389	64 170	67 617
Imputed social contributions	..	..	..	1 366	2 579	1 053	1 402	1 182	1 337	1 214
National Accounts: Taxes and all social contributions	..	..	..	34 710	63 352	47 614	53 185	62 571	65 507	68 831

.. Not available

Note: The personal income tax data shown for the country table for Ireland is different to the ESA2010 presentation as the expenditure component of the payable tax credits are excluded in accordance with the OECD Interpretative Guide.

The data for years 1965 to 1973 are on fiscal year basis (commencing on 1st April) and are therefore not strictly comparable with the data for later years, which are on a calendar year basis.

From 1998, data are on accrual basis.

Heading 1200: Capital gains taxes paid by corporations are included in heading 1210.

Heading 2100: Includes contributions by self-employed and certain voluntary contributions.

Heading 2200: Since 1976 income tax paid by corporations and corporation profits tax have been replaced by corporation tax.

Heading 5111: Includes arrears of the wholesale and turnover taxes.

Tax receipts in 1988 were inflated by the success of the new arrangements for assessment and collection of tax.These arrangements included an amnesty for tax arrears paid by 30th September. This amnesty waived penalities and interest charge tax. It resulted in payments of 631 millons of euros spread across the main tax headings.

Source: Annual Report of he Revenue Commissioners, Financial Accounts and National Income and Expenditure Accounts.

StatLink https://doi.org/10.1787/888934057001

Table 5.16. Israel: Detailed country table, 1965-2017

Million ILS

	1965	1980	1990	2000	2007	2010	2013	2015	2016	2017
Total tax revenue	..	..	..	**188 276**	**251 291**	**268 555**	**325 343**	**364 250**	**381 575**	**413 433**
1000 Taxes on income, profits and capital gains	..	..	..	**74 551**	**91 522**	**78 265**	**101 382**	**113 841**	**120 497**	**146 948**
1100 Of individuals	..	..	..	54 753	56 426	48 214	57 212	70 760	75 604	85 410
1110 On income and profits	..	..	..	53 698	55 205	47 550	55 782	68 280	72 964	79 410
On wages – deduction at source	..	..	..	45 278	45 507	40 159	46 359	53 962	58 218	62 430
On self employement income – deduction at source	..	..	..	2 655	3 676	3 135	3 891	4 880	4 453	5 243
On self employement income – other	..	..	..	5 764	6 022	4 256	5 532	9 438	10 293	11 737
1120 On capital gains	..	..	..	1 055	1 221	664	1 430	2 480	2 640	6 000
1200 Corporate	..	..	..	18 001	30 210	23 113	36 639	34 676	37 767	41 909
1210 On profits	..	..	..	16 109	27 582	22 291	33 939	33 476	36 667	40 049
deduction at source	..	..	..	1 991	2 550	2 271	2 611	3 075	2 902	3 309
In lieu of VAT on the profits of Financial Institutions	..	..	..	1 290	2 200	1 920	2 440	1 910	1 990	2 070
Other	..	..	..	12 828	22 832	18 100	28 888	28 491	31 775	34 670
1220 On capital gains	..	..	..	1 892	2 628	822	2 700	1 200	1 100	1 860
1300 Unallocable between 1100 and 1200	..	..	..	1 797	4 886	6 938	7 531	8 405	7 126	19 629
Tax deducted at the source on the capital market	..	..	..	1 797	4 886	6 938	7 531	8 405	7 126	19 629
2000 Social security contributions	..	..	..	**27 565**	**37 909**	**45 343**	**53 364**	**59 561**	**63 452**	**66 783**
2100 Employees	..	..	..	15 771	23 093	27 788	31 537	34 692	35 913	37 884
2110 On a payroll basis	..	..	..	15 771	23 093	27 788	31 537	34 692	35 913	37 884
2120 On an income tax basis	..	..	..	0	0	0	0	0	0	0
2200 Employers	..	..	..	8 182	9 960	11 427	15 026	17 247	19 453	20 596
2210 On a payroll basis	..	..	..	8 182	9 960	11 427	15 026	17 247	19 453	20 596
2220 On an income tax basis	..	..	..	0	0	0	0	0	0	0
2300 Self-employed or non-employed	..	..	..	3 612	4 856	6 128	6 802	7 622	8 085	8 303
2310 On a payroll basis	..	..	..	3 612	4 856	6 128	6 802	7 622	8 085	8 303
2320 On an income tax basis	..	..	..	0	0	0	0	0	0	0
2400 Unallocable between 2100, 2200 and 2300	..	..	..	0	0	0	0	0	0	0
2410 On a payroll basis	..	..	..	..	..	..	..	..	..	..
2420 On an income tax basis	..	..	..	..	..	..	..	..	..	..
3000 Taxes on payroll and workforce	..	..	..	**6 850**	**9 920**	**10 280**	**12 780**	**13 770**	**14 070**	**15 196**
Employers tax on the the non-profit sector other than govt	..	..	..	1 250	1 500	320	390	410	300	404
In lieu of VAT on the wage-bill in the non-profit sector	..	..	..	4 260	6 580	7 650	9 540	10 320	10 770	11 203
In lieu VAT on the wage-bill in Financial Institutions	..	..	..	1 340	1 840	2 310	2 850	3 040	3 000	3 589
4000 Taxes on property	..	..	..	**16 935**	**24 282**	**28 817**	**32 680**	**38 804**	**39 208**	**41 279**
4100 Recurrent taxes on immovable property	..	..	..	11 311	16 156	18 768	21 541	23 765	24 362	24 874
Land tax	..	..	..	442	52	48	59	44	18	21
4110 Households	..	..	..	0	0	0	0	0	0	0
4120 Others	..	..	..	10 869	16 104	18 720	21 483	23 721	24 344	24 853
4200 Recurrent taxes on net wealth	..	..	..	0	0	0	0	0	0	0
4210 Individual	..	..	..	..	..	..	..	..	..	..
4220 Corporate	..	..	..	..	..	..	..	..	..	..
4300 Estate, inheritance and gift taxes	..	..	..	0	0	0	0	0	0	0
4310 Estate and inheritance taxes	..	..	..	..	..	..	..	..	..	..
4320 Gift taxes	..	..	..	..	..	..	..	..	..	..
4400 Taxes on financial and capital transactions	..	..	..	3 181	3 555	4 071	4 532	6 732	6 599	6 642
Transaction tax on the buyer of real estate	..	..	..	1 972	3 084	4 024	4 513	6 731	6 593	6 638
Transaction tax on the seller of real estate	..	..	..	206	404	27	19	1	6	4
Stamp tax	..	..	..	1 003	67	20	0	0	0	0
4500 Non-recurrent taxes	..	..	..	2 443	4 572	5 979	6 607	8 307	8 247	9 763
4510 On net wealth	..	..	..	0	0	0	0	0	0	0
4520 Other non-recurrent taxes	..	..	..	2 443	4 572	5 979	6 607	8 307	8 247	9 763
Capital gains tax on real estate	..	..	..	2 443	4 572	5 979	6 607	8 307	8 247	9 763
4600 Other recurrent taxes on property	..	..	..	0	0	0	0	0	0	0
5000 Taxes on goods and services	..	..	..	**62 375**	**87 658**	**105 850**	**125 137**	**138 274**	**144 348**	**143 227**
5100 Taxes on production, sale, transfer, etc.	..	..	..	57 887	81 107	98 092	116 335	128 277	134 422	133 293
5110 General taxes	..	..	..	49 876	67 569	79 945	97 357	107 765	112 866	110 971
5111 Value added taxes	..	..	..	39 805	53 982	65 508	81 524	90 824	91 999	94 531
5112 Sales tax	..	..	..	10 071	13 587	14 437	15 833	16 941	20 867	16 440
On domestic production	..	..	..	662	287	291	457	450	313	290
On imports	..	..	..	9 409	13 300	14 146	15 376	16 491	20 554	16 150
5113 Other	..	..	..	0	0	0	0	0	0	0
5120 Taxes on specific goods and services	..	..	..	8 012	13 538	18 147	18 978	20 512	21 556	22 322
5121 Excise duties	..	..	..	6 595	11 323	15 458	16 680	17 642	18 267	19 312
On domestically refined fuel	..	..	..	5 666	10 590	14 637	15 876	17 008	17 679	18 757
On domestically processed tobacco products	..	..	..	929	733	821	804	634	588	555
5122 Profits of fiscal monopolies	..	..	..	0	0	0	0	0	0	0
5123 Customs and import duties	..	..	..	1 417	2 215	2 689	2 298	2 870	3 289	3 010
5124 Taxes on exports	..	..	..	0	0	0	0	0	0	0

	1965	1980	1990	2000	2007	2010	2013	2015	2016	2017
5125 Taxes on investment goods	..	..	..	0	0	0	0	0	0	0
5126 Taxes on specific services	..	..	..	0	0	0	0	0	0	0
5127 Other taxes on internat. trade and transactions	..	..	..	0	0	0	0	0	0	0
5128 Other taxes	..	..	..	0	0	0	0	0	0	0
5130 Unallocable between 5110 and 5120	..	..	..	0	0	0	0	0	0	0
5200 Taxes on use of goods and perform activities	..	..	..	4 488	6 551	7 758	8 803	9 997	9 927	9 934
5210 Recurrent taxes	..	..	..	4 488	6 551	7 758	8 803	9 997	9 927	9 934
5211 Paid by households: motor vehicles	..	..	..	1 436	1 895	2 274	2 872	3 179	3 396	3 623
5212 Paid by others: motor vehicles	..	..	..	479	632	758	957	1 060	1 132	1 208
5213 Paid in respect of other goods	..	..	..	2 574	4 025	4 726	4 973	5 759	5 399	5 104
Licences collected by the Ministry of Transportation	..	..	..	257	535	350	132	196	120	61
Licences collected by the Ministry of Communication	..	..	..	151	0	274	299	338	325	199
Licences collected by other ministries	..	..	..	1 587	2 605	2 990	3 227	3 781	3 467	3 320
Business and professional licences paid locally	..	..	..	528	799	1 011	1 190	1 317	1 355	1 386
Other local authority fees	..	..	..	51	86	101	125	128	133	138
5220 Non-recurrent taxes	..	..	..	0	0	0	0	0	0	0
5300 Unallocable between 5100 and 5200	..	..	..	0	0	0	0	0	0	0
6000 Other taxes	**..**	**..**	**..**	**0**	**0**	**0**	**0**	**0**	**0**	**0**
6100 Paid solely by business	..	..	..	..	..	..	..	..	..	..
6200 Other	..	..	..	..	..	..	..	..	..	..
Non-wastable tax credits										
Non-wastable tax credits against 1110	..	..	..	..	..	87	911	1 415	1 253	1 589
Tax expenditure component	..	..	..	..	0	3	32	67	70	0
Transfer component	..	..	..	..	0	84	879	1 348	1 183	1 589
Non-wastable tax credits against 1210	..	..	..	0	0	0	0	0	0	0
Tax expenditure component	..	..	..	0	0	0	0	0	0	0
Transfer component	..	..	..	0	0	0	0	0	0	0
Total tax revenue on cash basis	**..**	**..**	**..**	**188 276**	**251 291**	**268 555**	**325 343**	**364 250**	**381 575**	**413 433**
Total tax revenue on accrual basis	**..**	**..**	**..**	**..**	**..**	**..**	**..**	**..**	**..**	**..**
Conciliation with National Accounts										
Additional taxes included in National Accounts	..	..	..	0	0	0	0	0	0	0
Taxes excluded from National Accounts	..	..	..	..	..	..	..	..	..	..
Difference in treatment of tax credits	..	..	..	..	..	..	..	..	..	..
Capital transfer for uncollected revenue	..	..	..	..	..	..	..	..	..	..
Voluntary social security contributions	..	..	..	..	..	..	..	..	..	..
Miscellaneous differences	..	..	..	..	..	..	..	..	..	..
National Accounts: Taxes and actual social contributions	..	..	..	188 276	251 291	268 555	325 343	364 250	381 575	413 433
Imputed social contributions	..	..	..	6 173	7 132	8 204	9 086	9 182	9 100	9 214
National Accounts: Taxes and all social contributions	..	..	..	194 449	258 424	276 760	334 428	373 432	390 676	422 647

.. Not available
Note: Year ending 31st December.
Data are on a cash basis.
The statistical data for Israel are supplied by and under the resposibility of the relevant Israeli authorities. The use of such data by the OECD is without prejudice to the status of the Golan Heights, East Jerusalem and Israeli settlements in the West Bank under the terms of International law.
Source: Israel Central Bureau of Statistics and Israel Ministry of Finance.

StatLink https://doi.org/10.1787/888934057020

Table 5.17. Italy: Detailed country table, 1965-2017

Million EUR

	1965	1980	1990	2000	2007	2010	2013	2015	2016	2017
Total tax revenue	**5 505**	**60 422**	**265 116**	**503 096**	**671 189**	**671 912**	**706 829**	**708 768**	**714 911**	**727 790**
Total tax revenue exclusive of custom duties	..	..	..	**501 560**	**668 928**	**669 687**	**704 939**	**706 522**	**712 678**	**725 495**
1000 Taxes on income, profits and capital gains	**982**	**18 821**	**96 707**	**166 912**	**226 498**	**219 547**	**233 294**	**225 934**	**228 368**	**230 868**
1100 Of individuals	603	13 940	69 654	124 918	172 136	180 512	185 996	184 622	183 714	186 953
1110 On income and profits	603	13 796	68 786	124 233	172 122	180 505	185 991	184 619	183 710	186 948
Personal income tax	0	11 538	57 318	121 211	162 644	173 991	175 921	173 007	173 709	176 822
Local income tax paid by households	0	829	4 492	67	0	0	0	0	0	0
Tax on income from investiments (60%)	319	55	15	0	0	0	11	80	87	54
10% Surcharge on income	94	37	5	0	0	0	0	0	0	0
10% proportional surcharge	1	0	0	0	0	0	0	0	0	0
Withholding tax on company dividends paid by households	23	51	496	110	542	393	564	875	1 134	1 144
Law 1177 proportional surcharge (60%)	39	0	1	0	0	0	0	0	0	0
Direct taxes 5% proportional surcharge (60%)	0	8	72	0	0	0	0	0	0	0
Additional Treasury increase (60%)	23	6	1	0	0	0	0	0	0	0
Decree 1132 revenues (60%)	0	0	0	0	0	0	0	0	0	0
Tax on households	65	7	0	0	0	0	0	0	0	0
Rental value tax	2	0	0	0	0	0	0	0	0	0
Driving licence tax	1	0	0	0	0	0	0	0	0	0
Municipal surcharge on buildings (40%)	37	5	0	22	0	0	0	0	0	0
Withholding tax on income from deposits paid by households	0	1 206	6 223	2 823	8 402	5 440	8 994	10 076	8 158	8 280
Direct taxes refund (60%)	0	0	41	0	0	0	0	0	0	0
Other	0	53	123	0	534	681	501	581	622	648
1120 On capital gains	0	144	867	685	14	7	5	3	4	5
Tax on capital gains on land	..	0	0	0	0	0	0	0	0	0
Municipal capital gains tax on buildings paid by households (60%)	..	144	867	685	14	7	5	3	4	5
1200 Corporate	379	4 710	26 605	34 699	50 529	36 740	41 194	33 530	36 311	36 344
1210 On profits	379	4 494	26 027	34 242	50 520	36 736	41 190	33 528	36 309	36 341
Corporation tax	0	1 245	9 042	28 877	47 192	34 841	39 160	31 927	34 548	34 579
Municipal surcharge on buildings (60%)	37	8	0	32	0	0	0	0	0	0
Tax on income from investments (40%)	213	37	10	0	0	0	8	54	58	36
Company franchise and liabilities tax	88	12	2	0	0	0	0	0	0	0
Law 1177 proportional surcharge (40%)	26	0	0	0	0	0	0	0	0	0
Direct taxes 5% proportional surcharge (40%)	0	20	48	0	0	0	0	0	0	0
Decree 1132 revenues (40%)	0	0	0	0	0	0	0	0	0	0
Additional Treasury increase (40%)	15	4	0	0	0	0	0	0	0	0
Withholding tax on company dividends paid by firms	0	77	745	166	0	0	0	0	0	0
Withholding tax on income from deposits paid by firms	0	1 810	9 334	4 235	2 370	605	1 464	759	614	623
Local income tax paid by firms	0	1 245	6 738	100	15	13	12	12	8	15
Direct taxes refund (40%)	0	0	27	0	0	0	0	0	0	0
Other	0	36	82	832	943	1 277	546	776	1 081	1 088
1220 On capital gains	0	216	578	457	9	4	4	2	2	3
Municipal capital gains tax on buildings paid by firms (40%)	..	216	578	457	9	4	4	2	2	3
1300 Unallocable between 1100 and 1200	0	171	448	7 295	3 833	2 295	6 104	7 782	8 343	7 571
Refunds tax on income	..	-240	-1 768	-5 175	0	0	0	0	0	0
Other	..	412	2 216	12 470	3 833	2 295	6 104	7 782	8 343	7 571
2000 Social security contributions	**1 881**	**22 976**	**87 256**	**143 629**	**200 772**	**209 122**	**210 462**	**214 376**	**215 856**	**220 622**
2100 Employees	..	4 171	16 753	27 333	35 715	37 598	39 284	39 805	39 977	40 872
2110 On a payroll basis	..	..	..	27 333	35 715	37 598	39 284	39 805	39 977	40 872
2120 On an income tax basis	..	..	..	0	0	0	0	0	0	0
2200 Employers	..	17 152	62 540	99 904	137 924	144 281	141 629	143 273	143 989	147 305
2210 On a payroll basis	..	..	..	99 904	137 924	144 281	141 629	143 273	143 989	147 305
2220 On an income tax basis	..	..	..	0	0	0	0	0	0	0
2300 Self-employed or non-employed	..	1 654	7 962	16 392	27 133	27 243	29 549	31 298	31 890	32 445
2310 On a payroll basis	..	..	..	16 392	27 133	27 243	29 549	31 298	31 890	32 445
2320 On an income tax basis	..	..	..	0	0	0	0	0	0	0
2400 Unallocable between 2100, 2200 and 2300	1 881	0	0	0	0	0	0	0	0	0
2410 On a payroll basis	..	..	..	..	..	..	..	..	..	..
2420 On an income tax basis	..	..	..	..	..	..	..	..	..	..
3000 Taxes on payroll and workforce	**0**	**387**	**890**	**0**	**0**	**0**	**0**	**0**	**0**	**0**
Contributions to GESCAL	..	387	890	..	..	..	..	..	..	..
4000 Taxes on property	**397**	**2 248**	**5 983**	**23 360**	**32 646**	**32 441**	**43 883**	**46 259**	**46 902**	**44 864**

	1965	1980	1990	2000	2007	2010	2013	2015	2016	2017
4100 Recurrent taxes on immovable property	96	7	1	9 354	12 778	9 663	20 748	25 558	21 692	22 069
Income tax on landowners	2	0	0	0	0	0	0	0	0	0
Income tax on buildings	12	2	1	0	0	0	0	0	0	0
Income tax on luxury buildings	1	0	0	0	0	0	0	0	0	0
Surcharge on land (provincial)	16	0	0	0	0	0	0	0	0	0
Surcharge on land (municipal)	18	0	0	0	0	0	0	0	0	0
Surcharge on buildings (provincial)	26	2	0	0	0	0	0	0	0	0
Surcharge on buildings (municipal)	21	3	0	0	0	0	0	0	0	0
Municipal real estate tax	0	0	0	9 354	12 778	9 663	20 748	20 798	20 531	20 937
Tax on indivisible services (TASI)	0	0	0	0	0	0	0	4 760	1 161	1 132
4110 Households	..	..	..	..	..	..	..	..	..	..
4120 Others	..	..	..	..	..	..	..	..	..	..
4200 Recurrent taxes on net wealth	0	0	0	14	1	2 118	2 547	231	396	355
4210 Individual	..	..	..	5	0	0	0	0	0	0
4220 Corporate	..	..	..	9	1	2 118	2 547	231	396	355
4300 Estate, inheritance and gift taxes	47	128	376	1 005	149	483	622	674	736	815
Inheritance and gift duty	33	119	376	1 005	149	483	622	674	736	815
Estate duty	11	9	0	0	0	0	0	0	0	0
Proportional surcharge and premium	3	0	0	0	0	0	0	0	0	0
4310 Estate and inheritance taxes	..	..	..	..	..	..	..	..	..	..
4320 Gift taxes	..	..	..	..	..	..	..	..	..	..
4400 Taxes on financial and capital transactions	255	2 113	5 606	12 320	18 256	17 365	17 092	17 245	17 684	17 690
Registration tax	120	1 048	2 421	6 794	9 410	9 019	7 353	7 625	8 129	8 541
Mortgage taxes and land registry duties	22	190	469	1 067	2 525	2 071	1 841	1 529	1 613	1 723
5% proportional surcharge	6	0	0	0	0	0	0	0	0	0
Additional surcharge	4	0	0	0	0	0	0	0	0	0
Stamp duties and surcharges accruing on cadastral acts	104	751	2 185	4 459	6 321	6 275	7 898	7 600	7 526	6 969
Other	0	123	530	0	0	0	0	491	416	457
4500 Non-recurrent taxes	0	0	0	98	151	916	985	309	4 231	1 148
4510 On net wealth	..	..	..	0	0	0	0	0	0	0
4520 Other non-recurrent taxes	..	..	..	98	151	916	985	309	4 231	1 148
4600 Other recurrent taxes on property	0	0	0	569	1 311	1 896	1 889	2 242	2 163	2 787
5000 Taxes on goods and services	**2 173**	**15 990**	**74 280**	**140 316**	**169 608**	**176 638**	**185 320**	**191 881**	**201 318**	**206 879**
5100 Taxes on production, sale, transfer, etc.	2 037	15 251	67 083	125 745	152 930	158 550	162 707	169 851	176 394	181 484
Direct taxes refund	0	-73	-86	0	0	0	0	0	0	0
5110 General taxes	710	9 438	38 940	77 473	95 623	97 586	93 921	100 692	102 378	107 901
5111 Value added taxes	0	9 438	38 940	77 473	95 623	97 586	93 921	100 692	102 378	107 901
VAT	..	9 438	38 940	77 473	95 623	97 586	93 921	100 692	102 378	107 901
5112 Sales tax	0	0	0	0	0	0	0	0	0	0
5113 Other	710	0	0	0	0	0	0	0	0	0
General tax on receipts	662	..	..	..	..	..	..	..	..	..
Compensation tax on imported products	48	..	..	..	..	..	..	..	..	..
5120 Taxes on specific goods and services	1 327	5 886	28 048	48 272	57 307	60 964	68 786	69 159	74 016	73 583
5121 Excise duties	816	4 088	20 304	31 479	32 904	36 414	45 720	46 238	48 427	46 762
Duty on mineral oils	465	3 462	15 928	22 172	23 252	22 884	26 332	25 759	25 687	26 160
Duty on spirits	27	87	206	486	595	570	571	600	636	649
Duty on beer	12	54	172	242	489	476	532	633	657	693
Duty on sugars	22	25	68	120	0	5	10	5	5	5
Duty on electricity	20	51	2 018	3 079	3 034	7 152	13 542	15 246	17 002	14 709
Duty on bananas	9	53	97	0	0	0	0	0	0	0
Duty on coffee	31	60	74	0	0	0	0	0	0	0
Duty on cocoa	3	4	7	0	0	0	0	0	0	0
Duty on olive oil	0	0	0	0	0	0	0	0	0	0
Other duty	44	190	1 037	5 201	5 385	5 268	4 659	3 898	4 417	4 520
Alcohol, spirits, liquor	5	0	0	0	0	0	0	0	0	0
On matches and flints	13	22	47	0	0	0	0	0	0	0
Meat	26	0	0	0	0	0	0	0	0	0
In-bond surcharge	0	81	650	174	143	54	67	90	17	19
Combustible materials	39	0	0	0	0	0	0	0	0	0
Construction materials	30	0	0	0	0	0	0	0	0	0
Excise duty on sound and video	3	0	0	0	0	0	0	0	0	0
Tax on phonograph records	1	0	0	0	0	0	0	0	0	0
Stamp duty on playing cards	1	0	0	0	0	0	0	0	0	0
Other	66	0	0	5	6	5	7	7	6	7
5122 Profits of fiscal monopolies	303	1 033	3 248	7 718	10 440	10 983	10 683	10 711	10 715	10 524
Duty on tobacco	292	1 033	3 248	7 712	10 436	10 978	10 679	10 710	10 714	10 523
On salt	10	0	0	0	0	0	0	0	0	0
Duty on products of Monopoli di Stato	1	0	0	6	4	5	4	1	1	1

	1965	1980	1990	2000	2007	2010	2013	2015	2016	2017
5123 Customs and import duties	142	261	1 164	0	0	0	0	0	0	0
Common Customs tariff (CEE)	0	0	836	..	..	..	..	..	..	..
Customs and shipping duties	115	14	0	..	..	..	..	..	..	..
Administrative services duties	11	0	0	..	..	..	..	..	..	..
Tax on agriculture	15	228	207	..	..	..	..	..	..	..
Other duties	0	9	68	..	..	..	..	..	..	..
Compensatory amounts	0	9	53	..	..	..	..	..	..	..
5124 Taxes on exports	0	0	0	0	0	0	0	0	0	0
5125 Taxes on investment goods	0	0	0	0	0	0	0	0	0	0
5126 Taxes on specific services	67	483	3 141	9 029	13 932	13 567	12 383	12 210	14 107	14 024
Entertainment tax	20	59	167	118	68	58	42	40	40	42
Stamp duty	6	0	0	0	0	0	0	0	0	0
Tax on advertisements	6	56	168	389	392	384	424	405	446	451
Tax on lotto, lotteries, betting and Totocalcio game	3	123	617	4 164	7 144	7 983	7 088	7 488	9 273	9 240
Casino takings, special duties, etc.	0	0	0	158	152	192	130	112	134	116
Single tax on games of skill and betting-levied indirectly	9	74	476	487	405	242	85	116	102	123
Aerotaxi passengers tax	0	0	0	0	0	0	7	8	8	10
Local tax (including insurance)	23	171	1 714	3 713	5 771	4 708	4 607	3 835	4 104	4 042
Bank levy for the National Resolution Fund	0	0	0	0	..	..	..	206	0	0
5127 Other taxes on internat. trade and transactions	0	0	0	0	0	0	0	0	0	0
Special Duty on foreign payments and currency selling	..	..	..	..	..	..	..	..	..	..
5128 Other taxes	0	21	192	46	31	0	0	0	767	2 273
ECSC taxes and contributions on sugar and other levies	..	21	121	0	0	..	..	..	0	0
Other	..	0	70	46	31	..	..	..	0	0
Bank cont. to the unique European Resolution Fund	..	0	0	0	0	..	..	..	767	2 273
5130 Unallocable between 5110 and 5120	0	0	180	0	0	0	0	0	0	0
5200 Taxes on use of goods and perform activities	136	456	4 474	8 479	10 550	10 531	11 352	11 130	13 261	13 171
5210 Recurrent taxes	136	456	4 474	8 479	10 550	1 155	1 359	1 653	1 665	1 801
Public motor vehicle register tax	64	152	967	1 034	1 326	1 155	1 359	1 653	1 665	1 801
Tax on vehicles 5% proportional surcharge	3	13	450	0	0	0	0	0	0	0
Surcharge on diesel cars	0	66	683	0	0	0	0	0	0	0
Surcharge on gas cars	0	0	171	0	0	0	0	0	0	0
5211 Paid by households: motor vehicles	..	..	..	3 433	4 652	4 628	4 487	4 710	5 109	5 045
5212 Paid by others: motor vehicles	..	..	..	1 006	1 332	1 300	1 395	1 446	1 507	1 504
Motor vehicle duty paid by firms	..	..	..	1 006	1 332	1 300	1 395	1 446	1 507	1 504
5213 Paid in respect of other goods	67	225	2 203	3 006	3 240	3 448	4 111	3 321	4 980	4 821
Law 1177 proportional surcharge	22	0	0	0	0	0	0	0	0	0
Taxes on signs	2	4	0	0	0	0	0	0	0	0
Tax on dog tags	0	7	12	0	0	0	0	0	0	0
Tax on hunting and fishing	0	0	0	0	0	0	0	0	0	0
Duty on official franchises	43	215	2 191	3 006	3 240	3 448	4 111	3 321	2 868	2 879
Television tax (households)	0	0	0	0	0	0	0	0	2 112	1 942
5220 Non-recurrent taxes	0	0	0	0	0	0	0	0	0	0
Motor vehicles, airplanes	..	..	..	..	..	..	..	..	..	..
Pro-Friuli tax on vehicles	..	..	..	..	..	..	..	..	..	..
5300 Unallocable between 5100 and 5200	0	283	2 724	6 092	6 128	7 557	11 261	10 900	11 663	12 224
Indirect taxes refund	..	0	160	288	616	693	477	715	700	722
Other	..	283	2 564	5 804	5 512	6 864	10 784	10 185	10 963	11 502
6000 Other taxes	**72**	**0**	**0**	**27 343**	**39 404**	**31 939**	**31 980**	**28 072**	**20 234**	**22 262**
6100 Paid solely by business	0	..	..	27 343	39 404	31 939	31 980	28 072	20 234	22 262
6200 Other	72	..	..	0	0	0	0	0	0	0
Capital levies	2	..	..	..	..	..	..	..	..	..
Other taxes	71	..	..	..	..	..	..	..	..	..
Custom duties collected for the EU	**..**	**..**	**..**	**1 536**	**2 261**	**2 225**	**1 890**	**2 246**	**2 233**	**2 295**
Non-wastable tax credits										
Non-wastable tax credits against 1110	..	..	..	..	0	0	357	9 793	10 180	10 276
Tax expenditure component	..	..	..	..	..	-109	206	8 615	8 927	9 056
Transfer component	..	..	..	..	..	109	151	1 178	1 253	1 220
Non-wastable tax credits against 1210	..	..	..	..	0	0	2 401	4 866	2 401	0
Tax expenditure component	..	..	..	..	..	..	0	0	0	..
Transfer component	..	..	..	..	..	..	2 401	4 866	2 401	..
Total tax revenue on cash basis	**5 505**	**60 422**	**265 116**	**488 738**	**653 836**	**659 704**	**689 299**	**711 837**	**710 008**	**725 712**
Total tax revenue on accrual basis	**..**	**..**	**..**	**503 096**	**671 189**	**671 912**	**706 829**	**708 768**	**714 911**	**727 790**

	1965	1980	1990	2000	2007	2010	2013	2015	2016	2017
Conciliation with National Accounts										
Additional taxes included in National Accounts	..	..	..	0	0	0	0	0	0	0
Taxes excluded from National Accounts	..	..	..	-5 416	-5 470	-6 538	-9 786	-9 801	-9 965	-10 307
The tax for the urban solid waste disposal (TARSU)	..	..	..	-4 387	-4 443	-5 519	-8 363	-8 519	-8 584	-8 883
Other	..	..	..	-1 029	-1 027	-1 019	-1 423	-1 282	-1 381	-1 424
Difference in treatment of tax credits	..	..	..	0	0	-109	206	8 615	8 927	9 056
Capital transfer for uncollected revenue	..	..	..	0	0	0	0	0	0	0
Voluntary social security contributions	..	..	..	464	567	561	738	750	780	783
Miscellaneous differences	..	..	..	0	0	0	0	0	0	0
National Accounts: Taxes and actual social contributions	..	..	..	498 144	666 286	665 826	697 987	708 332	714 653	727 322
Imputed social contributions	..	..	..	3 884	3 980	3 984	4 093	3 938	4 021	4 111
National Accounts: Taxes and all social contributions	..	..	..	502 028	670 266	669 810	702 080	712 270	718 674	731 433

.. Not available

Note: The tax year ends in December 31th.

As from 2000, revenues data are computed on accrual basis.

As from 1997, revenues data are based on data provided to the European Union as for the Treaty of Maastricht excessive deficit procedure.

Section 6000: Regional Tax on Productive Activities (IRAP); it is a tax on the value of production therefore its taxable base is different from other groups tax bases.

Regarding the section "Taxes excluded National Accounts" the item "Others" includes: tax on the public areas utilization and tax on the collection and disposal of waste water.

Source: Ministero dell'economia e delle finanze; Istituto nazionale di statistica.

StatLink https://doi.org/10.1787/888934057039

Table 5.18. Japan: Detailed country table, 1965-2017

Billion JPY

	1965	1980	1990	2000	2007	2010	2013	2015	2016	2017
Total tax revenue	**6 172**	**62 443**	**130 843**	**136 236**	**146 248**	**132 484**	**146 405**	**163 533**	**164 963**	**171 751**
1000 Taxes on income, profits and capital gains	**2 708**	**28 800**	**65 682**	**47 398**	**53 174**	**40 034**	**47 534**	**50 969**	**50 448**	**52 658**
1100 Of individuals	1 338	15 180	36 394	28 677	28 600	24 663	28 150	30 847	30 670	32 325
1110 On income and profits	1 338	15 180	36 394	28 677	28 600	24 663	28 150	30 847	30 670	32 325
Income tax	970	10 800	25 996	18 789	16 080	12 984	15 865	18 178	17 978	19 276
Prefectural inhabitants tax	123	1 415	3 675	3 621	5 008	4 699	5 090	5 252	5 128	5 376
Municipal inhabitants tax	220	2 890	6 475	6 044	7 294	6 795	7 015	7 224	7 365	7 471
Enterprise tax	25	75	249	223	218	184	181	194	198	203
1120 On capital gains	0	0	0	0	0	0	0	0	0	0
1200 Corporate	1 370	13 620	29 288	18 721	24 573	15 372	19 384	20 122	19 778	20 333
1210 On profits	1 370	13 620	29 288	18 721	24 573	15 372	19 384	20 122	19 778	20 333
Corporation tax	927	8 923	18 384	11 747	14 744	8 968	11 698	10 832	10 332	11 995
Prefectural inhabitants tax	53	557	1 414	879	1 206	777	854	859	763	762
Municipal inhabitants tax	85	1 297	3 198	2 176	3 015	1 954	2 157	2 324	2 392	2 224
Enterprise tax	305	2 843	6 293	3 918	5 608	2 253	2 674	3 510	4 395	3 991
Local special corporate tax	0	0	0	0	0	1 420	2 001	2 081	1 782	1 858
Local corporate tax	0	0	0	0	0	0	0	516	629	654
1220 On capital gains	0	0	0	0	0	0	0	0	0	0
1300 Unallocable between 1100 and 1200	0	0	0	0	0	0	0	0	0	0
2000 Social security contributions	**1 344**	**18 178**	**34 613**	**47 968**	**53 325**	**54 461**	**59 803**	**64 465**	**66 614**	**68 562**
2100 Employees	446	6 393	13 895	19 830	21 975	23 593	25 984	28 224	29 311	30 340
2110 On a payroll basis	..	..	13 895	19 830	21 975	23 593	25 984	28 224	29 311	30 340
2120 On an income tax basis	..	..	0	0	0	0	0	0	0	0
2200 Employers	588	9 267	16 649	22 456	24 243	24 674	27 143	29 479	30 560	31 637
2210 On a payroll basis	..	..	16 649	22 456	24 243	24 674	27 143	29 479	30 560	31 637
2220 On an income tax basis	..	..	0	0	0	0	0	0	0	0
2300 Self-employed or non-employed	107	2 518	4 069	5 683	7 108	6 194	6 676	6 763	6 742	6 585
2310 On a payroll basis	..	..	4 069	5 683	7 108	6 194	6 676	6 763	6 742	6 585
2320 On an income tax basis	..	..	0	0	0	0	0	0	0	0
2400 Unallocable between 2100, 2200 and 2300	203	0	0	0	0	0	0	0	0	0
2410 On a payroll basis	..	..	..	..	..	..	..	..	..	..
2420 On an income tax basis	..	..	..	..	..	..	..	..	..	..
3000 Taxes on payroll and workforce	**0**	**0**	**0**	**0**	**0**	**0**	**0**	**0**	**0**	**0**
4000 Taxes on property	**498**	**5 114**	**12 296**	**14 294**	**13 138**	**12 878**	**12 940**	**13 400**	**13 772**	**14 073**
4100 Recurrent taxes on immovable property	319	3 326	7 099	10 414	9 949	10 225	9 882	10 005	10 165	10 323
Prefectural property tax	4	8	15	11	14	5	2	2	3	4
Municipal property tax	296	2 784	6 023	9 041	8 729	8 961	8 653	8 755	9 077	9 025
City planning tax	19	469	942	1 318	1 202	1 256	1 227	1 244	1 262	1 277
Special landholding tax	0	65	118	43	4	3	1	3	7	1
Water and land utilization tax	0	0	0	0	0	0	0	0	0	0
Land value tax	0	0	0	1	0	0	0	0	0	0
4110 Households	..	..	..	..	..	..	..	..	..	..
4120 Others	..	..	..	..	..	..	..	..	..	..
4200 Recurrent taxes on net wealth	0	0	0	0	0	0	0	0	0	0
4210 Individual	..	..	..	..	..	..	..	..	..	..
4220 Corporate	..	..	..	..	..	..	..	..	..	..
4300 Estate, inheritance and gift taxes	44	441	1 918	1 782	1 503	1 250	1 574	1 968	2 131	2 292
4310 Estate and inheritance taxes	34	375	..	..	..	..	..	..	..	..
Inheritance tax	34	375	..	..	..	..	..	..	..	..
4320 Gift taxes	10	65	..	..	..	..	..	..	..	..
Tax on gifts	10	65	..	..	..	..	..	..	..	..
4400 Taxes on financial and capital transactions	135	1 347	3 280	2 099	1 686	1 403	1 483	1 426	1 476	1 458
Bourse tax	3	15	41	0	0	0	0	0	0	0
Securities transaction	8	209	748	0	0	0	0	0	0	0
Bank of Japan note issue tax	0	0	0	0	0	0	0	0	0	0
Stamp revenues	83	841	1 894	1 532	1 202	1 024	1 126	1 050	1 079	1 052
Real property acquisition tax	41	282	596	567	485	379	357	377	397	407
4500 Non-recurrent taxes	0	0	0	0	0	0	0	0	0	0
4510 On net wealth	..	..	..	..	..	..	..	..	..	..
4520 Other non-recurrent taxes	..	..	..	..	..	..	..	..	..	..
4600 Other recurrent taxes on property	0	0	0	0	0	0	0	0	0	0
5000 Taxes on goods and services	**1 620**	**10 200**	**17 917**	**26 227**	**26 256**	**24 730**	**25 744**	**34 286**	**33 711**	**36 031**
5100 Taxes on production, sale, transfer, etc.	1 544	8 822	15 647	23 180	23 241	22 160	23 313	31 871	31 254	33 582
5110 General taxes	0	0	5 778	12 350	12 841	12 675	13 479	22 400	21 931	22 249
5111 Value added taxes	..	..	5 778	12 350	12 841	12 675	13 479	22 400	21 931	22 249
5112 Sales tax	..	..	0	0	0	0	0	0	0	0
5113 Other	..	..	0	0	0	0	0	0	0	0
5120 Taxes on specific goods and services	1 544	8 822	9 868	10 830	10 400	9 485	9 834	9 470	9 323	11 333

	1965	1980	1990	2000	2007	2010	2013	2015	2016	2017
5121 Excise duties	1 062	6 674	8 637	9 837	9 374	8 622	8 728	8 351	8 316	10 241
Liquor tax	353	1 424	1 935	1 816	1 524	1 389	1 371	1 338	1 320	1 304
Sugar excises	29	43	0	0	0	0	0	0	0	0
Local gasoline tax	46	278	361	296	302	294	275	264	261	256
Gasoline tax	254	1 547	2 007	2 769	2 820	2 750	2 574	2 465	2 434	2 396
Liquefied petroleum gas tax	0	30	31	28	27	24	21	18	17	17
Aviation fuel tax	0	58	76	104	104	89	67	66	66	67
Commodity tax	138	1 038	5	0	0	0	0	0	0	0
Playing-card tax	1	1	0	0	0	0	0	0	0	0
Prefectural tobacco tax	44	229	361	282	278	256	173	153	149	141
Municipal tobacco tax	73	402	636	865	853	788	983	936	911	862
Timber delivery tax	3	3	0	0	0	0	0	0	0	0
Mineral product tax	2	5	3	2	2	2	2	2	2	2
Electricity and gas tax	54	386	0	0	0	0	0	0	0	0
Diesel oil tax	65	447	834	1 208	1 034	918	943	925	933	949
Vehicle acquisition tax	0	270	613	464	425	192	193	137	146	190
Promotion of power resources development tax	0	109	295	375	352	349	328	316	320	326
Petroleum and coal tax	0	404	487	489	513	502	600	630	702	691
Tobacco tax	0	0	996	876	925	908	1 038	954	914	864
Special tobacco tax	0	0	0	264	214	163	161	148	141	134
5122 Profits of fiscal monopolies	179	808	0	0	0	0	0	0	0	0
Monopoly profits	179	808	..	..	..	..	..	..	..	..
5123 Customs and import duties	222	786	928	877	941	786	1 034	1 049	939	1 024
Customs duty	222	786	928	877	941	786	1 034	1 049	939	1 024
5124 Taxes on exports	0	0	0	0	0	0	0	0	0	0
5125 Taxes on investment goods	0	0	0	0	0	0	0	0	0	0
5126 Taxes on specific services	81	554	303	116	85	77	71	70	68	67
Travel tax	4	64	0	0	0	0	0	0	0	0
Admission tax	10	5	0	0	0	0	0	0	0	0
Local entertainment tax	10	74	0	0	0	0	0	0	0	0
Golf course utilization tax	0	0	90	81	60	55	49	48	46	45
Meal and lodging tax	56	398	0	0	0	0	0	0	0	0
Special local consumption tax	0	0	195	12	0	0	0	0	0	0
Bathing tax	1	13	18	23	25	22	22	23	22	23
5127 Other taxes on internat. trade and transactions	0	0	0	0	0	0	0	0	0	0
5128 Other taxes	0	0	0	0	0	0	0	0	0	0
5130 Unallocable between 5110 and 5120	0	0	0	0	0	0	0	0	0	0
5200 Taxes on use of goods and perform activities	76	1 378	2 270	3 047	3 015	2 570	2 431	2 416	2 457	2 450
5210 Recurrent taxes	69	1 358	2 250	3 027	2 993	2 548	2 409	2 393	2 435	2 427
Automobile tax	55	781	1 276	1 765	1 717	1 616	1 574	1 543	1 535	1 541
Light vehicle tax	13	43	88	125	164	178	189	200	238	249
Motor vehicle tonnage tax	0	527	881	1 134	1 110	753	643	649	660	637
Hunter licence tax	0	3	2	2	0	0	0	0	0	0
Hunting tax	0	3	2	1	2	2	2	1	1	1
Mine lot tax	1	1	1	1	0	0	0	0	0	0
5211 Paid by households: motor vehicles	..	..	..	..	..	..	..	..	..	0
5212 Paid by others: motor vehicles	..	..	..	..	..	..	..	..	..	0
5213 Paid in respect of other goods	..	..	..	..	..	..	..	..	..	0
5220 Non-recurrent taxes	7	20	20	20	22	21	22	22	22	22
5300 Unallocable between 5100 and 5200	0	0	0	0	0	0	0	0	0	0
6000 Other taxes	**2**	**151**	**335**	**348**	**356**	**381**	**384**	**413**	**418**	**427**
6100 Paid solely by business	0	139	288	324	313	330	348	361	366	371
Business office tax	..	139	288	324	313	330	348	361	366	371
6200 Other	2	12	47	24	43	52	36	52	52	56
Taxes not in local tax law	2	12	47	24	43	52	36	52	52	56
Other	0	0	0	0	0	0	0	0	0	0
Total tax revenue on cash basis	**6 172**	**62 443**	..	..	..	..	..	..	..	..
Total tax revenue on accrual basis	..	..	**130 843**	**136 236**	**146 248**	**132 484**	**146 405**	**163 533**	**164 963**	**171 751**
Conciliation with National Accounts										
Additional taxes included in National Accounts	..	..	..	..	..	..	..	..	..	..
Taxes excluded from National Accounts	..	..	..	..	..	..	..	..	..	..
Difference in treatment of tax credits	..	..	..	..	..	..	..	..	..	..
Capital transfer for uncollected revenue	..	..	..	..	..	..	..	..	..	..
Voluntary social security contributions	..	..	..	..	..	..	..	..	..	..
Miscellaneous differences	..	..	..	..	..	..	..	..	..	..
National Accounts: Taxes and actual social contributions	..	..	..	..	..	..	..	..	..	..
Imputed social contributions	..	..	..	..	..	..	..	..	..	..
National Accounts: Taxes and all social contributions	..	..	..	..	..	..	..	..	..	..

.. Not available

Note: Data are on a fiscal year basis beginning 1st April.
From 1990, data are on accrual basis.
The figures for different groups of taxes are reported on different reporting bases, namely: Social security contributions (heading 2000) : in principle accrual basis, Central government taxes : accrual basis (revenues accrued during the fiscal year plus cash receipts collected before the end of May (the end of April until 1977), Local government taxes : accrual basis (due to be paid during the fiscal year and cash receipts collected before the end of May).
The Japanese authorities take the view that the Enterprise tax (classified in 1100 and 1200) and the Mineral product tax (classified in 5121) should be classified in heading 6000 since under articles 72 and 519 of the Local Tax Law these taxes are regarded as levies on the business or mining activity itself.
Heading 2000 includes some unidentifiable voluntary contributions.
Heading 2300: Includes contibutions to the National pension, National Health Insurance and the Farmer's pension fund. Contributions to the Farmer's pension fund are not available for the years before 1999.
Heading 4100: Municipal property tax, includes Prefectural property tax from 1990 to 1994 because data is not available to provide a breakdown.
Heading 5121: Municipal tobacco tax, includes Prefectural tobacco tax from 1990 to 1994 because data is not available to provide a breakdown.
Heading 5121: In sub-item Petroleum and coal tax, the data before 2003 refer to petroleum tax.
Source: Tax Bureau, Ministry of Finance.

StatLink https://doi.org/10.1787/888934057058

Table 5.19. Korea: Detailed country table, 1965-2017

Billion KRW

	1965	1980	1990	2000	2007	2010	2013	2015	2016	2017
Total tax revenue	..	**6 687**	**37 262**	**136 295**	**258 571**	**295 968**	**347 332**	**393 559**	**430 752**	**465 470**
1000 Taxes on income, profits and capital gains	..	**1 704**	**12 203**	**39 254**	**82 239**	**82 905**	**101 792**	**119 151**	**134 503**	**149 420**
1100 Of individuals	..	766	7 440	19 950	43 276	42 098	53 311	67 600	75 711	83 121
1110 On income and profits	..	766	6 327	18 569	31 984	33 935	46 654	55 744	62 028	67 987
Income tax	..	0	0	0	0	0	0	0	0	0
Dividends and interest income tax	..	0	0	0	4 682	4 425	4 889	4 561	4 125	4 517
Wages and salaries income tax	..	0	0	0	14 124	15 517	21 931	27 055	30 994	34 034
Other income tax	..	0	0	0	2 607	2 986	3 432	4 467	5 346	5 333
Global income tax	..	661	4 723	16 128	6 151	6 369	10 901	12 784	14 348	16 049
Defence tax on income tax	..	105	938	0	0	0	0	0	0	0
Education tax on income tax	..	0	325	0	0	0	0	0	0	0
Rural dev. tax on interest, bus. Inc. & cap. gains relief	..	0	0	156	160	179	124	105	109	104
Inhabitant tax on income tax (local)	..	0	341	2 285	4 260	4 459	5 377	6 772	7 106	7 950
1120 On capital gains	..	0	1 113	1 381	11 292	8 163	6 657	11 856	13 683	15 134
Capital gains tax	..	..	1 113	1 381	11 292	8 163	6 657	11 856	13 683	15 134
1200 Corporate	..	738	4 757	19 271	38 963	40 807	48 481	51 551	58 792	66 299
1210 On profits	..	738	4 757	19 271	38 963	40 807	48 481	51 551	58 792	66 299
Corporation tax - withholding	..	..	677	8 577	8 360	9 095	12 176	12 317	11 986	11 990
Corporation tax - final returns	..	..	2 549	9 302	27 057	28 173	31 679	32 713	40 130	47 187
Defence tax on corporation tax	..	..	1 323	0	0	0	0	0	0	0
Inhabitant tax on corporation tax (local)	..	..	207	1 142	3 152	3 094	4 118	6 217	6 270	6 785
Rural development tax corporate income	..	..	0	251	394	445	508	304	406	337
Excess profit tax	..	0	0	0	0	0	0	0	0	0
1220 On capital gains	..	0	0	0	0	0	0	0	0	0
Capital gains tax	..	..	..	..	..	..	..	..	..	..
1300 Unallocable between 1100 and 1200	..	199	6	33	0	0	0	0	0	0
Business income tax	..	0	0	0	..	..	..	..	..	..
Real estate income tax	..	0	0	0	..	..	..	..	..	..
Defence tax on real estate & business income	..	0	0	0	..	..	..	..	..	..
Rural dev. tax on bus. inc. & cap. gains relief	..	0	0	30	..	..	..	..	..	..
Inhabitant tax before 1990 (local)	..	117	0	0	..	..	..	..	..	..
Farm land tax (local)	..	83	6	3	..	..	..	..	..	..
Inhabitant tax on farm land tax (local)	..	0	0	0	..	..	..	..	..	..
2000 Social security contributions	..	**73**	**3 760**	**22 759**	**53 588**	**69 090**	**91 596**	**104 693**	**112 658**	**119 676**
2100 Employees	..	0	1 464	8 578	21 773	28 213	38 396	44 281	48 077	51 125
Veterans' relief fund	..	0	0	0	0	0	0	0	0	0
Soldiers' annuity fund	..	0	0	0	0	0	0	0	0	0
Unemployment assurance	..	0	0	598	1 164	1 358	2 418	3 076	3 251	3 418
National welfare pension fund	..	0	429	4 325	9 338	11 004	13 890	15 821	16 862	17 864
Social benefit fund	..	0	0	0	0	0	0	0	0	0
Health Insurance	..	0	483	2 066	8 180	11 783	17 128	19 868	21 470	22 814
Teachers' pensions	..	0	86	279	581	868	1 077	1 125	1 410	1 507
Government employees pensions	..	0	406	1 144	2 202	2 878	3 435	3 876	4 533	4 934
Military personal pensions	..	0	60	166	308	322	448	515	551	588
2110 On a payroll basis	..	..	..	8 578	21 773	28 213	38 396	44 281	48 077	51 125
2120 On an income tax basis	..	..	..	0	0	0	0	0	0	0
2200 Employers	..	73	1 694	9 409	23 557	30 856	41 518	47 846	51 190	54 063
Ind. works' insurance fund	..	73	550	1 876	4 431	4 632	5 436	6 062	6 283	6 429
Soldiers' annuity fund	..	0	0	0	0	0	0	0	0	0
Pneumoconiosis fund	..	0	0	0	0	0	0	0	0	0
Unemployment insurance	..	0	0	1 449	2 474	2 860	4 545	5 499	5 790	6 082
Veterans' relief fund	..	0	0	0	0	0	0	0	0	0
National welfare pension fund	..	0	430	4 340	9 383	11 052	13 958	15 895	16 928	17 922
Social benefit fund	..	0	0	0	0	0	0	0	0	0
Health Insurance	..	0	658	1 547	6 844	11 718	16 826	19 493	21 074	22 397
Teachers' pensions	..	0	56	197	425	594	753	897	1 115	1 233
Government employees pensions	..	0	0	0	0	0	0	0	0	0
2210 On a payroll basis	..	..	..	9 409	23 557	30 856	41 518	47 846	51 190	54 063
2220 On an income tax basis	..	..	..	0	0	0	0	0	0	0
2300 Self-employed or non-employed	..	0	602	4 772	8 258	10 021	11 682	12 566	13 391	14 488
2310 On a payroll basis	..	..	0	0	0	0	0	0	0	0
2320 On an income tax basis	..	..	602	4 772	8 258	10 021	11 682	12 566	13 391	14 488
2400 Unallocable between 2100, 2200 and 2300	..	0	0	0	0	0	0	0	0	0
2410 On a payroll basis	..	..	..	..	..	..	..	..	..	..
2420 On an income tax basis	..	..	..	..	..	..	..	..	..	..
3000 Taxes on payroll and workforce	..	**34**	**153**	**258**	**619**	**714**	**981**	**1 122**	**1 293**	**1 376**
Workshop tax on workforce (local)	..	31	124	258	619	714	981	1 122	1 293	1 376
Vocational training promotion fund	..	3	29	0	0	0	0	0	0	0
4000 Taxes on property	..	**537**	**4 389**	**16 846**	**33 109**	**33 516**	**35 847**	**48 625**	**49 820**	**54 406**

	1965	1980	1990	2000	2007	2010	2013	2015	2016	2017
4100 Recurrent taxes on immovable property	..	183	980	3 385	9 196	9 270	10 809	12 486	13 095	14 319
Property tax (local)	..	119	227	728	3 755	4 817	8 267	9 294	9 930	10 662
City planning tax on urban real estate (local)	..	51	244	815	1 883	2 465	0	0	0	0
Community facilities tax (local)	..	13	86	341	543	650	912	1 351	1 450	1 513
Tax on excessive land holdings (local)	..	0	1	0	0	0	0	0	0	0
Tax on aggregate land holdings (local)	..	0	400	1 282	5	0	0	0	0	0
Rural dev. tax on local agg. land holdings tax	..	0	0	81	1	0	0	0	0	0
Tax on excessively increased land value	..	0	0	0	0	0	0	0	0	0
Comprehensive real estate tax	..	0	0	0	2 414	1 029	1 224	1 399	1 294	1 652
Rural dev. tax on comprehensive real estate tax	..	0	0	0	483	208	250	267	240	302
4110 Households	..	..	0	0	0	0	0	0	0	0
4120 Others	..	..	22	138	112	101	156	175	181	190
Workshop tax on property (local)	..	..	22	138	112	101	156	175	181	190
4200 Recurrent taxes on net wealth	..	0	0	0	0	0	0	0	0	0
4210 Individual	..	..	..	..	..	..	..	..	..	..
4220 Corporate	..	..	..	..	..	..	..	..	..	..
4300 Estate, inheritance and gift taxes	..	12	354	989	2 842	3 076	4 290	5 044	5 350	6 785
4310 Estate and inheritance taxes	..	5	85	449	1 059	1 203	1 587	1 944	1 995	2 342
Inheritance tax	..	3	71	449	1 059	1 203	1 587	1 944	1 995	2 342
Defence tax on inheritance tax	..	2	14	0	0	0	0	0	0	0
4320 Gift taxes	..	7	269	540	1 783	1 873	2 703	3 100	3 355	4 443
Gift tax	..	7	225	540	1 783	1 873	2 703	3 100	3 355	4 443
Defence tax on gift tax	..	0	44	0	0	0	0	0	0	0
4400 Taxes on financial and capital transactions	..	319	2 960	11 935	21 071	21 170	20 748	31 095	31 375	33 302
Registration tax (local)	..	122	1 378	4 528	7 254	7 370	1 312	1 831	1 708	1 608
Registration tax	..	0	0	0	0	0	0	0	0	0
Defence tax on registration tax	..	0	0	0	0	0	0	0	0	0
Rural dev. tax on local acquisition tax	..	0	0	246	627	632	874	969	954	1 028
Rural dev. tax on local registration tax	..	0	0	66	143	144	1	1	0	0
Securities transactions tax	..	0	224	2 736	3 469	3 667	3 077	4 670	4 468	4 508
Rural dev. tax on securities transaction tax	..	0	0	823	1 729	2 010	1 529	1 861	1 637	1 775
Acquisition tax (local)	..	163	1 165	3 148	7 261	6 825	13 318	20 810	21 702	23 487
Stamp tax	..	34	193	388	588	522	637	953	906	896
4500 Non-recurrent taxes	..	22	95	537	0	0	0	0	0	0
Asset revaluation tax	..	22	95	537	..	..	..	..	..	..
4510 On net wealth	..	..	..	..	..	..	..	..	..	..
4520 Other non-recurrent taxes	..	..	..	..	..	..	..	..	..	..
4600 Other recurrent taxes on property	..	0	0	0	0	0	0	0	0	0
5000 Taxes on goods and services	**..**	**4 190**	**16 497**	**52 271**	**80 861**	**99 769**	**106 717**	**110 326**	**121 197**	**129 065**
5100 Taxes on production, sale, transfer, etc.	..	4 114	16 024	50 023	78 414	96 573	99 970	103 254	113 644	121 293
5110 General taxes	..	1 471	6 964	23 212	40 942	51 800	59 105	60 162	68 229	74 361
5111 Value added taxes	..	1 471	6 964	23 212	40 942	51 800	59 105	60 162	68 229	74 361
Value added tax	..	1 471	6 964	23 212	40 942	51 800	59 105	60 162	68 229	74 361
5112 Sales tax	..	0	0	0	0	0	0	0	0	0
Business tax	..	..	..	..	..	..	..	..	..	..
5113 Other	..	0	0	0	0	0	0	0	0	0
5120 Taxes on specific goods and services	..	2 643	9 059	26 811	37 472	44 773	40 865	43 092	45 415	46 932
5121 Excise duties	..	1 029	4 924	18 155	27 880	31 340	27 661	31 857	34 762	35 779
Commodity tax	..	0	0	0	0	0	0	0	0	0
Defence tax on commodity tax	..	0	0	0	0	0	0	0	0	0
Liquor tax	..	298	1 022	1 963	2 268	2 878	2 947	3 228	3 209	3 035
Defence tax on liquor tax	..	78	0	0	0	0	0	0	0	0
Education tax on liquor tax	..	0	81	516	580	724	764	808	813	745
Textile tax	..	0	0	0	0	0	0	0	0	0
Petroleum tax	..	0	0	0	0	0	0	0	0	0
Transport tax on petrol products	..	0	0	8 404	11 464	13 970	13 248	14 055	15 303	15 553
Education tax on transport tax	..	0	0	1 247	1 715	2 133	1 895	2 154	2 289	2 320
Electricity and gas tax	..	0	0	0	0	0	0	0	0	0
Special excise tax	..	583	1 912	2 985	5 161	5 066	5 484	8 001	8 881	9 861
Defence tax on special excise tax	..	70	337	0	0	0	0	0	0	0
Education tax on special excise tax	..	0	0	498	607	501	485	515	463	602
Rural development on special excise tax	..	0	0	37	54	24	56	61	60	60
Tobacco sales tax (local)	..	0	0	0	0	0	0	0	0	0
Tobacco consumption tax (local)	..	0	1 572	2 251	2 761	2 875	2 782	3 035	3 744	3 603
Motor fuel tax (local)	..	0	0	254	3 270	3 169	0	0	0	0
5122 Profits of fiscal monopolies	..	510	0	0	0	0	0	0	0	0
Monopoly profit	..	510	..	..	..	..	..	..	..	..

	1965	1980	1990	2000	2007	2010	2013	2015	2016	2017
5123 Customs and import duties	..	1 014	3 692	5 936	7 690	11 046	11 012	8 907	8 434	8 938
Customs duties	..	762	2 765	5 800	7 411	10 666	10 562	8 495	8 045	8 529
Defence tax on customs duties	..	248	919	0	0	0	0	0	0	0
Special customs duties	..	0	0	0	0	0	0	0	0	0
Tonnage tax	..	0	0	0	0	0	0	0	0	0
Education tax on imports	..	0	7	99	234	336	429	390	366	382
Rural dev. tax on customs exemptions	..	0	0	37	45	44	21	22	23	27
Previous year receipts	..	4	0	0	0	0	0	0	0	0
5124 Taxes on exports	..	0	0	0	0	0	0	0	0	0
5125 Taxes on investment goods	..	0	0	0	0	0	0	0	0	0
5126 Taxes on specific services	..	90	444	2 720	1 902	2 387	2 192	2 328	2 219	2 215
Telephone tax	..	50	262	1 457	0	0	0	0	0	0
Defence tax on telephone tax	..	33	0	0	0	0	0	0	0	0
Entertainment tax	..	0	0	0	0	0	0	0	0	0
Defence tax on entertainment tax	..	0	0	0	0	0	0	0	0	0
Entertainment tax (local)	..	0	0	0	0	0	0	0	0	0
Travel tax	..	0	0	0	0	0	0	0	0	0
Admission tax	..	0	0	0	0	0	0	0	0	0
Defence tax on admission tax	..	0	0	0	0	0	0	0	0	0
Education tax on banking & insurance	..	0	108	473	721	951	938	1 004	951	959
Horse race tax (local)	..	3	56	566	864	1 068	1 042	1 089	1 060	1 051
Rural dev. tax on horse race tax	..	0	0	84	165	215	212	235	208	205
Butchery tax (local)	..	5	18	51	52	58	0	0	0	0
Regional development tax (local)	..	0	0	89	100	95	0	0	0	0
5127 Other taxes on internat. trade and transactions	..	0	0	0	0	0	0	0	0	0
5128 Other taxes	..	0	0	0	0	0	0	0	0	0
5130 Unallocable between 5110 and 5120	..	0	0	0	0	0	0	0	0	0
5200 Taxes on use of goods and perform activities	..	75	474	2 248	2 447	3 196	6 747	7 072	7 553	7 772
5210 Recurrent taxes	..	75	474	2 248	2 447	3 196	6 747	7 072	7 553	7 772
License tax (local)	..	18	48	241	77	76	0	0	0	0
Automobile tax (local)	..	57	426	2 007	2 370	3 120	6 747	7 072	7 553	7 772
5211 Paid by households: motor vehicles	..	..	..	..	..	..	..	..	..	..
5212 Paid by others: motor vehicles	..	..	..	..	..	..	..	..	..	..
5213 Paid in respect of other goods	..	..	..	..	..	..	..	..	..	..
5220 Non-recurrent taxes	..	0	0	0	0	0	0	0	0	0
5300 Unallocable between 5100 and 5200	..	0	0	0	0	0	0	0	0	0
6000 Other taxes	..	**150**	**259**	**4 907**	**8 155**	**9 974**	**10 399**	**9 642**	**11 281**	**11 527**
6100 Paid solely by business	..	0	0	0	0	0	0	0	0	0
6200 Other	..	150	259	4 907	8 155	9 974	10 399	9 642	11 281	11 527
Unallocable tax revenue	..	143	0	0	0	0	0	0	0	0
Previous year tax	..	0	213	1 474	2 965	4 449	4 774	3 435	4 147	4 389
Previous year tax (local)	..	6	47	474	672	654	601	392	868	715
Unallocable defence tax	..	0	0	-3	0	0	0	0	0	0
Education tax on local taxes	..	0	0	2 962	4 518	4 871	5 024	5 815	6 266	6 423
Total tax revenue on cash basis	..	**6 687**	**37 262**	**136 295**	**258 571**	**295 968**	**347 332**	**393 559**	**430 752**	**465 470**
Total tax revenue on accrual basis	..	..	..	..	..	..	..	..	..	..
Conciliation with National Accounts										
Additional taxes included in National Accounts	..	..	..	..	..	..	..	..	..	..
Taxes excluded from National Accounts	..	..	..	..	..	..	..	..	..	..
Difference in treatment of tax credits	..	..	..	..	..	..	..	..	..	..
Capital transfer for uncollected revenue	..	..	..	..	..	..	..	..	..	..
Voluntary social security contributions	..	..	..	..	..	..	..	..	..	..
Miscellaneous differences	..	..	..	..	..	..	..	..	..	..
National Accounts: Taxes and actual social contributions	..	..	..	..	..	..	..	..	..	..
Imputed social contributions	..	..	..	..	..	..	..	..	..	..
National Accounts: Taxes and all social contributions	..	..	..	..	..	..	..	..	..	..

.. Not available

Note: Year ending 31st December.

Data are on cash basis.

Heading 2000: From 1997 the contributions to the three funds (civil servant pension fund, private school teachers pension fund and medical insurance fund) are classified as security social contributions. The reasons for the change are that the contributions either became mandatory or the fund started to be managed by public authorities in that year, thereby meeting the OECD definition of social security contributions.

Heading 2200: From 2007, this includes long-term care insurance.

Source: Ministry of Finance and Economy, Ministry of Home Affairs.

StatLink https://doi.org/10.1787/888934057077

Table 5.20. Latvia: Detailed country table, 1965-2017

Million EUR

	1965	1980	1990	2000	2007	2010	2013	2015	2016	2017
Total tax revenue	..	..	..	**1 995**	**6 401**	**5 162**	**6 695**	**7 334**	**7 812**	**8 412**
Total tax revenue exclusive of customs duties	..	..	..	**1 995**	**6 364**	**5 137**	**6 667**	**7 294**	**7 765**	**8 366**
1000 Taxes on income, profits and capital gains	..	..	..	**480**	**1 857**	**1 292**	**1 690**	**1 833**	**2 011**	**2 204**
1100 Of individuals	..	..	..	376	1 287	1 116	1 320	1 445	1 587	1 777
1110 On income and profits	..	..	..	376	1 287	1 116	1 320	1 445	1 587	1 777
Personal income tax	..	..	..	376	1 287	1 116	1 320	1 445	1 532	1 712
Solidarity tax	..	..	..	0	0	0	0	0	55	65
1120 On capital gains	..	..	..	0	0	0	0	0	0	0
1200 Corporate	..	..	..	105	570	175	370	389	424	427
1210 On profits	..	..	..	105	570	175	370	389	424	427
1220 On capital gains	..	..	..	0	0	0	0	0	0	0
1300 Unallocable between 1100 and 1200	..	..	..	0	0	0	0	0	0	0
2000 Social security contributions	..	..	..	**669**	**1 774**	**1 554**	**1 933**	**2 030**	**2 067**	**2 259**
2100 Employees	..	..	..	167	479	389	531	585	530	627
2110 On a payroll basis	..	..	..	167	479	389	531	585	530	627
2120 On an income tax basis	..	..	..	0	0	0	0	0	0	0
2200 Employers	..	..	..	501	1 283	1 155	1 391	1 432	1 523	1 618
2210 On a payroll basis	..	..	..	501	1 283	1 155	1 391	1 432	1 523	1 618
2220 On an income tax basis	..	..	..	0	0	0	0	0	0	0
2300 Self-employed or non-employed	..	..	..	1	12	9	11	12	13	15
2310 On a payroll basis	..	..	..	1	12	9	11	12	13	15
2320 On an income tax basis	..	..	..	0	0	0	0	0	0	0
2400 Unallocable between 2100, 2200 and 2300	..	..	..	0	0	0	0	0	0	0
2410 On a payroll basis	..	..	..	..	..	..	..	..	..	..
2420 On an income tax basis	..	..	..	..	..	..	..	..	..	..
3000 Taxes on payroll and workforce	..	..	..	**0**	**4**	**3**	**3**	**3**	**3**	**3**
Risk duty of business	..	..	..	..	4	3	3	3	3	3
4000 Taxes on property	..	..	..	**76**	**195**	**157**	**221**	**246**	**268**	**278**
4100 Recurrent taxes on immovable property	..	..	..	63	106	128	173	197	220	228
4110 Households	..	..	..	0	0	0	22	24	32	35
4120 Others	..	..	..	63	106	128	151	173	188	193
Tax on property	..	..	..	63	106	128	151	173	188	193
Tax on land	..	..	..	0	0	0	0	0	0	0
4200 Recurrent taxes on net wealth	..	..	..	0	0	0	0	0	0	0
4210 Individual	..	..	..	..	..	..	..	..	..	..
4220 Corporate	..	..	..	..	..	..	..	..	..	..
4300 Estate, inheritance and gift taxes	..	..	..	0	3	3	5	7	8	9
4310 Estate and inheritance taxes	..	..	..	..	3	3	5	7	8	9
Duty for legacies and donations	..	..	..	..	0	2	3	4	5	6
Stamp duty for transactions made in Land Register in relation to legacies and donations	..	..	..	..	1	0	0	1	1	1
Duty for consolidation of ownership and legal cliens in Land Register anent legacies and donations	..	..	..	..	2	2	2	2	2	2
4320 Gift taxes	..	..	..	..	0	0	0	0	0	0
4400 Taxes on financial and capital transactions	..	..	..	13	86	26	43	42	40	41
Duties on transactions with privatization vouchers	..	..	..	0	0	0	0	0	0	0
Stamp duty for transactions made in Land Register, which have been collected from juridical persons, except legacies and donations	..	..	..	0	1	1	1	1	1	1
Duty for consolidation of ownership and legal liens in Land Register, which have been collected from juridical persons, except legacies and donations	..	..	..	4	27	13	17	18	17	17
Stamp duty for transactions made in Land Register, which have been collected from physical persons, except legacies and donations	..	..	..	1	8	1	2	2	2	2
Duty for consolidation of ownership and legal liens in Land Register, which have been collected from physical persons, except legacies and donations	..	..	..	7	51	11	23	20	21	21
4500 Non-recurrent taxes	..	..	..	0	0	0	0	0	0	0
4510 On net wealth	..	..	..	..	..	..	..	..	..	..
4520 Other non-recurrent taxes	..	..	..	..	..	..	..	..	..	..
4600 Other recurrent taxes on property	..	..	..	0	0	0	0	0	0	0
5000 Taxes on goods and services	..	..	..	**770**	**2 535**	**2 132**	**2 821**	**3 182**	**3 415**	**3 621**
5100 Taxes on production, sale, transfer, etc.	..	..	..	739	2 478	2 006	2 667	3 012	3 242	3 428
5110 General taxes	..	..	..	476	1 753	1 301	1 855	2 130	2 298	2 440
5111 Value added taxes	..	..	..	476	1 727	1 202	1 690	1 876	2 032	2 164
5112 Sales tax	..	..	..	0	0	0	0	31	29	31
Subsidised electricity tax	..	..	..	..	..	..	..	31	29	31
5113 Other	..	..	..	0	27	99	165	223	237	245
Mandatory procurement public service obligation fee	..	..	..	0	27	99	165	223	237	245
5120 Taxes on specific goods and services	..	..	..	262	725	705	812	882	944	989

	1965	1980	1990	2000	2007	2010	2013	2015	2016	2017
5121 Excise duties	..	..	..	232	626	645	742	807	874	913
Excise duty on alcoholic beverages	..	..	..	63	127	111	124	128	139	162
Excise duty on beer	..	..	..	4	15	25	24	27	32	37
Excise duty on oil products	..	..	..	124	359	360	388	428	467	484
Excise duty on tobacco	..	..	..	27	92	130	160	178	188	191
Excise duty on other products	..	..	..	14	32	18	24	25	25	15
Excise duty on coffee and non alcoholic beverages	..	..	..	6	8	13	14	14	14	15
Excise duty / Tax on cars and motorcycles	..	..	..	8	24	5	10	11	10	0
Excise duty on natural gas	..	..	..	0	0	1	22	20	22	19
Tax on electricity	..	..	..	0	1	1	1	2	1	5
5122 Profits of fiscal monopolies	..	..	..	0	0	0	0	0	0	0
5123 Customs and import duties	..	..	..	21	33	14	2	2	-3	3
Customs duties	..	..	..	21	3	0	0	0	-5	-1
Levies on imported agricultural products	..	..	..	0	2	0	0	0	0	0
Excise duty of imported goods for omission for free turnover	..	..	..	0	28	14	2	3	2	4
5124 Taxes on exports	..	..	..	0	0	0	0	0	0	0
5125 Taxes on investment goods	..	..	..	0	0	0	0	0	0	0
5126 Taxes on specific services	..	..	..	10	66	47	68	72	73	72
Taxes on lotteries and gambling	..	..	..	7	42	22	29	32	34	36
Financial stability fee	..	..	..	0	0	0	5	4	15	11
Passenger departure duty	..	..	..	3	0	0	0	0	0	0
Contributions to the EU Single Resolution Fund	..	..	..	0	0	0	0	8	7	7
Contributions to the fund for the protection of the insured	..	..	..	0	1	1	1	1	0	0
Contributions to the deposit guarantee fund	..	..	..	0	22	24	32	28	16	17
5127 Other taxes on internat. trade and transactions	..	..	..	0	0	0	0	0	0	..
5128 Other taxes	..	..	..	0	0	0	0	0	0	..
5130 Unallocable between 5110 and 5120	..	..	..	0	0	0	0	0	0	..
5200 Taxes on use of goods and perform activities	..	..	..	32	57	126	154	170	173	193
5210 Recurrent taxes	..	..	..	32	57	73	140	142	141	156
5211 Paid by households: motor vehicles	..	..	..	12	16	34	48	54	55	61
Vehicle tax for vehicles which have been registered on physical persons	..	..	..	0	0	0	48	54	55	61
Annual vehicle duty for vehicles which have been registered on physical persons	..	..	..	12	16	34	0	0	0	0
5212 Paid by others: motor vehicles	..	..	..	0	20	22	45	46	51	52
Tax on cars belonging to enterprises	..	..	..	..	0	0	21	20	22	22
Vehicle tax for vehicles which have been registered on judical persons	..	..	..	..	0	0	24	26	29	30
Annual vehicle duty for vehicles which have been registered on judical persons	..	..	..	..	20	22	0	0	0	0
5213 Paid in respect of other goods	..	..	..	20	21	17	47	42	35	43
Duty for keeping animals	..	..	..	0	0	0	0	0	0	0
Income from lease of reservoirs and fishing rights and non-production use of fishing rights (fishing cards)	..	..	..	0	0	0	1	1	1	1
Business and professional licences	..	..	..	5	6	4	27	20	17	17
State duties and payments for issue of special permits (licences) and registration of documents that commensurate correspondence of professional qualification	..	..	..	1	0	0	0	0	0	0
Lottery and gambling state duty	..	..	..	1	4	2	2	2	3	3
Gambling equipment marking duty	..	..	..	0	1	1	0	0	0	0
Payment for rental of commercial fishing rights	..	..	..	0	0	0	0	1	1	1
Lottery of goods and services organization duty	..	..	..	2	0	0	0	0	0	0
State duty for using numerative rights	..	..	..	0	0	0	0	0	0	0
State duty for keeping oil products` security reserves	..	..	..	0	0	0	24	16	13	12
Tax on natural resources	..	..	..	15	15	12	19	22	18	26
5220 Non-recurrent taxes	..	..	..	0	0	53	14	28	33	37
Revenue from state-owned greenhouse gas emission unit trade	..	..	..	..	..	53	14	0	0	0
Payment for emission quota trading	..	..	..	..	..	0	0	11	15	12
The fee for the appeal of procurement	..	..	..	..	..	0	0	0	0	0
Toll for the use of motorways	..	..	..	..	..	0	0	17	18	25
5300 Unallocable between 5100 and 5200	..	..	..	0	0	0	0	0	0	0
6000 Other taxes	**..**	**..**	**..**	**0**	**0**	**0**	**0**	**0**	**0**	**0**
6100 Paid solely by business	..	..	..	..	..	..	..	..	..	..
6200 Other	..	..	..	..	..	..	..	..	..	..
Custom duties collected for the EU	**..**	**..**	**..**	**..**	**37**	**25**	**28**	**40**	**47**	**46**
Total tax revenue on cash basis	**..**	**..**	**..**	**..**	**..**	**..**	**..**	**..**	**..**	**..**
Total tax revenue on accrual basis	**..**	**..**	**..**	**1 995**	**6 401**	**5 162**	**6 695**	**7 334**	**7 812**	**8 412**

	1965	1980	1990	2000	2007	2010	2013	2015	2016	2017
Conciliation with National Accounts										
Additional taxes included in National Accounts	..	..	..	14	1	1	0	0	0	0
Taxes excluded from National Accounts	..	..	..	0	0	0	0	0	0	0
Difference in treatment of tax credits	..	..	..	0	0	0	0	0	0	0
Capital transfer for uncollected revenue	..	..	..	0	0	0	0	0	0	0
Voluntary social security contributions	..	..	..	0	0	0	0	0	0	0
Miscellaneous differences	..	..	..	0	0	0	0	0	0	0
National Accounts: Taxes and actual social contributions	..	..	..	2 009	6 402	5 163	6 695	7 334	7 813	8 413
Imputed social contributions	..	..	..	12	51	36	59	80	87	97
National Accounts: Taxes and all social contributions	..	..	..	2 022	6 453	5 199	6 754	7 415	7 899	8 509

.. Not available

Note: Year ending 31st December.

Data on accrual basis.

Source: Ministry of Finance.

StatLink https://doi.org/10.1787/888934057096

Table 5.21. Lithuania: Detailed country table, 1965-2017

Million EUR

	1965	1980	1990	2000	2007	2010	2013	2015	2016	2017
Total tax revenue	..	..	..	**4 154**	**8 730**	**7 961**	**9 445**	**10 826**	**11 548**	**12 461**
Total tax revenue exclusive of customs duties	..	..	..	**4 154**	**8 669**	**7 909**	**9 377**	**10 727**	**11 452**	**12 360**
1000 Taxes on income, profits and capital gains	..	..	..	**1 111**	**2 625**	**1 281**	**1 726**	**2 013**	**2 175**	**2 258**
1100 Of individuals	..	..	..	1 020	1 891	1 005	1 250	1 440	1 548	1 627
1110 On income and profits	..	..	..	1 020	1 810	972	1 226	1 390	1 479	1 558
Tax on payroll and workforce	..	..	..	950	1 628	793	1 008	1 148	1 214	1 235
Tax on income from individual activities	..	..	..	40	81	36	48	55	66	79
Tax on capital income	..	..	..	31	102	143	170	187	199	243
1120 On capital gains	..	..	..	0	81	33	24	50	69	69
1200 Corporate	..	..	..	90	734	276	477	574	628	631
1210 On profits	..	..	..	90	734	276	477	574	628	631
1220 On capital gains	..	..	..	0	0	0	0	0	0	0
1300 Unallocable between 1100 and 1200	..	..	..	0	0	0	0	0	0	0
2000 Social security contributions	..	..	..	**1 362**	**2 643**	**3 293**	**3 791**	**4 338**	**4 714**	**5 170**
2100 Employees	..	..	..	107	233	641	763	873	972	1 071
2110 On a payroll basis	..	..	..	107	233	641	763	873	972	1 071
2120 On an income tax basis	..	..	..	0	0	0	0	0	0	0
2200 Employers	..	..	..	1 119	2 180	2 109	2 526	2 916	3 193	3 512
2210 On a payroll basis	..	..	..	1 119	2 180	2 109	2 526	2 916	3 193	3 512
2220 On an income tax basis	..	..	..	0	0	0	0	0	0	0
2300 Self-employed or non-employed	..	..	..	135	230	544	502	549	549	587
2310 On a payroll basis	..	..	..	135	230	544	502	549	549	587
2320 On an income tax basis	..	..	..	0	0	0	0	0	0	0
2400 Unallocable between 2100, 2200 and 2300	..	..	..	0	0	0	0	0	0	0
2410 On a payroll basis	..	..	..	..	..	..	..	..	..	..
2420 On an income tax basis	..	..	..	..	..	..	..	..	..	..
3000 Taxes on payroll and workforce	..	..	..	**0**	**0**	**0**	**0**	**0**	**0**	**0**
4000 Taxes on property	..	..	..	**62**	**83**	**103**	**97**	**126**	**127**	**129**
4100 Recurrent taxes on immovable property	..	..	..	61	82	102	96	125	126	127
4110 Households	..	..	..	3	6	7	8	17	17	25
4120 Others	..	..	..	58	76	95	88	108	109	102
Tax on land from corporations	..	..	..	3	8	9	10	10	11	5
Tax on immovable property	..	..	..	55	69	86	77	98	98	97
4200 Recurrent taxes on net wealth	..	..	..	0	0	0	0	0	0	0
4210 Individual	..	..	..	..	..	..	..	..	..	..
4220 Corporate	..	..	..	..	..	..	..	..	..	..
4300 Estate, inheritance and gift taxes	..	..	..	1	2	1	1	1	1	2
4310 Estate and inheritance taxes	..	..	..	1	2	1	1	1	1	2
4320 Gift taxes	..	..	..	0	0	0	0	0	0	0
4400 Taxes on financial and capital transactions	..	..	..	0	0	0	0	0	0	0
4500 Non-recurrent taxes	..	..	..	0	0	0	0	0	0	0
4510 On net wealth	..	..	..	..	..	..	..	..	..	..
4520 Other non-recurrent taxes	..	..	..	..	..	..	..	..	..	..
4600 Other recurrent taxes on property	..	..	..	0	0	0	0	0	0	0
5000 Taxes on goods and services	..	..	..	**1 619**	**3 317**	**3 232**	**3 762**	**4 249**	**4 436**	**4 803**
5100 Taxes on production, sale, transfer, etc.	..	..	..	1 556	3 238	3 149	3 685	4 176	4 359	4 721
5110 General taxes	..	..	..	1 086	2 339	2 183	2 611	2 913	3 052	3 336
5111 Value added taxes	..	..	..	1 005	2 330	2 180	2 611	2 889	3 028	3 310
5112 Sales tax	..	..	..	0	0	0	0	0	0	0
5113 Other	..	..	..	81	8	3	0	24	24	26
Deductions from revenue according to the RoL on the financing of road maintence and development	..	..	..	81	0	0	..	0	0	0
Deductions from revenue according to the RoL Forestry Law	..	..	..	0	0	0	..	24	24	26
Turnover tax on goods	..	..	..	0	0	0	..	0	0	0
Deductions from Ignalina nuclear power plant income generated by sales of electricity	..	..	..	0	8	3	..	0	0	0
Turnover tax on publications of erotic and violent nature	..	..	..	0	0	0	..	0	0	0
Turnover tax on motor cars	..	..	..	0	0	0	..	0	0	0
Turnover tax on goods containing ethyl	..	..	..	0	0	0	..	0	0	0
5120 Taxes on specific goods and services	..	..	..	470	899	966	1 073	1 263	1 307	1 385

	1965	1980	1990	2000	2007	2010	2013	2015	2016	2017
5121 Excise duties	..	..	..	428	835	903	996	1 165	1 236	1 339
Alcoholic beverages	..	..	..	10	2	10	12	6	7	13
Manufactured tabacco	..	..	..	41	121	170	209	270	291	286
Oil and other oil products	..	..	..	230	451	487	534	619	674	730
Electricity	..	..	..	2	0	3	3	4	3	2
Luxury cars	..	..	..	1	0	0	0	0	0	0
Sugar	..	..	..	25	13	1	7	1	1	1
Other former minor excises	..	..	..	5	0	0	0	0	0	0
Wine and sparkling wine	..	..	..	6	23	30	31	36	35	41
Beer	..	..	..	24	38	44	38	50	51	79
Other alcoholic beverages	..	..	..	84	186	158	162	179	173	187
5122 Profits of fiscal monopolies	..	..	..	0	0	0	0	0	0	0
5123 Customs and import duties	..	..	..	41	0	0	0	0	0	0
Taxes on international trades and transactions	..	..	..	41	..	..	..	..	..	..
Imported sugar tax	..	..	..	0	..	..	..	..	..	..
5124 Taxes on exports	..	..	..	0	0	0	0	0	0	0
5125 Taxes on investment goods	..	..	..	0	0	0	0	0	0	0
5126 Taxes on specific services	..	..	..	0	64	63	77	98	71	47
Tax on lotteries and gambling	..	..	..	..	9	8	12	15	14	16
Contributions to the Guarantee Fund	..	..	..	..	11	5	12	16	17	0
Deposit and investment insurance tax	..	..	..	..	43	48	52	56	33	22
Resolution Fund	..	..	..	..	0	0	0	10	7	7
Other taxes on specific services	..	..	..	..	0	1	2	1	1	1
5127 Other taxes on internat. trade and transactions	..	..	..	0	0	0	0	0	0	0
5128 Other taxes	..	..	..	0	0	0	0	0	0	0
5130 Unallocable between 5110 and 5120	..	..	..	0	0	0	0	0	0	0
5200 Taxes on use of goods and perform activities	..	..	..	64	80	83	78	74	77	81
5210 Recurrent taxes	..	..	..	64	80	83	78	74	77	81
5211 Paid by households: motor vehicles	..	..	..	0	0	0	0	0	0	0
5212 Paid by others: motor vehicles	..	..	..	7	30	13	31	32	34	34
Car registration taxes	..	..	..	0	0	0	15	15	15	15
Conveyance taxes	..	..	..	7	30	13	16	17	19	19
5213 Paid in respect of other goods	..	..	..	57	50	70	47	42	43	47
Pollution taxes	..	..	..	6	18	7	19	13	13	15
Payments by households for licences (not for business purposes)	..	..	..	5	3	6	2	2	2	2
Tax on market place	..	..	..	2	0	0	0	0	0	0
State-imposed fees and charges	..	..	..	34	22	44	6	5	5	6
Other taxes on production	..	..	..	10	6	13	21	22	23	24
5220 Non-recurrent taxes	..	..	..	0	0	0	0	0	0	0
5300 Unallocable between 5100 and 5200	..	..	..	0	0	0	0	0	0	0
6000 Other taxes	**..**	**..**	**..**	**0**	**0**	**0**	**0**	**0**	**0**	**0**
6100 Paid solely by business	..	..	..	..	..	..	..	..	..	..
6200 Other	..	..	..	..	..	..	..	..	..	..
Custom duties collected for the EU	**..**	**..**	**..**	**..**	**61**	**53**	**68**	**99**	**96**	**101**
Total tax revenue on cash basis	**..**	**..**	**..**	**..**	**..**	**..**	**..**	**..**	**..**	**..**
Total tax revenue on accrual basis	**..**	**..**	**..**	**4 154**	**8 730**	**7 961**	**9 445**	**10 826**	**11 548**	**12 461**
Conciliation with National Accounts										
Additional taxes included in National Accounts	..	..	..	0	0	0	0	0	0	0
Taxes excluded from National Accounts	..	..	..	0	0	0	0	0	0	0
Difference in treatment of tax credits	..	..	..	0	0	0	0	0	0	0
Capital transfer for uncollected revenue	..	..	..	-39	-9	-32	-17	-18	-14	-3
Voluntary social security contributions	..	..	..	0	2	2	3	2	2	2
Miscellaneous differences	..	..	..	0	0	0	0	0	0	0
National Accounts: Taxes and actual social contributions	..	..	..	4 115	8 723	7 932	9 430	10 811	11 536	12 460
Imputed social contributions	..	..	..	3	91	103	99	116	128	128
National Accounts: Taxes and all social contributions	..	..	..	4 118	8 814	8 035	9 529	10 927	11 664	12 588

.. Not available

Note: Year ending 31st December.

Data on an accrual basis.

Source: Ministry of Finance.

StatLink https://doi.org/10.1787/888934057115

Table 5.22. Luxembourg: Detailed country table, 1965-2017

Million EUR

	1965	1980	1990	2000	2007	2010	2013	2015	2016	2017
Total tax revenue	**266**	**1 543**	**3 671**	**8 521**	**13 416**	**15 025**	**17 806**	**19 271**	**20 221**	**21 405**
Total tax revenue exclusive of custom duties	**..**	**..**	**..**	**8 494**	**13 393**	**15 008**	**17 791**	**19 248**	**20 196**	**21 378**
1000 Taxes on income, profits and capital gains	**95**	**667**	**1 476**	**3 107**	**4 655**	**5 467**	**6 275**	**7 011**	**7 443**	**7 958**
1100 Of individuals	66	417	884	1 573	2 678	3 157	4 062	4 716	4 984	5 056
1110 On income and profits	66	417	884	1 573	2 678	3 157	4 062	4 716	4 984	5 056
Personal income tax - fixed by assessment	27	106	184	258	389	540	666	721	774	822
Supplementary solidarity income tax	0	10	41	37	59	74	268	305	322	329
Tax on wages and salaries	36	287	601	1 178	1 910	2 136	2 797	3 227	3 365	3 424
Withholding tax on income from capital	2	11	52	88	188	315	223	313	373	385
Special tax on company directors fees	1	2	5	11	20	26	38	44	53	48
Tax on certain income of non-residents	0	1	1	2	1	1	1	1	1	1
Tax withheld on savings income (non-residents)	0	0	0	0	51	33	40	0	0	0
Withholding tax on interest	0	0	0	0	60	31	28	20	22	33
Crisis tax	0	0	0	0	0	0	0	0	0	0
Temporary budgetary balance tax	0	0	0	0	0	0	0	85	74	13
1120 On capital gains	0	0	0	0	0	0	0	0	0	0
Tax on betting gains	..	..	..	..	..	..	..	..	..	..
1200 Corporate	29	250	592	1 533	1 977	2 311	2 213	2 295	2 459	2 902
1210 On profits	29	250	592	1 533	1 977	2 311	2 213	2 295	2 459	2 902
Corporation tax	18	168	376	1 031	1 381	1 646	1 530	1 569	1 620	1 951
Supplementary solidarity corporation tax	0	2	8	43	58	61	113	120	121	149
Trade tax	0	80	209	460	538	603	569	606	718	802
1220 On capital gains	0	0	0	0	0	0	0	0	0	0
1300 Unallocable between 1100 and 1200	0	0	0	0	0	0	0	0	0	0
2000 Social security contributions	**86**	**443**	**1 011**	**2 223**	**3 704**	**4 352**	**5 173**	**5 546**	**5 735**	**6 125**
2100 Employees	32	175	388	993	1 690	2 007	2 337	2 497	2 589	2 776
2110 On a payroll basis	..	175	388	993	1 690	2 007	2 337	2 497	2 589	2 776
2120 On an income tax basis	..	0	0	0	0	0	0	0	0	0
2200 Employers	49	243	494	963	1 577	1 875	2 168	2 334	2 406	2 555
2210 On a payroll basis	..	243	494	963	1 577	1 875	2 168	2 334	2 406	2 555
2220 On an income tax basis	..	0	0	0	0	0	0	0	0	0
2300 Self-employed or non-employed	5	25	129	266	437	471	667	715	740	793
2310 On a payroll basis	..	25	129	266	437	471	667	715	740	793
2320 On an income tax basis	..	0	0	0	0	0	0	0	0	0
2400 Unallocable between 2100, 2200 and 2300	0	0	0	0	0	0	0	0	0	0
2410 On a payroll basis	..	..	..	..	..	..	..	..	..	..
2420 On an income tax basis	..	..	..	..	..	..	..	..	..	..
3000 Taxes on payroll and workforce	**2**	**10**	**0**	**0**	**0**	**0**	**0**	**0**	**0**	**0**
Payroll tax	2	10	..	..	..	..	..	..	..	..
4000 Taxes on property	**16**	**87**	**309**	**910**	**1 294**	**1 062**	**1 296**	**1 715**	**1 874**	**2 065**
4100 Recurrent taxes on immovable property	4	9	14	21	27	29	33	36	37	38
Taxes on ownership of lands and buildings	4	9	14	21	27	29	33	36	37	38
4110 Households	..	..	..	..	..	..	..	..	..	..
4120 Others	..	..	..	..	..	..	..	..	..	..
4200 Recurrent taxes on net wealth	7	44	172	633	878	831	980	1 318	1 419	1 513
4210 Individual	0	0	0	0	0	0	0	0	0	0
Wealth tax	..	..	..	..	..	..	..	..	..	..
4220 Corporate	7	44	172	633	878	831	980	1 318	1 419	1 513
Wealth tax	2	15	58	152	172	208	269	385	509	521
Holding tax	3	29	114	481	706	622	710	933	910	992
4300 Estate, inheritance and gift taxes	1	5	11	23	47	50	72	74	86	111
4310 Estate and inheritance taxes	1	5	11	23	47	50	72	74	86	111
4320 Gift taxes	0	0	0	0	0	0	0	0	0	0
4400 Taxes on financial and capital transactions	4	30	112	232	343	152	212	287	332	404
Registration taxes	4	26	94	208	288	116	164	221	258	319
Mortgage taxes	1	3	9	12	29	21	28	39	46	56
Stamp duties	0	2	2	5	7	5	7	8	8	8
Tax on contruction in dense sectors	0	0	0	0	1	1	1	2	3	1
Tax on sale of real estate	0	0	6	7	17	8	10	16	16	18
Mortgage tax on salaries	0	0	1	1	1	1	1	1	1	1
Building permits	0	0	0	0	0	0	0	0	0	0
Infrastructure tax	0	0	0	0	0	0	0	0	0	0
Authorisation taxes on oil tanks	0	0	0	0	0	0	0	0	0	0
Tax on secondary residence	0	0	0	0	0	1	0	0	0	0
4500 Non-recurrent taxes	0	0	0	0	0	0	0	0	0	0
4510 On net wealth	..	..	..	..	..	..	..	..	..	..
4520 Other non-recurrent taxes	..	..	..	..	..	..	..	..	..	..
4600 Other recurrent taxes on property	0	0	0	0	0	0	0	0	0	0
5000 Taxes on goods and services	**66**	**336**	**866**	**2 243**	**3 726**	**4 104**	**5 025**	**4 949**	**5 110**	**5 204**

	1965	1980	1990	2000	2007	2010	2013	2015	2016	2017
5100 Taxes on production, sale, transfer, etc.	62	327	846	2 213	3 651	4 030	4 944	4 862	5 026	5 119
5110 General taxes	33	179	443	1 138	2 196	2 559	3 389	3 389	3 388	3 403
5111 Value added taxes	0	179	443	1 138	2 196	2 559	3 389	3 389	3 388	3 403
VAT own resources	..	18	75	92	50	41	49	45	48	66
5112 Sales tax	0	0	0	0	0	0	0	0	0	0
5113 Other	33	0	0	0	0	0	0	0	0	0
Turnover tax	33	..	..	..	..	..	..	..	..	..
5120 Taxes on specific goods and services	30	148	403	1 075	1 455	1 470	1 555	1 473	1 639	1 716
5121 Excise duties	26	134	365	1 036	1 394	1 401	1 484	1 374	1 414	1 449
Excise duties on mineral oils	1	1	10	100	135	145	197	184	179	185
Excise duties on tobacco (part on national production)	..	0	8	24	66	70	85	81	92	95
Autonomous excise duties on mineral oils	..	76	173	414	559	536	530	495	481	497
Tax on the consumption of national alcoholic beverages and spirits	1	5	19	20	21	20	25	28	36	38
Excise duties on tobacco	..	40	141	407	418	422	445	394	438	440
Supplementary tax on fuel	..	0	0	59	145	132	126	117	115	119
Tax on control of domestic fuel	..	0	0	2	3	3	2	2	2	2
Excise duty on liquefied petroleum	..	0	0	0	0	0	0	0	0	0
Excise duty on benzol	..	0	0	1	1	1	1	1	1	1
Excise duties on imported alcoholic beverages	..	3	5	5	6	5	7	8	10	10
Excise duties on beers (national production)	..	4	2	3	4	4	4	5	4	4
Excise duty on fermented fruit beverages	..	2	3	0	0	0	0	0	0	0
Excise duties on fermented sparkling beverages	..	0	1	0	0	0	0	0	0	0
Excise duty on sugar	..	0	1	0	0	0	0	0	0	0
Excise UEBL	..	0	0	0	0	0	0	0	0	0
Excise duties on nationally produced alcoholic beverages	..	1	1	0	0	0	0	0	0	0
Excise duty on Kyoto	..	0	0	0	37	62	62	58	56	58
Excise duty on alcopops	..	0	0	0	0	0	0	0	0	0
5122 Profits of fiscal monopolies	0	0	0	0	0	0	0	0	0	0
5123 Customs and import duties	1	5	11	0	1	0	0	0	0	0
Levies on imported agricultural products	1	0	0	0	1	0	0	0	0	0
Customs duty	0	0	0	0	0	0	0	0	0	0
Customs duty + mobiles + C.E.C.A. + anti-dumping	0	4	11	0	0	0	0	0	0	0
Agricultural compensatory amounts	0	0	0	0	0	0	0	0	0	0
5124 Taxes on exports	0	0	0	0	0	0	0	0	0	0
5125 Taxes on investment goods	0	0	0	0	0	0	0	0	0	0
5126 Taxes on specific services	2	6	22	39	60	69	70	98	225	267
Tax on betting stakes	0	0	0	0	0	0	0	0	0	0
Tax on insurance	1	5	15	23	32	40	45	46	49	60
Tax on transport	1	0	0	0	0	0	0	0	0	0
Tourist tax	0	0	1	1	2	2	2	3	3	3
Tax on national lottery	0	0	3	4	3	3	0	0	0	0
Tax on casino gambling	0	0	3	9	21	23	21	19	18	19
Tax on bank notes	0	0	1	2	2	1	2	0	0	0
Entertainment tax	0	1	0	0	0	0	0	2	2	2
Contributions to FGDL	0	0	0	0	0	0	0	0	77	79
Contributions to FRL	0	0	0	0	0	0	0	29	77	100
Special tax for insurers in the interest of the rescue service	0	0	0	0	0	0	0	0	0	5
5127 Other taxes on internat. trade and transactions	0	0	0	0	0	0	0	0	0	0
5128 Other taxes	0	4	4	0	0	0	1	1	0	0
C.E.C.A.	..	3	4	..	..	..	0	0	0	0
Co-responsibility tax on milk	..	1	0	..	..	..	1	1	0	0
Co-responsibility tax on cereals	..	0	0	..	..	..	0	0	0	0
5130 Unallocable between 5110 and 5120	0	0	0	0	0	0	0	0	0	0
5200 Taxes on use of goods and perform activities	3	9	20	30	75	75	80	86	83	85
5210 Recurrent taxes	3	8	18	28	68	68	72	71	70	69
5211 Paid by households: motor vehicles	2	4	9	16	39	39	40	41	40	40
5212 Paid by others: motor vehicles	1	4	7	11	26	26	27	28	27	27
5213 Paid in respect of other goods	0	0	1	2	2	3	4	3	3	3
Tax on licenced premises	0	0	0	0	1	1	1	1	1	1
Ship registration tax	0	0	0	1	1	1	2	1	1	1
Dog tax	0	0	1	1	1	1	1	1	1	1
Tax on peddling	0	0	0	0	0	0	0	0	0	0
Tax on ships	0	0	0	0	0	0	0	0	0	0
5220 Non-recurrent taxes	0	0	2	2	7	7	9	15	14	16
Emission permits	..	..	0	0	0	0	3	7	5	7
Car registration taxes	..	..	2	2	7	7	6	8	8	9
5300 Unallocable between 5100 and 5200	0	0	0	0	0	0	0	0	0	0
6000 Other taxes	**0**	**0**	**8**	**12**	**14**	**22**	**23**	**51**	**59**	**54**

	1965	1980	1990	2000	2007	2010	2013	2015	2016	2017
6100 Paid solely by business	..	0	6	11	13	21	21	28	34	27
Supplementary tax on electricity	..	0	0	2	2	2	2	2	2	2
Tax on distribution of electricity	..	0	3	4	1	1	1	1	1	1
Tax on production of electricity	..	0	2	2	1	1	1	0	6	0
Tax on natural gas consumption	..	0	0	0	3	9	11	4	5	4
Tax on enterprise register	..	0	1	1	0	0	0	0	0	0
Tax concerning foreign affairs departments	..	0	0	0	2	5	5	4	5	7
Chancellery stamps	..	0	1	2	4	3	2	1	1	1
VAT reclassified as tax on production	..	0	0	1	1	1	1	1	1	1
Under-compensation of VAT (flat rate system)	..	0	2	0	0	0	0	0	0	0
Tax on water	..	0	2	0	0	0	0	0	0	0
6200 Other	..	0	0	0	0	0	0	23	25	27
Custom duties collected for the EU	**..**	**..**	**..**	**27**	**23**	**18**	**15**	**23**	**25**	**27**
Non-wastable tax credits										
Non-wastable tax credits against 1110	..	..	..	..	..	..	..	198	198	196
Tax expenditure component	..	..	..	..	..	..	..	..	..	..
Transfer component	..	..	..	..	..	..	..	..	..	..
Total tax revenue on cash basis	**266**	**1 543**	**3 722**	**8 624**	**13 393**	**14 726**	**17 857**	**19 418**	**20 252**	**21 448**
Total tax revenue on accrual basis	**..**	**..**	**3 671**	**8 521**	**13 416**	**15 025**	**17 806**	**19 271**	**20 221**	**21 405**
Conciliation with National Accounts										
Additional taxes included in national accounts	..	..	0	0	0	0	0	0	0	0
Tax excluded from national accounts	..	..	0	0	0	0	0	0	0	0
Difference in treatment of tax credits	..	..	0	0	0	0	0	0	0	0
Capital transfer for uncollected revenue	..	..	0	0	0	0	0	0	0	0
Voluntary social security contributions	..	..	4	18	18	28	34	38	41	44
Miscellaneous differences	..	..	0	0	0	0	0	0	0	0
National Accounts: taxes and actual social contributions	..	..	3 674	8 539	13 434	15 053	17 840	19 309	20 262	21 449
Imputed social contributions	..	..	267	287	429	507	567	671	706	749
National Accounts: taxes and all social contributions	..	..	3 941	8 826	13 863	15 560	18 406	19 981	20 968	22 198

.. Not available

Note: The civil year ends December 31st.

From 1990 onwards, data are on an accrual basis.

Under the heading 2000, the difference between the total social security contributions and those collected by the social security parastatals corresponds to the levy for realignment of pensions operated on the remuneration and pensions of employees and former agents of P&T and BCEE; one of these establishments belonging to the "non-corporate and quasi-corporate sector" and the other to the "credit institutions sector".

Source: General account of the State.

StatLink https://doi.org/10.1787/888934057134

Table 5.23. Mexico: Detailed country table, 1965-2017

Million MXN

	1965	1980	1990	2000	2007	2010	2013	2015	2016	2017
Total tax revenue	..	**771**	**102 005**	**767 216**	**1 382 103**	**1 716 243**	**2 165 501**	**2 953 480**	**3 343 314**	**3 527 123**
1000 Taxes on income, profits and capital gains	..	**230**	**34 673**	**276 548**	**554 099**	**683 604**	**957 213**	**1 230 555**	**1 427 114**	**1 571 954**
1100 Of individuals	..	..	..	..	238 938	313 473	425 621	609 384	681 784	754 109
Tax on income of individuals	..	..	..	..	238 938	313 473	425 621	609 384	681 784	754 109
1110 On income and profits	..	..	..	..	..	..	..	..	..	..
1120 On capital gains	..	..	..	..	..	..	..	..	..	..
1200 Corporate	..	..	..	..	217 790	246 745	392 199	592 443	700 925	769 193
Tax on income of corporations	..	..	..	..	217 790	246 745	392 199	592 443	700 925	769 193
1210 On profits	..	..	..	..	..	..	..	..	..	..
1220 On capital gains	..	..	..	..	..	..	..	..	..	..
1300 Unallocable between 1100 and 1200	..	230	34 673	276 548	97 370	123 386	139 393	28 728	44 405	48 652
Tax on income	..	..	..	244 841	54 785	66 937	89 028	36 268	44 225	46 004
Tax on asset	..	..	..	13 913	15 670	-624	-1 325	-502	-918	-1 069
Credit on salary	..	..	..	17 794	23 177	9 708	1 274	993	1 144	1 036
Oil yields tax	..	..	..	0	3 738	2 296	3 210	0	0	0
IETU	..	..	..	0	0	45 069	47 205	-11 777	-4 039	-1 648
Imposed by activity exploration and extraction of hydrocarbon	..	..	..	0	0	0	0	3 746	3 994	4 330
2000 Social security contributions	..	**109**	**17 165**	**138 223**	**236 727**	**277 459**	**351 993**	**409 249**	**434 998**	**467 710**
2100 Employees	..	..	..	..	..	..	..	..	..	..
2110 On a payroll basis	..	..	..	..	..	..	..	..	..	..
2120 On an income tax basis	..	..	..	..	..	..	..	..	..	..
2200 Employers	..	..	..	..	..	..	..	..	..	..
2210 On a payroll basis	..	..	..	..	..	..	..	..	..	..
2220 On an income tax basis	..	..	..	..	..	..	..	..	..	..
2300 Self-employed or non-employed	..	..	..	..	..	..	..	..	..	..
2310 On a payroll basis	..	..	..	..	..	..	..	..	..	..
2320 On an income tax basis	..	..	..	..	..	..	..	..	..	..
2400 Unallocable between 2100, 2200 and 2300	..	109	17 165	138 223	236 727	277 459	351 993	409 249	434 998	467 710
2410 On a payroll basis	..	..	..	138 223	236 727	277 459	351 993	409 249	434 998	467 710
2420 On an income tax basis	..	..	..	0	0	0	0	0	0	0
3000 Taxes on payroll and workforce	..	**8**	**1 797**	**11 217**	**28 071**	**36 911**	**53 042**	**70 221**	**76 762**	**84 099**
Substitute tax on salary	..	..	..	0	0	0	0	0	0	0
Payroll tax	..	..	..	11 101	20 277	27 813	41 184	69 866	76 304	0
Tax on remuneration to the personal work	..	..	..	65	7 578	8 841	11 645	152	225	0
Tax on professions and fees	..	..	..	36	68	71	50	106	99	0
Tax on operations by contract	..	..	..	15	148	186	163	96	134	0
4000 Taxes on property	..	**15**	**1 914**	**13 964**	**33 161**	**38 955**	**46 238**	**57 673**	**63 273**	**67 836**
4100 Recurrent taxes on immovable property	..	10	1 036	9 948	19 425	25 724	31 338	37 961	40 357	44 680
4110 Households	..	0	0	0	0	0	0	0	0	0
4120 Others	..	10	1 036	9 948	19 425	25 724	31 338	37 961	40 357	44 680
Property tax	..	..	..	9 948	19 425	25 724	31 338	37 961	40 357	44 680
4200 Recurrent taxes on net wealth	..	0	0	0	0	0	0	0	0	0
4210 Individual	..	..	..	..	..	..	..	..	..	..
4220 Corporate	..	..	..	..	..	..	..	..	..	..
4300 Estate, inheritance and gift taxes	..	0	8	0	0	0	0	0	0	0
4310 Estate and inheritance taxes	..	..	8	..	..	..	..	..	..	..
4320 Gift taxes	..	..	0	..	..	..	..	..	..	..
4400 Taxes on financial and capital transactions	..	5	870	4 017	13 736	13 231	14 900	19 712	22 917	23 156
Alienation of immovable property	..	..	..	1 763	1 076	1 122	1 271	1 595	1 723	1 623
Transfer of ownership of real estate	..	..	..	2 236	8 147	5 027	4 518	6 671	9 593	7 016
Purchasing property	..	..	..	18	4 513	7 082	9 110	11 447	11 600	14 516
4500 Non-recurrent taxes	..	0	0	0	0	0	0	0	0	0
4510 On net wealth	..	..	..	..	..	..	..	..	..	..
4520 Other non-recurrent taxes	..	..	..	..	..	..	..	..	..	..
4600 Other recurrent taxes on property	..	0	0	0	0	0	0	0	0	0
5000 Taxes on goods and services	..	**395**	**44 837**	**319 612**	**513 140**	**651 915**	**715 811**	**1 141 170**	**1 295 653**	**1 283 049**
5100 Taxes on production, sale, transfer, etc.	..	388	44 171	310 325	491 928	630 123	696 150	1 120 610	1 274 738	1 262 770
5110 General taxes	..	121	26 635	189 606	409 013	504 509	556 794	707 213	791 700	816 048
5111 Value added taxes	..	120	26 635	189 606	409 013	504 509	556 794	707 213	791 700	816 048
5112 Sales tax	..	0	0	0	0	0	0	0	0	0
5113 Other	..	1	0	0	0	0	0	0	0	0
5120 Taxes on specific goods and services	..	265	17 519	120 720	82 915	125 614	139 356	413 397	483 038	446 722
5121 Excise duties	..	45	10 072	86 163	47 008	86 098	104 111	361 538	420 448	378 537
Special tax on production and services	..	..	..	81 544	41 532	81 427	97 860	354 294	411 390	367 834
Tax on new automobiles	..	..	..	4 619	5 476	4 671	6 252	7 244	9 058	10 703
Tax on luxury goods and services	..	..	..	0	0	0	0	0	0	0
5122 Profits of fiscal monopolies	..	0	0	0	0	0	0	0	0	0

	1965	1980	1990	2000	2007	2010	2013	2015	2016	2017
5123 Customs and import duties	..	45	6 998	33 285	33 344	26 602	32 324	45 366	51 889	53 793
Step customs officer	..	..	..	423	1 156	2 071	3 065	1 270	1 336	1 463
Import taxes	..	..	..	32 861	32 188	24 531	29 260	44 096	50 553	52 330
5124 Taxes on exports	..	2	75	4	3	0	1	1	0	0
Tax on exports	..	..	..	4	3	0	1	1	0	0
5125 Taxes on investment goods	..	0	0	0	0	0	0	0	0	0
5126 Taxes on specific services	..	8	132	1 042	2 146	10 958	-967	1 763	5 630	7 778
IDE	..	8	..	0	0	8 022	-5 988	-3 323	-1 262	-739
Tax on lodging	..	0	..	504	1 059	1 384	1 890	2 561	3 009	3 598
Public entertainment tax	..	0	..	240	365	462	566	689	858	839
Tax on lotteries, raffles and gambling	..	0	..	267	705	923	1 213	1 416	1 828	2 717
Tax on commercials	..	0	..	4	17	166	203	210	906	1 082
Various indirect taxes	..	0	..	28	0	1	1 149	209	291	282
5127 Other taxes on internat. trade and transactions	..	0	0	0	0	0	0	0	0	0
5128 Other taxes	..	165	242	226	414	1 956	3 886	4 730	5 070	6 613
Mining fees	..	..	..	226	414	1 956	3 886	4 730	5 070	6 613
5130 Unallocable between 5110 and 5120	..	2	17	0	0	0	0	0	0	0
5200 Taxes on use of goods and perform activities	..	7	666	9 287	21 212	21 793	19 661	20 560	20 915	20 279
5210 Recurrent taxes	..	7	666	9 287	21 212	21 793	19 661	20 560	20 915	20 279
5211 Paid by households: motor vehicles	..	3	567	8 878	20 692	21 319	19 174	19 880	20 192	19 530
Tax on motor vehicules	..	..	..	8 878	20 692	21 319	19 174	19 880	20 192	19 530
5212 Paid by others: motor vehicles	..	0	0	301	275	281	357	439	503	554
Tax on federal auto transport	..	..	..	301	275	281	357	439	503	554
5213 Paid in respect of other goods	..	4	99	108	246	193	130	240	220	194
Sport fishing	..	..	..	40	98	59	50	62	68	71
Sport hunting	..	..	..	3	0	0	0	0	0	0
Tax on commercial activities	..	..	..	63	147	50	26	64	46	28
Trade in books and magazines	..	..	..	0	0	0	3	1	1	0
Tax on industrial activities	..	..	..	2	0	82	49	93	78	77
Mining	..	..	..	0	0	1	1	21	28	18
5220 Non-recurrent taxes	..	0	0	0	0	0	0	0	0	0
5300 Unallocable between 5100 and 5200	..	0	0	0	0	0	0	0	0	0
6000 Other taxes	**..**	**14**	**1 619**	**7 651**	**16 905**	**27 398**	**41 204**	**44 612**	**45 514**	**52 475**
6100 Paid solely by business	..	0	0	0	0	0	0	0	0	0
6200 Other	..	14	1 619	7 651	16 905	27 398	41 204	44 612	45 514	52 475
Accessories	..	..	..	5 504	12 403	22 206	25 301	23 211	28 480	32 153
Unallocable between 1000 and 5000 caused in exercices fiscal previous liquidation slopes or of payment	..	..	..	374	222	30	1 618	4 168	329	281
Additional state and local taxes	..	..	..	1 773	4 280	5 162	14 285	17 232	16 705	20 042
Non-wastable tax credits										
Non-wastable tax credits against 1000	..	..	..	..	59 065	40 344	41 800	43 806	44 851	46 793
Tax expenditure component	..	..	..	..	35 888	30 635	40 526	42 813	43 707	45 757
Transfer component	..	..	..	..	23 177	9 708	1 274	993	1 144	1 036
Total tax revenue on cash basis	**..**	**771**	**102 005**	**767 216**	**1 382 103**	**1 716 243**	**2 165 501**	**2 953 480**	**3 343 314**	**3 527 123**
Total tax revenue on accrual basis	**..**	**..**	**..**	**..**	**..**	**..**	**..**	**..**	**..**	**..**
Conciliation with National Accounts										
Additional taxes included in National Accounts	..	..	..	..	..	..	..	..	..	..
Taxes excluded from National Accounts	..	..	..	..	..	..	..	..	..	..
Difference in treatment of tax credits	..	..	..	..	..	..	..	..	..	..
Capital transfer for uncollected revenue	..	..	..	..	..	..	..	..	..	..
Voluntary social security contributions	..	..	..	..	..	..	..	..	..	..
Miscellaneous differences	..	..	..	..	..	..	..	..	..	..
National Accounts: Taxes and actual social contributions	..	..	..	..	..	..	..	..	..	..
Imputed social contributions	..	..	..	..	..	..	..	..	..	..
National Accounts: Taxes and all social contributions	..	..	..	..	..	..	..	..	..	..

.. Not available

Note: Year ending 31st December.

Data are on cash basis.

Source: Ministry of Finance, Economic Department.

StatLink https://doi.org/10.1787/888934057153

Table 5.24. Netherlands: Detailed country table, 1965-2017

Million EUR

	1965	1980	1990	2000	2007	2010	2013	2015	2016	2017
Total tax revenue	**10 860**	**69 982**	**104 419**	**166 824**	**220 950**	**227 911**	**238 488**	**255 348**	**272 008**	**285 670**
Total tax revenue exclusive of custom duties	..	..	..	**165 514**	**219 271**	**226 179**	**236 732**	**253 082**	**269 655**	**283 250**
1000 Taxes on income, profits and capital gains	**3 884**	**22 998**	**33 689**	**43 256**	**62 463**	**63 581**	**59 085**	**70 849**	**73 993**	**85 761**
1100 Of individuals	3 008	18 383	25 806	25 116	41 414	48 992	44 830	52 405	50 292	61 571
1110 On income and profits	3 007	18 364	25 757	25 057	41 276	48 771	44 592	52 167	50 162	61 442
Income tax	1 359	2 895	2 455	-880	2 294	2 076	-1 337	-2 566	-5 111	-1 183
Wage tax	1 466	14 984	22 258	24 433	37 729	46 102	45 546	53 953	54 962	61 844
Dividend tax	123	486	1 044	1 504	1 253	593	383	780	311	781
Directors tax	14	0	0	0	0	0	0	0	0	0
Inhabited house tax	45	0	0	0	0	0	0	0	0	0
1120 On capital gains	1	18	50	59	138	221	238	238	130	129
Tax on games of chance	1	18	50	59	138	221	238	238	130	129
1200 Corporate	876	4 615	7 882	18 140	21 049	14 589	14 255	18 444	23 701	24 190
1210 On profits	876	4 615	7 882	18 140	21 049	14 589	14 255	18 444	23 701	24 190
Corporate income and dividend taxes	876	4 615	7 882	18 140	21 049	14 589	14 255	18 444	23 701	24 190
1220 On capital gains	0	0	0	0	0	0	0	0	0	0
1300 Unallocable between 1100 and 1200	0	0	0	0	0	0	0	0	0	0
2000 Social security contributions	**3 342**	**26 641**	**39 075**	**64 522**	**77 072**	**82 732**	**97 372**	**96 426**	**103 902**	**101 913**
2100 Employees	1 659	11 018	24 109	35 305	40 918	41 637	49 327	48 213	41 959	39 578
2110 On a payroll basis	..	..	..	35 305	40 918	41 637	49 327	48 213	41 959	39 578
2120 On an income tax basis	..	..	..	0	0	0	0	0	0	0
2200 Employers	1 371	12 465	7 837	18 671	25 925	29 351	31 603	34 614	36 595	37 720
2210 On a payroll basis	..	..	..	18 671	25 925	29 351	31 603	34 614	36 595	37 720
2220 On an income tax basis	..	..	..	0	0	0	0	0	0	0
2300 Self-employed or non-employed	311	3 158	7 129	10 546	10 229	11 744	16 442	13 599	25 348	24 615
2310 On a payroll basis	..	..	..	0	0	0	0	0	0	0
2320 On an income tax basis	..	..	..	10 546	10 229	11 744	16 442	13 599	25 348	24 615
2400 Unallocable between 2100, 2200 and 2300	0	0	0	0	0	0	0	0	0	0
2410 On a payroll basis	..	..	..	..	..	..	..	..	..	..
2420 On an income tax basis	..	..	..	..	..	..	..	..	..	..
3000 Taxes on payroll and workforce	**0**	**0**	**0**	**0**	**0**	**0**	**0**	**0**	**0**	**0**
4000 Taxes on property	**476**	**2 509**	**3 816**	**8 797**	**10 363**	**8 770**	**8 084**	**9 768**	**10 764**	**11 487**
4100 Recurrent taxes on immovable property	111	1 021	1 711	3 094	3 488	4 241	5 249	6 382	6 627	6 919
Municipal immovable property tax	-59	821	1 398	..	..	..	..	..	..	..
Other municipal taxes	66	5	18	..	..	..	..	..	..	..
Contributions polder boards	44	195	295	..	..	..	..	..	..	..
Tax on land	59	0	0	..	..	..	..	..	..	..
4110 Households	..	..	..	1 806	1 642	2 058	2 802	3 741	3 929	4 154
Municipal immovable property tax	..	..	..	1 651	1 368	1 553	1 754	1 882	1 923	1 975
Contributions polder boards	..	..	..	155	274	429	492	514	532	561
Levies on social housing corporations	..	..	..	0	0	76	556	1 345	1 474	1 618
4120 Others	..	..	..	1 288	1 846	2 183	2 447	2 641	2 698	2 765
Municipal immovable property tax	..	..	..	893	1 319	1 488	1 686	1 809	1 848	1 898
Contributions polder boards	..	..	..	395	527	695	761	832	850	867
4200 Recurrent taxes on net wealth	86	517	554	824	30	23	1	0	0	0
4210 Individual	86	517	554	824	30	23	1	..	..	..
Property tax of individuals	86	517	554	824	30	23	1	..	..	..
4220 Corporate	0	0	0	0	0	0	0	..	..	..
4300 Estate, inheritance and gift taxes	117	336	522	1 483	1 877	1 721	1 730	1 614	1 845	1 841
4310 Estate and inheritance taxes	..	304	472	1 303	1 877	1 721	1 730	1 614	1 845	1 841
Estate tax	..	0	0	0	0	0	0	0	0	0
Inheritance tax	..	304	472	1 303	1 877	1 721	1 730	1 614	1 845	1 841
4320 Gift taxes	..	32	50	180	0	0	0	0	0	0
4400 Taxes on financial and capital transactions	162	635	1 030	3 396	4 968	2 785	1 104	1 772	2 292	2 727
Stamp duties	44	0	0	0	0	0	0	0	0	0
Registration duties	118	0	0	0	0	0	0	0	0	0
Tax on legal transactions	0	635	1 030	0	0	0	0	0	0	0
Real estate transfer tax	0	0	0	2 804	4 925	2 785	1 104	1 772	2 292	2 727
Tax on capital formation	0	0	0	592	43	0	0	0	0	0
4500 Non-recurrent taxes	0	0	0	0	0	0	0	0	0	0
4510 On net wealth	..	..	..	..	..	..	..	..	..	..
4520 Other non-recurrent taxes	..	..	..	..	..	..	..	..	..	..
4600 Other recurrent taxes on property	0	0	0	0	0	0	0	0	0	0
5000 Taxes on goods and services	**3 110**	**17 675**	**27 585**	**48 162**	**68 405**	**70 134**	**71 068**	**75 623**	**80 282**	**83 232**
5100 Taxes on production, sale, transfer, etc.	2 943	16 204	25 067	43 561	61 994	62 515	63 274	67 049	71 559	74 399
5110 General taxes	1 344	11 081	17 216	28 857	42 884	42 674	42 459	44 922	47 896	49 893
5111 Value added taxes	0	11 081	17 216	28 849	42 873	42 654	42 424	44 879	47 849	49 833
5112 Sales tax	0	0	0	0	0	0	0	0	0	0

	1965	1980	1990	2000	2007	2010	2013	2015	2016	2017
5113 Other	1 344	0	0	8	11	20	35	43	47	60
Turnover tax	1 344	..	..	..	..	..	..	..	..	..
5120 Taxes on specific goods and services	1 600	5 123	7 850	14 704	19 110	19 841	20 815	22 127	23 663	24 506
5121 Excise duties	880	3 789	5 985	13 755	17 724	18 392	17 309	18 020	18 973	19 692
Excise on spirits	129	463	422	397	335	331	306	314	324	331
Excise on beer	34	123	259	263	310	389	413	451	446	447
Excise on sugar	45	9	27	0	0	0	0	0	0	0
Excise on tobacco	307	839	948	1 590	2 136	2 437	2 228	2 222	2 491	2 397
Excise on wine	14	82	91	173	257	304	348	354	358	346
Registration tax on motor vehicles	0	613	1 189	2 875	3 647	2 096	1 159	1 462	1 551	2 000
Excise on soft drinks	0	59	186	216	155	156	154	207	256	265
Levies for nuclear reactor	0	0	0	0	0	0	0	0	0	0
Excise on petrol	310	1 280	1 684	3 151	4 010	4 086	3 960	4 109	4 226	4 293
Excise on other mineral oils	41	295	808	2 139	2 965	3 573	3 630	3 757	3 862	3 875
Levies on air pollution	0	27	304	0	0	0	0	0	0	0
Taxes on pollution/resources	0	0	68	462	456	356	141	345	364	380
Levies on energy	0	0	0	2 387	3 333	4 250	4 856	4 679	4 967	5 213
Other excise duties and consumption taxes	0	0	0	0	0	0	0	0	0	0
Other environmental taxes	0	0	0	34	35	314	13	14	20	35
Strategic stockpile tax on mineral oils	0	0	0	68	85	100	101	106	108	110
5122 Profits of fiscal monopolies	0	0	0	0	0	0	0	0	0	0
5123 Customs and import duties	702	971	1 375	0	0	0	0	0	0	0
EU levies on food products	338	295	168	..	..	..	..	..	..	..
MCA levy	0	9	0	..	..	..	..	..	..	..
Remaining import duties	364	667	1 207	..	..	..	..	..	..	..
5124 Taxes on exports	0	0	0	0	0	0	0	0	0	0
5125 Taxes on investment goods	0	77	0	0	0	0	0	0	0	0
Selective investment regulation levy	..	77	..	..	..	..	..	..	..	..
5126 Taxes on specific services	16	222	372	662	1 041	1 213	3 253	3 751	4 447	4 571
Tax on fire insurance	2	0	0	0	0	0	0	0	0	0
Entertainment tax	14	0	0	0	0	0	0	0	0	0
Tax on insurances	0	209	340	512	807	861	2 343	2 375	2 464	2 486
Tourist tax	0	14	32	83	125	131	164	206	210	252
Tax on games of chance	0	0	0	67	109	221	239	238	350	340
Flight tax	0	0	0	0	0	0	0	0	0	0
Bank levies	0	0	0	0	0	0	507	478	921	948
Contribution to EU Single Resolution Fund	0	0	0	0	0	0	0	454	502	545
5127 Other taxes on internat. trade and transactions	0	0	0	0	0	0	0	0	0	0
5128 Other taxes	1	64	118	287	345	236	253	356	243	243
ESCC levy	1	5	0	0	0	0	0	0	0	0
Sugar contribution	0	23	36	0	0	0	0	0	0	0
Milk levy	0	36	82	0	0	0	0	0	0	0
EU levies on food products	0	0	0	273	345	236	253	356	243	243
Sugar storage duty	0	0	0	14	0	0	0	0	0	0
5130 Unallocable between 5110 and 5120	0	0	0	0	0	0	0	0	0	0
5200 Taxes on use of goods and perform activities	167	1 470	2 518	4 601	6 411	7 619	7 794	8 574	8 723	8 833
5210 Recurrent taxes	165	1 470	2 518	4 601	6 411	7 619	7 751	8 410	8 524	8 633
5211 Paid by households: motor vehicles	27	463	799	2 288	3 211	4 084	4 008	4 470	4 500	4 582
Motor vehicle tax	27	427	744	2 288	3 211	4 084	4 008	4 470	4 500	4 582
Motor vehicle licence	0	36	54	0	0	0	0	0	0	0
5212 Paid by others: motor vehicles	132	604	1 044	554	760	976	959	1 069	1 080	1 096
Motor vehicle tax	132	590	1 026	554	760	976	959	1 069	1 080	1 096
Motor vehicle licence	0	14	18	0	0	0	0	0	0	0
Heavy motor vehicle tax	0	0	0	0	0	0	0	0	0	0
5213 Paid in respect of other goods	6	404	676	1 759	2 440	2 559	2 784	2 871	2 944	2 955
Dog licences	3	23	27	40	54	59	67	65	67	61
Commuter tax	0	5	5	12	21	25	29	29	30	32
Levies on water pollution	1	372	644	1 003	1 220	1 127	1 182	1 212	1 244	1 257
Permission to sell spirits	2	5	0	0	0	0	0	0	0	0
Sewerage charges	0	0	0	650	1 094	1 304	1 463	1 531	1 584	1 597
Levies on manure surplus	0	0	0	18	-4	2	4	3	11	7
Noise nuisance tax civil aviation	0	0	0	36	55	42	39	31	8	1
5220 Non-recurrent taxes	2	0	0	0	0	0	43	164	199	200
Emission permits	..	..	..	..	..	..	43	164	199	200
5300 Unallocable between 5100 and 5200	0	0	0	0	0	0	0	0	0	0
6000 Other taxes	**48**	**159**	**254**	**777**	**968**	**962**	**1 123**	**416**	**714**	**857**
6100 Paid solely by business	48	159	254	410	322	326	139	0	0	0
Administrative levies	48	159	254	410	322	326	139	..	..	..
6200 Other	0	0	0	367	646	636	984	416	714	857
Employers tax	..	..	..	331	497	609	804	208	530	569
Tax revenue from Caribbean Netherlands	..	..	..	0	0	13	100	128	145	153
Other taxes on wealth	..	..	..	36	149	14	80	80	39	135

	1965	1980	1990	2000	2007	2010	2013	2015	2016	2017
Custom duties collected for the EU	**..**	**..**	**..**	**1 310**	**1 679**	**1 732**	**1 756**	**2 266**	**2 353**	**2 420**
Total tax revenue on cash basis	**10 860**	**69 982**	**104 419**	**165 503**	**..**	**..**	**..**	**..**	**..**	**..**
Total tax revenue on accrual basis	**..**	**..**	**..**	**166 824**	**220 950**	**227 911**	**238 488**	**255 348**	**272 008**	**285 670**
Conciliation with National Accounts										
Additional taxes included in National Accounts	..	..	..	1 400	0	0	0	0	0	0
Wage Tax reductions	..	..	..	1 400	..	..	..	..	..	..
Taxes excluded from National Accounts	..	..	..	0	0	0	0	0	0	0
Difference in treatment of tax credits	..	..	..	0	0	0	0	0	0	0
Capital transfer for uncollected revenue	..	..	..	0	0	0	0	0	0	0
Voluntary social security contributions	..	..	..	0	0	0	0	0	0	0
Miscellaneous differences	..	..	..	-70	0	0	0	0	0	0
National Accounts: Taxes and actual social contributions	..	..	..	168 154	220 950	227 911	238 488	255 348	272 008	285 670
Imputed social contributions	..	..	..	3 808	3 509	3 545	3 414	3 160	3 584	3 622
National Accounts: Taxes and all social contributions	..	..	..	171 962	224 459	231 456	241 902	258 508	275 592	289 292

.. Not available

Note: Year ending 31st December.

From 1999 data are on accrual basis.

Heading 2000: From 1998 the figures include some violuntary contributions and the breakdown between premiums paid by employees (2100) and by self-employed / non-employed has been estimated. This is also the case for the breakdown between premiums paid on a payroll or on an income tax basis for those years where both apply.

Heading 4100: From 1992, there was a structural break in the data for the 'municipal immovable property tax'. The tax ceased to be collected by the central government at that time and the figures are presented on a different type of statistical registration (no longer cash basis).

Heading 5110: Includes 358 millions of euros (1969) and 186 millions of euros (1970) in respect of deduction of turnover tax on stocks existing at 1st January 1969.

Heading 5213: Small amounts (less than 2.3 millions euros) of hunting and fishing licence receipts which should be classified here have been omitted.

Source: Social security contributions and local taxes: Central Bureau of Statistics.

Other taxes: Ministry of Finance.

StatLink https://doi.org/10.1787/888934057172

Table 5.25. New Zealand: Detailed country table, 1965-2017

Million NZD

	1965	1980	1990	2000	2007	2010	2013	2015	2016	2017
Total tax revenue	**1 001**	**7 594**	**27 471**	**39 765**	**64 046**	**62 310**	**72 187**	**81 500**	**86 601**	**92 661**
1000 Taxes on income, profits and capital gains	**606**	**5 299**	**16 370**	**23 861**	**40 308**	**33 494**	**39 415**	**44 724**	**48 134**	**51 505**
1100 Of individuals	394	4 679	13 177	17 126	26 965	23 519	26 555	30 298	31 869	35 020
1110 On income and profits	394	4 679	13 177	17 126	26 965	23 519	26 555	30 298	31 869	35 020
1120 On capital gains	0	0	0	0	0	0	0	0	0	0
1200 Corporate	207	589	1 780	4 914	9 069	7 609	10 344	11 407	13 461	13 584
1210 On profits	207	589	1 780	4 914	9 069	7 609	10 344	11 407	13 461	13 584
1220 On capital gains	0	0	0	0	0	0	0	0	0	0
1300 Unallocable between 1100 and 1200	5	31	1 413	1 821	4 274	2 366	2 516	3 019	2 804	2 901
NRWT	5	24	277	760	1 506	467	427	733	594	619
Property speculation	0	0	0	0	0	0	0	0	0	0
Absentee income tax	0	7	0	0	0	0	0	0	0	0
Interest	0	0	1 028	990	2 699	1 704	1 643	1 660	1 468	1 530
Dividends	0	0	83	71	69	195	446	626	742	752
Other	0	0	25	0	0	0	0	0	0	0
2000 Social security contributions	**0**	**0**	**0**	**0**	**0**	**0**	**0**	**0**	**0**	**0**
2100 Employees	0	0	0	0	0	0	0	0	0	0
2110 On a payroll basis	..	..	..	..	..	..	..	..	..	..
2120 On an income tax basis	..	..	..	..	..	..	..	..	..	..
2200 Employers	0	0	0	0	0	0	0	0	0	0
2210 On a payroll basis	..	..	..	..	..	..	..	..	..	..
2220 On an income tax basis	..	..	..	..	..	..	..	..	..	..
2300 Self-employed or non-employed	0	0	0	0	0	0	0	0	0	0
2310 On a payroll basis	..	..	..	..	..	..	..	..	..	..
2320 On an income tax basis	..	..	..	..	..	..	..	..	..	..
2400 Unallocable between 2100, 2200 and 2300	0	0	0	0	0	0	0	0	0	0
2410 On a payroll basis	..	..	..	..	..	..	..	..	..	..
2420 On an income tax basis	..	..	..	..	..	..	..	..	..	..
3000 Taxes on payroll and workforce	**0**	**0**	**0**	**0**	**0**	**0**	**0**	**0**	**0**	**0**
4000 Taxes on property	**116**	**602**	**1 880**	**2 112**	**3 417**	**4 119**	**4 585**	**5 046**	**5 257**	**5 543**
4100 Recurrent taxes on immovable property	84	515	1 722	2 049	3 322	4 031	4 492	4 962	5 178	5 436
Local govt rates and services	81	503	1 550	2 049	3 322	4 031	4 492	4 962	5 178	5 436
Land tax	3	12	172	0	0	0	0	0	0	0
4110 Households	..	..	0	..	..	..	..	..	..	..
4120 Others	..	..	172	..	..	..	..	..	..	..
4200 Recurrent taxes on net wealth	0	0	0	0	0	0	0	0	0	0
4210 Individual	..	..	..	..	..	..	..	..	..	..
4220 Corporate	..	..	..	..	..	..	..	..	..	..
4300 Estate, inheritance and gift taxes	23	39	80	2	3	2	0	0	0	0
4310 Estate and inheritance taxes	21	37	74	0	0	0	..	..	..	..
4320 Gift taxes	2	2	6	2	3	2	..	..	..	..
4400 Taxes on financial and capital transactions	9	48	78	61	92	86	93	84	79	107
Instrument duty	7	40	62	51	85	82	91	84	79	107
Cheque duty	2	8	16	10	7	4	2	0	0	0
4500 Non-recurrent taxes	0	0	0	0	0	0	0	0	0	0
4510 On net wealth	..	..	..	..	..	..	..	..	..	..
4520 Other non-recurrent taxes	..	..	..	..	..	..	..	..	..	..
4600 Other recurrent taxes on property	0	0	0	0	0	0	0	0	0	0
5000 Taxes on goods and services	**280**	**1 693**	**9 220**	**13 792**	**20 290**	**24 692**	**28 184**	**31 728**	**33 203**	**35 612**
5100 Taxes on production, sale, transfer, etc.	262	1 624	8 680	12 887	18 832	23 107	26 344	29 584	30 925	33 220
5110 General taxes	77	776	6 163	9 885	15 046	19 143	22 063	24 587	25 847	27 951
5111 Value added taxes	0	0	6 163	9 885	15 046	19 143	22 063	24 587	25 847	27 951
5112 Sales tax	77	776	0	0	0	0	0	0	0	0
Motor vehicles	..	231	..	..	..	..	..	..	..	..
Other sales tax	..	544	..	..	..	..	..	..	..	..
5113 Other	0	0	0	0	0	0	0	0	0	0
5120 Taxes on specific goods and services	186	849	2 517	3 002	3 786	3 964	4 281	4 997	5 078	5 269

	1965	1980	1990	2000	2007	2010	2013	2015	2016	2017
5121 Excise duties	124	548	1 929	2 148	1 627	1 782	1 854	2 280	2 231	2 214
On alcoholic beverages	37	84	411	436	573	622	650	672	684	699
Beer	33	64	0	201	290	207	250	262	265	265
Wine	0	0	0	100	163	181	204	216	218	227
Spirits	4	20	0	135	120	234	196	194	201	207
Tobacco	33	99	568	764	159	220	273	362	352	399
Motor vehicles	0	0	7	0	0	0	0	0	0	0
Refined sugar	2	0	0	0	0	0	0	0	0	0
CA petroleum fuels	0	140	835	810	819	872	865	1 185	1 137	1 057
NRF fuel excise	49	121	0	0	0	0	0	0	0	0
Local petroleum fuels	0	18	21	27	30	32	31	33	34	33
CA mileage tax	0	0	0	0	0	0	0	0	0	0
NRF mileage tax	3	0	0	0	0	0	0	0	0	0
Road user charges	0	68	0	0	0	0	0	0	0	0
Energy resources levy	0	20	87	111	46	36	35	28	24	26
5122 Profits of fiscal monopolies	0	0	0	0	0	0	0	0	0	0
5123 Customs and import duties	49	231	505	648	1 857	1 916	2 160	2 442	2 550	2 738
5124 Taxes on exports	0	0	0	0	0	0	0	0	0	0
5125 Taxes on investment goods	0	0	0	0	0	0	0	0	0	0
5126 Taxes on specific services	13	57	83	206	302	266	267	275	297	317
Lottery (national)	1	6	26	167	290	253	254	260	281	301
Lottery (overseas)	0	0	0	0	0	0	0	0	0	0
Racing	12	46	57	39	12	13	13	15	16	16
Film hire tax	0	1	0	0	0	0	0	0	0	0
Domestic air travel tax	0	3	0	0	0	0	0	0	0	0
5127 Other taxes on internat. trade and transactions	0	12	0	0	0	0	0	0	0	0
Foreign fishing vessels tax	..	0	..	..	..	..	..	..	..	..
Foreign travel tax	..	0	..	..	..	..	..	..	..	..
International departure tax	..	12	..	..	..	..	..	..	..	..
5128 Other taxes	0	0	0	0	0	0	0	0	0	0
5130 Unallocable between 5110 and 5120	0	0	0	0	0	0	0	0	0	0
5200 Taxes on use of goods and perform activities	18	69	539	905	1 458	1 585	1 840	2 144	2 278	2 392
5210 Recurrent taxes	18	69	539	905	1 458	1 585	1 840	2 144	2 278	2 392
Motor vehicle registration	7	47	154	181	226	172	187	214	223	227
Heavy traffic fees	8	0	285	532	851	1 016	1 205	1 381	1 469	1 551
Accident compensation levies	0	0	0	0	0	0	0	0	0	0
5211 Paid by households: motor vehicles	0	0	0	0	0	0	0	0	0	0
5212 Paid by others: motor vehicles	0	0	0	0	0	0	0	0	0	0
5213 Paid in respect of other goods	3	23	100	192	381	397	448	549	586	614
Local authority fees and charges	3	23	100	192	381	397	448	549	586	614
5220 Non-recurrent taxes	0	0	0	0	0	0	0	0	0	0
5300 Unallocable between 5100 and 5200	0	0	0	0	0	0	0	0	0	0
6000 Other taxes	**0**	**0**	**1**	**0**	**31**	**5**	**3**	**2**	**7**	**1**
6100 Paid solely by business	..	..	0	..	0	0	0	0	0	0
6200 Other	..	..	1	..	31	5	3	2	7	1
Non-wastable tax credits										
Non-wastable tax credits against 1110	..	..	..	1 057	2 568	2 794	2 582	2 352	2 313	2 195
Tax expenditure component	..	..	..	311	873	950	1 349	1 253	1 232	1 189
Transfer component	..	..	..	746	1 695	1 844	1 233	1 099	1 081	1 006
Non-wastable tax credits against 1210	..	..	..	0	0	0	0	0	0	0
Tax expenditure component	..	..	..	..	..	..	..	..	..	..
Transfer component	..	..	..	..	..	..	..	..	..	..
Total tax revenue on cash basis	**1 001**	**7 594**	**27 471**	**39 276**	**64 273**	**62 053**	**73 172**	**82 481**	**87 907**	**93 911**
Total tax revenue on accrual basis	**..**	**..**	**..**	**39 765**	**64 046**	**62 310**	**72 187**	**81 500**	**86 601**	**92 661**
Conciliation with National Accounts										
Additional taxes included in National Accounts	..	..	..	..	0	0	2 265	2 615	4 152	4 080
Taxes excluded from National Accounts	..	..	..	..	0	0	-4 955	-5 769	-7 111	-7 404
Difference in treatment of tax credits	..	..	..	..	873	950	1 349	1 253	1 232	1 189
Capital transfer for uncollected revenue	..	..	..	..	0	0	0	0	0	0
Voluntary social security contributions	..	..	..	..	0	0	0	0	0	0
Miscellaneous differences	..	..	..	..	0	0	461	-1 602	500	-81
National Accounts: Taxes and actual social contributions	..	..	..	..	64 919	63 260	71 307	77 997	85 374	90 445
Imputed social contributions	..	..	..	..	0	0	2 617	2 063	2 030	1 948
National Accounts: Taxes and all social contributions	..	..	..	..	64 919	63 260	73 924	80 060	87 404	92 393

.. Not available

Note: For the years before 1989 data are on a fiscal year basis ending 31st March. The figures provided for 1989 and onwards relate to the financial year ending 30th June of the following year.
From 1993, data are on accrual basis.
Heading 1000: Tax credits to exporters under the export incentives schemes are non-wastable, but that part of the excess of tax liability paid out to taxpayers is not identifiable.
Heading 1100: The figures up to 1969 include revenues collected by a social security income tax. The base of this tax was the same as the ordinary income tax base and the two have now been incorporated into a single income tax.
Heading 5121: From October 1986 incorporates that portion of the selective impost on wine, spirits, tobacco and motor vehicles which was formerly collected and reported as sales tax. The revenue collected on those imported goods which are subject to the equivalent of the domestic excise has been classified as excise duty. In this respect, there is a discontinuity between the excises recorded before and after October 1986.
Heading 5210: The other local authority licence fees include some small items which could be regarded as non-tax revenues.
Heading for non-wastable tax credits 1110 comprises four Family assistance tax credits. The total in item 1100 is net of the tax expenditure component but not net of the transfer component.
Source: Local Authorities Statistics, Department of Statistics, Wellington.

StatLink https://doi.org/10.1787/888934057191

Table 5.26. Norway: Detailed country table, 1965-2017

Million NOK

	1965	1980	1990	2000	2007	2010	2013	2015	2016	2017
Total tax revenue	**16 842**	**133 499**	**301 812**	**631 576**	**989 614**	**1 086 662**	**1 226 149**	**1 198 232**	**1 207 561**	**1 281 966**
1000 Taxes on income, profits and capital gains	**7 316**	**55 837**	**106 290**	**284 189**	**474 557**	**512 049**	**558 116**	**475 374**	**458 170**	**499 695**
1100 Of individuals	6 671	38 018	79 068	152 013	219 726	256 544	304 409	335 199	332 773	339 076
1110 On income and profits	6 671	38 018	79 068	152 013	219 726	256 544	304 409	335 199	332 773	339 076
Employee social security contributions	1 305	0	0	0	0	0	0	0	0	0
Income taxes	5 366	38 018	79 068	152 013	219 726	256 544	304 409	335 199	332 773	339 076
1120 On capital gains	0	0	0	0	0	0	0	0	0	0
1200 Corporate	645	17 819	27 222	132 176	254 831	255 505	253 707	140 175	125 397	160 619
1210 On profits	..	..	..	132 176	254 831	255 505	253 707	140 175	125 397	160 619
1220 On capital gains	..	..	..	0	0	0	0	0	0	0
1300 Unallocable between 1100 and 1200	0	0	0	0	0	0	0	0	0	0
2000 Social security contributions	**2 009**	**28 205**	**79 362**	**132 170**	**204 602**	**243 015**	**292 278**	**325 569**	**331 389**	**341 591**
2100 Employees	0	6 639	25 345	45 162	68 518	81 032	98 124	112 662	115 358	119 273
2110 On a payroll basis	..	..	..	45 162	68 518	81 032	98 124	112 662	115 358	119 273
2120 On an income tax basis	..	..	..	0	0	0	0	0	0	0
2200 Employers	1 716	20 454	50 116	79 242	124 307	148 060	177 275	191 362	193 755	199 302
2210 On a payroll basis	..	..	..	79 242	124 307	148 060	177 275	191 362	193 755	199 302
2220 On an income tax basis	..	..	..	0	0	0	0	0	0	0
2300 Self-employed or non-employed	293	1 112	3 901	7 766	11 777	13 923	16 879	21 545	22 276	23 016
2310 On a payroll basis	..	..	..	7 766	11 777	13 923	16 879	21 545	22 276	23 016
2320 On an income tax basis	..	..	..	0	0	0	0	0	0	0
2400 Unallocable between 2100, 2200 and 2300	0	0	0	0	0	0	0	0	0	0
2410 On a payroll basis	..	..	..	..	..	..	..	..	..	..
2420 On an income tax basis	..	..	..	..	..	..	..	..	..	..
3000 Taxes on payroll and workforce	**0**	**0**	**0**	**0**	**0**	**0**	**0**	**0**	**0**	**1 891**
4000 Taxes on property	**523**	**2 295**	**8 887**	**14 546**	**27 709**	**30 871**	**37 268**	**35 572**	**39 232**	**42 851**
4100 Recurrent taxes on immovable property	100	431	2 216	2 848	6 335	8 482	10 579	12 728	13 688	14 550
4110 Households	..	431	2 216	2 724	5 571	7 109	3 693	5 437	6 310	7 067
4120 Others	..	0	0	124	764	1 373	6 886	7 291	7 378	7 483
4200 Recurrent taxes on net wealth	341	1 450	5 118	7 703	13 244	14 144	17 134	14 123	16 749	18 965
4210 Individual	235	907	3 692	6 869	10 746	12 169	14 039	12 902	14 040	15 409
4220 Corporate	106	543	1 426	834	2 498	1 975	3 095	1 221	2 709	3 556
4300 Estate, inheritance and gift taxes	45	122	446	1 273	2 576	2 377	2 246	295	206	91
4310 Estate and inheritance taxes	..	122	446	1 273	2 576	2 377	2 246	295	206	91
4320 Gift taxes	..	0	0	0	0	0	0	0	0	0
4400 Taxes on financial and capital transactions	37	292	1 107	2 722	5 554	5 868	7 309	8 426	8 589	9 245
4500 Non-recurrent taxes	0	0	0	0	0	0	0	0	0	0
4510 On net wealth	..	..	..	..	..	..	..	..	..	..
4520 Other non-recurrent taxes	..	..	..	..	..	..	..	..	..	..
4600 Other recurrent taxes on property	0	0	0	0	0	0	0	0	0	0
5000 Taxes on goods and services	**6 928**	**47 154**	**107 262**	**200 671**	**282 746**	**300 727**	**338 487**	**361 717**	**378 770**	**395 938**
5100 Taxes on production, sale, transfer, etc.	6 720	45 882	102 901	185 921	266 124	284 947	321 606	342 432	358 841	376 576
5110 General taxes	3 622	24 350	56 656	124 985	189 424	201 802	235 771	256 028	270 085	284 705
5111 Value added taxes	0	24 350	56 656	124 166	188 705	201 184	234 941	255 181	269 215	282 784
Value added tax	..	24 350	56 656	124 166	188 705	201 184	234 941	255 181	269 215	282 784
5112 Sales tax	0	0	0	0	0	0	0	0	0	1 016
5113 Other	3 622	0	0	819	719	618	830	847	870	905
5120 Taxes on specific goods and services	3 098	21 532	46 245	60 936	76 700	83 145	85 835	86 404	88 756	91 871
5121 Excise duties	2 338	14 914	37 453	54 871	71 047	76 328	78 515	78 845	79 456	81 252
Stamp duty on tobacco	392	1 076	3 750	6 806	6 815	7 768	6 375	7 219	6 824	7 564
Taxes on spirits and wines	449	2 013	3 454	5 217	0	0	0	0	0	0
Excise on beer	162	605	2 195	3 650	0	0	0	0	0	0
Excise on petrol	480	2 310	7 057	9 756	8 132	7 373	6 417	5 711	5 491	5 597
Vehicles transfer tax	395	2 761	4 554	10 956	22 898	21 835	22 229	19 355	18 445	17 360
Chocolate and sweets	123	247	551	789	1 078	1 173	1 261	1 324	1 462	1 439
Sugar	0	0	217	230	192	196	201	206	203	206
Non-alcoholic beverages	38	120	487	1 113	1 024	1 739	1 803	1 972	2 031	2 111
Electric energy	89	1 515	3 414	5 091	7 079	8 110	8 656	9 233	10 795	11 575
Oil and gas products	0	3 703	8 729	88	92	98	108	103	110	109
Sales of radio and tv sets	0	163	220	920	0	0	0	0	0	0
Mineral oil	0	113	1 098	490	685	1 419	1 383	1 986	1 821	1 832
Cosmetics	0	0	0	159	0	0	0	0	0	0
Recording equipment	0	0	92	35	0	0	0	0	0	0
Others	210	288	1 635	1 249	1 821	1 965	2 060	2 535	2 666	2 737
Taxes on alcoholic beverages	0	0	0	0	10 338	11 317	12 602	12 969	13 580	13 638
Excise on diesel	0	0	0	4 802	6 424	8 653	10 507	10 267	9 563	9 924
Tax on Co2 emissions, petroleum sector excepted	0	0	0	3 520	4 469	4 682	4 913	5 965	6 465	7 160

	1965	1980	1990	2000	2007	2010	2013	2015	2016	2017
5122 Profits of fiscal monopolies	31	395	751	2 534	2 532	3 734	3 800	3 892	4 507	4 868
Profits state wine monopoly	31	30	67	41	32	44	36	0	0	0
Norsk tipping	0	365	684	2 493	2 500	3 690	3 764	3 892	4 507	4 868
5123 Customs and import duties	634	697	1 360	1 944	2 170	2 505	3 111	3 305	3 343	3 498
Customs revenue	615	689	1 305	1 944	2 170	2 505	3 111	3 305	3 343	3 498
Loading and lighthouse dues	11	0	0	0	0	0	0	0	0	0
Other import duties	8	8	55	0	0	0	0	0	0	0
5124 Taxes on exports	7	105	227	0	112	151	177	178	209	233
5125 Taxes on investment goods	0	4 274	4 454	0	0	0	0	0	0	0
5126 Taxes on specific services	88	195	1 233	1 386	131	114	140	138	1 193	1 972
Excise on race tracks	9	25	15	88	119	114	140	138	142	144
Taxes on specific services	34	49	150	1 298	0	0	0	0	1 051	1 828
Pengelotteriet (national lotteries)	45	121	462	0	0	0	0	0	0	0
Excise on lotto games	0	0	606	0	12	0	0	0	0	0
5127 Other taxes on internat. trade and transactions	0	0	0	0	0	0	0	0	0	0
5128 Other taxes	0	952	767	201	708	313	92	46	48	48
5130 Unallocable between 5110 and 5120	0	0	0	0	0	0	0	0	0	0
5200 Taxes on use of goods and perform activities	208	1 272	4 361	14 750	16 622	15 780	16 881	19 285	19 929	19 362
5210 Recurrent taxes	208	1 272	4 361	14 750	16 622	14 305	16 593	18 501	19 445	18 798
5211 Paid by households: motor vehicles	88	458	1 789	4 435	6 699	7 157	8 007	8 400	8 694	7 934
5212 Paid by others: motor vehicles	108	696	2 072	1 346	712	539	494	352	344	339
5213 Paid in respect of other goods	12	118	500	8 969	9 211	6 609	8 092	9 749	10 407	10 525
CO2 tax	0	0	0	3 047	3 385	2 166	3 293	4 906	5 116	5 223
Excise on pharmacies	6	32	59	105	153	80	78	99	108	94
Others	6	86	441	5 817	4 466	4 276	4 656	4 675	5 131	5 149
Tax on emissions of NOX	0	0	0	0	1 207	87	65	69	52	59
5220 Non-recurrent taxes	0	0	0	0	0	1 475	288	784	484	564
5300 Unallocable between 5100 and 5200	0	0	0	0	0	0	0	0	0	0
6000 Other taxes	**66**	**8**	**11**	**0**	**0**	**0**	**0**	**0**	**0**	**0**
6100 Paid solely by business	0	3	2	..	..	..	..	..	..	..
6200 Other	66	5	9	..	..	..	..	..	..	..
Non-wastable tax credits										
Non-wastable tax credits against 1210	..	..	..	..	994	1 229	1 576	2 959	3 630	3 990
Tax expenditure component	..	..	..	..	253	270	362	484	636	752
Transfer component	..	..	..	..	741	959	1 214	2 475	2 994	3 238
Total tax revenue on cash basis	**16 842**	**133 499**	**301 812**	**575 989**	**967 171**	**1 044 570**	**1 247 706**	**1 212 199**	**1 191 385**	**203 170**
Total tax revenue on accrual basis	**..**	**..**	**..**	**631 576**	**989 614**	**1 086 662**	**1 226 149**	**1 198 232**	**1 207 561**	**1 281 966**
Conciliation with National Accounts										
Additional taxes included in National Accounts	..	..	..	0	0	0	0	0	0	0
Taxes excluded from National Accounts	..	..	..	0	0	0	0	0	0	0
Difference in treatment of tax credits	..	..	..	0	253	270	362	484	636	752
Capital transfer for uncollected revenue	..	..	..	0	0	0	0	0	0	0
Voluntary social security contributions	..	..	..	0	0	0	0	0	0	0
Miscellaneous differences	..	..	..	0	0	0	0	0	0	0
National Accounts: Taxes and actual social contributions	..	..	..	631 576	989 867	1 086 932	1 226 511	1 198 716	1 208 197	1 282 718
Imputed social contributions	..	..	..	400	656	314	243	195	97	45
National Accounts: Taxes and all social contributions	..	..	..	631 976	990 523	1 087 246	1 226 754	1 198 911	1 208 294	1 282 763

.. Not available

Note: Year ending 31st December.

From 2000, data are on accrual basis.

Heading 5211: Up to 1971 this item contains motor vehicle licences paid by both households and enterprises.

Heading 5121: From 2005, taxes on alcoholic beverages include both 'taxes on spirits and wines' and 'excise on beer'.

Heading 5125: From 1998, revenue from taxes on investments goods is included in item 5121 "Others".

Source: Statistics Norway; National Accounts.

StatLink https://doi.org/10.1787/888934057210

Table 5.27. Poland: Detailed country table, 1965-2017
Million PLN

	1965	1980	1990	2000	2007	2010	2013	2015	2016	2017
Total tax revenue	..	..	..	**246 039**	**411 175**	**454 044**	**529 259**	**582 410**	**624 168**	**679 086**
Total tax revenue exclusive of custom duties	..	..	..	..	**409 415**	**452 417**	**527 282**	**579 587**	**620 876**	**675 601**
1000 Taxes on income, profits and capital gains	..	..	..	**50 268**	**93 795**	**91 026**	**103 567**	**117 078**	**124 251**	**137 481**
1100 Of individuals	..	..	..	32 415	61 471	62 901	74 216	83 974	90 071	99 121
Individual income tax	..	..	..	32 415	61 403	62 818	74 124	83 861	89 943	98 969
Tax on winnings from lottery or gambling	..	..	..	0	68	83	92	113	128	152
1110 On income and profits	..	..	..	..	..	..	..	..	..	..
1120 On capital gains	..	..	..	..	..	..	..	..	..	..
1200 Corporate	..	..	..	17 853	32 324	28 125	29 351	33 104	34 180	38 360
1210 On profits	..	..	..	..	..	..	..	..	..	..
1220 On capital gains	..	..	..	..	..	..	..	..	..	..
1300 Unallocable between 1100 and 1200	..	..	..	0	0	0	0	0	0	0
2000 Social security contributions	..	..	..	**96 386**	**140 086**	**156 026**	**202 629**	**223 531**	**236 292**	**254 968**
2100 Employees	..	..	..	42 357	51 929	60 247	75 747	88 557	97 132	105 817
2110 On a payroll basis	..	..	..	..	..	..	..	..	..	..
2120 On an income tax basis	..	..	..	..	..	..	..	..	..	..
2200 Employers	..	..	..	41 130	55 472	65 353	79 524	87 616	91 910	100 873
2210 On a payroll basis	..	..	..	..	..	..	..	..	..	..
2220 On an income tax basis	..	..	..	..	..	..	..	..	..	..
2300 Self-employed or non-employed	..	..	..	12 899	32 685	30 426	47 358	47 358	47 250	48 278
2310 On a payroll basis	..	..	..	..	..	..	..	..	..	..
2320 On an income tax basis	..	..	..	..	..	..	..	..	..	..
2400 Unallocable between 2100, 2200 and 2300	..	..	..	0	0	0	0	0	0	0
2410 On a payroll basis	..	..	..	..	..	..	..	..	..	..
2420 On an income tax basis	..	..	..	..	..	..	..	..	..	..
3000 Taxes on payroll and workforce	..	..	..	**1 628**	**3 081**	**3 720**	**3 998**	**4 028**	**4 173**	**4 485**
Rehabilitation fund contribution	..	..	..	1 508	2 860	3 370	3 633	3 621	3 742	4 020
Wage guarantee fund contribution	..	..	..	120	221	350	365	407	431	465
4000 Taxes on property	..	..	..	**10 584**	**17 116**	**19 068**	**23 120**	**24 637**	**25 612**	**27 101**
4100 Recurrent taxes on immovable property	..	..	..	8 404	13 515	16 399	20 747	22 206	22 723	23 783
Agricultural tax-local	..	..	..	720	906	969	1 666	1 579	1 499	1 487
Forest tax-local	..	..	..	96	157	165	228	230	296	295
Real estate tax-local	..	..	..	7 588	12 452	15 265	18 853	20 397	20 928	22 001
4110 Households	..	..	..	2 348	3 613	4 555	6 289	6 549	6 785	6 945
4120 Others	..	..	..	6 056	9 902	11 844	14 458	15 657	15 938	16 838
4200 Recurrent taxes on net wealth	..	..	..	0	0	0	0	0	0	0
4210 Individual	..	..	..	..	..	..	..	..	..	..
4220 Corporate	..	..	..	..	..	..	..	..	..	..
4300 Estate, inheritance and gift taxes	..	..	..	172	328	290	252	246	279	295
Inheritance and gift tax-local	..	..	..	172	328	290	252	246	279	295
4310 Estate and inheritance taxes	..	..	..	..	..	..	..	..	..	..
4320 Gift taxes	..	..	..	..	..	..	..	..	..	..
4400 Taxes on financial and capital transactions	..	..	..	2 008	3 273	2 379	2 121	2 185	2 610	3 023
Tax on civil law transactions and stamp tax	..	..	..	2 008	3 273	2 379	2 121	2 185	2 610	3 023
4500 Non-recurrent taxes	..	..	..	0	0	0	0	0	0	0
4510 On net wealth	..	..	..	..	..	..	..	..	..	..
4520 Other non-recurrent taxes	..	..	..	..	..	..	..	..	..	..
4600 Other recurrent taxes on property	..	..	..	0	0	0	0	0	0	0
5000 Taxes on goods and services	..	..	..	**86 880**	**154 813**	**181 983**	**192 943**	**209 666**	**229 626**	**250 580**
5100 Taxes on production, sale, transfer, etc.	..	..	..	84 885	150 093	175 207	187 498	201 701	221 529	243 209
5110 General taxes	..	..	..	51 615	97 848	109 717	116 607	125 836	134 554	154 656
5111 Value added taxes	..	..	..	51 615	97 848	109 717	116 607	125 836	134 554	154 656
5112 Sales tax	..	..	..	0	0	0	0	0	0	0
5113 Other	..	..	..	0	0	0	0	0	0	0
Turnover tax, of which:	..	..	..	..	..	..	..	..	..	..
On spirits	..	..	..	..	..	..	..	..	..	..
On fuels	..	..	..	..	..	..	..	..	..	..
On tobacco	..	..	..	..	..	..	..	..	..	..
5120 Taxes on specific goods and services	..	..	..	33 270	52 245	65 490	70 891	75 865	86 975	88 553

	1965	1980	1990	2000	2007	2010	2013	2015	2016	2017
5121 Excise duties	..	..	..	27 170	49 376	62 016	66 310	70 632	75 644	78 957
On domestic excise products, of which:	..	..	..	24 213	45 752	58 935	60 774	62 442	68 121	73 764
On spirits	..	..	..	4 309	5 000	6 154	7 393	6 655	7 343	7 727
On fuels	..	..	..	11 056	22 128	26 545	28 184	29 874	34 001	38 169
On tobacco	..	..	..	6 143	11 973	17 348	18 126	17 788	18 661	18 661
On beer	..	..	..	1 758	2 975	3 303	3 473	3 547	3 604	3 604
On wine	..	..	..	459	378	315	219	246	199	199
On other products	..	..	..	488	3 298	5 270	3 379	4 332	4 313	5 491
On imported excise products, of which:	..	..	..	2 957	3 624	3 081	5 536	8 190	7 523	5 193
On spirits	..	..	..	90	253	311	279	267	294	323
On fuels	..	..	..	2 031	2 045	1 051	3 481	5 650	4 494	1 915
On tobacco	..	..	..	18	214	114	62	86	84	51
On beer	..	..	..	26	12	14	43	53	58	56
On wine	..	..	..	71	106	133	149	139	161	159
On other products	..	..	..	721	994	1 458	1 522	1 995	2 432	2 689
5122 Profits of fiscal monopolies	..	..	..	0	0	0	0	0	0	0
5123 Customs and import duties	..	..	..	5 038	0	0	0	0	0	0
5124 Taxes on exports	..	..	..	0	0	0	0	0	0	0
5125 Taxes on investment goods	..	..	..	0	0	0	0	0	0	0
5126 Taxes on specific services	..	..	..	1 062	1 297	2 764	3 678	4 181	10 249	8 545
Taxes and payments of financial institutions	..	..	..	443	189	1 165	2 221	2 858	4 953	2 564
Gambling tax	..	..	..	619	1 108	1 599	1 457	1 323	1 421	1 632
Tax from some financial institutions	..	..	..	0	0	0	0	0	3 875	4 349
5127 Other taxes on internat. trade and transactions	..	..	..	0	0	0	0	0	0	0
5128 Other taxes	..	..	..	0	1 572	710	903	1 052	1 082	1 051
5130 Unallocable between 5110 and 5120	..	..	..	0	0	0	0	0	0	0
5200 Taxes on use of goods and perform activities	..	..	..	1 995	4 720	6 776	5 445	7 965	8 097	7 371
5210 Recurrent taxes	..	..	..	433	2 224	3 667	3 432	4 317	4 660	4 084
5211 Paid by households: motor vehicles	..	..	..	0	0	0	0	0	0	0
5212 Paid by others: motor vehicles	..	..	..	0	0	0	0	0	0	0
5213 Paid in respect of other goods	..	..	..	433	2 224	3 667	3 432	4 317	4 660	4 084
5220 Non-recurrent taxes	..	..	..	1 562	2 496	3 109	2 013	3 648	3 437	3 287
5300 Unallocable between 5100 and 5200	..	..	..	0	0	0	0	0	0	0
6000 Other taxes	**..**	**..**	**..**	**293**	**524**	**594**	**1 025**	**647**	**922**	**986**
Abolished taxes	..	..	..	..	..	..	..	..	..	..
6100 Paid solely by business	..	..	..	0	0	0	0	0	0	0
6200 Other	..	..	..	293	524	594	1 025	647	922	986
Custom duties collected for the EU	**..**	**..**	**..**	**..**	**1 760**	**1 627**	**1 977**	**2 823**	**3 292**	**3 485**
Total tax revenue on cash basis	**..**	**..**	**..**	**..**	**..**	**..**	**..**	**..**	**..**	**..**
Total tax revenue on accrual basis	**..**	**..**	**..**	**246 039**	**411 175**	**454 044**	**529 259**	**582 410**	**624 168**	**679 086**
Conciliation with National Accounts										
Additional taxes included in National Accounts	..	..	..	..	..	..	..	..	..	..
Taxes excluded from National Accounts	..	..	..	..	..	..	..	..	..	..
Difference in treatment of tax credits	..	..	..	..	..	..	..	..	..	..
Capital transfer for uncollected revenue	..	..	..	..	..	..	..	..	..	..
Voluntary social security contributions	..	..	..	..	..	..	..	..	..	..
Miscellaneous differences	..	..	..	..	..	..	..	..	..	..
National Accounts: Taxes and actual social contributions	..	..	..	246 039	411 175	454 044	529 259	582 410	624 168	679 086
Imputed social contributions	..	..	..	777	10 848	13 841	16 603	17 423	17 875	18 098
National Accounts: Taxes and all social contributions	..	..	..	252 943	422 023	467 885	545 862	599 833	642 043	697 184

.. Not available
Note: Year ending 31st December.
From 2002, data are on accrual basis.
Source: Ministry of Finance, Economic Department.

StatLink https://doi.org/10.1787/888934057229

Table 5.28. Portugal: Detailed country table, 1965-2017

Million EUR

	1965	1980	1990	2000	2007	2010	2013	2015	2016	2017
Total tax revenue	**99**	**1 798**	**14 825**	**39 888**	**55 829**	**54 708**	**58 015**	**61 938**	**63 634**	**67 027**
Total tax revenue exclusive of customs duties	..	..	..	**39 684**	**55 644**	**54 530**	**57 872**	**61 780**	**63 460**	**66 840**
1000 Taxes on income, profits and capital gains	**24**	**355**	**3 805**	**11 691**	**15 443**	**14 640**	**18 664**	**18 762**	**18 287**	**18 894**
1100 Of individuals	..	..	2 350	6 947	9 369	9 638	13 120	13 149	12 613	12 613
Individual income tax	..	..	2 350	6 947	9 369	9 638	13 120	13 149	12 613	12 613
1110 On income and profits	..	..	..	..	..	..	..	..	..	..
1120 On capital gains	..	..	..	..	..	..	..	..	..	..
1200 Corporate	..	..	1 182	4 744	6 073	4 919	5 545	5 614	5 674	6 281
Corporate income tax	..	..	1 088	4 457	5 760	4 653	5 327	5 405	5 399	5 956
Local corporate income tax ("Derrama")	..	..	84	287	313	266	217	208	275	325
Other	..	..	11	0	0	0	0	0	0	0
1210 On profits	..	..	..	..	..	..	..	..	..	..
1220 On capital gains	..	..	..	..	..	..	..	..	..	..
1300 Unallocable between 1100 and 1200	24	355	273	0	0	83	0	0	0	0
Tax on wages and professional income	2	93	9	..	..	0	..	..	..	..
Industrial tax	7	108	129	..	..	0	..	..	..	..
Tax on income from movable capital	2	71	1	..	..	0	..	..	..	..
Property income tax	3	23	17	..	..	0	..	..	..	..
Agricultural income tax	0	0	1	..	..	0	..	..	..	..
Complementary income ax	4	43	58	..	..	0	..	..	..	..
Tax on capital gains	0	3	1	..	..	83	..	..	..	..
Taxes abolished by DL 442-A/88 and DL 442-B/88	0	0	0	..	..	0	..	..	..	..
Other	6	15	58	..	..	0	..	..	..	..
2000 Social security contributions	**22**	**531**	**4 026**	**10 168**	**14 274**	**15 457**	**15 139**	**16 182**	**16 918**	**17 950**
2100 Employees	8	203	1 470	4 286	6 344	6 670	6 403	6 992	7 233	7 619
2110 On a payroll basis	8	203	1 470	4 286	6 344	6 670	6 403	6 992	7 233	7 619
Compulsory employee's social contributions	8	203	1 470	..	..	..	..	..	..	..
2120 On an income tax basis	0	0	0	0	0	0	0	0	0	0
2200 Employers	13	318	2 413	5 882	7 930	8 786	8 736	9 191	9 685	10 331
2210 On a payroll basis	13	318	2 413	5 882	7 930	8 786	8 736	9 191	9 685	10 331
Employers' social contributions	13	318	2 413	5 882	7 930	8 786	8 736	9 191	9 685	10 331
2220 On an income tax basis	0	0	0	0	0	0	0	0	0	0
2300 Self-employed or non-employed	0	10	143	0	0	0	0	0	0	0
Compulsory social contributions by self-employed	0	10	143	..	..	..	..	..	..	..
2310 On a payroll basis	..	..	..	..	..	..	..	..	..	..
2320 On an income tax basis	..	..	..	..	..	..	..	..	..	..
2400 Unallocable between 2100, 2200 and 2300	0	0	0	0	0	0	0	0	0	0
2410 On a payroll basis	..	..	..	..	..	..	..	..	..	..
2420 On an income tax basis	..	..	..	..	..	..	..	..	..	..
3000 Taxes on payroll and workforce	**1**	**47**	**0**	**0**	**0**	**0**	**0**	**0**	**0**	**0**
Contributions for Unemployment Fund	1	47	..	..	..	..	..	..	..	..
Stamp duty on wages and salaries	0	0	..	..	..	..	..	..	..	..
4000 Taxes on property	**5**	**26**	**402**	**1 468**	**2 284**	**1 935**	**1 906**	**2 303**	**2 356**	**2 644**
4100 Recurrent taxes on immovable property	0	0	133	508	1 008	1 101	1 337	1 529	1 503	1 589
Real estate tax	..	..	133	508	1 008	1 101	1 337	1 529	1 503	1 589
4110 Households	..	..	..	..	..	..	..	..	..	..
4120 Others	..	..	..	..	..	..	..	..	..	..
4200 Recurrent taxes on net wealth	0	0	0	0	0	0	0	0	0	0
4210 Individual	..	..	..	..	..	..	..	..	..	..
4220 Corporate	..	..	..	..	..	..	..	..	..	..
4300 Estate, inheritance and gift taxes	2	4	74	103	10	2	2	0	0	0
Inheritance and gift taxes	2	4	74	103	10	2	2	0	0	0
4310 Estate and inheritance taxes	..	..	..	..	..	..	..	..	..	..
4320 Gift taxes	..	..	..	..	..	..	..	..	..	..
4400 Taxes on financial and capital transactions	2	21	195	857	1 266	832	567	774	853	1 055
Real estate transfer tax	2	21	195	674	973	595	356	569	640	831
Stamp duty on registrations and mortgages	0	0	0	34	35	34	32	30	31	32
Stamp duty on the raising of capital	0	0	0	0	10	1	0	0	0	0
Stamp duty on real estate transactions	0	0	0	150	249	202	180	175	182	192
4500 Non-recurrent taxes	0	0	0	0	0	0	0	0	0	0
4510 On net wealth	..	..	..	..	..	..	..	..	..	..
4520 Other non-recurrent taxes	..	..	..	..	..	..	..	..	..	..
4600 Other recurrent taxes on property	0	0	0	0	0	0	0	0	0	0
5000 Taxes on goods and services	**47**	**837**	**6 555**	**16 069**	**23 225**	**22 004**	**21 684**	**23 924**	**25 254**	**26 785**
5100 Taxes on production, sale, transfer, etc.	44	810	6 440	15 634	22 550	21 246	20 470	22 838	24 025	25 495
5110 General taxes	0	290	2 906	9 733	14 333	13 527	13 710	15 368	15 767	16 809
5111 Value added taxes	0	0	2 899	9 733	14 333	13 527	13 710	15 368	15 767	16 809
VAT	..	..	2 899	9 733	14 333	13 527	13 710	15 368	15 767	16 809

	1965	1980	1990	2000	2007	2010	2013	2015	2016	2017
5112 Sales tax	0	290	7	0	0	0	0	0	0	0
General sales tax	..	290	7	..	..	..	..	..	..	..
5113 Other	0	0	0	0	0	0	0	0	0	0
5120 Taxes on specific goods and services	44	519	3 534	5 901	8 217	7 719	6 760	7 470	8 258	8 685
5121 Excise duties	15	295	2 052	4 501	5 940	5 665	4 675	5 209	5 808	6 125
Excise duties on tobacco	3	62	362	1 077	1 165	1 496	1 387	1 357	1 484	1 542
Excise duties on beer	1	0	55	90	100	82	76	75	81	86
Tax on motor vehicle sales	1	59	304	1 239	1 221	832	360	585	687	775
Tax on oil products	6	166	1 251	1 969	3 325	3 140	2 740	3 069	3 410	3 497
Excise duties on alcoholic beverages	0	0	23	126	128	114	109	115	132	140
Excise duties on alcohol	0	0	0	1	1	1	1	0	0	0
Tax on sugary soft drinks	0	0	0	0	0	0	0	0	0	70
Other	4	7	59	0	0	0	1	8	12	14
5122 Profits of fiscal monopolies	0	0	0	261	521	420	419	489	581	638
5123 Customs and import duties	21	96	511	1	1	1	0	0	0	0
Import levies	14	36	392	0	1	1	0	0	0	0
Import surtax	0	26	1	0	0	0	0	0	0	0
Other	6	34	119	0	0	0	0	0	0	0
5124 Taxes on exports	0	0	0	0	0	0	0	0	0	0
Taxes on Oporto wine exports	0	0	..	..	..	..	..	..	..	..
Other	0	0	..	..	..	..	..	..	..	..
5125 Taxes on investment goods	0	0	0	0	0	0	0	0	0	0
5126 Taxes on specific services	1	38	547	1 102	1 712	1 522	1 567	1 676	1 769	1 817
Tax on insurance premiums	0	6	47	131	170	215	200	218	230	244
Stamp duty on bank transactions	1	24	405	330	734	601	536	522	543	572
Stamp duty on debt related operations, interest and leasing of buildings	0	0	22	258	384	309	276	269	279	294
Stamp duty on insurance premiums	0	0	0	248	347	325	289	283	294	310
Bank levies	0	0	0	100	48	46	238	353	384	351
Other	2	8	73	34	29	25	29	30	39	46
5127 Other taxes on internat. trade and transactions	0	0	0	0	0	0	0	0	0	0
5128 Other taxes	6	91	424	36	43	111	99	96	100	105
Stamp taxes (miscellaneous)	6	91	424	36	43	111	99	96	100	105
Other	0	0	0	0	0	0	0	0	0	0
5130 Unallocable between 5110 and 5120	0	0	0	0	0	0	0	0	0	0
5200 Taxes on use of goods and perform activities	4	27	115	382	615	718	994	1 068	1 121	1 250
5210 Recurrent taxes	4	27	115	382	615	718	937	988	1 046	1 153
5211 Paid by households: motor vehicles	0	4	15	55	94	114	185	172	173	178
Local tax on vehicles	..	4	15	55	94	114	185	172	173	178
5212 Paid by others: motor vehicles	2	10	20	67	132	204	342	366	392	420
Local tax on vehicles	0	2	6	0	0	0	0	0	0	0
Road taxes	2	8	14	67	132	204	342	366	392	420
5213 Paid in respect of other goods	2	13	80	260	390	400	409	450	482	555
Gambling tax	0	3	72	110	140	143	107	108	123	170
Tax on the use, carrying and possession of weapons	0	0	1	3	6	4	7	5	5	11
Tax on motor vehicles - compensation	2	8	0	0	0	0	0	0	0	0
Hunting and fishery licenses	0	1	4	1	1	1	5	13	13	12
Fee for the use of water resources	0	0	0	0	2	13	13	19	19	20
Other	0	1	2	146	241	239	278	306	322	342
5220 Non-recurrent taxes	0	0	0	0	0	0	57	80	74	97
Special tax on motor vehicles	..	..	0	..	..	..	..	..	..	..
Emissions Permits	..	..	..	..	..	..	57	80	74	97
5300 Unallocable between 5100 and 5200	0	0	0	53	60	39	219	19	108	40
Miscellaneous taxes on production	..	..	..	53	60	39	219	19	108	40
6000 Other taxes	**0**	**3**	**37**	**288**	**417**	**495**	**479**	**608**	**644**	**568**
6100 Paid solely by business	0	2	17	107	217	225	234	354	406	285
General services and licenses granted to corporations	0	2	17	107	217	225	234	354	406	285
6200 Other	0	0	20	181	200	270	245	254	239	282
Fees collected by courts of justice	0	0	0	175	189	254	219	252	238	274
Miscellaneous taxes	0	0	20	5	11	17	25	1	1	8
Custom duties collected for the EU	**..**	**..**	**..**	**204**	**185**	**177**	**144**	**158**	**174**	**187**
Import duties	..	..	..	170	156	157	119	158	173	187
Agricultural levies	..	..	..	30	29	20	25	0	1	0
Levy on sugar and isoglucose	..	..	..	4	0	0	0	0	0	0
Total tax revenue on cash basis	**99**	**1 798**	**14 825**	**..**	**..**	**..**	**..**	**..**	**..**	**..**
Total tax revenue on accrual basis	**..**	**..**	**..**	**39 888**	**55 829**	**54 708**	**58 015**	**61 938**	**63 634**	**67 027**

	1965	1980	1990	2000	2007	2010	2013	2015	2016	2017
Conciliation with National Accounts										
Additional taxes included in National Accounts	..	..	..	0	0	0	0	0	0	0
Taxes excluded from National Accounts	..	..	..	0	0	0	0	0	0	0
Difference in treatment of tax credits	..	..	..	0	0	0	0	0	0	0
Capital transfer for uncollected revenue	..	..	..	0	0	0	0	0	0	0
Voluntary social security contributions	..	..	..	0	0	0	0	0	0	0
Miscellaneous differences	..	..	..	0	0	0	0	0	0	0
National Accounts: Taxes and actual social contributions	..	..	..	39 888	55 829	54 708	58 015	61 938	63 634	67 027
Imputed social contributions	..	..	..	3 292	5 592	5 906	5 310	4 601	4 707	4 735
National Accounts: Taxes and all social contributions	..	..	..	43 181	61 421	60 613	63 326	66 539	68 342	71 763

.. Not available

Note: Fiscal year ending 31 December.

From 1995, data are on accrual basis.

Source: Instituto Nacionale de Estatistica; Conta do Estado, Contas de Gerência dos Fundos e Serviços Autonomos da Administraçao Central; Estatisticas das Financas publicas; Relatorio do Instituto de Gestao Financeira da Seguranta Social, Contas de Gerência das Regioes Autonomas da Madeira e dos Atores.

StatLink https://doi.org/10.1787/888934057248

Table 5.29. Slovak Republic: Detailed country table, 1965-2017

Million EUR

	1965	1980	1990	2000	2007	2010	2013	2015	2016	2017
Total tax revenue	..	..	..	**10 626**	**18 417**	**18 972**	**22 456**	**25 388**	**26 266**	**28 089**
Total tax revenue exclusive of custom duties	..	..	..	..	**18 282**	**18 829**	**22 342**	**25 269**	**26 142**	**27 953**
1000 Taxes on income, profits and capital gains	..	..	..	**2 181**	**3 844**	**3 601**	**4 471**	**5 542**	**5 676**	**5 959**
1100 Of individuals	..	..	..	1 055	1 820	1 790	2 175	2 464	2 679	2 855
1110 On income and profits	..	..	..	1 055	1 820	1 790	2 175	2 464	2 679	2 855
Wages and salaries withholding	..	..	..	..	..	..	..	..	..	..
Of unicorporated individuals	..	..	..	..	..	..	..	..	..	..
1120 On capital gains	..	..	..	0	0	0	0	0	0	0
1200 Corporate	..	..	..	813	1 835	1 659	2 118	2 917	2 818	2 925
1210 On profits	..	..	..	..	..	..	..	..	..	..
1220 On capital gains	..	..	..	..	..	..	..	..	..	..
1300 Unallocable between 1100 and 1200	..	..	..	314	189	152	178	162	179	178
2000 Social security contributions	..	..	..	**4 409**	**7 244**	**8 154**	**9 847**	**10 861**	**11 426**	**12 325**
2100 Employees	..	..	..	901	1 700	2 077	2 238	2 410	2 644	2 941
Retirement	..	..	..	..	..	..	..	..	..	..
State employment policy	..	..	..	..	..	..	..	..	..	..
Health insurance	..	..	..	..	..	..	..	..	..	..
Sick leave	..	..	..	..	..	..	..	..	..	..
2110 On a payroll basis	..	..	..	901	1 700	2 077	2 238	2 410	2 644	2 941
2120 On an income tax basis	..	..	..	0	0	0	0	0	0	0
2200 Employers	..	..	..	2 850	3 914	4 579	5 556	6 283	6 467	7 198
Retirement	..	..	..	..	..	..	..	..	..	..
State employment policy	..	..	..	..	..	..	..	..	..	..
Health insurance	..	..	..	..	..	..	..	..	..	..
Sick leave	..	..	..	..	..	..	..	..	..	..
2210 On a payroll basis	..	..	..	2 850	3 914	4 579	5 556	6 283	6 467	7 198
2220 On an income tax basis	..	..	..	0	0	0	0	0	0	0
2300 Self-employed or non-employed	..	..	..	658	1 631	1 498	2 054	2 168	2 315	2 186
Retirement	..	..	..	..	..	..	..	..	..	..
State employment policy	..	..	..	..	..	..	..	..	..	..
Health insurance	..	..	..	..	..	..	..	..	..	..
Sick leave	..	..	..	..	..	..	..	..	..	..
2310 On a payroll basis	..	..	..	658	1 631	1 498	2 054	2 168	2 315	2 186
2320 On an income tax basis	..	..	..	0	0	0	0	0	0	0
2400 Unallocable between 2100, 2200 and 2300	..	..	..	0	0	0	0	0	0	0
2410 On a payroll basis	..	..	..	..	..	..	..	..	..	..
2420 On an income tax basis	..	..	..	..	..	..	..	..	..	..
3000 Taxes on payroll and workforce	..	..	..	**0**	**0**	**0**	**0**	**0**	**0**	**0**
4000 Taxes on property	..	..	..	**194**	**245**	**277**	**327**	**335**	**348**	**361**
4100 Recurrent taxes on immovable property	..	..	..	143	243	277	327	335	348	361
4110 Households	..	..	..	55	76	88	105	107	111	115
4120 Others	..	..	..	88	168	189	223	228	237	246
4200 Recurrent taxes on net wealth	..	..	..	0	0	0	0	0	0	0
4210 Individual	..	..	..	..	..	..	..	..	..	..
4220 Corporate	..	..	..	..	..	..	..	..	..	..
4300 Estate, inheritance and gift taxes	..	..	..	8	0	0	0	0	0	0
4310 Estate and inheritance taxes	..	..	..	3	0	0	0	0	0	..
4320 Gift taxes	..	..	..	5	0	0	0	0	0	..
4400 Taxes on financial and capital transactions	..	..	..	43	1	0	0	0	0	0
Real property transfer tax	..	..	..	30	1	0	0	0	0	0
4500 Non-recurrent taxes	..	..	..	0	0	0	0	0	0	0
4510 On net wealth	..	..	..	..	..	..	..	..	..	..
4520 Other non-recurrent taxes	..	..	..	..	..	..	..	..	..	..
4600 Other recurrent taxes on property	..	..	..	0	0	0	0	0	0	0
5000 Taxes on goods and services	..	..	..	**3 842**	**6 948**	**6 797**	**7 697**	**8 531**	**8 691**	**9 308**
5100 Taxes on production, sale, transfer, etc.	..	..	..	3 621	6 419	6 255	7 051	7 841	7 955	8 573
5110 General taxes	..	..	..	2 168	4 147	4 182	4 696	5 420	5 420	5 917
5111 Value added taxes	..	..	..	2 168	4 147	4 182	4 696	5 420	5 420	5 917
5112 Sales tax	..	..	..	0	0	0	0	0	0	0
5113 Other	..	..	..	0	0	0	0	0	0	0
5120 Taxes on specific goods and services	..	..	..	1 453	2 271	2 073	2 355	2 421	2 536	2 656

	1965	1980	1990	2000	2007	2010	2013	2015	2016	2017
5121 Excise duties	..	..	..	971	2 171	1 931	1 985	2 108	2 174	2 251
On hydrocarbon fuels and lubricants	..	..	..	617	1 118	1 032	1 045	1 139	1 194	1 230
On alcohol and liquers	..	..	..	143	201	197	201	205	209	212
On beer	..	..	..	43	66	56	56	57	57	57
On wine	..	..	..	12	4	4	4	4	5	4
On tobacco products	..	..	..	156	783	602	636	665	672	711
On electricity	..	..	..	0	0	16	17	13	12	11
On coal	..	..	..	0	0	1	1	0	0	0
On natural gas	..	..	..	0	0	24	25	23	25	26
5122 Profits of fiscal monopolies	..	..	..	0	0	0	0	0	0	0
5123 Customs and import duties	..	..	..	437	1	0	0	0	0	0
Customs duties	..	..	..	122	0	0	0	0	0	0
Import surcharges	..	..	..	315	0	0	0	0	0	0
Other customs revenues	..	..	..	0	0	0	0	0	0	0
5124 Taxes on exports	..	..	..	0	0	0	0	0	0	0
5125 Taxes on investment goods	..	..	..	0	0	0	6	2	2	3
5126 Taxes on specific services	..	..	..	45	99	142	364	310	360	403
5127 Other taxes on internat. trade and transactions	..	..	..	0	0	0	0	0	0	0
5128 Other taxes	..	..	..	0	0	0	0	0	0	0
5130 Unallocable between 5110 and 5120	..	..	..	0	0	0	0	0	0	0
5200 Taxes on use of goods and perform activities	..	..	..	219	424	409	495	538	581	575
5210 Recurrent taxes	..	..	..	219	372	384	466	470	495	500
5211 Paid by households: motor vehicles	..	..	..	0	0	0	0	0	0	0
5212 Paid by others: motor vehicles	..	..	..	76	124	127	153	142	145	150
5213 Paid in respect of other goods	..	..	..	143	248	257	313	328	350	350
5220 Non-recurrent taxes	..	..	..	0	53	25	29	68	86	75
5300 Unallocable between 5100 and 5200	..	..	..	2	105	134	151	153	155	160
6000 Other taxes	**..**	**..**	**..**	**0**	**0**	**0**	**0**	**0**	**0**	**0**
6100 Paid solely by business	..	..	..	..	..	..	..	..	..	..
6200 Other	..	..	..	..	..	..	..	..	..	..
Custom duties collected for the EU	**..**	**..**	**..**	**..**	**136**	**143**	**115**	**119**	**124**	**136**
Non-wastable tax credits										
Non-wastable tax credits against 1110	..	..	..	..	252	276	265	261	263	266
Tax expenditure component	..	..	..	..	..	..	..	..	..	..
Transfer component	..	..	..	..	..	..	..	..	..	..
Non-wastable tax credits against 1210	..	..	..	..	0	0	0	0	0	0
Tax expenditure component	..	..	..	..	..	..	..	..	..	..
Transfer component	..	..	..	..	..	..	..	..	..	..
Total tax revenue on cash basis	**..**	**..**	**..**	**10 821**	**17 993**	**18 322**	**21 934**	**25 555**	**26 146**	**27 437**
Total tax revenue on accrual basis	**..**	**..**	**..**	**10 626**	**18 417**	**18 972**	**22 456**	**25 388**	**26 266**	**28 089**
Conciliation with National Accounts										
Additional taxes included in National Accounts	..	..	..	53	33	47	0	43	10	10
Taxes excluded from National Accounts	..	..	..	0	-103	-131	-148	-149	-152	-157
Difference in treatment of tax credits	..	..	..	0	0	0	0	0	0	0
Capital transfer for uncollected revenue	..	..	..	0	0	0	0	0	0	0
Voluntary social security contributions	..	..	..	0	22	31	17	11	10	10
Miscellaneous differences	..	..	..	0	0	0	0	0	0	0
National Accounts: Taxes and actual social contributions	..	..	..	10 679	18 370	18 919	22 326	25 292	26 133	27 952
Imputed social contributions	..	..	..	19	80	139	142	171	181	189
National Accounts: Taxes and all social contributions	..	..	..	10 699	18 449	19 058	22 468	25 463	26 314	28 141

.. Not available

Note: Year ending 31st December.

Data are on accrual basis.

Source: Ministry of Finance.

StatLink https://doi.org/10.1787/888934057267

Table 5.30. Slovenia: Detailed country table, 1965-2017

Million EUR

	1965	1980	1990	2000	2007	2010	2013	2015	2016	2017
Total tax revenue	..	..	..	**6 924**	**13 030**	**13 376**	**13 199**	**14 118**	**14 732**	**15 598**
Total tax revenue exclusive of customs duties	..	..	..	..	**12 945**	**13 317**	**13 147**	**14 067**	**14 680**	**15 544**
1000 Taxes on income, profits and capital gains	..	..	..	**1 280**	**3 041**	**2 692**	**2 285**	**2 547**	**2 766**	**2 980**
1100 Of individuals	..	..	..	1 041	1 919	2 020	1 849	1 977	2 119	2 214
1110 On income and profits	..	..	..	1 039	1 916	2 017	1 847	1 974	2 116	2 211
Personal income tax	..	..	..	1 039	1 916	2 017	1 847	1 974	2 116	2 211
Special contribution for the reconstruction of the Posocje region	..	..	..	0	0	0	0	0	0	0
1120 On capital gains	..	..	..	2	3	3	3	3	3	3
Taxes on winnings from lottery and gambling	..	..	..	2	3	3	3	3	3	3
1200 Corporate	..	..	..	216	1 116	668	433	568	645	764
1210 On profits	..	..	..	216	1 116	668	433	568	645	764
1220 On capital gains	..	..	..	0	0	0	0	0	0	0
1300 Unallocable between 1100 and 1200	..	..	..	24	5	4	3	2	3	3
Tax on income - copy rights, patents and trademarks	..	..	..	24	5	4	2	2	3	2
Tax on profits due to changes in land use	..	..	..	0	0	0	0	0	0	0
2000 Social security contributions	..	..	..	**2 631**	**4 724**	**5 382**	**5 269**	**5 606**	**5 842**	**6 240**
2100 Employees	..	..	..	1 446	2 488	2 778	2 637	2 910	3 018	3 247
2110 On a payroll basis	..	..	..	1 446	2 488	2 778	2 637	2 910	3 018	3 247
2120 On an income tax basis	..	..	..	0	0	0	0	0	0	0
2200 Employers	..	..	..	1 008	1 844	2 063	2 022	2 135	2 240	2 408
2210 On a payroll basis	..	..	..	1 008	1 844	2 063	2 022	2 135	2 240	2 408
2220 On an income tax basis	..	..	..	0	0	0	0	0	0	0
2300 Self-employed or non-employed	..	..	..	177	392	541	610	561	584	585
2310 On a payroll basis	..	..	..	177	392	541	610	561	584	585
2320 On an income tax basis	..	..	..	0	0	0	0	0	0	0
2400 Unallocable between 2100, 2200 and 2300	..	..	..	0	0	0	0	0	0	0
2410 On a payroll basis	..	..	..	..	..	..	..	..	..	..
2420 On an income tax basis	..	..	..	..	..	..	..	..	..	..
3000 Taxes on payroll and workforce	..	..	..	**289**	**418**	**28**	**23**	**20**	**20**	**21**
Payroll tax	..	..	..	272	391	0	0	0	0	0
Tax on work contracts	..	..	..	18	27	28	23	20	20	21
4000 Taxes on property	..	..	..	**120**	**206**	**222**	**232**	**241**	**254**	**277**
4100 Recurrent taxes on immovable property	..	..	..	81	140	173	199	199	210	221
4110 Households	..	..	..	17	38	46	61	56	63	64
Property tax on weekend cottages	..	..	..	1	1	1	1	1	1	1
Compensation on the use of building ground - paid by individuals	..	..	..	16	37	45	48	56	62	63
Tax on immovable property of higher value	..	..	..	0	0	0	13	0	0	0
4120 Others	..	..	..	65	102	127	138	142	147	158
Property tax on buildings	..	..	..	2	3	3	4	4	4	5
Compensation on the use of building ground - paid by legal entities	..	..	..	63	100	124	134	139	143	153
4200 Recurrent taxes on net wealth	..	..	..	4	0	0	0	0	0	0
4210 Individual	..	..	..	0	..	..	..	..	..	..
4220 Corporate	..	..	..	4	..	..	..	..	..	..
Tax on balance wealth paid by banks	..	..	..	4	..	..	..	..	..	..
4300 Estate, inheritance and gift taxes	..	..	..	2	9	14	8	8	8	11
4310 Estate and inheritance taxes	..	..	..	..	..	..	..	..	..	..
4320 Gift taxes	..	..	..	..	..	..	..	..	..	..
4400 Taxes on financial and capital transactions	..	..	..	23	57	32	23	29	32	41
Taxes on the sale of immovable property - from legal entities	..	..	..	11	19	7	5	7	8	5
Taxes on the sale of immovable property - from individuals	..	..	..	12	38	25	18	23	23	36
4500 Non-recurrent taxes	..	..	..	10	0	2	1	4	5	3
4510 On net wealth	..	..	..	0	..	0	0	0	0	0
4520 Other non-recurrent taxes	..	..	..	10	..	2	1	4	5	3
Payments for the change of use of agricultural and forest land	..	..	..	10	..	0	1	2	4	2
Granting of easements and the creation of building rights	..	..	..	0	..	2	1	3	1	2
4600 Other recurrent taxes on property	..	..	..	0	0	0	0	0	0	0
Property tax on boats	..	..	..	0	0	0	0	0	0	0
5000 Taxes on goods and services	..	..	..	**2 602**	**4 556**	**4 994**	**5 337**	**5 653**	**5 797**	**6 026**
5100 Taxes on production, sale, transfer, etc.	..	..	..	2 481	4 341	4 779	4 996	5 275	5 414	5 623
5110 General taxes	..	..	..	1 641	2 916	2 927	3 048	3 221	3 319	3 483
5111 Value added taxes	..	..	..	1 610	2 916	2 927	3 048	3 221	3 319	3 483
Value added tax	..	..	..	1 598	2 898	2 924	3 044	3 217	3 314	3 479
Negative compensation of farmers in a VAT flat rate	..	..	..	12	18	3	4	5	4	4

	1965	1980	1990	2000	2007	2010	2013	2015	2016	2017
system										
5112 Sales tax	..	..	..	8	0	0	0	0	0	0
Customs duties paid by individuals	..	..	..	1	..	..	..	..	..	..
Special import duties and customs charges	..	..	..	7	..	..	..	..	..	..
5113 Other	..	..	..	23	0	0	0	0	0	0
Turnover tax on goods	..	..	..	11	..	..	..	..	..	..
Turnover tax on services	..	..	..	12	..	..	..	..	..	..
Special turnover tax on alcohol	..	..	..	0	..	..	..	..	..	..
5120 Taxes on specific goods and services	..	..	..	841	1 425	1 851	1 948	2 054	2 096	2 140
5121 Excise duties	..	..	..	581	1 196	1 555	1 579	1 626	1 670	1 707
Alcohol and alcoholic drinks	..	..	..	39	71	89	96	108	109	113
Mineral oil and gas	..	..	..	405	758	1 016	998	1 033	1 086	1 099
Tobacco	..	..	..	97	301	391	425	419	412	428
Duty free shops - alcohol and alcoholic drinks	..	..	..	3	0	0	0	0	0	0
Duty free shops - tobacco	..	..	..	17	0	0	0	0	0	0
Electric power and coal	..	..	..	0	4	19	31	34	34	32
Tax on the sales of new motor vehicles	..	..	..	18	60	40	26	26	23	28
Tax on the sales of used motor vehicles	..	..	..	2	2	0	0	0	0	0
Additional tax on motor vehicles	..	..	..	0	0	0	3	6	6	7
5122 Profits of fiscal monopolies	..	..	..	0	0	0	0	0	0	0
5123 Customs and import duties	..	..	..	158	0	0	0	0	0	0
Import duties	..	..	..	151	..	..	..	..	..	..
Levies on imported agricultural products	..	..	..	7	..	..	..	..	..	..
5124 Taxes on exports	..	..	..	0	0	0	0	0	0	0
5125 Taxes on investment goods	..	..	..	0	0	0	0	0	0	0
5126 Taxes on specific services	..	..	..	102	230	296	369	428	426	432
Tax on special gambling (gambling in casinos)	..	..	..	25	64	53	41	48	46	45
Tax on classical gambling (lottery...)	..	..	..	1	3	3	3	3	3	3
Special tax on slot machines	..	..	..	4	0	0	0	0	0	0
Tax on insurance services	..	..	..	37	65	69	65	82	85	90
Sojourn tax	..	..	..	3	7	7	8	11	12	14
Concessions	..	..	..	1	29	40	90	79	74	69
Concessions duties on special gambling (in casinos)	..	..	..	26	55	47	38	37	31	38
Fire protection tax	..	..	..	4	6	7	8	8	8	8
Tax on lottery tickets	..	..	..	0	0	0	3	17	16	16
Tax on financial services	..	..	..	0	0	0	32	57	57	59
FIHO, FSO	..	..	..	0	0	25	26	27	23	22
SOS	..	..	..	0	0	23	10	11	11	11
Tax on balance wealth paid by banks	..	..	..	0	0	0	18	2	0	0
Commodity reserve fund	..	..	..	0	0	21	27	32	32	32
Deposit guarantee Fund, Single Resolution Fund	..	..	..	0	0	0	0	16	29	26
5127 Other taxes on internat. trade and transactions	..	..	..	0	0	0	0	0	0	0
5128 Other taxes	..	..	..	0	0	0	0	0	0	0
Sugar levy	..	..	..	..	0	..	..	..	..	..
5130 Unallocable between 5110 and 5120	..	..	..	0	0	0	0	0	0	0
5200 Taxes on use of goods and perform activities	..	..	..	121	215	216	342	378	383	403
5210 Recurrent taxes	..	..	..	121	215	216	323	354	363	369
5211 Paid by households: motor vehicles	..	..	..	49	87	86	109	118	120	122
Registration fees on motor vehicles, boats and airplanes paid by individuals	..	..	..	49	87	86	109	118	120	122
5212 Paid by others: motor vehicles	..	..	..	12	21	20	24	27	28	30
Registration fees on motor vehicles, boats and airplanes paid by legal entities	..	..	..	12	21	20	24	27	28	30
Registration fees on tractors	..	..	..	0	0	0	0	0	0	0
5213 Paid in respect of other goods	..	..	..	59	107	110	189	209	215	218
Charges on the use of water	..	..	..	4	22	23	29	32	31	30
Taxes on waste pollution	..	..	..	7	10	3	4	3	2	2
Taxes on air pollution - caused by gas and hard fuels	..	..	..	3	8	10	10	13	13	15
Cont. of nuclear power plant to finance its de-composition	..	..	..	16	8	8	8	8	8	9
Indemnity for the restricted use of area on the territory of nuclear power plant	..	..	..	0	7	10	11	12	12	12
Taxes on air pollution	..	..	..	29	21	23	98	114	122	126
Special water tax	..	..	..	0	30	33	29	27	27	24
5220 Non-recurrent taxes	..	..	..	0	0	0	19	24	20	34
Emission permits	..	..	..	..	..	..	19	24	20	34
5300 Unallocable between 5100 and 5200	..	..	..	0	0	0	0	0	0	0
6000 Other taxes	**..**	**..**	**..**	**0**	**0**	**0**	**0**	**0**	**0**	**0**
6100 Paid solely by business	..	..	..	..	..	..	..	..	..	..
6200 Other	..	..	..	..	..	..	..	..	..	..
Custom duties collected for the EU	**..**	**..**	**..**	**..**	**85**	**59**	**52**	**52**	**53**	**54**
Total tax revenue on cash basis	**..**	**..**	**..**	**6 990**	**12 937**	**13 350**	**13 129**	**14 182**	**14 738**	**15 632**
Total tax revenue on accrual basis	**..**	**..**	**..**	**6 924**	**13 030**	**13 376**	**13 199**	**14 118**	**14 732**	**15 598**

	1965	1980	1990	2000	2007	2010	2013	2015	2016	2017
Conciliation with National Accounts										
Additional taxes included in National Accounts	..	..	..	0	0	87	90	94	94	94
Radio and television licence fee	..	..	..	..	..	87	90	94	94	94
Taxes excluded from National Accounts	..	..	..	0	0	0	0	0	0	0
Difference in treatment of tax credits	..	..	..	0	0	0	0	0	0	0
Capital transfer for uncollected revenue	..	..	..	0	0	0	0	0	0	0
Voluntary social security contributions	..	..	..	0	0	0	0	0	0	0
Miscellaneous differences	..	..	..	0	0	0	0	0	0	0
National Accounts: Taxes and actual social contributions	..	..	..	6 924	13 030	13 463	13 290	14 212	14 827	15 692
Imputed social contributions	..	..	..	39	80	99	117	118	125	132
National Accounts: Taxes and all social contributions	..	..	..	6 962	13 110	13 562	13 407	14 330	14 952	15 823

.. Not available

Note: Year ending 31st December.

Data are on accrual basis.

Source: Statistical Office of the Republic of Slovenia.

StatLink https://doi.org/10.1787/888934057286

Table 5.31. Spain: Detailed country table, 1965-2017

Million EUR

	1965	1980	1990	2000	2007	2010	2013	2015	2016	2017
Total tax revenue	**1 238**	**22 002**	**103 662**	**218 194**	**397 802**	**345 925**	**344 097**	**368 419**	**376 227**	**396 059**
Total tax revenue exclusive of custom duties	..	..	..	**217 223**	**396 080**	**344 416**	**342 782**	**366 616**	**374 356**	**394 129**
1000 Taxes on income, profits and capital gains	**304**	**5 714**	**31 763**	**61 769**	**132 909**	**97 241**	**100 546**	**104 662**	**105 908**	**113 417**
1100 Of individuals	177	4 481	22 527	41 851	81 267	75 745	78 343	78 673	80 347	86 341
Personal income tax	..	..	22 527	40 969	80 514	75 158	78 039	78 363	79 931	85 855
Income tax of non-residents	..	..	0	882	753	587	304	310	416	486
1110 On income and profits	..	..	..	..	..	..	..	..	..	..
1120 On capital gains	..	..	..	..	..	..	..	..	..	..
1200 Corporate	114	1 119	9 146	19 918	51 642	21 496	22 203	25 989	25 561	27 076
Corporate income tax	..	..	9 146	19 616	49 750	19 369	21 079	24 713	23 836	25 217
Income tax of non-residents (legal persons)	..	..	0	302	1 892	2 127	1 124	1 276	1 725	1 859
1210 On profits	..	..	..	..	..	..	..	..	..	..
Tax on commercial activity	..	..	..	..	..	..	..	..	..	..
Special tax 4 percent	..	..	..	..	..	..	..	..	..	..
Taxes on profits	..	..	..	..	..	..	..	..	..	..
1220 On capital gains	..	..	..	..	..	..	..	..	..	..
1300 Unallocable between 1100 and 1200	13	114	91	0	0	0	0	0	0	0
Local taxes	13	114	0	..	..	..	..	..	..	..
Other taxes	..	..	..	..	..	..	..	..	..	..
2000 Social security contributions	**350**	**10 682**	**36 722**	**76 046**	**128 715**	**129 733**	**117 929**	**123 470**	**127 523**	**134 698**
2100 Employees	81	2 376	5 976	12 336	20 582	20 512	16 697	18 839	19 642	20 669
2110 On a payroll basis	..	..	5 976	12 336	20 582	20 512	16 697	18 839	19 642	20 669
2120 On an income tax basis	..	..	0	0	0	0	0	0	0	0
2200 Employers	269	8 306	26 385	54 767	93 702	90 708	82 954	88 382	91 952	97 881
2210 On a payroll basis	..	..	26 385	54 767	93 702	90 708	82 954	88 382	91 952	97 881
2220 On an income tax basis	..	..	0	0	0	0	0	0	0	0
2300 Self-employed or non-employed	0	0	4 361	8 943	14 431	18 513	18 278	16 249	15 929	16 148
Self-employment	..	..	2 492	6 985	10 280	10 461	10 474	11 057	11 259	11 670
Unemployment	..	..	1 869	1 958	4 151	8 052	7 804	5 192	4 670	4 478
2310 On a payroll basis	..	..	..	..	..	..	..	..	..	..
2320 On an income tax basis	..	..	..	..	..	..	..	..	..	..
2400 Unallocable between 2100, 2200 and 2300	0	0	0	0	0	0	0	0	0	0
2410 On a payroll basis	..	..	..	..	..	..	..	..	..	..
2420 On an income tax basis	..	..	..	..	..	..	..	..	..	..
3000 Taxes on payroll and workforce	**0**	**0**	**0**	**0**	**0**	**0**	**0**	**0**	**0**	**0**
4000 Taxes on property	**79**	**1 004**	**5 718**	**14 033**	**32 537**	**22 841**	**24 676**	**28 155**	**28 819**	**29 648**
4100 Recurrent taxes on immovable property	6	41	1 478	3 990	7 302	9 685	11 845	12 624	12 861	13 161
Real State tax (IBI)/Real State tax surcharge	..	41	1 478	3 982	7 267	9 657	11 755	12 581	12 819	13 120
Special Real State tax for non-residents	..	0	0	8	7	7	8	4	5	8
Other taxes on property, land or building use	..	0	0	0	3	0	1	1	0	0
4110 Households	..	..	..	0	0	0	0	0	0	0
4120 Others	..	..	..	0	25	21	81	38	37	33
Tax on large commercial establishments	..	..	..	0	25	21	81	38	37	33
4200 Recurrent taxes on net wealth	0	107	637	1 414	2 484	694	2 080	1 944	2 043	2 159
4210 Individual	..	107	637	1 414	2 484	694	2 080	1 944	2 043	2 159
Wealth tax	..	..	637	1 200	2 059	110	1 370	1 184	1 257	1 348
Real State tax (unoccupied dwellings)	..	..	0	214	425	584	710	760	786	811
4220 Corporate	..	0	0	0	0	0	0	0	0	0
4300 Estate, inheritance and gift taxes	13	90	440	1 381	2 905	2 425	2 515	2 778	2 686	2 710
Inheritance and gift tax	..	..	440	1 381	2 905	2 425	2 515	2 778	2 686	2 710
4310 Estate and inheritance taxes	..	..	..	..	..	..	..	..	..	..
4320 Gift taxes	..	..	..	..	..	..	..	..	..	..
4400 Taxes on financial and capital transactions	60	767	2 478	6 140	17 399	8 228	5 657	7 255	7 490	8 585
Taxes on property transactions	60	767	2 478	6 140	17 399	8 228	5 657	7 255	7 490	8 585
4500 Non-recurrent taxes	0	0	646	1 108	2 447	1 809	2 579	3 554	3 739	3 033
Levy on "Revaluation of Reserve Account" Law 16/2012	..	..	..	..	..	..	386	..	..	..
4510 On net wealth	..	..	467	0	495	192	325	1 006	997	330
Tax on land holding gains	..	..	467	..	..	..	..	..	..	..
Urban use tax	..	..	..	..	495	192	90	73	64	96
Extraordinary resource of FGD	..	..	..	..	..	..	235	933	933	234
4520 Other non-recurrent taxes	..	..	179	1 108	1 952	1 617	1 868	2 548	2 742	2 703
Special duties	..	..	179	180	168	129	84	70	71	77
Land development contributions	..	..	0	223	368	225	71	61	80	55
Tax on the increase in value of urban terrains	..	..	0	705	1 416	1 263	1 711	2 417	2 591	2 571
Others	..	..	0	0	0	0	2	0	0	0
4600 Other recurrent taxes on property	0	0	38	0	0	0	0	0	0	0
5000 Taxes on goods and services	**506**	**4 553**	**29 437**	**65 372**	**101 907**	**94 078**	**99 555**	**110 140**	**111 938**	**116 241**
5100 Taxes on production, sale, transfer, etc.	503	4 552	26 732	59 278	93 343	86 720	91 643	101 884	103 478	107 566

	1965	1980	1990	2000	2007	2010	2013	2015	2016	2017
5110 General taxes	275	2 234	16 611	38 561	63 978	58 769	62 232	70 166	72 433	75 933
5111 Value added taxes	0	0	16 304	38 546	63 943	58 458	62 058	69 982	72 243	75 738
Value added tax (VAT)	..	..	16 304	37 806	62 672	57 649	60 951	68 601	70 705	74 107
Canary Islands general indirect tax	..	..	0	740	1 271	809	1 107	1 381	1 538	1 631
5112 Sales tax	0	0	0	15	35	311	174	184	190	195
Fees for RTVE (since 2010)	..	..	..	0	0	278	174	184	190	195
Fees from Nat. Commission of Telecomms. Market	..	..	..	15	35	33	0	0	0	0
5113 Other	275	2 234	307	0	0	0	0	0	0	0
Cascade tax	118	1 483	197	..	..	..	..	..	..	..
Excises on luxury expenditure	96	939	15	..	..	..	..	..	..	..
Other import duties	94	832	128	..	..	..	..	..	..	..
Refund of internal taxes	-33	-1 020	-33	..	..	..	..	..	..	..
5120 Taxes on specific goods and services	228	2 317	10 120	20 717	29 365	27 951	29 411	31 718	31 045	31 633
5121 Excise duties	69	1 239	6 048	18 013	25 608	24 439	24 602	25 990	25 804	26 384
Special excises	69	1 239	10	0	0	0	0	0	0	0
On beer	0	0	87	202	307	302	302	317	327	342
On wine	0	0	0	0	0	0	0	0	0	0
On alcohol	0	0	481	821	1 032	881	779	887	977	897
On hydrocarbon	0	0	4 222	9 997	11 785	10 904	11 918	12 478	12 994	13 156
On tobacco	0	0	1 123	4 505	7 250	8 028	7 126	7 212	7 137	7 130
On electricity bills	0	0	0	703	1 153	1 483	1 560	1 456	1 343	1 387
On carbon	0	0	0	0	0	0	148	308	243	315
Tax on retail sales of specific hydrocarbons	0	0	0	0	1 356	1 238	499	0	1	1
Tax on oil derived fuels	0	0	120	237	263	220	267	316	308	332
Petrol tax	0	0	0	6	5	5	13	22	24	25
Production and storage of electricity	0	0	0	0	0	0	1 278	1 610	1 287	1 511
Tax Greenhouse Effect Flourinated	0	0	0	0	0	0	0	99	96	123
Other taxes	0	0	5	18	23	18	19	20	21	20
Canary Islands taxes on national products	0	0	0	51	86	71	75	85	87	90
Taxes on national products in Ceuta and Melilla	0	0	0	108	110	105	103	115	112	115
Fees from the National Energy Commission	0	0	0	13	27	35	0	0	0	0
Contribution to the National Energy Efficiency Fund	0	0	0	0	0	366	150	207	207	207
Special tax on certain means of transport	0	0	0	1 323	2 159	736	325	358	406	481
Fee for use of continental waters for electricity production	0	0	0	0	0	0	0	453	202	197
Special duties and other taxes on imported products	0	0	0	29	52	47	40	47	32	32
Other taxes on products	0	0	0	0	0	0	0	0	0	23
5122 Profits of fiscal monopolies	66	132	546	0	0	0	0	0	0	0
Tobacco	21	77	0	..	..	..	..	..	..	..
Petroleum	45	55	546	..	..	..	..	..	..	..
5123 Customs and import duties	87	561	2 078	74	93	84	84	96	97	101
Import duties	87	561	1 394	0	0	0	0	0	0	0
Tax on Imports of Goods in the Canary Islands	0	0	137	33	51	44	45	53	55	58
Tax on Imports in Ceuta and Melilla	0	0	36	41	42	40	39	43	42	43
Customs duties collected for the EU	0	0	511	0	0	0	0	0	0	0
5124 Taxes on exports	0	0	0	0	0	0	0	0	0	0
5125 Taxes on investment goods	0	0	0	0	0	0	0	0	0	0
5126 Taxes on specific services	7	385	1 427	2 548	3 658	3 216	4 511	5 416	4 945	4 962
Taxes on betting and gambling	0	232	1 307	1 699	2 062	1 663	1 282	1 171	1 318	1 298
Taxes on other specific services	6	153	120	0	0	0	0	0	0	0
Taxes on insurance premiums	0	0	0	849	1 581	1 530	1 417	1 446	1 475	1 542
Tax on deposits of credit institution	0	0	0	0	15	23	236	422	447	414
Ordinary resource DGF	0	0	0	0	0	0	1 576	1 644	897	923
Tourist tax	0	0	0	0	0	0	0	43	82	109
EU SRF contribution	0	0	0	0	0	0	0	690	726	676
5127 Other taxes on internat. trade and transactions	0	0	0	0	0	0	0	0	0	0
5128 Other taxes	0	0	22	82	6	212	214	216	199	186
EU levies (excluding Customs duties collected for the EU)	..	..	22	77	-2	35	7	15	6	6
Others	..	..	0	5	8	8	20	34	33	33
Resource CORES	..	..	0	0	0	169	187	167	160	147
5130 Unallocable between 5110 and 5120	0	0	0	0	0	0	0	0	0	0
5200 Taxes on use of goods and perform activities	3	1	2 633	6 094	8 564	7 358	7 912	8 256	8 460	8 675
5210 Recurrent taxes	3	1	1 616	4 301	5 355	5 762	6 469	6 424	6 637	6 675
Other taxes on luxury expenses	..	..	..	2	7	4	3	3	3	4
5211 Paid by households: motor vehicles	..	0	461	1 129	1 698	1 810	1 876	1 729	1 867	1 838
Car registration tax	..	..	461	1 129	1 698	1 810	1 876	1 729	1 867	1 838
5212 Paid by others: motor vehicles	..	0	117	286	430	458	475	466	393	387
Car registration tax	..	..	117	286	430	458	475	466	393	387

	1965	1980	1990	2000	2007	2010	2013	2015	2016	2017
5213 Paid in respect of other goods	..	1	1 038	2 884	3 220	3 490	4 115	4 226	4 374	4 446
Hunting and fishing taxes	..	..	0	28	28	34	34	30	30	27
Economic activity tax	..	..	925	1 934	1 635	1 785	1 701	1 798	1 821	1 849
Economic activity tax. surchage	..	..	0	0	0	0	0	0	0	0
Advertising	..	..	27	0	0	0	0	0	0	0
Tax on environment and pollution	..	..	0	0	0	0	0	0	0	0
Other taxes on environment	..	..	0	42	131	142	625	563	605	610
Tax on effluent, use of hydrocarbon and mines	..	..	0	45	82	47	126	180	189	183
Other fees paid by households for licences	..	..	0	179	264	228	206	245	292	323
Compensation for local taxes	..	..	86	140	176	165	129	118	124	138
Vehicle inspection duty	..	..	0	6	18	17	20	19	21	23
Municipal fees for private use of public space	..	..	0	510	886	1 072	1 274	1 273	1 292	1 293
5220 Non-recurrent taxes	0	0	1 017	1 793	3 209	1 596	1 443	1 832	1 823	2 000
Tax and building permits	..	..	327	1 117	2 227	859	519	575	659	784
Urban licenses	..	..	0	451	490	260	157	200	231	284
Greenhouse gas emission trading	..	..	0	0	0	0	138	412	396	451
Parafiscal taxes	..	..	690	225	492	477	629	645	537	481
5300 Unallocable between 5100 and 5200	0	0	72	0	0	0	0	0	0	0
6000 Other taxes	**0**	**49**	**22**	**3**	**12**	**523**	**76**	**189**	**168**	**125**
6100 Paid solely by business	..	49	0	0	0	0	0	0	0	0
6200 Other	..	0	22	3	12	523	76	189	168	125
Fees on guarantees	..	..	..	0	0	515	0	0	0	0
Other taxes on production	..	..	..	3	12	8	76	189	168	125
Custom duties collected for the EU	**..**	**..**	**..**	**971**	**1 722**	**1 509**	**1 315**	**1 803**	**1 871**	**1 930**
Non-wastable tax credits										
Non-wastable tax credits against 1110	..	..	..	0	1 323	1 897	774	1 093	1 673	1 803
Tax expenditure component	..	..	..	..	522	729	432	546	765	828
Transfer component	..	..	..	..	801	1 168	342	547	908	975
Non-wastable tax credits against 1210	..	..	..	0	0	0	0	0	0	11
Tax expenditure component	..	..	..	0	0	0	0	0	0	11
Transfer component	..	..	..	0	0	0	0	0	0	0
Total tax revenue on cash basis	**1 238**	**22 002**	**103 662**	**213 976**	**391 946**	**337 383**	**342 417**	**365 916**	**375 233**	**393 770**
Total tax revenue on accrual basis	**..**	**..**	**..**	**218 194**	**397 802**	**345 925**	**344 097**	**368 419**	**376 227**	**396 059**
Conciliation with National Accounts										
Additional taxes included in National Accounts	..	..	..	0	0	0	0	0	0	0
Taxes excluded from National Accounts	..	..	..	0	0	0	0	0	0	0
Difference in treatment of tax credits	..	..	..	0	522	729	432	546	765	839
Capital transfer for uncollected revenue	..	..	..	-3 454	-4 837	-8 558	-6 501	-4 851	-3 794	-3 209
Voluntary social security contributions	..	..	..	0	0	0	2 209	1 170	1 149	1 133
Miscellaneous differences	..	..	..	0	0	0	0	0	0	0
National Accounts: Taxes and actual social contributions	..	..	..	214 740	393 487	338 096	340 237	365 296	374 364	394 835
Imputed social contributions	..	..	..	5 379	7 702	8 916	8 079	7 680	7 335	7 225
National Accounts: Taxes and all social contributions	..	..	..	220 119	401 189	347 012	348 316	372 976	381 699	402 060

.. Not available

Note: Year ending 31st December.

From 2000, data are on accrual basis.

From 1981 the figures take into account the classification procedures set out in the OECD Interpretative Guide. Consequently they are not completely comparable with the figures for earlier years though the amounts involved are quite small.

Heading 1000: Includes a tax on property 'Contribucion Rustica' which would be more appropriately classified in 4110, and the 'Licencia fiscal industrial and professionales' which, because it is a tax levied by reference to the size of the firm, energy input, etc, would be more appropriately classified in 6000. The data necessary to provide a breakdown is not available.

All subdivisions are estimated.

Heading 2300: Contributions paid by self-employed were shown under heading 2100 until 1982.

Heading 4100: Most of these receipts fall under 4110.

Heading 4400: In 1988 revenues from taxes on legal Acts issued by Autonomous Communities (Local) are included in 4400.

Heading 5121 comprises certain local levies which may include non-tax revenues.

Source: Informacion Estatistica del Ministerio de Hacienda (for national taxes).

Cuentas de las Administraciones Publicas (for local taxes and social security) both published by Secretaria General Tecnica del Ministerio de Hacienda.

StatLink https://doi.org/10.1787/888934057305

Table 5.32. Sweden: Detailed country table, 1965-2017

Million SEK

	1965	1980	1990	2000	2007	2010	2013	2015	2016	2017
Total tax revenue	**40 003**	**259 216**	**755 953**	**1 166 006**	**1 482 704**	**1 521 312**	**1 617 482**	**1 809 354**	**1 938 742**	**2 032 324**
Total tax revenue exclusive of custom duties	..	..	..	**1 162 556**	**1 477 605**	**1 515 899**	**1 612 505**	**1 803 111**	**1 932 699**	**2 026 099**
1000 Taxes on income, profits and capital gains	**21 956**	**112 730**	**314 797**	**475 304**	**573 698**	**539 715**	**559 026**	**649 780**	**697 616**	**736 949**
1100 Of individuals	19 500	106 376	291 146	387 531	457 760	423 915	459 078	525 901	577 111	608 328
1110 On income and profits	19 390	105 866	289 598	353 106	408 054	389 372	426 777	456 837	502 506	527 938
Coupon tax	9	44	233	2 040	6 306	3 047	4 108	4 615	5 718	6 398
Duties on foreign artists	4	3	3	50	86	89	-1	2	0	0
National income tax individual	8 676	31 682	70 755	32 486	44 326	42 595	44 664	52 480	57 839	62 697
Local income tax individual	9 294	78 134	220 072	336 304	479 068	522 850	581 934	635 719	669 579	700 078
Tax reduction individual	0	-3 997	-1 465	-18 872	-122 029	-179 890	-204 632	-236 613	-231 424	-241 976
Other	1 407	0	0	1 098	296	681	704	635	795	741
1120 On capital gains	110	510	1 548	34 425	49 707	34 543	32 301	69 064	74 605	80 391
Lottery prize tax	110	510	1 548	60	0	0	0	0	0	0
1200 Corporate	2 456	6 354	23 651	87 772	115 937	115 800	99 948	123 878	120 505	128 621
1210 On profits	2 456	6 354	23 651	87 772	115 937	115 800	99 948	123 878	120 505	128 621
Tax on profits not distributed	1	10	3	0	0	0	0	0	0	0
National income tax b.c. list	1 425	2 078	19 774	74 501	103 150	103 944	93 097	115 507	115 860	124 419
Local income tax b.c. list	1 030	4 266	0	0	0	0	0	0	0	0
Special tax on profits	0	0	3 874	0	0	0	0	0	0	0
Taxes on pension insurance savings	0	0	0	13 271	12 787	11 856	6 850	8 371	4 646	4 202
1220 On capital gains	0	0	0	0	0	0	0	0	0	0
1300 Unallocable between 1100 and 1200	0	0	0	0	0	0	0	0	0	0
2000 Social security contributions	**4 851**	**74 647**	**205 867**	**306 974**	**388 505**	**384 668**	**376 684**	**404 851**	**438 870**	**443 110**
2100 Employees	743	254	823	63 074	81 088	89 175	100 861	108 356	113 340	118 740
Health insurance fees	743	9	5	0	0	0	0	0	0	0
Unemployment insurance fees	0	245	818	0	0	0	0	0	0	0
Pension fees	0	0	0	63 074	81 088	89 175	100 861	108 356	113 340	118 740
2110 On a payroll basis	..	..	..	63 074	81 088	89 175	100 861	108 356	113 340	118 740
2120 On an income tax basis	..	..	..	0	0	0	0	0	0	0
2200 Employers	3 568	71 602	196 905	237 527	300 010	288 426	271 449	291 646	321 430	320 387
Survivors pension fees	0	20 343	44 181	14 847	19 611	20 362	15 693	17 305	18 954	11 983
Health insurance fees	717	26 005	58 334	74 097	100 979	71 292	58 365	64 332	78 540	74 389
Unemployment insurance fees	0	0	0	0	0	0	0	0	0	0
Labour market fees	0	982	12 516	45 975	48 471	55 443	39 007	37 926	41 632	43 924
Industrial injury insurance fees	132	1 201	4 663	12 030	7 844	8 146	4 022	4 431	4 856	3 422
Seamen's pension fees	0	10	26	30	0	0	0	0	0	0
Part pension fees	0	1 119	2 897	0	0	0	0	0	0	0
Supplementary pension fees	2 719	21 458	73 129	71 335	97 748	106 828	119 508	129 204	135 341	142 220
Parent insurance fees	0	484	1 159	19 215	25 356	26 355	34 854	38 448	42 108	44 448
2210 On a payroll basis	..	..	..	237 527	300 010	288 426	271 449	291 646	321 430	320 387
2220 On an income tax basis	..	..	..	0	0	0	0	0	0	0
2300 Self-employed or non-employed	540	2 791	8 139	5 618	8 391	7 468	5 607	5 058	5 058	4 819
Survivors pension fees	0	943	1 580	451	662	687	442	443	444	256
Health insurance fees	260	992	1 702	1 988	3 297	2 082	550	256	326	273
Industrial injury insurance fees	0	64	191	365	264	275	113	84	113	58
Parent insurance fees	0	58	106	573	856	888	960	603	663	625
Supplementary pension fees	280	734	4 560	2 241	3 312	3 536	3 542	3 672	3 514	3 606
Reduction	0	0	0	0	0	0	0	0	0	0
2310 On a payroll basis	..	..	..	5 618	8 391	7 468	5 607	5 058	5 058	4 819
2320 On an income tax basis	..	..	..	0	0	0	0	0	0	0
2400 Unallocable between 2100, 2200 and 2300	0	0	0	756	-984	-401	-1 233	-209	-958	-836
2410 On a payroll basis	..	..	..	756	-984	-401	-1 233	-209	-958	-836
2420 On an income tax basis	..	..	..	0	0	0	0	0	0	0
3000 Taxes on payroll and workforce	**13**	**6 759**	**18 686**	**50 106**	**83 279**	**107 515**	**172 170**	**194 121**	**203 432**	**233 192**
Special wage tax	0	61	0	22 391	30 225	33 090	36 832	40 283	43 640	45 977
Child care fees	0	4 740	13 080	0	0	0	0	0	0	0
Adult education fees	0	614	1 555	0	0	0	0	0	0	0
Building research fees	13	105	0	0	0	0	0	0	0	0
Labour welfare fees	0	257	2 033	0	0	0	0	0	0	0
Labour education fees	0	982	0	0	0	0	0	0	0	0
Labour market fees	0	0	0	112	156	219	7	-1	1	1
General wage fees	0	0	2 018	27 603	52 898	74 207	135 331	153 839	159 791	187 213
4000 Taxes on property	**712**	**2 424**	**26 630**	**39 890**	**36 228**	**36 509**	**41 182**	**43 852**	**46 254**	**45 472**
4100 Recurrent taxes on immovable property	10	16	8 946	23 286	25 899	26 402	31 596	32 444	33 445	32 876
4110 Households	0	0	3 877	13 321	13 474	11 593	13 422	13 320	13 548	13 999
Special tax on real estate	..	..	3 877	13 321	13 474	11 593	13 422	13 320	13 548	13 999
4120 Others	10	16	5 069	9 965	12 424	14 809	18 174	19 124	19 897	18 877
Forestry levy	10	16	423	22	34	18	37	19	14	15
Special tax on real estate	0	0	4 646	9 943	12 390	14 791	18 137	19 105	19 883	18 863

	1965	1980	1990	2000	2007	2010	2013	2015	2016	2017
4200 Recurrent taxes on net wealth	366	717	3 200	8 223	0	0	0	0	0	0
4210 Individual	361	702	3 135	8 043	..	..	..	..	..	..
4220 Corporate	5	15	65	180	..	..	..	..	..	..
4300 Estate, inheritance and gift taxes	155	545	1 433	2 549	23	9	-4	0	0	0
4310 Estate and inheritance taxes	143	495	1 118	2 088	15	9	-4	0	..	..
4320 Gift taxes	12	50	315	460	8	0	0	0	..	..
4400 Taxes on financial and capital transactions	181	1 146	13 051	5 833	10 305	10 097	9 590	11 408	12 809	12 596
Taxes on financial and capital transactions	181	1 146	6 946	4 878	9 414	8 968	8 913	10 895	12 331	12 138
Turnover tax on securities	0	0	6 105	0	0	0	0	0	0	0
Tax on life group insurances	0	0	0	955	891	1 129	678	513	478	458
4500 Non-recurrent taxes	0	0	0	0	0	0	0	0	0	0
4510 On net wealth	..	..	..	..	..	..	..	..	..	..
4520 Other non-recurrent taxes	..	..	..	..	..	..	..	..	..	..
4600 Other recurrent taxes on property	0	0	0	0	0	0	0	0	0	0
5000 Taxes on goods and services	**12 471**	**62 234**	**188 709**	**288 803**	**394 128**	**446 071**	**461 637**	**509 152**	**544 367**	**565 119**
5100 Taxes on production, sale, transfer, etc.	11 808	58 474	181 587	281 370	381 045	429 672	445 135	490 399	524 670	545 195
5110 General taxes	4 147	34 643	112 399	199 606	286 211	326 685	341 952	382 712	409 367	427 738
5111 Value added taxes	0	34 643	112 399	197 483	282 586	322 603	337 822	378 830	404 987	425 053
5112 Sales tax	4 147	0	0	0	0	0	0	0	0	0
5113 Other	0	0	0	2 123	3 625	4 082	4 130	3 882	4 379	2 685
5120 Taxes on specific goods and services	7 661	23 831	69 188	81 764	94 834	102 986	103 183	107 687	115 304	117 457
5121 Excise duties	5 953	19 941	55 332	70 313	84 873	91 470	88 168	91 572	95 506	97 927
Taxes on petrol and fuel	1 420	4 229	17 171	39 011	44 501	47 426	43 869	44 906	47 647	47 145
Special sales tax	390	585	1 098	0	0	0	0	0	0	0
Sales tax on motor vehicles	325	553	1 983	195	3	0	0	0	0	0
Tobacco tax	1 150	3 087	5 636	7 747	9 742	10 588	11 136	11 825	11 918	11 872
Tax on spirits	1 548	4 431	6 205	4 902	4 249	4 324	4 001	4 208	4 233	4 327
Tax on wine	149	930	2 922	3 567	4 001	4 589	4 887	5 654	5 724	5 985
Tax on beer and soft drinks	242	964	2 532	2 355	2 773	3 219	3 329	3 895	3 973	4 122
Tax on energy consumption	729	5 162	16 352	11 451	18 994	21 035	20 827	20 787	21 709	23 557
Taxes on electricity from certain sources	0	0	1 018	0	0	0	0	0	0	0
Tax on wastes	0	0	0	1 085	609	289	119	297	302	185
Tax on cassette tapes	0	0	194	0	0	0	0	0	0	0
Tax on video recorders	0	0	221	0	0	0	0	0	0	0
Tax on chemicals	0	0	..	..	..	..	..	..	..	735
5122 Profits of fiscal monopolies	72	204	332	3 641	3 952	5 068	5 385	5 001	5 112	4 974
Alcohol monopoly wholesale	23	116	98	0	0	0	0	0	0	0
Alcohol monopoly retailing	49	88	234	80	296	302	116	198	289	282
Gaming monopoly retailing	0	0	0	3 561	3 657	4 766	5 269	4 803	4 823	4 691
5123 Customs and import duties	1 419	2 433	8 308	0	0	0	0	0	0	0
Customs	1 080	1 300	3 115	..	..	..	..	..	..	..
Agricultural levies	339	1 133	5 193	..	..	..	..	..	..	..
5124 Taxes on exports	0	0	0	0	0	0	0	0	0	0
5125 Taxes on investment goods	0	0	40	0	0	0	0	0	0	0
Investment tax	..	..	40	..	..	..	..	..	..	..
5126 Taxes on specific services	217	1 253	5 176	6 472	4 341	5 745	9 072	10 587	14 269	14 150
Betting tax	79	223	616	0	0	0	0	0	0	0
Advertisement tax	0	202	1 073	1 116	657	335	244	200	201	170
Tax on gambling	0	69	88	1 245	1 315	1 378	1 309	1 353	1 455	1 485
Other specific services	138	656	2 938	4 111	2 369	4 031	7 520	9 034	12 613	12 496
Tax on charter travelling	0	103	461	0	0	0	0	0	0	0
Tax on air travel	..	..	..	..	..	..	..	..	..	..
5127 Other taxes on internat. trade and transactions	0	0	0	0	0	0	0	0	0	0
5128 Other taxes	0	0	0	1 339	1 668	703	559	527	417	406
5130 Unallocable between 5110 and 5120	0	0	0	0	0	0	0	0	0	0
5200 Taxes on use of goods and perform activities	663	3 760	7 122	7 433	13 083	16 400	16 502	18 752	19 696	19 924
5210 Recurrent taxes	663	3 760	7 122	7 433	13 083	16 400	16 502	18 752	19 696	19 924
5211 Paid by households: motor vehicles	336	1 241	2 003	4 969	7 451	8 550	8 275	10 897	10 082	10 884
5212 Paid by others: motor vehicles	313	2 476	5 055	2 464	5 632	7 850	8 227	7 855	9 614	9 040
5213 Paid in respect of other goods	14	43	64	0	0	0	0	0	0	0
5220 Non-recurrent taxes	0	0	0	0	0	0	0	0	0	0
5300 Unallocable between 5100 and 5200	0	0	0	0	0	0	0	0	0	0
6000 Other taxes	**0**	**422**	**1 264**	**1 479**	**1 768**	**1 421**	**1 806**	**1 356**	**2 159**	**2 257**
6100 Paid solely by business	..	0	0	0	0	0	0	0	0	0
6200 Other	..	422	1 264	1 479	1 768	1 421	1 806	1 356	2 159	2 257
Custom duties collected for the EU	**..**	**..**	**..**	**3 450**	**5 099**	**5 412**	**4 976**	**6 243**	**6 044**	**6 225**
Total tax revenue on cash basis	**40 003**	**259 216**	**755 953**	**1 144 233**	**1 465 382**	**1 496 374**	**1 611 798**	**1 768 413**	**..**	**..**
Total tax revenue on accrual basis	**..**	**..**	**..**	**1 166 006**	**1 482 704**	**1 521 312**	**1 617 482**	**1 809 354**	**1 938 742**	**2 032 324**

	1965	1980	1990	2000	2007	2010	2013	2015	2016	2017
Conciliation with National Accounts										
Additional taxes included in National Accounts	..	..	..	0	0	0	0	0	0	0
Taxes excluded from National Accounts	..	..	..	0	0	0	0	0	0	0
Difference in treatment of tax credits	..	..	..	0	0	0	0	0	0	0
Capital transfer for uncollected revenue	..	..	..	0	0	0	0	0	0	0
Voluntary social security contributions	..	..	..	8 108	13 903	14 884	15 881	16 697	17 986	19 225
Miscellaneous differences	..	..	..	0	0	0	0	0	0	0
National Accounts: Taxes and actual social contributions	..	..	..	1 174 114	1 496 607	1 536 196	1 633 363	1 826 051	1 956 728	2 051 549
Imputed social contributions	..	..	..	0	0	0	0	0	0	0
National Accounts: Taxes and all social contributions	..	..	..	1 174 114	1 496 607	1 536 196	1 633 363	1 826 051	1 956 728	2 051 549

.. Not available

Note: Year ending 31st December.

From 2000 data are on accrual basis.

Figures prior to 1970 are not strictly comparable with those of later years, though the amounts involved are insignificant.

Heading 1000: Receipts are on accrual and not on a cash basis for all years.

Heading 2000 includes some voluntary contributions.

Source: Monthly reports of central Government Revenues (unpublished) National Audit Bureau, Stockholm. Local Government Finance (SOS), Tax assessment statistics (SOS) , National Central Bureau of Statistics, Stockholm.National Accounts (Statistical Reports), National Bureau of Statistics, Stockholm.

StatLink https://doi.org/10.1787/888934057324

Table 5.33. Switzerland: Detailed country table, 1965-2017

Million CHF

	1965	1980	1990	2000	2007	2010	2013	2015	2016	2017
Total tax revenue	**11 237**	**46 385**	**85 367**	**127 572**	**151 923**	**163 017**	**173 557**	**181 466**	**183 981**	**191 040**
1000 Taxes on income, profits and capital gains	**4 616**	**21 022**	**40 203**	**56 411**	**69 790**	**74 439**	**79 271**	**84 376**	**85 680**	**90 394**
1100 Of individuals	3 748	18 056	27 824	37 948	47 994	51 835	53 803	56 377	57 072	57 817
1110 On income and profits	3 547	17 622	27 824	37 948	47 994	51 835	53 803	56 377	57 072	57 817
Direct federal tax	245	2 525	4 432	5 713	8 589	9 880	9 655	10 394	10 525	10 397
Military service exemption tax	35	103	135	163	138	155	163	173	174	175
Cantonal tax individuals	1 473	7 510	12 856	17 592	23 094	24 957	26 273	27 185	27 532	28 070
Municipal tax individuals	1 322	6 235	10 402	14 481	16 174	16 844	17 712	18 625	18 841	19 175
Withholding tax	358	1 249	0	0	0	0	0	0	0	0
Coupons	114	0	0	0	0	0	0	0	0	0
1120 On capital gains	201	434	0	0	0	0	0	0	0	0
Cantonal tax individuals	84	229	..	..	..	..	..	..	..	..
Municipal tax individuals	112	190	..	..	..	..	..	..	..	..
Direct federal tax	5	15	..	..	..	..	..	..	..	..
1200 Corporate	868	2 966	6 300	11 323	16 161	16 378	17 815	19 443	20 822	20 535
1210 On profits	801	2 818	6 300	11 323	16 161	16 378	17 815	19 443	20 822	20 535
Direct federal tax	153	781	2 214	4 928	6 800	8 006	8 698	9 731	10 532	10 547
Corporate cantonal tax	363	1 230	2 576	3 989	6 098	5 445	5 985	6 294	6 641	6 454
Corporate municipal tax	285	807	1 510	2 406	3 263	2 927	3 132	3 418	3 649	3 534
Withholding tax	0	0	0	0	0	0	0	0	0	0
1220 On capital gains	67	148	0	0	0	0	0	0	0	0
Corporate tax on gains	2	7	..	..	..	..	..	..	..	..
Corporate cantonal tax	28	77	..	..	..	..	..	..	..	..
Corporate municipal tax	37	64	..	..	..	..	..	..	..	..
1300 Unallocable between 1100 and 1200	0	0	6 079	7 140	5 635	6 226	7 653	8 556	7 786	12 042
Withholding tax	..	..	4 044	6 202	4 211	4 723	5 619	6 543	5 619	9 710
Property gains tax	..	..	2 035	938	1 424	1 502	2 033	2 014	2 167	2 332
Other	..	..	0	0	0	0	0	0	0	0
2000 Social security contributions	**1 670**	**10 844**	**19 892**	**30 750**	**34 949**	**38 369**	**42 654**	**44 073**	**44 527**	**44 998**
2100 Employees	716	4 833	9 312	14 385	16 356	17 573	19 710	20 436	20 627	20 887
2110 On a payroll basis	716	4 833	9 312	14 385	16 356	17 573	19 710	20 436	20 627	20 887
2120 On an income tax basis	0	0	0	0	0	0	0	0	0	0
2200 Employers	747	4 897	9 320	14 398	16 371	17 600	19 742	20 468	20 663	20 922
2210 On a payroll basis	747	4 897	9 320	14 398	16 371	17 600	19 742	20 468	20 663	20 922
2220 On an income tax basis	0	0	0	0	0	0	0	0	0	0
2300 Self-employed or non-employed	208	1 046	1 261	1 967	2 222	3 197	3 202	3 169	3 237	3 189
2310 On a payroll basis	209	1 046	1 261	1 967	2 222	3 197	3 202	3 169	3 237	3 189
2320 On an income tax basis	0	0	0	0	0	0	0	0	0	0
2400 Unallocable between 2100, 2200 and 2300	0	68	0	0	0	0	0	0	0	0
2410 On a payroll basis	..	68	..	..	..	..	..	..	..	..
2420 On an income tax basis	..	0	..	..	..	..	..	..	..	..
3000 Taxes on payroll and workforce	**0**	**0**	**0**	**0**	**0**	**0**	**0**	**0**	**0**	**0**
4000 Taxes on property	**1 108**	**3 830**	**7 586**	**12 333**	**12 223**	**12 402**	**12 037**	**13 126**	**13 531**	**14 439**
4100 Recurrent taxes on immovable property	78	304	447	735	895	968	1 052	1 138	1 203	1 270
4110 Households	78	304	447	735	895	968	1 052	1 138	1 203	1 270
Cantonal tax on buildings	20	71	125	187	265	286	303	349	391	342
Municipal tax on buildings	58	233	322	548	630	682	748	789	811	927
4120 Others	0	0	0	0	0	0	0	0	0	0
4200 Recurrent taxes on net wealth	692	2 201	3 382	5 254	7 002	7 105	7 403	8 083	8 688	9 002
4210 Individual	420	1 383	2 194	3 972	5 309	5 576	5 785	6 604	7 009	7 328
Cantonal wealth tax	206	739	1 232	2 241	3 145	3 324	3 532	4 044	4 238	4 508
Municipal wealth tax	214	644	962	1 731	2 164	2 252	2 253	2 560	2 771	2 820
4220 Corporate	272	818	1 188	1 282	1 693	1 529	1 617	1 479	1 679	1 673
Direct federal tax on capital	21	92	0	0	0	0	0	0	0	0
Cantonal tax on capital	142	436	760	821	1 107	969	1 032	947	1 080	1 093
Municipal tax on capital	109	290	428	461	586	561	585	531	599	580
4300 Estate, inheritance and gift taxes	142	393	896	1 215	869	974	966	1 088	1 148	1 191
4310 Estate and inheritance taxes	142	393	896	1 215	869	974	966	1 088	1 148	1 191
Cantonal inheritance tax	128	361	820	1 118	774	886	854	964	1 018	1 042
Municipal inheritance tax	14	32	76	97	96	88	112	124	130	149
4320 Gift taxes	0	0	0	0	0	0	0	0	0	0
4400 Taxes on financial and capital transactions	196	932	2 245	4 342	2 562	2 428	1 671	1 902	1 547	1 973
Cantonal transfer tax	48	245	115	144	182	182	185	177	184	191
Municipal transfer tax	21	103	39	52	42	50	52	52	52	60
Securities issuance	99	175	0	0	405	779	182	360	209	407
Securities trading	19	409	0	0	1 933	1 417	1 253	1 314	1 102	1 315
Currency effects	9	0	0	0	0	0	0	0	0	0
Securities issuance and trading	0	0	2 091	4 146	0	0	0	0	0	0
4500 Non-recurrent taxes	0	0	0	0	0	0	0	0	0	0

	1965	1980	1990	2000	2007	2010	2013	2015	2016	2017
4510 On net wealth	..	..	..	..	..	..	..	..	..	..
4520 Other non-recurrent taxes	..	..	..	..	..	..	..	..	..	..
4600 Other recurrent taxes on property	0	0	616	786	895	927	946	915	946	1 004
5000 Taxes on goods and services	**3 843**	**10 689**	**17 546**	**27 864**	**34 711**	**37 216**	**38 930**	**39 092**	**39 351**	**40 243**
5100 Taxes on production, sale, transfer, etc.	3 582	9 863	15 975	25 302	30 669	32 264	33 861	33 760	33 775	34 380
5110 General taxes	1 191	4 772	9 871	16 917	19 962	21 035	22 870	22 791	22 744	23 298
5111 Value added taxes	0	0	9 871	16 594	19 604	20 662	22 501	22 397	22 396	22 902
5112 Sales tax	1 191	4 772	0	323	358	373	369	393	349	396
Automobile duty	..	..	..	323	358	373	369	393	349	396
Other sales taxes	..	..	..	0	0	0	0	0	0	0
5113 Other	0	0	0	0	0	0	0	0	0	0
5120 Taxes on specific goods and services	2 391	5 091	6 058	8 337	10 663	11 191	10 936	10 901	10 960	11 011
5121 Excise duties	1 016	3 427	4 604	6 810	7 805	8 295	8 099	8 056	8 089	8 105
Beer tax	26	33	0	0	107	112	113	114	131	112
Excises on tobacco	190	634	15	32	2 247	2 417	2 354	2 255	2 186	2 195
Other price supplements	104	542	1 503	1 783	3	0	0	3	3	3
Fuel tax	467	955	1 334	2 975	3 076	3 110	3 034	2 864	2 848	2 791
Additional fuel tax	229	1 263	1 753	2 020	2 071	2 082	2 025	1 905	1 894	1 855
Road tax	0	0	0	0	0	0	0	0	0	0
Mineral oil tax on combustibles	0	0	0	0	20	20	23	19	17	18
Automobile duty	0	0	0	0	0	0	0	0	0	0
Tax on distilled spirits	0	0	0	1	281	296	292	279	279	282
Electricity consumption tax	0	0	0	0	0	259	258	617	731	847
5122 Profits of fiscal monopolies	158	472	0	0	0	0	0	0	0	0
Alcohol monopoly	111	354	..	..	..	..	..	..	..	..
Salt monopoly	16	25	..	..	..	..	..	..	..	..
Water monopoly	30	90	..	..	..	..	..	..	..	..
Other	1	3	..	..	..	..	..	..	..	..
5123 Customs and import duties	1 104	953	1 201	1 096	1 040	1 079	1 059	1 056	1 134	1 103
Import duties	972	923	1 201	1 096	1 040	1 079	1 059	1 056	1 134	1 103
Tobacco duty	114	6	0	0	0	0	0	0	0	0
Additional duties	18	24	0	0	0	0	0	0	0	0
5124 Taxes on exports	0	0	0	0	0	0	0	0	0	0
5125 Taxes on investment goods	0	0	0	0	0	0	0	0	0	0
5126 Taxes on specific services	113	239	253	431	1 818	1 816	1 778	1 789	1 737	1 804
Games in B casinos Confederation	2	2	2	37	449	381	308	272	274	273
Cantonal entertainment tax	17	37	23	27	39	101	73	67	68	66
Municipal entertainment tax	11	19	46	26	18	17	15	15	16	18
Other cantonal expenditure taxes	24	63	..	0	0	0	0	0	0	0
Other municipal expenditure taxes	19	6	..	0	0	0	0	0	0	0
Premium stamp duty	40	112	..	0	645	659	700	715	706	713
Lottery taxes	0	0	181	320	474	459	466	517	472	532
Other	0	0	0	20	193	199	216	204	202	201
5127 Other taxes on internat. trade and transactions	0	0	0	0	0	0	0	0	0	0
5128 Other taxes	0	0	0	0	0	0	0	0	0	0
5130 Unallocable between 5110 and 5120	0	0	46	47	44	38	55	68	71	72
5200 Taxes on use of goods and perform activities	261	826	1 570	2 562	4 043	4 952	5 069	5 332	5 576	5 862
5210 Recurrent taxes	261	826	1 570	2 562	4 043	4 952	5 069	5 328	5 572	5 858
5211 Paid by households: motor vehicles	152	501	1 075	1 573	1 845	1 953	1 977	2 074	2 109	2 136
Paid by households in respect of motor vehicles	..	..	921	1 336	1 580	1 667	1 685	1 768	1 801	1 819
Paid by households in respect of motorway tax sticker	..	..	154	237	265	286	292	306	308	317
5212 Paid by others: motor vehicles	76	251	431	799	1 901	2 092	2 093	2 054	2 059	2 249
Paid by others in respect of motor vehicles	..	..	367	686	395	417	421	442	450	455
Paid by others in respect of motorway tax sticker	..	..	39	59	66	72	73	77	77	79
Paid by others in respect of heavy vehicle charge	..	..	25	54	1 440	1 604	1 599	1 536	1 532	1 715
5213 Paid in respect of other goods	33	74	64	190	296	907	999	1 199	1 404	1 473
Hunting and fishing	9	20	..	0	0	0	0	0	0	0
Cantonal dog license	3	9	6	9	8	8	10	9	10	10
Municipal dog license	2	8	14	21	25	30	33	35	38	43
Cantonal inns	12	24	0	0	0	0	0	0	0	0
Cantonal royalties	5	12	0	0	0	0	0	0	0	0
Other	2	1	0	33	33	30	31	24	15	13
Environmental incentive fees	0	0	3	73	166	755	833	1 036	1 236	1 294
Royalties and concessions	0	0	42	53	64	84	93	94	105	114
5220 Non-recurrent taxes	0	0	0	0	0	0	0	5	4	5
5300 Unallocable between 5100 and 5200	0	0	0	0	0	0	0	0	0	0
6000 Other taxes	**0**	**0**	**140**	**215**	**249**	**590**	**664**	**799**	**891**	**966**
6100 Paid solely by business	..	..	42	65	75	274	300	342	344	337
6200 Other	..	..	98	151	174	316	364	457	547	629
Exemption tax	..	..	98	151	174	187	191	190	201	199
Other	..	..	..	..	..	130	173	267	346	431

	1965	1980	1990	2000	2007	2010	2013	2015	2016	2017
Total tax revenue on cash basis	**11 237**	**46 385**	..	..	..	..	..	..	..	..
Total tax revenue on accrual basis	..	..	**85 367**	**127 572**	**151 923**	**163 017**	**173 557**	**181 466**	**183 981**	**191 040**
Conciliation with National Accounts										
Additional taxes included in national accounts	..	..	0	0	0	0	0	0	0	0
Tax excluded from national accounts	..	..	0	0	0	0	0	0	0	0
Difference in treatment of tax credits	..	..	0	0	0	0	0	0	0	0
Capital transfer for uncollected revenue	..	..	-242	-733	-964	-1 101	-1 265	-1 061	-1 001	-874
Voluntary social security contributions	..	..	0	0	0	0	0	0	0	0
Miscellaneous differences	..	..	0	0	0	0	0	0	0	0
National Accounts: taxes and actual social contributions	..	..	85 126	126 839	150 959	161 916	172 292	180 405	182 980	190 167
Imputed social contributions	..	..	362	501	468	399	482	334	385	471
National Accounts: taxes and all social contributions	..	..	85 488	127 340	151 427	162 315	172 774	180 739	183 365	190 638

.. Not available

Note: Calendar year ending on 31 December.

The data is on an accrual basis.

The pre-1970 figures are not strictly comparable with those from the following years which were revised slightly.

"Parish taxes" are not reported in these statistics from 1985 onward.

In section 1100: payments made in consideration for exemption from military service could be classed under nontax receipts.

Section 2000 (Social security contributions) has been revised from 1985 onward to take account of the sectoring of government units adopted when switching to the ESA 95 system of accounts (currently ESA 2010). Consequently, health insurance contributions and those to the Swiss National Accident Insurance Fund are now excluded from section 2000.

Source: Financial Statistics, Federal Finance Administration.

StatLink https://doi.org/10.1787/888934057343

Table 5.34. Turkey: Detailed country table, 1965-2017

Million TRY

	1965	1980	1990	2000	2007	2010	2013	2015	2016	2017
Total tax revenue	**0**	**1**	**79**	**40 263**	**203 053**	**287 873**	**458 698**	**586 722**	**660 007**	**773 406**
1000 Taxes on income, profits and capital gains	**0**	**0**	**26**	**11 890**	**48 197**	**61 317**	**92 749**	**119 144**	**139 574**	**165 306**
1100 Of individuals	0	0	21	8 954	34 447	40 392	63 761	85 756	96 605	112 401
1110 On income and profits	0	0	21	8 954	34 447	40 392	63 761	85 756	96 605	112 401
Income tax	0	0	21	8 954	34 447	40 392	63 761	85 756	96 605	112 401
1120 On capital gains	0	0	0	0	0	0	0	0	0	0
1200 Corporate	0	0	5	2 935	13 751	20 925	28 988	33 388	42 970	52 906
1210 On profits	0	0	5	2 935	13 751	20 925	28 988	33 388	42 970	52 906
Corporation tax	0	0	5	2 935	13 751	20 925	28 988	33 388	42 970	52 906
1220 On capital gains	0	0	0	0	0	0	0	0	0	0
1300 Unallocable between 1100 and 1200	0	0	0	0	0	0	0	0	0	0
Fiscal balance tax	..	0	..	..	..	..	..	..	..	..
Capital gains tax on real estate sales	..	0	..	..	..	..	..	..	..	..
2000 Social security contributions	**0**	**0**	**15**	**7 543**	**44 052**	**71 696**	**125 871**	**170 282**	**190 247**	**226 720**
2100 Employees	0	0	6	2 712	17 867	26 934	49 831	64 214	72 850	86 410
2110 On a payroll basis	..	..	..	2 712	17 867	26 934	49 831	64 214	72 850	86 410
2120 On an income tax basis	..	..	..	0	0	0	0	0	0	0
2200 Employers	0	0	9	3 619	20 442	39 363	71 184	95 067	107 905	128 331
2210 On a payroll basis	..	..	..	3 619	20 442	39 363	71 184	95 067	107 905	128 331
2220 On an income tax basis	..	..	..	0	0	0	0	0	0	0
2300 Self-employed or non-employed	0	0	1	1 211	5 743	5 399	4 856	11 001	9 493	11 979
2310 On a payroll basis	..	..	..	1 211	5 743	5 399	4 856	11 001	9 493	11 979
2320 On an income tax basis	..	..	..	0	0	0	0	0	0	0
2400 Unallocable between 2100, 2200 and 2300	0	0	0	0	0	0	0	0	0	0
2410 On a payroll basis	..	..	..	..	..	..	..	..	..	..
2420 On an income tax basis	..	..	..	..	..	..	..	..	..	..
3000 Taxes on payroll and workforce	**0**	**0**	**0**	**0**	**0**	**0**	**0**	**0**	**0**	**0**
4000 Taxes on property	**0**	**0**	**2**	**1 272**	**7 621**	**11 684**	**21 280**	**28 582**	**31 873**	**34 857**
4100 Recurrent taxes on immovable property	0	0	0	191	1 464	2 669	3 847	5 882	6 729	6 809
Real estate tax	0	0	..	191	1 464	2 669	3 847	5 882	6 729	6 809
4110 Households	..	..	..	..	..	..	..	..	..	..
4120 Others	..	..	..	..	..	..	..	..	..	..
4200 Recurrent taxes on net wealth	0	0	0	0	0	0	0	0	0	0
4210 Individual	..	..	..	..	..	..	..	..	..	..
4220 Corporate	..	..	..	..	..	..	..	..	..	..
4300 Estate, inheritance and gift taxes	0	0	0	15	125	215	340	435	619	718
Gift and inheritance tax	0	0	0	15	125	215	340	435	619	718
4310 Estate and inheritance taxes	..	..	..	..	..	..	..	..	..	..
4320 Gift taxes	..	..	..	..	..	..	..	..	..	..
4400 Taxes on financial and capital transactions	0	0	2	1 065	6 032	8 800	17 093	22 265	24 525	27 331
Stamp tax	0	0	2	818	3 642	5 083	9 416	12 045	13 419	15 596
Real estate purchase tax	0	0	0	0	0	0	0	0	0	0
Title deed fees	0	0	0	207	2 000	3 329	7 072	9 530	10 381	10 970
Notary fees	0	0	0	40	389	388	606	690	724	765
4500 Non-recurrent taxes	0	0	0	0	0	0	0	0	0	0
4510 On net wealth	..	..	..	..	..	..	..	..	..	..
4520 Other non-recurrent taxes	..	..	..	..	..	..	..	..	..	..
4600 Other recurrent taxes on property	0	0	0	0	0	0	0	0	0	0
5000 Taxes on goods and services	**0**	**0**	**22**	**16 901**	**96 766**	**137 252**	**211 257**	**259 964**	**287 948**	**336 256**
5100 Taxes on production, sale, transfer, etc.	0	0	22	16 328	92 605	131 878	203 364	250 261	277 580	324 935
5110 General taxes	0	0	16	9 735	43 285	62 533	100 723	121 070	130 822	155 680
5111 Value added taxes	..	..	14	9 735	43 285	62 533	100 723	121 070	130 822	155 680
5112 Sales tax	..	..	0	0	0	0	0	0	0	0
5113 Other	..	..	1	0	0	0	0	0	0	0
5120 Taxes on specific goods and services	0	0	6	6 593	49 320	69 345	102 641	129 191	146 757	169 256
5121 Excise duties	0	0	1	4 718	39 111	57 285	85 462	105 922	120 399	138 338
Sales taxes	0	0	0	0	0	0	0	0	0	0
Domestic production tax	0	0	0	0	0	0	0	0	0	0
Domestic production tax on petrol	0	0	0	0	0	0	0	0	0	0
Production tax on monopoly goods	0	0	0	0	0	0	0	0	0	0
Sugar consumption taxes	0	0	0	0	0	0	0	0	0	0
Motor vehicles purchase tax (Total)	0	0	1	916	4 293	6 193	10 565	17 027	18 873	22 017
Motor vehicles purchase tax	0	0	..	498	4 293	6 193	10 565	17 027	18 873	22 017
Additional motor vehicle purchase tax	0	0	..	418	0	0	0	0	0	0
Revenue from other excises	0	0	0	533	12 765	19 395	29 739	38 066	45 230	52 718
Petroleum consumption tax	0	0	0	3 269	22 052	31 697	45 158	50 830	56 296	63 603
5122 Profits of fiscal monopolies	0	0	0	0	0	0	0	0	0	0

	1965	1980	1990	2000	2007	2010	2013	2015	2016	2017
5123 Customs and import duties	0	0	4	462	2 478	3 319	5 542	8 521	9 413	12 837
Customs duty	0	0	1	449	2 441	3 240	5 409	8 280	9 065	12 329
Customs duty on petrol	0	0	0	0	0	0	0	0	0	0
Production tax on imports	0	0	0	0	0	0	0	0	0	0
Production tax on petrol imports	0	0	0	0	0	0	0	0	0	0
Stamp duty on imports	0	0	2	0	0	0	0	0	0	0
Wharf duty	0	0	1	0	0	0	0	0	0	0
Other	0	0	0	13	37	80	133	240	348	508
5124 Taxes on exports	0	0	0	0	0	0	0	0	0	0
5125 Taxes on investment goods	0	0	0	0	0	0	0	0	0	0
5126 Taxes on specific services	0	0	1	997	7 686	4 005	6 853	10 014	11 968	14 262
Bank, insurance transaction tax	0	0	1	997	3 149	3 571	6 160	9 172	11 068	13 270
Transportation tax	0	0	0	0	0	0	0	0	0	0
PTT service tax	0	0	0	0	4 211	0	0	0	0	0
Tax on football pool	0	0	0	0	0	0	0	0	0	0
Lottery tax	0	0	0	0	327	434	692	842	900	993
5127 Other taxes on internat. trade and transactions	0	0	0	0	0	0	0	0	0	0
Foreign travel expenditures tax	0	0	..	..	..	..	..	..	..	..
5128 Other taxes	0	0	0	416	46	4 736	4 785	4 734	4 978	3 818
5130 Unallocable between 5110 and 5120	0	0	0	0	0	0	0	0	0	0
5200 Taxes on use of goods and perform activities	0	0	0	572	4 161	5 374	7 894	9 703	10 368	11 321
5210 Recurrent taxes	0	0	0	359	4 161	5 374	7 894	9 703	10 368	11 321
Motor vehicles tax	0	0	0	359	0	5 374	7 894	9 703	10 368	11 321
5211 Paid by households: motor vehicles	..	..	..	0	0	0	0	0	0	0
5212 Paid by others: motor vehicles	..	..	..	359	4 161	5 374	7 894	9 703	10 368	11 321
Motor vehicles tax	..	..	..	302	3 521	5 033	7 353	8 949	9 986	10 825
Traffic fees	..	..	..	58	640	341	540	754	382	496
5213 Paid in respect of other goods	..	..	..	0	0	0	0	0	0	0
5220 Non-recurrent taxes	0	0	0	213	0	0	0	0	0	0
Building construction tax	..	0	..	..	..	..	..	..	..	..
5300 Unallocable between 5100 and 5200	0	0	0	0	0	0	0	0	0	0
6000 Other taxes	**0**	**0**	**13**	**2 658**	**6 417**	**5 924**	**7 541**	**8 750**	**10 365**	**10 266**
6100 Paid solely by business	..	0	0	0	0	0	0	0	0	0
6200 Other	..	0	13	2 658	6 417	5 924	7 541	8 750	10 365	10 266
Funds	..	..	..	1 938	0	0	0	0	0	0
Vocatial Train Pro.F.	..	..	..	67	0	0	0	0	0	0
Tax penalties and fines	..	..	..	548	4 191	2 689	3 175	3 779	4 850	3 838
Municipalities revenue	..	..	..	106	2 227	3 235	4 366	4 971	5 515	6 429
Total tax revenue on cash basis	**0**	**1**	**79**	**40 263**	**203 053**	**287 873**	**458 698**	**586 722**	**660 007**	**773 406**
Total tax revenue on accrual basis	..	..	..	..	..	..	..	..	..	..
Conciliation with National Accounts										
Additional taxes included in National Accounts	..	..	..	..	..	..	..	..	..	..
Taxes excluded from National Accounts	..	..	..	..	..	..	..	..	..	..
Difference in treatment of tax credits	..	..	..	..	..	..	..	..	..	..
Capital transfer for uncollected revenue	..	..	..	..	..	..	..	..	..	..
Voluntary social security contributions	..	..	..	..	..	..	..	..	..	..
Miscellaneous differences	..	..	..	..	..	..	..	..	..	..
National Accounts: Taxes and actual social contributions	..	..	..	..	..	..	..	..	..	..
Imputed social contributions	..	..	..	..	..	..	..	..	..	..
National Accounts: Taxes and all social contributions	..	..	..	..	..	..	..	..	..	..

.. Not available

Note: From 1982 the data are based on the fiscal year ending 31st December. Before that the data are on a fiscal year basis beginning 1st March. Revenue is reported on a cash basis except for social security contributions which are reported on an assessment basis.

The figures under the local tax collections include taxes under "Municipalities Revenues Law" and Property tax. They also include transfers to the local authorities from central budget tax revenues under the revenue sharing system.

Heading 2000: Before 2003, contributions to some private social security schemes are included in this heading.

Source: Bulletin of national accounts and the Budget revenue Bulletin.

StatLink https://doi.org/10.1787/888934057362

Table 5.35. United Kingdom: Detailed country table, 1965-2017

Million GBP

	1965	1980	1990	2000	2007	2010	2013	2015	2016	2017
Total tax revenue	**10 945**	**81 153**	**202 368**	**358 654**	**508 148**	**514 132**	**567 150**	**609 653**	**644 555**	**681 855**
Total tax revenue exclusive of custom duties	..	..	..	**356 854**	**506 074**	**511 199**	**564 236**	**606 576**	**641 237**	**678 436**
1000 Taxes on income, profits and capital gains	**4 050**	**30 651**	**79 576**	**142 197**	**202 063**	**193 806**	**201 542**	**214 870**	**229 942**	**243 181**
1100 Of individuals	3 618	23 868	59 506	104 136	151 157	147 019	156 570	168 873	176 642	185 560
1110 On income and profits	3 615	23 376	57 614	101 925	147 309	144 502	152 668	163 291	169 582	177 182
Income tax	..	23 370	57 614	101 925	147 309	144 502	152 668	163 291	169 582	177 182
Surtax	..	6	0	0	0	0	0	0	0	0
1120 On capital gains	3	492	1 892	2 211	3 848	2 517	3 902	5 582	7 060	8 378
1200 Corporate	484	6 783	20 070	38 061	50 906	46 787	44 972	45 997	53 300	57 621
1210 On profits	484	6 510	18 994	35 730	47 615	45 911	43 935	44 882	52 022	56 372
Petroleum revenue tax	..	1 799	941	1 540	1 387	1 349	1 296	-552	-768	-634
Supplementary petroleum duty	..	0	0	0	0	0	0	0	0	0
Corporation tax	..	4 712	18 053	34 190	45 514	43 919	41 972	44 814	52 093	56 267
Corporation tax overspill relief	..	-1	0	0	0	0	0	0	0	0
Profits tax	..	0	0	0	0	0	0	0	0	0
Windfall tax	..	0	0	0	0	0	0	0	0	0
Betting tax	..	0	0	0	590	568	605	595	686	737
Non fossil fuel obligation levy	..	0	0	0	124	75	62	25	11	2
1220 On capital gains	0	273	1 076	2 331	3 291	876	1 037	1 115	1 278	1 249
1300 Unallocable between 1100 and 1200	-52	0	0	0	0	0	0	0	0	0
2000 Social security contributions	**1 685**	**13 531**	**34 457**	**60 252**	**93 210**	**97 346**	**106 085**	**114 067**	**121 900**	**130 595**
2100 Employees	770	5 228	13 296	24 175	36 585	38 703	41 481	44 454	47 304	50 411
2110 On a payroll basis	..	..	13 296	24 175	36 585	38 703	41 481	44 454	47 304	50 411
2120 On an income tax basis	..	..	0	0	0	0	0	0	0	0
2200 Employers	831	8 210	19 984	34 028	53 765	55 887	62 019	66 491	71 407	76 748
2210 On a payroll basis	..	..	19 984	34 028	53 765	55 887	62 019	66 491	71 407	76 748
2220 On an income tax basis	..	..	0	0	0	0	0	0	0	0
2300 Self-employed or non-employed	75	317	1 177	2 049	2 860	2 756	2 585	3 122	3 189	3 436
2310 On a payroll basis	..	..	1 177	2 049	2 860	2 756	2 585	3 122	3 189	3 436
2320 On an income tax basis	..	..	0	0	0	0	0	0	0	0
2400 Unallocable between 2100, 2200 and 2300	9	-224	0	0	0	0	0	0	0	0
2410 On a payroll basis	..	..	..	..	..	..	..	..	..	..
2420 On an income tax basis	..	..	..	..	..	..	..	..	..	..
3000 Taxes on payroll and workforce	**0**	**3 498**	**0**	**0**	**0**	**0**	**0**	**0**	**0**	**1 842**
Selective employment tax	..	0	..	..	..	..	..	..	..	..
National insurance surcharge	..	3 498	..	..	..	..	..	..	..	..
Apprenticeship Levy	..	0	..	..	..	..	..	..	..	1 842
4000 Taxes on property	**1 591**	**9 774**	**16 538**	**41 134**	**63 392**	**61 768**	**70 094**	**76 563**	**81 345**	**85 555**
4100 Recurrent taxes on immovable property	1 228	8 665	13 462	30 552	44 891	50 028	55 139	58 185	60 262	62 799
4110 Households	539	3 687	2 373	14 205	23 609	25 919	27 640	29 356	30 598	32 273
Northern Ireland rates paid to CG	..	37	113	141	265	335	409	384	372	362
Council tax	..	0	0	13 991	23 217	25 438	27 061	28 777	30 018	31 693
Rates paid to LA	..	3 650	2 260	73	127	146	170	195	208	218
4120 Others	689	4 978	11 089	16 347	21 282	24 109	27 499	28 829	29 664	30 526
National non-domestic rates	..	0	7 542	14 966	19 358	21 602	24 611	25 834	26 610	27 341
Rates paid to LA	..	4 925	2 869	149	267	497	567	600	629	675
Northern Ireland rates paid to CG	..	53	115	207	353	361	373	398	410	420
London Regional Transport levy	..	0	47	0	0	0	0	0	0	0
LA payments of NNDR	..	0	469	889	1 111	1 236	1 389	1 389	1 389	1 389
NPISH payments of NNDR	..	0	47	136	193	245	342	384	395	430
Crossrail Business rates supplement	..	0	0	0	0	168	217	224	231	271
4200 Recurrent taxes on net wealth	0	0	0	0	0	0	0	0	0	0
4210 Individual	..	..	..	..	..	..	..	..	..	..
4220 Corporate	..	..	..	..	..	..	..	..	..	..
4300 Estate, inheritance and gift taxes	287	479	1 321	2 215	3 867	2 642	3 379	4 442	4 801	5 382
4310 Estate and inheritance taxes	287	479	1 321	2 215	3 867	2 642	3 379	4 442	4 801	5 382
Death duties	..	423	1 278	2 156	3 764	2 592	3 293	4 359	4 703	5 283
Development land tax	..	42	6	0	0	0	0	0	0	0
Taxes on other capital transfers	..	14	37	59	50	50	50	50	50	50
Special tax on bank deposits	..	0	0	0	0	0	0	0	0	0
Betterment duty	..	0	0	0	0	0	0	0	0	0
Special charges	..	0	0	0	0	0	0	0	0	0
Special contribution	..	0	0	0	0	0	0	0	0	0
Equal pay on capital transfers	..	0	0	0	53	0	36	33	48	49
4320 Gift taxes	0	0	0	0	0	0	0	0	0	0
4400 Taxes on financial and capital transactions	76	630	1 755	8 367	14 634	9 098	11 540	13 789	16 023	17 099
Stamp duties	..	630	1 755	8 367	14 634	9 098	11 540	13 789	16 023	17 099
4500 Non-recurrent taxes	0	0	0	0	0	0	36	147	259	275
4510 On net wealth	..	..	..	..	..	..	..	..	..	..

	1965	1980	1990	2000	2007	2010	2013	2015	2016	2017
4520 Other non-recurrent taxes	..	..	..	0	0	0	36	147	259	275
4600 Other recurrent taxes on property	0	0	0	0	0	0	0	0	0	0
5000 Taxes on goods and services	**3 619**	**23 699**	**62 780**	**113 271**	**147 409**	**158 279**	**186 515**	**201 076**	**208 050**	**217 263**
5100 Taxes on production, sale, transfer, etc.	3 406	22 677	59 379	108 288	141 355	150 838	178 932	193 633	200 465	209 481
5110 General taxes	647	11 897	34 136	64 302	92 051	95 946	118 044	129 443	133 856	141 336
5111 Value added taxes	0	11 897	34 136	64 302	92 051	95 946	118 044	129 443	133 856	141 336
Value added tax	..	11 893	33 620	64 202	92 025	95 865	118 234	129 327	133 857	141 590
Adj. to VAT contribution	..	4	516	100	26	81	-190	116	-1	-254
Purchase tax	..	0	0	0	0	0	0	0	0	0
5112 Sales tax	647	0	0	0	0	0	0	0	0	0
5113 Other	0	0	0	0	0	0	0	0	0	0
5120 Taxes on specific goods and services	2 759	10 780	25 243	43 986	49 304	54 892	60 888	64 190	66 609	68 145
5121 Excise duties	2 383	8 616	19 707	37 315	40 427	45 454	46 588	47 294	47 951	48 697
Beer	..	1 029	2 220	2 813	3 042	3 278	3 337	3 294	3 288	3 443
Wines, spirits, cider and perry	..	1 513	2 627	3 751	5 008	6 075	7 063	7 385	7 578	8 151
Tobacco	..	2 735	5 541	7 666	7 862	9 076	9 479	9 190	9 087	9 122
Hydrocarbon oil	..	3 327	9 302	23 041	24 512	27 013	26 697	27 415	27 989	27 973
Other excise duties	..	12	17	0	0	0	0	0	0	0
Sugar levy	..	12	..	44	3	12	12	10	9	8
Soft Drinks Levy	..	..	..	0	0	0	0	0	0	0
5122 Profits of fiscal monopolies	0	0	0	0	0	0	0	0	0	0
5123 Customs and import duties	343	1 109	1 837	286	448	125	128	142	145	145
Custom duties	..	0	0	0	0	0	0	0	0	0
Import duties	..	855	1 722	0	0	0	0	0	0	0
Agricultural levies	..	254	115	286	338	0	0	0	0	0
Temporary charges of import	..	0	0	0	0	0	0	0	0	0
British Transport Police	..	0	0	0	110	125	128	142	145	145
5124 Taxes on exports	0	-1	36	0	0	0	0	0	0	0
Levies on exports	..	-1	36	..	..	..	..	..	..	..
5125 Taxes on investment goods	0	0	0	0	0	0	0	0	0	0
5126 Taxes on specific services	33	456	1 022	5 826	6 523	7 292	11 601	13 620	15 203	15 663
Betting and gaming	..	456	1 022	1 522	959	1 092	1 538	2 053	2 329	2 235
National Lottery contributions to fund	..	0	0	1 590	1 310	1 625	1 644	1 713	1 713	1 713
Air passenger duty	..	0	0	940	1 883	2 094	2 960	3 119	3 150	3 398
Insurance premium tax	..	0	0	1 707	2 306	2 401	3 018	3 294	4 827	5 670
Bank Levy - Stability Fee Scheme	..	0	0	0	0	0	2 352	3 363	3 111	2 568
Light Dues	..	0	0	67	65	80	89	78	73	79
5127 Other taxes on internat. trade and transactions	0	0	0	0	0	0	0	0	0	0
5128 Other taxes	0	600	2 641	559	1 906	2 021	2 571	3 134	3 310	3 640
Fossil fuel levy	..	0	875	56	0	0	0	0	0	0
European coal and steel levy	..	21	11	0	0	0	0	0	0	0
Gas levy	..	12	291	0	0	0	0	0	0	0
Car tax	..	83	1 464	0	0	0	0	0	0	0
Landfill tax	..	484	0	461	877	1 065	1 191	1 028	1 024	904
Climate change levy	..	0	0	0	690	666	1 098	1 752	1 881	1 878
Aggregates levy	..	0	0	0	339	290	282	354	405	375
Hydro benefit	..	0	0	42	0	0	0	0	0	0
Renewable energy obligations	..	0	0	0	0	0	0	0	0	0
Channel 4 advertising formula	..	0	0	0	0	0	0	0	0	0
Milk super levy	..	0	0	0	0	0	0	0	0	0
Contracts for Difference	..	0	0	0	0	0	0	0	0	483
5130 Unallocable between 5110 and 5120	0	0	0	0	0	0	0	0	0	0
5200 Taxes on use of goods and perform activities	212	1 378	3 401	4 983	6 054	7 441	7 583	7 443	7 585	7 782
5210 Recurrent taxes	212	1 378	3 401	4 983	6 054	7 441	7 583	7 443	7 585	7 719
5211 Paid by households: motor vehicles	118	729	1 841	2 996	4 096	4 561	4 312	3 823	3 784	4 012
Motor vehicle duty	..	726	1 837	2 992	4 096	4 561	4 312	3 823	3 784	4 012
Boat licences	..	3	4	4	0	0	0	0	0	0
5212 Paid by others: motor vehicles	74	588	1 134	1 614	1 288	1 279	1 789	2 076	2 205	2 214
Motor vehicle levy	..	588	1 134	1 614	1 288	1 279	1 789	2 076	2 205	2 214
5213 Paid in respect of other goods	20	61	426	373	670	1 601	1 482	1 544	1 596	1 493
IBA levy	..	..	134	0	0	0	0	0	0	0
Telecommunications regulator fees	..	..	7	12	17	12	0	0	0	0
Gas regulator fees	..	..	2	0	0	0	0	0	0	0
Electricity regulator fees	..	..	5	0	0	0	0	0	0	0
Water regulator fees	..	..	6	11	11	12	24	27	24	24
Rail regulator fees	..	..	0	14	12	12	12	12	12	12
Company registration surplus fees	..	..	12	0	0	0	0	0	0	0
Consumer and credit act fees	..	..	163	119	281	480	480	480	480	480
Levy funded bodies	..	..	97	217	349	1 040	922	970	1 019	915
1936 Tithe Act payments	..	..	0	0	0	0	0	0	0	0
Recurrent taxes paid in respect of other goods	..	..	0	0	0	45	44	55	61	62

	1965	1980	1990	2000	2007	2010	2013	2015	2016	2017
5220 Non-recurrent taxes	0	0	0	0	0	0	0	0	0	63
Immigration Skills Charge	..	..	..	..	..	..	..	..	..	63
5300 Unallocable between 5100 and 5200	1	-356	0	0	0	0	0	0	0	0
6000 Other taxes	**0**	**0**	**9 017**	**0**	**0**	**0**	**0**	**0**	**0**	**0**
6100 Paid solely by business	..	..	0	..	..	..	..	..	..	..
6200 Other	..	..	9 017	..	..	..	..	..	..	..
Community charge	..	..	9 017	..	..	..	..	..	..	..
Custom duties collected for the EU	**..**	**..**	**..**	**1 800**	**2 074**	**2 933**	**2 914**	**3 077**	**3 318**	**3 419**
Non-wastable tax credits										
Non-wastable tax credits against 1110	..	..	7 454	4 651	20 031	28 880	29 710	28 539	27 430	25 940
Tax expenditure component	..	..	6 973	1 233	4 414	5 542	2 538	2 571	2 471	2 336
Transfer component	..	..	481	3 418	15 617	23 338	27 172	25 968	24 959	23 604
Non-wastable tax credits against 1210	..	..	0	1	762	1 260	1 470	2 226	2 652	3 574
Tax expenditure component	..	..	..	0	549	947	979	800	919	1 192
Transfer component	..	..	..	1	213	313	491	1 426	1 733	2 382
Total tax revenue on cash basis	**10 945**	**81 153**	**202 400**	**355 355**	**507 907**	**507 888**	**559 762**	**599 136**	**632 643**	**667 362**
Total tax revenue on accrual basis	**..**	**..**	**202 368**	**358 654**	**508 148**	**514 132**	**567 150**	**609 653**	**644 555**	**681 855**
Conciliation with National Accounts										
Additional taxes included in National Accounts	..	..	1 323	2 062	4 072	4 731	5 816	7 261	8 082	8 861
Taxes excluded from National Accounts	..	..	0	0	0	0	0	0	0	0
Difference in treatment of tax credits	..	..	6 973	1 233	4 963	6 489	3 517	3 371	3 390	3 528
Capital transfer for uncollected revenue	..	..	0	0	0	0	0	0	0	0
Voluntary social security contributions	..	..	3 288	8 103	18 629	21 217	22 438	25 025	25 903	26 678
Miscellaneous differences	..	..	0	0	0	0	0	0	0	0
National Accounts: Taxes and actual social contributions	..	..	213 952	370 052	535 812	546 569	598 921	645 310	681 930	720 147
Imputed social contributions	..	..	3 966	4 192	1 360	1 530	1 293	1 563	1 622	1 199
National Accounts: Taxes and all social contributions	..	..	217 918	374 244	537 172	548 099	600 214	646 873	683 552	721 346

.. Not available

Note: Year ending 31st December.

From 1990 data are on accrual basis.

Corporate income tax revenues for the United Kingdom are based on data provided in July; this was prior to revisions made to the historic Corporation tax data in September, so the revisions are not reflected here. For the latest UK Corporation tax data, please see www.gov.uk/government/statistics/corporation-tax-statistics-2019 the main revisions are explained on page 13 of https://assets.publishing.service.gov.uk/government/uploads/system/uploads/attachment_data/file/833371/Aug19_Receipts_NS_Bulletin_Final.odt.

Heading 1210: The corporate tax figures include company income tax from 1990 onwards.

Heading 2000: Includes some voluntary contributions which cannot be separately identified.

Heading 6200: The community charge replaced domestic rates in Scotland in April 1989 and was extended to England and Wales in April 1990. This tax has been classified in heading 6200 as it is a lump-sum tax levied on each adult in a household (domestic rates are classified in heading 4100). Headings for non-wastable tax credits 1110 and 1210 are consistent with the guidelines, and the figures in the data are treated accordingly. The following method is adopted separately for Working Families 'Tax Credit and Disabled Persons Tax Credit' paid from 1999 to 2003. For each calendar, a random sample of awards over-lapping the quarter is taken. Each recipient family's income tax liability for the fiscal year within which the quarter falls is calculated , based on the earned income reported for the award (uprated to the middle of the overlap period). And the result multiplied by the number of days in the overlap period divided by 365. The tax expenditure component is defined as the minimum of this amount and the total amount of award paid in the overlap period. The total amount of award paid and the tax expenditure component are each summed over the sample cases, and the ratio is taken as the tax expenditure ration for the quarter. From 2003, the equivalent breakdown for Child and Working tax credits is based on household survey data. Survey data is used to estimate the breakdown into the tax expenditure and the transfer components for the other smaller tax credits.

Source: National Income and Expenditure; Central Statistical Office; Annual reports of Her Majesty's Revenue and Customs.

StatLink https://doi.org/10.1787/888934057381

Table 5.36. United States: Detailed country table, 1965-2017

Million USD

	1965	1980	1990	2000	2007	2010	2013	2015	2016	2017
Total tax revenue	**167 022**	**730 672**	**1 552 413**	**2 900 519**	**3 868 612**	**3 517 144**	**4 291 752**	**4 765 481**	**4 841 950**	**5 227 338**
1000 Taxes on income, profits and capital gains	**80 284**	**364 137**	**701 731**	**1 453 865**	**1 865 205**	**1 488 699**	**2 016 390**	**2 311 432**	**2 325 796**	**2 363 093**
1100 Of individuals	52 894	285 513	584 733	1 224 538	1 479 085	1 223 218	1 664 074	1 925 528	1 944 820	2 025 518
1110 On income and profits	50 401	272 879	552 859	1 088 967	1 326 736	1 163 737	1 556 113	1 750 034	1 805 073	1 826 591
Individual income tax federal	46 492	233 269	449 239	895 677	1 062 755	910 874	1 235 275	1 409 861	1 456 929	1 477 863
Individual income tax state and local govt.	3 909	39 610	103 620	193 290	263 981	252 863	320 838	340 173	348 144	348 727
1120 On capital gains	2 493	12 634	31 874	135 571	152 349	59 481	107 961	175 494	139 747	198 927
Capital gains federal	2 300	10 800	25 900	111 507	122 036	46 557	85 702	141 381	112 794	160 949
Capital gains tax state and local govt.	193	1 834	5 974	24 064	30 313	12 924	22 259	34 113	26 953	37 979
1200 Corporate	27 390	78 624	116 998	229 327	386 119	265 481	352 316	385 904	380 976	337 575
1210 On profits	26 745	73 586	106 134	170 835	330 597	239 340	313 172	338 390	330 632	293 228
Corporate income tax federal	24 861	60 525	85 736	144 590	281 040	197 785	265 274	289 021	283 877	247 250
Corporate income tax state and local govt.	1 884	13 061	20 398	26 245	49 556	41 555	47 898	49 369	46 755	45 978
1220 On capital gains	645	5 038	10 864	58 492	55 523	26 141	39 144	47 514	50 344	44 347
Capital gains tax corp. federal	600	4 143	8 776	49 506	47 200	21 602	33 157	40 582	43 225	37 393
Capital gains tax corp. state and local govt.	45	895	2 088	8 986	8 323	4 539	5 987	6 932	7 119	6 954
1300 Unallocable between 1100 and 1200	0	0	0	0	0	0	0	0	0	0
2000 Social security contributions	**22 192**	**159 763**	**396 972**	**683 104**	**907 357**	**917 409**	**1 030 099**	**1 126 111**	**1 153 645**	**1 204 453**
2100 Employees	8 459	67 022	173 860	305 555	400 941	406 404	456 777	502 663	517 031	542 924
Federal insurance contribution Act tax	8 084	66 221	..	..	..	..	..	..	..	..
Less refund federal	-192	-507	..	..	..	..	..	..	..	..
Railroad retirement taxes federal	322	590	..	..	..	..	..	..	..	..
Fed. hosp. insur. recpts from railroad retir.	0	111	..	..	..	..	..	..	..	..
Unemployment state tax federal	20	127	..	..	..	..	..	..	..	..
Temp. disability insurance state and local	225	480	..	..	..	..	..	..	..	..
2110 On a payroll basis	..	..	..	..	..	..	..	..	..	..
2120 On an income tax basis	..	..	..	..	..	..	..	..	..	..
2200 Employers	12 703	87 019	204 102	343 184	456 602	461 702	519 064	562 307	574 322	598 241
Federal insurance contributions act tax	7 802	64 768	..	..	..	..	..	..	..	..
Railroad retirement taxes federal	314	1 722	..	..	..	..	..	..	..	..
Fed. hosp. insur. recpts from railroad retir.	0	111	..	..	..	..	..	..	..	..
Military service credit federal	14	652	..	..	..	..	..	..	..	..
Old-age dis. hosp. insur. fed. employer contr.	282	1 453	..	..	..	..	..	..	..	..
Unemployment state tax federal	3 032	11 788	..	..	..	..	..	..	..	..
Federal unemployment tax Act	615	3 246	..	..	..	..	..	..	..	..
Railroad unempl. insurance Act tax federal	152	175	..	..	..	..	..	..	..	..
Workmen's compensation state and local	484	3 039	..	..	..	..	..	..	..	..
Temp. disability insurance state and local	8	65	..	..	..	..	..	..	..	..
2210 On a payroll basis	..	..	..	..	..	..	..	..	..	..
2220 On an income tax basis	..	..	..	..	..	..	..	..	..	..
2300 Self-employed or non-employed	1 030	5 722	19 010	34 365	49 814	49 303	54 258	61 141	62 292	63 288
Federal old-age survivors trust	0	4 250	..	..	..	..	..	..	..	..
Federal disability insurance trust	1 030	733	..	..	..	..	..	..	..	..
Federal hospital insurance trust	0	739	..	..	..	..	..	..	..	..
2310 On a payroll basis	..	..	..	..	..	..	..	..	..	..
2320 On an income tax basis	..	..	..	..	..	..	..	..	..	..
2400 Unallocable between 2100, 2200 and 2300	0	0	0	0	0	0	0	0	0	0
2410 On a payroll basis	..	..	..	..	..	..	..	..	..	..
2420 On an income tax basis	..	..	..	..	..	..	..	..	..	..
3000 Taxes on payroll and workforce	**0**	**0**	**0**	**0**	**285**	**2 285**	**1 591**	**1 745**	**1 876**	**2 050**
4000 Taxes on property	**26 529**	**77 913**	**182 408**	**299 546**	**463 052**	**473 422**	**503 220**	**536 146**	**559 055**	**837 718**
4100 Recurrent taxes on immovable property	22 918	68 499	161 533	254 669	403 688	438 588	456 790	487 751	508 386	532 221
4110 Households	8 548	28 975	..	..	..	..	..	..	..	..
Property tax state and local	8 548	28 975	..	..	..	..	..	..	..	..
Other	0	0	..	..	..	..	..	..	..	..
4120 Others	14 370	39 524	..	..	..	..	..	..	..	..
Property tax state and local	14 370	39 524	..	..	..	..	..	..	..	..
Other	0	0	..	..	..	..	..	..	..	..
4200 Recurrent taxes on net wealth	0	0	0	0	0	0	0	0	0	0
4210 Individual	..	..	..	..	..	..	..	..	..	..
4220 Corporate	..	..	..	..	..	..	..	..	..	..
4300 Estate, inheritance and gift taxes	3 447	8 425	15 755	35 640	31 927	19 699	26 178	25 394	25 298	28 118
4310 Estate and inheritance taxes	3 080	8 149	..	..	..	..	..	..	..	..
Estate tax less refund federal	2 427	6 181	..	..	..	..	..	..	..	..
Estate tax state and local govt.	653	1 968	..	..	..	..	..	..	..	..
4320 Gift taxes	367	276	..	..	..	..	..	..	..	..
Gift tax less refund federal	289	209	..	..	..	..	..	..	..	..
Gift tax calculate state and local govt.	78	67	..	..	..	..	..	..	..	..

	1965	1980	1990	2000	2007	2010	2013	2015	2016	2017
4400 Taxes on financial and capital transactions	164	989	2 148	4 389	20 503	7 460	12 171	14 549	16 499	18 159
Interest equalisation tax federal	15	0	..	..	..	..	..	..	..	..
Document and stock transfer state and local	149	989	2 148	4 389	20 503	7 460	12 171	14 549	16 499	18 159
4500 Non-recurrent taxes	0	0	0	0	0	0	0	0	0	250 000
4510 On net wealth	..	..	..	..	..	..	..	..	..	250 000
4520 Other non-recurrent taxes	..	..	..	..	..	..	..	..	..	..
4600 Other recurrent taxes on property	0	0	2 972	4 848	6 934	7 675	8 081	8 452	8 872	9 220
5000 Taxes on goods and services	**38 017**	**128 844**	**271 301**	**464 004**	**632 713**	**635 329**	**740 452**	**790 048**	**801 578**	**820 024**
5100 Taxes on production, sale, transfer, etc.	33 300	111 810	235 233	404 093	540 291	546 710	640 249	693 108	703 852	717 817
5110 General taxes	8 016	51 328	125 575	221 358	301 403	295 123	343 853	372 261	380 932	395 700
5111 Value added taxes	0	0	0	0	0	0	0	0	0	0
5112 Sales tax	8 016	51 328	125 575	221 358	301 403	295 123	343 853	372 261	380 932	395 700
General sales - general receipts state and local	7 981	51 328	125 575	221 358	301 403	295 123	343 853	372 261	380 932	395 700
Other state and local	35	0	0	0	0	0	0	0	0	0
5113 Other	0	0	0	0	0	0	0	0	0	0
5120 Taxes on specific goods and services	25 284	60 482	109 658	182 735	238 888	251 587	296 396	320 847	322 920	322 117
5121 Excise duties	21 209	45 471	64 953	108 600	137 373	146 582	154 390	156 747	158 927	160 858
Alcohol taxes federal govt.	3 689	5 601	5 228	7 281	8 571	8 848	9 026	9 515	9 827	9 985
Tobacco taxes federal govt.	2 142	2 443	4 217	6 741	8 377	17 487	15 830	14 266	13 914	13 629
Airport, airway, highway federal	3 559	6 411	0	0	0	0	0	0	0	0
Manufacturer's excise taxes federal govt.	2 867	6 122	0	0	0	0	0	0	0	0
Sugar tax federal govt.	97	0	0	0	0	0	0	0	0	0
Other taxes excise federal govt.	889	2	0	0	0	0	0	0	0	0
Undistributed tax deposits federal government	-11	152	0	0	0	0	0	0	0	0
Other taxes excise and undist. fed.govt. -	0	0	13 316	32 005	31 747	26 913	33 746	35 288	36 052	36 608
Less special tax liquor occupations federal	-22	-21	0	0	0	0	0	0	0	0
Other federal (refunds)	-7	-32	0	0	0	0	0	0	0	0
Alcohol taxes state and local govt.	949	2 642	3 577	4 485	5 684	6 197	6 706	7 142	7 180	7 359
Tobacco taxes state and local govt.	1 386	3 874	6 009	8 726	16 433	18 611	18 464	17 977	18 514	19 128
Public utilities state and local govt.	871	5 888	11 814	17 989	27 879	28 892	28 544	27 878	27 714	27 114
Motor fuel taxes state and local govt.	4 331	9 822	20 792	31 373	38 682	39 634	42 074	44 681	45 726	47 035
Other state and local taxes	469	2 295	0	0	0	0	0	0	0	0
Coal tonnage tax federal govt.	0	272	0	0	0	0	0	0	0	0
Hazardous substances tax federal	0	0	0	0	0	0	0	0	0	0
Transportation fuels tax federal	0	0	0	0	0	0	0	0	0	0
Boat fuels and equipment tax federal	0	0	0	0	0	0	0	0	0	0
Waste site deposits tax federal	0	0	0	0	0	0	0	0	0	0
Leaking underground storage federal	0	0	0	0	0	0	0	0	0	0
Vaccine injury compens. federal	0	0	0	0	0	0	0	0	0	0
Ozone depletion tax federal	0	0	0	0	0	0	0	0	0	0
Oil spill liability federal	0	0	0	0	0	0	0	0	0	0
Luxury tax federal govt.	0	0	0	0	0	0	0	0	0	0
5122 Profits of fiscal monopolies	275	608	..	..	..	..	..	..	..	..
Liquor store revenue state and local govt.	1 447	3 200	..	..	..	..	..	..	..	..
Liquor store expend. state and local govt.	-1 172	-2 592	..	..	..	..	..	..	..	..
5123 Customs and import duties	1 442	7 436	17 490	21 123	28 793	28 603	35 468	38 146	37 558	38 539
Custom duties federal	1 442	7 436	17 490	21 123	28 793	28 603	35 468	38 146	37 558	38 539
Petroleum import fees federal govt.	0	0	0	0	0	0	0	0	0	0
5124 Taxes on exports	0	0	0	0	0	0	0	0	0	0
5125 Taxes on investment goods	0	0	0	0	0	0	0	0	0	0
5126 Taxes on specific services	2 358	6 967	8 895	13 857	23 639	23 642	26 899	30 187	32 027	33 865
Amusements state and local govt.	23	234	671	3 668	7 105	7 082	7 784	8 188	8 367	8 540
Parimutuels state and local govt.	386	731	659	326	328	206	193	189	189	185
Transportation of persons federal	126	1 601	0	0	0	0	0	0	0	0
Transport of property	0	92	0	0	0	0	0	0	0	0
General and toll telephone federal	1 079	1 118	0	0	0	0	0	0	0	0
Foreign insurance policies federal	0	75	0	0	0	0	0	0	0	0
Insurance state and local govt.	744	3 113	7 565	9 863	16 206	16 354	18 922	21 810	23 471	25 140
Employee pension plans federal	0	3	0	0	0	0	0	0	0	0
Inland waterway tax federal	0	0	0	0	0	0	0	0	0	0
Ship departure tax federal	0	0	0	0	0	0	0	0	0	0
5127 Other taxes on internat. trade and transactions	0	0	0	0	0	0	0	0	0	0
5128 Other taxes	0	0	18 320	39 155	49 083	52 760	79 639	95 767	94 408	88 855
5130 Unallocable between 5110 and 5120	0	0	0	0	0	0	0	0	0	0
5200 Taxes on use of goods and perform activities	4 717	17 034	36 068	59 910	92 422	88 619	100 203	96 940	97 726	102 207
5210 Recurrent taxes	3 490	9 501	21 262	37 114	68 547	66 440	70 557	74 600	76 878	79 388
5211 Paid by households: motor vehicles	1 211	3 370	8 104	11 409	14 996	16 294	17 781	18 767	19 257	19 726
Motor vehicle regis. license st. and loc.	1 056	2 981	..	..	..	..	..	..	..	..
Motor vehicle oper. license st. and loc.	152	389	..	..	..	..	..	..	..	..
Other motor vehicle	3	0	..	..	..	..	..	..	..	..

	1965	1980	1990	2000	2007	2010	2013	2015	2016	2017
5212 Paid by others: motor vehicles	937	2 343	3 564	6 688	8 484	9 108	10 071	10 661	11 000	11 303
Motor vehicle regis. license st. and loc.	937	2 343	..	..	..	..	..	..	..	..
Motor vehicle oper. license st. and loc.	0	0	..	..	..	..	..	..	..	..
5213 Paid in respect of other goods	1 342	3 788	9 594	19 017	45 067	41 038	42 705	45 172	46 621	48 359
Misc. fees permit license federal	19	0	0	0	0	0	0	0	0	0
Special tax liquor occupations federal	22	21	0	0	0	0	0	0	0	0
Use tax of certain vehicles federal	99	277	0	0	0	0	0	0	0	0
Use of internat. travel facilities federal	0	92	0	0	0	0	0	0	0	0
Use tax of aircraft federal	0	21	0	0	0	0	0	0	0	0
Corporation in general license st. and loc.	528	1 388	3 147	6 736	10 658	9 473	7 560	6 560	6 702	6 790
Alcoholic beverage license tax st. and loc.	133	179	264	308	608	596	899	819	831	877
Public utilities license tax st. and loc.	30	130	270	395	1 903	1 468	1 432	1 647	1 783	1 905
Amusements license taxes st. and loc.	7	69	202	196	966	638	604	763	672	697
Occupation and business license st. and loc.	349	1 113	3 512	7 651	16 484	17 812	19 284	20 449	21 103	21 600
Wagering occupation tax federal	7	12	0	0	0	0	0	0	0	0
Other license taxes st. and loc.	10	69	229	521	8 939	6 606	8 211	9 338	9 995	10 769
Hunting and fishing license taxes st. and loc.	138	417	82	112	146	151	155	161	160	161
Other	0	0	0	0	0	0	0	0	0	0
5220 Non-recurrent taxes	1 227	7 533	14 806	22 796	23 875	22 179	29 645	22 340	20 848	22 819
Severance state and local govt.	503	4 167	5 224	5 285	12 895	11 751	18 266	9 621	7 395	8 758
Poll taxes state and local govt.	9	0	0	0	0	0	0	0	0	0
Other taxes state and local govt.	715	3 366	9 582	17 511	10 980	10 428	11 379	12 719	13 453	14 061
5300 Unallocable between 5100 and 5200	0	0	0	0	0	0	0	0	0	0
6000 Other taxes	**0**	**15**	**0**	**0**	**0**	**0**	**0**	**0**	**0**	**0**
6100 Paid solely by business	..	0	..	..	..	..	..	..	..	..
6200 Other	..	15	..	..	..	..	..	..	..	..
Non-wastable tax credits										
Non-wastable tax credits against 1110	..	..	6 155	36 511	90 439	171 630	158 160	156 656	165 120	176 520
Tax expenditure component	..	..	1 800	9 602	35 910	69 870	41 560	42 826	44 110	48 950
Transfer component	..	..	4 355	26 909	54 529	101 760	116 600	113 830	121 010	127 570
Non-wastable tax credits against 1210	..	..	..	..	..	250	630	577	510	470
Tax expenditure component	..	..	..	..	..	240	610	527	450	410
Transfer component	..	..	..	..	..	10	20	50	60	60
Unallocable transfer component	..	..	..	..	..	2 420	4 280	4 890	4 350	4 740
Total tax revenue on cash basis	**167 022**	**730 672**	**..**	**..**	**3 842 190**	**3 380 068**	**4 156 852**	**4 702 756**	**4 757 319**	**4 882 711**
Total tax revenue on accrual basis	**..**	**..**	**1 552 413**	**2 900 519**	**3 868 612**	**3 517 144**	**4 291 752**	**4 765 481**	**4 841 950**	**5 227 338**
Conciliation with National Accounts										
Additional taxes included in National Accounts	..	..	..	..	..	..	..	..	..	..
Taxes excluded from National Accounts	..	..	..	..	..	..	..	..	..	..
Difference in treatment of tax credits	..	..	..	..	..	..	..	..	..	..
Capital transfer for uncollected revenue	..	..	..	..	..	..	..	..	..	..
Voluntary social security contributions	..	..	11 719	22 562	51 635	61 833	69 903	74 886	82 208	90 166
Miscellaneous differences	..	..	..	..	..	..	..	..	..	..
National Accounts: Taxes and actual social contributions	..	..	1 564 132	2 923 081	3 920 247	3 578 977	4 361 655	4 840 367	4 924 158	5 317 504
Imputed social contributions	..	..	3 384	3 727	7 134	9 428	9 438	9 570	9 153	9 147
National Accounts: Taxes and all social contributions	..	..	1 567 516	2 926 808	3 927 381	3 588 405	4 371 093	4 849 937	4 933 311	5 326 651

.. Not available

Note: From 1990, data are on a year ending 31st December basis. For years up to and including 1976 the dated covered fiscal years ending 30th June. Between 1977 and 1989, Federal government data covered fiscal years ending 30th September and State & Local government data covered fiscal years ending 30th June.

From 1990, data are on accrual basis. There are no separate estimates for the State and Local capital gains tax revenues.

Heading 5121: In 1994 through 1996, some Federal excise taxes formerly shown separately were included in 'Other taxes,excises and undistributed, Federal government'.

Source: Federal estimates are derived from the US Budget, the Final Monthly Treasury Statement and the Annual Report of the US Treasury Department. The State and Local estimates are derived from Government Finances, published by the Bureau of the Census.

StatLink https://doi.org/10.1787/888934057400

5.2. Memorandum tables

Table 5.37 shows different sources for financing social benefits, beyond compulsory social security contributions reported in section 5.1. In addition, this table shows also data on other taxes, on voluntary contributions to government and on compulsory contributions to private sector.

Table 5.38 shows social security contributions and payroll taxes paid by government. During the revision of the Interpretative Guide in 1984, the question arose of how to treat taxes paid by government. The two most prominent examples of such taxes are social security contributions and payroll taxes paid by government in respect of its employees. After a long discussion it was decided that the data shown in this publication should continue to include taxes paid by government (see §5 of the Interpretative Guide in annex A).

Whilst it was recognised that for certain purposes (e.g. to show the cash flow to the government sector from the private sector) it would be appropriate to eliminate taxes paid by one sector of government to another or tax payments between different units of the same sector of government, the view was taken that to record tax flows in the context of the economy as a whole required that taxes paid by government should be included in the data. This treatment ensures that the different resource flows of an economy, including the calculation of the output of government, are measured consistently in after-tax units. Nevertheless, it was decided that data on identifiable taxes paid by government should be separately identified in a memorandum item and this is the purpose of the country tables which follow.

The data that are reproduced in the following tables refer to actual compulsory payments made by general government in respect of their employees. Fictive, voluntary and imputed contributions are excluded from these data. The definitions of social security contributions, payroll taxes and general government are those set out in §35 to §41, §42 and §3 to §4 of the Interpretative Guide. Information on the other taxes paid by government (namely property taxes and consumption taxes) is not available in most countries, although it is believed that in all countries taxes based upon payroll are the most important taxes paid by government. In many cases, the data are estimates and are not always constructed on a basis consistent with that used in the main tables.

Table 5.37. Financing social benefits

Memorandum item on the financing of social security benefits

	1965	1980	1990	2000	2007	2010	2013	2015	2016	2017
Australia, million AUD										
Contribution under 2000 heading	..	..	..	..	..	..	..	..	..	..
Other taxes	..	..	..	..	..	..	..	..	..	..
Voluntary contributions to government	..	..	..	..	..	..	..	..	..	..
Compulsory contributions to private sector	..	..	..	..	..	..	..	..	..	..
Total	**0**	**0**	**0**	**0**	**0**	**0**	**0**	**0**	**0**	**0**
Austria, million EUR										
Contribution under 2000 heading	1 548	9 200	17 763	30 510	38 453	41 423	46 845	49 867	51 827	53 917
Other taxes	0	0	0	0	0	0	0	0	0	0
Voluntary contributions to government	32	135	141	206	256	339	299	321	321	318
Compulsory contributions to private sector	0	0	0	0	0	0	0	0	0	0
Total	**1 580**	**9 335**	**17 904**	**30 716**	**38 709**	**41 762**	**47 144**	**50 188**	**52 148**	**54 235**
Belgium, million EUR										
Contribution under 2000 heading	2 018	10 798	23 386	34 636	45 659	50 447	56 355	58 628	57 931	59 594
Other taxes	0	171	644	5 375	13 659	16 772	18 390	12 347	13 041	16 920
Voluntary contributions to government	0	41	52	54	55	62	74	72	72	73
Compulsory contributions to private sector	0	0	0	0	0	0	0	0	0	0
Total	**2 018**	**11 009**	**24 082**	**40 065**	**59 372**	**67 281**	**74 819**	**71 046**	**71 044**	**76 587**
Canada, million CAD										
Contribution under 2000 heading	854	10 649	29 653	53 109	73 722	76 787	90 394	96 371	98 954	99 346
Other taxes	1 199	0	0	0	0	0	0	0	0	0
Voluntary contributions to government	0	0	0	0	0	0	0	0	0	0
Compulsory contributions to private sector	0	0	0	0	0	0	0	0	0	0
Total	**2 053**	**10 649**	**29 653**	**53 109**	**73 722**	**76 787**	**90 394**	**96 371**	**98 954**	**99 346**
Chile, million CLP										
Contribution under 2000 heading	..	..	159 559	576 758	1 148 647	1 493 987	1 968 973	2 252 489	2 441 419	2 627 558
Other taxes	..	..	0	0	0	0	0	0	0	0
Voluntary contributions to government	..	..	0	0	0	0	0	0	0	0
Compulsory contributions to private sector	..	..	328 102	2 021 631	3 808 658	5 408 703	7 583 251	8 914 415	9 648 757	10 263 722
Total	**..**	**..**	**487 661**	**2 598 389**	**4 957 305**	**6 902 690**	**9 552 224**	**11 166 904**	**12 090 176**	**12 891 280**
Czech Republic, million CZK										
Contribution under 2000 heading	..	..	..	341 544	573 417	576 029	603 072	659 743	699 604	757 183
Other taxes	..	..	..	0	0	0	0	0	0	0
Voluntary contributions to government	..	..	..	1 099	974	661	337	386	418	463
Compulsory contributions to private sector	..	..	..	2 837	5 757	6 094	6 424	6 741	7 109	7 585
Total	**..**	**..**	**..**	**345 480**	**580 148**	**582 784**	**609 833**	**666 871**	**707 132**	**765 231**
Denmark, million DKK										
Contribution under 2000 heading	690	710	101	8 453	1 286	1 815	1 618	1 378	1 197	1 060
Other taxes	0	0	0	0	0	0	0	0	0	0
Voluntary contributions to government	0	1 673	8 087	16 633	17 061	17 192	14 655	14 721	14 833	14 891
Compulsory contributions to private sector	145	554	1 278	1 445	4 526	3 847	3 068	2 964	2 822	2 779
Total	**835**	**2 937**	**9 466**	**26 531**	**22 873**	**22 854**	**19 341**	**19 063**	**18 852**	**18 730**
Estonia, million EUR										
Contribution under 2000 heading	..	..	..	674	1 683	1 879	2 077	2 290	2 429	2 636
Other taxes	..	..	..	0	0	0	0	0	0	0
Voluntary contributions to government	..	..	..	0	0	0	0	0	0	0
Compulsory contributions to private sector	..	..	..	1	341	38	268	389	412	429
Total	**..**	**..**	**..**	**674**	**2 024**	**1 918**	**2 346**	**2 679**	**2 841**	**3 065**
Finland, million EUR										
Contribution under 2000 heading	93	2 776	10 012	15 756	21 384	22 648	25 632	26 639	27 641	27 000
Other taxes	47	22	0	404	0	0	0	0	0	0
Voluntary contributions to government	0	262	632	236	228	254	270	303	308	302
Compulsory contributions to private sector	0	123	426	508	631	577	668	645	613	597
Total	**140**	**3 183**	**11 070**	**16 904**	**22 243**	**23 479**	**26 570**	**27 587**	**28 562**	**27 899**

	1965	1980	1990	2000	2007	2010	2013	2015	2016	2017
France, million EUR										
Contribution under 2000 heading	8 804	76 235	191 141	231 875	307 663	323 816	356 934	370 375	375 441	387 443
Other taxes	0	895	2 950	81 001	127 511	137 383	162 838	170 210	171 620	176 209
Voluntary contributions to government	0	0	0	0	0	0	0	0	0	0
Compulsory contributions to private sector	0	0	0	0	0	0	0	0	0	0
Total	**8 804**	**77 130**	**194 091**	**312 876**	**435 174**	**461 199**	**519 772**	**540 585**	**547 061**	**563 652**
Germany, million EUR										
Contribution under 2000 heading	19 876	98 659	170 449	299 440	320 594	353 955	392 295	424 633	445 013	466 470
Other taxes	0	0	0	0	0	0	0	0	0	0
Voluntary contributions to government	1 946	8 441	13 002	23 329	20 930	6 442	7 354	8 226	8 781	9 324
Compulsory contributions to private sector	107	690	1 462	6 120	8 243	9 386	10 444	11 202	11 615	11 699
Total	**21 929**	**107 791**	**184 914**	**328 889**	**349 767**	**369 783**	**410 093**	**444 061**	**465 409**	**487 493**
Greece, million EUR										
Contribution under 2000 heading	37	485	3 466	14 284	24 940	24 748	19 354	18 807	19 313	20 746
Other taxes	8	0	0	0	0	0	0	0	0	0
Voluntary contributions to government	0	0	0	0	0	0	0	0	0	0
Compulsory contributions to private sector	0	0	0	0	0	0	0	0	0	0
Total	**44**	**485**	**3 466**	**14 284**	**24 940**	**24 748**	**19 354**	**18 807**	**19 313**	**20 746**
Hungary, million HUF										
Contribution under 2000 heading	..	..	..	1 506 755	3 402 194	3 184 209	3 745 638	4 293 731	4 613 936	4 704 101
Other taxes	..	..	..	188 413	85 058	74 035	245 746	293 773	317 075	316 775
Voluntary contributions to government	..	..	..	1 273	1 762	1 585	1 503	1 229	1 235	1 163
Compulsory contributions to private sector	..	..	..	62 836	190 331	279 814	0	0	0	0
Total	**..**	**..**	**..**	**1 759 277**	**3 679 344**	**3 539 643**	**3 992 887**	**4 588 733**	**4 932 246**	**5 022 039**
Iceland, million ISK										
Contribution under 2000 heading	5	102	3 607	19 680	39 594	63 599	69 899	79 707	85 370	89 649
Other taxes	0	1 047	20 571	26 732	52 444	77 472	90 895	97 987	108 570	133 273
Voluntary contributions to government	0	0	0	0	0	0	0	0	0	0
Compulsory contributions to private sector	0	459	13 454	48 847	118 117	95 438	117 903	139 792	277 894	243 733
Total	**5**	**1 608**	**37 632**	**95 260**	**210 155**	**236 509**	**278 697**	**317 486**	**471 834**	**466 655**
Ireland, million EUR										
Contribution under 2000 heading	21	578	1 729	3 947	8 126	8 442	9 019	10 218	10 717	11 439
Other taxes	0	0	0	0	0	0	0	0	0	0
Voluntary contributions to government	0	0	0	0	0	0	0	0	0	0
Compulsory contributions to private sector	0	0	0	0	0	0	0	0	0	0
Total	**21**	**578**	**1 729**	**3 947**	**8 126**	**8 442**	**9 019**	**10 218**	**10 717**	**11 439**
Israel, million ILS										
Contribution under 2000 heading	..	..	..	27 565	37 909	45 343	53 364	59 561	63 452	66 783
Other taxes	..	..	..	0	0	0	0	0	0	0
Voluntary contributions to government	..	..	..	0	0	0	0	0	0	0
Compulsory contributions to private sector	..	..	..	0	0	9 100	22 400	28 700	30 700	34 000
Total	**..**	**..**	**..**	**27 565**	**37 909**	**54 443**	**75 764**	**88 261**	**94 152**	**100 783**
Italy, million EUR										
Contribution under 2000 heading	1 881	22 976	87 256	143 629	200 772	209 122	210 462	214 376	215 856	220 622
Other taxes	0	0	0	0	0	0	0	0	0	0
Voluntary contributions to government	0	0	0	464	567	561	738	750	780	783
Compulsory contributions to private sector	0	0	0	0	0	0	0	0	0	0
Total	**1 881**	**22 976**	**87 256**	**144 093**	**201 339**	**209 683**	**211 200**	**215 126**	**216 636**	**221 405**
Japan, billion JPY										
Contribution under 2000 heading	1 344	18 178	34 613	47 968	53 325	54 461	59 803	64 465	66 614	68 562
Other taxes	0	0	0	0	0	0	0	0	0	0
Voluntary contributions to government	0	0	0	0	0	0	0	0	0	0
Compulsory contributions to private sector	0	0	0	0	0	0	0	0	0	0
Total	**1 344**	**18 178**	**34 613**	**47 968**	**53 325**	**54 461**	**59 803**	**64 465**	**66 614**	**68 562**
Korea, billion KRW										
Contribution under 2000 heading	..	73	3 760	22 759	53 588	69 090	91 596	104 693	112 658	119 676
Other taxes	..	0	0	0	0	0	0	0	0	0
Voluntary contributions to government	..	0	0	0	0	0	0	0	0	0
Compulsory contributions to private sector	..	0	0	0	0	0	0	0	0	0
Total	**..**	**73**	**3 760**	**22 759**	**53 588**	**69 090**	**91 596**	**104 693**	**112 658**	**119 676**

	1965	1980	1990	2000	2007	2010	2013	2015	2016	2017
Latvia, million EUR										
Contribution under 2000 heading	..	..	..	669	1 774	1 554	1 933	2 030	2 067	2 259
Other taxes	..	..	..	12	51	36	59	80	87	97
Voluntary contributions to government	..	..	..	0	0	0	0	0	0	0
Compulsory contributions to private sector	..	..	..	0	0	0	0	0	0	0
Total	**..**	**..**	**..**	**682**	**1 825**	**1 590**	**1 992**	**2 111**	**2 154**	**2 356**
Lithuania, million EUR										
Contribution under 2000 heading	..	..	..	1 362	2 643	3 293	3 791	4 338	4 714	5 170
Other taxes	..	..	..	0	0	0	0	0	0	0
Voluntary contributions to government	..	..	..	0	2	2	3	2	2	2
Compulsory contributions to private sector	..	..	..	0	247	95	149	140	156	173
Total	**..**	**..**	**..**	**1 362**	**2 892**	**3 391**	**3 943**	**4 480**	**4 872**	**5 345**
Luxembourg, million EUR										
Contribution under 2000 heading	86	443	1 011	2 223	3 704	4 352	5 173	5 545	5 735	6 125
Other taxes	0	0	0	0	0	0	0	0	0	0
Voluntary contributions to government	0	0	4	18	18	28	34	38	41	44
Compulsory contributions to private sector	0	0	0	0	0	0	0	0	0	0
Total	**86**	**443**	**1 015**	**2 240**	**3 722**	**4 380**	**5 206**	**5 583**	**5 776**	**6 169**
Mexico, million MXN										
Contribution under 2000 heading	..	109	17 165	138 223	236 727	277 459	351 993	409 249	434 998	467 710
Other taxes	..	0	0	0	0	0	0	0	0	0
Voluntary contributions to government	..	0	0	0	0	0	0	0	0	0
Compulsory contributions to private sector	..	25	3 840	67 352	144 331	146 110	168 111	206 824	224 804	243 726
Total	**..**	**134**	**21 005**	**205 575**	**381 057**	**423 569**	**520 104**	**616 073**	**659 803**	**711 436**
Netherlands, million EUR										
Contribution under 2000 heading	3 342	26 641	39 075	64 522	77 072	82 732	97 372	96 426	103 902	101 913
Other taxes	0	0	0	0	0	0	0	0	0	0
Voluntary contributions to government	168	1 139	163	0	0	0	0	0	0	0
Compulsory contributions to private sector	1 266	7 642	5 727	37 088	..	..	..	..	..	..
Total	**4 776**	**35 422**	**44 965**	**101 610**	**77 072**	**82 732**	**97 372**	**96 426**	**103 902**	**101 913**
New Zealand, million NZD										
Contribution under 2000 heading	..	..	..	..	..	..	..	..	..	..
Other taxes	..	..	..	..	..	..	..	..	..	..
Voluntary contributions to government	..	..	..	..	..	..	..	..	..	..
Compulsory contributions to private sector	..	..	..	..	..	..	..	..	..	..
Total	**0**	**0**	**0**	**0**	**0**	**0**	**0**	**0**	**0**	**0**
Norway, million NOK										
Contribution under 2000 heading	2 009	28 205	79 362	132 170	204 602	243 015	292 278	325 569	331 389	341 591
Other taxes	1 305	4 256	0	0	0	0	0	0	0	0
Voluntary contributions to government	0	0	0	0	0	0	0	0	0	0
Compulsory contributions to private sector	0	242	339	0	0	0	0	0	0	0
Total	**3 314**	**32 703**	**79 701**	**132 170**	**204 602**	**243 015**	**292 278**	**325 569**	**331 389**	**341 591**
Poland, million PLN										
Contribution under 2000 heading	..	..	..	96 386	140 086	156 026	202 629	223 531	236 292	254 968
Other taxes	..	..	..	0	0	0	0	0	0	0
Voluntary contributions to government	..	..	..	0	0	0	0	0	0	0
Compulsory contributions to private sector	..	..	..	0	0	0	0	0	0	0
Total	**..**	**..**	**..**	**96 386**	**140 086**	**156 026**	**202 629**	**223 531**	**236 292**	**254 968**
Portugal, million EUR										
Contribution under 2000 heading	22	531	4 026	10 168	14 274	15 457	15 139	16 182	16 918	17 950
Other taxes	0	1	29	434	658	698	970	994	781	797
Voluntary contributions to government	0	0	0	0	0	0	0	0	0	0
Compulsory contributions to private sector	0	0	0	0	0	0	0	0	0	0
Total	**22**	**532**	**4 055**	**10 602**	**14 932**	**16 154**	**16 109**	**17 176**	**17 699**	**18 747**
Slovak Republic, million EUR										
Contribution under 2000 heading	..	..	..	4 409	7 244	8 154	9 847	10 861	11 426	12 325
Other taxes	..	..	..	0	0	0	0	0	0	0
Voluntary contributions to government	..	..	..	0	22	31	17	11	10	10
Compulsory contributions to private sector	..	..	..	0	701	719	385	413	435	504
Total	**..**	**..**	**..**	**4 409**	**7 968**	**8 904**	**10 249**	**11 284**	**11 871**	**12 839**

	1965	1980	1990	2000	2007	2010	2013	2015	2016	2017
Slovenia, million EUR										
Contribution under 2000 heading	..	..	..	2 631	4 724	5 382	5 269	5 606	5 842	6 240
Other taxes	..	..	..	0	0	0	0	0	0	0
Voluntary contributions to government	..	..	..	0	0	0	0	0	0	0
Compulsory contributions to private sector	..	..	..	0	0	0	0	0	0	0
Total	**..**	**..**	**..**	**2 631**	**4 724**	**5 382**	**5 269**	**5 606**	**5 842**	**6 240**
Spain, million EUR										
Contribution under 2000 heading	350	10 682	36 722	76 046	128 715	129 733	117 929	123 470	127 523	134 698
Other taxes	0	49	0	0	0	0	0	0	0	0
Voluntary contributions to government	0	0	0	0	0	0	2 209	1 170	1 149	1 133
Compulsory contributions to private sector	0	0	0	0	0	0	0	0	0	0
Total	**350**	**10 731**	**36 722**	**76 046**	**128 715**	**129 733**	**120 138**	**124 640**	**128 672**	**135 831**
Sweden, million SEK										
Contribution under 2000 heading	4 851	74 647	205 867	306 974	388 505	384 668	376 684	404 851	438 870	443 110
Other taxes	1 407	0	0	0	0	0	0	0	0	0
Voluntary contributions to government	0	0	0	8 108	13 903	14 884	15 881	16 697	17 986	19 225
Compulsory contributions to private sector	0	0	0	0	0	0	0	0	0	0
Total	**6 258**	**74 647**	**205 867**	**315 082**	**402 408**	**399 552**	**392 565**	**421 548**	**456 856**	**462 335**
Switzerland, million CHF										
Contribution under 2000 heading	1 670	10 844	19 892	30 750	34 949	38 369	42 654	44 073	44 527	44 998
Other taxes	336	778	1 176	4 509	6 342	6 644	7 850	7 815	7 568	7 722
Voluntary contributions to government	95	431	0	0	0	0	0	0	0	0
Compulsory contributions to private sector	2 505	9 674	20 797	29 532	41 478	45 527	49 473	52 991	54 796	56 934
Total	**4 606**	**21 727**	**41 865**	**64 791**	**82 769**	**90 541**	**99 977**	**104 878**	**106 892**	**109 655**
Turkey, million TRY										
Contribution under 2000 heading	0	0	15	7 543	44 052	71 696	125 871	170 282	190 247	226 720
Other taxes	0	0	0	0	0	0	0	0	0	0
Voluntary contributions to government	0	0	0	0	0	0	0	0	0	0
Compulsory contributions to private sector	0	0	0	0	0	0	0	0	0	0
Total	**0**	**0**	**15**	**7 543**	**44 052**	**71 696**	**125 871**	**170 282**	**190 247**	**226 720**
United Kingdom, million GBP										
Contribution under 2000 heading	1 685	13 531	34 457	60 252	93 210	97 346	106 085	114 067	121 900	130 595
Other taxes	0	0	0	0	0	0	0	0	0	0
Voluntary contributions to government	0	11	3 288	8 103	18 629	21 217	22 438	25 025	25 903	26 678
Compulsory contributions to private sector	1 148	13 350	7 945	8 308	9 969	9 656	6 074	5 495	2 058	48
Total	**2 833**	**26 892**	**45 690**	**76 663**	**121 808**	**128 219**	**134 597**	**144 587**	**149 861**	**157 321**
United States, million USD										
Contribution under 2000 heading	22 192	159 763	396 972	683 104	907 357	917 409	1 030 099	1 126 111	1 153 645	1 204 453
Other taxes	0	0	0	0	0	0	0	0	0	0
Voluntary contributions to government	488	3 407	11 719	22 562	51 635	61 833	69 903	74 886	82 208	90 166
Compulsory contributions to private sector	0	0	0	0	0	0	0	0	0	0
Total	**22 680**	**163 170**	**408 691**	**705 666**	**958 992**	**979 242**	**1 100 002**	**1 200 997**	**1 235 853**	**1 294 619**

.. Not available

StatLink https://doi.org/10.1787/888934057419

Table 5.38. Social security contributions and payroll taxes paid by government

	1965	1980	1990	2000	2007	2010	2013	2015	2016	2017
Australia, million AUD										
2000 Social security contributions										
Federal or Central government	..	..	..	..	..	..	..	..	..	..
State/Regional	..	..	..	..	..	..	..	..	..	..
Local government	..	..	..	..	..	..	..	..	..	..
Social Security Funds	..	..	..	..	..	..	..	..	..	..
Total	**0**	**0**	**0**	**0**	**0**	**0**	**0**	**0**	**0**	**0**
3000 Taxes on payroll and workforce										
Federal or Central government	0	4	0	0	0	0	0	0	0	0
State/Regional	15	302	0	0	0	0	0	0	0	0
Local government	0	0	2	19	41	31	37	38	39	42
Social Security Funds	0	0	0	0	0	0	0	0	0	0
Multi-jurisdictional (University) sector[1]	..	..	..	..	..	..	..	..	..	..
Total	**15**	**306**	**92**	**301**	**496**	**579**	**702**	**765**	**796**	**840**
2000+3000 Total	**15**	**306**	**92**	**301**	**496**	**579**	**702**	**765**	**796**	**840**
Austria, million EUR[2]										
2000 Social security contributions										
Federal or Central government	48	230	337	620	1 244	1 532	1 664	1 825	1 936	2 036
State/Regional	13	166	337	692	988	1 179	1 255	1 376	1 454	1 531
Local government	17	145	292	699	1 036	1 277	1 379	1 515	1 579	1 622
Social Security Funds	11	79	48	176	203	226	250	264	277	279
Total	**88**	**619**	**1 015**	**2 186**	**3 471**	**4 213**	**4 547**	**4 980**	**5 246**	**5 467**
3000 Taxes on payroll and workforce										
Federal or Central government	0	49	134	186	337	533	558	624	632	621
State/Regional	0	48	74	232	351	458	485	492	500	496
Local government	1	29	79	301	262	359	396	428	433	424
Social Security Funds	0	0	39	44	51	55	61	65	66	67
Total	**1**	**125**	**326**	**763**	**1 000**	**1 405**	**1 500**	**1 609**	**1 632**	**1 609**
2000+3000 Total	**89**	**745**	**1 341**	**2 949**	**4 471**	**5 618**	**6 047**	**6 589**	**6 878**	**7 076**
Belgium, million EUR										
2000 Social security contributions										
Federal or Central government	..	536	211	259	434	494	531	721	715	744
State/Regional	..	0	614	1 218	1 600	1 786	1 984	2 338	2 330	2 424
Local government	..	434	768	1 376	2 151	2 621	3 602	3 960	4 022	4 184
Social Security Funds	..	89	176	252	308	361	418	418	406	423
Total	**..**	**1 059**	**1 769**	**3 105**	**4 493**	**5 261**	**6 535**	**7 437**	**7 473**	**7 774**
3000 Taxes on payroll and workforce										
Federal or Central government	..	..	..	..	..	..	..	..	..	..
State/Regional	..	..	..	..	..	..	..	..	..	..
Local government	..	..	..	..	..	..	..	..	..	..
Social Security Funds	..	..	..	..	..	..	..	..	..	..
Total	**..**	**0**	**0**	**0**	**0**	**0**	**0**	**0**	**0**	**0**
2000+3000 Total	**..**	**1 059**	**1 769**	**3 105**	**4 493**	**5 261**	**6 535**	**7 437**	**7 473**	**7 774**
Canada, million CAD										
2000 Social security contributions										
Federal or Central government	..	..	..	944	1 198	1 397	1 449	1 515	1 543	1 575
State/Regional	..	..	..	3 023	4 269	5 071	5 825	6 349	6 376	6 433
Local government	..	..	..	2 225	2 806	3 390	3 912	4 205	4 362	4 401
Social Security Funds	..	..	..	0	0	0	0	0	0	0
Total	**..**	**..**	**..**	**6 192**	**8 273**	**9 857**	**11 186**	**12 070**	**12 281**	**12 409**
3000 Taxes on payroll and workforce										
Federal or Central government	..	..	..	0	0	0	0	0	0	0
State/Regional	..	..	..	173	234	328	362	362	367	375
Local government	..	..	..	0	0	0	0	0	0	0
Social Security Funds	..	..	..	0	0	0	0	0	0	0
Total	**..**	**..**	**..**	**173**	**234**	**328**	**362**	**362**	**367**	**375**
2000+3000 Total	**..**	**..**	**..**	**6 365**	**8 507**	**10 185**	**11 548**	**12 432**	**12 648**	**12 784**

	1965	1980	1990	2000	2007	2010	2013	2015	2016	2017
Chile, million CLP										
2000 Social security contributions										
Federal or Central government	..	..	..	43 210	107 911	148 006	186 652	205 125	221 395	236 530
State/Regional	..	..	..	..	..	..	..	..	..	..
Local government	..	..	..	11 317	30 218	41 518	51 114	63 603	76 825	82 601
Social Security Funds	..	..	..	106	263	449	550	600	743	801
Total	**..**	**..**	**..**	**54 633**	**138 392**	**189 974**	**238 315**	**269 328**	**298 964**	**319 933**
3000 Taxes on payroll and workforce										
Federal or Central government	..	..	..	..	..	..	..	..	..	..
State/Regional	..	..	..	..	..	..	..	..	..	..
Local government	..	..	..	..	..	..	..	..	..	..
Social Security Funds	..	..	..	..	..	..	..	..	..	..
Total	**..**	**..**	**..**	**..**	**..**	**..**	**..**	**..**	**..**	**..**
2000+3000 Total	**..**	**..**	**..**	**54 633**	**138 392**	**189 974**	**238 315**	**269 328**	**298 964**	**319 933**
Czech Republic, million CZK										
2000 Social security contributions										
Federal or Central government	..	..	..	28 050	44 437	45 439	46 360	37 553	39 814	43 564
State/Regional	..	..	..	..	..	..	..	..	..	..
Local government	..	..	..	5 660	8 253	9 394	9 448	41 954	44 261	47 919
Social Security Funds	..	..	..	510	791	938	881	975	1 009	1 056
Total	**..**	**..**	**..**	**34 220**	**53 481**	**55 771**	**56 689**	**80 482**	**85 085**	**92 538**
3000 Taxes on payroll and workforce										
Federal or Central government	..	..	..	..	..	..	..	..	..	..
State/Regional	..	..	..	..	..	..	..	..	..	..
Local government	..	..	..	..	..	..	..	..	..	..
Social Security Funds	..	..	..	..	..	..	..	..	..	..
Total	**..**	**..**	**..**	**0**	**0**	**0**	**0**	**0**	**0**	**0**
2000+3000 Total	**..**	**..**	**..**	**34 220**	**53 481**	**55 771**	**56 689**	**80 482**	**85 085**	**92 538**
Denmark, million DKK										
2000 Social security contributions										
Federal or Central government	..	179	..	..	..	..	..	..	..	..
State/Regional	..	..	..	..	..	..	..	..	..	..
Local government	..	0	..	..	..	..	..	..	..	..
Social Security Funds	..	0	..	..	..	..	..	..	..	..
Total	**..**	**179**	**0**	**0**	**0**	**0**	**0**	**0**	**0**	**0**
3000 Taxes on payroll and workforce										
Federal or Central government	..	..	..	..	..	..	..	..	..	..
State/Regional	..	..	..	..	..	..	..	..	..	..
Local government	..	..	..	..	..	..	..	..	..	..
Social Security Funds	..	..	..	..	..	..	..	..	..	..
Total	**..**	**0**	**0**	**0**	**0**	**0**	**0**	**0**	**0**	**0**
2000+3000 Total	**..**	**179**	**0**	**0**	**0**	**0**	**0**	**0**	**0**	**0**
Estonia, million EUR										
2000 Social security contributions										
Federal or Central government	..	..	..	129	257	315	368	451	469	486
State/Regional	..	..	..	..	..	..	..	..	..	..
Local government	..	..	..	48	156	175	206	235	252	277
Social Security Funds	..	..	..	0	3	41	24	24	41	64
Total	**..**	**..**	**..**	**177**	**417**	**532**	**598**	**710**	**762**	**827**
3000 Taxes on payroll and workforce										
Federal or Central government	..	..	..	..	..	..	..	..	..	..
State/Regional	..	..	..	..	..	..	..	..	..	..
Local government	..	..	..	..	..	..	..	..	..	..
Social Security Funds	..	..	..	..	..	..	..	..	..	..
Total	**..**	**..**	**..**	**0**	**0**	**0**	**0**	**0**	**0**	**0**
2000+3000 Total	**..**	**..**	**..**	**177**	**417**	**532**	**598**	**710**	**762**	**827**

	1965	1980	1990	2000	2007	2010	2013	2015	2016	2017
Finland, million EUR										
2000 Social security contributions										
Federal or Central government	..	61	196	908	1 057	1 137	1 226	1 220	1 100	997
State/Regional	..	..	..	..	..	..	..	..	..	..
Local government	..	170	1 709	2 786	4 061	4 352	4 881	4 868	4 867	4 327
Social Security Funds	..	9	33	75	88	90	102	109	112	118
Total	**..**	**239**	**1 938**	**3 769**	**5 206**	**5 579**	**6 209**	**6 197**	**6 079**	**5 442**
3000 Taxes on payroll and workforce										
Federal or Central government	..	1	..	..	..	..	..	..	..	..
State/Regional	..	..	..	..	..	..	..	..	..	..
Local government	..	4	..	..	..	..	..	..	..	..
Social Security Funds	..	0	..	..	..	..	..	..	..	..
Total	**..**	**5**	**0**	**0**	**0**	**0**	**0**	**0**	**0**	**0**
2000+3000 Total	**..**	**245**	**1 938**	**3 769**	**5 206**	**5 579**	**6 209**	**6 197**	**6 079**	**5 442**
France, million EUR										
2000 Social security contributions										
Federal or Central government	..	3 816	8 063	10 466	12 426	12 841	12 825	12 999	13 241	13 880
State/Regional	..	..	..	..	..	..	..	..	..	..
Local government	..	2 369	5 542	10 372	15 925	18 065	20 050	21 553	21 852	22 414
Social Security Funds	..	2 594	6 940	10 827	14 035	15 427	16 614	17 399	17 455	17 963
Total	**..**	**8 779**	**20 545**	**31 665**	**42 386**	**46 333**	**49 489**	**51 951**	**52 548**	**54 257**
3000 Taxes on payroll and workforce										
Federal or Central government	..	836	494	854	1 558	1 611	1 697	1 768	1 796	1 892
State/Regional	..	..	..	..	..	..	..	..	..	..
Local government	..	27	107	324	549	698	791	852	875	916
Social Security Funds	..	629	2 234	3 413	4 531	5 028	5 374	5 522	5 522	5 624
Total	**..**	**1 492**	**2 835**	**4 591**	**6 638**	**7 337**	**7 862**	**8 142**	**8 193**	**8 432**
2000+3000 Total	**..**	**10 271**	**23 380**	**36 256**	**49 024**	**53 670**	**57 351**	**60 093**	**60 741**	**62 689**
Germany, million EUR										
2000 Social security contributions										
Federal or Central government	775	1 324	2 376	1 559	1 398	1 674	1 641	1 782	1 802	1 983
State/Regional	293	2 611	4 647	5 359	5 831	6 524	6 963	7 470	7 814	8 150
Local government	325	3 140	5 791	6 992	8 435	9 626	10 136	10 933	11 662	12 222
Social Security Funds	1 495	456	767	1 828	2 182	2 495	2 678	2 915	3 013	3 100
Total	**2 887**	**7 531**	**13 581**	**15 738**	**17 846**	**20 319**	**21 419**	**23 101**	**24 291**	**25 455**
3000 Taxes on payroll and workforce										
Federal or Central government	..	..	..	..	..	..	..	..	..	..
State/Regional	..	..	..	..	..	..	..	..	..	..
Local government	..	..	..	..	..	..	..	..	..	..
Social Security Funds	..	..	..	..	..	..	..	..	..	..
Total	**0**	**0**	**0**	**0**	**0**	**0**	**0**	**0**	**0**	**0**
2000+3000 Total	**2 887**	**7 531**	**13 581**	**15 738**	**17 846**	**20 319**	**21 419**	**23 101**	**24 291**	**25 455**
Greece, million EUR										
2000 Social security contributions										
Federal or Central government	..	..	124	1 542	2 888	3 217	2 372	2 337	2 345	1 282
State/Regional	..	..	..	..	..	..	..	..	..	..
Local government	..	..	0	0	0	0	0	0	0	0
Social Security Funds	..	..	0	200	440	387	350	265	318	355
Total	**..**	**..**	**124**	**1 742**	**3 328**	**3 604**	**2 722**	**2 602**	**2 663**	**1 637**
3000 Taxes on payroll and workforce										
Federal or Central government	..	..	..	..	..	..	..	..	..	..
State/Regional	..	..	..	..	..	..	..	..	..	..
Local government	..	..	..	..	..	..	..	..	..	..
Social Security Funds	..	..	..	..	..	..	..	..	..	..
Total	**..**	**..**	**0**	**0**	**0**	**0**	**0**	**0**	**0**	**0**
2000+3000 Total	**..**	**..**	**124**	**1 742**	**3 328**	**3 604**	**2 722**	**2 602**	**2 663**	**1 637**

	1965	1980	1990	2000	2007	2010	2013	2015	2016	2017
Hungary, million HUF										
2000 Social security contributions										
Federal or Central government	..	..	..	148 251	293 684	255 557	449 428	529 471	556 687	535 993
State/Regional	..	..	..	..	..	..	..	..	..	..
Local government	..	..	..	173 475	343 306	278 385	124 111	147 861	161 082	149 461
Social Security Funds	..	..	..	4 936	8 052	6 656	2 781	3 058	2 794	1 922
Total	**..**	**..**	**..**	**326 661**	**645 042**	**540 597**	**576 320**	**680 389**	**720 563**	**687 375**
3000 Taxes on payroll and workforce										
Federal or Central government	..	..	..	13 901	7 287	1 011	12 435	13 706	15 342	16 067
State/Regional	..	..	..	..	..	..	..	..	..	..
Local government	..	..	..	25 990	11 928	3 254	4 224	3 327	3 498	3 770
Social Security Funds	..	..	..	406	162	8	101	0	102	96
Total	**..**	**..**	**..**	**40 297**	**19 377**	**4 273**	**16 760**	**17 033**	**18 942**	**19 933**
2000+3000 Total	**..**	**..**	**..**	**366 958**	**664 420**	**544 870**	**593 080**	**697 422**	**739 505**	**707 308**
Iceland, million ISK										
2000 Social security contributions										
Federal or Central government	..	..	..	..	..	..	..	..	..	..
State/Regional	..	..	..	..	..	..	..	..	..	..
Local government	..	..	..	..	..	..	..	..	..	..
Social Security Funds	..	..	..	..	..	..	..	..	..	..
Total	**..**	**..**	**..**	**..**	**..**	**..**	**..**	**..**	**..**	**..**
3000 Taxes on payroll and workforce										
Federal or Central government	..	..	..	..	..	..	..	..	..	..
State/Regional	..	..	..	..	..	..	..	..	..	..
Local government	..	..	..	..	..	..	..	..	..	..
Social Security Funds	..	..	..	..	..	..	..	..	..	..
Total	**..**	**..**	**..**	**..**	**..**	**..**	**..**	**..**	**..**	**..**
2000+3000 Total	**..**	**..**	**..**	**..**	**..**	**..**	**..**	**..**	**..**	**..**
Ireland, million EUR										
2000 Social security contributions										
Federal or Central government	..	21	65	166	460	395	426	497	532	574
State/Regional	..	..	..	..	..	..	..	..	..	..
Local government	..	25	83	277	862	805	799	932	998	1 077
Social Security Funds	..	0	1	4	6	6	6	6	6	6
Total	**..**	**46**	**149**	**447**	**1 328**	**1 205**	**1 231**	**1 435**	**1 536**	**1 657**
3000 Taxes on payroll and workforce										
Federal or Central government	..	..	..	..	..	..	..	..	..	..
State/Regional	..	..	..	..	..	..	..	..	..	..
Local government	..	..	..	..	..	..	..	..	..	..
Social Security Funds	..	..	..	..	..	..	..	..	..	..
Total	**..**	**0**	**0**	**0**	**0**	**0**	**0**	**0**	**0**	**0**
2000+3000 Total	**..**	**46**	**149**	**447**	**1 328**	**1 205**	**1 231**	**1 435**	**1 536**	**1 657**
Israel, million ILS										
2000 Social security contributions										
Federal or Central government	..	..	..	840	1 030	1 180	1 550	1 780	2 000	2 120
State/Regional	..	..	..	..	..	..	..	..	..	..
Local government	..	..	..	280	340	390	510	590	660	700
Social Security Funds	..	..	..	0	0	0	0	0	0	0
Total	**..**	**..**	**..**	**1 120**	**1 370**	**1 570**	**2 060**	**2 370**	**2 660**	**2 820**
3000 Taxes on payroll and workforce										
Federal or Central government	..	..	..	2 330	3 600	4 180	5 220	5 650	5 890	6 130
State/Regional	..	..	..	..	..	..	..	..	..	..
Local government	..	..	..	660	880	960	1 190	1 290	1 350	1 400
Social Security Funds	..	..	..	0	0	0	0	0	0	0
Total	**..**	**..**	**..**	**2 990**	**4 480**	**5 140**	**6 410**	**6 940**	**7 240**	**7 530**
2000+3000 Total	**..**	**..**	**..**	**4 110**	**5 850**	**6 710**	**8 470**	**9 310**	**9 900**	**10 350**

	1965	1980	1990	2000	2007	2010	2013	2015	2016	2017
Italy, million EUR										
2000 Social security contributions										
Federal or Central government	..	..	..	0	0	0	0	0	0	0
State/Regional	..	..	..	..	..	..	..	..	..	..
Local government	..	..	..	0	0	0	0	0	0	0
Social Security Funds	..	..	..	36 679	47 394	50 627	49 827	49 251	49 881	50 628
Total	**..**	**..**	**..**	**36 679**	**47 394**	**50 627**	**49 827**	**49 251**	**49 881**	**50 628**
3000 Taxes on payroll and workforce										
Federal or Central government	..	..	..	..	..	..	..	..	..	..
State/Regional	..	..	..	..	..	..	..	..	..	..
Local government	..	..	..	..	..	..	..	..	..	..
Social Security Funds	..	..	..	..	..	..	..	..	..	..
Total	**..**	**..**	**..**	**0**	**0**	**0**	**0**	**0**	**0**	**0**
2000+3000 Total	**..**	**..**	**..**	**36 679**	**47 394**	**50 627**	**49 827**	**49 251**	**49 881**	**50 628**
Japan, billion JPY										
2000 Social security contributions										
Federal or Central government	..	..	507	732	766	758	810	881	897	908
State/Regional	..	..	..	..	..	..	..	..	..	..
Local government	..	..	1 510	2 168	2 216	2 223	2 392	2 524	2 562	2 555
Social Security Funds	..	..	0	0	0	0	0	0	0	0
Total	**..**	**..**	**2 017**	**2 900**	**2 982**	**2 981**	**3 202**	**3 405**	**3 459**	**3 463**
3000 Taxes on payroll and workforce										
Federal or Central government	..	..	..	..	..	..	..	..	..	..
State/Regional	..	..	..	..	..	..	..	..	..	..
Local government	..	..	..	..	..	..	..	..	..	..
Social Security Funds	..	..	..	..	..	..	..	..	..	..
Total	**..**	**..**	**0**	**0**	**0**	**0**	**0**	**0**	**0**	**0**
2000+3000 Total	**..**	**..**	**2 017**	**2 900**	**2 982**	**2 981**	**3 202**	**3 405**	**3 459**	**3 463**
Korea, billion KRW										
2000 Social security contributions										
Federal or Central government	..	..	..	..	..	..	..	..	..	..
State/Regional	..	..	..	..	..	..	..	..	..	..
Local government	..	..	..	..	..	..	..	..	..	..
Social Security Funds	..	..	..	..	..	..	..	..	..	..
Total	**..**	**..**	**..**	**..**	**..**	**..**	**..**	**..**	**..**	**..**
3000 Taxes on payroll and workforce										
Federal or Central government	..	..	..	..	..	..	..	..	..	..
State/Regional	..	..	..	..	..	..	..	..	..	..
Local government	..	..	..	..	..	..	..	..	..	..
Social Security Funds	..	..	..	..	..	..	..	..	..	..
Total	**..**	**..**	**..**	**..**	**..**	**..**	**..**	**..**	**..**	**..**
2000+3000 Total	**..**	**..**	**..**	**..**	**..**	**..**	**..**	**..**	**..**	**..**
Latvia, million EUR										
2000 Social security contributions										
Federal or Central government	..	..	..	..	..	..	..	..	..	..
State/Regional	..	..	..	..	..	..	..	..	..	..
Local government	..	..	..	..	..	..	..	..	..	..
Social Security Funds	..	..	..	..	..	..	..	..	..	..
Total	**..**	**..**	**..**	**40**	**156**	**174**	**228**	**262**	**230**	**252**
3000 Taxes on payroll and workforce										
Federal or Central government	..	..	..	..	..	..	..	..	..	..
State/Regional	..	..	..	..	..	..	..	..	..	..
Local government	..	..	..	..	..	..	..	..	..	..
Social Security Funds	..	..	..	..	..	..	..	..	..	..
Total	**..**	**..**	**..**	**0**	**0**	**0**	**0**	**0**	**0**	**0**
2000+3000 Total	**..**	**..**	**..**	**40**	**156**	**174**	**228**	**262**	**230**	**252**

	1965	1980	1990	2000	2007	2010	2013	2015	2016	2017
Lithuania, million EUR										
2000 Social security contributions										
Federal or Central government	..	..	..	179	327	334	395	426	454	479
State/Regional	..	..	..	..	..	..	..	..	..	..
Local government	..	..	..	174	294	350	347	374	395	414
Social Security Funds	..	..	..	5	14	16	15	16	16	16
Total	**..**	**..**	**..**	**358**	**635**	**700**	**756**	**816**	**865**	**909**
3000 Taxes on payroll and workforce										
Federal or Central government	..	..	..	..	..	..	..	..	..	..
State/Regional	..	..	..	..	..	..	..	..	..	..
Local government	..	..	..	..	..	..	..	..	..	..
Social Security Funds	..	..	..	..	..	..	..	..	..	..
Total	**..**	**..**	**..**	**0**	**0**	**0**	**0**	**0**	**0**	**0**
2000+3000 Total	**..**	**..**	**..**	**358**	**635**	**700**	**756**	**816**	**865**	**909**
Luxembourg, million EUR										
2000 Social security contributions										
Federal or Central government	..	..	257	273	413	491	548	651	684	725
State/Regional	..	..	..	..	..	..	..	..	..	..
Local government	..	..	2	4	4	4	4	4	4	4
Social Security Funds	..	..	7	11	12	12	15	17	18	20
Total	**..**	**..**	**267**	**287**	**429**	**507**	**567**	**671**	**706**	**749**
3000 Taxes on payroll and workforce										
Federal or Central government	..	..	..	..	..	..	..	..	..	..
State/Regional	..	..	..	..	..	..	..	..	..	..
Local government	..	..	..	..	..	..	..	..	..	..
Social Security Funds	..	..	..	..	..	..	..	..	..	..
Total	**..**	**..**	**0**	**0**	**0**	**0**	**0**	**0**	**0**	**0**
2000+3000 Total	**..**	**..**	**267**	**287**	**429**	**507**	**567**	**671**	**706**	**749**
Mexico, million MXN										
2000 Social security contributions										
Federal or Central government	..	25	2 952	44 879	94 251	103 440	126 518	145 329	150 386	159 491
State/Regional	..	0	0	0	0	0	0	0	0	0
Local government	..	0	0	0	0	0	0	0	0	0
Social Security Funds	..	0	0	0	0	0	0	0	0	0
Total	**..**	**25**	**2 952**	**44 879**	**94 251**	**103 440**	**126 518**	**145 329**	**150 386**	**159 491**
3000 Taxes on payroll and workforce										
Federal or Central government	..	..	..	..	..	..	..	..	..	..
State/Regional	..	..	..	..	..	..	..	..	..	..
Local government	..	..	..	..	..	..	..	..	..	..
Social Security Funds	..	..	..	..	..	..	..	..	..	..
Total	**..**	**0**	**0**	**0**	**0**	**0**	**0**	**0**	**0**	**0**
2000+3000 Total	**..**	**25**	**2 952**	**44 879**	**94 251**	**103 440**	**126 518**	**145 329**	**150 386**	**159 491**
Netherlands, million EUR										
2000 Social security contributions										
Federal or Central government	63	1 366	286	..	..	..	..	..	..	..
State/Regional	..	..	..	..	..	..	..	..	..	..
Local government	0	0	0	..	..	..	..	..	..	..
Social Security Funds	7	91	59	..	..	..	..	..	..	..
Total	**70**	**1 457**	**345**	**2 006**	**4 310**	**..**	**..**	**..**	**..**	**..**
3000 Taxes on payroll and workforce										
Federal or Central government	..	..	..	..	..	..	..	..	..	..
State/Regional	..	..	..	..	..	..	..	..	..	..
Local government	..	..	..	..	..	..	..	..	..	..
Social Security Funds	..	..	..	..	..	..	..	..	..	..
Total	**0**	**0**	**0**	**0**	**0**	**0**	**0**	**0**	**0**	**0**
2000+3000 Total	**70**	**1 457**	**345**	**2 006**	**4 310**	**0**	**0**	**0**	**0**	**0**

	1965	1980	1990	2000	2007	2010	2013	2015	2016	2017
New Zealand, million NZD										
2000 Social security contributions										
Federal or Central government	..	..	..	..	..	..	..	..	..	..
State/Regional	..	..	..	..	..	..	..	..	..	..
Local government	..	..	..	..	..	..	..	..	..	..
Social Security Funds	..	..	..	..	..	..	..	..	..	..
Total	**0**	**0**	**0**	**0**	**0**	**0**	**0**	**0**	**0**	**0**
3000 Taxes on payroll and workforce										
Federal or Central government	..	..	..	..	..	..	..	..	..	..
State/Regional	..	..	..	..	..	..	..	..	..	..
Local government	..	..	..	..	..	..	..	..	..	..
Social Security Funds	..	..	..	..	..	..	..	..	..	..
Total	**0**	**0**	**0**	**0**	**0**	**0**	**0**	**0**	**0**	**0**
2000+3000 Total	**0**	**0**	**0**	**0**	**0**	**0**	**0**	**0**	**0**	**0**
Norway, million NOK										
2000 Social security contributions										
Federal or Central government	..	1 242	2 859	11 895	30 530	36 609	44 540	52 914	51 886	54 686
State/Regional	..	..	..	..	..	..	..	..	..	..
Local government	..	4 538	11 964	24 831	32 096	40 979	53 062	59 454	61 195	63 628
Social Security Funds	..	1 222	3 064	0	0	0	0	0	0	0
Total	**..**	**7 002**	**17 887**	**36 726**	**62 626**	**77 588**	**97 602**	**112 368**	**113 081**	**118 314**
3000 Taxes on payroll and workforce										
Federal or Central government	..	..	..	..	..	..	..	..	..	..
State/Regional	..	..	..	..	..	..	..	..	..	..
Local government	..	..	..	..	..	..	..	..	..	..
Social Security Funds	..	..	..	..	..	..	..	..	..	..
Total	**..**	**0**	**0**	**0**	**0**	**0**	**0**	**0**	**0**	**0**
2000+3000 Total	**..**	**7 002**	**17 887**	**36 726**	**62 626**	**77 588**	**97 602**	**112 368**	**113 081**	**118 314**
Poland, million PLN										
2000 Social security contributions										
Federal or Central government	..	..	..	4 566	6 023	6 643	8 231	9 839	10 597	11 096
State/Regional	..	..	..	..	..	..	..	..	..	..
Local government	..	..	..	6 756	9 856	11 411	13 638	14 384	15 210	16 009
Social Security Funds	..	..	..	279	426	499	514	517	550	590
Total	**..**	**..**	**..**	**11 601**	**16 305**	**18 553**	**22 383**	**24 740**	**26 357**	**27 695**
3000 Taxes on payroll and workforce										
Federal or Central government	..	..	..	..	..	..	..	..	..	..
State/Regional	..	..	..	..	..	..	..	..	..	..
Local government	..	..	..	..	..	..	..	..	..	..
Social Security Funds	..	..	..	..	..	..	..	..	..	..
Total	**..**	**..**	**..**	**0**	**0**	**0**	**0**	**0**	**0**	**0**
2000+3000 Total	**..**	**..**	**..**	**11 601**	**16 305**	**18 553**	**22 383**	**24 740**	**26 357**	**27 695**
Portugal, million EUR										
2000 Social security contributions										
Federal or Central government	..	0	0	0	..	..	..	..	..	..
State/Regional	..	..	..	..	..	..	..	..	..	..
Local government	..	0	33	197	..	..	..	..	..	..
Social Security Funds	..	4	0	0	..	..	..	..	..	..
Total	**..**	**4**	**33**	**197**	**0**	**0**	**0**	**0**	**0**	**0**
3000 Taxes on payroll and workforce										
Federal or Central government	..	..	..	..	..	..	..	..	..	..
State/Regional	..	..	..	..	..	..	..	..	..	..
Local government	..	..	..	..	..	..	..	..	..	..
Social Security Funds	..	..	..	..	..	..	..	..	..	..
Total	**..**	**0**	**0**	**0**	**0**	**0**	**0**	**0**	**0**	**0**
2000+3000 Total	**..**	**4**	**33**	**197**	**0**	**0**	**0**	**0**	**0**	**0**

	1965	1980	1990	2000	2007	2010	2013	2015	2016	2017
Slovak Republic, million EUR										
2000 Social security contributions										
Federal or Central government	..	..	..	489	602	785	936	1 033	1 069	1 120
State/Regional	..	..	..	..	..	..	..	..	..	..
Local government	..	..	..	130	427	493	562	650	691	739
Social Security Funds	..	..	..	22	26	44	32	36	38	40
Total	**..**	**..**	**..**	**642**	**1 055**	**1 322**	**1 530**	**1 719**	**1 798**	**1 899**
3000 Taxes on payroll and workforce										
Federal or Central government	..	..	..	..	..	..	..	..	..	..
State/Regional	..	..	..	..	..	..	..	..	..	..
Local government	..	..	..	..	..	..	..	..	..	..
Social Security Funds	..	..	..	..	..	..	..	..	..	..
Total	**..**	**..**	**..**	**0**	**0**	**0**	**0**	**0**	**0**	**0**
2000+3000 Total	**..**	**..**	**..**	**642**	**1 055**	**1 322**	**1 530**	**1 719**	**1 798**	**1 899**
Slovenia, million EUR										
2000 Social security contributions										
Federal or Central government	..	..	..	161	333	402	402	375	402	422
State/Regional	..	..	..	..	..	..	..	..	..	..
Local government	..	..	..	86	175	195	197	189	203	212
Social Security Funds	..	..	..	3	7	8	7	6	7	7
Total	**..**	**..**	**..**	**250**	**515**	**604**	**606**	**571**	**612**	**641**
3000 Taxes on payroll and workforce										
Federal or Central government	..	..	..	55	76	6	7	7	7	7
State/Regional	..	..	..	..	..	..	..	..	..	..
Local government	..	..	..	29	36	3	4	4	4	4
Social Security Funds	..	..	..	1	2	0	0	0	0	0
Total	**..**	**..**	**..**	**85**	**114**	**9**	**11**	**11**	**11**	**11**
2000+3000 Total	**..**	**..**	**..**	**335**	**629**	**613**	**617**	**582**	**623**	**652**
Spain, million EUR										
2000 Social security contributions										
Federal or Central government	..	387	989	1 401	1 960	2 196	2 008	2 228	2 268	2 325
State/Regional	..	2	0	4 411	9 426	11 002	10 218	11 243	11 689	12 464
Local government	..	252	1 819	2 524	4 098	4 781	4 617	4 797	4 779	4 802
Social Security Funds	..	396	1 202	1 284	484	527	498	496	496	491
Total	**..**	**1 037**	**4 010**	**9 620**	**15 968**	**18 506**	**17 341**	**18 764**	**19 232**	**20 082**
3000 Taxes on payroll and workforce										
Federal or Central government	..	..	..	..	..	..	..	..	..	..
State/Regional	..	..	..	..	..	..	..	..	..	..
Local government	..	..	..	..	..	..	..	..	..	..
Social Security Funds	..	..	..	..	..	..	..	..	..	..
Total	**..**	**0**	**0**	**0**	**0**	**0**	**0**	**0**	**0**	**0**
2000+3000 Total	**..**	**1 037**	**4 010**	**9 620**	**15 968**	**18 506**	**17 341**	**18 764**	**19 232**	**20 082**
Sweden, million SEK										
2000 Social security contributions										
Federal or Central government	..	7 543	12 430	21 153	25 164	24 729	24 595	25 707	27 582	27 612
State/Regional	..	..	..	..	..	..	..	..	..	..
Local government	..	18 149	49 298	66 215	83 877	82 141	78 774	85 373	93 760	95 132
Social Security Funds	..	0	0	0	0	0	0	0	0	0
Total	**..**	**25 692**	**61 728**	**87 367**	**109 040**	**106 870**	**103 370**	**111 079**	**121 342**	**122 744**
3000 Taxes on payroll and workforce										
Federal or Central government	..	..	1 527	3 453	5 394	6 912	11 242	12 326	12 785	14 531
State/Regional	..	..	..	..	..	..	..	..	..	..
Local government	..	..	6 060	10 808	17 980	22 958	36 005	40 935	43 461	50 064
Social Security Funds	..	..	0	0	0	0	0	0	0	0
Total	**..**	**0**	**7 587**	**14 261**	**23 374**	**29 870**	**47 247**	**53 261**	**56 246**	**64 596**
2000+3000 Total	**..**	**25 692**	**69 315**	**101 628**	**132 414**	**136 740**	**150 616**	**164 340**	**177 588**	**187 340**

	1965	1980	1990	2000	2007	2010	2013	2015	2016	2017
Switzerland, million CHF										
2000 Social security contributions										
Federal or Central government	13	91	224	293	375	439	485	489	504	522
State/Regional	34	380	770	971	1 296	1 524	1 699	1 767	1 797	1 858
Local government	22	270	460	595	745	823	867	911	940	952
Social Security Funds	2	21	4	14	18	23	25	26	26	26
Total	**71**	**762**	**1 458**	**1 873**	**2 434**	**2 809**	**3 075**	**3 193**	**3 266**	**3 359**
3000 Taxes on payroll and workforce										
Federal or Central government	..	..	..	..	..	..	..	..	..	..
State/Regional	..	..	..	..	..	..	..	..	..	..
Local government	..	..	..	..	..	..	..	..	..	..
Social Security Funds	..	..	..	..	..	..	..	..	..	..
Total	**0**	**0**	**0**	**0**	**0**	**0**	**0**	**0**	**0**	**0**
2000+3000 Total	**71**	**762**	**1 458**	**1 873**	**2 434**	**2 809**	**3 075**	**3 193**	**3 266**	**3 359**
Turkey, million TRY										
2000 Social security contributions										
Federal or Central government	..	..	9	3 619	20 442	39 363	71 184	95 067	107 905	128 331
State/Regional	..	..	..	..	..	..	..	..	..	..
Local government	..	..	0	0	0	0	0	0	0	0
Social Security Funds	..	..	0	0	0	0	0	0	0	0
Total	**..**	**..**	**9**	**3 619**	**20 442**	**39 363**	**71 184**	**95 067**	**107 905**	**128 331**
3000 Taxes on payroll and workforce										
Federal or Central government	..	..	..	..	..	..	..	..	..	..
State/Regional	..	..	..	..	..	..	..	..	..	..
Local government	..	..	..	..	..	..	..	..	..	..
Social Security Funds	..	..	..	..	..	..	..	..	..	..
Total	**..**	**..**	**0**	**0**	**0**	**0**	**0**	**0**	**0**	**0**
2000+3000 Total	**..**	**..**	**9**	**3 619**	**20 442**	**39 363**	**71 184**	**95 067**	**107 905**	**128 331**
United Kingdom, million GBP										
2000 Social security contributions										
Federal or Central government	87	920	2 134	3 122	5 897	6 421	7 054	7 824	8 546	9 301
State/Regional	..	..	..	..	..	..	..	..	..	..
Local government	83	926	1 957	2 913	4 908	5 311	4 669	4 542	4 669	4 785
Social Security Funds	0	0	0	0	0	0	0	0	0	0
Total	**170**	**1 846**	**4 091**	**6 035**	**10 805**	**11 732**	**11 723**	**12 366**	**13 215**	**14 086**
3000 Taxes on payroll and workforce										
Federal or Central government	..	360	..	..	..	..	..	..	..	..
State/Regional	..	..	..	..	..	..	..	..	..	..
Local government	..	410	..	..	..	..	..	..	..	..
Social Security Funds	..	0	..	..	..	..	..	..	..	..
Total	**0**	**770**	**0**	**0**	**0**	**0**	**0**	**0**	**0**	**0**
2000+3000 Total	**170**	**2 616**	**4 091**	**6 035**	**10 805**	**11 732**	**11 723**	**12 366**	**13 215**	**14 086**
United States, million USD										
2000 Social security contributions										
Federal or Central government	301	2 053	9 059	11 323	19 628	25 434	25 938	26 722	26 852	27 616
State/Regional	699	7 585	19 802	32 814	44 061	45 936	46 832	49 359	50 802	52 250
Local government	0	0	0	0	0	0	0	0	0	0
Social Security Funds	0	0	0	0	0	0	0	0	0	0
Total	**1 000**	**9 638**	**28 861**	**44 137**	**63 689**	**71 370**	**72 770**	**76 081**	**77 654**	**79 866**
3000 Taxes on payroll and workforce										
Federal or Central government	..	..	..	..	..	..	..	..	..	..
State/Regional	..	..	..	..	..	..	..	..	..	..
Local government	..	..	..	..	..	..	..	..	..	..
Social Security Funds	..	..	..	..	..	..	..	..	..	..
Total	**0**	**0**	**0**	**0**	**0**	**0**	**0**	**0**	**0**	**0**
2000+3000 Total	**1 000**	**9 638**	**28 861**	**44 137**	**63 689**	**71 370**	**72 770**	**76 081**	**77 654**	**79 866**

.. Not available

1. The multi-jurisdictional sector contains units where jurisdiction is shared between two or more governments, or classification of a unit to a jurisdiction is otherwise unclear. The main type of units currently falling into this category is public universities.

2. There is a break in the series in 1990. The data are based on ESA 2010 from that year onwards.

StatLink https://doi.org/10.1787/888934057438

6 Tax revenues by subsectors of general government

Chapter 6 provides comparative information on tax revenues by subsectors of general government as well as summary information for each OECD country.

6.1. Comparative tables 1975, 1995, 2000 and 2017

This part of the Report presents comparative data on tax revenues by level of government. The tax data have been attributed to the sub-sectors of general government identified in section A.12 of the Interpretative Guide (see Annex A) and the attribution criteria used are those set out in that guide.

The column "supranational" reports the customs duties collected by the twenty-three EU member states on behalf of the European Union.

In this section, the averages for 2016 have been calculated excluding the one-off revenues from stability contributions in Iceland.

Table 6.1. Tax revenues of sub-sectors of general government as % of total tax revenue (Federal/regional countries)

	Total				Supranational			
	1975	1995	2005	2017	1975	1995	2005	2017
Federal countries								
Australia	100.0	100.0	100.0	100.0	..	..	..	..
Austria	100.0	100.0	100.0	100.0	..	0.4	0.4	0.4
Belgium	100.0	100.0	100.0	100.0	1.4	1.0	0.9	1.0
Canada	100.0	100.0	100.0	100.0	..	..	..	..
Germany	100.0	100.0	100.0	100.0	1.2	0.6	0.5	0.6
Mexico	..	100.0	100.0	100.0	..	..	..	..
Switzerland[1]	100.0	100.0	100.0	100.0	..	..	..	..
United States	100.0	100.0	100.0	100.0	..	..	..	..
Unweighted average	100.0	100.0	100.0	100.0	1.3	0.7	0.6	0.7
Regional country								
Spain[1, 2]	100.0	100.0	100.0	100.0	..	0.5	0.4	0.7

	Central government				State or Regional government			
	1975	1995	2005	2017	1975	1995	2005	2017
Federal countries								
Australia	80.1	77.5	82.2	80.6	15.7	19.0	14.9	16.0
Austria	51.7	64.7	67.2	65.8	10.6	1.8	1.6	1.6
Belgium	65.3	60.1	58.3	51.4	..	1.8	5.1	10.8
Canada	47.6	39.1	44.5	40.9	32.5	37.1	37.9	39.8
Germany	33.5	31.4	30.5	29.5	22.3	21.6	21.5	23.5
Mexico	..	73.9	76.1	81.1	..	2.8	3.2	4.1
Switzerland[1]	30.7	31.2	35.2	36.5	27.0	24.3	25.3	24.6
United States	45.4	41.4	40.9	44.5	19.5	20.0	20.1	18.3
Unweighted average	50.6	52.4	54.4	53.8	21.3	16.1	16.2	17.3
Regional country								
Spain[1, 2]	48.2	51.5	44.9	41.3	..	4.7	14.0	15.2

	Local government				Social Security Funds			
	1975	1995	2005	2017	1975	1995	2005	2017
Federal countries								
Australia	4.2	3.4	2.9	3.4	0.0	0.0	0.0	0.0
Austria	12.4	4.1	3.1	3.0	25.3	29.0	27.7	29.2
Belgium	4.4	4.8	4.8	4.9	28.8	32.2	30.9	32.0
Canada	9.9	9.8	9.2	10.3	10.0	14.0	8.4	9.1
Germany	9.0	7.4	7.8	8.6	34.0	39.0	39.8	37.9
Mexico	..	1.5	1.6	1.6	..	21.8	19.0	13.3
Switzerland[1]	20.3	17.7	15.9	15.3	22.0	26.8	23.7	23.6
United States	14.7	13.3	14.6	14.2	20.5	25.2	24.4	23.0
Unweighted average	10.7	7.8	7.5	7.7	20.1	23.5	21.7	21.0
Regional country								
Spain[1, 2]	4.3	8.6	8.2	9.7	47.5	34.7	32.5	33.1

.. Not available

1. The total tax revenue has been reduced by the amount of any capital transfer that represents uncollected taxes. The capital transfer has been allocated between tax headings in proportion to the reported tax revenue.
2. Spain is constitutionally a non-federal country but has a highly decentralised political structure.

StatLink https://doi.org/10.1787/888934057457

Table 6.2. Tax revenues of sub-sectors of general government as % of total tax revenue (Unitary countries)

	Supranational				Central government			
	1975	1995	2005	2017	1975	1995	2005	2017
Chile	..	..	..	..	..	89.9	89.0	86.3
Czech Republic	..	..	0.5	0.5	..	57.7	55.6	55.4
Denmark[1]	1.0	0.5	0.4	0.3	69.1	68.4	69.2	73.2
Estonia	..	..	0.7	0.6	..	84.3	83.0	82.0
Finland	..	0.4	0.2	0.3	56.0	46.6	51.8	48.4
France[1]	0.7	0.4	0.2	0.4	51.2	42.6	39.7	34.2
Greece	..	0.6	0.4	0.5	67.1	66.4	64.5	67.4
Hungary	..	..	0.3	0.3	..	63.8	62.7	62.4
Iceland	..	..	..	..	81.3	79.2	77.1	73.5
Ireland	2.3	1.5	0.5	0.6	77.4	83.1	84.9	82.5
Israel	..	..	..	..	..	79.6	76.3	76.2
Italy	..	0.4	0.3	0.6	53.2	62.7	52.3	53.6
Japan	..	..	..	..	45.5	41.2	37.9	37.4
Korea	..	..	..	..	89.0	69.2	61.5	57.0
Latvia	..	..	0.7	0.6	..	43.5	54.2	53.2
Lithuania[1]	..	..	0.7	0.9	..	71.7	67.5	56.4
Luxembourg	0.8	0.4	0.2	0.6	63.6	66.5	68.2	67.5
Netherlands	1.5	1.3	0.9	1.1	58.9	56.0	60.6	60.2
New Zealand	..	..	..	..	92.3	94.7	94.7	93.4
Norway	..	..	..	..	50.6	58.4	86.7	84.1
Poland	..	..	0.4	0.5	..	61.2	50.1	49.2
Portugal	..	0.8	0.3	0.5	65.4	72.3	68.6	72.9
Slovak Republic	..	..	0.5	0.5	..	62.5	58.6	55.0
Slovenia	..	..	0.3	0.4	..	51.8	55.9	50.7
Sweden	..	0.4	0.3	0.3	51.3	46.9	56.4	52.4
Turkey	..	..	..	..	..	75.1	69.9	61.2
United Kingdom	1.0	1.0	0.5	0.5	70.5	77.5	76.2	75.5
Unweighted average	1.2	0.7	0.4	0.5	65.2	65.7	65.7	63.8

	Local government				Social Security Funds			
	1975	1995	2005	2017	1975	1995	2005	2017
Chile	..	6.5	6.5	7.8	..	3.6	4.5	5.9
Czech Republic	..	0.9	1.1	1.1	..	41.4	42.8	43.0
Denmark[1]	29.8	31.1	30.4	26.4	0.1	0.0	0.1	0.0
Estonia	..	0.8	1.2	0.9	..	14.9	15.1	16.6
Finland	23.5	22.3	20.7	23.5	20.4	30.8	27.2	27.8
France[1]	7.6	10.9	11.4	13.3	40.6	46.0	48.6	52.1
Greece	3.4	2.0	2.2	2.4	29.5	31.1	32.9	29.6
Hungary	..	2.5	6.2	5.8	..	33.6	30.7	31.5
Iceland	18.7	20.8	22.9	26.5	0.0	0.0	0.0	0.0
Ireland	7.3	2.7	2.2	2.2	13.1	12.7	12.4	14.7
Israel	..	6.4	7.6	7.6	..	14.0	16.1	16.2
Italy	0.9	5.4	16.6	15.5	45.9	31.5	30.8	30.3
Japan	25.6	25.2	25.2	22.7	29.0	33.6	36.9	39.9
Korea	10.1	18.7	17.4	17.3	0.9	12.1	21.2	25.7
Latvia	..	19.5	16.7	19.2	..	36.9	28.4	26.9
Lithuania[1]	..	2.3	1.5	1.2	..	26.1	30.3	41.5
Luxembourg	6.7	6.5	4.5	4.1	29.0	26.6	27.2	27.9
Netherlands	1.2	3.1	4.0	3.0	38.4	39.5	34.5	35.7
New Zealand	7.7	5.3	5.3	6.6	0.0	0.0	0.0	0.0
Norway	22.4	19.6	13.3	15.9	27.0	22.0	0.0	0.0
Poland	..	8.5	12.7	12.7	..	30.3	36.9	37.5
Portugal	0.0	5.4	6.7	7.1	34.6	21.5	24.4	19.5
Slovak Republic	..	1.3	2.6	1.9	..	36.2	38.3	42.5
Slovenia	..	6.3	7.4	9.4	..	41.9	36.4	39.6
Sweden	29.2	30.9	32.1	35.3	19.5	21.8	11.1	12.1
Turkey	..	12.8	7.6	9.5	..	12.1	22.4	29.3
United Kingdom	11.1	3.7	4.7	4.9	17.5	17.8	18.6	19.2
Unweighted average	12.8	10.4	10.8	11.2	21.6	23.6	23.3	24.6

.. Not available

1. The total tax revenue has been reduced by the amount of any capital transfer that represents uncollected taxes. The capital transfer has been allocated between tax headings in proportion to the reported tax revenue.

StatLink https://doi.org/10.1787/888934057476

Table 6.3. Main central government tax revenues as % of GDP at market prices (Federal/regional countries)

	1000 Income & profits			2000+3000 Social security & payroll[3]			4000 Property		
	1975	1995	2017	1975	1995	2017	1975	1995	2017
Federal countries									
Australia	14.2	15.7	16.8	0.1	0.6	0.1	0.1	0.0	0.1
Austria	6.0	10.4	11.5	3.1	4.3	4.0	0.6	0.4	0.3
Belgium	14.2	14.6	12.9	0.5	0.6	0.0	1.0	0.6	0.5
Canada	10.3	9.8	9.7	0.0	0.0	1.0	0.0	0.0	0.0
Germany	4.9	4.8	5.0	0.0	0.0	0.0	0.2	0.0	0.0
Mexico	..	3.3	7.2	..	0.0	0.0	..	0.0	0.0
Switzerland[1]	2.1	2.6	4.6	0.0	0.0	0.0	0.3	0.4	0.3
United States	9.7	9.8	9.9	0.0	0.0	0.0	0.3	0.2	1.4
Unweighted average	8.8	8.9	9.7	0.5	0.7	0.6	0.3	0.2	0.3
Regional country									
Spain[1, 2]	3.5	8.5	5.6	0.0	0.4	0.3	1.1	0.1	0.0

	5110 General taxes			5120 Specific goods and services			Other taxes		
	1975	1995	2017	1975	1995	2017	1975	1995	2017
Federal countries									
Australia	1.7	2.5	3.6	4.2	3.2	2.1	0.0	0.1	0.4
Austria	5.0	7.6	7.7	3.9	2.9	3.0	0.1	1.0	1.0
Belgium	6.3	6.5	6.8	3.0	2.8	2.6	0.4	0.6	0.0
Canada	1.9	2.3	1.9	2.5	1.4	0.8	0.1	0.0	0.0
Germany	3.4	3.5	3.5	3.1	3.1	2.5	0.0	0.0	0.1
Mexico	..	2.2	3.7	..	1.6	2.0	..	0.4	0.2
Switzerland[1]	2.0	3.1	3.5	2.6	1.8	1.5	0.0	0.1	0.5
United States	0.0	0.0	0.0	1.2	1.0	0.7	0.0	0.0	0.0
Unweighted average	2.9	3.5	3.8	2.9	2.2	1.9	0.1	0.3	0.3
Regional country									
Spain[1, 2]	2.5	4.4	5.7	1.5	2.6	2.1	0.0	0.0	0.1

.. Not available

Note: Excluding social security contributions accruing to social security funds.

1. The total tax revenue has been reduced by the amount of any capital transfer that represents uncollected taxes. The capital transfer has been allocated between tax headings in proportion to the reported tax revenue.
2. Spain is constitutionally a non-federal country but has a highly decentralised political structure.
3. These comprise only social security contributions accruing to central government.

StatLink https://doi.org/10.1787/888934057495

Table 6.4. Main central government tax revenues as % of GDP at market prices (Unitary countries)

	1000 Income & profits			2000+3000 Social security & payroll			4000 Property		
	1975	1995	2017	1975	1995	2017	1975	1995	2017
Chile	..	4.6	6.9	..	0.5	0.3	..	0.6	0.4
Czech Republic	..	8.7	7.7	..	0.0	0.0	..	0.2	0.3
Denmark[1]	12.2	15.8	18.2	0.1	0.3	0.3	0.8	0.7	0.5
Estonia	..	10.8	7.2	..	6.9	5.7	..	0.1	0.0
Finland	7.1	6.6	6.0	0.8	0.0	0.0	0.7	0.5	0.8
France[1]	5.6	5.6	5.8	0.7	1.1	0.5	0.6	0.8	1.1
Greece	2.4	5.9	8.9	0.0	0.4	0.0	1.8	1.1	2.2
Hungary	..	8.5	7.2	..	1.3	1.6	..	0.2	0.6
Iceland	3.1	5.9	10.5	2.0	2.5	3.7	0.7	1.6	0.4
Ireland	8.4	12.8	9.8	0.2	0.5	0.7	0.7	0.7	0.8
Israel	..	12.4	11.6	..	1.7	1.2	..	1.4	0.9
Italy	5.1	13.0	11.4	0.0	0.1	0.0	0.8	1.4	1.4
Japan	6.2	6.4	6.2	0.0	0.0	..	0.6	1.1	0.6
Korea	3.3	5.4	7.8	0.0	0.0	0.0	0.6	0.6	1.0
Latvia	..	1.7	3.1	..	0.0	0.0	..	0.1	0.2
Lithuania[1]	..	8.3	5.4	..	0.0	0.0	..	0.0	0.0
Luxembourg	12.0	11.9	12.9	0.1	0.1	0.3	1.4	2.4	3.6
Netherlands	13.1	10.2	11.6	0.0	0.0	0.0	0.7	0.9	0.8
New Zealand	20.0	21.8	17.8	0.0	0.0	0.0	0.7	0.2	0.0
Norway	3.8	7.0	9.8	0.8	0.6	10.4	0.4	0.4	0.5
Poland	..	9.5	4.2	..	0.2	0.2	..	0.0	0.0
Portugal	3.3	7.4	9.1	0.5	1.8	3.0	0.5	0.3	0.2
Slovak Republic	..	10.1	7.0	..	0.4	0.5	..	0.1	0.0
Slovenia	..	4.5	4.4	..	0.5	0.2	..	0.0	0.0
Sweden	8.3	3.8	0.8	1.7	3.6	9.4	0.4	1.2	0.6
Turkey	..	4.1	4.7	..	0.0	0.0	..	0.5	0.8
United Kingdom	15.3	10.9	11.9	0.0	0.0	0.1	0.6	1.9	2.6
Unweighted average	8.1	8.7	8.4	0.4	0.8	1.5	0.7	0.7	0.8

	5110 General taxes			5120 Specific goods and services			Other taxes		
	1975	1995	2017	1975	1995	2017	1975	1995	2017
Chile	..	7.4	8.4	..	3.3	1.7	..	-0.1	-0.4
Czech Republic	..	5.8	7.7	..	4.5	3.3	..	0.9	0.4
Denmark[1]	6.4	9.1	9.5	5.2	5.3	3.9	0.7	0.7	1.2
Estonia	..	9.6	9.1	..	2.8	4.4	..	0.2	0.4
Finland	5.6	7.7	9.1	5.8	5.4	4.5	0.1	0.4	0.6
France[1]	8.1	7.3	6.6	2.8	3.0	1.7	0.2	0.2	0.1
Greece	3.4	5.9	8.2	4.3	4.7	4.5	0.7	0.7	2.4
Hungary	..	7.3	9.9	..	8.5	4.1	..	0.2	0.4
Iceland	8.4	9.2	8.9	9.5	4.3	3.0	0.2	0.9	1.1
Ireland	4.1	6.7	4.4	7.6	5.0	2.2	0.6	0.6	0.7
Israel	..	10.6	8.7	..	1.5	1.8	..	0.7	0.7
Italy	3.5	5.3	5.8	3.4	4.0	3.7	0.3	0.4	0.3
Japan	0.0	1.4	3.2	2.3	1.5	1.6	0.2	0.2	0.1
Korea	1.9	3.4	3.9	6.9	3.4	2.4	0.6	0.5	0.3
Latvia	..	8.4	9.0	..	2.7	3.6	..	0.0	0.7
Lithuania[1]	..	8.2	7.9	..	3.0	3.3	..	0.3	0.1
Luxembourg	3.8	4.3	6.2	2.4	4.3	2.9	0.2	0.2	0.2
Netherlands	5.4	6.0	6.8	2.5	3.0	3.2	0.6	0.8	0.9
New Zealand	2.7	8.1	9.7	4.0	3.0	1.8	0.3	0.6	0.6
Norway	8.0	8.5	8.6	6.2	6.2	2.8	0.5	0.7	0.5
Poland	..	6.1	7.8	..	6.3	4.4	..	0.2	0.2
Portugal	2.1	6.2	7.9	5.5	5.3	4.1	0.5	0.3	0.8
Slovak Republic	..	8.2	7.0	..	4.9	3.1	..	0.9	0.7
Slovenia	..	11.3	8.1	..	3.2	4.8	..	0.3	0.9
Sweden	4.7	8.8	9.3	4.1	3.6	2.6	0.7	0.3	0.5
Turkey	..	4.4	4.4	..	0.9	4.9	..	2.5	0.4
United Kingdom	3.2	5.6	6.9	4.6	4.0	3.3	0.4	0.5	0.4
Unweighted average	4.5	7.1	7.5	4.8	4.0	3.2	0.4	0.5	0.6

.. Not available

Note: Excluding social security contributions accruing to social security funds.

1. The total tax revenue has been reduced by the amount of any capital transfer that represents uncollected taxes. The capital transfer has been allocated between tax headings in proportion to the reported tax revenue.

StatLink https://doi.org/10.1787/888934057514

Table 6.5. Main central government taxes as % of total tax revenues of central government (Federal/regional countries)

	1000 Income & profits			1100 Individuals			1200 Corporate			2000+3000 Social security & payroll		
	1975	1995	2017	1975	1995	2017	1975	1995	2017	1975	1995	2017
Federal countries												
Australia	69.9	71.4	73.0	54.5	52.4	50.0	15.5	19.0	23.0	0.3	2.6	0.3
Austria	32.2	39.2	41.9	25.0	31.1	32.0	6.9	4.8	8.8	16.5	16.2	14.6
Belgium	56.0	57.0	56.6	45.5	47.9	38.5	10.5	9.0	18.1	2.0	2.2	0.1
Canada	69.4	72.5	72.6	46.7	57.7	52.6	20.9	13.0	17.3	0.0	0.0	7.3
Germany	42.3	41.9	45.1	37.0	38.7	39.8	5.2	3.2	5.3	0.0	0.0	0.0
Mexico	..	44.1	55.0	..	..	26.4	..	..	26.9	..	0.0	0.0
Switzerland[1]	30.2	32.3	44.2	24.0	17.6	15.2	6.3	8.3	15.1	0.0	0.0	0.0
United States	86.5	89.2	82.6	64.9	70.7	70.4	21.6	18.5	12.2	0.0	0.0	0.0
Unweighted average	55.2	56.0	58.9	42.5	45.1	40.6	12.4	10.8	15.8	2.7	2.6	2.8
Regional country												
Spain[1, 2]	40.6	52.8	40.0	26.3	42.3	24.3	14.3	10.5	15.7	0.0	2.7	2.1

	4000 Property			5110 General taxes			5120 Specific goods and services			Other taxes		
	1975	1995	2017	1975	1995	2017	1975	1995	2017	1975	1995	2017
Federal countries												
Australia	0.6	0.0	0.4	8.3	11.2	15.5	20.8	14.4	9.2	0.1	0.3	1.7
Austria	3.0	1.4	1.2	26.7	28.5	27.8	20.9	10.9	10.7	0.7	3.8	3.8
Belgium	3.8	2.5	2.1	24.8	25.3	29.7	11.7	10.8	11.6	1.7	2.2	0.0
Canada	0.0	0.0	0.0	12.8	16.9	14.0	17.0	10.6	6.2	0.7	0.0	0.0
Germany	1.9	0.1	0.1	29.1	31.1	31.6	26.7	26.9	22.1	0.0	0.0	1.1
Mexico	..	0.0	0.0	..	30.0	28.5	..	21.2	15.3	..	4.8	1.2
Switzerland[1]	4.1	5.3	2.5	28.3	38.3	33.4	37.3	22.6	14.9	0.0	1.5	5.0
United States	2.4	1.8	11.7	0.0	0.0	0.0	10.8	9.0	5.6	0.2	0.0	0.0
Unweighted average	2.3	1.4	2.2	18.6	22.7	22.6	20.8	15.8	12.0	0.5	1.6	1.6
Regional country												
Spain[1, 2]	12.3	0.5	0.3	29.0	27.5	41.3	17.8	16.3	15.4	0.3	0.2	1.0

.. Not available

Note: Excluding social security contributions accruing to social security funds.

1. The total tax revenue has been reduced by the amount of any capital transfer that represents uncollected taxes. The capital transfer has been allocated between tax headings in proportion to the reported tax revenue.

2. Spain is constitutionally a non-federal country but has a highly decentralised political structure.

StatLink https://doi.org/10.1787/888934057533

Table 6.6. Main central government taxes as % of total tax revenues of central government (Unitary countries)

	1000 Income & profits			1100 Individuals			1200 Corporate			2000+3000 Social security & payroll		
	1975	1995	2017	1975	1995	2017	1975	1995	2017	1975	1995	2017
Chile	..	28.1	40.0	..	5.8	11.2	..	17.3	24.5	..	3.2	1.6
Czech Republic	..	43.3	40.0	..	22.1	20.7	..	21.2	19.3	..	0.0	0.0
Denmark[1]	48.1	49.8	54.3	43.4	37.6	40.1	4.7	7.2	9.8	0.2	0.9	0.8
Estonia	..	35.6	27.0	..	27.7	21.2	..	7.9	5.8	..	22.6	21.4
Finland	35.3	32.0	28.6	31.0	26.0	19.6	4.3	6.0	9.0	4.1	0.1	0.0
France[1]	31.0	31.3	36.6	20.7	19.9	21.9	10.1	11.4	14.8	3.8	6.4	3.3
Greece	18.9	31.2	33.7	12.7	17.2	23.7	5.0	11.8	7.4	0.3	2.2	0.2
Hungary	..	32.8	30.1	..	25.3	21.4	..	7.0	8.7	..	4.9	6.7
Iceland	13.1	24.2	38.0	10.6	20.4	22.9	2.5	3.8	11.1	8.5	10.2	13.5
Ireland	38.8	48.6	52.7	32.5	38.5	37.8	6.2	10.1	14.9	0.9	2.0	3.5
Israel	..	43.9	46.6	..	33.3	27.1	..	10.0	13.3	..	5.9	4.8
Italy	39.0	53.9	50.7	27.7	41.4	39.9	11.3	13.8	8.9	0.0	0.5	0.0
Japan	67.2	60.5	52.6	37.8	35.5	30.0	29.4	25.0	22.6	0.0	0.0	..
Korea	24.7	40.5	50.8	9.6	24.2	28.3	10.0	15.8	22.4	0.0	0.0	0.0
Latvia	..	12.9	18.6	..	0.0	9.1	..	12.9	9.5	..	0.0	0.1
Lithuania[1]	..	42.0	32.1	..	31.6	23.1	..	10.4	9.0	..	0.0	0.0
Luxembourg	60.0	51.3	49.6	43.2	33.2	35.0	16.8	18.0	14.5	0.7	0.6	1.1
Netherlands	58.7	48.7	49.9	45.6	34.2	35.8	13.1	14.5	14.1	0.0	0.0	0.0
New Zealand	72.1	64.7	59.5	58.8	47.5	40.4	12.8	12.5	15.7	0.0	0.0	0.0
Norway	19.2	30.0	30.1	16.1	16.9	15.2	3.2	13.0	14.9	4.0	2.7	31.9
Poland	..	42.5	25.0	..	31.0	16.0	..	11.4	9.0	..	1.1	1.3
Portugal	26.7	34.8	36.2	..	24.9	24.3	..	9.9	11.9	3.8	8.3	12.1
Slovak Republic	..	40.9	38.6	..	14.3	18.5	..	23.9	18.9	..	1.7	2.5
Slovenia	..	22.9	23.8	..	19.8	14.1	..	2.6	9.7	..	2.5	1.1
Sweden	41.7	17.9	3.5	37.9	5.6	-8.6	3.8	12.4	12.1	8.5	17.0	40.5
Turkey	..	32.9	30.7	..	25.1	20.9	..	7.8	9.8	..	0.0	0.0
United Kingdom	63.5	47.7	47.2	56.8	37.2	36.1	8.8	10.4	11.2	0.0	0.0	0.4
Unweighted average	41.1	38.7	38.0	32.3	25.8	23.9	9.5	12.2	13.1	2.2	3.4	5.6

	4000 Property			5110 General taxes			5120 Specific goods and services			Other taxes		
	1975	1995	2017	1975	1995	2017	1975	1995	2017	1975	1995	2017
Chile	..	3.7	2.4	..	45.1	48.2	..	20.3	9.9	..	-0.4	-2.1
Czech Republic	..	1.2	1.3	..	28.8	39.7	..	22.4	16.8	..	4.2	2.1
Denmark[1]	3.0	2.1	1.5	25.4	28.5	28.2	20.5	16.6	11.7	2.8	2.2	3.5
Estonia	..	0.3	0.0	..	31.5	33.9	..	9.3	16.2	..	0.6	1.6
Finland	3.4	2.6	3.6	27.9	37.3	43.5	28.5	26.0	21.4	0.7	1.9	2.9
France[1]	3.2	4.2	7.0	45.1	40.6	41.6	15.5	16.7	10.6	1.4	0.8	0.8
Greece	14.1	6.1	8.4	26.9	31.5	31.3	33.9	25.2	17.2	5.9	3.8	9.2
Hungary	..	0.8	2.7	..	27.9	41.5	..	32.6	17.3	..	0.9	1.7
Iceland	2.8	6.4	1.5	35.1	37.8	32.4	39.5	17.6	10.7	1.0	3.8	3.8
Ireland	3.2	2.6	4.5	19.0	25.4	23.8	35.4	19.1	11.9	2.8	2.4	3.7
Israel	..	4.8	3.6	..	37.5	35.2	..	5.5	7.1	..	2.4	2.7
Italy	5.9	5.7	6.2	26.9	22.0	25.6	26.2	16.5	16.2	2.0	1.5	1.3
Japan	6.0	10.1	5.2	0.0	13.2	27.2	24.7	14.3	14.0	2.1	1.9	1.0
Korea	4.7	4.4	6.4	14.2	25.8	25.3	51.8	25.6	15.9	4.6	3.7	1.7
Latvia	..	0.8	1.0	..	65.3	54.5	..	21.0	21.7	..	0.1	4.1
Lithuania[1]	..	0.0	0.0	..	41.3	47.4	..	15.2	19.6	..	1.5	0.9
Luxembourg	7.1	10.2	13.9	19.1	18.6	23.6	11.9	18.6	11.1	1.2	0.8	0.8
Netherlands	3.0	4.2	3.6	24.4	28.8	29.0	11.1	14.4	13.6	2.8	3.9	3.9
New Zealand	2.6	0.7	0.1	9.8	24.0	32.3	14.4	8.9	6.0	1.2	1.7	2.1
Norway	2.3	1.6	1.5	40.5	36.3	26.4	31.7	26.5	8.5	2.4	3.0	1.6
Poland	..	0.0	0.0	..	27.3	46.3	..	28.3	26.5	..	0.9	1.0
Portugal	3.8	1.2	0.7	17.1	29.1	31.4	44.3	25.0	16.4	4.4	1.6	3.2
Slovak Republic	..	0.5	0.0	..	33.2	38.3	..	20.0	17.0	..	3.6	3.7
Slovenia	..	0.2	0.0	..	57.0	44.1	..	15.9	26.3	..	1.5	4.7
Sweden	2.2	5.8	2.7	23.4	41.3	40.2	20.7	16.6	11.0	3.6	1.4	2.1
Turkey	..	3.7	5.2	..	36.1	29.0	..	7.0	32.2	..	20.3	2.9
United Kingdom	2.4	8.1	10.2	13.4	24.6	27.5	19.0	17.4	13.2	1.8	2.2	1.5
Unweighted average	4.4	3.4	3.5	23.0	33.2	35.1	26.8	18.6	15.6	2.5	2.7	2.4

.. Not available

Note: Excluding social security contributions accruing to social security funds.

1. The total tax revenue has been reduced by the amount of any capital transfer that represents uncollected taxes. The capital transfer has been allocated between tax headings in proportion to the reported tax revenue.

StatLink https://doi.org/10.1787/888934057552

Table 6.7. Main state government tax revenues as % of GDP at market prices (Federal/regional countries)

	1000 Income & profits			2000 Social security			3000 Payroll			4000 Property		
	1975	1995	2017	1975	1995	2017	1975	1995	2017	1975	1995	2017
Federal countries												
Australia	0.0	0.0	0.0	0.0	0.0	0.0	1.4	1.4	1.3	1.1	1.5	1.9
Austria	1.7	0.3	0.3	0.1	0.2	0.1	0.0	0.1	0.1	0.1	0.0	0.0
Belgium[1]	..	0.0	2.3	..	0.0	0.1	..	0.0	0.0	..	0.6	1.7
Canada	4.4	6.3	6.1	0.0	0.0	0.7	0.0	0.8	0.7	0.2	0.8	0.6
Germany[1]	4.8	4.1	4.7	0.0	0.0	0.0	0.0	0.0	0.0	0.5	0.5	0.6
Mexico	..	0.0	0.0	..	0.0	0.0	..	0.1	0.4	..	0.1	0.1
Switzerland[2]	4.7	4.8	5.3	0.0	0.0	0.0	0.0	0.0	0.0	0.9	1.0	1.2
United States	1.5	2.1	2.0	0.0	0.0	0.0	0.0	0.0	0.0	0.2	0.2	0.2
Unweighted average	2.9	2.2	2.6	0.0	0.0	0.1	0.2	0.3	0.3	0.5	0.6	0.8
Regional country												
Spain[1, 2, 3]	..	0.1	3.6	..	0.0	0.0	..	0.0	0.0	..	0.9	1.0

	5110 General taxes			5120 Specific goods and services			5200 Taxes on use of goods			6000 Other taxes		
	1975	1995	2017	1975	1995	2017	1975	1995	2017	1975	1995	2017
Federal countries												
Australia	0.0	0.0	0.0	0.6	0.9	0.7	0.9	1.6	0.7	0.0	0.0	0.0
Austria	1.3	0.0	0.0	0.5	0.1	0.1	0.2	0.0	0.1	0.0	0.0	0.0
Belgium[1]	..	0.0	0.0	..	0.0	0.2	..	0.2	0.6	..	0.0	0.0
Canada	2.0	2.5	2.8	1.7	2.0	1.7	1.8	0.5	0.5	0.0	0.0	0.0
Germany[1]	1.7	2.8	3.2	0.2	0.1	0.1	0.5	0.4	0.2	0.0	0.0	0.0
Mexico	..	0.0	..	..	0.0	0.0	..	0.0	0.1	..	0.0	0.0
Switzerland[2]	0.0	0.0	0.0	0.1	0.1	0.1	0.4	0.4	0.4	0.0	0.0	0.0
United States	1.5	1.8	1.6	1.1	0.9	0.8	0.5	0.4	0.3	0.0	0.0	0.0
Unweighted average	1.1	0.9	1.1	0.7	0.5	0.5	0.7	0.4	0.4	0.0	0.0	0.0
Regional country												
Spain[1, 2, 3]	..	0.1	0.2	..	0.3	0.3	..	0.0	0.0	..	0.0	0.0

.. Not available

1. Payments to the European Union are excluded from these comparisons.
2. The total tax revenue has been reduced by the amount of any capital transfer that represents uncollected taxes. The capital transfer has been allocated between tax headings in proportion to the reported tax revenue.
3. Spain is constitutionally a non-federal country but has a highly decentralised political structure.

StatLink https://doi.org/10.1787/888934057571

Table 6.8. Main local government tax revenues as % of GDP at market prices (Federal/regional countries)

	1000 Income & profits			2000 Social security			3000 Payroll			4000 Property		
	1975	1995	2017	1975	1995	2017	1975	1995	2017	1975	1995	2017
Federal countries												
Australia	0.0	0.0	0.0	0.0	0.0	0.0	0.0	0.0	0.0	1.1	1.0	1.0
Austria	1.7	0.0	0.0	0.1	0.1	0.1	0.5	0.8	0.9	0.5	0.2	0.2
Belgium[1]	1.1	1.4	0.8	0.0	0.0	0.0	0.0	0.0	0.0	0.3	0.4	1.2
Canada	0.0	0.0	0.0	0.0	0.0	0.0	0.0	0.0	0.0	2.7	2.9	3.3
Germany[1]	2.1	2.1	2.6	0.0	0.0	0.0	0.3	0.0	0.0	0.6	0.5	0.4
Mexico	..	0.0	0.0	..	0.0	0.0	..	0.0	0.0	..	0.1	0.2
Switzerland[2]	3.9	3.8	3.5	0.0	0.0	0.0	0.0	0.0	0.0	0.7	0.6	0.7
United States	0.2	0.2	0.2	0.0	0.0	0.0	0.0	0.0	0.0	3.0	2.6	2.7
Unweighted average	1.3	1.0	0.9	0.0	0.0	0.0	0.1	0.1	0.1	1.3	1.0	1.2
Regional country												
Spain[1, 2, 3]	0.4	0.5	0.5	0.0	0.0	0.0	0.0	0.0	0.0	0.1	0.8	1.5

	5110 General taxes			5120 Specific goods and services			5200 Taxes on use of goods			6000 Other taxes		
	1975	1995	2017	1975	1995	2017	1975	1995	2017	1975	1995	2017
Federal countries												
Australia	0.0	0.0	0.0	0.0	0.0	0.0	0.0	0.0	..	0.0	0.0	0.0
Austria	0.9	0.0	0.0	0.6	0.3	0.0	0.0	0.1	0.1	0.1	0.0	0.0
Belgium[1]	0.0	0.0	0.0	0.3	0.1	0.1	0.0	0.0	0.0	0.0	0.0	0.0
Canada	0.0	0.0	0.0	0.0	0.0	0.0	0.1	0.0	0.0	0.3	0.4	0.0
Germany[1]	0.0	0.0	0.2	0.0	0.0	0.0	0.0	0.0	0.0	0.0	0.0	0.0
Mexico	..	0.0	..	..	0.0	0.0	..	0.0	0.0	..	0.0	0.1
Switzerland[2]	0.0	0.0	0.0	0.0	0.0	0.0	0.0	0.0	0.0	0.0	0.0	0.1
United States	0.3	0.4	0.5	0.1	0.2	0.2	0.1	0.2	0.2	0.0	0.0	0.0
Unweighted average	0.2	0.0	0.1	0.1	0.1	0.0	0.0	0.0	0.0	0.1	0.1	0.0
Regional country												
Spain[1, 2, 3]	0.2	0.4	0.5	0.0	0.1	0.2	0.0	0.9	0.6	0.0	0.0	0.0

.. Not available

1. Payments to the European Union are excluded from these comparisons.

2. The total tax revenue has been reduced by the amount of any capital transfer that represents uncollected taxes. The capital transfer has been allocated between tax headings in proportion to the reported tax revenue.

3. Spain is constitutionally a non-federal country but has a highly decentralised political structure.

StatLink https://doi.org/10.1787/888934057590

Table 6.9. Main state government taxes as % of total tax revenues of state government (Federal/regional countries)

	1000 Income & profits			2000 Social security			3000 Payroll			4000 Property		
	1975	1995	2017	1975	1995	2017	1975	1995	2017	1975	1995	2017
Federal countries												
Australia	0.0	0.0	0.0	0.0	0.0	0.0	35.3	25.1	29.0	26.6	28.1	41.4
Austria	44.2	42.3	47.1	1.8	24.0	19.8	0.0	10.2	8.5	1.8	2.4	2.1
Belgium[1]	..	4.7	47.3	..	0.0	1.1	..	0.0	0.0	..	70.4	36.0
Canada	43.6	48.7	46.7	0.0	0.0	5.3	0.0	6.0	5.1	2.3	6.0	4.9
Germany[1]	62.8	51.9	52.9	0.0	0.0	0.0	0.0	0.0	0.0	6.2	6.1	6.7
Mexico	..	0.0	0.0	..	0.0	0.0	..	45.3	58.3	..	44.5	18.1
Switzerland[2]	77.7	76.9	76.1	0.0	0.0	0.0	0.0	0.0	0.0	14.3	16.3	16.9
United States	31.6	38.8	41.6	0.0	0.0	0.0	0.0	0.0	0.2	4.1	4.2	3.3
Unweighted average	43.3	32.9	39.0	0.3	3.0	3.3	5.9	10.8	12.6	9.2	22.3	16.2
Regional country												
Spain[1, 2, 3]	..	8.6	69.4	..	0.0	0.0	..	0.0	0.0	..	58.9	20.0

	5110 General taxes			5120 Specific goods and services			5200 Taxes on use of goods			6000 Other taxes		
	1975	1995	2017	1975	1995	2017	1975	1995	2017	1975	1995	2017
Federal countries												
Australia	0.0	0.0	0.0	16.0	17.3	14.7	22.0	29.5	14.9	0.0	0.0	0.0
Austria	33.9	0.0	0.0	13.5	12.2	10.7	4.4	5.0	7.6	0.4	3.9	4.2
Belgium[1]	..	0.0	0.0	..	3.5	3.7	..	21.4	11.9	..	0.0	0.0
Canada	19.6	19.9	21.3	16.8	15.5	12.9	17.8	3.8	3.8	0.0	0.0	0.0
Germany[1]	21.8	35.4	36.6	2.8	1.8	1.1	6.4	4.7	2.8	0.0	0.0	0.0
Mexico	..	0.0	..	..	0.3	5.0	..	6.4	13.6	..	3.5	5.0
Switzerland[2]	0.0	0.0	0.0	1.5	0.9	1.3	6.4	5.7	5.0	0.0	0.1	0.7
United States	30.8	33.2	31.7	23.6	16.1	16.3	10.0	7.8	6.9	0.0	0.0	0.0
Unweighted average	17.7	11.1	12.8	12.4	8.5	8.2	11.2	10.5	8.3	0.1	0.9	1.2
Regional country												
Spain[1, 2, 3]	..	9.2	3.3	..	20.9	6.3	..	2.5	0.9	..	0.0	0.0

.. Not available

1. Payments to the European Union are excluded from these comparisons.
2. The total tax revenue has been reduced by the amount of any capital transfer that represents uncollected taxes. The capital transfer has been allocated between tax headings in proportion to the reported tax revenue.
3. Spain is constitutionally a non-federal country but has a highly decentralised political structure.

StatLink https://doi.org/10.1787/888934057609

Table 6.10. Main local government taxes as % of total tax revenues of local governments (Federal/regional countries)

	1000 Income & profits			2000 Social security			3000 Payroll			4000 Property		
	1975	1995	2017	1975	1995	2017	1975	1995	2017	1975	1995	2017
Federal countries												
Australia	0.0	0.0	0.0	0.0	0.0	0.0	0.0	0.0	0.0	100.0	100.0	100.0
Austria	38.9	1.5	0.0	1.3	8.6	5.5	11.5	49.9	68.5	11.2	13.2	15.1
Belgium[1]	66.3	71.3	35.4	2.6	1.9	0.2	0.0	0.0	0.0	15.0	19.0	57.6
Canada	0.0	0.0	0.0	0.0	0.0	0.0	0.0	0.0	0.0	88.3	85.7	97.3
Germany[1]	69.4	79.5	79.4	0.0	0.0	0.0	9.0	0.0	0.0	20.3	19.3	13.2
Mexico	..	0.5	0.0	..	0.0	0.0	..	0.2	0.0	..	77.5	74.6
Switzerland[2]	85.5	84.4	81.2	0.0	0.0	0.0	0.0	0.0	0.0	14.3	14.2	16.3
United States	4.3	5.8	5.8	0.0	0.0	0.0	0.0	0.0	0.0	81.9	72.9	72.0
Unweighted average	37.8	30.4	25.2	0.5	1.3	0.7	2.9	6.3	9.8	47.3	50.2	55.8
Regional country												
Spain[1, 2, 3]	57.3	19.8	16.3	0.0	0.0	0.0	0.0	0.0	0.0	8.5	29.7	44.7

	5110 General taxes			5120 Specific goods and services			5200 Taxes on use of goods			6000 Other taxes		
	1975	1995	2017	1975	1995	2017	1975	1995	2017	1975	1995	2017
Federal countries												
Australia	0.0	0.0	0.0	0.0	0.0	0.0	0.0	0.0	..	0.0	0.0	0.0
Austria	19.7	0.0	0.0	14.1	19.5	2.0	1.0	5.2	5.9	2.4	2.0	3.0
Belgium[1]	0.0	0.0	0.0	14.6	6.9	6.6	1.5	0.9	0.2	0.0	0.0	0.0
Canada	0.2	0.1	0.1	0.2	0.0	0.1	2.1	1.2	1.4	9.2	12.9	1.0
Germany[1]	0.0	0.0	5.8	0.5	0.5	1.0	0.4	0.3	0.3	0.4	0.3	0.2
Mexico	..	0.0	..	..	16.4	2.5	..	0.2	0.0	..	5.1	22.9
Switzerland[2]	0.0	0.0	0.0	0.2	0.2	0.1	0.1	0.2	0.3	0.0	0.9	1.9
United States	7.1	10.8	12.6	3.6	4.8	4.7	3.1	5.6	5.0	0.0	0.0	0.0
Unweighted average	3.8	1.4	2.6	4.7	6.0	2.1	1.2	1.7	1.9	1.7	2.6	3.6
Regional country												
Spain[1, 2, 3]	31.0	15.5	16.6	3.2	2.6	5.0	0.0	32.3	17.3	0.0	0.1	0.1

.. Not available

1. Payments to the European Union are excluded from these comparisons.
2. The total tax revenue has been reduced by the amount of any capital transfer that represents uncollected taxes. The capital transfer has been allocated between tax headings in proportion to the reported tax revenue.
3. Spain is constitutionally a non-federal country but has a highly decentralised political structure.

StatLink https://doi.org/10.1787/888934057628

Table 6.11. Main local government tax revenues as % of GDP at market prices (Unitary countries)

	1000 Income & profits			4000 Property			5110 General taxes		
	1975	1995	2017	1975	1995	2017	1975	1995	2017
Chile	..	0.0	0.0	..	0.5	0.7	..	0.0	0.0
Czech Republic[1]	..	0.0	0.0	..	0.2	0.2	..	0.0	0.0
Denmark[1, 2]	9.5	13.5	10.8	1.5	1.0	1.3	0.0	0.0	0.0
Estonia[1]	..	0.0	0.0	..	0.3	0.2	..	0.0	0.0
Finland[1]	8.5	9.5	9.4	0.0	0.4	0.8	0.0	0.0	0.0
France[1, 2]	0.0	0.0	0.0	1.2	2.2	3.3	0.0	0.0	0.0
Greece	0.1	0.0	0.0	0.0	0.5	0.9	0.1	0.0	0.0
Hungary[1]	..	0.0	0.0	..	0.3	0.4	..	0.7	1.7
Iceland	3.6	4.6	7.9	0.8	1.2	1.7	0.0	0.6	0.0
Ireland[1]	0.0	0.0	0.0	2.0	0.7	0.5	0.0	..	..
Israel	..	0.0	0.0	..	2.1	2.4	..	0.0	0.0
Italy[1]	0.2	0.6	1.9	0.0	0.8	1.2	..	0.0	0.5
Japan	2.8	3.4	3.4	1.3	2.1	2.0	0.0	0.0	0.9
Korea	0.3	0.4	0.9	0.8	2.1	2.2	0.0	0.0	0.4
Latvia	..	4.9	5.1	..	0.9	0.8	..	0.0	0.0
Lithuania[2]	..	0.0	0.0	..	0.3	0.3	..	..	0.0
Luxembourg[1]	1.6	2.1	1.5	0.2	0.1	0.1	0.0	0.0	0.0
Netherlands[1]	0.1	0.0	0.0	0.2	0.7	0.7	0.0	0.0	0.0
New Zealand	0.0	0.0	0.0	2.1	1.7	1.9	0.0	0.0	0.0
Norway	8.0	7.1	5.3	0.4	0.8	0.8	0.0	0.0	0.0
Poland[1]	..	1.4	2.7	..	1.3	1.4	..	0.0	..
Portugal[1]	0.0	0.3	0.6	0.0	0.7	1.2	0.0	0.4	0.3
Slovak Republic[1]	..	0.0	0.0	..	0.4	0.4	..	0.0	0.0
Slovenia[1]	..	1.8	2.5	..	0.5	0.6	..	0.0	0.0
Sweden[1]	11.3	14.1	15.3	0.0	0.0	0.4	0.0	0.0	0.0
Turkey	..	0.6	0.6	..	0.0	0.3	..	0.6	0.6
United Kingdom[1]	0.0	0.0	0.0	3.8	1.1	1.6	0.0	0.0	0.0
Unweighted average	2.9	2.4	2.5	0.9	0.9	1.0	0.0	0.1	0.2

	5120 Specific goods and services			5200 Taxes on use of goods			Other taxes		
	1975	1995	2017	1975	1995	2017	1975	1995	2017
Chile	..	0.2	0.2	..	0.5	0.7	..	0.0	0.0
Czech Republic[1]	..	0.0	0.0	..	0.1	0.2	..	0.0	0.0
Denmark[1, 2]	0.0	0.0	0.0	..	..	..	0.0	0.0	0.0
Estonia[1]	..	0.0	0.0	..	0.0	0.0	..	0.0	0.0
Finland[1]	0.0	0.0	0.0	0.0	0.0	0.0	0.0	0.0	0.0
France[1, 2]	0.1	0.3	1.2	0.1	0.3	0.2	1.2	1.8	1.5
Greece	0.2	0.1	0.1	0.1	0.0	0.0	0.1	0.0	0.0
Hungary[1]	..	0.0	0.0	..	0.0	0.1	..	0.0	0.0
Iceland	0.4	0.0	0.0	0.0	0.0	0.3	0.6	0.0	0.0
Ireland[1]	0.0	..	..	0.0	..	..	0.0	0.1	0.0
Israel	..	0.0	0.0	..	0.1	0.1	..	0.0	0.0
Italy[1]	..	0.2	0.5	0.0	0.3	0.5	0.0	0.3	1.9
Japan	0.8	0.6	0.4	0.3	0.3	0.3	0.0	0.1	0.1
Korea	0.2	0.6	0.3	0.2	0.4	0.4	0.0	0.1	0.5
Latvia	..	0.0	0.0	..	0.0	0.0	..	0.0	0.0
Lithuania[2]	..	..	0.0	..	0.3	0.0	..	0.0	0.0
Luxembourg[1]	0.0	0.0	0.0	0.0	0.0	0.0	0.3	0.0	0.0
Netherlands[1]	0.0	0.0	0.0	0.1	0.4	0.4	0.0	0.0	0.0
New Zealand	0.2	0.0	0.0	0.1	0.2	0.2	0.0	0.0	0.0
Norway	0.0	0.0	0.0	0.0	0.0	0.1	0.3	0.0	0.0
Poland[1]	..	0.0	..	..	0.4	0.2	..	0.0	0.1
Portugal[1]	0.0	0.1	0.2	0.0	0.1	0.1	0.0	0.0	0.0
Slovak Republic[1]	..	0.1	0.0	..	0.0	0.0	..	0.0	0.2
Slovenia[1]	..	0.1	0.1	..	0.0	0.1	..	0.0	0.0
Sweden[1]	0.0	0.0	0.0	0.0	0.0	0.0	0.0	0.0	0.0
Turkey	..	0.1	0.5	..	0.0	0.1	..	0.7	0.2
United Kingdom[1]	0.0	0.0	0.0	0.0	..	..	0.0	0.0	0.0
Unweighted average	0.1	0.1	0.1	0.1	0.1	0.2	0.2	0.1	0.2

.. Not available

1. Payments to the European Union are excluded from these comparisons.

2. The total tax revenue has been reduced by the amount of any capital transfer that represents uncollected taxes. The capital transfer has been allocated between tax headings in proportion to the reported tax revenue.

StatLink https://doi.org/10.1787/888934057647

Table 6.12. Main local government tax revenues as % of total tax revenues of local governments (Unitary countries)

	1000 Income & profits			1100 Individuals			1200 Corporate			4000 Property		
	1975	1995	2017	1975	1995	2017	1975	1995	2017	1975	1995	2017
Chile	..	0.0	0.0	..	0.0	0.0	..	0.0	0.0	..	45.0	42.6
Czech Republic[1]	..	0.0	0.0	..	0.0	0.0	..	0.0	0.0	..	76.7	57.2
Denmark[1, 2]	86.3	93.3	89.3	86.3	93.3	89.3	0.0	0.0	0.0	13.7	6.7	10.7
Estonia[1]	..	0.0	0.0	..	0.0	0.0	..	0.0	0.0	..	90.5	81.9
Finland[1]	99.8	95.4	92.1	89.9	85.2	83.9	9.9	10.2	8.3	0.0	4.5	7.8
France[1, 2]	0.0	0.0	0.0	0.0	0.0	0.0	0.0	0.0	0.0	46.0	47.8	53.2
Greece	16.5	0.0	0.0	11.0	0.0	0.0	0.0	0.0	0.0	6.6	83.4	93.2
Hungary[1]	..	0.0	0.0	..	0.0	0.0	..	0.0	0.0	..	28.9	19.3
Iceland	65.1	71.9	80.1	62.0	71.9	80.1	3.1	0.0	0.0	15.3	19.3	16.6
Ireland[1]	0.0	0.0	0.0	0.0	..	..	0.0	..	..	100.0	87.9	93.1
Israel	..	0.0	0.0	..	0.0	0.0	..	0.0	0.0	..	94.1	95.2
Italy[1]	80.0	27.6	29.4	48.0	0.7	27.7	32.0	0.5	1.5	17.5	38.6	18.4
Japan	54.8	52.7	48.5	26.3	30.5	33.5	28.5	22.2	15.0	24.9	31.6	27.6
Korea	23.0	11.1	18.3	0.0	7.4	9.9	0.0	3.7	8.4	54.5	58.5	46.6
Latvia	..	83.8	84.8	..	83.8	84.8	..	0.0	0.0	..	15.5	14.1
Lithuania[2]	..	0.0	0.0	..	..	..	..	..	..	..	51.6	86.5
Luxembourg[1]	74.6	92.8	92.1	0.0	0.0	0.0	74.6	92.8	92.1	9.3	5.9	6.7
Netherlands[1]	15.4	0.0	0.0	15.4	0.0	0.0	0.0	0.0	0.0	54.2	59.9	61.9
New Zealand	0.0	0.0	0.0	0.0	0.0	0.0	0.0	0.0	0.0	89.1	89.9	89.4
Norway	91.9	89.7	86.0	86.3	81.6	86.0	5.7	8.2	0.0	5.2	9.7	12.9
Poland[1]	..	45.5	62.7	..	41.1	52.9	..	4.4	9.8	..	40.6	31.4
Portugal[1]	50.0	21.8	25.3	..	11.1	16.0	..	10.7	9.4	0.0	42.5	48.3
Slovak Republic[1]	..	0.0	0.0	..	0.0	0.0	..	0.0	..	..	83.3	66.6
Slovenia[1]	..	75.8	75.0	..	74.9	75.0	..	0.0	0.0	..	20.7	18.8
Sweden[1]	99.6	99.7	97.6	91.5	99.7	97.6	8.2	0.0	0.0	0.0	0.0	2.4
Turkey	..	28.1	27.2	..	21.4	18.3	..	6.7	8.9	..	2.0	13.9
United Kingdom[1]	0.0	0.0	0.0	0.0	0.0	0.0	0.0	0.0	0.0	100.0	100.0	100.0
Unweighted average	47.3	32.9	33.6	34.4	28.1	30.2	10.8	6.4	6.4	33.5	45.7	45.0

	5110 General taxes			5120 Specific goods and services			5200 Taxes on use of goods			Other taxes		
	1975	1995	2017	1975	1995	2017	1975	1995	2017	1975	1995	2017
Chile	..	0.0	0.0	..	15.1	14.8	..	40.0	42.5	..	0.0	0.0
Czech Republic[1]	..	0.0	0.0	..	2.5	1.8	..	20.8	40.9	..	0.0	0.0
Denmark[1, 2]	0.0	0.0	0.0	0.0	0.0	0.0	..	..	..	0.0	0.0	0.0
Estonia[1]	..	2.0	0.0	..	0.9	8.5	..	6.7	9.5	..	0.0	0.0
Finland[1]	0.0	0.0	0.0	0.1	0.0	0.0	0.1	0.1	0.0	0.0	0.0	0.1
France[1, 2]	0.0	0.0	0.0	4.8	7.4	19.7	3.2	6.9	3.2	46.0	37.9	23.8
Greece	9.0	6.0	0.6	32.9	10.3	5.3	18.7	0.4	0.9	16.3	0.0	0.0
Hungary[1]	..	63.5	75.5	..	1.3	1.6	..	4.5	3.6	..	1.8	0.0
Iceland	0.0	8.8	0.0	7.9	0.0	0.0	0.0	0.0	3.3	11.7	0.0	0.0
Ireland[1]	0.0	..	..	0.0	..	..	0.0	..	..	0.0	12.1	6.9
Israel	..	0.0	0.0	..	0.0	0.0	..	5.9	4.8	..	0.0	0.0
Italy[1]	..	0.0	7.2	..	7.3	7.3	2.5	13.8	8.2	0.0	12.7	29.5
Japan	0.0	0.0	12.2	15.1	9.6	6.0	4.9	5.0	4.6	0.2	1.0	1.1
Korea	0.0	0.0	9.0	11.7	16.1	5.8	10.8	11.5	9.7	0.0	2.8	10.6
Latvia	..	0.0	0.0	..	0.0	0.5	..	0.7	0.6	..	0.0	0.0
Lithuania[2]	..	..	0.0	..	..	0.0	..	48.4	13.5	..	0.0	0.0
Luxembourg[1]	0.0	0.0	0.0	0.9	0.9	0.9	0.0	0.2	0.2	15.2	0.2	0.2
Netherlands[1]	0.0	0.2	0.7	2.7	1.4	2.9	27.7	38.6	34.4	0.0	0.0	0.0
New Zealand	0.0	0.0	0.0	6.7	1.8	0.5	4.2	8.3	10.1	0.0	0.0	0.0
Norway	0.0	0.0	0.0	0.0	0.0	0.0	0.0	0.6	1.1	2.9	0.0	0.0
Poland[1]	..	0.0	..	..	0.0	..	..	12.4	4.7	..	1.5	1.1
Portugal[1]	0.0	22.5	13.9	0.0	8.8	6.3	50.0	4.0	5.6	0.0	0.4	0.6
Slovak Republic[1]	..	0.0	0.0	..	10.3	2.8	..	1.0	1.1	..	5.4	29.5
Slovenia[1]	..	0.0	0.0	..	2.8	3.7	..	0.0	2.4	..	0.8	0.0
Sweden[1]	0.0	0.0	0.0	0.3	0.3	0.0	0.1	0.0	0.0	0.0	0.0	0.0
Turkey	..	30.8	25.2	..	6.0	22.8	..	0.5	2.1	..	32.7	8.7
United Kingdom[1]	0.0	0.0	0.0	0.0	0.0	0.0	0.0	..	..	0.0	0.0	0.0
Unweighted average	0.6	5.4	5.8	5.5	4.1	4.5	8.1	9.6	8.6	5.8	4.0	4.2

.. Not available

1. Payments to the European Union are excluded from these comparisons.

2. The total tax revenue has been reduced by the amount of any capital transfer that represents uncollected taxes. The capital transfer has been allocated between tax headings in proportion to the reported tax revenue.

StatLink https://doi.org/10.1787/888934057666

6.2. Country tables 1975, 1985, 1995, 2005 and 2017

This part of the Report presents detailed country information on tax revenues by level of government. The data have been attributed to the sub-sectors of general government identified in section A.12 of the Interpretative Guide (see Annex A) and the attribution criteria used are those set out in that guide.

Table 6.13. Australia, tax revenues by sub-sectors of government

Million AUD

	Federal government					State/Regional				
	1975	1995	2005	2015	2017	1975	1995	2005	2015	2017
1000 Taxes on income, profits and capital gains	**11 831**	**82 615**	**175 695**	**262 357**	**310 041**	**0**	**0**	**0**	**0**	**0**
1100 Of individuals	9 213	60 602	118 239	191 747	212 520	..	..	..	..	..
1200 Corporate	2 618	22 013	57 456	70 610	97 521	..	..	..	..	..
1300 Unallocable between 1100 and 1200	0	0	0	0	0	0	0	0	0	0
2000 Social security contributions	**0**	**0**	**0**	**0**	**0**	**0**	**0**	**0**	**0**	**0**
2100 Employees	0	0	0	0	0	0	0	0	0	0
2200 Employers	0	0	0	0	0	0	0	0	0	0
2300 Self-employed or non-employed	0	0	0	0	0	0	0	0	0	0
2400 Unallocable between 2100, 2200 and 2300	0	0	0	0	0	0	0	0	0	0
3000 Taxes on payroll and workforce	**54**	**3 065**	**369**	**670**	**1 107**	**1 171**	**7 120**	**13 095**	**22 684**	**24 413**
4000 Taxes on property	**103**	**8**	**14**	**15**	**1 542**	**883**	**7 988**	**16 940**	**33 006**	**34 869**
4100 Recurrent taxes on immovable property	12	0	0	0	..	217	1 840	4 559	10 473	12 222
4200 Recurrent taxes on net wealth	0	0	0	0	0	0	0	0	0	0
4300 Estate, inheritance and gift taxes	87	0	0	0	0	227	0	0	0	0
4400 Taxes on financial and capital transactions	4	8	14	15	1 542	439	6 148	12 381	22 533	22 647
4500 Non-recurrent taxes	0	0	0	0	0	0	0	0	0	0
4600 Other recurrent taxes on property	0	0	0	0	0	0	0	0	0	0
5000 Taxes on goods and services	**4 932**	**30 004**	**69 360**	**104 590**	**112 113**	**1 262**	**13 295**	**14 479**	**23 408**	**24 978**
5100 Taxes on production, sale, transfer, etc	4 919	29 613	67 822	98 301	104 950	532	4 923	8 188	11 884	12 390
5110 General taxes	1 408	12 970	40 086	61 815	65 700	0	0	0	0	0
5120 Taxes on specific goods and services	3 511	16 643	27 736	36 486	39 250	532	4 923	8 188	11 884	12 390
5130 Unallocable between 5110 and 5120	0	0	0	0	0	0	0	0	0	0
5200 Taxes on use of goods and perform activities	13	391	1 538	6 289	7 163	730	8 372	6 291	11 524	12 588
5300 Unallocable between 5100 and 5200	0	0	0	0	0	0	0	0	0	0
6000 Other taxes	**0**	**0**	**0**	**0**	**0**	**0**	**0**	**0**	**0**	**0**
6100 Paid solely by business	..	..	..	..	..	..	..	..	..	..
6200 Other	..	..	..	..	..	..	..	..	..	..
Total tax revenue	**16 920**	**115 692**	**245 438**	**367 632**	**424 803**	**3 316**	**28 403**	**44 514**	**79 098**	**84 260**

	Local government					Social Security Funds				
	1975	1995	2005	2015	2017	1975	1995	2005	2015	2017
1000 Taxes on income, profits and capital gains	**0**	**0**	**0**	**0**	**0**	**0**	**0**	**0**	**0**	**0**
1100 Of individuals	..	..	..	..	..	..	..	..	..	..
1200 Corporate	..	..	..	..	..	..	..	..	..	..
1300 Unallocable between 1100 and 1200	0	0	0	0	0	0	0	0	0	0
2000 Social security contributions	**0**	**0**	**0**	**0**	**0**	**0**	**0**	**0**	**0**	**0**
2100 Employees	0	0	0	0	0	0	0	0	0	0
2200 Employers	0	0	0	0	0	0	0	0	0	0
2300 Self-employed or non-employed	0	0	0	0	0	0	0	0	0	0
2400 Unallocable between 2100, 2200 and 2300	0	0	0	0	0	0	0	0	0	0
3000 Taxes on payroll and workforce	**0**	**0**	**0**	**0**	**0**	**0**	**0**	**0**	**0**	**0**
4000 Taxes on property	**883**	**5 134**	**8 726**	**16 620**	**18 122**	**0**	**0**	**0**	**0**	**0**
4100 Recurrent taxes on immovable property	883	5 134	8 726	16 620	18 122	..	..	..	..	..
4200 Recurrent taxes on net wealth	0	0	0	0	0	..	..	..	..	..
4300 Estate, inheritance and gift taxes	0	0	0	0	0	..	..	..	..	..
4400 Taxes on financial and capital transactions	0	0	0	0	0	..	..	..	..	..
4500 Non-recurrent taxes	0	0	0	0	0	..	..	..	..	..
4600 Other recurrent taxes on property	0	0	0	0	0	..	..	..	..	..
5000 Taxes on goods and services	**0**	**0**	**0**	**0**	**0**	**0**	**0**	**0**	**0**	**0**
5100 Taxes on production, sale, transfer, etc	0	0	0	0	0	0	0	0	0	0
5110 General taxes	0	0	0	0	0	0	0	0	0	0
5120 Taxes on specific goods and services	0	0	0	0	0	0	0	0	0	0
5130 Unallocable between 5110 and 5120	0	0	0	0	..	0	0	0	0	..
5200 Taxes on use of goods and perform activities	0	0	0	0	0	0	0	0	0	0
5300 Unallocable between 5100 and 5200	0	0	0	0	..	0	0	0	0	..
6000 Other taxes	**0**	**0**	**0**	**0**	**0**	**0**	**0**	**0**	**0**	**0**
6100 Paid solely by business	..	..	..	..	..	..	..	..	..	..
6200 Other	..	..	..	..	..	..	..	..	..	..
Total tax revenue	**883**	**5 134**	**8 726**	**16 620**	**18 122**	**0**	**0**	**0**	**0**	**0**

.. Not available

StatLink https://doi.org/10.1787/888934057685

Table 6.14. Austria, tax revenues by sub-sectors of government

Million EUR

	Federal government					State/Regional				
	1975	1995	2005	2015	2017	1975	1995	2005	2015	2017
1000 Taxes on income, profits and capital gains	**3 064**	**18 452**	**28 781**	**43 419**	**42 572**	**865**	**547**	**742**	**1 081**	**1 157**
1100 Of individuals	2 381	14 649	22 126	34 606	32 510	834	459	637	941	1 011
1200 Corporate	655	2 267	5 341	7 519	8 971	31	88	104	141	146
1300 Unallocable between 1100 and 1200	27	1 536	1 313	1 295	1 091	0	0	0	0	0
2000 Social security contributions	**352**	**4 243**	**5 720**	**7 547**	**8 038**	**34**	**311**	**409**	**496**	**487**
2100 Employees	225	2 379	2 978	3 911	4 161	34	310	395	465	456
2200 Employers	127	1 830	2 498	3 350	3 597	0	0	0	0	0
2300 Self-employed or non-employed	0	34	243	286	280	0	1	14	31	31
2400 Unallocable between 2100, 2200 and 2300	0	0	0	0	0	0	0	0	0	0
3000 Taxes on payroll and workforce	**1 217**	**3 394**	**4 384**	**6 861**	**6 836**	**0**	**132**	**156**	**203**	**210**
4000 Taxes on property	**282**	**655**	**801**	**1 247**	**1 188**	**35**	**31**	**36**	**44**	**51**
4100 Recurrent taxes on immovable property	18	32	32	43	51	15	31	36	44	51
4200 Recurrent taxes on net wealth	226	58	0	0	0	10	0	0	0	0
4300 Estate, inheritance and gift taxes	24	82	140	12	1	10	0	0	0	0
4400 Taxes on financial and capital transactions	14	483	629	1 116	1 110	0	0	0	0	0
4500 Non-recurrent taxes	0	0	0	76	27	0	0	0	0	0
4600 Other recurrent taxes on property	0	0	0	0	0	0	0	0	0	0
5000 Taxes on goods and services	**4 554**	**19 894**	**29 646**	**39 720**	**42 514**	**1 013**	**222**	**234**	**362**	**448**
5100 Taxes on production, sale, transfer, etc	4 549	18 639	27 613	36 693	39 245	926	158	139	216	262
5110 General taxes	2 545	13 436	19 421	26 282	28 312	662	0	0	0	0
5120 Taxes on specific goods and services	1 991	5 159	8 148	10 408	10 929	264	158	139	216	262
5130 Unallocable between 5110 and 5120	14	44	45	4	4	0	0	0	0	0
5200 Taxes on use of goods and perform activities	5	1 255	2 033	3 027	3 269	87	64	95	146	186
5300 Unallocable between 5100 and 5200	0	0	0	0	0	0	0	0	0	0
6000 Other taxes	**52**	**486**	**699**	**517**	**551**	**8**	**50**	**61**	**93**	**103**
6100 Paid solely by business	..	..	..	..	..	..	..	..	..	..
6200 Other	..	..	..	..	..	..	..	..	..	..
Total tax revenue	**9 521**	**47 124**	**70 031**	**99 311**	**101 699**	**1 955**	**1 294**	**1 638**	**2 279**	**2 456**

	Local government					Social Security Funds				
	1975	1995	2005	2015	2017	1975	1995	2005	2015	2017
1000 Taxes on income, profits and capital gains	**887**	**46**	**0**	**0**	**0**	**0**	**0**	**0**	**0**	**0**
1100 Of individuals	771	19	0	0	0	..	..	..	..	..
1200 Corporate	115	26	0	0	0	..	..	..	..	..
1300 Unallocable between 1100 and 1200	0	0	0	0	0	..	..	..	..	..
2000 Social security contributions	**29**	**258**	**267**	**266**	**258**	**4 667**	**21 173**	**28 912**	**41 557**	**45 134**
2100 Employees	29	207	240	241	234	1 840	8 110	10 751	15 499	16 867
2200 Employers	0	50	27	26	24	2 375	10 912	14 037	19 906	21 665
2300 Self-employed or non-employed	0	0	0	0	0	453	2 151	4 125	6 153	6 602
2400 Unallocable between 2100, 2200 and 2300	0	0	0	0	0	0	0	0	0	0
3000 Taxes on payroll and workforce	**262**	**1 492**	**2 035**	**2 977**	**3 192**	**0**	**0**	**0**	**0**	**0**
4000 Taxes on property	**254**	**395**	**539**	**675**	**703**	**0**	**0**	**0**	**0**	**0**
4100 Recurrent taxes on immovable property	139	395	539	675	703	..	..	..	..	..
4200 Recurrent taxes on net wealth	35	0	0	0	0	..	..	..	..	..
4300 Estate, inheritance and gift taxes	0	0	0	0	0	..	..	..	..	..
4400 Taxes on financial and capital transactions	81	0	0	0	0	..	..	..	..	..
4500 Non-recurrent taxes	0	0	0	0	0	..	..	..	..	..
4600 Other recurrent taxes on property	0	0	0	0	0	..	..	..	..	..
5000 Taxes on goods and services	**792**	**738**	**302**	**353**	**366**	**0**	**0**	**0**	**0**	**0**
5100 Taxes on production, sale, transfer, etc	769	582	134	96	91	..	..	..	..	..
5110 General taxes	448	0	0	0	0	..	..	..	..	..
5120 Taxes on specific goods and services	321	582	134	96	91	..	..	..	..	..
5130 Unallocable between 5110 and 5120	0	0	0	0	0	..	..	..	..	..
5200 Taxes on use of goods and perform activities	24	155	168	258	275	..	..	..	..	..
5300 Unallocable between 5100 and 5200	0	0	0	0	0	..	..	..	..	..
6000 Other taxes	**55**	**60**	**103**	**127**	**142**	**0**	**0**	**0**	**0**	**0**
6100 Paid solely by business	..	..	..	..	..	..	..	..	..	..
6200 Other	..	..	..	..	..	..	..	..	..	..
Total tax revenue	**2 279**	**2 987**	**3 246**	**4 398**	**4 661**	**4 667**	**21 173**	**28 912**	**41 557**	**45 134**

.. Not available

Note: Excluding customs duties collected on behalf of the European Union.

StatLink https://doi.org/10.1787/888934057704

Table 6.15. Belgium, tax revenues by sub-sectors of government

Million EUR

	Federal government					State/Regional				
	1975	1995	2005	2015	2017	1975	1995	2005	2015	2017
1000 Taxes on income, profits and capital gains	**8 534**	**30 899**	**45 809**	**57 132**	**56 809**	**..**	**79**	**0**	**4 283**	**9 947**
1100 Of individuals	6 929	25 973	35 956	43 438	38 619	..	79	..	4 283	9 947
1200 Corporate	1 596	4 885	9 811	13 643	18 127	..	0	..	0	0
1300 Unallocable between 1100 and 1200	10	41	42	51	63	..	0	..	0	0
2000 Social security contributions	**299**	**1 181**	**1 904**	**2 334**	**67**	**..**	**0**	**38**	**11**	**230**
2100 Employees	264	854	1 125	1 372	0	..	..	10	3	220
2200 Employers	36	228	608	713	67	..	..	27	8	10
2300 Self-employed or non-employed	0	99	171	249	0	..	..	0	0	0
2400 Unallocable between 2100, 2200 and 2300	0	0	0	0	0	..	..	0	0	0
3000 Taxes on payroll and workforce	**0**	**0**	**0**	**0**	**0**	**..**	**0**	**0**	**0**	**0**
4000 Taxes on property	**583**	**1 340**	**873**	**1 861**	**2 063**	**..**	**1 168**	**4 669**	**7 086**	**7 580**
4100 Recurrent taxes on immovable property	12	25	41	41	45	..	83	192	249	252
4200 Recurrent taxes on net wealth	0	8	189	661	929	..	0	0	0	0
4300 Estate, inheritance and gift taxes	178	42	0	0	0	..	647	1 749	3 002	3 131
4400 Taxes on financial and capital transactions	393	1 193	521	596	602	..	438	2 728	3 763	4 198
4500 Non-recurrent taxes	0	73	123	563	487	..	0	0	72	0
4600 Other recurrent taxes on property	0	0	0	0	0	..	0	0	0	0
5000 Taxes on goods and services	**5 813**	**20 791**	**29 790**	**38 631**	**41 388**	**..**	**412**	**2 044**	**2 678**	**3 289**
5100 Taxes on production, sale, transfer, etc	5 562	19 607	29 548	38 611	41 363	..	58	76	227	781
5110 General taxes	3 776	13 734	21 340	27 578	29 763	..	0	0	0	0
5120 Taxes on specific goods and services	1 785	5 872	8 208	11 034	11 601	..	58	76	227	781
5130 Unallocable between 5110 and 5120	0	0	0	0	0	..	0	0	0	0
5200 Taxes on use of goods and perform activities	249	1 178	234	10	10	..	355	1 968	2 451	2 508
5300 Unallocable between 5100 and 5200	3	6	8	9	15	..	0	0	0	0
6000 Other taxes	**0**	**0**	**0**	**0**	**0**	**..**	**0**	**68**	**40**	**0**
6100 Paid solely by business	..	..	..	..	..	..	..	0	0	0
6200 Other	..	..	..	..	..	..	..	68	40	0
Total tax revenue	**15 230**	**54 211**	**78 376**	**99 958**	**100 327**	**..**	**1 659**	**6 819**	**14 097**	**21 046**

	Local government					Social Security Funds				
	1975	1995	2005	2015	2017	1975	1995	2005	2015	2017
1000 Taxes on income, profits and capital gains	**683**	**3 058**	**2 249**	**3 052**	**3 355**	**0**	**335**	**825**	**1 106**	**1 209**
1100 Of individuals	675	3 058	2 249	3 052	3 355	..	335	825	1 106	1 209
1200 Corporate	8	0	0	0	0	..	0	0	0	0
1300 Unallocable between 1100 and 1200	0	0	0	0	0	..	0	0	0	0
2000 Social security contributions	**27**	**81**	**23**	**26**	**20**	**6 709**	**28 289**	**39 256**	**56 257**	**59 277**
2100 Employees	27	81	20	19	20	1 749	8 268	11 558	15 568	17 502
2200 Employers	0	0	3	6	0	4 347	17 556	24 332	35 479	35 944
2300 Self-employed or non-employed	0	0	0	0	0	612	2 465	3 366	5 211	5 831
2400 Unallocable between 2100, 2200 and 2300	0	0	0	0	0	0	0	0	0	0
3000 Taxes on payroll and workforce	**0**	**0**	**0**	**0**	**0**	**0**	**0**	**5**	**8**	**8**
4000 Taxes on property	**154**	**815**	**3 599**	**5 142**	**5 458**	**0**	**121**	**229**	**318**	**293**
4100 Recurrent taxes on immovable property	154	815	3 599	5 142	5 458	..	0	0	0	0
4200 Recurrent taxes on net wealth	0	0	0	0	0	..	0	0	0	0
4300 Estate, inheritance and gift taxes	0	0	0	0	0	..	0	0	0	0
4400 Taxes on financial and capital transactions	0	0	0	0	0	..	0	0	0	0
4500 Non-recurrent taxes	0	0	0	0	0	..	0	0	0	0
4600 Other recurrent taxes on property	0	0	0	0	0	..	121	229	318	293
5000 Taxes on goods and services	**166**	**332**	**523**	**715**	**644**	**14**	**330**	**1 237**	**1 575**	**1 728**
5100 Taxes on production, sale, transfer, etc	150	295	437	694	622	14	330	1 237	1 575	1 728
5110 General taxes	0	0	0	0	0	0	29	373	219	194
5120 Taxes on specific goods and services	150	295	437	694	622	14	301	865	1 356	1 534
5130 Unallocable between 5110 and 5120	0	0	0	0	0	0	0	0	0	0
5200 Taxes on use of goods and perform activities	16	37	87	22	22	0	0	0	0	0
5300 Unallocable between 5100 and 5200	0	0	0	0	0	0	0	0	0	0
6000 Other taxes	**0**	**0**	**0**	**0**	**0**	**0**	**0**	**0**	**0**	**0**
6100 Paid solely by business	..	..	..	..	..	..	..	..	..	..
6200 Other	..	..	..	..	..	..	..	..	..	..
Total tax revenue	**1 029**	**4 286**	**6 394**	**8 935**	**9 477**	**6 723**	**29 075**	**41 552**	**59 264**	**62 514**

.. Not available

Note: Excluding customs duties collected on behalf of the European Union.

StatLink https://doi.org/10.1787/888934057723

Table 6.16. Canada, tax revenues by sub-sectors of government

Million CAD

	Federal government					State/Regional				
	1975	1995	2005	2015	2017	1975	1995	2005	2015	2017
1000 Taxes on income, profits and capital gains	**19 047**	**82 237**	**140 013**	**191 684**	**208 461**	**8 165**	**52 373**	**78 331**	**123 157**	**130 405**
1100 Of individuals	12 822	65 384	102 366	143 315	150 989	6 074	43 428	62 435	96 989	100 103
1200 Corporate	5 741	14 739	32 197	41 726	49 769	2 091	8 944	15 896	26 168	30 302
1300 Unallocable between 1100 and 1200	484	2 114	5 450	6 643	7 703	0	0	0	0	0
2000 Social security contributions	**0**	**0**	**17 936**	**23 603**	**20 851**	**0**	**0**	**11 759**	**13 892**	**14 900**
2100 Employees	..	..	7 429	9 772	8 623	..	..	1 858	1 128	1 278
2200 Employers	..	..	10 507	13 831	12 228	..	..	9 901	12 764	13 622
2300 Self-employed or non-employed	..	..	0	0	0	..	..	0	0	0
2400 Unallocable between 2100, 2200 and 2300	..	..	0	0	0	..	..	0	0	0
3000 Taxes on payroll and workforce	**0**	**0**	**0**	**0**	**0**	**0**	**6 498**	**9 230**	**13 256**	**14 331**
4000 Taxes on property	**13**	**0**	**0**	**0**	**0**	**428**	**6 492**	**9 298**	**11 809**	**13 647**
4100 Recurrent taxes on immovable property	0	..	..	0	0	85	2 960	2 934	5 410	5 838
4200 Recurrent taxes on net wealth	0	..	..	..	..	200	2 914	3 456	372	440
4300 Estate, inheritance and gift taxes	13	..	..	..	..	143	3	0	268	304
4400 Taxes on financial and capital transactions	0	..	..	..	..	0	0	1 965	3 912	5 693
4500 Non-recurrent taxes	0	..	..	..	..	0	615	943	1 847	1 372
4600 Other recurrent taxes on property	0	..	..	..	..	0	0	0	0	0
5000 Taxes on goods and services	**8 180**	**31 160**	**48 551**	**53 837**	**57 991**	**10 128**	**42 076**	**67 537**	**95 284**	**106 215**
5100 Taxes on production, sale, transfer, etc	8 180	31 136	48 506	53 797	57 953	6 800	37 961	61 316	86 822	95 607
5110 General taxes	3 504	19 167	35 069	36 958	40 222	3 664	21 328	33 353	53 572	59 646
5120 Taxes on specific goods and services	4 676	11 969	13 437	16 839	17 731	3 136	16 633	27 963	33 250	35 961
5130 Unallocable between 5110 and 5120	0	0	0	0	0	0	0	0	..	..
5200 Taxes on use of goods and perform activities	0	24	45	40	38	3 328	4 115	6 221	8 462	10 608
5300 Unallocable between 5100 and 5200	0	0	0	0	0	0	0	0	0	0
6000 Other taxes	**198**	**0**	**0**	**0**	**0**	**0**	**0**	**0**	**0**	**0**
6100 Paid solely by business	0	..	..	0	0	..	..	..	0	0
6200 Other	198	..	..	0	0	..	..	..	0	0
Total tax revenue	**27 438**	**113 397**	**206 500**	**269 124**	**287 303**	**18 721**	**107 439**	**176 156**	**257 398**	**279 498**

	Local government					Social Security Funds				
	1975	1995	2005	2015	2017	1975	1995	2005	2015	2017
1000 Taxes on income, profits and capital gains	**0**	**0**	**0**	**0**	**0**	**0**	**0**	**0**	**0**	**0**
1100 Of individuals	..	..	..	0	0	..	..	..	0	0
1200 Corporate	..	..	..	0	0	..	..	..	0	0
1300 Unallocable between 1100 and 1200	..	..	..	..	..	..	..	..	..	..
2000 Social security contributions	**0**	**0**	**0**	**0**	**0**	**5 787**	**40 559**	**38 834**	**58 876**	**63 595**
2100 Employees	..	..	..	..	..	2 142	15 028	18 328	27 785	30 016
2200 Employers	..	..	..	..	..	3 527	24 765	18 328	27 785	30 016
2300 Self-employed or non-employed	..	..	..	..	..	118	766	2 177	3 307	3 563
2400 Unallocable between 2100, 2200 and 2300	..	..	..	..	..	0	0	0	0	0
3000 Taxes on payroll and workforce	**0**	**0**	**0**	**0**	**0**	**0**	**0**	**0**	**0**	**0**
4000 Taxes on property	**5 018**	**24 415**	**40 495**	**65 969**	**70 374**	**0**	**0**	**0**	**0**	**0**
4100 Recurrent taxes on immovable property	4 770	23 150	37 409	57 241	61 001	..	..	..	0	0
4200 Recurrent taxes on net wealth	0	0	0	0	0	..	..	..	..	..
4300 Estate, inheritance and gift taxes	0	0	0	0	0	..	..	..	..	..
4400 Taxes on financial and capital transactions	0	0	375	1 063	1 246	..	..	..	..	..
4500 Non-recurrent taxes	248	1 265	2 711	7 665	8 127	..	..	..	..	..
4600 Other recurrent taxes on property	0	0	0	0	0	..	..	..	..	..
5000 Taxes on goods and services	**142**	**406**	**833**	**1 149**	**1 189**	**0**	**0**	**0**	**0**	**0**
5100 Taxes on production, sale, transfer, etc	22	51	104	126	161	..	..	..	..	..
5110 General taxes	10	40	88	63	70	..	..	..	..	..
5120 Taxes on specific goods and services	12	11	16	63	91	..	..	..	..	..
5130 Unallocable between 5110 and 5120	0	0	0	0	0	..	..	..	..	..
5200 Taxes on use of goods and perform activities	120	355	729	1 023	1 028	..	..	..	0	0
5300 Unallocable between 5100 and 5200	0	0	0	0	0	..	..	..	0	0
6000 Other taxes	**525**	**3 662**	**1 483**	**748**	**745**	**0**	**0**	**0**	**0**	**0**
6100 Paid solely by business	437	2 946	541	0	0	..	..	..	0	0
6200 Other	88	716	942	748	745	..	..	..	0	0
Total tax revenue	**5 685**	**28 483**	**42 811**	**67 866**	**72 308**	**5 787**	**40 559**	**38 834**	**58 876**	**63 595**

.. Not available

StatLink https://doi.org/10.1787/888934057742

Table 6.17. Chile, tax revenues by sub-sectors of government

Million CLP

	Central government					State/Regional				
	1975	1995	2005	2015	2017	1975	1995	2005	2015	2017
1000 Taxes on income, profits and capital gains	..	**1 359 694**	**5 171 293**	**11 840 521**	**12 516 154**	..	..	..	..	..
1100 Of individuals	..	281 293	738 620	3 199 876	3 500 023	..	..	..	..	..
1200 Corporate	..	836 725	3 155 480	6 839 133	7 658 420	..	..	..	..	..
1300 Unallocable between 1100 and 1200	..	241 676	1 277 193	1 801 512	1 357 711	..	..	..	..	..
2000 Social security contributions	..	**155 855**	**287 422**	**434 658**	**506 019**	..	..	..	..	..
2100 Employees	..	142 001	249 526	370 744	432 377	..	..	..	..	..
2200 Employers	..	13 854	37 896	63 914	73 643	..	..	..	..	..
2300 Self-employed or non-employed	..	0	0	0	0	..	..	..	..	..
2400 Unallocable between 2100, 2200 and 2300	..	0	0	0	0	..	..	..	..	..
3000 Taxes on payroll and workforce	..	**0**	**0**	**0**	**0**	..	..	..	..	..
4000 Taxes on property	..	**181 432**	**490 120**	**379 603**	**738 311**	..	..	..	..	..
4100 Recurrent taxes on immovable property	..	13 044	4 909	15 249	17 289	..	..	..	..	..
4200 Recurrent taxes on net wealth	..	0	0	0	0	..	..	..	..	..
4300 Estate, inheritance and gift taxes	..	13 245	23 184	92 236	202 376	..	..	..	..	..
4400 Taxes on financial and capital transactions	..	155 143	462 027	272 118	518 645	..	..	..	..	..
4500 Non-recurrent taxes	..	0	0	0	0	..	..	..	..	..
4600 Other recurrent taxes on property	..	0	0	0	0	..	..	..	..	..
5000 Taxes on goods and services	..	**3 179 304**	**6 831 482**	**16 181 720**	**18 227 989**	..	..	..	..	..
5100 Taxes on production, sale, transfer, etc	..	3 169 645	6 811 389	16 129 953	18 175 736	..	..	..	..	..
5110 General taxes	..	2 187 602	5 391 285	13 273 958	15 069 540	..	..	..	..	..
5120 Taxes on specific goods and services	..	982 043	1 420 104	2 855 995	3 106 196	..	..	..	..	..
5130 Unallocable between 5110 and 5120	..	0	0	0	0	..	..	..	..	..
5200 Taxes on use of goods and perform activities	..	9 659	20 094	51 767	52 254	..	..	..	..	..
5300 Unallocable between 5100 and 5200	..	0	0	0	0	..	..	..	..	..
6000 Other taxes	..	**-29 554**	**-85 954**	**-579 308**	**-714 253**	..	..	..	..	..
6100 Paid solely by business	..	0	0	0	0	..	..	..	..	..
6200 Other	..	-29 554	-85 954	-579 308	-714 253	..	..	..	..	..
Total tax revenue	..	**4 846 730**	**12 694 362**	**28 257 194**	**31 274 220**	..	..	..	..	..

	Local government					Social Security Funds				
	1975	1995	2005	2015	2017	1975	1995	2005	2015	2017
1000 Taxes on income, profits and capital gains	..	**0**	**0**	**0**	**0**	..	**0**	**0**	**0**	**0**
1100 Of individuals	..	0	0	0	0	..	0	0	0	0
1200 Corporate	..	0	0	0	0	..	0	0	0	0
1300 Unallocable between 1100 and 1200	..	0	0	0	0	..	0	0	0	0
2000 Social security contributions	..	**0**	**0**	**0**	**0**	..	**193 269**	**644 295**	**1 817 831**	**2 121 539**
2100 Employees	..	..	..	..	..	..	193 269	644 295	1 817 831	2 121 539
2200 Employers	..	..	..	..	..	..	0	0	0	0
2300 Self-employed or non-employed	..	..	..	..	..	..	0	0	0	0
2400 Unallocable between 2100, 2200 and 2300	..	..	..	..	..	..	0	0	0	0
3000 Taxes on payroll and workforce	..	**0**	**0**	**0**	**0**	..	**0**	**0**	**0**	**0**
4000 Taxes on property	..	**157 193**	**411 656**	**1 041 671**	**1 211 906**	..	**0**	**0**	**0**	**0**
4100 Recurrent taxes on immovable property	..	157 193	411 656	1 041 671	1 211 906	..	..	..	..	..
4200 Recurrent taxes on net wealth	..	0	0	0	0	..	..	..	..	..
4300 Estate, inheritance and gift taxes	..	0	0	0	0	..	..	..	..	..
4400 Taxes on financial and capital transactions	..	0	0	0	0	..	..	..	..	..
4500 Non-recurrent taxes	..	0	0	0	0	..	..	..	..	..
4600 Other recurrent taxes on property	..	0	0	0	0	..	..	..	..	..
5000 Taxes on goods and services	..	**192 325**	**514 952**	**1 415 658**	**1 630 892**	..	**0**	**0**	**0**	**0**
5100 Taxes on production, sale, transfer, etc	..	52 690	140 703	385 532	421 444	..	..	..	..	..
5110 General taxes	..	0	0	0	0	..	..	..	..	..
5120 Taxes on specific goods and services	..	52 690	140 703	385 532	421 444	..	..	..	..	..
5130 Unallocable between 5110 and 5120	..	0	0	0	0	..	..	..	..	..
5200 Taxes on use of goods and perform activities	..	139 635	374 249	1 030 126	1 209 448	..	..	..	..	..
5300 Unallocable between 5100 and 5200	..	0	0	0	0	..	..	..	..	..
6000 Other taxes	..	**0**	**0**	**0**	**0**	..	**0**	**0**	**0**	**0**
6100 Paid solely by business	..	..	..	..	..	..	..	..	..	..
6200 Other	..	..	..	..	..	..	..	..	..	..
Total tax revenue	..	**349 518**	**926 608**	**2 457 329**	**2 842 798**	..	**193 269**	**644 295**	**1 817 831**	**2 121 539**

.. Not available

StatLink https://doi.org/10.1787/888934057761

Table 6.18. Czech Republic, tax revenues by sub-sectors of government

Million CZK

	Central government[1]					State/Regional				
	1975	1995	2005	2015	2017	1975	1995	2005	2015	2017
1000 Taxes on income, profits and capital gains	..	**137 616**	**273 549**	**329 768**	**390 566**	..	..	..	..	..
1100 Of individuals	..	70 361	137 937	164 678	202 244	..	..	..	..	..
1200 Corporate	..	67 255	135 611	165 090	188 322	..	..	..	..	..
1300 Unallocable between 1100 and 1200	..	0	0	0	0	..	..	..	..	..
2000 Social security contributions	..	**0**	**0**	**0**	**0**	..	..	..	..	..
2100 Employees	..	..	..	..	..	..	..	..	..	..
2200 Employers	..	..	..	..	..	..	..	..	..	..
2300 Self-employed or non-employed	..	..	..	..	..	..	..	..	..	..
2400 Unallocable between 2100, 2200 and 2300	..	..	..	..	..	..	..	..	..	..
3000 Taxes on payroll and workforce	..	**0**	**0**	**0**	**0**	..	..	..	..	..
4000 Taxes on property	..	**3 857**	**8 050**	**11 607**	**13 092**	..	..	..	..	..
4100 Recurrent taxes on immovable property	..	0	5	20	25	..	..	..	..	..
4200 Recurrent taxes on net wealth	..	0	0	0	0	..	..	..	..	..
4300 Estate, inheritance and gift taxes	..	393	728	20	13	..	..	..	..	..
4400 Taxes on financial and capital transactions	..	3 464	7 317	11 566	13 054	..	..	..	..	..
4500 Non-recurrent taxes	..	0	0	0	0	..	..	..	..	..
4600 Other recurrent taxes on property	..	0	0	0	0	..	..	..	..	..
5000 Taxes on goods and services	..	**175 869**	**343 554**	**505 085**	**571 225**	..	..	..	..	..
5100 Taxes on production, sale, transfer, etc	..	162 913	325 662	487 086	551 685	..	..	..	..	..
5110 General taxes	..	91 673	215 118	333 274	387 537	..	..	..	..	..
5120 Taxes on specific goods and services	..	71 240	110 544	153 812	164 148	..	..	..	..	..
5130 Unallocable between 5110 and 5120	..	0	0	0	0	..	..	..	..	..
5200 Taxes on use of goods and perform activities	..	12 956	17 892	17 999	19 540	..	..	..	..	..
5300 Unallocable between 5100 and 5200	..	0	0	0	0	..	..	..	..	..
6000 Other taxes	..	**545**	**55**	**387**	**904**	..	..	..	..	..
6100 Paid solely by business	..	0	0	0	0	..	..	..	..	..
6200 Other	..	545	55	387	904	..	..	..	..	..
Total tax revenue	..	**317 887**	**625 207**	**846 847**	**975 787**	..	..	..	..	..

	Local government					Social Security Funds				
	1975	1995	2005	2015	2017	1975	1995	2005	2015	2017
1000 Taxes on income, profits and capital gains	..	**0**	**0**	**0**	**0**	..	**0**	**0**	**0**	**0**
1100 Of individuals	..	0	0	0	0	..	0	0	0	0
1200 Corporate	..	0	0	0	0	..	0	0	0	0
1300 Unallocable between 1100 and 1200	..	0	0	0	..	..	0	0	0	..
2000 Social security contributions	..	**0**	**0**	**0**	**0**	..	**227 871**	**481 626**	**659 743**	**757 183**
2100 Employees	..	..	..	..	..	..	54 536	108 316	133 878	155 827
2200 Employers	..	..	..	..	..	..	148 342	307 618	417 778	483 437
2300 Self-employed or non-employed	..	..	..	..	..	..	24 993	65 692	108 088	117 919
2400 Unallocable between 2100, 2200 and 2300	..	..	..	..	..	..	0	0	0	0
3000 Taxes on payroll and workforce	..	**0**	**0**	**0**	**0**	..	**0**	**0**	**0**	**0**
4000 Taxes on property	..	**3 778**	**4 987**	**10 313**	**10 758**	..	**0**	**0**	**0**	**0**
4100 Recurrent taxes on immovable property	..	3 778	4 987	10 313	10 758	..	..	..	..	..
4200 Recurrent taxes on net wealth	..	0	0	0	0	..	..	..	..	..
4300 Estate, inheritance and gift taxes	..	0	0	0	0	..	..	..	..	..
4400 Taxes on financial and capital transactions	..	0	0	0	0	..	..	..	..	..
4500 Non-recurrent taxes	..	0	0	0	0	..	..	..	..	..
4600 Other recurrent taxes on property	..	0	0	0	0	..	..	..	..	..
5000 Taxes on goods and services	..	**1 150**	**7 395**	**7 749**	**8 048**	..	**0**	**0**	**0**	**0**
5100 Taxes on production, sale, transfer, etc	..	124	199	292	348	..	..	..	..	..
5110 General taxes	..	0	0	0	0	..	..	..	..	..
5120 Taxes on specific goods and services	..	124	199	292	348	..	..	..	..	..
5130 Unallocable between 5110 and 5120	..	0	0	0	0	..	..	..	..	..
5200 Taxes on use of goods and perform activities	..	1 026	7 196	7 457	7 701	..	..	..	..	..
5300 Unallocable between 5100 and 5200	..	0	0	0	0	..	..	..	..	..
6000 Other taxes	..	**0**	**0**	**0**	**0**	..	**0**	**0**	**0**	**0**
6100 Paid solely by business	..	..	..	..	..	..	..	..	..	..
6200 Other	..	..	..	..	..	..	..	..	..	..
Total tax revenue	..	**4 928**	**12 382**	**18 063**	**18 806**	..	**227 871**	**481 626**	**659 743**	**757 183**

.. Not available

Note: Excluding customs duties collected on behalf of the European Union.

1. Tax revenues of the regions are reported under the heading of central government up to and including 1995 and under local government thereafter.

StatLink https://doi.org/10.1787/888934057780

Table 6.19. Denmark, tax revenues by sub-sectors of government

Million DKK

	Central government					State/Regional				
	1975	1995	2005	2015	2017	1975	1995	2005	2015	2017
1000 Taxes on income, profits and capital gains	**28 694**	**164 962**	**258 922**	**384 883**	**399 164**	**..**	**..**	**..**	**..**	**..**
1100 Of individuals	25 904	124 613	167 082	304 329	294 952	..	..	..	..	..
1200 Corporate	2 790	23 803	54 597	57 723	71 928	..	..	..	..	..
1300 Unallocable between 1100 and 1200	0	16 546	37 244	22 832	32 284	..	..	..	..	..
2000 Social security contributions	**143**	**562**	**1 180**	**836**	**737**	**..**	**..**	**..**	**..**	**..**
2100 Employees	0	559	1 177	826	729	..	..	..	..	..
2200 Employers	142	3	3	10	8	..	..	..	..	..
2300 Self-employed or non-employed	0	0	0	0	0	..	..	..	..	..
2400 Unallocable between 2100, 2200 and 2300	0	0	0	0	0	..	..	..	..	..
3000 Taxes on payroll and workforce	**0**	**2 262**	**2 907**	**5 894**	**5 494**	**..**	**..**	**..**	**..**	**..**
4000 Taxes on property	**1 779**	**7 094**	**11 801**	**11 084**	**10 793**	**..**	**..**	**..**	**..**	**..**
4100 Recurrent taxes on immovable property	16	170	0	0	0	..	..	..	..	..
4200 Recurrent taxes on net wealth	414	930	0	0	0	..	..	..	..	..
4300 Estate, inheritance and gift taxes	336	2 372	3 154	5 177	4 368	..	..	..	..	..
4400 Taxes on financial and capital transactions	936	3 584	8 613	5 907	6 426	..	..	..	..	..
4500 Non-recurrent taxes	77	38	34	0	0	..	..	..	..	..
4600 Other recurrent taxes on property	0	0	0	0	0	..	..	..	..	..
5000 Taxes on goods and services	**29 014**	**156 578**	**253 352**	**301 504**	**319 205**	**..**	**..**	**..**	**..**	**..**
5100 Taxes on production, sale, transfer, etc	27 338	149 393	239 951	277 791	293 774	..	..	..	..	..
5110 General taxes	15 117	94 368	154 654	191 479	207 768	..	..	..	..	..
5120 Taxes on specific goods and services	12 221	55 026	85 298	86 312	86 006	..	..	..	..	..
5130 Unallocable between 5110 and 5120	0	0	0	..	..	..	..	..	..	..
5200 Taxes on use of goods and perform activities	1 676	4 739	9 379	16 537	16 895	..	..	..	..	..
5300 Unallocable between 5100 and 5200	0	2 446	4 021	7 177	8 536	..	..	..	..	..
6000 Other taxes	**0**	**0**	**203**	**320**	**272**	**..**	**..**	**..**	**..**	**..**
6100 Paid solely by business	..	..	203	320	272	..	..	..	..	..
6200 Other	..	..	0	0	0	..	..	..	..	..
Total tax revenue	**59 630**	**331 457**	**528 366**	**704 520**	**735 664**	**..**	**..**	**..**	**..**	**..**

	Local government					Social Security Funds				
	1975	1995	2005	2015	2017	1975	1995	2005	2015	2017
1000 Taxes on income, profits and capital gains	**22 171**	**140 762**	**214 581**	**220 815**	**236 796**	**0**	**0**	**0**	**0**	**0**
1100 Of individuals	22 170	140 758	214 581	220 815	236 796	..	..	..	..	..
1200 Corporate	1	5	0	0	0	..	..	..	..	..
1300 Unallocable between 1100 and 1200	0	0	0	0	0	..	..	..	..	..
2000 Social security contributions	**0**	**0**	**0**	**0**	**0**	**58**	**0**	**529**	**542**	**323**
2100 Employees	..	..	..	0	0	0	..	0	0	0
2200 Employers	..	..	..	0	0	58	..	529	542	323
2300 Self-employed or non-employed	..	..	..	0	0	0	..	0	0	0
2400 Unallocable between 2100, 2200 and 2300	..	..	..	0	0	0	..	0	0	0
3000 Taxes on payroll and workforce	**0**	**0**	**0**	**0**	**0**	**0**	**0**	**0**	**0**	**0**
4000 Taxes on property	**3 518**	**10 155**	**17 466**	**28 085**	**28 465**	**0**	**0**	**0**	**0**	**0**
4100 Recurrent taxes on immovable property	3 518	10 155	17 466	28 085	28 465	..	..	..	..	..
4200 Recurrent taxes on net wealth	0	0	0	0	0	..	..	..	..	..
4300 Estate, inheritance and gift taxes	0	0	0	0	0	..	..	..	..	..
4400 Taxes on financial and capital transactions	0	0	0	0	0	..	..	..	..	..
4500 Non-recurrent taxes	0	0	0	0	0	..	..	..	..	..
4600 Other recurrent taxes on property	0	0	0	0	0	..	..	..	..	..
5000 Taxes on goods and services	**0**	**0**	**0**	**0**	**0**	**0**	**0**	**0**	**0**	**0**
5100 Taxes on production, sale, transfer, etc	0	..	..	..	..	..	..	..	..	..
5110 General taxes	0	..	..	..	..	..	..	..	..	..
5120 Taxes on specific goods and services	0	..	..	..	..	..	..	..	..	..
5130 Unallocable between 5110 and 5120	0	0	0	..	..	..	..	..	..	..
5200 Taxes on use of goods and perform activities	..	..	..	..	..	..	..	..	..	..
5300 Unallocable between 5100 and 5200	0	0	0	0	0	..	..	..	..	..
6000 Other taxes	**0**	**0**	**0**	**0**	**0**	**0**	**0**	**0**	**0**	**0**
6100 Paid solely by business	..	..	..	..	..	..	..	..	..	..
6200 Other	..	..	..	..	..	..	..	..	..	..
Total tax revenue	**25 689**	**150 918**	**232 047**	**248 900**	**265 260**	**58**	**0**	**529**	**542**	**323**

.. Not available

Note: Excluding customs duties collected on behalf of the European Union.

StatLink https://doi.org/10.1787/888934057799

Table 6.20. Estonia, tax revenues by sub-sectors of government

Million EUR

	Central government					State/Regional				
	1975	1995	2005	2015	2017	1975	1995	2005	2015	2017
1000 Taxes on income, profits and capital gains	..	**301**	**782**	**1 607**	**1 710**	..	..	..	..	..
1100 Of individuals	..	234	622	1 182	1 344	..	..	..	..	..
1200 Corporate	..	67	160	424	366	..	..	..	..	..
1300 Unallocable between 1100 and 1200	..	0	0	0	0	..	..	..	..	..
2000 Social security contributions	..	**191**	**636**	**1 181**	**1 354**	..	..	..	..	..
2100 Employees	..	0	0	0	0	..	..	..	..	..
2200 Employers	..	191	636	1 169	1 342	..	..	..	..	..
2300 Self-employed or non-employed	..	0	0	12	13	..	..	..	..	..
2400 Unallocable between 2100, 2200 and 2300	..	0	0	0	0	..	..	..	..	..
3000 Taxes on payroll and workforce	..	**0**	**0**	**0**	**0**	..	..	..	..	..
4000 Taxes on property	..	**3**	**0**	**0**	**0**	..	..	..	..	..
4100 Recurrent taxes on immovable property	..	3	..	..	..	..	..	..	..	..
4200 Recurrent taxes on net wealth	..	0	..	..	..	..	..	..	..	..
4300 Estate, inheritance and gift taxes	..	0	..	..	..	..	..	..	..	..
4400 Taxes on financial and capital transactions	..	0	..	..	..	..	..	..	..	..
4500 Non-recurrent taxes	..	0	..	..	..	..	..	..	..	..
4600 Other recurrent taxes on property	..	0	..	..	..	..	..	..	..	..
5000 Taxes on goods and services	..	**350**	**1 385**	**2 864**	**3 279**	..	..	..	..	..
5100 Taxes on production, sale, transfer, etc	..	345	1 348	2 790	3 178	..	..	..	..	..
5110 General taxes	..	266	908	1 872	2 148	..	..	..	..	..
5120 Taxes on specific goods and services	..	79	440	918	1 030	..	..	..	..	..
5130 Unallocable between 5110 and 5120	..	0	0	0	0	..	..	..	..	..
5200 Taxes on use of goods and perform activities	..	5	37	74	100	..	..	..	..	..
5300 Unallocable between 5100 and 5200	..	0	0	0	0	..	..	..	..	..
6000 Other taxes	..	**0**	**0**	**0**	**0**	..	..	..	..	..
6100 Paid solely by business	..	..	..	..	..	..	..	..	..	..
6200 Other	..	..	..	..	..	..	..	..	..	..
Total tax revenue	..	**845**	**2 803**	**5 651**	**6 343**	..	..	..	..	..

	Local government					Social Security Funds				
	1975	1995	2005	2015	2017	1975	1995	2005	2015	2017
1000 Taxes on income, profits and capital gains	..	**0**	**0**	**0**	**0**	..	**0**	**0**	**0**	**0**
1100 Of individuals	..	0	0	0	0	..	0	0	0	0
1200 Corporate	..	0	0	0	0	..	0	0	0	0
1300 Unallocable between 1100 and 1200	..	0	0	0	0	..	0	0	0	0
2000 Social security contributions	..	**0**	**0**	**0**	**0**	..	**149**	**511**	**1 110**	**1 282**
2100 Employees	..	..	..	..	..	..	0	31	99	112
2200 Employers	..	..	..	..	..	..	143	466	1 002	1 161
2300 Self-employed or non-employed	..	..	..	..	..	..	6	14	8	8
2400 Unallocable between 2100, 2200 and 2300	..	..	..	..	..	..	0	0	0	0
3000 Taxes on payroll and workforce	..	**0**	**0**	**0**	**0**	..	**0**	**0**	**0**	**0**
4000 Taxes on property	..	**7**	**32**	**58**	**58**	..	**0**	**0**	**0**	**0**
4100 Recurrent taxes on immovable property	..	7	32	58	58	..	..	..	..	..
4200 Recurrent taxes on net wealth	..	0	0	0	0	..	..	..	..	..
4300 Estate, inheritance and gift taxes	..	0	0	0	0	..	..	..	..	..
4400 Taxes on financial and capital transactions	..	0	0	0	0	..	..	..	..	..
4500 Non-recurrent taxes	..	0	0	0	0	..	..	..	..	..
4600 Other recurrent taxes on property	..	0	0	0	0	..	..	..	..	..
5000 Taxes on goods and services	..	**1**	**7**	**11**	**13**	..	**0**	**0**	**0**	**0**
5100 Taxes on production, sale, transfer, etc	..	0	2	4	6	..	..	..	..	..
5110 General taxes	..	0	0	0	0	..	..	..	..	..
5120 Taxes on specific goods and services	..	0	2	4	6	..	..	..	..	..
5130 Unallocable between 5110 and 5120	..	0	0	0	0	..	..	..	..	..
5200 Taxes on use of goods and perform activities	..	1	5	7	7	..	..	..	..	..
5300 Unallocable between 5100 and 5200	..	0	0	0	0	..	..	..	..	..
6000 Other taxes	..	**0**	**0**	**0**	**0**	..	**0**	**0**	**0**	**0**
6100 Paid solely by business	..	..	..	..	..	..	..	..	..	..
6200 Other	..	..	..	..	..	..	..	..	..	..
Total tax revenue	..	**8**	**40**	**69**	**70**	..	**149**	**511**	**1 110**	**1 282**

.. Not available

Note: Excluding customs duties collected on behalf of the European Union.

StatLink https://doi.org/10.1787/888934057818

Table 6.21. Finland, tax revenues by sub-sectors of government

Million EUR

	Central government					State/Regional				
	1975	1995	2005	2015	2017	1975	1995	2005	2015	2017
1000 Taxes on income, profits and capital gains	**1 304**	**6 538**	**12 885**	**12 127**	**13 413**	..	..	..	..	..
1100 Of individuals	1 146	5 320	8 791	9 248	9 175	..	..	..	..	..
1200 Corporate	157	1 219	4 094	2 879	4 238	..	..	..	..	..
1300 Unallocable between 1100 and 1200	0	0	0	0	0	..	..	..	..	..
2000 Social security contributions	**0**	**25**	**0**	**0**	**0**	..	..	..	..	..
2100 Employees	..	0	..	..	..	..	..	..	..	..
2200 Employers	..	25	..	..	..	..	..	..	..	..
2300 Self-employed or non-employed	..	0	..	..	..	..	..	..	..	..
2400 Unallocable between 2100, 2200 and 2300	..	0	..	..	..	..	..	..	..	..
3000 Taxes on payroll and workforce	**153**	**0**	**0**	**0**	**0**	..	..	..	..	..
4000 Taxes on property	**127**	**534**	**1 169**	**1 414**	**1 685**	..	..	..	..	..
4100 Recurrent taxes on immovable property	0	0	0	0	0	..	..	..	..	..
4200 Recurrent taxes on net wealth	33	35	129	0	0	..	..	..	..	..
4300 Estate, inheritance and gift taxes	14	167	486	631	909	..	..	..	..	..
4400 Taxes on financial and capital transactions	80	331	554	783	776	..	..	..	..	..
4500 Non-recurrent taxes	0	0	0	0	0	..	..	..	..	..
4600 Other recurrent taxes on property	0	0	0	0	0	..	..	..	..	..
5000 Taxes on goods and services	**2 099**	**13 239**	**21 768**	**29 722**	**31 762**	..	..	..	..	..
5100 Taxes on production, sale, transfer, etc	2 082	12 936	21 178	28 666	30 453	..	..	..	..	..
5110 General taxes	1 030	7 621	13 748	18 974	20 404	..	..	..	..	..
5120 Taxes on specific goods and services	1 052	5 314	7 430	9 692	10 049	..	..	..	..	..
5130 Unallocable between 5110 and 5120	0	0	0	0	0	..	..	..	..	..
5200 Taxes on use of goods and perform activities	16	304	590	1 056	1 309	..	..	..	..	..
5300 Unallocable between 5100 and 5200	0	0	0	0	0	..	..	..	..	..
6000 Other taxes	**10**	**91**	**68**	**81**	**61**	..	..	..	..	..
6100 Paid solely by business	0	0	0	0	0	..	..	..	..	..
6200 Other	10	91	68	81	61	..	..	..	..	..
Total tax revenue	**3 693**	**20 427**	**35 890**	**43 344**	**46 921**	..	..	..	..	..

	Local government					Social Security Funds				
	1975	1995	2005	2015	2017	1975	1995	2005	2015	2017
1000 Taxes on income, profits and capital gains	**1 547**	**9 313**	**13 574**	**20 244**	**20 991**	**0**	**0**	**0**	**0**	**0**
1100 Of individuals	1 393	8 320	12 420	18 576	19 102	..	..	..	..	..
1200 Corporate	154	994	1 154	1 668	1 889	..	..	..	..	..
1300 Unallocable between 1100 and 1200	0	0	0	0	0	..	..	..	..	..
2000 Social security contributions	**0**	**0**	**23**	**15**	**14**	**1 347**	**13 492**	**18 856**	**26 624**	**26 986**
2100 Employees	..	..	4	4	4	278	2 536	3 460	6 360	7 463
2200 Employers	..	..	19	11	10	990	9 447	14 108	18 221	17 575
2300 Self-employed or non-employed	..	..	0	0	0	79	1 509	1 288	2 043	1 948
2400 Unallocable between 2100, 2200 and 2300	..	..	0	0	0	0	0	0	0	0
3000 Taxes on payroll and workforce	**0**	**0**	**0**	**0**	**0**	**0**	**0**	**0**	**0**	**0**
4000 Taxes on property	**0**	**441**	**725**	**1 603**	**1 774**	**0**	**0**	**0**	**0**	**0**
4100 Recurrent taxes on immovable property	0	441	725	1 603	1 774	..	..	..	..	..
4200 Recurrent taxes on net wealth	0	0	0	0	0	..	..	..	..	..
4300 Estate, inheritance and gift taxes	0	0	0	0	0	..	..	..	..	..
4400 Taxes on financial and capital transactions	0	0	0	0	0	..	..	..	..	..
4500 Non-recurrent taxes	0	0	0	0	0	..	..	..	..	..
4600 Other recurrent taxes on property	0	0	0	0	0	..	..	..	..	..
5000 Taxes on goods and services	**3**	**7**	**8**	**2**	**2**	**0**	**0**	**0**	**0**	**0**
5100 Taxes on production, sale, transfer, etc	1	1	4	1	1	..	..	..	..	..
5110 General taxes	0	0	0	0	0	..	..	..	..	..
5120 Taxes on specific goods and services	1	1	4	1	1	..	..	..	..	..
5130 Unallocable between 5110 and 5120	0	0	0	0	0	..	..	..	..	..
5200 Taxes on use of goods and perform activities	2	6	4	1	1	..	..	..	..	..
5300 Unallocable between 5100 and 5200	0	0	0	0	0	..	..	..	..	..
6000 Other taxes	**0**	**0**	**0**	**0**	**0**	**0**	**0**	**0**	**0**	**0**
6100 Paid solely by business	..	..	..	..	..	..	..	..	..	..
6200 Other	..	..	..	..	..	..	..	..	..	..
Total tax revenue	**1 550**	**9 761**	**14 330**	**21 864**	**22 781**	**1 347**	**13 492**	**18 856**	**26 624**	**26 986**

.. Not available

Note: Excluding customs duties collected on behalf of the European Union.

StatLink https://doi.org/10.1787/888934057837

Table 6.22. France, tax revenues by sub-sectors of government

Million EUR

	Central government					State/Regional				
	1975	1995	2005	2015	2017	1975	1995	2005	2015	2017
1000 Taxes on income, profits and capital gains	**13 106**	**69 134**	**98 623**	**121 529**	**133 516**	**..**	**..**	**..**	**..**	**..**
1100 Of individuals	8 743	43 963	56 862	75 366	79 725	..	..	..	..	..
1200 Corporate	4 282	25 172	41 761	46 163	53 791	..	..	..	..	..
1300 Unallocable between 1100 and 1200	80	0	0	0	0	..	..	..	..	..
2000 Social security contributions	**419**	**3 733**	**5 796**	**7 941**	**8 336**	**..**	**..**	**..**	**..**	**..**
2100 Employees	419	3 733	4 812	6 048	6 699	..	..	..	..	..
2200 Employers	0	0	984	1 893	1 637	..	..	..	..	..
2300 Self-employed or non-employed	0	0	0	0	0	..	..	..	..	..
2400 Unallocable between 2100, 2200 and 2300	0	0	0	0	0	..	..	..	..	..
3000 Taxes on payroll and workforce	**1 194**	**10 299**	**13 117**	**4 796**	**3 707**	**..**	**..**	**..**	**..**	**..**
4000 Taxes on property	**1 372**	**9 196**	**16 021**	**23 374**	**25 611**	**..**	**..**	**..**	**..**	**..**
4100 Recurrent taxes on immovable property	26	1 849	2 106	3 112	3 310	..	..	..	..	..
4200 Recurrent taxes on net wealth	0	1 309	3 053	5 224	5 068	..	..	..	..	..
4300 Estate, inheritance and gift taxes	616	4 261	9 006	12 317	14 344	..	..	..	..	..
4400 Taxes on financial and capital transactions	731	1 777	1 856	2 721	2 889	..	..	..	..	..
4500 Non-recurrent taxes	0	0	0	0	0	..	..	..	..	..
4600 Other recurrent taxes on property	0	0	0	..	..	..	..	..	..	..
5000 Taxes on goods and services	**26 154**	**127 617**	**165 674**	**175 528**	**192 028**	**..**	**..**	**..**	**..**	**..**
5100 Taxes on production, sale, transfer, etc	25 618	126 699	163 729	173 782	190 084	..	..	..	..	..
5110 General taxes	19 077	89 768	127 096	141 371	151 443	..	..	..	..	..
5120 Taxes on specific goods and services	6 540	36 931	36 633	32 411	38 641	..	..	..	..	..
5130 Unallocable between 5110 and 5120	0	0	0	..	..	..	..	..	..	..
5200 Taxes on use of goods and perform activities	536	918	1 945	1 746	1 944	..	..	..	..	..
5300 Unallocable between 5100 and 5200	..	..	..	..	..	..	..	..	..	..
6000 Other taxes	**49**	**924**	**3 522**	**1 898**	**1 113**	**..**	**..**	**..**	**..**	**..**
6100 Paid solely by business	32	871	3 502	1 892	1 107	..	..	..	..	..
6200 Other	17	53	21	6	6	..	..	..	..	..
Total tax revenue	**42 294**	**220 903**	**302 753**	**335 066**	**364 311**	**..**	**..**	**..**	**..**	**..**

	Local government					Social Security Funds				
	1975	1995	2005	2015	2017	1975	1995	2005	2015	2017
1000 Taxes on income, profits and capital gains	**0**	**0**	**0**	**20**	**18**	**0**	**14 997**	**80 173**	**112 983**	**118 174**
1100 Of individuals	0	0	0	13	11	0	14 997	80 173	112 978	118 174
1200 Corporate	0	0	0	7	7	0	0	0	5	0
1300 Unallocable between 1100 and 1200	0	0	0	0	0	0	0	0	0	0
2000 Social security contributions	**0**	**0**	**0**	**0**	**0**	**33 089**	**217 995**	**275 433**	**362 434**	**379 107**
2100 Employees	..	..	..	..	..	6 683	65 964	65 369	87 719	94 211
2200 Employers	..	..	..	..	..	24 236	135 892	190 090	246 280	257 054
2300 Self-employed or non-employed	..	..	..	..	..	2 170	16 139	19 975	28 435	27 842
2400 Unallocable between 2100, 2200 and 2300	..	..	..	..	..	0	0	0	0	0
3000 Taxes on payroll and workforce	**299**	**2 529**	**5 437**	**9 278**	**10 275**	**107**	**36**	**1 767**	**20 500**	**21 733**
4000 Taxes on property	**2 876**	**27 105**	**44 534**	**68 949**	**75 378**	**0**	**0**	**0**	**0**	**0**
4100 Recurrent taxes on immovable property	2 626	23 117	35 989	57 331	60 842	..	..	..	..	..
4200 Recurrent taxes on net wealth	..	0	0	0	0	..	..	..	..	..
4300 Estate, inheritance and gift taxes	0	0	0	0	0	..	..	..	..	..
4400 Taxes on financial and capital transactions	250	3 988	8 545	11 618	14 536	..	..	..	..	..
4500 Non-recurrent taxes	0	0	0	0	0	..	..	..	..	..
4600 Other recurrent taxes on property	..	..	..	..	..	..	..	..	..	..
5000 Taxes on goods and services	**496**	**8 056**	**14 708**	**31 014**	**32 502**	**301**	**5 708**	**12 776**	**36 159**	**35 940**
5100 Taxes on production, sale, transfer, etc	297	4 168	12 233	26 769	27 906	301	5 429	12 393	35 202	34 966
5110 General taxes	0	0	0	0	0	248	1 810	4 271	15 569	14 911
5120 Taxes on specific goods and services	297	4 168	12 233	26 769	27 906	53	3 620	8 122	19 633	20 055
5130 Unallocable between 5110 and 5120	..	..	..	..	..	..	..	..	..	..
5200 Taxes on use of goods and perform activities	198	3 888	2 475	4 245	4 596	0	279	383	957	974
5300 Unallocable between 5100 and 5200	..	..	..	..	..	..	..	..	..	..
6000 Other taxes	**2 577**	**18 971**	**22 334**	**22 093**	**23 393**	**0**	**0**	**0**	**568**	**362**
6100 Paid solely by business	2 577	18 970	22 334	22 093	23 393	..	..	..	568	362
6200 Other	0	1	0	0	0	..	..	..	0	0
Total tax revenue	**6 248**	**56 661**	**87 013**	**131 354**	**141 566**	**33 497**	**238 737**	**370 149**	**532 644**	**555 316**

.. Not available

Note: Excluding customs duties collected on behalf of the European Union.

StatLink https://doi.org/10.1787/888934057856

Table 6.23. Germany, tax revenues by sub-sectors of government

Million EUR

	Federal government					State/Regional				
	1975	1995	2005	2015	2017	1975	1995	2005	2015	2017
1000 Taxes on income, profits and capital gains	**26 782**	**90 688**	**89 383**	**143 653**	**164 077**	**26 428**	**77 258**	**83 503**	**133 852**	**152 860**
1100 Of individuals	23 469	83 710	77 468	129 712	144 796	23 267	71 598	70 916	118 806	132 616
1200 Corporate	3 314	6 978	11 915	13 941	19 281	3 160	5 659	12 587	15 046	20 244
1300 Unallocable between 1100 and 1200	0	0	0	0	0	0	0	0	0	0
2000 Social security contributions	**0**	**0**	**0**	**0**	**0**	**0**	**0**	**0**	**0**	**0**
2100 Employees	..	..	..	..	..	..	..	..	..	..
2200 Employers	..	..	..	..	..	..	..	..	..	..
2300 Self-employed or non-employed	..	..	..	..	..	..	..	..	..	..
2400 Unallocable between 2100, 2200 and 2300	..	..	..	..	..	..	..	..	..	..
3000 Taxes on payroll and workforce	**0**	**0**	**0**	**0**	**0**	**0**	**0**	**0**	**0**	**0**
4000 Taxes on property	**1 225**	**175**	**0**	**324**	**382**	**2 606**	**9 080**	**8 985**	**17 537**	**19 253**
4100 Recurrent taxes on immovable property	0	0	..	0	0	0	0	0	0	0
4200 Recurrent taxes on net wealth	920	147	..	324	382	1 993	4 163	97	-2	0
4300 Estate, inheritance and gift taxes	0	0	..	0	0	271	1 815	4 097	6 290	6 114
4400 Taxes on financial and capital transactions	305	28	..	0	0	342	3 102	4 791	11 249	13 139
4500 Non-recurrent taxes	0	0	..	0	0	0	0	0	0	0
4600 Other recurrent taxes on property	0	0	..	0	0	0	0	0	0	0
5000 Taxes on goods and services	**35 370**	**125 377**	**147 967**	**199 426**	**199 130**	**13 082**	**62 564**	**75 007**	**107 912**	**116 891**
5100 Taxes on production, sale, transfer, etc	35 370	125 377	147 967	188 858	195 566	10 371	55 506	66 334	99 781	108 898
5110 General taxes	18 458	67 178	74 361	110 451	115 002	9 194	52 783	62 851	96 751	105 765
5120 Taxes on specific goods and services	16 913	58 200	73 170	78 115	80 280	1 177	2 723	3 483	3 030	3 133
5130 Unallocable between 5110 and 5120	0	0	436	292	284	0	0	0	0	0
5200 Taxes on use of goods and perform activities	0	0	0	10 568	3 564	2 711	7 058	8 673	8 131	7 993
5300 Unallocable between 5100 and 5200	0	0	0	0	0	0	0	0	0	0
6000 Other taxes	**0**	**0**	**-1**	**0**	**1**	**0**	**0**	**0**	**0**	**0**
6100 Paid solely by business	..	..	0	..	0	..	..	..	..	..
6200 Other	..	..	-1	0	1	..	..	..	0	0
Total tax revenue	**63 378**	**216 240**	**237 349**	**343 403**	**363 590**	**42 116**	**148 902**	**167 495**	**259 301**	**289 004**

	Local government					Social Security Funds				
	1975	1995	2005	2015	2017	1975	1995	2005	2015	2017
1000 Taxes on income, profits and capital gains	**11 819**	**40 295**	**46 725**	**73 882**	**83 668**	**0**	**0**	**0**	**0**	**0**
1100 Of individuals	9 931	33 761	31 261	50 328	56 657	..	..	..	..	..
1200 Corporate	1 888	6 534	15 464	23 554	27 011	..	..	..	..	..
1300 Unallocable between 1100 and 1200	0	0	0	0	0	..	..	..	..	..
2000 Social security contributions	**0**	**0**	**0**	**0**	**0**	**64 290**	**268 052**	**310 301**	**424 633**	**466 470**
2100 Employees	..	..	..	..	..	28 106	117 916	135 775	188 972	209 593
2200 Employers	..	..	..	..	..	34 609	133 120	149 191	199 153	216 423
2300 Self-employed or non-employed	..	..	..	..	..	1 575	17 016	25 335	36 508	40 454
2400 Unallocable between 2100, 2200 and 2300	..	..	..	..	..	0	0	0	0	0
3000 Taxes on payroll and workforce	**1 533**	**0**	**0**	**0**	**0**	**0**	**0**	**0**	**0**	**0**
4000 Taxes on property	**3 461**	**9 794**	**10 247**	**13 215**	**13 965**	**0**	**0**	**0**	**0**	**0**
4100 Recurrent taxes on immovable property	2 122	7 027	10 247	13 215	13 965	..	..	..	..	..
4200 Recurrent taxes on net wealth	911	2 615	0	0	0	..	..	..	..	..
4300 Estate, inheritance and gift taxes	0	0	0	0	0	..	..	..	..	..
4400 Taxes on financial and capital transactions	428	151	0	0	0	..	..	..	..	..
4500 Non-recurrent taxes	0	0	0	0	0	..	..	..	..	..
4600 Other recurrent taxes on property	0	0	0	0	0	..	..	..	..	..
5000 Taxes on goods and services	**162**	**448**	**3 395**	**5 947**	**7 540**	**0**	**0**	**0**	**0**	**0**
5100 Taxes on production, sale, transfer, etc	94	271	3 136	5 615	7 182	..	..	..	..	..
5110 General taxes	0	0	2 909	4 734	6 134	..	..	..	..	..
5120 Taxes on specific goods and services	94	271	227	881	1 048	..	..	..	..	..
5130 Unallocable between 5110 and 5120	0	0	0	0	0	..	..	..	..	..
5200 Taxes on use of goods and perform activities	68	176	259	332	358	..	..	..	..	..
5300 Unallocable between 5100 and 5200	0	0	0	0	0	..	..	..	..	..
6000 Other taxes	**67**	**130**	**79**	**216**	**251**	**0**	**0**	**0**	**0**	**0**
6100 Paid solely by business	0	0	0	0	0	..	..	..	..	..
6200 Other	67	130	79	216	251	..	..	..	..	..
Total tax revenue	**17 042**	**50 666**	**60 446**	**93 260**	**105 424**	**64 290**	**268 052**	**310 301**	**424 633**	**466 470**

.. Not available

Note: Excluding customs duties collected on behalf of the European Union.

StatLink https://doi.org/10.1787/888934057875

Table 6.24. Greece, tax revenues by sub-sectors of government

Million EUR

	Central government					State/Regional				
	1975	1995	2005	2015	2017	1975	1995	2005	2015	2017
1000 Taxes on income, profits and capital gains	**64**	**5 456**	**16 101**	**14 895**	**15 956**	**..**	**..**	**..**	**..**	**..**
1100 Of individuals	43	3 011	8 719	10 146	11 218	..	..	..	..	..
1200 Corporate	17	2 067	6 487	3 800	3 510	..	..	..	..	..
1300 Unallocable between 1100 and 1200	4	378	895	949	1 228	..	..	..	..	..
2000 Social security contributions	**0**	**380**	**1 048**	**745**	**71**	**..**	**..**	**..**	**..**	**..**
2100 Employees	..	380	1 031	744	71	..	..	..	..	..
2200 Employers	..	0	17	1	0	..	..	..	..	..
2300 Self-employed or non-employed	..	0	0	0	0	..	..	..	..	..
2400 Unallocable between 2100, 2200 and 2300	..	0	0	0	0	..	..	..	..	..
3000 Taxes on payroll and workforce	**1**	**0**	**0**	**0**	**0**	**..**	**..**	**..**	**..**	**..**
4000 Taxes on property	**47**	**1 060**	**2 263**	**3 931**	**3 979**	**..**	**..**	**..**	**..**	**..**
4100 Recurrent taxes on immovable property	1	0	0	3 046	3 057	..	..	..	..	..
4200 Recurrent taxes on net wealth	0	138	284	180	182	..	..	..	..	..
4300 Estate, inheritance and gift taxes	5	274	258	134	154	..	..	..	..	..
4400 Taxes on financial and capital transactions	41	641	1 469	509	577	..	..	..	..	..
4500 Non-recurrent taxes	0	0	73	0	0	..	..	..	..	..
4600 Other recurrent taxes on property	0	7	179	62	9	..	..	..	..	..
5000 Taxes on goods and services	**224**	**10 586**	**21 526**	**25 292**	**27 286**	**..**	**..**	**..**	**..**	**..**
5100 Taxes on production, sale, transfer, etc	205	9 953	19 454	21 011	23 068	..	..	..	..	..
5110 General taxes	90	5 504	13 605	13 017	14 815	..	..	..	..	..
5120 Taxes on specific goods and services	114	4 413	5 772	7 901	8 133	..	..	..	..	..
5130 Unallocable between 5110 and 5120	0	36	77	93	120	..	..	..	..	..
5200 Taxes on use of goods and perform activities	20	385	1 780	3 187	3 426	..	..	..	..	..
5300 Unallocable between 5100 and 5200	0	248	292	1 094	792	..	..	..	..	..
6000 Other taxes	**0**	**0**	**0**	**0**	**0**	**..**	**..**	**..**	**..**	**..**
6100 Paid solely by business	..	..	..	..	..	..	..	..	..	..
6200 Other	..	..	..	..	..	..	..	..	..	..
Total tax revenue	**337**	**17 482**	**40 938**	**44 863**	**47 292**	**..**	**..**	**..**	**..**	**..**

	Local government					Social Security Funds				
	1975	1995	2005	2015	2017	1975	1995	2005	2015	2017
1000 Taxes on income, profits and capital gains	**3**	**0**	**0**	**0**	**0**	**0**	**0**	**0**	**9**	**9**
1100 Of individuals	2	..	..	..	..	0	0	0	9	9
1200 Corporate	0	0	0	0	0	0	0	0	0	0
1300 Unallocable between 1100 and 1200	1	0	0	0	0	0	0	0	0	0
2000 Social security contributions	**0**	**0**	**0**	**0**	**0**	**148**	**7 991**	**20 288**	**18 062**	**20 675**
2100 Employees	..	..	..	..	..	62	4 181	10 206	10 351	12 130
2200 Employers	..	..	..	..	..	62	3 810	10 082	7 711	8 545
2300 Self-employed or non-employed	..	..	..	..	..	0	0	0	0	0
2400 Unallocable between 2100, 2200 and 2300	..	..	..	..	..	24	0	0	0	0
3000 Taxes on payroll and workforce	**0**	**0**	**0**	**0**	**0**	**0**	**0**	**0**	**0**	**0**
4000 Taxes on property	**1**	**447**	**1 208**	**1 449**	**1 580**	**0**	**66**	**361**	**38**	**0**
4100 Recurrent taxes on immovable property	0	180	420	546	596	..	32	83	0	0
4200 Recurrent taxes on net wealth	0	267	788	903	984	..	0	0	0	0
4300 Estate, inheritance and gift taxes	0	0	0	0	0	..	0	0	0	0
4400 Taxes on financial and capital transactions	0	0	0	0	0	..	34	278	38	0
4500 Non-recurrent taxes	0	0	0	0	0	..	0	0	0	0
4600 Other recurrent taxes on property	0	0	0	0	0	..	0	0	0	0
5000 Taxes on goods and services	**10**	**89**	**197**	**96**	**116**	**0**	**124**	**248**	**240**	**99**
5100 Taxes on production, sale, transfer, etc	7	87	185	82	101	..	102	195	224	96
5110 General taxes	2	32	26	3	11	..	86	85	170	79
5120 Taxes on specific goods and services	6	55	159	79	90	..	16	110	47	1
5130 Unallocable between 5110 and 5120	0	0	0	0	0	..	0	0	7	16
5200 Taxes on use of goods and perform activities	3	2	12	14	15	..	22	53	16	3
5300 Unallocable between 5100 and 5200	0	0	0	0	0	..	0	0	0	0
6000 Other taxes	**0**	**0**	**0**	**0**	**0**	**0**	**0**	**0**	**0**	**0**
6100 Paid solely by business	..	..	..	..	..	..	..	..	..	..
6200 Other	..	..	..	..	..	..	..	..	..	..
Total tax revenue	**17**	**536**	**1 405**	**1 545**	**1 696**	**148**	**8 181**	**20 897**	**18 349**	**20 783**

.. Not available

Note: Excluding customs duties collected on behalf of the European Union.

StatLink https://doi.org/10.1787/888934057894

Table 6.25. Hungary, tax revenues by sub-sectors of government

Million HUF

	Central government					State/Regional				
	1975	1995	2005	2015	2017	1975	1995	2005	2015	2017
1000 Taxes on income, profits and capital gains	..	**498 608**	**1 915 178**	**2 311 932**	**2 750 166**	..	..	..	..	..
1100 Of individuals	..	383 744	1 449 552	1 698 410	1 951 837	..	..	..	..	..
1200 Corporate	..	106 259	465 626	613 522	798 329	..	..	..	..	..
1300 Unallocable between 1100 and 1200	..	8 605	0	0	0	..	..	..	..	..
2000 Social security contributions	..	**69 554**	**235 148**	**148 044**	**353 194**	..	..	..	..	..
2100 Employees	..	18 468	53 611	144 868	351 991	..	..	..	..	..
2200 Employers	..	51 086	175 013	3 176	1 203	..	..	..	..	..
2300 Self-employed or non-employed	..	0	0	0	0	..	..	..	..	..
2400 Unallocable between 2100, 2200 and 2300	..	0	6 524	0	0	..	..	..	..	..
3000 Taxes on payroll and workforce	..	**5 474**	**39 459**	**189 051**	**262 886**	..	..	..	..	..
4000 Taxes on property	..	**11 463**	**63 007**	**292 950**	**247 658**	..	..	..	..	..
4100 Recurrent taxes on immovable property	..	0	0	55 906	55 042	..	..	..	..	..
4200 Recurrent taxes on net wealth	..	0	0	136 282	53 392	..	..	..	..	..
4300 Estate, inheritance and gift taxes	..	1 364	7 678	7 373	9 393	..	..	..	..	..
4400 Taxes on financial and capital transactions	..	10 099	55 329	93 389	129 831	..	..	..	..	..
4500 Non-recurrent taxes	..	0	0	0	0	..	..	..	..	..
4600 Other recurrent taxes on property	..	0	0	0	0	..	..	..	..	..
5000 Taxes on goods and services	..	**924 906**	**2 869 329**	**5 104 320**	**5 483 307**	..	..	..	..	..
5100 Taxes on production, sale, transfer, etc	..	919 500	2 853 878	4 996 899	5 364 857	..	..	..	..	..
5110 General taxes	..	423 954	1 972 998	3 483 251	3 787 356	..	..	..	..	..
5120 Taxes on specific goods and services	..	495 546	880 880	1 513 648	1 577 501	..	..	..	..	..
5130 Unallocable between 5110 and 5120	..	0	0	0	0	..	..	..	..	..
5200 Taxes on use of goods and perform activities	..	5 406	15 451	107 421	118 450	..	..	..	..	..
5300 Unallocable between 5100 and 5200	..	0	0	0	0	..	..	..	..	..
6000 Other taxes	..	**8 901**	**44 873**	**42 803**	**37 690**	..	..	..	..	..
6100 Paid solely by business	..	..	23 710	21 294	22 798	..	..	..	..	..
6200 Other	..	..	0	0	0	..	..	..	..	..
Total tax revenue	..	**1 518 905**	**5 166 993**	**8 089 100**	**9 134 901**	..	..	..	..	..

	Local government					Social Security Funds				
	1975	1995	2005	2015	2017	1975	1995	2005	2015	2017
1000 Taxes on income, profits and capital gains	..	**0**	**173**	**45**	**35**	..	**0**	**26 307**	**116 453**	**123 376**
1100 Of individuals	..	0	173	45	35	..	0	26 307	116 453	123 376
1200 Corporate	..	0	0	0	0	..	0	0	0	0
1300 Unallocable between 1100 and 1200	..	0	0	0	0	..	0	0	0	0
2000 Social security contributions	..	**0**	**0**	**0**	**0**	..	**778 467**	**2 452 562**	**4 145 687**	**4 350 907**
2100 Employees	..	..	..	..	..	..	116 824	530 098	1 639 617	1 992 717
2200 Employers	..	..	..	..	..	..	632 478	1 894 306	2 476 925	2 327 797
2300 Self-employed or non-employed	..	..	..	..	..	..	27 466	2 080	0	0
2400 Unallocable between 2100, 2200 and 2300	..	..	..	..	..	..	1 699	26 078	29 145	30 393
3000 Taxes on payroll and workforce	..	**1 075**	**1 153**	**0**	**0**	..	**0**	**44 397**	**10 283**	**12 757**
4000 Taxes on property	..	**17 531**	**123 929**	**145 002**	**163 016**	..	**0**	**0**	**0**	**0**
4100 Recurrent taxes on immovable property	..	6 068	58 836	145 002	163 016	..	..	..	..	..
4200 Recurrent taxes on net wealth	..	0	0	0	0	..	..	..	..	..
4300 Estate, inheritance and gift taxes	..	1 364	7 932	0	0	..	..	..	..	..
4400 Taxes on financial and capital transactions	..	10 099	57 162	0	0	..	..	..	..	..
4500 Non-recurrent taxes	..	0	0	0	0	..	..	..	..	..
4600 Other recurrent taxes on property	..	0	0	0	0	..	..	..	..	..
5000 Taxes on goods and services	..	**41 970**	**388 385**	**625 570**	**683 177**	..	**0**	**0**	**103 105**	**118 015**
5100 Taxes on production, sale, transfer, etc	..	39 240	337 935	594 855	652 333	..	..	..	103 105	118 015
5110 General taxes	..	38 472	334 077	584 380	638 731	..	..	..	29 882	34 171
5120 Taxes on specific goods and services	..	768	3 858	10 475	13 602	..	..	..	73 223	83 844
5130 Unallocable between 5110 and 5120	..	0	0	0	0	..	..	..	0	0
5200 Taxes on use of goods and perform activities	..	2 730	50 450	30 715	30 844	..	..	..	0	0
5300 Unallocable between 5100 and 5200	..	0	0	0	0	..	..	..	0	0
6000 Other taxes	..	**0**	**0**	**0**	**0**	..	**21 605**	**9 616**	**14 021**	**9 891**
6100 Paid solely by business	..	..	..	..	..	..	..	..	..	..
6200 Other	..	..	..	..	..	..	..	..	..	..
Total tax revenue	..	**60 576**	**513 641**	**770 617**	**846 228**	..	**800 072**	**2 532 882**	**4 389 549**	**4 614 946**

.. Not available

Note: Excluding customs duties collected on behalf of the European Union.

StatLink https://doi.org/10.1787/888934057913

Table 6.26. Iceland, tax revenues by sub-sectors of government

Million ISK

	Central government					State/Regional				
	1975	1995	2005	2015	2017	1975	1995	2005	2015	2017
1000 Taxes on income, profits and capital gains	**68**	**27 156**	**105 705**	**210 536**	**274 572**	..	..	..	..	..
1100 Of individuals	55	22 914	70 944	127 535	165 012	..	..	..	..	..
1200 Corporate	13	4 242	20 297	52 544	79 993	..	..	..	..	..
1300 Unallocable between 1100 and 1200	0	0	14 464	30 457	29 566	..	..	..	..	..
2000 Social security contributions	**17**	**11 452**	**32 777**	**79 707**	**89 649**	..	..	..	..	..
2100 Employees	0	460	..	..	..	..	..	..	..	..
2200 Employers	17	10 992	..	..	..	..	..	..	..	..
2300 Self-employed or non-employed	0	0	..	..	..	..	..	..	..	..
2400 Unallocable between 2100, 2200 and 2300	0	0	32 777	79 707	89 649	..	..	..	..	..
3000 Taxes on payroll and workforce	**27**	**0**	**324**	**6 638**	**7 946**	..	..	..	..	..
4000 Taxes on property	**15**	**7 198**	**13 340**	**8 786**	**10 784**	..	..	..	..	..
4100 Recurrent taxes on immovable property	0	47	0	178	190	..	..	..	..	..
4200 Recurrent taxes on net wealth	5	3 191	2 887	657	346	..	..	..	..	..
4300 Estate, inheritance and gift taxes	0	389	866	2 919	4 268	..	..	..	..	..
4400 Taxes on financial and capital transactions	9	3 571	9 073	4 327	4 581	..	..	..	..	..
4500 Non-recurrent taxes	0	0	248	362	528	..	..	..	..	..
4600 Other recurrent taxes on property	0	0	266	343	871	..	..	..	..	..
5000 Taxes on goods and services	**392**	**66 356**	**168 295**	**259 996**	**322 292**	..	..	..	..	..
5100 Taxes on production, sale, transfer, etc	387	62 140	157 941	250 095	311 200	..	..	..	..	..
5110 General taxes	182	42 358	113 897	183 674	233 951	..	..	..	..	..
5120 Taxes on specific goods and services	205	19 782	44 044	66 421	77 249	..	..	..	..	..
5130 Unallocable between 5110 and 5120	0	0	0	0	0	..	..	..	..	..
5200 Taxes on use of goods and perform activities	5	4 216	10 354	9 901	11 092	..	..	..	..	..
5300 Unallocable between 5100 and 5200	0	0	0	0	0	..	..	..	..	..
6000 Other taxes	**0**	**0**	**1 504**	**38 364**	**16 448**	..	..	..	..	..
6100 Paid solely by business	..	..	565	32 477	10 331	..	..	..	..	..
6200 Other	..	..	939	5 887	6 117	..	..	..	..	..
Total tax revenue	**519**	**112 162**	**321 944**	**604 026**	**721 691**	..	..	..	..	..

	Local government					Social Security Funds				
	1975	1995	2005	2015	2017	1975	1995	2005	2015	2017
1000 Taxes on income, profits and capital gains	**78**	**21 170**	**74 455**	**170 443**	**207 996**	**0**	**0**	**0**	**0**	**0**
1100 Of individuals	74	21 170	74 455	170 443	207 996	..	..	..	..	..
1200 Corporate	4	0	0	0	0	..	..	..	..	..
1300 Unallocable between 1100 and 1200	0	0	0	0	0	..	..	..	..	..
2000 Social security contributions	**0**	**0**	**0**	**0**	**0**	**0**	**0**	**0**	**0**	**0**
2100 Employees	..	..	..	..	..	..	..	..	..	..
2200 Employers	..	..	..	..	..	..	..	..	..	..
2300 Self-employed or non-employed	..	..	..	..	..	..	..	..	..	..
2400 Unallocable between 2100, 2200 and 2300	..	..	..	..	..	..	..	..	..	..
3000 Taxes on payroll and workforce	**0**	**0**	**0**	**0**	**0**	**0**	**0**	**0**	..	..
4000 Taxes on property	**18**	**5 674**	**13 931**	**34 701**	**43 174**	**0**	**0**	**0**	**0**	**0**
4100 Recurrent taxes on immovable property	18	5 674	13 931	34 701	43 174	..	..	..	..	..
4200 Recurrent taxes on net wealth	0	0	0	0	0	..	..	..	..	..
4300 Estate, inheritance and gift taxes	0	0	0	0	0	..	..	..	..	..
4400 Taxes on financial and capital transactions	0	0	0	0	0	..	..	..	..	..
4500 Non-recurrent taxes	0	0	0	0	0	..	..	..	..	..
4600 Other recurrent taxes on property	0	0	0	0	0	..	..	..	..	..
5000 Taxes on goods and services	**9**	**2 585**	**6 904**	**2 832**	**8 503**	**0**	**0**	**0**	**0**	**0**
5100 Taxes on production, sale, transfer, etc	9	2 585	0	0	0	..	..	..	..	..
5110 General taxes	0	2 585	0	0	0	..	..	..	..	..
5120 Taxes on specific goods and services	9	0	0	0	0	..	..	..	..	..
5130 Unallocable between 5110 and 5120	0	0	0	0	0	..	0	0	0	0
5200 Taxes on use of goods and perform activities	0	0	6 904	2 832	8 503	..	0	0	0	0
5300 Unallocable between 5100 and 5200	0	0	0	0	0	..	..	..	..	..
6000 Other taxes	**14**	**0**	**93**	**0**	**0**	**0**	**0**	**0**	**0**	**0**
6100 Paid solely by business	14	..	93	0	0	..	..	0	0	0
6200 Other	0	..	0	0	0	..	..	0	0	0
Total tax revenue	**119**	**29 429**	**95 383**	**207 976**	**259 673**	**0**	**0**	**0**	**0**	**0**

.. Not available

StatLink https://doi.org/10.1787/888934057932

Table 6.27. Ireland, tax revenues by sub-sectors of government

Million EUR

	Central government					State/Regional				
	1975	1995	2005	2015	2017	1975	1995	2005	2015	2017
1000 Taxes on income, profits and capital gains	**456**	**7 022**	**20 080**	**26 044**	**29 078**	..	..	..	..	..
1100 Of individuals	382	5 563	14 568	19 167	20 876	..	..	..	..	..
1200 Corporate	73	1 458	5 511	6 873	8 198	..	..	..	..	..
1300 Unallocable between 1100 and 1200	0	0	0	4	4	..	..	..	..	..
2000 Social security contributions	**11**	**87**	**217**	**1 568**	**1 502**	..	..	..	..	..
2100 Employees	10	87	217	1 568	1 502	..	..	..	..	..
2200 Employers	0	0	0	0	0	..	..	..	..	..
2300 Self-employed or non-employed	1	0	0	0	0	..	..	..	..	..
2400 Unallocable between 2100, 2200 and 2300	0	0	0	0	0	..	..	..	..	..
3000 Taxes on payroll and workforce	**0**	**209**	**332**	**357**	**431**	..	..	..	..	..
4000 Taxes on property	**37**	**370**	**2 741**	**2 530**	**2 473**	..	..	..	..	..
4100 Recurrent taxes on immovable property	0	15	0	475	477	..	..	..	..	..
4200 Recurrent taxes on net wealth	5	0	0	169	0	..	..	..	..	..
4300 Estate, inheritance and gift taxes	17	76	255	401	448	..	..	..	..	..
4400 Taxes on financial and capital transactions	15	279	2 486	1 484	1 547	..	..	..	..	..
4500 Non-recurrent taxes	0	0	0	0	0	..	..	..	..	..
4600 Other recurrent taxes on property	0	0	0	0	0	..	..	..	..	..
5000 Taxes on goods and services	**671**	**6 763**	**19 122**	**19 781**	**21 706**	..	..	..	..	..
5100 Taxes on production, sale, transfer, etc	639	6 419	18 106	17 834	19 697	..	..	..	..	..
5110 General taxes	223	3 666	12 373	11 956	13 111	..	..	..	..	..
5120 Taxes on specific goods and services	416	2 753	5 733	5 878	6 585	..	..	..	..	..
5130 Unallocable between 5110 and 5120	0	0	0	0	0	..	..	..	..	..
5200 Taxes on use of goods and perform activities	33	344	1 015	1 947	2 009	..	..	..	..	..
5300 Unallocable between 5100 and 5200	0	0	0	0	0	..	..	..	..	..
6000 Other taxes	**0**	**0**	**0**	**12**	**8**	..	..	..	..	..
6100 Paid solely by business	..	..	..	0	0	..	..	..	..	..
6200 Other	..	..	0	12	8	..	..	..	..	..
Total tax revenue	**1 175**	**14 451**	**42 492**	**50 292**	**55 198**	..	..	..	..	..

	Local government					Social Security Funds				
	1975	1995	2005	2015	2017	1975	1995	2005	2015	2017
1000 Taxes on income, profits and capital gains	**0**	**0**	**0**	**0**	**0**	**0**	**0**	**0**	**0**	**0**
1100 Of individuals	..	..	..	..	..	..	..	..	..	..
1200 Corporate	..	..	..	..	..	..	..	..	..	..
1300 Unallocable between 1100 and 1200	0	..	..	..	..	0	..	..	..	..
2000 Social security contributions	**0**	**56**	**90**	**126**	**100**	**198**	**2 215**	**6 212**	**8 524**	**9 836**
2100 Employees	..	56	90	126	100	73	576	1 397	1 853	2 138
2200 Employers	..	0	0	0	0	125	1 528	4 427	6 211	7 177
2300 Self-employed or non-employed	..	0	0	0	0	0	111	388	460	522
2400 Unallocable between 2100, 2200 and 2300	..	0	0	0	0	0	0	0	0	0
3000 Taxes on payroll and workforce	**0**	**0**	**0**	**0**	**0**	**0**	**0**	**0**	**0**	**0**
4000 Taxes on property	**110**	**408**	**1 020**	**1 389**	**1 349**	..	**0**	**0**	**0**	**0**
4100 Recurrent taxes on immovable property	110	408	1 020	1 389	1 349	..	..	..	..	..
4200 Recurrent taxes on net wealth	0	0	0	0	0	..	..	..	..	..
4300 Estate, inheritance and gift taxes	0	0	0	0	0	..	..	..	..	..
4400 Taxes on financial and capital transactions	0	0	0	0	0	..	..	..	..	..
4500 Non-recurrent taxes	0	0	0	0	0	..	..	..	..	..
4600 Other recurrent taxes on property	0	0	0	0	0	..	..	..	..	..
5000 Taxes on goods and services	**0**	**0**	**0**	**0**	**0**	**0**	**0**	**0**	**0**	**0**
5100 Taxes on production, sale, transfer, etc	..	..	..	..	..	0	..	..	..	..
5110 General taxes	..	..	..	..	..	0	0	0	0	0
5120 Taxes on specific goods and services	..	..	..	..	..	0	..	..	..	..
5130 Unallocable between 5110 and 5120	0	0	0	0	0	0	0	0	0	0
5200 Taxes on use of goods and perform activities	..	..	..	..	..	0	0	0	0	0
5300 Unallocable between 5100 and 5200	0	..	..	..	..	0	..	..	..	..
6000 Other taxes	**0**	**0**	**0**	**0**	**0**	**0**	**0**	**0**	**0**	**0**
6100 Paid solely by business	..	..	..	..	..	..	..	..	..	..
6200 Other	..	..	..	..	..	..	..	..	..	..
Total tax revenue	**110**	**464**	**1 110**	**1 515**	**1 449**	**198**	**2 215**	**6 212**	**8 524**	**9 836**

.. Not available

Note: Excluding customs duties collected on behalf of the European Union. The personal income tax data shown for the country table for Ireland is different to the ESA2010 presentation as the expenditure component of the payable tax credits are excluded in accordance with the OECD Interpretative Guide.

StatLink https://doi.org/10.1787/888934057951

Table 6.28. Israel, tax revenues by sub-sectors of government

Million ILS

	Central government					State/Regional				
	1975	1995	2005	2015	2017	1975	1995	2005	2015	2017
1000 Taxes on income, profits and capital gains	..	**37 422**	**73 082**	**113 841**	**146 948**	..	..	..	..	..
1100 Of individuals	..	28 399	47 062	70 760	85 410	..	..	..	..	..
1200 Corporate	..	8 514	21 909	34 676	41 909	..	..	..	..	..
1300 Unallocable between 1100 and 1200	..	509	4 111	8 405	19 629	..	..	..	..	..
2000 Social security contributions	..	**0**	**0**	**0**	**0**	..	..	..	..	..
2100 Employees	..	..	..	..	..	..	..	..	..	..
2200 Employers	..	..	..	..	..	..	..	..	..	..
2300 Self-employed or non-employed	..	..	..	..	..	..	..	..	..	..
2400 Unallocable between 2100, 2200 and 2300	..	..	..	..	..	..	..	..	..	..
3000 Taxes on payroll and workforce	..	**5 007**	**9 920**	**13 770**	**15 196**	..	..	..	..	..
4000 Taxes on property	..	**4 122**	**5 547**	**10 593**	**11 276**	..	..	..	..	..
4100 Recurrent taxes on immovable property	..	786	322	44	21	..	..	..	..	..
4200 Recurrent taxes on net wealth	..	0	0	0	0	..	..	..	..	..
4300 Estate, inheritance and gift taxes	..	0	0	0	0	..	..	..	..	..
4400 Taxes on financial and capital transactions	..	2 049	3 591	6 732	6 642	..	..	..	..	..
4500 Non-recurrent taxes	..	1 287	1 634	3 817	4 613	..	..	..	..	..
4600 Other recurrent taxes on property	..	0	0	0	0	..	..	..	..	..
5000 Taxes on goods and services	..	**38 673**	**75 932**	**136 829**	**141 703**	..	..	..	..	..
5100 Taxes on production, sale, transfer, etc	..	36 637	70 741	128 277	133 293	..	..	..	..	..
5110 General taxes	..	31 975	59 374	107 765	110 971	..	..	..	..	..
5120 Taxes on specific goods and services	..	4 662	11 367	20 512	22 322	..	..	..	..	..
5130 Unallocable between 5110 and 5120	..	0	0	0	0	..	..	..	..	..
5200 Taxes on use of goods and perform activities	..	2 036	5 191	8 552	8 410	..	..	..	..	..
5300 Unallocable between 5100 and 5200	..	0	0	0	0	..	..	..	..	..
6000 Other taxes	..	**0**	**0**	**0**	**0**	..	..	..	..	..
6100 Paid solely by business	..	..	..	..	..	..	..	..	..	..
6200 Other	..	..	..	..	..	..	..	..	..	..
Total tax revenue	..	**85 224**	**164 481**	**275 033**	**315 123**	..	..	..	..	..
	Local government					Social Security Funds				
	1975	1995	2005	2015	2017	1975	1995	2005	2015	2017
1000 Taxes on income, profits and capital gains	..	**0**	**0**	**0**	**0**	..	**0**	**0**	**0**	**0**
1100 Of individuals	..	0	0	0	0	..	0	0	0	0
1200 Corporate	..	0	0	0	0	..	0	0	0	0
1300 Unallocable between 1100 and 1200	..	0	0	0	0	..	0	0	0	0
2000 Social security contributions	..	**0**	**0**	**0**	**0**	..	**14 958**	**34 597**	**59 561**	**66 783**
2100 Employees	..	..	..	..	..	..	7 953	19 720	34 692	37 884
2200 Employers	..	..	..	..	..	..	4 672	10 679	17 247	20 596
2300 Self-employed or non-employed	..	..	..	..	..	..	2 334	4 198	7 622	8 303
2400 Unallocable between 2100, 2200 and 2300	..	..	..	..	..	..	0	0	0	0
3000 Taxes on payroll and workforce	..	**0**	**0**	**0**	**0**	..	**0**	**0**	**0**	**0**
4000 Taxes on property	..	**6 445**	**15 689**	**28 210**	**30 003**	..	**0**	**0**	**0**	**0**
4100 Recurrent taxes on immovable property	..	5 489	13 962	23 721	24 853	..	..	..	..	..
4200 Recurrent taxes on net wealth	..	0	0	0	0	..	..	..	..	..
4300 Estate, inheritance and gift taxes	..	0	0	0	0	..	..	..	..	..
4400 Taxes on financial and capital transactions	..	0	0	0	0	..	..	..	..	..
4500 Non-recurrent taxes	..	956	1 727	4 490	5 150	..	..	..	..	..
4600 Other recurrent taxes on property	..	0	0	0	0	..	..	..	..	..
5000 Taxes on goods and services	..	**401**	**763**	**1 445**	**1 524**	..	**0**	**0**	**0**	**0**
5100 Taxes on production, sale, transfer, etc	..	0	0	0	0	..	..	..	..	..
5110 General taxes	..	0	0	0	0	..	..	..	..	..
5120 Taxes on specific goods and services	..	0	0	0	0	..	..	..	..	..
5130 Unallocable between 5110 and 5120	..	0	0	0	0	..	..	..	..	..
5200 Taxes on use of goods and perform activities	..	401	763	1 445	1 524	..	..	..	..	..
5300 Unallocable between 5100 and 5200	..	0	0	0	0	..	..	..	..	..
6000 Other taxes	..	**0**	**0**	**0**	**0**	..	**0**	**0**	**0**	**0**
6100 Paid solely by business	..	..	..	..	..	..	..	..	..	..
6200 Other	..	..	..	..	..	..	..	..	..	..
Total tax revenue	..	**6 846**	**16 452**	**29 656**	**31 527**	..	**14 958**	**34 597**	**59 561**	**66 783**

.. Not available

Note: The statistical data for Israel are supplied by and under the responsibility of the relevant Israeli authorities. The use of such data by the OECD is without prejudice to the status of the Golan Heights, East Jerusalem and Israeli settlements in the West Bank under the terms of international law.

StatLink https://doi.org/10.1787/888934057970

Table 6.29. Italy, tax revenues by sub-sectors of government

Million EUR

	Central government					State/Regional				
	1975	1995	2005	2015	2017	1975	1995	2005	2015	2017
1000 Taxes on income, profits and capital gains	**3 897**	**128 458**	**165 580**	**195 451**	**197 740**	..	..	..	..	..
1100 Of individuals	2 767	98 695	131 047	156 320	155 673	..	..	..	..	..
1200 Corporate	1 131	32 890	31 969	31 421	34 703	..	..	..	..	..
1300 Unallocable between 1100 and 1200	0	-3 127	2 564	7 710	7 364	..	..	..	..	..
2000 Social security contributions	**0**	**0**	**0**	**0**	**0**	..	..	..	..	..
2100 Employees	..	..	..	..	..	..	..	..	..	..
2200 Employers	..	..	..	..	..	..	..	..	..	..
2300 Self-employed or non-employed	..	..	..	..	..	..	..	..	..	..
2400 Unallocable between 2100, 2200 and 2300	..	..	..	..	..	..	..	..	..	..
3000 Taxes on payroll and workforce	**0**	**1 136**	**0**	**0**	**0**	..	..	..	..	..
4000 Taxes on property	**587**	**13 546**	**15 717**	**22 226**	**24 104**	..	..	..	..	..
4100 Recurrent taxes on immovable property	4	0	0	3 892	3 775	..	..	..	..	..
4200 Recurrent taxes on net wealth	0	4 494	0	231	355	..	..	..	..	..
4300 Estate, inheritance and gift taxes	39	587	56	638	778	..	..	..	..	..
4400 Taxes on financial and capital transactions	544	8 464	13 794	16 310	16 652	..	..	..	..	..
4500 Non-recurrent taxes	0	0	1 322	303	1 076	..	..	..	..	..
4600 Other recurrent taxes on property	0	0	545	852	1 468	..	..	..	..	..
5000 Taxes on goods and services	**5 506**	**95 323**	**123 870**	**157 330**	**168 011**	..	..	..	..	..
5100 Taxes on production, sale, transfer, etc	5 306	92 042	121 824	154 713	162 948	..	..	..	..	..
5110 General taxes	2 685	52 531	80 619	93 282	99 812	..	..	..	..	..
5120 Taxes on specific goods and services	2 621	39 245	41 205	61 431	63 136	..	..	..	..	..
5130 Unallocable between 5110 and 5120	0	323	0	0	0	..	..	..	..	..
5200 Taxes on use of goods and perform activities	200	2 802	1 535	2 191	3 886	..	..	..	..	..
5300 Unallocable between 5100 and 5200	0	479	511	426	1 177	..	..	..	..	..
6000 Other taxes	**1**	**0**	**0**	**0**	**0**	..	..	..	..	..
6100 Paid solely by business	0	..	..	..	..	..	..	..	..	..
6200 Other	1	..	..	..	..	..	..	..	..	..
Total tax revenue	**9 991**	**238 462**	**305 167**	**375 007**	**389 855**	..	..	..	..	..

	Local government					Social Security Funds				
	1975	1995	2005	2015	2017	1975	1995	2005	2015	2017
1000 Taxes on income, profits and capital gains	**134**	**5 658**	**18 494**	**30 483**	**33 128**	**0**	**0**	**0**	**0**	**0**
1100 Of individuals	81	145	16 995	28 302	31 280	..	..	..	..	..
1200 Corporate	54	97	1 491	2 109	1 641	..	..	..	..	..
1300 Unallocable between 1100 and 1200	0	5 416	8	72	207	..	..	..	..	..
2000 Social security contributions	**0**	**0**	**0**	**0**	**0**	**8 607**	**119 612**	**179 362**	**214 376**	**220 622**
2100 Employees	..	..	..	..	..	1 692	23 036	31 998	39 805	40 872
2200 Employers	..	..	..	..	..	6 915	79 716	125 099	143 273	147 305
2300 Self-employed or non-employed	..	..	..	..	..	0	16 860	22 265	31 298	32 445
2400 Unallocable between 2100, 2200 and 2300	..	..	..	..	..	0	0	0	0	0
3000 Taxes on payroll and workforce	**0**	**0**	**0**	**0**	**0**	**0**	**0**	**0**	**0**	**0**
4000 Taxes on property	**29**	**7 915**	**13 484**	**24 033**	**20 760**	**0**	**0**	**0**	**0**	**0**
4100 Recurrent taxes on immovable property	29	7 449	11 736	21 666	18 294	..	..	..	..	..
4200 Recurrent taxes on net wealth	0	0	0	0	0	..	..	..	..	..
4300 Estate, inheritance and gift taxes	0	0	5	36	37	..	..	..	..	..
4400 Taxes on financial and capital transactions	0	466	904	935	1 038	..	..	..	..	..
4500 Non-recurrent taxes	0	0	481	6	72	..	..	..	..	..
4600 Other recurrent taxes on property	0	0	358	1 390	1 319	..	..	..	..	..
5000 Taxes on goods and services	**4**	**6 941**	**30 231**	**34 551**	**36 595**	**0**	**0**	**0**	**0**	**0**
5100 Taxes on production, sale, transfer, etc	0	1 505	17 114	15 138	16 263	..	..	..	..	..
5110 General taxes	..	0	4 698	7 410	8 089	..	..	..	..	..
5120 Taxes on specific goods and services	..	1 505	12 416	7 728	8 174	..	..	..	..	..
5130 Unallocable between 5110 and 5120	..	0	0	0	0	..	..	..	..	..
5200 Taxes on use of goods and perform activities	4	2 838	7 512	8 939	9 285	..	..	..	..	..
5300 Unallocable between 5100 and 5200	0	2 597	5 605	10 474	11 047	..	..	..	..	..
6000 Other taxes	**0**	**0**	**34 690**	**28 072**	**22 262**	**0**	**0**	**0**	**0**	**0**
6100 Paid solely by business	..	..	34 690	28 072	22 262	..	..	..	..	..
6200 Other	..	..	0	0	0	..	..	..	..	..
Total tax revenue	**168**	**20 514**	**96 899**	**117 139**	**112 745**	**8 607**	**119 612**	**179 362**	**214 376**	**220 622**

.. Not available

Note: Excluding customs duties collected on behalf of the European Union.

StatLink https://doi.org/10.1787/888934057989

Table 6.30. Japan, tax revenues by sub-sectors of government

Billion JPY

	Central government					State/Regional				
	1975	1995	2005	2015	2017	1975	1995	2005	2015	2017
1000 Taxes on income, profits and capital gains	**9 747**	**33 255**	**29 975**	**31 607**	**33 783**	..	..	..	..	..
1100 Of individuals	5 482	19 515	16 702	18 178	19 276	..	..	..	..	..
1200 Corporate	4 265	13 740	13 274	13 429	14 507	..	..	..	..	..
1300 Unallocable between 1100 and 1200	0	0	0	0	0	..	..	..	..	..
2000 Social security contributions	**0**	**0**	**0**	**0**	**0**	..	..	..	..	..
2100 Employees	..	..	..	..	..	..	..	..	..	..
2200 Employers	..	..	..	..	..	..	..	..	..	..
2300 Self-employed or non-employed	..	..	..	..	..	..	..	..	..	..
2400 Unallocable between 2100, 2200 and 2300	..	..	..	..	..	..	..	..	..	..
3000 Taxes on payroll and workforce	**0**	**0**	**0**	**0**	**0**	..	..	..	..	..
4000 Taxes on property	**871**	**5 561**	**2 735**	**3 018**	**3 344**	..	..	..	..	..
4100 Recurrent taxes on immovable property	0	406	0	0	..	..	..	..	..	..
4200 Recurrent taxes on net wealth	0	0	0	0	0	..	..	..	..	..
4300 Estate, inheritance and gift taxes	310	2 690	1 566	1 968	2 292	..	..	..	..	..
4400 Taxes on financial and capital transactions	561	2 464	1 169	1 050	1 052	..	..	..	..	..
4500 Non-recurrent taxes	0	0	0	0	0	..	..	..	..	..
4600 Other recurrent taxes on property	0	0	0	0	0	..	..	..	..	..
5000 Taxes on goods and services	**3 888**	**16 147**	**19 580**	**25 345**	**27 158**	..	..	..	..	..
5100 Taxes on production, sale, transfer, etc	3 579	15 083	18 424	24 673	26 499	..	..	..	..	..
5110 General taxes	0	7 238	10 583	17 426	17 514	..	..	..	..	..
5120 Taxes on specific goods and services	3 579	7 845	7 840	7 247	8 985	..	..	..	..	..
5130 Unallocable between 5110 and 5120	0	0	0	0	0	..	..	..	..	..
5200 Taxes on use of goods and perform activities	309	1 065	1 157	671	659	..	..	..	..	..
5300 Unallocable between 5100 and 5200	0	0	0	0	0	..	..	..	..	..
6000 Other taxes	**0**	**0**	**0**	**0**	**0**	..	..	..	..	..
6100 Paid solely by business	..	..	..	..	0	..	..	..	..	..
6200 Other	..	..	..	..	0	..	..	..	..	..
Total tax revenue	**14 506**	**54 963**	**52 290**	**59 969**	**64 284**	..	..	..	..	..

	Local government					Social Security Funds				
	1975	1995	2005	2015	2017	1975	1995	2005	2015	2017
1000 Taxes on income, profits and capital gains	**4 472**	**17 752**	**16 655**	**19 362**	**18 875**	**0**	**0**	**0**	**0**	**0**
1100 Of individuals	2 147	10 283	8 520	12 669	13 049	..	..	..	..	..
1200 Corporate	2 325	7 470	8 135	6 693	5 826	..	..	..	..	..
1300 Unallocable between 1100 and 1200	0	0	0	0	0	..	..	..	..	..
2000 Social security contributions	**0**	**0**	**0**	**0**	**0**	**9 253**	**44 794**	**50 848**	**64 465**	**68 562**
2100 Employees	..	..	..	..	..	3 436	18 404	20 982	28 224	30 340
2200 Employers	..	..	..	..	..	4 825	21 432	23 154	29 479	31 637
2300 Self-employed or non-employed	..	..	..	..	..	992	4 958	6 712	6 763	6 585
2400 Unallocable between 2100, 2200 and 2300	..	..	..	..	..	0	0	0	0	0
3000 Taxes on payroll and workforce	**0**	**0**	**0**	**0**	**0**	**0**	**0**	**0**	**0**	**0**
4000 Taxes on property	**2 029**	**10 653**	**10 593**	**10 382**	**10 730**	**0**	**0**	**0**	**0**	**0**
4100 Recurrent taxes on immovable property	1 848	9 865	10 116	10 005	10 323	..	..	..	..	..
4200 Recurrent taxes on net wealth	0	0	0	0	0	..	..	..	..	..
4300 Estate, inheritance and gift taxes	0	0	0	0	0	..	..	..	..	..
4400 Taxes on financial and capital transactions	181	788	477	377	407	..	..	..	..	..
4500 Non-recurrent taxes	0	0	0	0	0	..	..	..	..	..
4600 Other recurrent taxes on property	0	0	0	0	0	..	..	..	..	..
5000 Taxes on goods and services	**1 636**	**4 941**	**7 206**	**8 942**	**8 873**	**0**	**0**	**0**	**0**	**0**
5100 Taxes on production, sale, transfer, etc	1 234	3 245	5 299	7 198	7 083	..	..	..	..	..
5110 General taxes	0	0	2 551	4 974	4 735	..	..	..	..	..
5120 Taxes on specific goods and services	1 234	3 245	2 747	2 223	2 348	..	..	..	..	..
5130 Unallocable between 5110 and 5120	0	0	0	0	0	..	..	..	..	..
5200 Taxes on use of goods and perform activities	402	1 697	1 907	1 744	1 790	..	..	..	..	..
5300 Unallocable between 5100 and 5200	0	0	0	0	0	..	..	..	..	..
6000 Other taxes	**20**	**329**	**351**	**413**	**427**	**0**	**0**	**0**	**0**	**0**
6100 Paid solely by business	15	307	297	361	371	..	..	..	..	..
6200 Other	5	22	54	52	56	..	..	..	..	..
Total tax revenue	**8 157**	**33 675**	**34 805**	**39 099**	**38 906**	**9 253**	**44 794**	**50 848**	**64 465**	**68 562**

.. Not available

StatLink https://doi.org/10.1787/888934058008

Table 6.31. Korea, tax revenues by sub-sectors of government

Billion KRW

	Central government					State/Regional				
	1975	1995	2005	2015	2017	1975	1995	2005	2015	2017
1000 Taxes on income, profits and capital gains	**344**	**23 000**	**55 109**	**106 162**	**134 685**	..	..	..	..	..
1100 Of individuals	134	13 713	24 766	60 828	75 171	..	..	..	..	..
1200 Corporate	139	8 988	30 343	45 334	59 514	..	..	..	..	..
1300 Unallocable between 1100 and 1200	71	300	0	0	0	..	..	..	..	..
2000 Social security contributions	**0**	**0**	**0**	**0**	**0**	..	..	..	..	..
2100 Employees	..	..	..	..	..	..	..	..	..	..
2200 Employers	..	..	..	..	..	..	..	..	..	..
2300 Self-employed or non-employed	..	..	..	..	..	..	..	..	..	..
2400 Unallocable between 2100, 2200 and 2300	..	..	..	..	..	..	..	..	..	..
3000 Taxes on payroll and workforce	**0**	**0**	**0**	**0**	**0**	..	..	..	..	..
4000 Taxes on property	**65**	**2 482**	**6 769**	**15 164**	**16 946**	..	..	..	..	..
4100 Recurrent taxes on immovable property	0	106	535	1 666	1 954	..	..	..	..	..
4200 Recurrent taxes on net wealth	0	0	0	0	0	..	..	..	..	..
4300 Estate, inheritance and gift taxes	11	1 029	1 873	5 044	6 785	..	..	..	..	..
4400 Taxes on financial and capital transactions	49	1 258	4 363	8 454	8 207	..	..	..	..	..
4500 Non-recurrent taxes	5	89	-2	0	0	..	..	..	..	..
4600 Other recurrent taxes on property	0	0	0	0	0	..	..	..	..	..
5000 Taxes on goods and services	**920**	**29 170**	**63 480**	**93 127**	**109 365**	..	..	..	..	..
5100 Taxes on production, sale, transfer, etc	920	29 170	63 480	93 127	109 365	..	..	..	..	..
5110 General taxes	198	14 637	36 118	54 159	67 087	..	..	..	..	..
5120 Taxes on specific goods and services	722	14 533	27 362	38 968	42 278	..	..	..	..	..
5130 Unallocable between 5110 and 5120	0	0	0	0	0	..	..	..	..	..
5200 Taxes on use of goods and perform activities	0	0	0	0	0	..	..	..	..	..
5300 Unallocable between 5100 and 5200	0	0	0	0	0	..	..	..	..	..
6000 Other taxes	**64**	**2 121**	**2 108**	**3 435**	**4 389**	..	..	..	..	..
6100 Paid solely by business	0	0	0	0	0	..	..	..	..	..
6200 Other	64	2 121	2 108	3 435	4 389	..	..	..	..	..
Total tax revenue	**1 393**	**56 774**	**127 466**	**217 888**	**265 385**	..	..	..	..	..

	Local government					Social Security Funds				
	1975	1995	2005	2015	2017	1975	1995	2005	2015	2017
1000 Taxes on income, profits and capital gains	**36**	**1 704**	**5 500**	**12 989**	**14 735**	**0**	**0**	**0**	**0**	**0**
1100 Of individuals	0	1 137	2 804	6 772	7 950	..	..	..	..	..
1200 Corporate	0	565	2 696	6 217	6 785	..	..	..	..	..
1300 Unallocable between 1100 and 1200	36	3	0	0	0	..	..	..	..	..
2000 Social security contributions	**0**	**0**	**0**	**0**	**0**	**13**	**9 913**	**43 902**	**104 693**	**119 676**
2100 Employees	..	..	..	..	..	0	4 539	17 632	44 281	51 125
2200 Employers	..	..	..	..	..	13	3 918	18 486	47 846	54 063
2300 Self-employed or non-employed	..	..	..	..	..	0	1 456	7 784	12 566	14 488
2400 Unallocable between 2100, 2200 and 2300	..	..	..	..	..	0	0	0	0	0
3000 Taxes on payroll and workforce	**0**	**237**	**514**	**1 122**	**1 376**	**0**	**0**	**0**	**0**	**0**
4000 Taxes on property	**87**	**8 960**	**17 928**	**33 461**	**37 460**	**0**	**0**	**0**	**0**	**0**
4100 Recurrent taxes on immovable property	45	2 636	4 495	10 820	12 365	..	..	..	..	..
4200 Recurrent taxes on net wealth	0	0	0	0	0	..	..	..	..	..
4300 Estate, inheritance and gift taxes	0	0	0	0	0	..	..	..	..	..
4400 Taxes on financial and capital transactions	42	6 324	13 433	22 641	25 095	..	..	..	..	..
4500 Non-recurrent taxes	0	0	0	0	0	..	..	..	..	..
4600 Other recurrent taxes on property	0	0	0	0	0	..	..	..	..	..
5000 Taxes on goods and services	**36**	**4 218**	**7 561**	**17 199**	**19 700**	**0**	**0**	**0**	**0**	**0**
5100 Taxes on production, sale, transfer, etc	19	2 464	5 589	10 127	11 928	..	..	..	..	..
5110 General taxes	0	0	0	6 003	7 274	..	..	..	..	..
5120 Taxes on specific goods and services	19	2 464	5 589	4 124	4 654	..	..	..	..	..
5130 Unallocable between 5110 and 5120	0	0	0	0	0	..	..	..	..	..
5200 Taxes on use of goods and perform activities	17	1 754	1 972	7 072	7 772	..	..	..	..	..
5300 Unallocable between 5100 and 5200	0	0	0	0	0	..	..	..	..	..
6000 Other taxes	**0**	**198**	**4 474**	**6 207**	**7 138**	**0**	**0**	**0**	**0**	**0**
6100 Paid solely by business	..	0	0	0	0	..	..	..	..	..
6200 Other	..	198	4 474	6 207	7 138	..	..	..	..	..
Total tax revenue	**159**	**15 316**	**35 977**	**70 978**	**80 409**	**13**	**9 913**	**43 902**	**104 693**	**119 676**

.. Not available

StatLink https://doi.org/10.1787/888934058027

Table 6.32. Latvia, tax revenues by sub-sectors of government

Million EUR

	Central government					State/Regional				
	1975	1995	2005	2015	2017	1975	1995	2005	2015	2017
1000 Taxes on income, profits and capital gains	**..**	**68**	**453**	**677**	**833**	**..**	**..**	**..**	**..**	**..**
1100 Of individuals	..	0	195	289	405	..	..	..	..	..
1200 Corporate	..	68	258	389	427	..	..	..	..	..
1300 Unallocable between 1100 and 1200	..	0	0	0	..	..	..	..	..	..
2000 Social security contributions	**..**	**0**	**0**	**0**	**0**	**..**	**..**	**..**	**..**	**..**
2100 Employees	..	..	..	..	..	..	..	..	..	..
2200 Employers	..	..	..	..	..	..	..	..	..	..
2300 Self-employed or non-employed	..	..	..	..	..	..	..	..	..	..
2400 Unallocable between 2100, 2200 and 2300	..	..	..	..	..	..	..	..	..	..
3000 Taxes on payroll and workforce	**..**	**0**	**4**	**3**	**3**	**..**	**..**	**..**	**..**	**..**
4000 Taxes on property	**..**	**4**	**48**	**44**	**44**	**..**	**..**	**..**	**..**	**..**
4100 Recurrent taxes on immovable property	..	0	0	0	0	..	..	..	..	..
4200 Recurrent taxes on net wealth	..	0	0	0	0	..	..	..	..	..
4300 Estate, inheritance and gift taxes	..	0	0	3	3	..	..	..	..	..
4400 Taxes on financial and capital transactions	..	4	48	42	41	..	..	..	..	..
4500 Non-recurrent taxes	..	0	0	0	0	..	..	..	..	..
4600 Other recurrent taxes on property	..	0	0	0	..	..	..	..	..	..
5000 Taxes on goods and services	**..**	**453**	**1 553**	**3 156**	**3 596**	**..**	**..**	**..**	**..**	**..**
5100 Taxes on production, sale, transfer, etc	..	453	1 510	2 997	3 413	..	..	..	..	..
5110 General taxes	..	343	1 002	2 130	2 440	..	..	..	..	..
5120 Taxes on specific goods and services	..	110	508	867	973	..	..	..	..	..
5130 Unallocable between 5110 and 5120	..	0	0	0	..	..	..	..	..	..
5200 Taxes on use of goods and perform activities	..	1	43	159	184	..	..	..	..	..
5300 Unallocable between 5100 and 5200	..	0	0	0	0	..	..	..	..	..
6000 Other taxes	**..**	**0**	**0**	**0**	**0**	**..**	**..**	**..**	**..**	**..**
6100 Paid solely by business	..	..	..	..	..	..	..	..	..	..
6200 Other	..	..	..	..	..	..	..	..	..	..
Total tax revenue	**..**	**525**	**2 058**	**3 881**	**4 476**	**..**	**..**	**..**	**..**	**..**

	Local government					Social Security Funds				
	1975	1995	2005	2015	2017	1975	1995	2005	2015	2017
1000 Taxes on income, profits and capital gains	**..**	**197**	**538**	**1 156**	**1 372**	**..**	**0**	**0**	**0**	**0**
1100 Of individuals	..	197	538	1 156	1 372	..	..	..	..	..
1200 Corporate	..	0	0	0	0	..	..	..	..	..
1300 Unallocable between 1100 and 1200	..	0	0	0	0	..	..	..	..	..
2000 Social security contributions	**..**	**0**	**0**	**0**	**0**	**..**	**445**	**1 079**	**2 030**	**2 259**
2100 Employees	..	..	..	..	..	..	12	292	585	627
2200 Employers	..	..	..	..	..	..	433	781	1 432	1 618
2300 Self-employed or non-employed	..	..	..	..	..	..	1	7	12	15
2400 Unallocable between 2100, 2200 and 2300	..	..	..	..	..	..	0	0	0	0
3000 Taxes on payroll and workforce	**..**	**0**	**0**	**0**	**0**	**..**	**0**	**0**	**0**	**0**
4000 Taxes on property	**..**	**37**	**88**	**197**	**228**	**..**	**0**	**0**	**4**	**6**
4100 Recurrent taxes on immovable property	..	37	88	197	228	..	..	..	..	..
4200 Recurrent taxes on net wealth	..	0	0	0	0	..	..	..	..	..
4300 Estate, inheritance and gift taxes	..	0	0	0	0	..	..	0	4	6
4400 Taxes on financial and capital transactions	..	0	0	0	0	..	..	..	..	..
4500 Non-recurrent taxes	..	0	0	0	0	..	..	..	..	..
4600 Other recurrent taxes on property	..	0	0	0	0	..	..	..	..	..
5000 Taxes on goods and services	**..**	**2**	**8**	**18**	**18**	**..**	**0**	**0**	**0**	**0**
5100 Taxes on production, sale, transfer, etc	..	0	5	7	8	..	..	..	..	..
5110 General taxes	..	0	0	0	0	..	..	..	..	..
5120 Taxes on specific goods and services	..	0	5	7	8	..	..	..	..	..
5130 Unallocable between 5110 and 5120	..	0	0	0	..	..	..	..	..	..
5200 Taxes on use of goods and perform activities	..	2	3	11	9	..	..	..	..	..
5300 Unallocable between 5100 and 5200	..	0	0	0	0	..	..	..	..	..
6000 Other taxes	**..**	**0**	**0**	**0**	**0**	**..**	**0**	**0**	**0**	**0**
6100 Paid solely by business	..	..	..	..	..	..	..	..	..	..
6200 Other	..	..	..	..	..	..	..	..	..	..
Total tax revenue	**..**	**236**	**634**	**1 371**	**1 617**	**..**	**445**	**1 079**	**2 034**	**2 266**

.. Not available

Note: Excluding customs duties collected on behalf of the European Union.

StatLink https://doi.org/10.1787/888934058046

Table 6.33. Lithuania, tax revenues by sub-sectors of government

Million EUR

	Central government					State/Regional				
	1975	1995	2005	2015	2017	1975	1995	2005	2015	2017
1000 Taxes on income, profits and capital gains	..	**646**	**1 871**	**2 013**	**2 258**	..	..	..	..	..
1100 Of individuals	..	487	1 435	1 440	1 627	..	..	..	..	..
1200 Corporate	..	160	437	574	631	..	..	..	..	..
1300 Unallocable between 1100 and 1200	..	0	0	0	0	..	..	..	..	..
2000 Social security contributions	..	**0**	**0**	**0**	**0**	..	..	..	..	..
2100 Employees	..	..	..	..	..	..	..	..	..	..
2200 Employers	..	..	..	..	..	..	..	..	..	..
2300 Self-employed or non-employed	..	..	..	..	..	..	..	..	..	..
2400 Unallocable between 2100, 2200 and 2300	..	..	..	..	..	..	..	..	..	..
3000 Taxes on payroll and workforce	..	**0**	**0**	**0**	**0**	..	..	..	..	..
4000 Taxes on property	..	**0**	**0**	**1**	**1**	..	..	..	..	..
4100 Recurrent taxes on immovable property	..	..	..	1	1	..	..	..	..	..
4200 Recurrent taxes on net wealth	..	..	..	0	0	..	..	..	..	..
4300 Estate, inheritance and gift taxes	..	..	..	0	0	..	..	..	..	..
4400 Taxes on financial and capital transactions	..	..	..	0	0	..	..	..	..	..
4500 Non-recurrent taxes	..	..	..	0	0	..	..	..	..	..
4600 Other recurrent taxes on property	..	..	..	0	..	..	..	..	..	..
5000 Taxes on goods and services	..	**892**	**2 273**	**4 220**	**4 775**	..	..	..	..	..
5100 Taxes on production, sale, transfer, etc	..	869	2 235	4 164	4 714	..	..	..	..	..
5110 General taxes	..	635	1 584	2 913	3 336	..	..	..	..	..
5120 Taxes on specific goods and services	..	234	651	1 252	1 377	..	..	..	..	..
5130 Unallocable between 5110 and 5120	..	0	0	0	0	..	..	..	..	..
5200 Taxes on use of goods and perform activities	..	24	38	56	61	..	..	..	..	..
5300 Unallocable between 5100 and 5200	..	0	0	0	0	..	..	..	..	..
6000 Other taxes	..	**0**	**0**	**0**	**0**	..	..	..	..	..
6100 Paid solely by business	..	..	..	..	..	..	..	..	..	..
6200 Other	..	..	..	..	..	..	..	..	..	..
Total tax revenue	..	**1 539**	**4 145**	**6 235**	**7 034**	..	..	..	..	..

	Local government					Social Security Funds				
	1975	1995	2005	2015	2017	1975	1995	2005	2015	2017
1000 Taxes on income, profits and capital gains	..	**0**	**0**	**0**	**0**	..	**0**	**0**	**0**	**0**
1100 Of individuals	..	..	..	..	..	..	..	..	..	..
1200 Corporate	..	..	..	..	..	..	..	..	..	..
1300 Unallocable between 1100 and 1200	..	..	..	..	..	..	..	..	..	..
2000 Social security contributions	..	**0**	**0**	**0**	**0**	..	**559**	**1 864**	**4 338**	**5 170**
2100 Employees	..	..	..	..	..	..	17	154	873	1 071
2200 Employers	..	..	..	..	..	..	537	1 522	2 916	3 512
2300 Self-employed or non-employed	..	..	..	..	..	..	4	188	549	587
2400 Unallocable between 2100, 2200 and 2300	..	..	..	..	..	..	0	0	0	0
3000 Taxes on payroll and workforce	..	**0**	**0**	**0**	**0**	..	**0**	**0**	**0**	**0**
4000 Taxes on property	..	**25**	**72**	**125**	**128**	..	**0**	**0**	**0**	**0**
4100 Recurrent taxes on immovable property	..	25	71	124	126	..	..	..	..	..
4200 Recurrent taxes on net wealth	..	0	0	0	0	..	..	..	..	..
4300 Estate, inheritance and gift taxes	..	0	1	1	2	..	..	..	..	..
4400 Taxes on financial and capital transactions	..	0	0	0	0	..	..	..	..	..
4500 Non-recurrent taxes	..	0	0	0	0	..	..	..	..	..
4600 Other recurrent taxes on property	..	0	0	0	0	..	..	..	..	..
5000 Taxes on goods and services	..	**23**	**17**	**18**	**20**	..	**0**	**0**	**0**	**0**
5100 Taxes on production, sale, transfer, etc	..	0	0	0	0	..	..	..	..	..
5110 General taxes	..	..	..	..	..	..	..	..	..	..
5120 Taxes on specific goods and services	..	..	..	..	..	..	..	..	..	..
5130 Unallocable between 5110 and 5120	..	..	..	..	..	..	..	..	..	..
5200 Taxes on use of goods and perform activities	..	23	17	18	20	..	..	..	..	..
5300 Unallocable between 5100 and 5200	..	0	0	0	0	..	..	..	..	..
6000 Other taxes	..	**0**	**0**	**0**	**0**	..	**0**	**0**	**0**	**0**
6100 Paid solely by business	..	..	..	..	..	..	..	..	..	..
6200 Other	..	..	..	..	..	..	..	..	..	..
Total tax revenue	..	**48**	**89**	**143**	**148**	..	**559**	**1 864**	**4 338**	**5 170**

.. Not available

Note: Excluding customs duties collected on behalf of the European Union.

StatLink https://doi.org/10.1787/888934058065

Table 6.34. Luxembourg, tax revenues by sub-sectors of government

Million EUR

	Central government					State/Regional				
	1975	1995	2005	2015	2017	1975	1995	2005	2015	2017
1000 Taxes on income, profits and capital gains	**353**	**1 873**	**3 454**	**6 405**	**7 156**	..	..	..	..	..
1100 Of individuals	254	1 214	2 162	4 716	5 056	..	..	..	..	..
1200 Corporate	99	659	1 293	1 689	2 100	..	..	..	..	..
1300 Unallocable between 1100 and 1200	0	0	0	0	0	..	..	..	..	..
2000 Social security contributions	**4**	**20**	**89**	**150**	**159**	..	..	..	..	..
2100 Employees	3	15	89	150	159	..	..	..	..	..
2200 Employers	0	0	0	0	0	..	..	..	..	..
2300 Self-employed or non-employed	1	5	0	0	0	..	..	..	..	..
2400 Unallocable between 2100, 2200 and 2300	0	0	0	0	0	..	..	..	..	..
3000 Taxes on payroll and workforce	**0**	**0**	**0**	**0**	**0**	..	..	..	..	..
4000 Taxes on property	**42**	**371**	**928**	**1 661**	**2 007**	..	..	..	..	..
4100 Recurrent taxes on immovable property	0	0	0	0	0	..	..	..	..	..
4200 Recurrent taxes on net wealth	21	268	698	1 318	1 513	..	..	..	..	..
4300 Estate, inheritance and gift taxes	3	15	44	74	111	..	..	..	..	..
4400 Taxes on financial and capital transactions	18	88	186	269	384	..	..	..	..	..
4500 Non-recurrent taxes	0	0	0	0	0	..	..	..	..	..
4600 Other recurrent taxes on property	0	0	0	0	0	..	..	..	..	..
5000 Taxes on goods and services	**189**	**1 384**	**3 255**	**4 909**	**5 095**	..	..	..	..	..
5100 Taxes on production, sale, transfer, etc	182	1 361	3 216	4 824	5 011	..	..	..	..	..
5110 General taxes	112	680	1 826	3 389	3 403	..	..	..	..	..
5120 Taxes on specific goods and services	70	680	1 390	1 435	1 608	..	..	..	..	..
5130 Unallocable between 5110 and 5120	0	0	0	0	0	..	..	..	..	..
5200 Taxes on use of goods and perform activities	7	23	39	85	84	..	..	..	..	..
5300 Unallocable between 5100 and 5200	0	0	0	0	0	..	..	..	..	..
6000 Other taxes	**0**	**6**	**11**	**27**	**25**	..	..	..	..	..
6100 Paid solely by business	..	6	10	27	25	..	..	..	..	..
6200 Other	..	0	0	0	0	..	..	..	..	..
Total tax revenue	**588**	**3 655**	**7 737**	**13 151**	**14 442**	..	..	..	..	..

	Local government					Social Security Funds				
	1975	1995	2005	2015	2017	1975	1995	2005	2015	2017
1000 Taxes on income, profits and capital gains	**46**	**331**	**460**	**606**	**802**	**0**	**0**	**0**	**0**	**0**
1100 Of individuals	0	0	0	0	0	..	..	..	..	..
1200 Corporate	46	331	460	606	802	..	..	..	..	..
1300 Unallocable between 1100 and 1200	0	0	0	0	0	..	..	..	..	..
2000 Social security contributions	**0**	**0**	**0**	**0**	**0**	**268**	**1 464**	**3 084**	**5 396**	**5 966**
2100 Employees	..	..	..	..	..	102	578	1 321	2 347	2 618
2200 Employers	..	..	..	..	..	150	685	1 375	2 334	2 555
2300 Self-employed or non-employed	..	..	..	..	..	16	200	388	715	793
2400 Unallocable between 2100, 2200 and 2300	..	..	..	..	..	0	0	0	0	0
3000 Taxes on payroll and workforce	**9**	**0**	**0**	**0**	**0**	**0**	**0**	**0**	**0**	**0**
4000 Taxes on property	**6**	**21**	**35**	**54**	**58**	**0**	**0**	**0**	**0**	**0**
4100 Recurrent taxes on immovable property	6	17	26	36	38	..	..	..	..	..
4200 Recurrent taxes on net wealth	0	0	0	0	0	..	..	..	..	..
4300 Estate, inheritance and gift taxes	0	0	0	0	0	..	..	..	..	..
4400 Taxes on financial and capital transactions	0	4	10	18	20	..	..	..	..	..
4500 Non-recurrent taxes	0	0	0	0	0	..	..	..	..	..
4600 Other recurrent taxes on property	0	0	0	0	0	..	..	..	..	..
5000 Taxes on goods and services	**1**	**4**	**8**	**10**	**10**	**0**	**0**	**0**	**0**	**0**
5100 Taxes on production, sale, transfer, etc	1	3	7	8	8	..	..	..	..	..
5110 General taxes	0	0	0	0	0	..	..	..	..	..
5120 Taxes on specific goods and services	1	3	7	8	8	..	..	..	..	..
5130 Unallocable between 5110 and 5120	0	0	0	0	0	..	..	..	..	..
5200 Taxes on use of goods and perform activities	0	1	1	1	1	..	..	..	..	..
5300 Unallocable between 5100 and 5200	0	0	0	0	0	..	..	..	..	..
6000 Other taxes	**0**	**1**	**2**	**1**	**1**	**0**	**0**	**0**	**0**	**0**
6100 Paid solely by business	..	1	2	1	1	..	..	..	..	..
6200 Other	..	0	0	0	0	..	..	..	..	..
Total tax revenue	**62**	**357**	**505**	**671**	**871**	**268**	**1 464**	**3 084**	**5 396**	**5 966**

.. Not available

Note: Excluding customs duties collected on behalf of the European Union.

StatLink https://doi.org/10.1787/888934058084

Table 6.35. Mexico, tax revenues by sub-sectors of government

Million MXN

	Federal government					State/Regional				
	1975	1995	2005	2015	2017	1975	1995	2005	2015	2017
1000 Taxes on income, profits and capital gains	..	**76 148**	**402 036**	**1 230 555**	**1 571 954**	..	**1**	**0**	**0**	**0**
1100 Of individuals	..	..	195 869	609 384	754 109	..	..	..	..	..
1200 Corporate	..	..	135 840	592 443	769 193	..	..	..	..	..
1300 Unallocable between 1100 and 1200	..	76 148	70 327	28 728	48 652	..	1	..	..	..
2000 Social security contributions	..	**0**	**0**	**0**	**0**	..	**0**	**0**	**0**	**0**
2100 Employees	..	..	..	..	..	..	..	..	..	..
2200 Employers	..	..	..	..	..	..	..	..	..	..
2300 Self-employed or non-employed	..	..	..	..	..	..	..	..	..	..
2400 Unallocable between 2100, 2200 and 2300	..	..	..	..	..	..	..	..	..	..
3000 Taxes on payroll and workforce	..	**0**	**0**	**0**	**0**	..	**2 976**	**20 429**	**70 221**	**84 099**
4000 Taxes on property	..	**0**	**0**	**0**	**0**	..	**2 927**	**10 905**	**22 481**	**26 068**
4100 Recurrent taxes on immovable property	..	..	..	..	..	..	2 198	6 544	14 245	15 567
4200 Recurrent taxes on net wealth	..	..	..	..	..	..	0	0	0	0
4300 Estate, inheritance and gift taxes	..	..	..	..	..	..	2	0	0	0
4400 Taxes on financial and capital transactions	..	..	..	..	..	..	727	4 361	8 235	10 501
4500 Non-recurrent taxes	..	..	..	..	..	..	0	0	0	0
4600 Other recurrent taxes on property	..	..	..	..	..	..	0	0	0	0
5000 Taxes on goods and services	..	**91 452**	**416 533**	**1 116 026**	**1 254 879**	..	**441**	**2 124**	**24 355**	**26 786**
5100 Taxes on production, sale, transfer, etc	..	88 372	401 580	1 115 525	1 254 253	..	22	1 364	4 357	7 141
5110 General taxes	..	51 785	318 432	707 213	816 048	..	0	0	0	..
5120 Taxes on specific goods and services	..	36 587	83 148	408 312	438 205	..	22	1 364	4 357	7 141
5130 Unallocable between 5110 and 5120	..	0	0	0	0	..	0	0	0	0
5200 Taxes on use of goods and perform activities	..	3 080	14 954	501	626	..	419	760	19 998	19 646
5300 Unallocable between 5100 and 5200	..	0	0	0	0	..	0	0	0	0
6000 Other taxes	..	**5 149**	**8 616**	**27 379**	**32 433**	..	**228**	**1 537**	**6 489**	**7 209**
6100 Paid solely by business	..	0	0	0	0	..	0	0	0	0
6200 Other	..	5 149	8 616	27 379	32 433	..	228	1 537	6 489	7 209
Total tax revenue (collecting government)	..	**172 749**	**827 186**	**2 373 960**	**2 859 266**	..	**6 573**	**34 995**	**123 545**	**144 162**
Adjustment[1]	..	**-49 115**	**-278 892**	**-629 130**	**-772 418**	..	**39 225**	**218 291**	**494 239**	**608 485**
Total tax revenue (beneficiary government)	..	**123 634**	**548 294**	**1 744 830**	**2 086 849**	..	**45 798**	**253 286**	**617 784**	**752 647**

	Local government					Social Security Funds				
	1975	1995	2005	2015	2017	1975	1995	2005	2015	2017
1000 Taxes on income, profits and capital gains	..	**16**	**0**	**0**	**0**	..	**0**	**0**	**0**	**0**
1100 Of individuals	..	..	..	..	..	..	..	..	..	..
1200 Corporate	..	..	..	..	..	..	..	..	..	..
1300 Unallocable between 1100 and 1200	..	16	..	..	..	..	..	..	..	..
2000 Social security contributions	..	**0**	**0**	**0**	**0**	..	**50 871**	**206 551**	**409 249**	**467 710**
2100 Employees	..	..	..	..	..	..	..	..	..	..
2200 Employers	..	..	..	..	..	..	..	..	..	..
2300 Self-employed or non-employed	..	..	..	..	..	..	..	..	..	..
2400 Unallocable between 2100, 2200 and 2300	..	..	..	..	..	..	50 871	206 551	409 249	467 710
3000 Taxes on payroll and workforce	..	**6**	**32**	**1**	**0**	..	**0**	**0**	**0**	**0**
4000 Taxes on property	..	**2 702**	**15 891**	**35 193**	**41 768**	..	**0**	**0**	**0**	**0**
4100 Recurrent taxes on immovable property	..	1 854	10 098	23 715	29 113	..	..	..	..	..
4200 Recurrent taxes on net wealth	..	0	0	0	0	..	..	..	..	..
4300 Estate, inheritance and gift taxes	..	0	0	0	0	..	..	..	..	..
4400 Taxes on financial and capital transactions	..	848	5 793	11 477	12 655	..	..	..	..	..
4500 Non-recurrent taxes	..	0	0	0	0	..	..	..	..	..
4600 Other recurrent taxes on property	..	0	0	0	0	..	..	..	..	..
5000 Taxes on goods and services	..	**582**	**288**	**789**	**1 384**	..	**0**	**0**	**0**	**0**
5100 Taxes on production, sale, transfer, etc	..	575	214	728	1 376	..	..	..	..	..
5110 General taxes	..	0	0	0	..	..	..	..	..	..
5120 Taxes on specific goods and services	..	572	214	728	1 376	..	..	..	..	..
5130 Unallocable between 5110 and 5120	..	3	0	0	0	..	..	..	..	..
5200 Taxes on use of goods and perform activities	..	7	74	61	7	..	..	..	..	..
5300 Unallocable between 5100 and 5200	..	0	0	0	0	..	..	..	..	..
6000 Other taxes	..	**179**	**1 539**	**10 743**	**12 833**	..	**0**	**0**	**0**	**0**
6100 Paid solely by business	..	0	0	0	0	..	..	..	..	..
6200 Other	..	179	1 539	10 743	12 833	..	..	..	..	..
Total tax revenue (collecting government)	..	**3 485**	**17 750**	**46 726**	**55 985**	..	**50 871**	**206 551**	**409 249**	**467 710**
Adjustment[1]	..	**9 890**	**60 601**	**134 892**	**163 933**	..	**0**	**0**	**0**	**0**
Total tax revenue (beneficiary government)	..	**13 375**	**78 351**	**181 617**	**219 918**	..	**50 871**	**206 551**	**409 249**	**467 710**

.. Not available

1. This adjustment is for taxes collected by Federal government in which States and Local governments have a share. Sub-central government's shares cannot be identified by type of tax.

StatLink https://doi.org/10.1787/888934058103

Table 6.36. Netherlands, tax revenues by sub-sectors of government

Million EUR

	Central government					State/Regional				
	1975	1995	2005	2015	2017	1975	1995	2005	2015	2017
1000 Taxes on income, profits and capital gains	**15 075**	**33 520**	**52 640**	**70 849**	**85 761**	..	..	..	..	..
1100 Of individuals	11 713	23 557	33 905	52 405	61 571	..	..	..	..	..
1200 Corporate	3 361	9 963	18 735	18 444	24 190	..	..	..	..	..
1300 Unallocable between 1100 and 1200	0	0	0	0	0	..	..	..	..	..
2000 Social security contributions	**0**	**0**	**0**	**0**	**0**	..	..	..	..	..
2100 Employees	..	..	..	..	..	..	..	..	..	..
2200 Employers	..	..	..	..	..	..	..	..	..	..
2300 Self-employed or non-employed	..	..	..	..	..	..	..	..	..	..
2400 Unallocable between 2100, 2200 and 2300	..	..	..	..	..	..	..	..	..	..
3000 Taxes on payroll and workforce	**0**	**0**	**0**	**0**	**0**	..	..	..	..	..
4000 Taxes on property	**767**	**2 880**	**6 235**	**4 731**	**6 186**	..	..	..	..	..
4100 Recurrent taxes on immovable property	50	0	0	1 345	1 618	..	..	..	..	..
4200 Recurrent taxes on net wealth	231	671	60	0	0	..	..	..	..	..
4300 Estate, inheritance and gift taxes	163	773	1 709	1 614	1 841	..	..	..	..	..
4400 Taxes on financial and capital transactions	323	1 436	4 466	1 772	2 727	..	..	..	..	..
4500 Non-recurrent taxes	0	0	0	0	0	..	..	..	..	..
4600 Other recurrent taxes on property	0	0	0	0	0	..	..	..	..	..
5000 Taxes on goods and services	**9 716**	**31 892**	**57 116**	**70 161**	**79 185**	..	..	..	..	..
5100 Taxes on production, sale, transfer, etc	9 113	29 728	54 658	65 990	73 299	..	..	..	..	..
5110 General taxes	6 257	19 832	36 950	44 879	49 833	..	..	..	..	..
5120 Taxes on specific goods and services	2 856	9 896	17 708	21 111	23 466	..	..	..	..	..
5130 Unallocable between 5110 and 5120	0	0	0	0	0	..	..	..	..	..
5200 Taxes on use of goods and perform activities	604	2 164	2 458	4 171	5 886	..	..	..	..	..
5300 Unallocable between 5100 and 5200	0	0	0	0	0	..	..	..	..	..
6000 Other taxes	**109**	**491**	**989**	**416**	**857**	..	..	..	..	..
6100 Paid solely by business	109	448	372	0	0	..	..	..	..	..
6200 Other	0	43	617	416	857	..	..	..	..	..
Total tax revenue	**25 667**	**68 783**	**116 980**	**146 157**	**171 989**	..	..	..	..	..

	Local government					Social Security Funds				
	1975	1995	2005	2015	2017	1975	1995	2005	2015	2017
1000 Taxes on income, profits and capital gains	**77**	**0**	**0**	**0**	**0**	**0**	**0**	**0**	**0**	**0**
1100 Of individuals	77	0	0	0	0	0	0	0	0	0
1200 Corporate	0	0	0	0	0	0	0	0	0	0
1300 Unallocable between 1100 and 1200	0	0	0	0	0	0	0	0	0	0
2000 Social security contributions	**0**	**0**	**0**	**0**	**0**	**16 732**	**48 532**	**66 547**	**96 426**	**101 913**
2100 Employees	..	..	..	..	..	7 139	32 795	35 383	48 213	39 578
2200 Employers	..	..	..	..	..	7 687	5 941	20 595	34 614	37 720
2300 Self-employed or non-employed	..	..	..	..	..	1 905	9 796	10 569	13 599	24 615
2400 Unallocable between 2100, 2200 and 2300	..	..	..	..	..	0	0	0	0	0
3000 Taxes on payroll and workforce	**0**	**0**	**0**	**0**	**0**	**0**	**0**	**0**	**0**	**0**
4000 Taxes on property	**272**	**2 287**	**4 341**	**5 037**	**5 301**	**0**	**0**	**0**	**0**	**0**
4100 Recurrent taxes on immovable property	272	2 287	4 341	5 037	5 301	..	..	..	..	..
4200 Recurrent taxes on net wealth	0	0	0	0	0	..	..	..	..	..
4300 Estate, inheritance and gift taxes	0	0	0	0	0	..	..	..	..	..
4400 Taxes on financial and capital transactions	0	0	0	0	0	..	..	..	..	..
4500 Non-recurrent taxes	0	0	0	0	0	..	..	..	..	..
4600 Other recurrent taxes on property	0	0	0	0	0	..	..	..	..	..
5000 Taxes on goods and services	**153**	**1 533**	**3 330**	**4 652**	**3 259**	**0**	**0**	**0**	**0**	**0**
5100 Taxes on production, sale, transfer, etc	14	59	118	249	312	..	..	..	..	..
5110 General taxes	0	6	10	43	60	..	..	..	..	..
5120 Taxes on specific goods and services	14	53	108	206	252	..	..	..	..	..
5130 Unallocable between 5110 and 5120	0	0	0	0	0	..	..	..	..	..
5200 Taxes on use of goods and perform activities	139	1 474	3 212	4 403	2 947	..	..	..	..	..
5300 Unallocable between 5100 and 5200	0	0	0	0	0	..	..	..	..	..
6000 Other taxes	**0**	**0**	**0**	**0**	**0**	**0**	**0**	**0**	**0**	**0**
6100 Paid solely by business	..	..	..	..	..	..	..	..	..	..
6200 Other	..	..	..	..	..	..	..	..	..	..
Total tax revenue	**502**	**3 820**	**7 671**	**9 689**	**8 560**	**16 732**	**48 532**	**66 547**	**96 426**	**101 913**

.. Not available

Note: Excluding customs duties collected on behalf of the European Union.

StatLink https://doi.org/10.1787/888934058122

Table 6.37. New Zealand, tax revenues by sub-sectors of government

Million NZD

	Central government					State/Regional				
	1975	1995	2005	2015	2017	1975	1995	2005	2015	2017
1000 Taxes on income, profits and capital gains	**2 296**	**21 253**	**37 379**	**44 724**	**51 505**	..	..	..	..	..
1100 Of individuals	1 874	15 626	24 373	30 298	35 020	..	..	..	..	..
1200 Corporate	407	4 122	9 957	11 407	13 584	..	..	..	..	..
1300 Unallocable between 1100 and 1200	16	1 505	3 049	3 019	2 901	..	..	..	..	..
2000 Social security contributions	**0**	**0**	**0**	**0**	**0**	..	..	..	..	..
2100 Employees	..	..	..	..	..	..	..	..	..	..
2200 Employers	..	..	..	..	..	..	..	..	..	..
2300 Self-employed or non-employed	..	..	..	..	..	..	..	..	..	..
2400 Unallocable between 2100, 2200 and 2300	..	..	..	..	..	..	..	..	..	..
3000 Taxes on payroll and workforce	**0**	**0**	**0**	**0**	**0**	..	..	..	..	..
4000 Taxes on property	**83**	**218**	**86**	**84**	**107**	..	..	..	..	..
4100 Recurrent taxes on immovable property	3	-1	0	0	0	..	..	..	..	..
4200 Recurrent taxes on net wealth	0	0	0	0	0	..	..	..	..	..
4300 Estate, inheritance and gift taxes	54	3	3	0	0	..	..	..	..	..
4400 Taxes on financial and capital transactions	25	216	83	84	107	..	..	..	..	..
4500 Non-recurrent taxes	0	0	0	0	0	..	..	..	..	..
4600 Other recurrent taxes on property	0	0	0	0	0	..	..	..	..	..
5000 Taxes on goods and services	**807**	**11 395**	**18 744**	**31 146**	**34 965**	..	..	..	..	..
5100 Taxes on production, sale, transfer, etc	770	10 833	17 792	29 551	33 187	..	..	..	..	..
5110 General taxes	311	7 895	14 133	24 587	27 951	..	..	..	..	..
5120 Taxes on specific goods and services	459	2 938	3 659	4 964	5 236	..	..	..	..	..
5130 Unallocable between 5110 and 5120	0	0	0	0	0	..	..	..	..	..
5200 Taxes on use of goods and perform activities	37	562	952	1 595	1 778	..	..	..	..	..
5300 Unallocable between 5100 and 5200	0	0	0	0	0	..	..	..	..	..
6000 Other taxes	**0**	**0**	**14**	**2**	**1**	..	..	..	..	..
6100 Paid solely by business	..	..	0	0	0	..	..	..	..	..
6200 Other	..	..	14	2	1	..	..	..	..	..
Total tax revenue	**3 186**	**32 866**	**56 223**	**75 956**	**86 578**	..	..	..	..	..
	Local government					Social Security Funds				
	1975	1995	2005	2015	2017	1975	1995	2005	2015	2017
1000 Taxes on income, profits and capital gains	**0**	**0**	**0**	**0**	**0**	**0**	**0**	**0**	**0**	**0**
1100 Of individuals	0	0	0	0	0	0	0	0	0	0
1200 Corporate	0	0	0	0	0	0	0	0	0	0
1300 Unallocable between 1100 and 1200	0	0	0	0	0	0	0	0	0	0
2000 Social security contributions	**0**	**0**	**0**	**0**	**0**	**0**	**0**	**0**	**0**	**0**
2100 Employees	..	..	..	..	..	..	..	..	..	..
2200 Employers	..	..	..	..	..	..	..	..	..	..
2300 Self-employed or non-employed	..	..	..	..	..	..	..	..	..	..
2400 Unallocable between 2100, 2200 and 2300	..	..	..	..	..	..	..	..	..	..
3000 Taxes on payroll and workforce	**0**	**0**	**0**	**0**	**0**	**0**	**0**	**0**	**0**	**0**
4000 Taxes on property	**237**	**1 646**	**2 825**	**4 962**	**5 436**	**0**	**0**	**0**	**0**	**0**
4100 Recurrent taxes on immovable property	237	1 646	2 825	4 962	5 436	..	..	..	..	..
4200 Recurrent taxes on net wealth	0	0	0	0	0	..	..	..	..	..
4300 Estate, inheritance and gift taxes	0	0	0	0	0	..	..	..	..	..
4400 Taxes on financial and capital transactions	0	0	0	0	0	..	..	..	..	..
4500 Non-recurrent taxes	0	0	0	0	0	..	..	..	..	..
4600 Other recurrent taxes on property	0	0	0	0	0	..	..	..	..	..
5000 Taxes on goods and services	**29**	**184**	**310**	**582**	**647**	**0**	**0**	**0**	**0**	**0**
5100 Taxes on production, sale, transfer, etc	18	33	30	33	33	..	..	..	..	..
5110 General taxes	0	0	0	0	0	..	..	..	..	..
5120 Taxes on specific goods and services	18	33	30	33	33	..	..	..	..	..
5130 Unallocable between 5110 and 5120	0	0	0	0	0	..	..	..	..	..
5200 Taxes on use of goods and perform activities	11	151	280	549	614	..	..	..	..	..
5300 Unallocable between 5100 and 5200	0	0	0	0	0	..	..	..	..	..
6000 Other taxes	**0**	**0**	**0**	**0**	**0**	**0**	**0**	**0**	**0**	**0**
6100 Paid solely by business	..	..	..	..	..	..	..	..	..	..
6200 Other	..	..	..	..	..	..	..	..	..	..
Total tax revenue	**266**	**1 830**	**3 135**	**5 544**	**6 083**	**0**	**0**	**0**	**0**	**0**

.. Not available

StatLink https://doi.org/10.1787/888934058141

Table 6.38. Norway, tax revenues by sub-sectors of government

Million NOK

	Central government[1]					State/Regional				
	1975	1995	2005	2015	2017	1975	1995	2005	2015	2017
1000 Taxes on income, profits and capital gains	**6 495**	**67 402**	**316 851**	**314 792**	**324 701**	..	..	..	..	..
1100 Of individuals	5 424	38 059	87 503	174 617	164 082	..	..	..	..	..
1200 Corporate	1 071	29 343	229 348	140 175	160 619	..	..	..	..	..
1300 Unallocable between 1100 and 1200	0	0	0	0	0	..	..	..	..	..
2000 Social security contributions	**1 341**	**6 013**	**173 151**	**325 569**	**341 591**	..	..	..	..	..
2100 Employees	331	1 233	58 320	112 662	119 273	..	..	..	..	..
2200 Employers	1 010	4 780	104 794	191 362	199 302	..	..	..	..	..
2300 Self-employed or non-employed	0	0	10 037	21 545	23 016	..	..	..	..	..
2400 Unallocable between 2100, 2200 and 2300	0	0	0	0	0	..	..	..	..	..
3000 Taxes on payroll and workforce	**0**	**0**	**0**	**0**	**1 891**	..	..	..	..	..
4000 Taxes on property	**771**	**3 497**	**11 406**	**13 760**	**16 542**	..	..	..	..	..
4100 Recurrent taxes on immovable property	0	0	228	1 551	939	..	..	..	..	..
4200 Recurrent taxes on net wealth	490	1 172	4 741	3 488	6 267	..	..	..	..	..
4300 Estate, inheritance and gift taxes	146	975	1 768	295	91	..	..	..	..	..
4400 Taxes on financial and capital transactions	135	1 350	4 669	8 426	9 245	..	..	..	..	..
4500 Non-recurrent taxes	0	0	0	0	0	..	..	..	..	..
4600 Other recurrent taxes on property	0	0	0	0	0	..	..	..	..	..
5000 Taxes on goods and services	**25 056**	**148 081**	**232 822**	**359 737**	**393 711**	..	..	..	..	..
5100 Taxes on production, sale, transfer, etc	24 367	141 401	220 898	342 432	376 576	..	..	..	..	..
5110 General taxes	13 670	81 772	153 820	256 028	284 705	..	..	..	..	..
5120 Taxes on specific goods and services	10 697	59 629	67 078	86 404	91 871	..	..	..	..	..
5130 Unallocable between 5110 and 5120	0	0	0	0	0	..	..	..	..	..
5200 Taxes on use of goods and perform activities	689	6 680	11 924	17 305	17 135	..	..	..	..	..
5300 Unallocable between 5100 and 5200	0	0	0	0	0	..	..	..	..	..
6000 Other taxes	**130**	**15**	**0**	**0**	**0**	..	..	..	..	..
6100 Paid solely by business	124	1	..	..	..	..	..	..	..	..
6200 Other	6	14	..	..	..	..	..	..	..	..
Total tax revenue	**33 793**	**225 008**	**734 230**	**1 013 858**	**1 078 436**	..	..	..	..	..

	Local government					Social Security Funds				
	1975	1995	2005	2015	2017	1975	1995	2005	2015	2017
1000 Taxes on income, profits and capital gains	**13 725**	**67 978**	**100 512**	**160 582**	**174 994**	**2 728**	**0**	**0**	**0**	**0**
1100 Of individuals	12 877	61 784	100 512	160 582	174 994	2 728	..	..	..	..
1200 Corporate	848	6 194	0	0	0	0	..	..	..	..
1300 Unallocable between 1100 and 1200	0	0	0	0	0	0	..	..	..	..
2000 Social security contributions	**0**	**0**	**0**	**0**	**0**	**15 224**	**84 563**	**0**	**0**	**0**
2100 Employees	..	..	..	..	..	2 949	30 417	..	..	..
2200 Employers	..	..	..	..	..	11 315	48 396	..	..	..
2300 Self-employed or non-employed	..	..	..	..	..	960	5 750	..	..	..
2400 Unallocable between 2100, 2200 and 2300	..	..	..	..	..	0	0	..	..	..
3000 Taxes on payroll and workforce	**0**	**0**	**0**	**0**	**0**	**0**	**0**	**0**	**0**	**0**
4000 Taxes on property	**772**	**7 352**	**10 283**	**21 812**	**26 309**	**0**	**0**	**0**	**0**	**0**
4100 Recurrent taxes on immovable property	278	2 792	4 324	11 177	13 611	..	..	..	..	..
4200 Recurrent taxes on net wealth	494	4 560	5 959	10 635	12 698	..	..	..	..	..
4300 Estate, inheritance and gift taxes	0	0	0	0	0	..	..	..	..	..
4400 Taxes on financial and capital transactions	0	0	0	0	0	..	..	..	..	..
4500 Non-recurrent taxes	0	0	0	0	0	..	..	..	..	..
4600 Other recurrent taxes on property	0	0	0	0	0	..	..	..	..	..
5000 Taxes on goods and services	**0**	**431**	**2 281**	**1 980**	**2 227**	**51**	**267**	**0**	**0**	**0**
5100 Taxes on production, sale, transfer, etc	0	0	0	0	0	51	267	..	..	..
5110 General taxes	0	0	0	0	0	0	0	..	..	..
5120 Taxes on specific goods and services	0	0	0	0	0	51	267	..	..	..
5130 Unallocable between 5110 and 5120	0	0	0	0	0	0	0	..	..	..
5200 Taxes on use of goods and perform activities	0	431	2 281	1 980	2 227	0	0	..	..	..
5300 Unallocable between 5100 and 5200	0	0	0	0	0	0	0	..	..	..
6000 Other taxes	**432**	**0**	**0**	**0**	**0**	**0**	**0**	**0**	**0**	**0**
6100 Paid solely by business	0	..	..	..	..	..	..	..	..	..
6200 Other	432	..	..	..	..	..	..	..	..	..
Total tax revenue	**14 929**	**75 761**	**113 076**	**184 374**	**203 530**	**18 003**	**84 830**	**0**	**0**	**0**

.. Not available

1. The Norwegian National Insurance has been integrated into the Central government sector from the year 2000 onwards.

StatLink https://doi.org/10.1787/888934058160

Table 6.39. Poland, tax revenues by sub-sectors of government

Million PLN

	Central government					State/Regional				
	1975	1995	2005	2015	2017	1975	1995	2005	2015	2017
1000 Taxes on income, profits and capital gains	**..**	**32 774**	**40 398**	**71 381**	**83 426**	**..**	**..**	**..**	**..**	**..**
1100 Of individuals	..	23 937	24 518	45 462	53 500	..	..	..	..	..
1200 Corporate	..	8 837	15 880	25 919	29 926	..	..	..	..	..
1300 Unallocable between 1100 and 1200	..	0	0	0	0	..	..	..	..	..
2000 Social security contributions	**..**	**0**	**0**	**0**	**0**	**..**	**..**	**..**	**..**	**..**
2100 Employees	..	..	..	..	..	..	..	..	..	..
2200 Employers	..	..	..	..	..	..	..	..	..	..
2300 Self-employed or non-employed	..	..	..	..	..	..	..	..	..	..
2400 Unallocable between 2100, 2200 and 2300	..	..	..	..	..	..	..	..	..	..
3000 Taxes on payroll and workforce	**..**	**831**	**2 555**	**4 028**	**4 485**	**..**	**..**	**..**	**..**	**..**
4000 Taxes on property	**..**	**0**	**0**	**0**	**0**	**..**	**..**	**..**	**..**	**..**
4100 Recurrent taxes on immovable property	..	..	..	..	..	..	..	..	..	..
4200 Recurrent taxes on net wealth	..	..	..	..	..	..	..	..	..	..
4300 Estate, inheritance and gift taxes	..	..	..	..	..	..	..	..	..	..
4400 Taxes on financial and capital transactions	..	..	..	..	..	..	..	..	..	..
4500 Non-recurrent taxes	..	..	..	..	..	..	..	..	..	..
4600 Other recurrent taxes on property	..	..	..	..	..	..	..	..	..	..
5000 Taxes on goods and services	**..**	**43 483**	**120 438**	**205 456**	**246 414**	**..**	**..**	**..**	**..**	**..**
5100 Taxes on production, sale, transfer, etc	..	42 863	120 036	201 630	243 136	..	..	..	..	..
5110 General taxes	..	21 051	75 783	125 836	154 656	..	..	..	..	..
5120 Taxes on specific goods and services	..	21 812	44 253	75 794	88 480	..	..	..	..	..
5130 Unallocable between 5110 and 5120	..	0	0	0	..	..	..	..	..	..
5200 Taxes on use of goods and perform activities	..	620	402	3 826	3 278	..	..	..	..	..
5300 Unallocable between 5100 and 5200	..	0	0	0	0	..	..	..	..	..
6000 Other taxes	**..**	**99**	**18**	**0**	**0**	**..**	**..**	**..**	**..**	**..**
6100 Paid solely by business	..	0	0	..	0	..	..	..	..	..
6200 Other	..	99	18	..	..	..	..	..	..	..
Total tax revenue	**..**	**77 187**	**163 409**	**280 865**	**334 325**	**..**	**..**	**..**	**..**	**..**

	Local government					Social Security Funds				
	1975	1995	2005	2015	2017	1975	1995	2005	2015	2017
1000 Taxes on income, profits and capital gains	**..**	**4 896**	**23 093**	**45 697**	**54 055**	**..**	**0**	**0**	**0**	**0**
1100 Of individuals	..	4 427	17 916	38 512	45 621	..	..	..	..	..
1200 Corporate	..	469	5 177	7 185	8 434	..	..	..	..	..
1300 Unallocable between 1100 and 1200	..	0	0	0	0	..	..	..	..	..
2000 Social security contributions	**..**	**0**	**0**	**0**	**0**	**..**	**38 260**	**120 296**	**223 531**	**254 968**
2100 Employees	..	..	..	..	..	..	16 486	49 644	88 557	105 817
2200 Employers	..	..	..	..	..	..	19 097	46 256	87 616	100 873
2300 Self-employed or non-employed	..	..	..	..	..	..	2 677	24 396	47 358	48 278
2400 Unallocable between 2100, 2200 and 2300	..	..	..	..	..	..	0	0	0	0
3000 Taxes on payroll and workforce	**..**	**0**	**0**	**0**	**0**	**..**	**0**	**0**	**0**	**0**
4000 Taxes on property	**..**	**4 370**	**14 723**	**24 637**	**27 101**	**..**	**0**	**0**	**0**	**0**
4100 Recurrent taxes on immovable property	..	3 579	12 718	22 206	23 783	..	..	..	..	..
4200 Recurrent taxes on net wealth	..	0	0	0	0	..	..	..	..	..
4300 Estate, inheritance and gift taxes	..	44	242	246	295	..	..	..	..	..
4400 Taxes on financial and capital transactions	..	747	1 763	2 185	3 023	..	..	..	..	..
4500 Non-recurrent taxes	..	0	0	0	0	..	..	..	..	..
4600 Other recurrent taxes on property	..	0	0	0	0	..	..	..	..	..
5000 Taxes on goods and services	**..**	**1 340**	**3 368**	**4 139**	**4 093**	**..**	**0**	**0**	**0**	**0**
5100 Taxes on production, sale, transfer, etc	..	0	0	0	0	..	..	..	..	..
5110 General taxes	..	..	..	..	..	..	..	..	..	..
5120 Taxes on specific goods and services	..	..	..	..	..	..	..	..	..	..
5130 Unallocable between 5110 and 5120	..	..	..	..	..	..	..	..	..	..
5200 Taxes on use of goods and perform activities	..	1 340	3 368	4 139	4 093	..	..	..	..	..
5300 Unallocable between 5100 and 5200	..	0	0	0	0	..	..	..	..	..
6000 Other taxes	**..**	**158**	**278**	**647**	**986**	**..**	**0**	**0**	**0**	**0**
6100 Paid solely by business	..	0	0	0	0	..	..	..	..	..
6200 Other	..	158	278	647	986	..	..	..	..	..
Total tax revenue	**..**	**10 764**	**41 462**	**75 120**	**86 235**	**..**	**38 260**	**120 296**	**223 531**	**254 968**

.. Not available

Note: Excluding customs duties collected on behalf of the European Union.

StatLink https://doi.org/10.1787/888934058179

Table 6.40. Portugal, tax revenues by sub-sectors of government

Million EUR

	Central government					State/Regional				
	1975	1995	2005	2015	2017	1975	1995	2005	2015	2017
1000 Taxes on income, profits and capital gains	**81**	**6 557**	**11 506**	**17 516**	**17 688**	..	..	..	..	..
1100 Of individuals	..	4 691	7 757	12 316	11 854	..	..	..	..	..
1200 Corporate	..	1 866	3 705	5 199	5 834	..	..	..	..	..
1300 Unallocable between 1100 and 1200	81	0	43	0	0	..	..	..	..	..
2000 Social security contributions	**0**	**1 560**	**1 887**	**5 304**	**5 901**	..	..	..	..	..
2100 Employees	..	941	1 629	5 106	5 710	..	..	..	..	..
2200 Employers	..	619	259	198	191	..	..	..	..	..
2300 Self-employed or non-employed	..	0	0	0	0	..	..	..	..	..
2400 Unallocable between 2100, 2200 and 2300	..	0	0	0	0	..	..	..	..	..
3000 Taxes on payroll and workforce	**12**	**0**	**0**	**0**	**0**	..	..	..	..	..
4000 Taxes on property	**12**	**226**	**261**	**196**	**347**	..	..	..	..	..
4100 Recurrent taxes on immovable property	0	0	0	0	131	..	..	..	..	..
4200 Recurrent taxes on net wealth	0	0	0	0	0	..	..	..	..	..
4300 Estate, inheritance and gift taxes	4	57	25	0	0	..	..	..	..	..
4400 Taxes on financial and capital transactions	7	169	236	196	215	..	..	..	..	..
4500 Non-recurrent taxes	0	0	0	0	0	..	..	..	..	..
4600 Other recurrent taxes on property	0	0	0	0	0	..	..	..	..	..
5000 Taxes on goods and services	**198**	**10 402**	**19 638**	**21 618**	**24 390**	..	..	..	..	..
5100 Taxes on production, sale, transfer, etc	187	10 195	19 220	20 787	23 373	..	..	..	..	..
5110 General taxes	52	5 481	11 846	13 745	15 352	..	..	..	..	..
5120 Taxes on specific goods and services	135	4 714	7 374	7 043	8 021	..	..	..	..	..
5130 Unallocable between 5110 and 5120	0	0	0	0	0	..	..	..	..	..
5200 Taxes on use of goods and perform activities	12	178	375	812	977	..	..	..	..	..
5300 Unallocable between 5100 and 5200	0	30	43	18	40	..	..	..	..	..
6000 Other taxes	**2**	**98**	**252**	**583**	**537**	..	..	..	..	..
6100 Paid solely by business	1	18	160	346	276	..	..	..	..	..
6200 Other	0	81	92	237	261	..	..	..	..	..
Total tax revenue	**304**	**18 844**	**33 544**	**45 216**	**48 862**	..	..	..	..	..

	Local government					Social Security Funds				
	1975	1995	2005	2015	2017	1975	1995	2005	2015	2017
1000 Taxes on income, profits and capital gains	**0**	**307**	**725**	**1 246**	**1 206**	**0**	**0**	**0**	**0**	**0**
1100 Of individuals	..	156	298	832	759	..	..	..	..	..
1200 Corporate	..	151	427	414	447	..	..	..	..	..
1300 Unallocable between 1100 and 1200	0	0	0	0	0	..	..	..	..	..
2000 Social security contributions	**0**	**2**	**7**	**19**	**10**	**161**	**5 267**	**11 100**	**10 860**	**12 039**
2100 Employees	..	2	7	19	10	62	2 100	4 053	1 867	1 899
2200 Employers	..	0	0	0	0	97	3 167	7 047	8 993	10 140
2300 Self-employed or non-employed	..	0	0	0	0	2	0	0	0	0
2400 Unallocable between 2100, 2200 and 2300	..	0	0	0	0	0	0	0	0	0
3000 Taxes on payroll and workforce	**0**	**0**	**0**	**0**	**0**	**0**	**0**	**0**	**0**	**0**
4000 Taxes on property	**0**	**599**	**1 532**	**2 107**	**2 297**	**0**	**0**	**0**	**0**	**0**
4100 Recurrent taxes on immovable property	..	310	827	1 529	1 458	..	..	..	..	..
4200 Recurrent taxes on net wealth	..	0	0	0	0	..	..	..	..	..
4300 Estate, inheritance and gift taxes	..	0	1	0	0	..	..	..	..	..
4400 Taxes on financial and capital transactions	..	289	704	578	839	..	..	..	..	..
4500 Non-recurrent taxes	..	0	0	0	0	..	..	..	..	..
4600 Other recurrent taxes on property	..	0	0	0	0	..	..	..	..	..
5000 Taxes on goods and services	**0**	**499**	**971**	**1 128**	**1 228**	**0**	**335**	**823**	**1 179**	**1 037**
5100 Taxes on production, sale, transfer, etc	0	442	837	872	961	..	335	823	1 179	1 031
5110 General taxes	0	318	563	629	660	..	276	592	994	797
5120 Taxes on specific goods and services	0	124	273	243	301	..	59	231	184	234
5130 Unallocable between 5110 and 5120	0	0	0	0	0	..	0	0	0	0
5200 Taxes on use of goods and perform activities	0	57	133	256	267	..	0	0	0	6
5300 Unallocable between 5100 and 5200	0	0	1	0	0	..	0	0	0	0
6000 Other taxes	**0**	**3**	**28**	**11**	**18**	**0**	**1**	**3**	**14**	**12**
6100 Paid solely by business	..	0	25	9	9	..	0	0	0	0
6200 Other	..	3	3	3	9	..	1	3	14	12
Total tax revenue	**0**	**1 410**	**3 262**	**4 511**	**4 760**	**161**	**5 603**	**11 926**	**12 053**	**13 088**

.. Not available

Note: Excluding customs duties collected on behalf of the European Union.

StatLink https://doi.org/10.1787/888934058198

Table 6.41. Slovak Republic, tax revenues by sub-sectors of government

Million EUR

	Central government					State/Regional				
	1975	1995	2005	2015	2017	1975	1995	2005	2015	2017
1000 Taxes on income, profits and capital gains	..	**1 993**	**2 968**	**5 542**	**5 959**	..	..	..	..	..
1100 Of individuals	..	695	1 496	2 464	2 855	..	..	..	..	..
1200 Corporate	..	1 166	1 345	2 917	2 925	..	..	..	..	..
1300 Unallocable between 1100 and 1200	..	132	128	162	178	..	..	..	..	..
2000 Social security contributions	..	**85**	**240**	**253**	**387**	..	..	..	..	..
2100 Employees	..	10	104	58	91	..	..	..	..	..
2200 Employers	..	75	136	195	295	..	..	..	..	..
2300 Self-employed or non-employed	..	0	0	0	1	..	..	..	..	..
2400 Unallocable between 2100, 2200 and 2300	..	0	0	0	0	..	..	..	..	..
3000 Taxes on payroll and workforce	..	**0**	**0**	**0**	**0**	..	..	..	..	..
4000 Taxes on property	..	**27**	**28**	**0**	**0**	..	..	..	..	..
4100 Recurrent taxes on immovable property	..	8	9	0	0	..	..	..	..	..
4200 Recurrent taxes on net wealth	..	0	0	0	0	..	..	..	..	..
4300 Estate, inheritance and gift taxes	..	2	1	0	0	..	..	..	..	..
4400 Taxes on financial and capital transactions	..	16	18	0	0	..	..	..	..	..
4500 Non-recurrent taxes	..	0	0	0	0	..	..	..	..	..
4600 Other recurrent taxes on property	..	0	0	0	0	..	..	..	..	..
5000 Taxes on goods and services	..	**2 766**	**5 995**	**8 349**	**9 109**	..	..	..	..	..
5100 Taxes on production, sale, transfer, etc	..	2 589	5 749	7 829	8 540	..	..	..	..	..
5110 General taxes	..	1 616	3 880	5 420	5 917	..	..	..	..	..
5120 Taxes on specific goods and services	..	973	1 870	2 408	2 624	..	..	..	..	..
5130 Unallocable between 5110 and 5120	..	0	0	0	0	..	..	..	..	..
5200 Taxes on use of goods and perform activities	..	177	244	521	569	..	..	..	..	..
5300 Unallocable between 5100 and 5200	..	0	2	0	0	..	..	..	..	..
6000 Other taxes	..	**0**	**0**	**0**	**0**	..	..	..	..	..
6100 Paid solely by business	..	..	..	..	..	..	..	..	..	..
6200 Other	..	..	..	..	..	..	..	..	..	..
Total tax revenue	..	**4 870**	**9 231**	**14 145**	**15 456**	..	..	..	..	..
	Local government					**Social Security Funds**				
	1975	1995	2005	2015	2017	1975	1995	2005	2015	2017
1000 Taxes on income, profits and capital gains	..	**0**	**0**	**0**	**0**	..	**0**	**0**	**0**	**0**
1100 Of individuals	..	..	..	..	..	..	..	..	..	..
1200 Corporate	..	..	..	..	..	..	..	..	..	..
1300 Unallocable between 1100 and 1200	..	..	..	..	..	..	..	..	..	..
2000 Social security contributions	..	**0**	**0**	**0**	**0**	..	**2 817**	**6 037**	**10 607**	**11 938**
2100 Employees	..	..	..	0	0	..	540	1 377	2 352	2 850
2200 Employers	..	..	..	0	0	..	1 774	3 356	6 087	6 904
2300 Self-employed or non-employed	..	..	..	0	0	..	503	1 304	2 168	2 184
2400 Unallocable between 2100, 2200 and 2300	..	..	..	0	0	..	0	0	0	0
3000 Taxes on payroll and workforce	..	**0**	**0**	**0**	**0**	..	**0**	**0**	**0**	**0**
4000 Taxes on property	..	**84**	**220**	**335**	**361**	..	**0**	**0**	**0**	**0**
4100 Recurrent taxes on immovable property	..	72	220	335	361	..	..	..	..	..
4200 Recurrent taxes on net wealth	..	0	0	0	0	..	..	..	..	..
4300 Estate, inheritance and gift taxes	..	0	0	0	0	..	..	..	..	..
4400 Taxes on financial and capital transactions	..	12	0	0	0	..	..	..	..	..
4500 Non-recurrent taxes	..	0	0	0	0	..	..	..	..	..
4600 Other recurrent taxes on property	..	0	0	0	0	..	..	..	..	..
5000 Taxes on goods and services	..	**17**	**198**	**182**	**181**	..	**0**	**0**	**0**	**0**
5100 Taxes on production, sale, transfer, etc	..	10	9	12	15	..	..	..	..	..
5110 General taxes	..	0	0	0	0	..	..	..	..	..
5120 Taxes on specific goods and services	..	10	9	12	15	..	..	..	..	..
5130 Unallocable between 5110 and 5120	..	0	0	0	0	..	..	..	..	..
5200 Taxes on use of goods and perform activities	..	1	94	17	6	..	..	..	..	..
5300 Unallocable between 5100 and 5200	..	6	95	153	160	..	..	..	..	..
6000 Other taxes	..	**0**	**0**	**0**	**0**	..	**0**	**0**	**0**	**0**
6100 Paid solely by business	..	..	..	..	..	..	..	..	..	..
6200 Other	..	..	..	..	..	..	..	..	..	..
Total tax revenue	..	**101**	**418**	**517**	**542**	..	**2 817**	**6 037**	**10 607**	**11 938**

.. Not available

Note: Excluding customs duties collected on behalf of the European Union.

StatLink https://doi.org/10.1787/888934058217

Table 6.42. Slovenia, tax revenues by sub-sectors of government

Million EUR

	Central government					State/Regional				
	1975	1995	2005	2015	2017	1975	1995	2005	2015	2017
1000 Taxes on income, profits and capital gains	..	**479**	**1 828**	**1 528**	**1 884**	..	..	..	..	..
1100 Of individuals	..	413	1 029	958	1 118	..	..	..	..	..
1200 Corporate	..	54	795	568	764	..	..	..	..	..
1300 Unallocable between 1100 and 1200	..	12	5	2	3	..	..	..	..	..
2000 Social security contributions	..	**38**	**42**	**59**	**67**	..	..	..	..	..
2100 Employees	..	20	24	31	35	..	..	..	..	..
2200 Employers	..	17	15	23	26	..	..	..	..	..
2300 Self-employed or non-employed	..	1	3	5	6	..	..	..	..	..
2400 Unallocable between 2100, 2200 and 2300	..	0	0	0	0	..	..	..	..	..
3000 Taxes on payroll and workforce	..	**14**	**521**	**20**	**21**	..	..	..	..	..
4000 Taxes on property	..	**5**	**3**	**2**	**2**	..	..	..	..	..
4100 Recurrent taxes on immovable property	..	0	0	0	0	..	..	..	..	..
4200 Recurrent taxes on net wealth	..	0	3	0	0	..	..	..	..	..
4300 Estate, inheritance and gift taxes	..	0	0	0	0	..	..	..	..	..
4400 Taxes on financial and capital transactions	..	0	0	0	0	..	..	..	..	..
4500 Non-recurrent taxes	..	5	0	2	2	..	..	..	..	..
4600 Other recurrent taxes on property	..	0	0	0	0	..	..	..	..	..
5000 Taxes on goods and services	..	**1 554**	**3 805**	**5 541**	**5 927**	..	..	..	..	..
5100 Taxes on production, sale, transfer, etc	..	1 524	3 624	5 202	5 559	..	..	..	..	..
5110 General taxes	..	1 192	2 467	3 221	3 483	..	..	..	..	..
5120 Taxes on specific goods and services	..	332	1 156	1 981	2 076	..	..	..	..	..
5130 Unallocable between 5110 and 5120	..	0	0	0	0	..	..	..	..	..
5200 Taxes on use of goods and perform activities	..	31	181	339	368	..	..	..	..	..
5300 Unallocable between 5100 and 5200	..	0	0	0	0	..	..	..	..	..
6000 Other taxes	..	**0**	**0**	**0**	**0**	..	..	..	..	..
6100 Paid solely by business	..	..	..	..	..	..	..	..	..	..
6200 Other	..	..	..	..	..	..	..	..	..	..
Total tax revenue	..	**2 090**	**6 199**	**7 150**	**7 901**	..	..	..	..	..

	Local government					Social Security Funds				
	1975	1995	2005	2015	2017	1975	1995	2005	2015	2017
1000 Taxes on income, profits and capital gains	..	**194**	**559**	**1 019**	**1 096**	..	**0**	**0**	**0**	**0**
1100 Of individuals	..	192	556	1 019	1 096	..	..	..	..	..
1200 Corporate	..	0	0	0	0	..	..	..	..	..
1300 Unallocable between 1100 and 1200	..	2	2	0	0	..	..	..	..	..
2000 Social security contributions	..	**0**	**0**	**0**	**0**	..	**1 690**	**4 042**	**5 547**	**6 173**
2100 Employees	..	..	..	..	..	..	810	2 122	2 879	3 212
2200 Employers	..	..	..	..	..	..	802	1 572	2 112	2 382
2300 Self-employed or non-employed	..	..	..	..	..	..	78	348	556	579
2400 Unallocable between 2100, 2200 and 2300	..	..	..	..	..	..	0	0	0	0
3000 Taxes on payroll and workforce	..	**2**	**0**	**0**	**0**	..	**0**	**0**	**0**	**0**
4000 Taxes on property	..	**53**	**167**	**239**	**275**	..	**0**	**0**	**0**	**0**
4100 Recurrent taxes on immovable property	..	37	122	199	221	..	..	..	..	..
4200 Recurrent taxes on net wealth	..	0	0	0	0	..	..	..	..	..
4300 Estate, inheritance and gift taxes	..	1	5	8	11	..	..	..	..	..
4400 Taxes on financial and capital transactions	..	12	40	29	41	..	..	..	..	..
4500 Non-recurrent taxes	..	3	0	3	2	..	..	..	..	..
4600 Other recurrent taxes on property	..	0	0	0	0	..	..	..	..	..
5000 Taxes on goods and services	..	**7**	**91**	**96**	**90**	..	**0**	**0**	**0**	**0**
5100 Taxes on production, sale, transfer, etc	..	7	43	57	55	..	..	..	..	..
5110 General taxes	..	0	0	0	0	..	..	..	..	..
5120 Taxes on specific goods and services	..	7	43	57	55	..	..	..	..	..
5130 Unallocable between 5110 and 5120	..	0	0	0	0	..	..	..	..	..
5200 Taxes on use of goods and perform activities	..	0	48	39	35	..	..	..	..	..
5300 Unallocable between 5100 and 5200	..	0	0	0	0	..	..	..	..	..
6000 Other taxes	..	**0**	**0**	**0**	**0**	..	**0**	**0**	**0**	**0**
6100 Paid solely by business	..	..	..	..	..	..	..	..	..	..
6200 Other	..	..	..	..	..	..	..	..	..	..
Total tax revenue	..	**256**	**817**	**1 354**	**1 461**	..	**1 690**	**4 042**	**5 547**	**6 173**

.. Not available

Note: Excluding customs duties collected on behalf of the European Union.

StatLink https://doi.org/10.1787/888934058236

Table 6.43. Spain, tax revenues by sub-sectors of government

Million EUR

	Federal government					State/Regional				
	1975	1995	2005	2015	2017	1975	1995	2005	2015	2017
1000 Taxes on income, profits and capital gains	**1 388**	**39 836**	**72 595**	**64 215**	**65 395**	**..**	**588**	**19 503**	**34 814**	**41 753**
1100 Of individuals	897	31 927	38 102	39 436	39 712	..	457	19 104	34 600	41 464
1200 Corporate	490	7 909	34 493	24 779	25 683	..	131	399	214	289
1300 Unallocable between 1100 and 1200	1	0	0	0	0	..	0	0	0	0
2000 Social security contributions	**0**	**2 027**	**3 027**	**3 505**	**3 446**	**..**	**0**	**0**	**0**	**0**
2100 Employees	..	1 017	1 369	1 541	1 465	..	..	..	..	..
2200 Employers	..	1 010	1 658	1 964	1 981	..	..	..	..	..
2300 Self-employed or non-employed	..	0	0	0	0	..	..	..	..	..
2400 Unallocable between 2100, 2200 and 2300	..	0	0	0	0	..	..	..	..	..
3000 Taxes on payroll and workforce	**0**	**0**	**0**	**0**	**0**	**..**	**0**	**0**	**0**	**0**
4000 Taxes on property	**421**	**404**	**78**	**1 186**	**438**	**..**	**4 050**	**19 273**	**10 597**	**12 034**
4100 Recurrent taxes on immovable property	1	6	6	4	8	..	0	27	39	33
4200 Recurrent taxes on net wealth	0	167	37	32	56	..	419	1 251	1 001	1 147
4300 Estate, inheritance and gift taxes	56	1	25	211	134	..	835	2 315	2 453	2 458
4400 Taxes on financial and capital transactions	364	230	10	6	6	..	2 796	15 680	7 104	8 396
4500 Non-recurrent taxes	0	0	0	933	234	..	0	0	0	0
4600 Other recurrent taxes on property	0	0	0	0	0	..	0	0	0	0
5000 Taxes on goods and services	**1 609**	**33 234**	**72 725**	**89 805**	**94 307**	**..**	**2 239**	**7 378**	**5 750**	**6 359**
5100 Taxes on production, sale, transfer, etc	1 599	33 047	72 078	88 306	92 809	..	2 070	7 056	5 214	5 807
5110 General taxes	990	20 732	52 660	62 527	67 569	..	633	1 455	1 824	1 998
5120 Taxes on specific goods and services	608	12 315	19 418	25 779	25 240	..	1 437	5 601	3 390	3 809
5130 Unallocable between 5110 and 5120	0	0	0	0	0	..	0	0	0	0
5200 Taxes on use of goods and perform activities	10	187	647	1 499	1 498	..	169	322	536	552
5300 Unallocable between 5100 and 5200	0	0	0	0	0	..	0	0	0	0
6000 Other taxes	**0**	**0**	**0**	**101**	**60**	**..**	**0**	**1**	**19**	**26**
6100 Paid solely by business	0	..	..	0	0	..	..	0	0	0
6200 Other	0	..	..	101	60	..	..	1	19	26
Total tax revenue	**3 418**	**75 501**	**148 425**	**158 812**	**163 646**	**..**	**6 877**	**46 155**	**51 180**	**60 172**

	Local government					Social Security Funds				
	1975	1995	2005	2015	2017	1975	1995	2005	2015	2017
1000 Taxes on income, profits and capital gains	**175**	**2 514**	**4 892**	**5 633**	**6 269**	**0**	**0**	**0**	**0**	**0**
1100 Of individuals	131	2 137	3 426	4 637	5 165	..	..	..	..	..
1200 Corporate	0	377	1 466	996	1 104	..	..	..	..	..
1300 Unallocable between 1100 and 1200	44	0	0	0	0	..	..	..	..	..
2000 Social security contributions	**0**	**0**	**0**	**0**	**0**	**3 367**	**50 834**	**107 626**	**119 965**	**131 252**
2100 Employees	..	..	..	..	..	645	7 611	16 164	17 298	19 204
2200 Employers	..	..	..	..	..	2 722	35 702	78 557	86 418	95 900
2300 Self-employed or non-employed	..	..	..	..	..	0	7 521	12 905	16 249	16 148
2400 Unallocable between 2100, 2200 and 2300	..	..	..	..	..	0	0	0	0	0
3000 Taxes on payroll and workforce	**0**	**0**	**0**	**0**	**0**	**0**	**0**	**0**	**0**	**0**
4000 Taxes on property	**26**	**3 759**	**8 869**	**16 372**	**17 176**	**0**	**0**	**0**	**0**	**0**
4100 Recurrent taxes on immovable property	26	2 754	6 038	12 581	13 120	..	0	0	0	0
4200 Recurrent taxes on net wealth	0	177	431	911	956	..	0	0	0	0
4300 Estate, inheritance and gift taxes	0	19	79	114	118	..	0	0	0	0
4400 Taxes on financial and capital transactions	0	166	423	145	183	..	0	0	0	0
4500 Non-recurrent taxes	0	643	1 898	2 621	2 799	..	0	0	0	0
4600 Other recurrent taxes on property	0	0	0	0	0	..	0	0	0	0
5000 Taxes on goods and services	**104**	**6 389**	**13 440**	**13 895**	**14 899**	**0**	**0**	**0**	**0**	**0**
5100 Taxes on production, sale, transfer, etc	104	2 293	6 576	7 674	8 274	..	..	..	..	..
5110 General taxes	95	1 958	4 718	5 815	6 366	..	..	..	..	..
5120 Taxes on specific goods and services	10	335	1 858	1 859	1 908	..	..	..	..	..
5130 Unallocable between 5110 and 5120	0	0	0	0	0	..	0	0	0	0
5200 Taxes on use of goods and perform activities	0	4 096	6 864	6 221	6 625	..	0	0	0	0
5300 Unallocable between 5100 and 5200	0	0	0	0	0	..	0	0	0	0
6000 Other taxes	**0**	**8**	**6**	**69**	**39**	**0**	**..**	**..**	**..**	**..**
6100 Paid solely by business	..	0	0	0	0	..	0	0	0	0
6200 Other	..	8	6	69	39	..	0	0	0	0
Total tax revenue	**305**	**12 670**	**27 207**	**35 969**	**38 383**	**3 367**	**50 834**	**107 626**	**119 965**	**131 252**

.. Not available

Note: Excluding customs duties collected on behalf of the European Union.

StatLink https://doi.org/10.1787/888934058255

Table 6.44. Sweden, tax revenues by sub-sectors of government

Million SEK

	Central government					State/Regional				
	1975	1995	2005	2015	2017	1975	1995	2005	2015	2017
1000 Taxes on income, profits and capital gains	**28 216**	**72 342**	**94 015**	**14 061**	**36 871**	..	..	..	..	..
1100 Of individuals	25 626	22 541	-7 974	-109 818	-91 750	..	..	..	..	..
1200 Corporate	2 590	49 801	101 989	123 878	128 621	..	..	..	..	..
1300 Unallocable between 1100 and 1200	0	0	0	0	0	..	..	..	..	..
2000 Social security contributions[1]	**0**	**50 560**	**212 964**	**180 723**	**198 078**	..	..	..	..	..
2100 Employees	..	0	0	0	0	..	..	..	..	..
2200 Employers	..	49 222	209 370	179 056	197 212	..	..	..	..	..
2300 Self-employed or non-employed	..	1 338	4 639	1 875	1 701	..	..	..	..	..
2400 Unallocable between 2100, 2200 and 2300	..	0	-1 044	-209	-836	..	..	..	..	..
3000 Taxes on payroll and workforce	**5 723**	**17 800**	**62 432**	**194 121**	**233 192**	..	..	..	..	..
4000 Taxes on property	**1 469**	**23 260**	**40 116**	**27 917**	**28 534**	..	..	..	..	..
4100 Recurrent taxes on immovable property	11	15 263	25 139	16 509	15 937	..	..	..	..	..
4200 Recurrent taxes on net wealth	647	3 583	4 998	0	0	..	..	..	..	..
4300 Estate, inheritance and gift taxes	335	1 388	1 092	0	0	..	..	..	..	..
4400 Taxes on financial and capital transactions	476	3 026	8 887	11 408	12 596	..	..	..	..	..
4500 Non-recurrent taxes	0	0	0	0	0	..	..	..	..	..
4600 Other recurrent taxes on property	0	0	0	0	0	..	..	..	..	..
5000 Taxes on goods and services	**31 985**	**237 720**	**353 163**	**509 119**	**565 085**	..	..	..	..	..
5100 Taxes on production, sale, transfer, etc	29 820	233 671	342 144	490 367	545 161	..	..	..	..	..
5110 General taxes	15 806	166 557	250 470	382 712	427 738	..	..	..	..	..
5120 Taxes on specific goods and services	14 014	67 114	91 674	107 655	117 423	..	..	..	..	..
5130 Unallocable between 5110 and 5120	0	0	0	0	0	..	..	..	..	..
5200 Taxes on use of goods and perform activities	2 165	4 049	11 019	18 752	19 924	..	..	..	..	..
5300 Unallocable between 5100 and 5200	0	0	0	0	0	..	..	..	..	..
6000 Other taxes	**260**	**1 438**	**1 347**	**1 356**	**2 257**	..	..	..	..	..
6100 Paid solely by business	0	0	0	0	..	..	..	..	..	..
6200 Other	260	1 438	1 347	1 356	2 257	..	..	..	..	..
Total tax revenue	**67 653**	**403 120**	**764 039**	**927 296**	**1 064 017**	..	..	..	..	..

	Local government					Social Security Funds				
	1975	1995	2005	2015	2017	1975	1995	2005	2015	2017
1000 Taxes on income, profits and capital gains	**38 415**	**265 068**	**435 577**	**635 719**	**700 078**	**0**	**0**	**0**	**0**	**0**
1100 Of individuals	35 269	265 068	435 577	635 719	700 078	..	..	..	..	..
1200 Corporate	3 146	0	0	0	0	..	..	..	..	..
1300 Unallocable between 1100 and 1200	0	0	0	0	0	..	..	..	..	..
2000 Social security contributions[1]	**0**	**0**	**0**	**0**	**0**	**25 756**	**186 992**	**151 019**	**224 129**	**245 032**
2100 Employees	..	..	..	..	..	0	28 989	74 178	108 356	118 740
2200 Employers	..	..	..	..	..	24 203	154 154	74 377	112 589	123 174
2300 Self-employed or non-employed	..	..	..	..	..	1 553	3 849	2 464	3 183	3 118
2400 Unallocable between 2100, 2200 and 2300	..	..	..	..	..	0	0	0	0	0
3000 Taxes on payroll and workforce	**0**	**0**	**0**	**0**	**0**	**0**	**0**	**0**	**0**	**0**
4000 Taxes on property	**0**	**0**	**0**	**15 935**	**16 939**	**0**	**0**	**0**	**0**	**0**
4100 Recurrent taxes on immovable property	..	..	..	15 935	16 939	..	..	..	..	..
4200 Recurrent taxes on net wealth	..	..	..	0	0	..	..	..	..	..
4300 Estate, inheritance and gift taxes	..	..	..	0	0	..	..	..	..	..
4400 Taxes on financial and capital transactions	..	..	..	0	0	..	..	..	..	..
4500 Non-recurrent taxes	..	..	..	0	0	..	..	..	..	..
4600 Other recurrent taxes on property	..	..	..	0	0	..	..	..	..	..
5000 Taxes on goods and services	**149**	**786**	**0**	**0**	**0**	**0**	**0**	**0**	**0**	**0**
5100 Taxes on production, sale, transfer, etc	119	732	0	0	0	..	..	..	..	..
5110 General taxes	0	0	0	0	0	..	..	..	..	..
5120 Taxes on specific goods and services	119	732	0	0	0	..	..	..	..	..
5130 Unallocable between 5110 and 5120	0	0	0	0	0	..	..	..	..	..
5200 Taxes on use of goods and perform activities	30	54	0	0	0	..	..	..	..	..
5300 Unallocable between 5100 and 5200	0	0	0	0	0	..	..	..	..	..
6000 Other taxes	**0**	**0**	**0**	**0**	**0**	**0**	**0**	**0**	**0**	**0**
6100 Paid solely by business	..	..	..	..	..	..	..	..	..	..
6200 Other	..	..	..	..	..	..	..	..	..	..
Total tax revenue	**38 564**	**265 854**	**435 577**	**651 654**	**717 017**	**25 756**	**186 992**	**151 019**	**224 129**	**245 032**

.. Not available

Note: Excluding customs duties collected on behalf of the European Union.

1. From 1985, social security contributions are classified using the SNA definition of Social security Funds which means that a proportion of these payments are shown under the heading of Central Government. Prior to that year, all such payments were classified under the heading of Social Security.

StatLink https://doi.org/10.1787/888934058274

Table 6.45. Switzerland, tax revenues by sub-sectors of government

Million CHF

	Federal government					State/Regional				
	1975	1995	2005	2015	2017	1975	1995	2005	2015	2017
1000 Taxes on income, profits and capital gains	**3 422**	**10 468**	**16 341**	**26 841**	**30 829**	**7 756**	**19 408**	**26 544**	**34 686**	**35 790**
1100 Of individuals	2 712	5 699	7 823	10 567	10 572	6 342	16 182	21 289	27 185	28 070
1200 Corporate	710	2 678	4 519	9 731	10 547	1 414	2 628	4 627	6 294	6 454
1300 Unallocable between 1100 and 1200	0	2 092	4 000	6 543	9 710	0	598	628	1 207	1 266
2000 Social security contributions	**0**	**0**	**0**	**0**	**0**	**0**	**0**	**0**	**0**	**0**
2100 Employees	..	..	..	..	..	..	..	..	..	..
2200 Employers	..	..	..	..	..	..	..	..	..	..
2300 Self-employed or non-employed	..	..	..	..	..	..	..	..	..	..
2400 Unallocable between 2100, 2200 and 2300	..	..	..	..	..	..	..	..	..	..
3000 Taxes on payroll and workforce	**0**	**0**	**0**	**0**	**0**	**0**	**0**	**0**	**0**	**0**
4000 Taxes on property	**463**	**1 703**	**2 703**	**1 674**	**1 722**	**1 428**	**4 116**	**5 523**	**7 191**	**7 941**
4100 Recurrent taxes on immovable property	0	0	0	0	0	60	162	230	349	342
4200 Recurrent taxes on net wealth	89	0	0	0	0	988	2 467	3 683	4 992	5 601
4300 Estate, inheritance and gift taxes	0	0	0	0	0	270	974	824	964	1 042
4400 Taxes on financial and capital transactions	374	1 703	2 703	1 674	1 722	110	103	157	177	191
4500 Non-recurrent taxes	0	0	0	0	0	0	0	0	0	0
4600 Other recurrent taxes on property	0	0	0	0	0	0	411	629	709	765
5000 Taxes on goods and services	**7 431**	**20 257**	**28 941**	**36 076**	**37 114**	**795**	**1 706**	**2 373**	**2 883**	**2 974**
5100 Taxes on production, sale, transfer, etc	7 431	19 763	27 114	33 093	33 692	154	266	447	604	621
5110 General taxes	3 205	12 428	18 429	22 791	23 298	0	0	0	0	0
5120 Taxes on specific goods and services	4 226	7 335	8 685	10 302	10 394	154	236	410	584	599
5130 Unallocable between 5110 and 5120	0	0	0	0	0	0	29	37	20	22
5200 Taxes on use of goods and perform activities	0	494	1 827	2 983	3 422	641	1 440	1 927	2 280	2 353
5300 Unallocable between 5100 and 5200	0	0	0	0	0	0	0	0	0	0
6000 Other taxes	**0**	**0**	**0**	**0**	**75**	**0**	**19**	**23**	**230**	**322**
6100 Paid solely by business	..	..	..	..	0	..	6	7	64	64
6200 Other	..	..	..	..	75	..	13	16	165	258
Total tax revenue	**11 316**	**32 428**	**47 986**	**64 590**	**69 740**	**9 979**	**25 249**	**34 462**	**44 990**	**47 027**

	Local government					Social Security Funds				
	1975	1995	2005	2015	2017	1975	1995	2005	2015	2017
1000 Taxes on income, profits and capital gains	**6 403**	**15 575**	**18 091**	**22 849**	**23 775**	**0**	**0**	**0**	**0**	**0**
1100 Of individuals	5 398	13 340	15 326	18 625	19 175	..	..	..	..	..
1200 Corporate	1 005	1 624	2 316	3 418	3 534	..	..	..	..	..
1300 Unallocable between 1100 and 1200	0	611	450	806	1 066	..	..	..	..	..
2000 Social security contributions	**0**	**0**	**0**	**0**	**0**	**8 111**	**27 831**	**32 318**	**44 073**	**44 998**
2100 Employees	..	..	..	..	..	3 589	13 021	15 125	20 436	20 887
2200 Employers	..	..	..	..	..	3 618	13 032	15 139	20 468	20 922
2300 Self-employed or non-employed	..	..	..	..	..	840	1 778	2 053	3 169	3 189
2400 Unallocable between 2100, 2200 and 2300	..	..	..	..	..	64	0	0	0	0
3000 Taxes on payroll and workforce	**0**	**0**	**0**	**0**	**0**	**0**	**0**	**0**	**0**	**0**
4000 Taxes on property	**1 068**	**2 614**	**3 251**	**4 262**	**4 776**	**0**	**0**	**0**	**0**	**0**
4100 Recurrent taxes on immovable property	182	443	588	789	927	..	..	..	..	..
4200 Recurrent taxes on net wealth	809	1 873	2 393	3 091	3 401	..	..	..	..	..
4300 Estate, inheritance and gift taxes	27	89	79	124	149	..	..	..	..	..
4400 Taxes on financial and capital transactions	50	42	38	52	60	..	..	..	..	..
4500 Non-recurrent taxes	0	0	0	0	0	..	..	..	..	..
4600 Other recurrent taxes on property	0	168	153	206	240	..	..	..	..	..
5000 Taxes on goods and services	**22**	**97**	**78**	**133**	**155**	**0**	**0**	**0**	**0**	**0**
5100 Taxes on production, sale, transfer, etc	17	55	26	63	67	..	..	..	..	..
5110 General taxes	0	0	0	0	0	..	..	..	..	..
5120 Taxes on specific goods and services	17	29	20	15	18	..	..	..	..	..
5130 Unallocable between 5110 and 5120	0	25	6	48	50	..	..	..	..	..
5200 Taxes on use of goods and perform activities	5	42	52	70	87	..	..	..	..	..
5300 Unallocable between 5100 and 5200	0	0	0	0	0	..	..	..	..	..
6000 Other taxes	**0**	**164**	**223**	**569**	**569**	**0**	**0**	**0**	**0**	**0**
6100 Paid solely by business	..	49	67	277	273	..	..	..	..	..
6200 Other	..	115	156	292	297	..	..	..	..	..
Total tax revenue	**7 493**	**18 451**	**21 643**	**27 813**	**29 275**	**8 111**	**27 831**	**32 318**	**44 073**	**44 998**

.. Not available

StatLink https://doi.org/10.1787/888934058293

Table 6.46. Turkey, tax revenues by sub-sectors of government

Million TRY

	Central government					State/Regional				
	1975	1995	2005	2015	2017	1975	1995	2005	2015	2017
1000 Taxes on income, profits and capital gains	**..**	**433**	**30 324**	**104 699**	**145 307**	**..**	**..**	**..**	**..**	**..**
1100 Of individuals	..	330	20 458	75 426	98 935	..	..	..	..	..
1200 Corporate	..	103	9 866	29 272	46 372	..	..	..	..	..
1300 Unallocable between 1100 and 1200	..	0	0	0	0	..	..	..	..	..
2000 Social security contributions	**..**	**0**	**0**	**0**	**0**	**..**	**..**	**..**	**..**	**..**
2100 Employees	..	..	..	..	..	..	..	..	..	..
2200 Employers	..	..	..	..	..	..	..	..	..	..
2300 Self-employed or non-employed	..	..	..	..	..	..	..	..	..	..
2400 Unallocable between 2100, 2200 and 2300	..	..	..	..	..	..	..	..	..	..
3000 Taxes on payroll and workforce	**..**	**0**	**0**	**0**	**0**	**..**	**..**	**..**	**..**	**..**
4000 Taxes on property	**..**	**49**	**3 626**	**20 211**	**24 620**	**..**	**..**	**..**	**..**	**..**
4100 Recurrent taxes on immovable property	..	0	0	0	0	..	..	..	..	..
4200 Recurrent taxes on net wealth	..	0	0	0	0	..	..	..	..	..
4300 Estate, inheritance and gift taxes	..	1	78	379	630	..	..	..	..	..
4400 Taxes on financial and capital transactions	..	29	3 548	19 832	23 990	..	..	..	..	..
4500 Non-recurrent taxes	..	19	0	0	0	..	..	..	..	..
4600 Other recurrent taxes on property	..	0	0	0	0	..	..	..	..	..
5000 Taxes on goods and services	**..**	**574**	**71 956**	**231 227**	**299 432**	**..**	**..**	**..**	**..**	**..**
5100 Taxes on production, sale, transfer, etc	..	567	69 266	222 702	289 671	..	..	..	..	..
5110 General taxes	..	475	30 343	107 451	137 136	..	..	..	..	..
5120 Taxes on specific goods and services	..	92	38 923	115 251	152 534	..	..	..	..	..
5130 Unallocable between 5110 and 5120	..	0	0	0	0	..	..	..	..	..
5200 Taxes on use of goods and perform activities	..	8	2 691	8 526	9 761	..	..	..	..	..
5300 Unallocable between 5100 and 5200	..	0	0	0	0	..	..	..	..	..
6000 Other taxes	**..**	**259**	**4 181**	**3 779**	**3 838**	**..**	**..**	**..**	**..**	**..**
6100 Paid solely by business	..	0	0	0	0	..	..	..	..	..
6200 Other	..	259	4 181	3 779	3 838	..	..	..	..	..
Total tax revenue	**..**	**1 316**	**110 088**	**359 915**	**473 197**	**..**	**..**	**..**	**..**	**..**

	Local government					Social Security Funds				
	1975	1995	2005	2015	2017	1975	1995	2005	2015	2017
1000 Taxes on income, profits and capital gains	**..**	**63**	**4 011**	**14 445**	**19 999**	**..**	**0**	**0**	**0**	**0**
1100 Of individuals	..	48	2 706	10 330	13 465	..	..	..	..	..
1200 Corporate	..	15	1 305	4 116	6 534	..	..	..	..	..
1300 Unallocable between 1100 and 1200	..	0	0	0	0	..	..	..	..	..
2000 Social security contributions	**..**	**0**	**0**	**0**	**0**	**..**	**212**	**35 321**	**170 282**	**226 720**
2100 Employees	..	..	..	..	..	..	82	12 128	64 214	86 410
2200 Employers	..	..	..	..	..	..	110	16 132	95 067	128 331
2300 Self-employed or non-employed	..	..	..	..	..	..	19	7 061	11 001	11 979
2400 Unallocable between 2100, 2200 and 2300	..	..	..	..	..	..	0	0	0	0
3000 Taxes on payroll and workforce	**..**	**0**	**0**	**0**	**0**	**..**	**0**	**0**	**0**	**0**
4000 Taxes on property	**..**	**4**	**1 627**	**8 371**	**10 237**	**..**	**0**	**0**	**0**	**0**
4100 Recurrent taxes on immovable property	..	0	1 148	5 882	6 809	..	..	..	..	..
4200 Recurrent taxes on net wealth	..	0	0	0	0	..	..	..	..	..
4300 Estate, inheritance and gift taxes	..	0	10	56	88	..	..	..	..	..
4400 Taxes on financial and capital transactions	..	4	469	2 433	3 341	..	..	..	..	..
4500 Non-recurrent taxes	..	0	0	0	0	..	..	..	..	..
4600 Other recurrent taxes on property	..	0	0	0	0	..	..	..	..	..
5000 Taxes on goods and services	**..**	**84**	**5 649**	**28 737**	**36 825**	**..**	**0**	**0**	**0**	**0**
5100 Taxes on production, sale, transfer, etc	..	82	5 295	27 560	35 264	..	..	..	..	..
5110 General taxes	..	69	4 014	13 619	18 543	..	..	..	..	..
5120 Taxes on specific goods and services	..	13	1 281	13 940	16 721	..	..	..	..	..
5130 Unallocable between 5110 and 5120	..	0	0	0	0	..	..	..	..	..
5200 Taxes on use of goods and perform activities	..	1	354	1 177	1 560	..	..	..	..	..
5300 Unallocable between 5100 and 5200	..	0	0	0	0	..	..	..	..	..
6000 Other taxes	**..**	**73**	**721**	**4 971**	**6 429**	**..**	**0**	**0**	**0**	**0**
6100 Paid solely by business	..	0	0	0	0	..	..	..	..	..
6200 Other	..	73	721	4 971	6 429	..	..	..	..	..
Total tax revenue	**..**	**224**	**12 008**	**56 525**	**73 490**	**..**	**212**	**35 321**	**170 282**	**226 720**

.. Not available

StatLink https://doi.org/10.1787/888934058312

Table 6.47. United Kingdom, tax revenues by sub-sectors of government

Million GBP

	Central government					State/Regional				
	1975	1995	2005	2015	2017	1975	1995	2005	2015	2017
1000 Taxes on income, profits and capital gains	**16 716**	**92 147**	**177 672**	**214 870**	**243 181**	..	..	..	..	..
1100 Of individuals	14 936	71 973	130 135	168 873	185 560	..	..	..	..	..
1200 Corporate	2 310	20 174	47 537	45 997	57 621	..	..	..	..	..
1300 Unallocable between 1100 and 1200	-530	0	0	0	0	..	..	..	..	..
2000 Social security contributions	**0**	**0**	**0**	**0**	**0**	..	..	..	..	..
2100 Employees	..	..	..	..	..	..	..	..	..	..
2200 Employers	..	..	..	..	..	..	..	..	..	..
2300 Self-employed or non-employed	..	..	..	..	..	..	..	..	..	..
2400 Unallocable between 2100, 2200 and 2300	..	..	..	..	..	..	..	..	..	..
3000 Taxes on payroll and workforce	**-1**	**0**	**0**	**0**	**1 842**	..	..	..	..	..
4000 Taxes on property	**619**	**15 730**	**32 583**	**46 620**	**52 423**	..	..	..	..	..
4100 Recurrent taxes on immovable property	44	12 369	19 523	28 389	29 942	..	..	..	..	..
4200 Recurrent taxes on net wealth	0	0	0	0	0	..	..	..	..	..
4300 Estate, inheritance and gift taxes	307	1 441	3 150	4 442	5 382	..	..	..	..	..
4400 Taxes on financial and capital transactions	266	1 920	9 910	13 789	17 099	..	..	..	..	..
4500 Non-recurrent taxes	2	0	0	0	0	..	..	..	..	..
4600 Other recurrent taxes on property	0	0	0	0	0	..	..	..	..	..
5000 Taxes on goods and services	**8 982**	**85 507**	**135 553**	**201 066**	**217 255**	..	..	..	..	..
5100 Taxes on production, sale, transfer, etc	8 502	81 175	130 157	193 623	209 473	..	..	..	..	..
5110 General taxes	3 515	47 539	83 444	129 443	141 336	..	..	..	..	..
5120 Taxes on specific goods and services	4 987	33 636	46 713	64 180	68 137	..	..	..	..	..
5130 Unallocable between 5110 and 5120	0	0	..	..	..	..	..	..	..	..
5200 Taxes on use of goods and perform activities	698	4 332	5 396	7 443	7 782	..	..	..	..	..
5300 Unallocable between 5100 and 5200	-218	0	0	0	0	..	..	..	..	..
6000 Other taxes	**0**	**0**	**0**	**0**	**0**	..	..	..	..	..
6100 Paid solely by business	..	..	..	..	..	..	..	..	..	..
6200 Other	..	..	..	..	..	..	..	..	..	..
Total tax revenue	**26 316**	**193 384**	**345 808**	**462 556**	**514 701**	..	..	..	..	..

	Local government					Social Security Funds				
	1975	1995	2005	2015	2017	1975	1995	2005	2015	2017
1000 Taxes on income, profits and capital gains	**0**	**0**	**0**	**0**	**0**	**0**	**0**	**0**	**0**	**0**
1100 Of individuals	0	0	0	0	0	0	0	0	0	0
1200 Corporate	0	0	0	0	0	0	0	0	0	0
1300 Unallocable between 1100 and 1200	0	0	0	0	0	0	0	0	0	0
2000 Social security contributions	**0**	**0**	**0**	**0**	**0**	**6 540**	**44 397**	**84 459**	**114 067**	**130 595**
2100 Employees	..	..	..	..	..	2 562	18 646	35 159	44 454	50 411
2200 Employers	..	..	..	..	..	4 068	24 210	46 475	66 491	76 748
2300 Self-employed or non-employed	..	..	..	..	..	195	1 541	2 825	3 122	3 436
2400 Unallocable between 2100, 2200 and 2300	..	..	..	..	..	-285	0	0	0	0
3000 Taxes on payroll and workforce	**0**	**0**	**0**	**0**	**0**	**0**	**0**	**0**	**0**	**0**
4000 Taxes on property	**4 127**	**9 303**	**21 255**	**29 943**	**33 132**	**0**	**0**	**0**	**0**	**0**
4100 Recurrent taxes on immovable property	3 978	9 303	21 255	29 796	32 857	..	..	..	..	..
4200 Recurrent taxes on net wealth	0	0	0	0	0	..	..	..	..	..
4300 Estate, inheritance and gift taxes	0	0	0	0	0	..	..	..	..	..
4400 Taxes on financial and capital transactions	0	0	0	0	0	..	..	..	..	..
4500 Non-recurrent taxes	0	0	0	147	275	..	..	..	..	..
4600 Other recurrent taxes on property	149	0	0	0	0	..	..	..	..	..
5000 Taxes on goods and services	**0**	**0**	**0**	**0**	**0**	**0**	**0**	**0**	**0**	**0**
5100 Taxes on production, sale, transfer, etc	..	..	..	..	..	..	..	..	..	..
5110 General taxes	..	..	..	..	..	..	..	..	..	..
5120 Taxes on specific goods and services	..	..	..	..	..	..	..	..	..	..
5130 Unallocable between 5110 and 5120	..	..	..	..	..	..	..	..	..	..
5200 Taxes on use of goods and perform activities	..	..	..	..	..	..	..	..	..	..
5300 Unallocable between 5100 and 5200	..	..	..	..	..	..	..	..	..	..
6000 Other taxes	**0**	**0**	**0**	**0**	**0**	**0**	**0**	**0**	**0**	**0**
6100 Paid solely by business	..	..	..	..	..	..	..	..	..	..
6200 Other	..	..	..	..	..	..	..	..	..	..
Total tax revenue	**4 127**	**9 303**	**21 255**	**29 943**	**33 132**	**6 540**	**44 397**	**84 459**	**114 067**	**130 595**

.. Not available

Note: Excluding customs duties collected on behalf of the European Union.

StatLink https://doi.org/10.1787/888934058331

Table 6.48. United States, tax revenues by sub-sectors of government

Million USD

	Federal government					State/Regional				
	1975	1995	2005	2015	2017	1975	1995	2005	2015	2017
1000 Taxes on income, profits and capital gains	**163 072**	**750 144**	**1 268 412**	**1 880 845**	**1 923 455**	**25 509**	**157 598**	**275 728**	**390 538**	**396 851**
1100 Of individuals	122 386	594 213	948 921	1 551 242	1 638 812	..	128 429	226 576	342 445	352 391
1200 Corporate	40 686	155 931	319 490	329 603	284 643	..	29 169	49 152	48 093	44 460
1300 Unallocable between 1100 and 1200	0	0	0	0	0	..	0	0	0	0
2000 Social security contributions	**0**	**0**	**0**	**0**	**0**	**0**	**0**	**0**	**0**	**0**
2100 Employees	..	..	..	..	..	..	..	..	..	..
2200 Employers	..	..	..	..	..	..	..	..	..	..
2300 Self-employed or non-employed	..	..	..	..	..	..	..	..	..	..
2400 Unallocable between 2100, 2200 and 2300	..	..	..	..	..	..	..	..	..	..
3000 Taxes on payroll and workforce	**0**	**0**	**0**	**0**	**0**	**0**	**0**	**0**	**1 745**	**2 050**
4000 Taxes on property	**4 613**	**14 948**	**24 989**	**20 191**	**273 151**	**3 284**	**16 880**	**28 808**	**28 998**	**31 868**
4100 Recurrent taxes on immovable property	0	0	0	0	0	1 451	7 240	9 037	12 040	13 127
4200 Recurrent taxes on net wealth	0	0	0	0	0	0	0	0	0	0
4300 Estate, inheritance and gift taxes	4 611	14 948	24 989	20 191	23 151	1 418	5 061	5 322	5 065	4 867
4400 Taxes on financial and capital transactions	2	0	0	0	0	415	2 386	11 711	8 246	9 897
4500 Non-recurrent taxes	0	0	0	0	250 000	0	0	0	0	0
4600 Other recurrent taxes on property	0	0	0	0	0	0	2 193	2 738	3 647	3 977
5000 Taxes on goods and services	**20 773**	**75 553**	**99 411**	**140 371**	**131 464**	**52 032**	**232 033**	**377 795**	**499 671**	**524 112**
5100 Taxes on production, sale, transfer, etc	20 442	75 553	99 411	140 371	131 464	43 960	200 495	323 137	435 708	458 668
5110 General taxes	0	0	0	0	0	24 916	135 132	218 917	287 573	302 626
5120 Taxes on specific goods and services	20 442	75 553	99 411	140 371	131 464	19 044	65 363	104 220	148 135	156 042
5130 Unallocable between 5110 and 5120	0	0	0	0	0	0	0	0	0	0
5200 Taxes on use of goods and perform activities	331	0	0	0	0	8 072	31 538	54 658	63 963	65 444
5300 Unallocable between 5100 and 5200	0	0	0	0	0	0	0	0	0	0
6000 Other taxes	**0**	**0**	**0**	**0**	**0**	**0**	**0**	**0**	**0**	**0**
6100 Paid solely by business	..	..	..	..	..	..	..	..	..	..
6200 Other	..	..	..	..	..	..	..	..	..	..
Total tax revenue	**188 458**	**840 645**	**1 392 812**	**2 041 407**	**2 328 070**	**80 825**	**406 511**	**682 331**	**920 952**	**954 881**

	Local government					Social Security Funds				
	1975	1995	2005	2015	2017	1975	1995	2005	2015	2017
1000 Taxes on income, profits and capital gains	**2 635**	**15 795**	**28 272**	**40 049**	**42 787**	**0**	**0**	**0**	**0**	**0**
1100 Of individuals	..	13 308	22 481	31 841	34 315	..	..	..	..	..
1200 Corporate	..	2 487	5 791	8 208	8 472	..	..	..	..	..
1300 Unallocable between 1100 and 1200	..	0	0	0	0	..	..	..	..	..
2000 Social security contributions	**0**	**0**	**0**	**0**	**0**	**85 039**	**510 476**	**831 410**	**1 126 111**	**1 204 453**
2100 Employees	..	..	..	..	..	36 382	221 800	362 829	502 663	542 924
2200 Employers	..	..	..	..	..	45 241	261 805	423 936	562 307	598 241
2300 Self-employed or non-employed	..	..	..	..	..	3 416	26 871	44 645	61 141	63 288
2400 Unallocable between 2100, 2200 and 2300	..	..	..	..	..	0	0	0	0	0
3000 Taxes on payroll and workforce	**0**	**0**	**0**	**0**	**0**	**0**	**0**	**0**	**0**	**0**
4000 Taxes on property	**50 040**	**197 392**	**359 344**	**486 957**	**532 699**	**0**	**0**	**0**	**0**	**0**
4100 Recurrent taxes on immovable property	50 040	195 339	342 203	475 711	519 094	..	..	..	..	..
4200 Recurrent taxes on net wealth	0	0	0	0	0	..	..	..	..	..
4300 Estate, inheritance and gift taxes	0	30	114	138	100	..	..	..	..	..
4400 Taxes on financial and capital transactions	0	50	13 570	6 303	8 262	..	..	..	..	..
4500 Non-recurrent taxes	0	0	0	0	0	..	..	..	..	..
4600 Other recurrent taxes on property	0	1 973	3 457	4 805	5 243	..	..	..	..	..
5000 Taxes on goods and services	**8 389**	**57 507**	**108 696**	**150 006**	**164 448**	**0**	**0**	**0**	**0**	**0**
5100 Taxes on production, sale, transfer, etc	6 518	42 269	76 976	117 029	127 685	..	..	..	..	..
5110 General taxes	4 322	29 316	53 842	84 688	93 074	..	..	..	..	..
5120 Taxes on specific goods and services	2 196	12 953	23 134	32 341	34 611	..	..	..	..	..
5130 Unallocable between 5110 and 5120	0	0	0	0	0	..	..	..	..	..
5200 Taxes on use of goods and perform activities	1 871	15 238	31 720	32 977	36 763	..	..	..	..	..
5300 Unallocable between 5100 and 5200	0	0	0	0	0	..	..	..	..	..
6000 Other taxes	**0**	**0**	**0**	**0**	**0**	**0**	**0**	**0**	**0**	**0**
6100 Paid solely by business	..	..	..	..	..	..	..	..	..	..
6200 Other	..	..	..	..	..	..	..	..	..	..
Total tax revenue	**61 064**	**270 695**	**496 313**	**677 012**	**739 934**	**85 039**	**510 476**	**831 410**	**1 126 111**	**1 204 453**

.. Not available

StatLink https://doi.org/10.1787/888934058350

Annex A. The OECD Classification of Taxes and Interpretative Guide

Table of Contents

A.1 the OECD Classification of Taxes

1. **1000. Taxes on income, profits and capital gains**
    - 1100. Taxes on income, profits and capital gains of individuals
        - 1110. On income and profits
        - 1120. On capital gains
    - 1200. Corporate taxes on income, profits and capital gains
        - 1210. On income and profits
        - 1220. On capital gains
    - 1300. Unallocable as between 1100 and 1200
2. **2000. Social security contributions**
    - 2100. Employees
        - 2110. On a payroll basis
        - 2120. On an income tax basis
    - 2200. Employers
        - 2210. On a payroll basis
        - 2220. On an income tax basis
    - 2300. Self-employed or non-employed
        - 2310. On a payroll basis
        - 2320. On an income tax basis
    - 2400. Unallocable as between 2100, 2200 and 2300
        - 2410. On a payroll basis
        - 2420. On an income tax basis
3. **3000. Taxes on payroll and workforce**
4. **4000. Taxes on property**
    - 4100. Recurrent taxes on immovable property
        - 4110. Households
        - 4120. Other
    - 4200. Recurrent taxes on net wealth
        - 4210. Individual
        - 4220. Corporate
    - 4300. Estate, inheritance and gift taxes
        - 4310. Estate and inheritance taxes
        - 4320. Gift taxes

4400. Taxes on financial and capital transactions

4500. Other non-recurrent taxes on property

4510. On net wealth

4520. Other non-recurrent taxes

4600. Other recurrent taxes on property

5. **5000. Taxes on goods and services**

5100. Taxes on production, sale, transfer, leasing and delivery of goods and rendering of services

5110. General taxes

5111. Value added taxes

5112. Sales taxes

5113. Turnover and other general taxes on goods and services

5120. Taxes on specific goods and services

5121. Excises

5122. Profits of fiscal monopolies

5123. Customs and import duties

5124. Taxes on exports

5125. Taxes on investment goods

5126 . Taxes on specific services

5127. Other taxes on international trade and transactions

5128. Other taxes on specific goods and services

5130. Unallocable as between 5110 and 5120

5200. Taxes on use of goods, or on permission to use goods or perform activities

5210. Recurrent taxes

5211. Paid by households in respect of motor vehicles

5212. Paid by others in respect of motor vehicles

5213. Other recurrent taxes

5220. Non-recurrent taxes

5300. Unallocable as between 5100 and 5200

6. **6000. Other taxes**

6100. Paid solely by business

6200. Paid by other than business or unidentifiable

A.2 Coverage

General criteria

1. In the OECD classification the term "taxes" is confined to compulsory unrequited payments to general government. Taxes are unrequited in the sense that benefits provided by government to taxpayers are not normally in proportion to their payments.

2. The term "tax" does not include fines, penalties and compulsory loans paid to government. Borderline cases between tax and non-tax revenues in relation to certain fees and charges are discussed in §11–14.

3. General government consists of the central administration, agencies whose operations are under its effective control, state and local governments and their administrations, certain social security schemes and autonomous governmental entities, excluding public enterprises. This definition of government follows that of the 2008 *System of National Accounts* (SNA).[1] In that publication, the general government sector and its sub-sectors are defined in Chapter 4, paragraphs 4.117 to 4.165.

4. Extra-budgetary units are part of the general government system. These are general government entities with individual budgets that are not fully covered by the main or general budget. These entities operate under the authority or control of a central, state, or local government. Extra-budgetary entities may have their own revenue sources, which may be supplemented by grants (transfers) from the general budget or from other sources. Even though their budgets may be subject to approval by the legislature, similar to that of budgetary accounts, they have discretion over the volume and composition of their spending. Such entities may be established to carry out specific government functions, such as road construction, or the nonmarket production of health or education services. Budgetary arrangements vary widely across countries, and various terms are used to describe these entities, but they are often referred to as "extra-budgetary funds" or "decentralised agencies."

5. Compulsory payments to supra-national bodies and their agencies are no longer included as taxes as from 1998, with some exceptions. However, custom duties collected by EU member states on behalf of the European Union are still identified as memorandum items and included in overall tax revenue amounts in the country tables (Chapter 5) of the country in which they are collected. (See §99). In countries where the church forms part of general government church taxes are included, provided they meet the criteria set out in §1 above. As the data refer to receipts of general government, levies paid to non-government bodies, welfare agencies or social insurance schemes outside general government, trade unions or trade associations, even where such levies are compulsory, are excluded. Compulsory payments to general government earmarked for such bodies are, however, included, provided that the government is not simply acting in an agency capacity.[2] Profits from fiscal monopolies are distinguished from those of other public enterprises and are treated as taxes because they reflect the exercise of the taxing power of the state by the use of monopoly powers (see §65–67), as are profits received by the government from the purchase and sale of foreign exchange at different rates (see §74).

6. Taxes paid by governments (e.g., social security contributions and payroll taxes paid by governments in their capacity as an employer, consumption taxes on their purchases or taxes on their property) are not excluded from the data provided. However, where it is possible to identify the amounts of revenue involved,[3] they are shown in Table 5.38 of this Report.

7. The relationship between this classification and that of the System of National Accounts (SNA) is set out in Sections A.9 and A.11 below. Because of the differences between the two classifications, the data shown in national accounts are sometimes calculated or classified differently from the practice set out in this guide. These and other differences are mentioned where appropriate (e.g., in §30 below) but it is not possible to refer to all of them. There may also be some differences between this classification and

that employed domestically by certain national administrations (e.g., see §12 below), so that OECD and national statistics data may not always be consistent: any such differences, however, are likely to be very slight in terms of amounts of revenues involved.

Social security contributions

8. Compulsory social security contributions, as defined in §39, and paid to general government, are treated here as tax revenues. Being compulsory payments to general government they clearly resemble taxes. They may, however, differ from other taxes in that the receipt of social security benefits depends, in most countries, upon appropriate contributions having been made, although the size of the benefits is not necessarily related to the amount of the contributions. Better comparability between countries is obtained by treating social security contributions as taxes, but they are listed under a separate heading so that they can be distinguished in any analysis.

9. The strict dividing line between tax revenues (compulsory unrequited payments to general government) and non-tax compulsory payments (NTCPs) (payments that are either requited or made to other institutions) is clearly defined. However, within the range of different compulsory payments to governments existing across countries, it is not always straightforward in practice to decide whether specific payments are either taxes or NTCPs. For example, compulsory pension savings that are controlled by general government and that accumulate on an individual account earning a market return or a rate that compensates for inflation would at first sight be categorised as NTCPs as opposed to taxes. However, even these payments might still be 'unrequited' and therefore classify as taxes instead of NTCPs (for example if these pension savings are not paid out when the taxpayer dies before reaching the pension age and the funds are then used to provide a minimum pension to all taxpayers that are insured). These issues result in the social security revenue figures reported for most countries being based on the premise that all types of compulsory payments to general government are judged to some extent to have a re-distributional element. It should be noted that this conclusion is based on a typically broad interpretation of the term 'unrequited' in the tax definition.

10. Social security contributions which are either voluntary or not payable to general government (see §1) are not treated as taxes, though in some countries, as indicated in the country footnotes, there are difficulties in completely eliminating voluntary contributions and certain compulsory payments to the private sector from the revenue figures. Imputed social security contributions are also not treated as taxes.

Fees, user charges and licence fees

11. Apart from vehicle licence fees, which are universally regarded as taxes, it is not easy to distinguish between those fees and user charges which are to be treated as taxes and those which are not, since, whilst a fee or charge is levied in connection with a specific service or activity, the strength of the link between the fee and the service provided may vary considerably, as may the relation between the amount of the fee and the cost of providing the service. Where the recipient of a service pays a fee clearly related to the cost of providing the service, the levy may be regarded as requited and under the definition of §1 would not be considered as a tax. In the following cases, however, a levy could be considered as 'unrequited':

- *a)* where the charge greatly exceeds the cost of providing the service;
- *b)* where the payer of the levy is not the receiver of the benefit (e.g., a fee collected from slaughterhouses to finance a service which is provided to farmers);
- *c)* where government is not providing a specific service in return for the levy which it receives even though a licence may be issued to the payer (e.g., where the government grants a hunting, fishing or shooting licence which is not accompanied by the right to use a specific area of government land);

d) where benefits are received only by those paying the levy but the benefits received by each individual are not necessarily in proportion to his payments (e.g., a milk marketing levy paid by dairy farmers and used to promote the consumption of milk).

12. In marginal cases, however, the application of the criteria set out in §1 can be particularly difficult. The solution adopted — given the desirability of international uniformity and the relatively small amounts of revenue usually involved — is to follow the predominant practice among tax administrations rather than to allow each country to adopt its own view as to whether such levies are regarded as taxes or as non-tax revenue.[4]

13. A list of the main fees and charges in question and their normal[5] treatment in this publication is as follows:

Non-tax revenues:	court fees; driving licence fees; harbour fees; passport fees; radio and television licence fees where public authorities provide the service
Taxes within heading 5200	permission to perform such activities as distributing films; hunting, fishing and shooting; providing entertainment or gambling facilities; selling alcohol or tobacco; permission to own dogs or to use or own motor vehicles or guns; severance taxes

14. In practice it may not always be possible to isolate tax receipts from non-tax revenue receipts when they are recorded together. If it is estimated that the bulk of the receipts derive from non-tax revenues, the whole amount involved is treated as a non-tax revenue; otherwise, such government receipts are included and classified according to the rules provided in §32 below.

Royalties

15. The ownership of subsoil assets in the form of deposits of minerals or fossil fuels (coal, oil, or natural gas) depends upon the way in which property rights are defined by law and also on international agreements in the case of deposits below international waters. In some cases, either the ground below which the mineral deposits are located, the deposits themselves or both may belong to a local or central government unit.

16. In such cases, these general government units may grant leases to other institutional units that permit them to extract these deposits over a specified period of time in return for a payment or series of payments. These payments are often described as 'royalties' but they are essentially rent that accrues to owners of natural resources in return for putting these assets at the disposal of other units for specified periods of time. The rent may take the form of periodic payments of fixed amounts, irrespective of the rate of extraction, or, more commonly, they may be a function of the quantity, volume, or value of the asset extracted. Enterprises engaged in exploration on government land may make payments to general government units in exchange for the right to undertake test drilling or otherwise investigate the existence and location of subsoil assets. Such payments are also recorded as rents even though no extraction may take place. These payments are therefore classified as non-tax revenues.

17. The same principles apply when other institutional units are granted leases that permit them to fell timber in natural forests on land owned by general government units. These payments are also classified as non-tax revenues.

18. These rents or royalties paid to general government should not be confused with taxes on income and profits, severance taxes, business licenses, or other taxes. If the payments are levied on the profits from the extraction activity, then they should be classified as taxes on incomes, profits and gains (1000). In addition, any severance payments that are imposed on the extraction of minerals and fossil fuels from reserves owned privately or by another government should be classified as taxes. Payments related to the gross value of production should be classified as other taxes on goods and services (5128). Payments for

a license or permit to conduct extraction operations should be classified as taxes on use of goods and on permission to use goods or perform activities (5213).

Fines and penalties

19. In principle, fines and penalties charged on overdue taxes or penalties imposed for the attempted evasion of taxes should not be recorded as tax revenues. However it may not be possible to separate payments of fines or other penalties from the revenues from the taxes to which they relate. In this case the fines and penalties relating to a particular tax are recorded together with the revenues from that tax and fines and penalties paid with revenue from unidentifiable taxes are classified as other taxes in Category 6000. Fines not relating to tax offences (e.g., for parking offences), or not identifiable as relating to tax offences, are also not treated as tax revenues.

A.3 Basis of reporting

Accrual reporting

20. The data reported in this publication for recent years are predominantly recorded on an accrual basis, i.e. recorded at the time that the tax liability was created. Further information is provided in the footnotes to the country table in Chapter 5 of the Report.

21. However, data for earlier years are still predominantly recorded on a cash basis, i.e. at the time at which the payment was received by government. Thus, for example, taxes withheld by employers in one year but paid to the government in the following year and taxes due in one year but actually paid in the following year are both included in the receipts of the second year. Corrective transactions, such as refunds, repayments and drawbacks, are deducted from gross revenues of the period in which they are made.

22. Data on tax revenues are recorded without offsets for the administrative expenses connected with tax collection. Similarly, where the proceeds of tax are used to subsidise particular members of the community, the subsidy is not deducted from the yield of the tax, though the tax may be shown net of subsidies in the national records of some countries.

23. As regards fiscal monopolies (heading 5122), only the amount actually transferred to the government is included in government revenues. However, if any expenditures of fiscal monopolies are considered to be government expenditures (e.g., social expenditures undertaken by fiscal monopolies at the direction of the government) they are added back for the purpose of arriving at tax revenue figures (see §65 below).

The distinction between tax and expenditure provisions

24. Because this publication is concerned only with the revenue side of government operations, no account being taken of the expenditure side, a distinction has to be made between tax and expenditure provisions. Normally there is no difficulty in making this distinction as expenditures are made outside the tax system and the tax accounts and under legislation separate from the tax legislation. In borderline cases, cash flow is used to distinguish between tax provisions and expenditure provisions. Insofar as a provision affects the flow of tax payments from the taxpayer to the government, it is regarded as a tax provision and is taken into account in the data shown in this publication. A provision which does not affect this flow is seen as an expenditure provision and is disregarded in the data recorded in this publication.[6]

25. Tax allowances, exemptions and deductions against the tax base clearly affect the amount of tax paid to the government and are therefore considered as tax provisions. At the other extreme, those subsidies which cannot be offset against tax liability and which are clearly not connected with the

assessment process, do not reduce tax revenues as recorded in this publication. Tax credits are amounts deductible from tax payable (as distinct from deductions from the tax base). Two types of tax credits are distinguished, those (referred to here as wastable tax credits) which are limited to the amount of the tax liability and therefore cannot give rise to a payment by the authorities to the taxpayer, and those (referred to as non-wastable tax credits) which are not so limited, so that the excess of the credit over the tax liability can be paid to the taxpayer.[7] A wastable tax credit, like a tax allowance, clearly affects the amount of tax paid to the government, and is therefore considered as a tax provision. The practice followed for non-wastable tax credits[8] is to distinguish between the 'tax expenditure component',[9] which is that portion of the credit that is used to reduce or eliminate a taxpayer's liability, and the 'transfer component', which is the portion that exceeds the taxpayer's liability and is paid to that taxpayer. Reported tax revenues should be reduced by the amount of the tax expenditure component but not by the amount of the transfer component. In addition, the amounts of the tax expenditure and transfer components should be reported as memorandum items in the country tables. Countries that are unable to distinguish between the tax expenditure and transfer components should indicate whether or not the tax revenues have been reduced by the total of these components, and provide any available estimates of the amounts of the two components. Further information is given in Chapter 1 of the Report, which illustrates the effect of alternative treatments of non-wastable tax credits on tax to GDP.

Calendar and fiscal years

26. National authorities whose fiscal years do not correspond to the calendar year show data, where possible, on a calendar year basis to permit maximum comparability with the data of other countries. There remain a few countries where data refer to fiscal years. For these the GDP data used in the comparative tables also correspond to the fiscal years.

A.4 General classification criteria

The main classification criteria

27. The classification of receipts among the main headings (1000, 2000, 3000, 4000, 5000 and 6000) is generally governed by the base on which the tax is levied: 1000 income, profits and capital gains; 2000 and 3000 earnings, payroll or number of employees; 4000 property; 5000 goods and services; 6000 multiple bases, other bases or unidentifiable bases. Where a tax is calculated on more than one base, the receipts are, where possible, split among the various headings (see §32 and §81). The headings 4000 and 5000 cover not only taxes where the tax base is the property, goods or services themselves but also certain related taxes. Thus, taxes on the transfer of property are included in 4400[10] and taxes on the use of goods or on permission to perform activities in 5200. In headings 4000 and 5000 a distinction is made in certain sub-headings between recurrent and non-recurrent taxes: recurrent taxes are defined as those levied at regular intervals (usually annually) and non-recurrent taxes are levied once and for all (see also §47 to §50, §53, §54 and §79 for particular applications of this distinction).

28. Earmarking of a tax for specific purposes does not affect the classification of tax receipts. However, as explained in §39 on the classification of social security contributions, the conferment of an entitlement to social benefits is crucial to the definition of the 2000 main heading.

29. The way that a tax is levied or collected (e.g., by use of stamps) does not affect classification.

Classification of taxpayers

30. In certain sub-headings distinctions are made between different categories of taxpayers. These distinctions vary from tax to tax:

a) Between individuals and corporations in relation to income and net wealth taxes

The basic distinction is that corporation income taxes, as distinct from individual income taxes, are levied on the corporation as an entity, not on the individuals who own it, and without regard to the personal circumstances of these individuals. The same distinction applies to net wealth taxes on corporations and those on individuals. Taxes paid on the profits of partnerships and the income of institutions, such as life insurance or pension funds, are classified according to the same rule. They are classified as corporate taxes (1200) if they are charged on the partnership or institution as an entity without regard to the personal circumstances of the owners. Otherwise, they are treated as individual taxes (1100). Usually, there is different legislation for the corporation taxes and for the individual taxes.[11] The distinction made here between individuals and corporations does not follow the sector classification between households, enterprises, and so on of the System of National Accounts for income and outlay accounts. The SNA classification requires certain unincorporated businesses[12] to be excluded from the household sector and included with non-financial enterprises and financial institutions. The tax on the profits of these businesses, however, cannot always be separated from the tax on the other income of their owners, or can be separated only on an arbitrary basis. No attempt at this separation is made here and the whole of the individual income tax is shown together without regard to the nature of the income chargeable.

b) Between households and others in relation to taxes on immovable property

Here the distinction is that adopted by the SNA for the production and consumption expenditure accounts. The distinction is between households as consumers (i.e. excluding non-incorporated business) on the one hand and producers on the other hand. However, taxes on dwellings occupied by households, whether paid by owner-occupiers, tenants or landlords, are classified under households. This follows the common distinction made between taxes on domestic property versus taxes on business property. Some countries are not, however, in a position to make this distinction.

c) Between households and others in relation to motor vehicle licences

Here the distinction is between households as consumers on the one hand and producers on the other, as in the production and consumption expenditure accounts of the SNA.

d) Between business and others in relation to the residual taxes (6000)

The distinction is the same as in c) above between producers on the one hand and households as consumers on the other hand. Taxes which are included under the heading 6000 because they involve more than one tax base or because the tax base does not fall within any of the previous categories but which are identifiable as levyable only on producers and not on households are included under 'business'. The rest of the taxes which are included under the heading 6000 are shown as 'other' or non-identified.

Surcharges

31. Receipts from surcharges in respect of particular taxes are usually classified with the receipts from the relevant tax whether or not the surcharge is temporary. If, however, the surcharge has a characteristic which would render it classifiable in a different heading of the OECD list, receipts from the surcharge are classified under that heading separately from the relevant tax.

Unidentifiable tax receipts and residual sub-headings

32. .A number of cases arise where taxes cannot be identified as belonging entirely to a heading or sub-heading of the OECD classification and the following practices are applied in such cases:

a) The heading is known, but it is not known how receipts should be allocated between sub-headings: receipts are classified in the appropriate residual sub-heading (1300, 2400, 4520, 4600, 5130, 5300 or 6200).

b) It is known that the bulk of receipts from a group of taxes (usually local taxes) is derived from taxes within a particular heading or sub-heading, but some of the taxes in the group whose amount cannot be precisely ascertained may be classifiable in other headings or sub-headings: receipts are shown in the heading or sub-heading under which most of the receipts fall.

c) Neither the heading nor sub-heading of a tax (usually local) can be identified: the tax is classified in 6200 unless it is known that it is a tax on business in which case it is classified in 6100.

A.5 Commentaries on items of the list

1000 — Taxes on income, profits and capital gains

33. This heading covers taxes levied on the net income or profits (i.e. gross income minus allowable tax reliefs) of individuals and enterprises. Also covered are taxes levied on the capital gains of individuals and enterprises, and gains from gambling.

34. Included in the heading are:

a) taxes levied predominantly on income or profits, though partially on other bases. Taxes on various bases which are not predominantly income or profits are classified according to the principles laid down in §32 and §81;

b) taxes on property, which are levied on a presumed or estimated income as part of an income tax (see also §47(a), (c) and (d));

c) compulsory payments to social security fund contributions that are levied on income but do not confer an entitlement to social benefits. When such contributions do confer an entitlement to social benefits, they are included in heading 2000 (see §39);

d) receipts from integrated scheduler income tax systems are classified as a whole in this heading, even though certain of the scheduler taxes may be based upon gross income and may not take into account the personal circumstances of the taxpayer.

35. The main subdivision of this heading is between levies on individuals (1100) and those on corporate enterprises (1200). Under each subdivision a distinction is made between taxes on income and profits (1110 and 1210), and taxes on capital gains (1120 and 1220). If certain receipts cannot be identified as appropriate to either 1100 or 1200, or if in practice this distinction cannot be made (e.g., because there are no reliable data on the recipients of payments from which withholding taxes are deducted) they are classified in 1300 as not-allocable.

Treatment of credits under imputation systems

36. Under imputation systems of corporate income tax, a company's shareholders are wholly or partly relieved of their liability to income tax on dividends paid by the company out of income or profits liable to corporate income tax. In countries with such systems,[13] part of the tax on the company's profits is available to provide relief against the shareholders' own tax liability. The relief to the shareholder takes the form of a tax credit, the amount of which may be less than, equal to, or more than the shareholder's overall tax liability. If the tax credit exceeds this tax liability the excess may be payable to the shareholder. As this type of tax credit is an integral part of the imputation system of corporate income tax, any payment to the shareholders is treated as a repayment of tax and not as expenditure (compare the treatment of other tax credits described in §25).

37. As the tax credit under imputation systems (even when exceeding tax liability) is to be regarded as a tax provision, the question arises whether it should be deducted from individual income tax receipts (1110) or corporate income tax receipts (1210). In this Report, the full amount of corporate income tax paid is shown under 1210 and no imputed tax is included under 1110. Thus, the full amount of the credit reduces the amount of 1110 whether the credit results in a reduction of personal income tax liability or whether an actual refund is made because the credit exceeds the income tax liability. (Where, however, such tax credits are deducted from corporation tax in respect of dividends paid to corporations the amounts are deducted from the receipts of 1210).

1120 and 1220 — Taxes on capital gains

38. These sub-headings comprise taxes imposed on capital gains, 1120 covering those levied on the gains of individuals and 1220 those levied on the gains of corporate enterprises, where receipts from such taxes can be separately identified. In many countries this is not the case and the receipts from such taxes are then classified with those from the income tax. Heading 1120 also includes taxes on gains from gambling.

2000 — Social security contributions

39. Classified here are all compulsory payments that confer an entitlement to receive a (contingent) future social benefit. Such payments are usually earmarked to finance social benefits and are often paid to institutions of general government that provide such benefits. However, such earmarking is not part of the definition of social security contributions and is not required for a tax to be classified here. However, conferment of an entitlement is required for a tax to be classified under this heading. So, levies on income or payroll that are earmarked for social security funds but do not confer an entitlement to benefit are excluded from this heading and shown under personal income taxes (1100) or taxes on payroll and workforce (3000). Taxes on other bases, such as goods and services, which are earmarked for social security benefits are not shown here but are classified according to their respective bases because they generally confer no entitlement to social security benefits.

40. Contributions for the following types of social security benefits would, *inter alia*, be included: unemployment insurance benefits and supplements, accident, injury and sickness benefits, old-age, disability and survivors' pensions, family allowances, reimbursements for medical and hospital expenses or provision of hospital or medical services. Contributions may be levied on both employees and employers.

41. Contributions may be based on earnings or payroll ('on a payroll basis') or on net income after deductions and exemptions for personal circumstances ('on an income tax basis'), and the revenues from the two bases should be separately identified if possible. However, where contributions to a general social security scheme are on a payroll basis, but the contributions of particular groups (such as the self-employed) cannot be assessed on this basis and net income is used as a proxy for gross earnings, the receipts may still be classified as being on a payroll basis. In principle, this heading excludes voluntary contributions paid to social security schemes. When separately identifiable these are shown in the memorandum item on the financing of social security benefits. In practice, however, they cannot always be separately identified from compulsory contributions, in which case they are included in this heading.

42. Contributions to social insurance schemes which are not institutions of general government and to other types of insurance schemes, provident funds, pension funds, friendly societies or other saving schemes are not considered as social security contributions. Provident funds are arrangements under which the contributions of each employee and of the corresponding employer on his/her behalf are kept in a separate account earning interest and withdrawable under specific circumstances. Pension funds are separately organised schemes negotiated between employees and employers and carry provisions for

different contributions and benefits, sometimes more directly tied to salary levels and length of service than under social security schemes. When contributions to these schemes are compulsory or quasi-compulsory (e.g., by virtue of agreement with professional and union organisations) they are shown in the memorandum item (refer to Table 5.37 of the Report).

43. Contributions by government employees and by governments in respect of their employees, to social security schemes classified within general government are included in this heading. Contributions to separate schemes for government employees, which can be regarded as replacing general social security schemes, are also regarded as taxes.[14] Where, however, a separate scheme is not seen as replacing a general scheme and has been negotiated between the government, in its role as an employer, and its employees, it is not regarded as social security and contributions to it are not regarded as taxes, even though the scheme may have been established by legislation.

44. This heading excludes 'imputed' contributions, which correspond to social benefits paid directly by employers to their employees or former employees or to their representatives (e.g., when employers are legally obliged to pay sickness benefits for a certain period).

45. Contributions are divided into those of employees (2100), employers (2200), and self-employed or non-employed (2300), and then further sub-divided according to the basis on which they are levied. Employees are defined for this purpose as all persons engaged in activities of business units, government bodies, private non-profit institutions, or other paid employment, except the proprietors and their unpaid family members in the case of unincorporated businesses. Members of the armed forces are included, irrespective of the duration and type of their service, if they contribute to social security schemes. The contributions of employers are defined as their payments on account of their employees to social security schemes. Where employees or employers are required to continue the payment of social security contributions when the employee becomes unemployed these contributions, data permitting, are shown in 2100 and 2200 respectively. Accordingly, the sub-heading 2300 is confined to contributions paid by the self-employed and by those outside of the labour force (e.g., disabled or retired individuals).

3000 — Taxes on payroll and workforce

46. These consist of taxes payable by enterprises assessed either as a proportion of the wages or salaries paid or as a fixed amount per person employed. They do not include compulsory social security contributions paid by employers or any taxes paid by employees themselves out of their wages or salaries

4000 — Taxes on property

47. This heading covers recurrent and non-recurrent taxes on the use, ownership or transfer of property. These include taxes on immovable property or net wealth, taxes on the change of ownership of property through inheritance or gift and taxes on financial and capital transactions. The following kinds of tax are excluded from this heading:

- *a)* taxes on capital gains resulting from the sale of a property (1120 or 1220);
- *b)* taxes on the use of goods or on permission to use goods or perform activities (5200); see §76;
- *c)* taxes on immovable property levied on the basis of a presumed net income which take into account the personal circumstances of the taxpayer. They are classified as income taxes along with taxes on income and capital gains derived from property (1100);
- *d)* taxes on the use of property for residence, where the tax is payable by either proprietor or tenant and the amount payable is a function of the user's personal circumstances (pay, dependants, and so on). They are classified as taxes on income (1100);

e) taxes on building in excess of permitted maximum density, taxes on the enlargement, construction or alteration of certain buildings beyond a permitted value and taxes on building construction. They are classified as taxes on permission to perform activities (5200);

f) taxes on the use of one's own property for special trading purposes like selling alcohol, tobacco, meat or for exploitation of land resources (e.g., United States severance taxes). They are classified as taxes on permission to perform activities (5200).

4100 — Recurrent taxes on immovable property

48. This sub-heading covers taxes levied regularly in respect of the use or ownership of immovable property.

- these taxes are levied on land and buildings;
- they can be in the form of a percentage of an assessed property value based on a national rental income, sales price, or capitalised yield; or in terms of other characteristics of real property, (for example size or location) from which a presumed rent or capital value can be derived.
- such taxes can be levied on proprietors, tenants, or both. They can also be paid by one level of government to another level of government in respect of property under the jurisdiction of the latter.
- debts are not taken into account in the assessment of these taxes, and they differ from taxes on net wealth in this respect.

49. Taxes on immovable property are further sub-divided into those paid by households (4110) and those paid by other entities (4120), according to the criteria set out in §30(*b*) above.

4200 — Recurrent taxes on net wealth

50. This sub-heading covers taxes levied regularly (in most cases annually) on net wealth, i.e. taxes on a wide range of movable and immovable property, net of debt. It is sub-divided into taxes paid by individuals (4210) and taxes paid by corporate enterprises (4220) according to the criteria set out in §30(*a*) above. If separate figures exist for receipts paid by institutions, the tax payments involved are added to those paid by corporations.

4300 — Estate, inheritance and gift taxes

51. This sub-heading is divided into taxes on estates and inheritances (4310) and taxes on gifts (4320).[15] Estate taxes are charged on the amount of the total estate whereas inheritance taxes are charged on the shares of the individual recipients; in addition the latter may take into account the relationship of the individual recipients to the deceased.

4400 — Taxes on financial and capital transactions

52. This sub-heading comprises, *inter alia*, taxes on the issue, transfer, purchase and sale of securities, taxes on cheques, and taxes levied on specific legal transactions such as validation of contracts and the sale of immovable property. The heading does not include:

a) taxes on the use of goods or property or permission to perform certain activities (5200);

b) fees paid to cover court charges, charges for birth, marriage or death certificates, which are normally regarded as non-tax revenues (see §11);

c) taxes on capital gains (1000);

d) recurrent taxes on immovable property (4100);

e) recurrent taxes on net wealth (4200);

f) once-and-for-all levies on property or wealth (4500).

4500 — Other non-recurrent taxes on property16

53. This sub-heading covers once-and-for-all, as distinct from recurrent, levies on property. It is divided into taxes on net wealth (4510) and other non-recurrent taxes on property (4520). Heading 4510 would include taxes levied to meet emergency expenditures, or for redistribution purposes. Heading 4520 would cover taxes levied to take account of increases in land value due to permission given to develop or provision of additional local facilities by general government, any taxes on the revaluation of capital and once-and-for-all taxes on particular items of property.

4600 — Other recurrent taxes on property

54. These rarely exist in OECD member countries, but the heading would include taxes on goods such as cattle, jewellery, windows, and other external signs of wealth.

5000 — Taxes on goods and services

55. All taxes and duties levied on the production, extraction, sale, transfer, leasing or delivery of goods, and the rendering of services (5100), or in respect of the use of goods or permission to use goods or to perform activities (5200) are included here. The heading thus covers:

a) multi-stage cumulative taxes;

b) general sales taxes — whether levied at manufacture/production, wholesale or retail level;

c) value-added taxes;

d) excises;

e) taxes levied on the import and export of goods;

f) taxes levied in respect of the use of goods and taxes on permission to use goods, or perform certain activities;

g) taxes on the extraction, processing or production of minerals and other products.

56. Borderline cases between this heading and heading 4000 (taxes on property) and 6100 (other taxes on business) are referred to in §47, §52 and §78. Residual sub-headings (5300) and (5130) cover tax receipts which cannot be allocated between 5100 and 5200 and between 5110 and 5120, respectively; see §32.

5100 — Taxes on the production, sale, transfer, leasing and delivery of goods and rendering of services

57. This sub-heading consists of all taxes, levied on transactions in goods and services on the basis of their intrinsic characteristics (e.g., value, weight of tobacco, strength of alcohol, and so on) as distinct from taxes imposed on the use of goods, or permission to use goods or perform activities, which fall under 5200.

5110 — General taxes on goods and services

58. This sub-heading includes all taxes, other than import and export duties (5123 and 5124), levied on the production, leasing, transfer, delivery or sales of a wide range of goods and/or the rendering of a wide range of services, irrespective of whether they are domestically produced or imported and irrespective of the stage of production or distribution at which they are levied. It thus covers value-added taxes, sales taxes and multi-stage cumulative taxes. Receipts from border adjustments in respect of such taxes when

goods are imported are added to gross receipts for this category, and repayments of such taxes when goods are exported are deducted. These taxes are subdivided into 5111 value-added taxes, 5112 sales taxes, 5113 turnover and other general taxes on goods and services.

59. Borderline cases arise between this heading and taxes on specific goods (5120) when taxes are levied on a large number of goods, for example, the United Kingdom purchase tax (repealed in 1973) and the Japanese commodity tax (repealed in 1988). In conformity with national views, the former United Kingdom purchase tax is classified as a general tax (5112) and the former Japanese commodity tax as excises (5121).

5111 — Value-added taxes

60. All general consumption taxes charged on value-added are classified in this sub-heading, irrespective of the method of deduction and the stages at which the taxes are levied. In practice, all OECD countries with value-added taxes normally allow immediate deduction of taxes on purchases by all but the final consumer and impose tax at all stages. In some countries the heading may include certain taxes, such as those on financial and insurance activities, either because receipts from them cannot be identified separately from those from the value-added tax, or because they are regarded as an integral part of the value-added tax, even though similar taxes in other countries might be classified elsewhere (e.g., 5126 as taxes on services or 4400 as taxes on financial and capital transactions).

5112 — Sales taxes

61. All general taxes levied at one stage only, whether at manufacturing or production, wholesale or retail stage are classified here.

5113 — Turnover and other general taxes on goods and services

62. These are multi-stage cumulative taxes and taxes where elements of consumption taxes are combined with multistage taxes. These taxes are levied each time a transaction takes place without deduction for taxes paid on inputs. Multi-stage taxes can be combined with elements of value-added or sales taxes.

5120 — Taxes on specific goods and services

63. Excises, profits generated and transferred from fiscal monopolies, and customs and imports duties as well as taxes on exports, foreign exchange transactions, investment goods and betting stakes and special taxes on services, which do not form part of a general tax of 5110, are included in this category.

5121 — Excises

64. Excises are taxes levied as a product specific unit tax on a predefined limited range of goods. Excises are usually levied at differentiated rates on nonessential or luxury goods, alcoholic beverages, tobacco, and energy. Excises may be imposed at any stage of production or distribution and are usually assessed as a specific charge per unit based on characteristics by reference to the value, weight, strength, or quantity of the product. Included are special taxes on individual products such as sugar, sugar beets, matches, and chocolates; taxes levied at varying rates on a certain range of goods; and taxes levied on tobacco goods, alcoholic drinks, motor fuels, and hydrocarbon oils. If a tax collected principally on imported goods also applies, or would apply, under the same law to comparable domestically produced goods, then the revenue from this tax is classified as arising from excises rather than from import duties. This principle applies even if there is no comparable domestic production or no possibility of such production. Taxes on the use of utilities such as water, electricity, gas, and energy are regarded as excises rather than taxes on

specific services (5126). Excises exclude those taxes that are levied as general taxes on goods and services (5110); profits of fiscal monopolies (5122); customs and other import duties (5123); or taxes on exports (5124).

5122 — Profits of fiscal monopolies

65. This sub-heading covers that part of the profits of fiscal monopolies which is transferred to general government or which is used to finance any expenditures considered to be government expenditures (see §23). Amounts are shown when they are transferred to general government or used to make expenditures considered to be government expenditures.

66. Fiscal monopolies reflect the exercise of the taxing power of government by the use of monopoly powers. Fiscal monopolies are non-financial public enterprises exercising a monopoly in most cases over the production or distribution of tobacco, alcoholic beverages, salt, matches, playing cards and petroleum or agricultural products (i.e. on the kind of products which are likely to be, alternatively or additionally, subject to the excises of 5121), to raise the government revenues which in other countries are gathered through taxes on dealings in such commodities by private business units. The government monopoly may be at the production stage or, as in the case of government-owned and controlled liquor stores, at the distribution stage.

67. Fiscal monopolies are distinguished from public utilities such as rail transport, electricity, post offices, and other communications, which may enjoy a monopoly or quasi-monopoly position but where the primary purpose is normally to provide basic services rather than to raise revenue for government. Transfers from such other public enterprises to the government are considered as non-tax revenues. The traditional concept of fiscal monopoly is not generally extended to include state lotteries, the profits of which are usually accordingly regarded as non-tax revenues. However, they can be included as tax revenues if the prime reason for their operation is to raise revenues to finance government expenditure. Fiscal monopoly profits are distinguished from export and import monopoly profits (5127) transferred from marketing boards or other enterprises dealing with international trade.

5123 — Customs and other import duties

68. Taxes, stamp duties and surcharges restricted by law to imported products are included here. Also included are levies on imported agricultural products which are imposed in member countries of the European Union and amounts paid by certain of these countries under the Monetary Compensation Accounts (MCA) system.[16] Starting from 1998, customs duties collected by European Union member states on behalf of the European Union are no longer reported under this heading in the country tables (in Chapter 5 of the Report). Excluded here are taxes collected on imports as part of a general tax on goods and services, or an excise applicable to both imported and domestically produced goods.

5124 — Taxes on exports

69. In the 1970s, export duties were levied in Australia, Canada and Portugal as a regular measure and they have been used in Finland for counter-cyclical purposes. Some member countries of the European Union pay, as part of the MCA system, a levy on exports (see note 16 to §68). Where these amounts are identifiable, they are shown in this heading. This heading does not include repayments of general consumption taxes or excises or customs duties on exported goods, which should be deducted from the gross receipts under 5110, 5121 or 5123, as appropriate.

5125 — Taxes on investment goods

70. This sub-heading covers taxes on investment goods, such as machinery. These taxes may be imposed for a number of years or temporarily for counter-cyclical purposes. Taxes on industrial inputs which are also levied on consumers [e.g., the Swedish energy tax which is classified under (5121)] are not included here.

5126 — Taxes on specific services

71. All taxes assessed on the payment for specific services, such as taxes on insurance premiums, banking services, gambling and betting stakes (e.g., from horse races, football pools, lottery tickets), transport, entertainment, restaurant and advertising charges, fall into this category. Taxes levied on the gross income of companies providing the service (e.g., gross insurance premiums or gambling stakes received by the company) are also classified under this heading. Tax revenues from bank levies and payments to deposit insurance and financial stability schemes are provisionally included here for the 2012 edition. The detailed classification is set out in §108.

72. Excluded from this sub-heading are:

- *a)* taxes on services forming part of a general tax on goods and services (5110);
- *b)* taxes on electricity, gas and energy (5121 as excises);
- *c)* taxes on individual gains from gambling (1120 as taxes on capital gains of individuals and non-corporate enterprises) and lump-sum taxes on the transfer of private lotteries or on the permission to set up lotteries (5200);[17]
- *d)* taxes on cheques and on the issue, transfer or redemption of securities (4400 as taxes on financial and capital transactions).

5127 — Other taxes on international trade and transactions

73. This sub-heading covers revenue received by the government from the purchase and sale of foreign exchange at different rates. When the government exercises monopoly powers to extract a margin between the purchase and sales price of foreign exchange, other than to cover administrative costs, the revenue derived constitutes a compulsory levy exacted in indeterminate proportions from both purchaser and seller of foreign exchange. It is the common equivalent of an import duty and export duty levied in a single exchange rate system or of a tax on the sale or purchase of foreign exchange. Like the profits of fiscal monopolies and import or export monopolies transferred to government, it represents the exercise of monopoly powers for tax purposes and is included in tax revenues.

74. The sub-heading covers also the profits of export or import monopolies, which do not however exist in OECD countries, taxes on purchase or sale of foreign exchange, and any other taxes levied specifically on international trade or transactions.

5128 — Other taxes on specific goods and services

75. This item includes taxes on the extraction of minerals, fossil fuels and other exhaustible resources from deposits owned privately or by another government together with any other unidentifiable receipts from taxes on specific goods and services. Taxes on the extraction of exhaustible resources are usually a fixed amount per unit of quality or weight, but can be a percentage of value. The taxes are recorded when the resources are extracted. Payments from the extraction of exhaustible resources from deposits owned by the government unit receiving the payment are classified as rent.

5200 — Taxes on use of goods or on permission to use goods or perform activities

76. This sub-heading covers taxes which are levied in respect of the use of goods as distinct from taxes on the goods themselves. Unlike the latter taxes – reported under 5100 –, they are not assessed on the value of the goods but usually as fixed amounts. Taxes on permission to use goods or to perform activities are also included here, as are pollution taxes not based upon the value of particular goods. It is sometimes difficult to distinguish between compulsory user charges and licence fees which are regarded as taxes and those which are excluded as non-tax revenues. The criteria which are employed are noted in §11–12.

77. Although the sub-heading refers to the 'use' of goods, registration of ownership rather than use may be what generates liability to tax, so that the taxes of this heading may apply to the ownership of animals or goods rather than their use (e.g., race horses, dogs and motor vehicles) and may apply even to unusable goods (e.g., unusable motor vehicles or guns).

78. Borderline cases arise with:

a) taxes on the permission to perform business activities which are levied on a combined income, payroll or turnover base and, accordingly, are classified following the rules in §81;

b) taxes on the ownership or use of property of headings 4100, 4200 and 4600. The heading 4100 is confined to taxes on the ownership or tenancy of immovable property and – unlike the taxes of 5200 – they are related to the value of the property. The net wealth taxes and taxes on chattels of 4200 and 4600 respectively are confined to the ownership rather than the use of assets, apply to groups of assets rather than particular goods and again are related to the value of the assets,

5210 — Recurrent taxes on use of goods and on permission to use goods or perform activities

79. The principal characteristic of taxes classified here is that they are levied at regular intervals and that they are usually fixed amounts. The most important item in terms of revenue receipts is vehicle licence taxes. This sub-heading also covers taxes on permission to hunt, shoot, fish or to sell certain products and taxes on the ownership of dogs and on the performance of certain services, provided that they meet the criteria set out in §11–12. The sub-divisions of 5210 are user taxes on motor vehicles paid by households (5211) and those paid by others (5212). Sub-heading 5213 covers dog licences and user charges for permission to perform activities such as selling meat or liquor when the levies are on a recurring basis. It also covers recurrent general licences for hunting, shooting and fishing where the right to carry out these activities is not granted as part of a normal commercial transaction (e.g., the granting of the licence is not accompanied by the right to use a specific area which is owned by government).

5220 — Non-recurrent taxes on use of goods and on permission to use goods or perform activities

80. This section covers non-recurrent taxes levied on the use of goods or on permission to use goods or perform activities and taxes levied each time goods are used. It includes taxes levied on the emission or discharge into the environment of noxious gases, liquids or other harmful substances.

- Payments for tradable emission permits issued by governments under cap and trade schemes should be recorded here at the time the emissions occur. No revenue should be recorded for permits that governments issue free of charge. The accrual basis of recording means that there can be a timing difference between the cash being received by government for the permits and the time the emission occurs. In the national accounts, this timing gives rise to a financial liability for government during the period.

- Payments made for the collection and disposal of waste or noxious substances by public authorities should be excluded as they constitute a sale of services to enterprises.

81. Other taxes falling under heading 5200 that are not levied recurrently are also included here. Thus, once-and-for-all payments for permission to sell liquor or tobacco or to set up betting shops are included provided they meet the criteria set out in §11–12.

6000 — Other taxes

82. Taxes levied on a base, or bases, other than those described under headings 1000, 3000, 4000 and 5000, or on bases of which cannot be considered to be related to any one of these headings, are included here. Where taxes are levied on a multiple base and it is possible to estimate the receipts related to each base the separate amounts are included under the appropriate headings. If separate amounts cannot be estimated and it is known that most of the receipts are derived from one base, the whole of the receipts are classified according to that base. Otherwise, they are classified here. Other revenues included here are presumptive taxes not included elsewhere in the classification system, taxes on individuals in the form of a poll tax or capitation tax, stamp taxes not related to financial and capital transactions nor falling exclusively on a single category of transaction, expenditure taxes where personal deductions or exemptions are applied and unidentifiable tax receipts. A subdivision is made between taxes levied wholly or predominantly on business (6100) and those levied on others (6200).

A.6 Conciliation with National Accounts

83. This section of the tables provides a re-conciliation between the OECD calculation of total tax revenues and the total of all taxes and social contributions paid to general government as recorded in the country's National Accounts. Where the country is a member of the European Union (EU), the comparison is between the OECD calculation of total tax revenues and the sum of tax revenues and social contributions recorded in the combination of the general government and the institutions of the EU sectors of the National Accounts.

A.7 Memorandum item on the financing of social security benefits

84. In view of the varying relationship between taxation and social security contributions and the cases referred to in §39 to §45, a memorandum item collects together all payments earmarked for social security-type benefits, other than voluntary payments to the private sector. Data are presented as follows (refer Table 5.37 of the Report):

a) Taxes of 2000 series.

b) Taxes earmarked for social security benefits.

c) Voluntary contributions to the government.

d) Compulsory contributions to the private sector.

Guidance on the breakdown of (a) to (d) above is provided in §39 to §45.

A.8 Memorandum item on identifiable taxes paid by government

85. Identifiable taxes actually paid by government are presented in a memorandum item classified by the main headings of the OECD classification of taxes. In the vast majority of countries, only social security contributions and payroll taxes paid by government can be identified. These are, however, usually the most important taxes paid by governments (refer to Table 5.38 of the Report).

A.9 Relation of OECD classification of taxes to national accounting systems

86. A system of national accounts (SNA) seeks to provide a coherent framework for recording and presenting the main flows relating respectively to production, consumption, accumulation and external transactions of a given economic area, usually a country or a major region within a country. Government revenues are an important part of the transactions recorded in SNA. The final version of the 2008 SNA was jointly published by five international organisations: the United Nations, the International Monetary Fund, the European Union, the Organisation for Economic Co-operation and Development, and the World Bank in August 2009. The *System* is a comprehensive, consistent and flexible set of macroeconomic accounts. It is designed for use in countries with market economies, whatever their stage of economic development, and also in countries in transition to market economies. The important parts of the SNA's conceptual framework and its definitions of the various sectors of the economy have been reflected in the OECD's classification of taxes.

87. There are, however, some differences between the OECD classification of taxes and SNA concepts that are listed below. They arise because the aim of the former is to provide the maximum disaggregation of statistical data on what are generally regarded as taxes by tax administrations.

a) OECD includes compulsory social security contributions paid to general government in total tax revenues. Imputed and voluntary contributions plus those paid to private funds are not treated as taxes (§8 and §10 above);

b) there are different points of view on whether or not some levies and fees are classified as taxes (§11 and §12 above);

c) OECD excludes imputed taxes or subsidies resulting from the operation of official multiple exchange rates or from the central bank paying a rate of interest on required reserves that is different from other market rates;

d) there are differences in the treatment of non-wastable tax credits

88. As noted in §1 and §2, headings 1000 to 6000 of the OECD list of taxes cover all unrequited payments to general government, other than compulsory loans and fines. Such unrequited payments including fines, but excluding compulsory loans can be obtained from adding together the following figures in the 2008 SNA

- value-added type taxes (D.211);
- taxes and duties on imports, excluding VAT (D.212);
- export taxes (D.213);
- taxes on products, excluding VAT, import and export taxes (D.214);
- other taxes on production (D.29);
- taxes on income (D.51);
- other current taxes (D.59);
- social contributions (D.61), excluding voluntary contributions;
- capital taxes (D.91).

A.10 The OECD classification of taxes and the International Monetary Fund (GFS) system

89. The coverage and valuation of tax revenues in the GFS system and the 2008 SNA are very similar. Therefore, the differences between the OECD classification and that of the 2008 SNA (see §87 above) also apply to the GFS. In addition the International Monetary Fund subdivides the OECD 5000 heading

into section IV (Domestic Taxes on Goods and Services) and section V (Taxes on International Trade and Transactions). This reflects the fact that while the latter usually yield insignificant amounts of revenue in OECD countries, this is not the case in many non-OECD countries.

A.11 Comparison of the OECD classification of taxes with other international classifications

90. The table below describes an item by item comparison of the OECD classification of taxes and the classifications used in the following:

- *a)* System of National Accounts (2008 SNA);
- *b)* European System of Accounts (2010 ESA);
- *c)* IMF Government Finance Statistics Manual (GFSM2014).

91. These comparisons represent those that would be expected to apply in the majority of cases. However in practice some flexibility should be used in their application. This is because in particular cases, countries can adopt varying approaches to the classification of revenues in National Accounts.

				OECD Classification	2008 SNA	2010 ESA	GFSM2014
1000				Taxes on income, profits and capital gains			
	1100			Individuals			
		1110		Income and profits	D51-8.61a	D51A	1111
		1120		Capital gains	D51-8.61c, d	D51C, D	1111
	1200			Corporations			
		1210		Income and profits	D51-8.61b	D51B	1112
		1220		Capital gains	D51-8.61c	D51C	1112
	1300			Unallocable as between 1100 and 1200			1113
2000				Social security contributions			
	2100			Employees	D613-8.85	D613	1211
	2200			Employers	D611-8.83	D611	1212
	2300			Self-employed, non-employed	D613-8.85	D613	1213
	2400			Unallocable as between 2100, 2200 and 2300			1214
3000				Taxes on payroll and workforce	D29-7.97a	D29C	112
4000				Taxes on property			
	4100			Recurrent taxes on immovable property			
		4110		Households	D59-8.63a	D59A	1131
		4120		Other	D29-7.97b	D29A	1131
	4200			Recurrent net wealth taxes			
		4210		Individual	D59-8.63b	D59A	1132
		4220		Corporations	D59-8.63b	D59A	1132
	4300			Estate, inheritance and gift taxes			
		4310		Estate and inheritance taxes	D91-10.207b	D91A	1133
		4320		Gift taxes	D91-10.207b	D91A	1133
	4400			Taxes on financial and capital transactions	D59-7.96d; D29-7.97e	D214B, C	114114; 1161
	4500			Other non-recurrent taxes on property	D91-10.207a	D91B	1135
	4600			Other recurrent taxes on property	D59-8.63c	D59A	1136
5000				Taxes on goods and services			
	5100			Taxes on production, sale and transfer of goods and services			
		5110		General taxes on goods and services			
			5111	Value-added taxes	D211-7.89	D211; D29G	11411

			5112	Sales taxes	D2122-7.94a; D214-7.96a	D21224; D214I	11412
			5113	Other general taxes on goods and services	D214-7.96a	D214I	11413
		5120		Taxes on specific goods and services			
			5121	Excises	D2122-7.94b; D214-7.96b	D21223; D214A, B, D	1142
			5122	Profits of fiscal monopolies	D214-7.96e	D214J	1143
			5123	Customs and other import duties	D2121-7.93	D2121; D21221, 2	1151
			5124	On exports	D213-7.95a	D214K	1152-4
			5125	On investment goods			
			5126	On specific services	D2122-7.94c; D214-7.96c	D21225; D214E, F, G, H; D29F	1144; 1156
			5127	Other taxes on international trade and transactions	D2122-7.94d D29-7.95b D29-7.97g D59-8.64d	D21226; D29D; D59E	1153; 1155-6
			5128	Other taxes on specific goods and services			1146
		5130		Unallocable between 5110 and 5120			
	5200			Taxes on use of goods and on permission to use goods or perform activities			
		5210		Recurrent taxes on use of goods and on permission to use goods or perform activities			
			5211	Motor vehicle taxes households	D59-8.64c	D59D	11451
			5212	Motor vehicles taxes others	D29-7.97d	D214D; D29B	11451
			5213	Other recurrent taxes on use of goods and on permission to use goods or perform activities	D29-7.97c, d, f D59-8.64c	D29B, E, F; D59D	11452
		5220		Non-recurrent taxes on permission to use goods or perform activities			11452
	5300			Unallocable as between 5100 and 5200			
6000				Other taxes			
	6100			Payable solely by business			1161
	6200			Payable by other than business, or unidentifiable	D59-8.64a, b	D59B, C	1162

A.12 Attribution of tax revenues by sub-sectors of general government

92. The OECD classification requires a breakdown of tax revenues by sub-sectors of government. The definition of each sub-sector and the criteria to be used to attribute tax revenues between these sub-sectors are set out below. They follow the guidance of the 2008 SNA and GFSM 2014.

Sub-sectors of general government to be identified

a) Central government

93. The central government sub-sector includes all governmental departments, offices, establishments and other bodies which are agencies or instruments of the central authority whose competence extends over the whole territory, with the exception of the administration of social security funds. Central government therefore has the authority to impose taxes on all resident and non-resident units engaged in economic activities within the country.

b) State, provincial or regional government

94. This sub-sector consists of intermediate units of government exercising a competence at a level below that of central government. It includes all such units operating independently of central government

in a part of a country's territory encompassing a number of smaller localities, with the exception of the administration of social security funds. In unitary countries, regional governments may be considered to have a separate existence where they have substantial autonomy to raise a significant proportion of their revenues from sources within their control and their officers are independent of external administrative control in the actual operation of the unit's activities.

95. At present, federal countries comprise the majority of cases where revenues attributed to intermediate units of government are identified separately. Spain is the only unitary country in this position. In the remaining unitary countries, regional revenues are included with those of local governments.

c) Local government

96. This sub-sector includes all other units of government exercising an independent competence in part of the territory of a country, with the exception of the administration of social security funds. It encompasses various urban and/or rural jurisdictions (e.g., local authorities, municipalities, cities, boroughs, districts).

d) Social security funds

97. Social security funds form a separate sub-sector of general government. The social security sub-sector is defined in the 2008 SNA by the following extracts from paragraphs 4.124 to 4.126 and 4.147:

"Social security schemes are social insurance schemes covering the community as a whole or large section of the community that are imposed and controlled by government units. The schemes cover a wide variety of programmes, providing benefits in cash or in kind for old age, invalidity or death, survivors, sickness and maternity, work injury, unemployment, family allowance, health care, etc. There is not necessarily a direct link between the amount of the contribution paid by an individual and the benefits he or she may receive." (Paragraph 4.124).

"When social security schemes are separately organised from the other activities of government units and hold their assets and liabilities separately from the latter and engage in financial transactions on their own account they qualify as institutional units that are described as social security funds." (Paragraph 4.125).

"The amounts raised, and paid out, in social security contributions and benefits may be deliberately varied in order to achieve objectives of government policy that have no direct connection with the concept of social security as a scheme to provide social benefits to members of the community. They may be raised or lowered in order to influence the level of aggregate demand in the economy, for example. Nevertheless, so long as they remain separately constituted funds, they must be treated as separate institutional units in the SNA. (Paragraph 4.126).

> *"The social security funds sub-sector (of general government) consists of the social security funds operating at all levels of government. Such funds are social insurance schemes covering the community as a whole or large section of the community that are imposed by government units." (Paragraph 4.147).*

98. This definition of social security funds is followed in the OECD classification with the two following exceptions which are excluded

- Schemes imposed by government and operated by bodies outside the general government sector, as defined in §3 of this manual; and
- Schemes to which all contributions are voluntary.

Supra-national Authorities

99. This sub-sector covers the revenue-raising operations of supra-national authorities within a country. In practice, the only relevant supra-national authority in the OECD area is that of the institutions of the European Union (EU). As from 1998, supra-national authorities are no longer included in the

Revenue Statistics, to achieve consistency with the SNA definition of general government which excludes them. For example, income taxes and social security contributions collected by European Institutions and paid by European civil servants who are resident of EU member countries should not be included. However the specific levies paid by the member states of the EU continue to be included in total tax revenues and they are shown under this heading.

Criteria to be used for the attribution of tax revenues

100. When a government collects taxes and pays them over in whole or in part to other governments, it is necessary to determine whether the revenues should be considered to be those of the collecting government which it distributes to others as grants, or those of the beneficiary governments which the collecting government receives and passes on only as their agent. The criteria to be used in the attribution of revenues are set out in §101 to §104 which replicate paragraphs 3.70 to 3.73 from the 2008 SNA.

101. In general, a tax is attributed to the government unit that

a) exercises the authority to impose the tax (either as a principal or through the delegated authority of the principal),

b) has final discretion to set and vary the rate of the tax

102. Where an amount is collected by one government for and on behalf of another government, and the latter government has the authority to impose the tax, and set and vary its rate, then the former is acting as an agent for the latter and the tax is reassigned. Any amount retained by the collecting government as a collection charge should be treated as a payment for a service. Any other amount retained by the collecting government, such as under a tax-sharing arrangement, should be treated as a current grant. If the collecting government was delegated the authority to set and vary the rate, then the amount collected should be treated as tax revenue of this government.

103. Where different governments jointly and equally set the rate of a tax and jointly and equally decide on the distribution of the proceeds, with no individual government having ultimate overriding authority, then the tax revenues are attributed to each government according to its respective share of the proceeds. If an arrangement allows one government unit to exercise ultimate overriding authority, then all of the tax revenue is attributed to that unit.

104. There may also be the circumstance where a tax is imposed under the constitutional or other authority of one government, but other governments individually set the tax rate in their jurisdictions. The proceeds of the tax generated in each respective government's jurisdiction are attributed as tax revenues of that government.

Levies paid by member states of the European Union

105. The levies paid by the member states of the EU take the form specific levies which include

a) custom duties and levies on agricultural goods (5123),

b) gross monetary compensation accounts (5123 if relating to imports and 5124 if relating to exports); and

c) Steel, coal, sugar and milk levies (5128).

106. The custom duties collected by member states on behalf of the EU are recorded

- on a gross of collection fee basis;
- using figures adjusted so that duties are shown on a 'final destination' as opposed to a 'country of first entry' basis where such adjustments can be made. These adjustments concern in particular duties collected at important (sea) ports. Although the EU duties are collected by the authorities of

the country of first entry, when possible these duties should be excluded from the revenue of the collecting country and be included in the revenue of the country of final destination

107. This is the specific EU levy that most clearly conforms to the attribution criterion described in §99 above. Consequently as from 1998, these amounts are footnoted as a memorandum item to the EU member state country tables (in Chapter 5) and no longer shown under heading 5123. However the figures are included in the total tax revenue figures on the top line for all the relevant years shown in the tables.

A.13 Provisional classification of revenues from bank levies and payments to deposit insurance and financial stability schemes

108. The OECD have adopted the following interim approach to reporting revenue from bank levies plus deposit insurance and stability fees for the 2012 and subsequent editions of *OECD Revenue Statistics*. It is recommended that the amounts should be recorded under category 5126.

- Compulsory payments of stability fees, bank levies and deposit insurance should generally be treated as tax revenues where the payments are made to General Government and allocated to the governments' consolidated or general funds so that the Government is free to make immediate use of the money for the purposes that it chooses. This principle would apply regardless of whether the Government is promising to make payments to guarantee the banks' customer deposits in some future contingency.
- If the compulsory payments are made to general government and placed in funds that are earmarked to be entirely channelled back to the sector of the economy that comprises the companies that are subject to the payment, they would still generally be treated as tax revenues on the grounds that the funds would be available for the government and would reduce its budget deficit, the fee is unrequited for an individual entity and the amounts raised could be unrelated to any eventual pay out to depositors or expenditure on wider support for the financial sector.
- Payments to made to the smaller long-standing schemes for insuring 'retail' deposits, where the payment levels are consistent with the costs of insurance should be classified as fee for service.
- Any payments which involve governments realising the assets of a failed institution or receiving a priority claim on its assets in liquidation in order to fund payments of compensation to customers for their lost deposits would be treated as a fee for a service as opposed to tax revenues.
- Compulsory payments that are made to funds operated outside the government sector and non-state institutions backed by the deposit takers and all payments to voluntary schemes should not be treated as tax revenues.

Notes

1. All references to SNA are to the 2008 edition.

2. See section A.12 of this guide for a discussion of the concept of agency capacity.

3. It is usually possible to identify amounts of social security contributions and payroll taxes, but not other taxes paid by government.

4. If, however, a levy which is considered as non-tax revenue by most countries is regarded as a tax — or raises substantial revenue — in one or more countries, the amounts collected are footnoted at the end of the relevant country tables, even though the amounts are not included in total tax revenues.

5. Names, however, can frequently be misleading. For example, though a passport fee would normally be considered a non-tax revenue, if a supplementary levy on passports (as is the case in Portugal) were imposed in order to raise substantial amounts of revenue relative to the cost of providing the passport, the levy would be regarded as a tax under 5200.

6. A more detailed explanation of this distinction can be found in the special feature, 'Current issues in reporting tax revenues', in the 2001 edition of the *Revenue Statistics*.

7. Sometimes the terms 'non-refundable' and 'refundable' are used, but it may be considered illogical to talk of 'refundable' when nothing has been paid.

8. A different treatment, however, is accorded to non-wastable tax credits under imputation systems of corporate income tax (§36–38).

9. This is not strictly a true tax expenditure in the formal sense. Such tax expenditures require identification of a benchmark tax system for each country or, preferably, a common international benchmark. In practice it has not been possible to reach agreement on a common international benchmark.

10. Unless based on the profit made on a sale, in which case they would be classified as capital gains taxes under 1120 or 1220.

11. In some countries the same legislation applies to both individual and corporate enterprises for particular taxes on income. However, the receipts from such taxes are usually allocable between individuals and enterprises and can therefore be shown in the appropriate sub-heading.

12. For example, "...sufficiently self-contained and independent that they behave in the same way as corporations.......(including) keeping a complete set of accounts" (2008 SNA, section 4.44).

13. In Canada — a country also referred to as having an imputation system — the (wastable) tax credit for the shareholder is in respect of domestic corporation tax deemed to have been paid whether or not a corporation tax liability has arisen. As there is no integral connection between the corporation tax liability and the credit given against income tax under such systems, these credits for dividends are treated, along with other tax credits, on the lines described in §25.

14. This may also apply where a scheme for government employees existed prior to the introduction of a general social security scheme.

15. In the 2008 SNA these are regarded as capital transfers and not as taxes (see section A.8).

16. This is the system by which the European Union adjusts for differences between the exchange rates used to determine prices under the Common Market Agricultural Policy and actual exchange rates. Payments under the system may relate to imports or exports and where these amounts are separately identifiable they are shown under the appropriate heading (5123 or 5124). In this Report, these amounts are shown gross (i.e. without deducting any subsidies paid out under the MCA system).

17. Transfers of profits of State lotteries are regarded as non-tax revenues (see also §67).

www.ingramcontent.com/pod-product-compliance
Lightning Source LLC
Chambersburg PA
CBHW061158240926
51846CB00006B/1045